READINGS IN LATER
CHINESE PHILOSOPHY

READINGS IN LATER CHINESE PHILOSOPHY
Han Dynasty to the 20th Century

Edited by

Justin Tiwald

and

Bryan W. Van Norden

Hackett Publishing Company, Inc.
Indianapolis/Cambridge

17 16 15 14   1 2 3 4 5 6 7

For further information, please address
  Hackett Publishing Company, Inc.
  P.O. Box 44937
  Indianapolis, Indiana 46244-0937

  www.hackettpublishing.com

Interior and cover designs by Elizabeth L. Wilson
Composition by Graphic Composition Inc., Bogart, Georgia

Library of Congress Cataloging-in-Publication Data

Readings in later Chinese philosophy / edited by Justin Tiwald and Bryan W. Van Norden.
    pages cm
  Includes bibliographical references and index.
  ISBN 978-1-62466-190-7 (pbk.) — ISBN 978-1-62466-191-4 (cloth)
  1. Philosophy, Chinese. I. Tiwald, Justin, editor. II. Van Norden, Bryan W. (Bryan
William), editor.
  B125.R43 2014
  181'.11—dc23   2014007385

The paper used in this publication meets the minimum requirements of American National
Standard for Information Sciences—Permanence of Paper for Printed Library Materials,
ANSI Z39.48-1984.

∞

To P. J. Ivanhoe,
mentor and friend.

CONTENTS

PREFACE

This book is intended to provide translations of a sampling of Chinese philosophical texts from the Han dynasty to the beginning of the 20th century. One might question whether there is a need for a new anthology such as this, given the availability of Wing-tsit Chan's *A Source Book in Chinese Philosophy* (Princeton: Princeton University Press, 1963). Chan's anthology is an impressive achievement that introduced generations of readers to some of the world's most fascinating texts. However, even the most outstanding translation will begin to seem dated after 50 years. We have diverged from Chan in terms of both focus and interpretive approach. In addition, among the most pressing needs is to have an anthology that brings Chinese thinking about gender and the experience of women into view. Finally, the Anglophone world is long overdue for an anthology of Chinese philosophy that uses the now dominant Hanyu Pinyin system of Romanization, so that readers can match the names and terminology with those that they find in other academic resources on China.

There is nothing privileged or exclusive about our decision to focus on philosophical texts. Some scholars and teachers may prefer to introduce Chinese traditional culture through poetry, belles lettres, essays, material culture, art, or a variety of other avenues, and there are excellent one-volume introductory anthologies for these purposes. Furthermore, given the richness of the Chinese philosophical tradition, and the immense span of time we survey, it is inevitable that there will be substantial gaps in our coverage, and disagreements with our choice of texts, authors, and topics. In general, we have been guided by the following principles:

- We have selected texts that have been influential; that we believe readers will find philosophically interesting; and that can be understood as engaging in a common dialogue, particularly over issues regarding ethical cultivation, human nature, virtue, government, and the underlying structure of the universe.
- We have tried to provide translations that are reader friendly, especially for contemporary students, general audiences, and scholars who do not read Chinese.
- We have made an effort to present many of our key texts in formats similar to those encountered by generations of Chinese intellectuals; for example, readers of this anthology will study the *Analects,* the sayings of Confucius and his disciples, accompanied by the commentary of Zhu Xi, whose interpretation was literally committed to memory by generations of Chinese.

- We have made a special effort to maintain consistency in translating key terms. Precisely because our selections are part of an ongoing dialogue, we want readers to be able to trace subtle intellectual influences over time, and see what key terms and phrases are in dispute.

- It is a commonplace among post-classical Chinese thinkers to quote from a shared body of established, classical texts. Many of their philosophical differences take the form of disputes about the meanings of those shared texts. For this reason, in addition to consistency in translating key terms, we have taken pains to ensure that classical passages are translated consistently no matter where they appear, except where a consistent translation obscures an interpreter's point. This and the preceding desideratum have required us to modify parts of the translations we have reprinted, and our contributing translators should not be held responsible for whatever infelicities or errors we may have introduced.

- We have generally tried to avoid gratuitously novel translations, but we have not hesitated to break new ground where we feel that previous translations are misleading, or fail to do justice to the complexity of the debate. For example, we have used "Pattern" instead of "principle" for *lǐ* 理, one of the key terms in Buddhist and Neo-Confucian thought. "Principle" would suggest to many readers a generalization that can be explicitly stated in words (like the "Principle of Least Action" of Newtonian physics). "Pattern" does a better job of suggesting a structure that is sometimes compared to a kind of web, and other times compared to the grain in a piece of wood. More controversially, in place of the common translations "investigating things" and "above form" for *géwù* 格物 and *xíng ér shàng* 形而上, we have used "getting a handle on things" and "above with respect to form," because the latter are neutral among the competing interpretations of these phrases offered by Zhu Xi, Lu Xiangshan, and Wang Yangming.

Textual interpretation is a topic about which informed, responsible scholars can defensibly disagree. We are sure that we have also made outright errors. We look forward to learning from our readers. As Wang Yangming observed, "all those who attack my failings are my teachers. How could I not receive such admonitions joyfully and take them to heart?"[1]

For feedback on drafts as various points, we would like to thank Feng Qingwen, Li Yunfeng, Wong Sum-lung, Lisa Wilcut, Ellen Zhang, and Jennifer Church. We are very grateful to all of our contributors for their hard work and their willingness to share their talents with us. David Elstein and Philip J. Ivanhoe also gave detailed feedback on some of the other contributions.

---

1. Wang Yangming, "Encouraging Goodness through Reproof," from *Essential Instructions for Students at Longchang*, in this volume, Part III, Selection 44.2.

We would like to give special thanks to our editor at Hackett Publishing, Deborah Wilkes, who has been a wise guide; Megan Wilson, our editorial assistant, who has saved us from as many embarrassing errors as any human could; and Jennifer White, part of the next generation of scholars of Chinese thought, who acted as our editorial assistant and served as an active member of the Mengzi Reading Group, which gave invaluable feedback. We are grateful to our students—past, present, and future—because through the dialogue that constitutes teaching, all participants grow. Finally, we owe a special debt of gratitude to one of our contributors, P. J. Ivanhoe, to whom this anthology is dedicated. P. J. was a mentor to each of us. Of course, like Xunzi in relation to Hanfeizi and Li Si, he cannot be held morally responsible for how his students turned out.

Justin Tiwald, San Francisco, CA
Bryan W. Van Norden, Poughkeepsie, NY

Tomb Painting, Han Dynasty.

PART I: HAN THOUGHT

The classic Chinese novel, *Romance of the Three Kingdoms,* famously opens with the line, "The empire, long divided, must unite; long united, must divide." This is perhaps the most accurate generalization we can make about Chinese history, which is characterized by long periods of strong centralized rule, alternating with periods of disunity. Centralized rule has always been perceived as the ideal, in part because the periods of unity often coincide with peace, prosperity, and cultural efflorescence. In contrast, disunity typically entails incessant warfare, crime, famine, and the threat of subjugation by "barbarians."

Traditional Chinese thinkers understood this cycle in moral terms. *Heaven* brings unity to the world by awarding a *mandate* to rule to someone with outstanding *Virtue.* This sage becomes the emperor who founds a dynasty, which lasts as long as its rulers continue to rule in accordance with Virtue. However, when the Virtue of the line of rulers decays, resulting in the dissatisfaction and rebelliousness of the common people, the mandate will be stripped from the dynasty and given to another Virtuous dynasty-founding sage. We see these themes illustrated in the traditional view of Chinese history, a view which had a profound influence on Han dynasty thought and provided many of the figures who became cultural reference points throughout later Chinese literature.[1]

The Three Sovereigns and the Five Emperors

Supposedly, the earliest humans had a precarious existence, living in fear of wild animals, subsisting day to day on whatever they could forage, and sleeping in dangerous tree houses or drafty caves. They had no technology or culture. Human life gradually improved and civilization developed through the actions of a series of sages, the earliest of whom are referred to as the Three Sovereigns and the Five Emperors. The first and second of the Three Sovereigns were Fú Xī 伏羲 and his wife, Nǚwā 女媧. Fu Xi taught people the technology required to hunt with weapons and fish with traps. He also taught people to cook their food; created the institution of marriage; and developed the trigrams, the earliest part of the *Changes,* a work of divination that would come to have great

---

1. This is an introduction to how Chinese thinkers understood their own history, not what that history actually was. For a scholarly contemporary view of Chinese history, see Harold M. Tanner, *China: A History* (Indianapolis: Hackett Publishing, 2009). There are also variations even among traditional Chinese accounts of ancient history. See, for example, Michael Puett, *The Ambiguity of Creation* (Stanford: Stanford University Press, 2002).

1

significance in later Chinese cosmology.[2] Legends say that Nüwa was responsible for even more amazing feats than was her husband, such as keeping the Heavens from collapsing by repairing them when they were damaged. The third of the Three Sovereigns was Shén Nóng 神農, whose name means "Divine Farmer." Shen Nong discovered how to plant crops and domesticate animals. He also was a pioneer of Chinese medicine.

The first of the Five Emperors was the Yellow Emperor, Huáng Dì 黃帝. He instituted armies and criminal sanctions to protect the people from external and internal threats. The second and third of the Five Emperors were the Yellow Emperor's descendants Zhuānxū 顓頊 and Emperor Kù 帝嚳. Yáo 堯 was the fourth of the Five Emperors. In addition to being a benevolent and wise ruler, he is associated with discovering the rudiments of astronomy and the regularity of the seasons, important knowledge for any agricultural civilization. Seeking an able minister to help him govern, Yao heard about Shùn 舜, a simple farmer who was renowned for his great filial piety. Shun was so successful as Yao's prime minister that, when Yao passed away, Shun became emperor (the last of the Five Emperors) as a result of the people's acclaim. Shun, in turn, appointed an able person, Yǔ 禹, to be his prime minister. Yu worked tirelessly and successfully on flood control and irrigation projects. As a result, in a parallel with the previous succession, his abilities led the people to treat him as the new emperor upon Shun's death.

The Three Dynasties

Yu is not counted among the Five Emperors, but this does not indicate any lesser prestige. Yu is distinct because, upon his death, Yu's son succeeded him as emperor, thereby establishing the first Chinese dynasty, the Xià 夏. The Xia dynasty was followed by the Shāng 商 and then the Zhōu 周, together constituting the Three Dynasties, the earliest in Chinese history.

The Three Dynasties set the pattern for the later Chinese understanding of dynastic creation and decay. In each of these dynasties we have a sage who is given a mandate (*mìng* 命) by Heaven (*Tiān* 天) to rule. (Because of this intimate relationship between Heaven and the ruler, a ruler is often referred to as the "Son of Heaven.") "Heaven" can refer to the sky or the place where the spirits of the ancestors dwell, but at least as important in Chinese history is the tendency to view Heaven as a higher power, which may or may not be treated as anthropomorphic (depending on the views of the philosopher in question). Heaven does not bestow the mandate capriciously. It gives it to a sage with outstanding Virtue (*dé* 德). "Virtue" refers both to excellences of character (especially benevolence and humility) and to a kind of ethical charisma that results from the possession of these excellences. People willingly follow someone with

---

2. See the *Changes*, in Part I, Selection 9 and Selection 10.

Virtue, without the need for coercion. As Kongzi (Confucius) famously said, "The Virtue of the gentleman is like the wind; the Virtue of the petty person is like the grass. When the wind moves over the grass, the grass is sure to bend."[3] Consequently, Heaven's choice for a ruler corresponds to the overall satisfaction of the common people. When the common people are happy (well-fed, orderly, and eager to follow the emperor), this is an indication of Heaven's approval of the ruler. When the people are unhappy (hungry, beset by bandits, rebellious), this is a sign of Heaven's disapproval. As the *Documents* says, "Heaven sees as my people see; Heaven hears as my people hear."[4] Some thinkers also emphasize the importance of divine signs and omens. Auspicious wonders show Heaven's approval, while inauspicious prodigies show its disapproval. Of course, whether to interpret any given anomaly as positive or negative was often a matter of debate: "A double rainbow! What does it mean?!"

In the normal order of things, a sagacious ruler founds a dynasty, bringing prosperity and order to society, but in a way that is largely non-coercive. The people willingly and joyfully follow him. However, over the centuries there is a gradual decline in the quality of the rulers, with a corresponding increase in social disorder, dissatisfaction, and disaffection. The decline is typically nonlinear: great emperors will arise to temporarily restore a dynasty to its greatness. Eventually, though, a dynasty will reach its nadir, and an evil last ruler will inspire full-fledged revolt against his atrocities, leading to the arrival of a sage who will found the next dynasty.

As we noted, Yu was the virtuous founder of the Xia dynasty. This dynasty was brought to an end centuries later by the evil Tyrant Jié 桀. The sage-king Tāng 湯 overthrew Jie and then founded the Shang dynasty. Like the Xia before it, the Shang gradually decayed: the evil last ruler of the Shang was Tyrant Zhòu 紂. The name of the dynasty that succeeded the Shang is also Romanized as "Zhou." To keep them straight in English, "Zhou" without qualification will refer to the dynasty, while the last ruler of the Shang will always be called "Tyrant Zhou." Tyrant Zhou

> kept the wise in obscurity and the vicious in office. The poor people in this situation, carrying their children and leading their wives, made their moan to Heaven, and even fled away, but were apprehended again.[5]

In contrast, King Wén 文, the leader of the Zhou people,

> was able to make bright his Virtue and be careful in the use of punishments. He did not dare to show any contempt to the widower and widows. He

---

3. *Analects* 12.19.

4. *Documents, Documents of Yu,* "Shun Dian." Translations from the *Documents* taken, with modifications, from James Legge, *The Chinese Classics, Volume 3, The Shoo King* (London: Trübner, 1865).

5. *Documents, Documents of Zhou,* "Shao Gao."

appointed those worthy of appointment and revered those worthy of reverence. . . . His fame ascended up to the High Ancestor, who approved of him. Heaven then gave a great charge to King Wen to exterminate the great dynasty of Shang and receive its great mandate.[6]

So the suffering people of Tyrant Zhou "made their moan to Heaven," which stripped him of the mandate and gave it to King Wen, leader of the Zhou people, because he "was able to make bright his Virtue." However, out of loyalty, humility, and love of peace, King Wen did not rebel against Tyrant Zhou. It was King Wen's son, King Wǔ 武, who finally led the conquest of the Shang. King Wu's rule over the newly founded Zhou dynasty was short-lived, though. He died of natural causes a few years later, and was succeeded by his son, King Chéng 成. King Cheng was only a child at the time, and having a minor on the throne immediately after the founding of a dynasty was a precarious situation. King Cheng's regent was his uncle, the Duke of Zhou (Zhōu Gōng 周公). It must have been tempting for the Duke of Zhou to seize the throne for himself. However, the Duke of Zhou supported King Cheng with loyalty and wisdom throughout his life. Because of this, he came to be regarded as a paragon of Virtue among later Confucians. The names of the emperors Fu Xi, Nüwa, Shen Nong, the Yellow Emperor, Yao, Shun, and Yu; the kings Tang, Wen, Wu, and Cheng; and the Duke of Zhou will appear repeatedly in Chinese history as paragons of wise and benevolent rule, while Tyrant Jie and Tyrant Zhou are bywords for viciousness.

    The Zhou succumbed to the same gradual decay that affects all dynasties. By the eighth century BCE, the Zhou king was a mere figurehead. Real power lay in the hands of the dukes and other nobles who governed the various states into which China was divided. In the absence of centralized authority, the states schemed against one another, formed and then broke alliances, and frequently engaged in interstate warfare. The common people suffered horribly: they were robbed and assaulted by brigands that the governments could not control, they were taxed to exhaustion by rulers who wanted to supply their armies and feed their own greed, and the planting and harvesting of crops was interrupted by invading armies or forced government labor. As is so often the case, a chaotic and desperate situation stimulated philosophical thought as intellectuals struggled to find a solution to the problems their society faced. What these Chinese thinkers were looking for was the *dào* 道, which we render in English as "Way." In the period that this book covers, "Way" has two primary senses: the "Way" can refer to (1) *the right way to live one's life and organize society,* or it can refer to (2) some sort of *ultimate metaphysical entity that is responsible for the way the world is and the way that it ought to be.*

---

6. *Documents, Documents of Zhou,* "Kang Gao."

Kongzi (Confucius) and His Works

Perhaps the most famous Chinese thinker who encouraged his contemporaries to return to the Way was Kǒngzǐ 孔子 (551–479 BCE; better known in the West by the Latinization of his name, "Confucius"). One of our major sources of information about Kongzi's views is the *Analects,* a collection of sayings and brief dialogues, mostly attributed to "the Master" himself.[7] The *Analects* was composed by Kongzi's immediate disciples, but Kongzi himself is said to have had a hand in the composition or editing of four of the *Five Classics,* which became central to Confucian education:

1. The *Odes* (also known in English as the *Songs* or *Classic of Poetry*) is an anthology of poetry that was already ancient by the time of Kongzi. Kongzi edited the *Odes* into its current form, and used it as a teaching tool, helping his disciples to see the hidden moral meanings in its poems.

2. The *Documents* (also referred to as the *History* or *Classic of History*) is a collection of historical documents (generally speeches or proclamations), supposedly dating back to the time of Emperor Yao and up to the early Zhou dynasty. As with the *Odes,* Kongzi is said to have edited the *Documents.*

3. The *Spring and Autumn Annals* is a terse historical chronicle covering the years 722–481, written from the perspective of Kongzi's home state of Lu. Representative of the content of the *Spring and Autumn Annals* is its second entry, which reads (in full), "The Duke and Yifu of Zhu made a treaty in Mie." No context is provided to explain the content of the treaty or its significance. According to tradition, the cryptic nature of the work is due to the fact that Kongzi wrote the *Spring and Autumn Annals* and subtly encoded in its statements his moral judgments of the actions described.[8]

4. The *Changes* (also called the *I Ching* or *Classic of Changes*) is both a divination manual and a philosophical work. The body of the work (supposedly developed over time by Fu Xi, King Wen, and the Duke of Zhou) consists of prognostications correlated with hexagrams. A hexagram is a set of six lines, each of which may be broken or unbroken (e.g., ䷀ or ䷁). There are sixty-four possible hexagrams, and each one represents the dynamic state of a particular situation. In addition, the *Changes* include appendices (also called "Wings"), which are attributed to Kongzi. The most philosophically important of the appendices are perhaps the "Great Appendix" (Dàzhuàn 大傳, also called the "Ap-

---

7. For a partial translation, see Zhu Xi, *Collected Commentaries on the* Analects, in Part III, Selection 34. For a complete translation, see Edward Slingerland, trans., *Confucius Analects: With Selections from Traditional Commentaries* (Indianapolis: Hackett Publishing, 2003).

8. For an example of this view, see Dong Zhongshu, "An In-Depth Examination into Names and Designations," in Part I, Selection 1.

pended Statements," Xìcí 繫辭) and the "Explanation of the Trigrams" (Shuō guà 說卦), which set out a philosophical view according to which the broken and unbroken lines of the *Changes* correspond to *yīn* 陰 and *yáng* 陽, complementary opposites that are the fundamental principles of Heaven and Earth.[9]

5. The *Rites* (also known as the *Record of Rites*) is largely a collection of detailed rules for performing various rituals. However, mixed in are a few chapters on philosophical topics. In particular, two brief chapters from the *Rites* would be singled out in later Chinese history as particularly important: the *Great Learning* and the *Mean*.[10]

It was traditionally believed that there existed at one time a sixth classic:

6. The *Music* (also known as the *Classic of Music*), referred to in some ancient texts, but no longer extant by the Han dynasty. Nonetheless, later Confucians would sometimes refer to it by its title, resulting in a list of Six Classics.

As we shall see over the course of this volume, Kongzi and his teachings have meant different things to different people over China's long history. However, among the common themes of Confucianism (all evident in the *Analects*) are rule by moral suasion rather than force, reverence for tradition, the importance of the family and filial piety, the need for ritual, and the transformative potential of ethical education.

Other Philosophers in the Classical Period: Daoists, Mohists, Yangists, Legalists, and Later Confucians

Lǎozǐ 老子, the semi-mythical founder of Daoism and the author of the *Dàodéjīng* 道德經, is said to have been a contemporary of Kongzi.[11] Legend holds that Laozi was a scribe in the Zhou dynasty archives, but one who did not take the writings of the ancients very seriously, describing them as mere "words" of those whose "bones have already decayed."[12] Like Confucianism, Daoism

---

9. See Selections on *Yin* and *Yang*, "Great Appendix," and "Explanation of the Trigrams," in Part I, Selections 7, 9, and 10.

10. See Zhu Xi, *Collected Commentaries on the* Great Learning, and *Collected Commentaries on the* Mean, in Part III, Selection 33 and 36.

11. For three interpretations of the *Daodejing*, see Philip J. Ivanhoe, trans., *The Daodejing of Laozi* (Indianapolis: Hackett Publishing, 2003); Victor Mair, trans., *Tao Te Ching* (New York: Bantam, 1990); and Richard John Lynn, trans., *The Classic of the Way and Virtue* (New York: Columbia University Press, 2004).

12. "Laozi's Biography" by Sima Qian (*Shiji* 63), in Mark Csikszentmihalyi, trans., *Readings in Han Chinese Thought* (Indianapolis: Hackett Publishing, 2006), p. 103.

defies easy summary. However, many Daoists were critical of what they saw as the artificiality of Confucian rituals and the potential for hypocrisy present in the effort to self-consciously become Virtuous, or to make others Virtuous. Thus, Laozi supposedly chastised Kongzi: "Dispense with your arrogant airs and many desires, your showy appearance, and your excessive ambitions."[13] Daoism later developed into a full-fledged religious tradition, sometimes called "Huang-Lao Daoism," during the Han dynasty. Huang-Lao Daoism stressed the effort to achieve immortality via meditative practices and elixirs. In addition, some Daoists claimed to have magical abilities. (*Romance of the Three Kingdoms* depicts Daoist adepts winning battles through their magic.)

Kongzi and Laozi, living near the end of the Spring and Autumn Period, were traditionally seen as the founders of the two greatest native Chinese philosophical traditions, Confucianism and Daoism. However, philosophical debate intensified during the Warring States Period (403–221 BCE), a time of even more severe inter- and intra-state conflict. This era is sometimes called the period of the Hundred Schools of Philosophy because of the diversity of views. For our purposes, six philosophers are worthy of note: Mengzi, Xunzi, Yang Zhu, Mozi, Zhuangzi, and Hanfeizi. Mengzi and Xunzi were Confucians who disagreed about the proper way to interpret the teachings of Kongzi. Mengzi famously claimed that human nature is good, while Xunzi stated that it is bad. Xunzi's view was perhaps closer to what became the orthodox view in the Han dynasty, but the Neo-Confucian philosophers of the Tang and later dynasties declared Mengzi's view orthodox.[14]

In describing his own intellectual context, Mengzi (fourth century BCE) wailed, "The doctrines of Yang Zhu and Mozi fill the world!"[15] These thinkers represented two extremes among those opposed to Confucianism. Yang Zhu advocated pure self-interest, while Mozi supported "impartial caring" for everyone, regardless of whether they were kin or strangers. Mengzi argued that Yang Zhu's view undermined our obligations to our rulers, while Mozi's view undermined filial piety. Later Confucians would draw parallels between Yang Zhu's view and Daoism, arguing that the quest for immortality that some Daoists pursued was ultimately selfish. Similarly, Mozi's "impartial caring" was likened to the "universal compassion" that led Buddhists to abandon their families to become celibate monks or nuns.[16]

Whereas Mengzi was deemed the "Second Sage" of Confucianism (second in importance only to Kongzi himself), Zhuangzi enjoyed a similar status in

---

13. Csikszentmihalyi, *Readings in Han Chinese Thought*, p. 103.

14. See Han Yu, "On Reading Xunzi," in Part III, Selection 21, and Zhu Xi, *Collected Commentaries on the* Mengzi, in Part III, Selection 35.

15. *Mengzi* 3B9.

16. As we explain in the Introduction to Part II, Buddhism came to China during the Han dynasty, but did not become philosophically important until after the fall of the Han.

Daoism. Although contemporary scholars note many areas of disagreement between the *Daodejing* and the eponymous *Zhuangzi,* Zhuangzi has traditionally
been seen as the faithful expositor of Laozi's worldview. Hanfeizi was a critic of
both Confucianism and Daoism, and the most articulate defender of the philosophy known as Legalism. Synthesizing the views attributed to Lord Shang
and Shen Buhai, Hanfeizi argued that the way for a ruler to get and maintain
power was to establish clear duties for government bureaucrats and clear laws
for the common people, and to enforce them with lavish rewards for compliance
and severe penalties for disobedience. Confucians have traditionally criticized
Legalism for the inflexibility of its rules and the severity of its punishments.[17]

During the Warring States Period, the state of Qín 秦 gradually increased in
power, until it conquered the last of its rivals in 221 BCE, establishing a new
dynasty. The "First Emperor" of Qin has always been controversial. Influenced
by Legalism, he centralized power and established clear laws that were strictly
enforced. The efficiency of his state and the discipline of his army were no doubt
significant factors in his eventual victory. After the conquest, the First Emperor
standardized weights and measures as well as the forms of Chinese characters.
He ordered construction of an early version of the Great Wall and was buried
with an army of clay statues, equipped with real weapons and modeled after his
actual honor guard. However, Chinese historians have generally criticized the
First Emperor for the draconian nature of his laws, for burning all books of philosophy other than Legalist ones, and for supposedly burying alive Confucian
scholars who dared to criticize his rule. However we evaluate it, the Qin dynasty
was short-lived, and rebels brought it to its knees in 207 BCE.

The Han Dynasty

After several years of fighting among claimants to the throne, the Hàn 漢 dynasty was established in 202 BCE and (except for a brief interregnum) lasted
until 220 CE. Within a century, Confucianism became official state ideology.
One of the central figures in the victory of Confucianism was Dǒng Zhòngshū
董仲舒. Dong convinced Emperor Wu (r. 140–87 BCE) of the political value of
Confucianism as a system for bringing order to the common people and justifying strong centralized rule. As a result of Dong's influence, government specialists were established in each of the *Five Classics*, and an Imperial University was
established, which focused on Confucian teachings. Government officials were,
at least in theory, expected to study in this university and pass its examinations.

---

17. For readings from these Spring and Autumn and Warring States period philosophers, see
Philip J. Ivanhoe and Bryan W. Van Norden, eds., *Readings in Classical Chinese Philosophy,*
2nd ed. (Indianapolis: Hackett Publishing, 2005). For more detailed explanations of their
views, see Bryan W. Van Norden, *Introduction to Classical Chinese Philosophy* (Indianapolis:
Hackett Publishing, 2011).

However, the version of Confucianism espoused by Dong Zhongshu and patronized by the Han emperors was very syncretic, combining Confucianism with elements of Daoism, Legalism, and other schools of thought. In addition, not everyone subscribed to Confucianism. Sima Qian was the author of the first official dynastic history, *Records of the Historian*. Chinese and Western scholars have long recognized that this work implies criticisms of Confucianism that were sufficiently subtle to escape the notice of careless readers (such as Emperor Wu).[18] In addition, Sima Qian's father, Sima Tan, was an avowed Daoist, and the *Records of the Historian* includes his essay, "On the Six Schools of Thought," which argues that Confucianism, Mohism, Legalism, the School of Names, and the Yin-yang School each have their strong and weak points, but Daoism is the school of thought that is most encompassing and best.

The selections in Part I give you some sense for which ideas from the Han dynasty were most influential in the long run. The doctrines of Dong Zhongshu, Yang Xiong, and Wang Fu are representative of Confucian political and ethical views. The excerpts from the *Changes* and the selections on *qi*, on *yin* and *yang*, and on the Five Phases introduce cosmological concepts that were to become central to all of traditional Chinese thought. To illustrate traditional concepts of gender, we provide the famous biography of Mengzi's mother, and, in its entirety, *Lessons for Women*, a work in which the distinguished Han-era historian Ban Zhao explicates her view of feminine roles.

---

18. See Steven Durrant, *The Cloudy Mirror* (Albany: State University of New York Press, 1995).

Confucian Political and Ethical Philosophy

Decorative Sculpture of an Offering Table.

1. Dong Zhongshu, "An In-Depth Investigation into Names and Designations"

From *Luxuriant Dew of the Spring and Autumn Annals* 35
translation by Mark Csikszentmihalyi
and Bryan W. Van Norden[1]

Dǒng Zhòngshū 董仲舒 *(c. 198–c. 104 BCE), whereas today identified with the resurgence of the study of the Confucian classics and with the rise of correlative thinking that linked events in the human and natural realms, was known in his day primarily as an exegete and devotee of the* Spring and Autumn Annals *(Chūnqiū* 春秋*), the terse chronicle thought to have been compiled by Kongzi, and its* Gongyang Commentary *(Gōngyáng zhuàn* 公羊傳*). The extant work attributed to Dong, the* Luxuriant Dew of the Spring and Autumn Annals *(Chūnqiū fánlù* 春秋繁露*), has seventeen parts containing 123 chapter titles, of which seventy-nine chapters survive.*

---

1. The first three paragraphs of this selection are translated by Bryan W. Van Norden. The remaining four paragraphs are reprinted with modifications from Mark Csikszentmihalyi, trans., *Readings in Han Chinese Thought* (Indianapolis: Hackett Publishing, 2006), pp. 7–9.

Many scholars cite the way the text elaborates underlying connections between Heaven and Earth and provides a cosmological explanation for the authority of the ruler, and on that basis identify Dong as the first writer to provide a religious rationale for the new governmental structures of imperial China. Because of its diverse content and its inconsistencies with historical descriptions of Dong's views in the standard histories, there is speculation that some chapters of the Luxuriant Dew of the Spring and Autumn Annals *may not have been written by Dong.* — Tr.

The beginning of putting the world in order lies in carefully distinguishing what is most important. The beginning of distinguishing what is most important lies in an in-depth examination of names and designations. Names [and designations] are the major divisions of the great Pattern.[2] . . .

Names are more numerous than designations. One *designates* the whole, and *names* the distinctions and differentiations. One *designates* the general in outline, and *names* the details and specifics. The specifics distinguish the activities. What is general refers to the larger whole. For example, offerings to the ghosts and spirits have one designation: "sacrifices." But the various sacrifices have their own names: in spring it is called the "vernal," in summer it is called the "aestival," in the fall it is called the "autumnal," and in winter it is called the "hibernal." . . .

The present generation is ignorant about human nature, giving various teachings about it. Why do they not try to examine the name "nature"? Does not the name "nature" (*xìng* 性) mean "birth" (*shēng* 生)?[3] The capacity that one naturally has at birth is what is called the "nature." The nature is one's mere potential. If we examine the nature using the name "good," does it apply exactly? Since it cannot apply exactly, how could we say that one's mere potential is good? The name "nature" does not apply to anything beyond one's mere potential; if it deviates from the mere potential by as much as a hair's breadth, then it is simply not the nature anymore. One may not fail to examine this carefully. The *Spring and Autumn Annals* rectifies names in accordance with the Pattern that differentiates things.[4] It names things in accordance with what they actually are, not making so much as a hair's breadth mistake. Hence, when it named the "meteorites falling, numbering five," it put the word "five" last, while when it described

---

2. The term "Pattern" (*li* 理) refers to the underlying structure of the world. It becomes a key term in later Buddhism and Neo-Confucianism. See Fazang, "Essay on the Golden Lion," in Part II, Selection 15, and Zhu Xi, *Categorized Conversations,* in Part III, Selection 32.—Eds.

3. This paragraph illustrates Dong's belief that the structure of Chinese characters is the key to understanding their deep meaning.—Eds.

4. This is a reference to *Analects* 13.3, in which Kongzi says that his first task if he were to be put into a position of governmental authority would be rectifying names.—Eds.

the "six fishhawks flying backwards," it put the word "six" first.[5] The Sage was this precise in rectifying names. The expressions about the five meteorites and the six fishhawks illustrate the saying that "the gentleman simply guards against arbitrariness in speech. That is all."[6]

Nature may be compared to the rice plant, and goodness may be compared to the rice kernel. The rice kernel comes out of the rice plant, but the rice plant cannot completely produce the rice kernel. Goodness comes out of a person's nature, but that nature cannot completely produce goodness. Both goodness and the rice kernel are things that humans have inherited from Heaven and are completed externally, rather than entirely being a matter of what Heaven has brought to completion internally.[7]

What Heaven creates reaches a limit and then stops. Everything prior to that point is called its "Heavenly nature," and everything past that point is called "human affairs." Affairs are external to a person's nature, but if you do not attend to them you will not develop Virtue.

The designation for "the people" [mín 民] is taken from the term "asleep" [míng 瞑]. If the people's nature is already good, then why are they designated as asleep? Speaking in terms of a person who is sleeping, without support he or she will stumble and fall or behave wildly. How could this be considered good? A person's nature has something resembling eyes. Lying down in the dark with closed eyes, one awaits awakening in order to see. When one is not yet awake, it is possible to say one has the mere potential for seeing, but it cannot be called seeing. Now, the nature of the myriad people is that they have the mere potential but have not yet awakened, and they may be likened to a sleeper who is waiting to be awakened. It is only after educating the people that they will become good. When not yet awake, it is possible to say they have the mere potential for goodness, but they cannot be called good. The idea is comparable to a person's eyes when asleep and when awake.

---

5. These anomalies are recorded in *Spring and Autumn Annals*, Duke Xi, Year 16. The *Gongyang Commentary on the Spring and Autumn Annals* explains that the objects were first identified as meteorites and only then was their number determined, so the number was provided last, while in the case of the fishhawks it was initially clear how many birds there were, and only then that they were fishhawks in particular, so the number was given first. This is representative of the intensive reading scholars like Dong subjected the *Spring and Autumn Annals* to, in order to decode the hidden meanings that Kongzi supposedly indicated by subtle word choices.—Eds.

6. Quoting Kongzi from *Analects* 13.3.

7. Dong here uses an analogy to argue that human nature is not good, but does have a potential for goodness within it. This potential can only be realized by extensive education and socialization. The issue of whether human nature is good, bad, indifferent, or varied has been debated extensively in Chinese thought. See Han Yu, "On Human Nature," and *Mengzi* 6A6, in Part III, Selection 22 and Selection 35.—Eds.

By making the mind tranquil and carefully examining such words [as "people" and "asleep"], this all may be comprehended. Heaven creates people with a nature that is asleep, not yet awake. They are given a designation following the model of what Heaven created, and are called "the people." This is the way of speaking of the people [*min*] because they are as if asleep [*ming*]. It is only once we follow their names and designations and penetrate into the Pattern behind them that we may grasp it.

2. Dong Zhongshu, "The Way of the King Links Up the Three"

From *Luxuriant Dew of the Spring and Autumn Annals* 44
translation by Sharon Sanderovitch

The title of this chapter is explained in its first paragraph's elaboration of the significance of the graph for "king" (wáng 王) with its three horizontal lines representing Heaven, Earth, and humankind, and the king as the vertical line that links the three together.[8] *A central theme is the providential concern of Heaven for humankind, and the development of a cosmological justification for ethical knowledge—in Dong's terminology a matching of the "Pattern of humans" (rénlǐ 人理) with the "Way of Heaven" (Tiāndào 天道).*[9]*—Tr.*

The ancients who created the written language denoted "king" by linking together the center of three [horizontal] lines [with a single vertical stroke]. The three lines represent Heaven, Earth, and humankind. That which connects their centers, links up their paths. Linking them up by grasping the central points of Heaven, Earth, and humankind and having them connect—who besides a king would be competent for such a task? Therefore, the king is none other than the executor of Heaven's [Way]. He carries through its seasonal [changes] and thereby brings them to completion; he emulates its mandate and applies it to succor the people; he models its procedures and uses them in instituting affairs; he follows the Way of Heaven and uses it as a point of departure; he follows the

---

8. See the introduction to the previous selection on Dong Zhongshu and the *Luxuriant Dew of the Spring and Autumn Annals.*—Eds.

9. This selection thus includes an example of "Pattern (*lǐ* 理)," a term which later comes to have great significance in Buddhist and Neo-Confucian thought. See Fazang, "Essay on the Golden Lion," in Part II, Selection 15, and Zhu Xi, *Categorized Conversations,* in Part III, Selection 32.—Eds.

purpose of Heaven and returns to it in benevolence.[10] The excellence of benevolence is in Heaven; Heaven *is* benevolence.

Heaven covers and nurtures the myriad things. Once they are transformed, it gives birth to them. It provides them nourishment and thus brings them to completion. Its accomplishments are endless; when they conclude it begins again. In every instance, what it advances comes back to benefit humankind. Observe Heaven's intentions and you will find inexhaustible benevolence. When a person receives his mandate from Heaven, that person takes up Heaven's benevolence and thereby turns benevolent. Thus, the mandate a person receives includes both reverence towards Heaven and affection between fathers, sons, and siblings. It possesses thoughts of conscientiousness and faithfulness, charity and kindness. It contains acts of propriety and righteousness, honesty and yielding. It has judgments of right and wrong, defiance and compliance. As human cultural accomplishments shine forth and they deepen, as their knowledge grows and it expands, it is only the Way of humans that is capable of matching Heaven's.

Heaven constantly makes caring and benefiting people its intention, nourishing and cultivating its task. Spring, autumn, winter, and summer are all its instruments. A king, too, constantly makes the care and benefit of the people of the world his intention, and the security and happiness of the generation his task. Like and dislike, joy and anger, are all at his disposal. Thus, a ruler's likes and dislikes, joy and anger, are Heaven's spring, summer, autumn, and winter in the way that they stir transformations and so create accomplishments by way of warmth, chill, cold, and heat. Heaven issues forth these phenomena in this way: if they are seasonally appropriate, then the yearly harvest will be good; if they are seasonally inappropriate, the yearly harvest will be poor. As for the issuing forth of these four by the human ruler: if it is righteous, the age is well-ordered; if it is unrighteous, the age is chaotic. Therefore, an ordered age and a good yearly harvest depend on the same procedure; a chaotic age and a poor yearly harvest are likewise a result of the same procedure. It is therefore evident that the Pattern of humans matches the Way of Heaven.[11]

---

10. Reading *zhì* 治 ("govern") as *yán* 沿 ("follow along").

11. For more of this chapter, see Selections on *Qi,* in Part I, Selection 6.

3. Dong Zhongshu, "The Necessity for Benevolence and Wisdom"

From *Luxuriant Dew of the Spring and Autumn Annals* 30
translation by Yun-Ling Wang

"The Necessity for Benevolence and Wisdom" has three sections: a discussion of the importance of benevolence and wisdom for talented people, a short disquisition on the rationale for Heaven-sent punishments, and a section directly attributed to Dong Zhongshu that uses classical allusions to explain how such punishments are evidence of Heaven's care for humankind. — Tr.

Nothing is more immediate than benevolence, and nothing is more urgent than wisdom. A person who lacks benevolence, but has courage and ability is similar to a lunatic holding a sharp weapon. One who lacks wisdom but has eloquence and astuteness is similar to someone riding a fast horse but unsure which direction to go. Hence a person who is neither benevolent nor wise but who has ability may well use that ability in the service of crazy or deviant thoughts, or to support aberrant and defiant conduct. It will end up being just enough to intensify his mistakes and aggravate his bad actions. For such a person will be energetic enough to cover his mistakes, defensive enough to deceive others, astute enough to perplex simpletons, eloquent enough to disguise his errors, obstinate enough to misapply legal guidelines, and fierce enough to reject remonstration. Such flaws are not due to a lack of ability, but rather from applying it inappropriately and managing it without righteousness.

One who has a corrupt mind should never be extended privileges; one whose nature is obtuse should never be given military power. What the *Analects* called "one who does not understand others" probably refers to people who fail to differentiate between the above types of people.[12] Being benevolent while lacking wisdom, one will be caring but unable to differentiate between others; being wise while lacking benevolence, one will be clever but unable to do good. Therefore benevolence is a means to care for one's fellow human beings, and wisdom is a means to alleviate their injuries.

What is meant by "benevolence"? A benevolent man is merciful and cares for people. He is respectful and cordial, and is not contentious. His likes and dislikes are appropriate. He has no harmful or depraved thoughts, and is not motivated by envy. Feelings of jealousy never arise, nor do regretful or sorrowful sentiments. He takes no crafty or deviant actions, and has no aberrant or defiant

---

12. Probably a reference to *Analects* 20.3, which ends: "If one does not understand speech, then one has no way to understand others."

conduct. Therefore his mind is relaxed, his intentions are tranquil, his temperament is balanced; his wants are restrained, his actions are uncomplicated, and his conduct is principled. Hence he can be tranquil and uncomplicated, harmonious and well-ordered without being contentious.[13] One who does all this may be called "benevolent."

What is meant by "wisdom"? It is to first speak and then live up to what you have said. Whenever one wants to decide what to do or what not to do, one always, by means of wisdom, first plans it out and only then takes action. If one's plans are correct, then one's goals will be achieved. One's actions will be appropriate, so one's conduct will be successful, and one's reputation reflects glory on one's person. There will be benefits but no trouble, the blessings will reach one's children and grandchildren, and one's Virtue will reach down to the common people. King Tang of Shang and King Wu of Zhou are examples of this. However, if one's plans are erroneous, then one's goals will not be achieved. One's actions will be inappropriate, so one's conduct will be unsuccessful, and one's reputation will be ruined. Harm will reach one's person, one's lineage will be extinguished due to a lack of descendants. One's group will be broken up, one's clan will be destroyed, and the state will perish. Tyrant Jie of Xia and the Tyrant Zhou of Shang are examples of this.

Therefore it is said that nothing is more urgent than wisdom. The wise person foresees fortune and misfortune from far away, recognizing benefits and harm ahead of time. As soon as objects move he understands their transformations; as soon as things arise he knows the path that they will take. Seeing the beginning, he knows the end. When he speaks, none dare make noise. Whatever he sets up cannot be abolished. What course he has adopted, cannot be abandoned. There is no contradiction between what he did before and what he does later, as he follows reasons from the beginning to the end. His thinking can withstand repeated examinations, and what he has accomplished cannot be abandoned. His words are few but sufficient, concise but comprehensive, simple but expressive, and brief but complete. While he speaks few words, nothing can be added to them, and when he uses many, not a single word could be omitted. His movements are exactly appropriate to human relations and his words suitable for priority matters. One who does all this may be called "wise."

Generally speaking, things between Heaven and Earth are of the following kinds: when there is an extraordinary change, it is called a "calamity," while a minor one is called an "omen."[14] Omens often occur first and then are followed with calamities. An omen is a condemnation from Heaven while a calamity is the punishment of Heaven. When Heaven condemns someone but that person

---

13. "Well-ordered," here is the term later translated as "Pattern," which becomes a key technical term in later Buddhist and Neo-Confucian philosophy.—Eds.

14. We have chosen to translate *yì* 異 as "calamity," and *zāi* 災 as "omen." However, a more literal rendering would be "abnormality" and "disaster," respectively.—Eds.

does not learn the lesson, Heaven will then terrify that person with its punishment. The *Odes* says, "Be terrified of the punishment of Heaven."[15] It generally conveys what is addressed here.

The root of omens and calamities is entirely caused by the faults of the state. As soon as the faults of the state start to sprout, Heaven sends down omens and misfortunes to condemn and warn the state. After condemning and warning the state, if the state does not realize that they should change their ways, Heaven will then put abnormalities and calamities on display to alert and frighten the state. Only if it alerts and frightens the state and the state still does not realize that it has cause for terror and fear will catastrophes and ill-fortune arrive. Based on this, one can now understand the benevolence of Heaven's intentions, and that Heaven does not want to harm humans.

Dong comments as follows:

> Omens and calamities are used to manifest Heaven's intentions. Heaven intends certain things that it wants or does not want. People should then examine themselves internally about what Heaven wants and does not want, and use it to reprimand their minds; they should observe their actions externally, and use it to locate portents in the state. Therefore, one who knows Heaven's intentions from omens and calamities lives in fear of them but does not detest them. Such a person believes that "Heaven wants to rectify our mistakes, and remedy our faults, so Heaven uses this method to inform me of them."
>
> According to the principles of the *Spring and Autumn Annals*, a state in which those in high position change the tradition or alter customs as a response to experiencing natural disasters is called a "fortunate state." Kongzi said, "Among the boons bestowed by Heaven, one is the severe punishment for doing something immoral."[16] Because no omens appeared in Heaven and no signs appeared on the Earth, King Zhuang of Chu prayed to the mountain and rivers and said, "Is Heaven planning to annihilate me? Heaven neither tells me my mistakes nor severely punishes my transgressions!" Looking at it from this perspective, the omens of Heaven arrive as responses to human misconduct, while calamities make obvious things that are worthy of concern. They indicate the things that Heaven wants to remedy, and so are things that the *Spring and Autumn Annals* only considers to be good fortune. This is why King Zhuang prayed for and requested them. Sagacious lords and worthy rulers are delighted to accept remonstration from their loyal subjects, so why are they not more willing to accept condemnation from Heaven!

---

15. *Odes* 272.

16. This quotation is not attested in the *Analects* or other early sources.

4. Yang Xiong, "Putting Learning into Practice"

From *Model Sayings* 1
translation by Mark Csikszentmihalyi[17]

The Model Sayings *(Fǎyán 法言), by Yáng Xióng (揚雄, 53 BCE–
18 CE), is a collection of short dialogues explicitly patterned on the* Analects,
the sayings attributed to Kongzi and his disciples.[18] *Historically, Yang has
been both excoriated for his penchant for imitation and celebrated for his
ability to craft elaborate works in a classical style. As a philosopher, Yang
reacted against the eclectic influences that he saw as diluting the classical message of Kongzi. Yang explained that he wrote the* Model Sayings
*to reestablish the primacy of the teachings of Kongzi in an age deluded by
the heterodox teachings of the "many masters."*[19] *As with the* Analects, *each
chapter title of the* Model Sayings *is composed of the first two characters
of the chapter itself, and both works are primarily concerned with self-
cultivation and the exceptional characteristics of the sage. — Tr.*

1. Putting learning into practice is supreme. Putting it into words comes next.
Teaching it to others comes after that. Anyone who does none of these is simply
an unexceptional person.

2. Was not the Way of Heaven located in Kongzi? Once Kongzi's carriage
came to a halt, was it not parked among the Classical Studies scholars?[20] If we
would like to get his teachings rolling again, nothing could be better than using
the Classical Studies scholars as metal mouths with wooden tongues![21]

3. Someone said: "Learning confers no advantage, for of what use is it to
one's basic substance?"

Yang replied: "You have not thought about this enough. Now, a person with
a knife grinds it, and a person with jade polishes it. If one neither grinds nor

---

17. Translation reprinted with modifications from Mark Csikszentmihalyi, trans., *Readings in
Han Chinese Thought* (Indianapolis: Hackett Publishing, 2006), pp. 16–22.

18. For the *Analects,* see Part III, Selection 34.—Eds.

19. *Hanshu* 87b.3580. [This led Han Yu, many centuries later, to praise Yang Xiong as one of
the few comparatively "pure" Confucians of the past. See Han Yu, "On Reading Xunzi," in
Part III, Selection 21.—Eds.]

20. "Classical Studies" is *rú* 儒, the term conventionally translated as "Confucian."—Eds.

21. *Analects* 3.24 quotes a border official as telling Kongzi's disciples: "The world has been
without the Way for a long while, but Heaven is going to use [Kongzi] as the wooden clapper
of [its] bell." Yang combines this metaphor with that of Kongzi's carriage, which symbolizes
the teaching of the master's doctrines.

polishes these things, of what use are they? Their basic substance is a matter for sharpening and polishing. To do otherwise is to inhibit one's substance."

4. When the caterpillar dies and it encounters the wasp, the wasp prays over it, saying: "Become like me, become like me." After a while, it does come to resemble the wasp! How quickly did the seventy disciples come to resemble Kongzi![22]

5. One who can learn in order to cultivate it, think in order to refine it, make friends in order to sharpen it, gain a reputation in order to exalt it, be tireless in order to follow it to the end—such a person may be said to "love learning."[23]

6. Someone said: "People today speak of casting gold. Is it possible to cast gold?"

Yang replied: "I have heard that 'those who have seen a gentleman ask about casting people, not about casting gold.'"

Someone said: "Is it possible to cast people?"

Yang replied: "Kongzi cast Yan Hui."[24]

Surprised, someone said: "How praiseworthy! I asked about casting gold, and heard about casting people!"

7. Learning is the means by which one cultivates one's nature. Seeing, listening, speaking, appearance, and thought are all parts of one's nature. If one learns, then [these faculties will] all become correct. If one fails, then they will all become bad.

8. The teacher! The teacher! [The teacher] is the fate of the child. To work at learning is not as good as working to find a teacher. The teacher is what molds and shapes people. Molds that do not mold, patterns that do not pattern—there are indeed many of these.

9. A market may only run along a single alley, but one will find different intentions there. A book may only run a single roll of bamboo slips, but one will find different explanations of it. In a market that runs along a single alley, one should set a single price. For a book that runs a single roll of bamboo slips, one should set up a single teacher.

10. Study! Studying the incorrect may defeat the correct, but how much the more may studying the correct defeat the incorrect. Ah! The learner must simply investigate the correct.

Someone said: "How can one know the correct and study it?"

---

22. Certain species of wasp use the caterpillars of moths as food for their young. After the wasp injects its eggs into the host caterpillar, the eggs grow into larvae and eat the host. It was long believed that the wasp transformed the caterpillar into its own kind. Here, Yang uses this as a metaphor for the ethical transformation of Kongzi's disciples.—Eds.

23. Kongzi singled out his most talented disciple, Yan Hui, as one who "loved learning." See Cheng Yi, "What Kind of Learning Was It that Yanzi Loved?" in Part III, Selection 28.—Eds.

24. See the previous note on Yan Hui.—Eds.

Yang replied: "If one sees the sun and moon then one knows the myriad stars are small. If one looks up to the Sage [i.e., Kongzi] then one knows other theories are lesser ones."[25]

11. Someone asked about progress [in ethical cultivation]. Yang replied: "It is like water."

Someone said: "Is that because it flows day and night?"

Yang said: "That's it! When it fills in a place and then progresses onward, is this not true of water?"[26]

Someone asked about the gradual advancement of wild geese.

Yang said: "If it is not a place they are willing to go, then they don't go. If it is not a place they are willing to stay, then they don't stay. Their gradual advancement is like that of water."

Someone asked about the gradual advancement of trees.

Yang said: "Fixed at the base but gradually advancing upward—this is the case with trees. In this they are also like water."

12. Learning is the means to seek to become a gentleman. There are those who seek and never find it, but there has never been a person who found it without seeking.

13. "Horses that aspire to be fast are the same type of horse as fast horses, and people who train to become like Yan Hui are the same kind of person as Yan Hui."

Someone asked: "Is it easy to become the kind of person that Yan Hui was?"

Yang said: "One aspires to it and then attains it."

14. Someone said: "Another piece of writing may say the same thing as a classic, but people today will not respect it. Would you still approve of studying it?"

Yang said: "I would approve."

Someone suddenly laughed and said: "It is necessary to [study] the questions and categories according to which one will be examined!"[27]

Yang said: "'A great person studies for the sake of the Way, a petty person studies for the sake of profit.' Are you doing it for the sake of the Way or for the sake of profit?"

Someone said: "If one plows but does not harvest, or hunts but does not feast on anything, may this be said to plow or to hunt?"[28]

Yang said: "If one plows the Way and attains the Way, if one hunts Virtue

---

25. This borrows a metaphor from the disciple Zigong in *Analects* 19.23: "The worthiness of others is like a small hill that may be surmounted. Kongzi is like the sun or the moon in that he cannot be surmounted."

26. This is an echo of *Analects* 9.17.—Eds.

27. A form of the civil service examinations (a key route to government power) was set up during the Han, and Yang Xiong was an early critic of those who studied simply to pass the examinations, rather than learning to improve their characters.—Eds.

28. Plowing without harvesting is a metaphor for studying without taking office.

and attains Virtue, this is harvesting and feasting. I have never yet seen Shen and Chen [stars from two ends of the sky] next to one another. This is the reason that the gentleman values the transformation to goodness. Isn't one who is transformed to goodness the same kind of person as the Sage? The hundred rivers study the sea and reach the sea; the hills study the mountains yet are unable to reach them. This is why I dislike those who 'draw a line.'"29

15. A group of people who only eat with one another are simply like a flock of crows in wasting grain. To be matched with a person but not in mind is to be a surface match; to be a companion but not in mind is to be a surface companion.

16. Someone said: "The way you earn your livelihood is not as lucrative as that of [the wealthy] Dan Gui."

Yang said: "I have heard that when gentlemen are talking together, then they speak of benevolence and righteousness. When merchants are talking together, they talk about money and profit.30 Is his [way] so lucrative? Is his [way] so lucrative?"

Someone said: "You, my elder, have nothing with which to nourish yourself, and nothing with which to bury yourself after death. Why is this?"

Yang said: "Nourishing oneself with what one has on hand is the epitome of nourishing, just as conducting a burial with what one has is the epitome of burial."

17. Someone said: "Is having the wealth of Yi Dun to [use in] the exercise of filial piety not the best? Yan Hui's [parents] must have starved."

Yang said: "Others supply [their parents] with the coarsest they possess, whereas Yan Hui supplied his with his most refined. Others used what was incorrect, but Yan Hui used what was authentic. Was it Yan who was poor? Was it Yan who was poor?"

18. Someone said: "If I were to wear a red cord holding my metal [seal], my joy would be immeasurable."31

Yang said: "The joy of wearing a red cord holding a metal [seal] is nothing compared to Yanzi's joy.32 Yanzi's joy was internal. The joy of a red ribbon holding the metal seal is external."

Someone said: "Let me ask for the details of his frequently dire straits."

Yang said: "If Yan Hui did not have Kongzi, even were he to have had the rest of the world, it would not have been sufficient for him to be joyful."33

---

29. This is a reference to a passage in which Kongzi condemns a disciple who arbitrarily sets limits to his own ethical development. See *Analects* 6.12, in Part III, Selection 34.—Eds.

30. Yang uses a paraphrase of *Analects* 4.16: "The gentleman's understanding lies in righteousness, while the petty man's understanding lies in profit."

31. The red cord and the metal seal are insignia of government office.—Eds.

32. Yanzi, literally Master Yan, is another way of referring to Yan Hui.—Eds.

33. Yan Hui was praised for being joyful even in poverty. See *Analects* 6.11, in Part III, Selection 34.—Eds.

"Then, did he also have any regrets?"

Yang said: "Yan Hui regretted how far Kongzi's level of development 'loomed above' him."[34]

Someone noted with surprise: "This regret, is it not exactly what made him happy?"

19. Yang said: "Giving instruction and establishing the Way did not stop with Kongzi, and engaging in study that carried on his endeavor did not stop with Yan Hui."

Someone said: "In establishing the Way, Kongzi cannot reflect for us, and in carrying on the endeavor, Yan Hui cannot give us his strength."

Yang said: "If you do not yourself reflect, then who is there to do it for you?"

5. Wang Fu, "Acculturation through Virtue"

From *Discussions of a Recluse*
translation by Mark Csikszentmihalyi

This chapter of Wáng Fú's 王符 *(d. c. 163 CE) Discussions of a Recluse (Qiánfū lùn* 潛夫論*) weaves together historical allusions and quotations of the classics into an essay that encapsulates many important aspects of Han psychology and politics.[35] "Acculturation through Virtue" yokes traditional thinking about the ruler's transformative moral influence to newer theories of the mutual influence of like categories (often called "echo and response between Heaven and humankind" or tiānrén gǎnyìng* 天人感應*) and the embodiment of moral dispositions to create a characteristically Han reflection on ethics and politics. — Tr.*

Out of all the different ways of governing people that have been used by the rulers of men, none is greater than the Way or more vigorous than Virtue; none is better than teaching or more spiritual than acculturation. The Way is how you manage people and Virtue is how you embrace them; teaching is how you make people understand, and acculturation is how you cause them to achieve.

Every person has a nature, feelings, acculturations and customs. Their feelings and natures are part of their minds, and so are fundamental. Their

---

34. This is a reference to *Analects* 9.11, in which Yan Hui describes how demanding the Way of Kongzi is, but also notes that Kongzi is such a skillful teacher that, "even if I wanted to give up I cannot."—Eds.

35. A book-length study and partial translation of the text is Anne Behnke Kinney, *The Art of the Han Essay: Wang Fu's Ch'ien-Fu Lun* (Phoenix: Arizona State University Center for Asian Research, 1990).

acculturations and customs are expressed in their actions, and so are secondary. The secondary is a product of the fundamental, just as actions arise from the mind. This is why the best rulers order the age by putting fundamentals first, and only then are concerned with what is secondary. They are cautious about minds first and only then are concerned with whether their actions accord with the Pattern. If the essence of mind is correct, then corruption and evil intentions have no place to come into being, and heterodoxies gain no support.

Now, acculturation can alter the minds of the people in the same way that good government can alter their bodies. If one applies government by Virtue to the people, then the more healthy, beautiful, strong and long-lived they will become. If one applies governing by vice to the people, then the more deformed, disabled, terminally ill, and short-lived they will become. This is why the *Documents* praises "completing the mandate given by Heaven" and criticizes "suffering an early death."[36]

When a state's government does damage to those who are clear-sighted, then its people will develop eye disorders.[37] When its government does damage to those who are sharp-eared, then its people will develop hearing problems. When its government does damage to the wise, then its people perish young of accidental death. Now, even if a person's physical form and skeleton are strong, they will still be altered by the nature of the government. How much the more would this be the case if one's mind and *qi* are too subtle to be nourished?[38]

The *Odes* says: "So thick are the rushes at the roadside, / the sheep and oxen do not walk over them. / Their roots and their stems, / their leaves are lush." It also says: "The hawk flies into the sky, / the fish jump in the depths of the sea. / Content is the gentleman, / how can he but influence others?"[39] [Zhou dynasty ancestor] Duke Liu had such generous Virtue that his kindness reached to the plants, sheep, oxen, and other animals. Moreover, each generated a response of Virtue, such that the benevolent could not bear to tread on living grass. How much more could an ordinary person not become acculturated?

When a gentleman cultivates his Virtue of contentment such that above it reaches to the flying birds, and below it reaches to the fish in the depths of the sea, no one is not happy and joyous. How could an official or ordinary person not become benevolent?

---

36. *Documents, Documents of Zhou*, "Great Plan," where the former is one of the "five sources of happiness" and the latter is one of the "six extreme evils." [See the "Great Plan," in Part I, Selection 8, Selections on the Five Phases, which translates these phrases somewhat differently.—Eds.]

37. I have left out a number of lines of the traditional edition of this chapter that are between the parallel sentences beginning "When a state's government does damage to those who are clear-sighted" and "When its government does damage to those who are sharp-eared."

38. See Selections on *Qi*, in Part I, Selection 6.—Eds.

39. *Odes* 246 and 239.

The sage is deeply cognizant of this, and so works to correct himself in order to serve as a standard for others, to be a clear model of ritual and righteousness in order to instruct others. Sages harmonize virtuous *qi* prior to birth, and correct external ceremonies from when they first began to laugh. When people are in utero, they join in finding their proper place and so reach completion; when they are born they stand erect and straight and so mature. This is how they reach the point that their minds are benevolent and righteous, and their intentions honorable. Their bones lengthen and their vessels have good circulation, all thrive inside the body, devoid of muddy and dirty *qi* or desires that are corrupt.

Though one might end up on the other side of the hinterlands or down in the darkest depths, in the end one would still not act contrary to the rituals. Though one could be thrown into a fatal situation, or placed in a forest of knives and spears, in the end one would not think to preserve oneself at all costs. If the actions of one's contemporaries are all of this kind, then why would it be necessary to punish disruptive people for what succeeds or fails?

"The transports of Heaven above have neither sound nor smell; / If one's ceremonies use King Wen as their model, / then the myriad states will trust you as leader."[40] This explains why the Ji clan [that ruled the Zhou] was celebrated and praised by people in the past and used as exemplars by those who came later.

This is the reason that the highest level of sage did not work to govern human affairs, but rather worked to govern their minds. This is why [Kongzi] said: "In hearing legal cases I am like any other person. What is necessary is to make it so there are no legal cases," and "lead them with Virtue, and order them with ritual."[41] If he works to make his feelings more generous and understanding, and so working on his duties, the people will take care of those close to them and not harbor intentions to injure one another. In their actions, they will think of their duty and never have thoughts of evil. A situation like this may neither be achieved through laws and statutes, not forced on people through the threat of punishment, but rather is something that is the product of instruction and acculturation.[42]

The sages deeply revered Virtuous rituals and disparaged punishments. That is why Shun first admonished Xie by "respectfully bestowing the five teachings," and afterwards charged Gao Yao with administering the "five disfiguring punishments" and the "three levels of banishment."[43] This is why in all cases in which laws were promulgated, it was not done in order to sniff out the shortcomings of the people and apply capital punishment to their more extreme errors, but rather to prevent their avarice and rescue them from disaster, restraining them from the vicious so they can accept the correct Way.

---

40. *Odes* 235.

41. Quoting *Analects* 12.13 and 2.3.

42. This paragraph has been moved from earlier in the traditional text.

43. *Documents, Documents of Yu,* "Canon of Shun."

The *Odes* says: "This is the constant that people cleave to. / They are fond of this beautiful Virtue."[44] So the people's minds are like farmers' fields. If they encounter harmonious *qi* then they will become lush and abundant, but if their source of water dries up they will wither and die. When a people inherit good culture, then their minds will be those of officers and gentlemen. However, when they grapple with bad government, then their thoughts will turn to treachery and rebellion.

Therefore, those who are good at nourishing the people of Heaven are like an expert making fermented soybeans. This person will store it according to the season and appropriate to the temperature outdoors. He ends up with a cellar full of tasty bean sauce. But someone who is bad at making it will end up with a cellar full of useless muck. Now, the world in every direction is akin to a cellar, and the black-haired people who inhabit it are like the bean seedlings. Their "changes and transformations, speech and action,"[45] are purely a matter of the future. If they encounter quality officials then they will be all faithful and conscientious, acting with benevolence and generosity. However, if they meet bad officials then they will be all crafty and evil, and their conduct will be ignorant. As conscientiousness and acts of generosity accumulate, an era of Great Peace will arise. As craftiness and acts of ignorance accumulate, things will fall into peril.

This is why sagely emperors and clear-sighted kings all valued acculturation by Virtue, and denigrated the fear of punishment. Virtue has always been the way that one cultivates oneself, while fear is the way that one governs others. Those who are "the loftiest of the wise" or "the most lowly of the ignorant" are few, and most people are close to the mean.[46] The birth of these ordinary people is like the smelting of metal by using a bamboo mold to change its shape. Whether it is smelted into a circular or square shape, whether it ends up thick or thin, is wholly determined by the mold.

This is the reason that the moral quality of an age and the depth of its customs all rest with its leader.

- The best leader is a Sage able to harmonize *qi* in a way that acculturates the minds of the people and corrects moral standards so that they lead their subordinates. This is why every household and its neighbor contained people worthy of commission as officials. Yao and Shun were at this level.[47]
- The next best embodied the Way and Virtue, and valued kindness and caring. They praised education and training, and revered ritual

---

44. *Odes* 260. Compare *Mengzi* 6A6, in Part III, Selection 35.—Eds.

45. *Changes*, "Great Appendix," II.12. This expression is used to talk about how the sages came to know how to read the present to know the future using the hexagrams.

46. *Analects* 17.3, in Part III, Selection 34.—Eds.

47. On these and the other historical figures mentioned below, see the Introduction to Part I.—Eds.

propriety and yielding. This is how they were able to rid the people of bellicosity, and were able to set up unused laws. Wen and Wu were at this level.

- The next best made known their likes and dislikes, and publicized their penal laws and prohibitions. They made rewards and punishments fair and eliminated selfishness. This is how they could cause their people to avoid things that are crafty and evil and be attracted to those that promote the public good. It is how they imparted a Pattern on the weak and disordered to make them strong and well-governed. The flourishing period [of the early Zhou dynasty] was an example of this.

- Those who govern the people of the world who dwell in filth and give free rein to their feelings, are inattentive to the affairs of their people while caught up in wine and music. They hang with wild youth while keeping their distance from the worthy and talented, stay close to flatterers while avoiding truth-tellers. They increase taxes so they can reward those who have done nothing; following their moods they do injury to the innocent. This is how they managed to disorder their government and lose their people, benefit themselves while dooming their state. Kings You and Li were examples of this.[48]

Kongzi said, "Even when walking in a group of three people, the others may certainly be my teachers. I see what is good in them and emulate it, and what is not and correct those points in myself."[49] The *Odes* praises "Using the example of the Shang [kings] as a mirror," and "being able to seek good fortune on one's own."[50] So with Sincerity the ruler of an age can affect the world in every direction, can promote those contemporaries who have nothing but magnanimous feelings and are devoid of petty vices, so that each one promotes the public interest ahead of their private wants. This is how the customs under Fu Xi and Shen Nong may reappear in the present, and how unicorns, dragons and phoenixes may once again find places to settle.

---

48. Li and You were notoriously bad kings whose misrule helped bring the Western Zhou dynasty to an end.—Eds.

49. *Analects* 7.22.

50. *Mao* 235. In the context of the *Odes*, both these quotations relate to the importance of the Mandate of Heaven that authorizes the ruler, but here those phrases are not quoted.

Cosmology

6. Selections on *Qi*

Qì 氣 *is a central cosmological notion in Chinese thought, but is one of the most difficult for Westerners to fully grasp. As the selection below from the* Huainanzi *indicates, qi is the fundamental "stuff" out of which everything condenses. It is therefore tempting to identify it with the Western notion of "matter." However, qi is unlike matter as conceived of by classical physics in that it is self-generating and self-moving; qi is also unlike the mass-energy of contemporary physics in that it is not conceptualized as quantized. (Perhaps the closest Western equivalent is the* apeiron, *"Boundless," referred to by the pre-Socratic philosopher Anaximander.[1]) Although qi is the most fundamental stuff of the universe, it can also manifest as specific types. Different works will give different characterizations of what these types of qi are, but the selection below from the* Zuo Commentary on the Spring and Autumn Annals *is a typical example. Finally, as the quotation below from the* Analects *illustrates, qi is closely associated with human emotional and physical states. "Qi" has been translated in a variety of ways, including "psychophysical stuff," "material force," "vital energy," and "ether." Each of these translations brings out some aspects of the concept of qi but not others. Consequently, we have chosen to simply Romanize the term in this anthology. —Eds.*

"Lesson on the Configuration of Heaven," *Huainanzi* 3
translation by Bryan W. Van Norden

The Way first created vacuity. Vacuity created space and time. Space and time created *qi*. There was a boundary between the clear, subtle *qi* that rose to become Heaven, and the heavy, turbid *qi* that congealed to become Earth. Because it was quite easy for the clear, subtle *qi* to unite, but very difficult for the heavy and turbid *qi* to congeal, Heaven was completed first and Earth was only fixed afterward. The most refined *qi* became *yin* and *yang*.[2] The most refined *yin* and

---

1. Benjamin Schwartz, *The World of Thought in Ancient China* (Cambridge, MA: Harvard University Press, 1985), p. 183.

2. See Selections on *Yin* and *Yang,* in Part I, Selection 7.

yang became the four seasons. The dispersed *qi* of the four seasons became the myriad things. The accumulated *yang* of hot *qi* created fire, and the most refined fiery *qi* became the Sun. The accumulated *yin* of cold *qi* became water, and the most refined of watery *qi* became the Moon. The refined excess of the Sun and the Moon became the stars and planets. Heaven accepted the Sun, Moon, stars, and planets, while Earth accepted bodies of water and land.

Zuo Commentary on the Spring and Autumn Annals, Duke Zhao, Year 1
translation by James Legge[3]

The marquis of Jin was ill and asked the help of a physician from Qin, and the earl sent one to see him, who said, "The disease cannot be cured. It is said that, when one becomes intimate with women, the chamber disease can become like insanity. The illness of the Marquis is not caused by spirits nor by food. It is that obsession which has destroyed his mind. Your outstanding minister will also die; it is not the will of Heaven to preserve him."

The marquis said, "So may one not be intimate with women?"

The physician replied, "Yes, but relations with them must be regulated. The ancient kings indicated by their music how all other things should be regulated. Hence there are the five regular intervals. Either slow or quick, from beginning to end, they blend with one another. Each note rests in the exact intermediate place; and when the five are thus determined, no further exercise on the instruments is permitted. Thus the gentleman does not listen to music with licentious notes, pleasing the ears but injurious to the mind, where the rules of equable harmony are forgotten. So it is with all things. When they come to this, they should stop; if they do not do so, it produces disease. The gentleman plays the zither to illustrate his observance of rules, and not merely to delight his mind.

"Similarly, Heaven has six *qi*, which descend and create the five tastes, are expressed in the five colors, and are verified in the five notes; but when they are in excess, they produce the six diseases. Those six *qi* are called *yin*, *yang*, wind, rain, obscurity, and brightness. In their separation, they form the four seasons; in their order, they form the five periods. When any of them is in excess, there ensues calamity. An excess of the *yin* leads to diseases of cold; of the *yang*, to diseases of heat; of wind, to diseases of the extremities; of rain, to diseases of the belly; of obscurity, to diseases of obsession; of brightness, to diseases of the mind. The desire for a woman is something *yang* that should be done in darkness. If this be done to excess, disease is produced of internal heat and utter

---

3. Reprinted with modifications from James Legge, *The Chinese Classics, Volume 5, The Ch'un ts'ew, with the Tso chuen* (London: Trübner, 1872).

delusion. Was it possible for your lordship, paying no regard to moderation or to time, not to come to this?"

Analects 16.7
translation by Bryan W. Van Norden

Kongzi said, "The gentleman guards against three things. When he is young and the *qi* of his blood is not settled, he guards against lust. When he becomes mature and the *qi* of his blood is vigorous, he guards against combativeness. When he is old and the *qi* of his blood has declined, he guards against acquisitiveness."

Dong Zhongshu, "The Way of the
King Links Up the Three"
From *Luxuriant Dew of the Spring and Autumn Annals* 44
translation by Sharon Sanderovitch

This is the continuation of the selection from the Luxuriant Dew of the Spring and Autumn Annals *translated earlier (Part I, Selection 2). The following section frames the obligations of the ruler in terms of a correlative cosmology in which the ruler's emotions correspond to the seasons. By manifesting emotions appropriately (e.g., being angry only at those who deserve it, taking joy only in the good) the king helps maintain the natural order of the cosmos, ensuring good harvests and avoiding natural disasters. —Eds.*

The manifestations of joy and anger, grief and delight, are of the same type as chill and warmth, cold and heat.[4] The *qi* of joy functions as warmth and serves as spring. The *qi* of anger functions to chill [the world] and serves as autumn. The *qi* of delight functions as the Sun [literally, Great Yang] and serves as summer. The *qi* of grief functions as the Moon [literally, Great Yin] and serves as winter. These four types of *qi* are possessed by both Heaven and humans. They are not something one can raise on one's own. Therefore, they can be regulated but cannot be stopped. Regulate them, and one will achieve compliance. Stop them up and one will reap chaos.

Human beings are born from Heaven, and undergo transformation from Heaven: the *qi* of joy is derived from spring; the *qi* of delight is derived from summer; the *qi* of anger is derived from autumn; and the *qi* of grief is derived

---

4. I have removed a clause that seems out of place from the beginning of this paragraph.

from winter. These are the emotions of the four kinds of *qi*.[5] Each of the four limbs has its designated place—so do the four seasons. Cold and heat cannot change places—neither can the body's limbs. When limbs change their places, we call it a person who will die prematurely.[6] When cold and heat change their places, we call it a failed harvest. When joy and anger change their places, we call it a chaotic age.

An enlightened king corrects his joy to match the spring; corrects his anger to match the autumn; corrects his delight to match the summer; and corrects his grief to match the winter. Superiors and inferiors all emulate this, and thereby adopt the Way of Heaven. The *qi* of spring is loving; the *qi* of autumn is stern; the *qi* of summer is delight; the *qi* of winter is grief. With the *qi* of love one gives birth to things; with the *qi* of sternness one gets results; with the *qi* of delight one cultivates life; with the *qi* of grief one mourns the deceased—these are Heaven's intentions. For this reason, the *qi* of spring is warm and with it Heaven gives care and life to all things; the *qi* of autumn is chilly and with it Heaven shows sternness and brings things to completion; the *qi* of summer is mildly hot, and with it Heaven delights and nourishes things; the *qi* of winter is cold, and with it Heaven grieves and stores things away. The spring governs birth; the summer governs nourishment; the autumn governs harvesting; the winter governs storage. After birth, one channels one's delight into providing nourishment; after death, one channels one's grief into providing burial—this is being a parent or a child. Therefore, the operation of the four seasons is the same as the Way of father and son; the intention of Heaven and Earth is the same as the proper relationship between sovereign and minister; the principle of *yin* and *yang* is the same as the laws of the sage.[7] *Yin* is the *qi* of punishment; *yang* is the *qi* of virtue. *Yin* begins in autumn; *yang* begins in spring.

The word "spring" (*chūn* 春) sounds like "cheerful" (*chǔn chǔn* 惷惷). The word "autumn" (*qiū* 秋) sounds like "sorrowful" (*qiū qiū* 湫湫). "Cheerful" is the appearance of joy and delight. "Sorrowful" is the state of sadness and sorrow. Thus, spring is joy, summer is delight, autumn is sadness, and winter is sorrow: sorrow over death and delight in life. With summer to nurture [that which was born in the] spring, and with winter to store up [that which was harvested in the] autumn—this is the intention of the Great Man. Therefore, to first show care and only then sternness, to delight in life and grieve over death, is the proper [Way] of Heaven. People inherit this from Heaven. Heaven inherently has this, and the human body is the same.

The human ruler stands in the position in charge of life and death, so shares with Heaven the power of transformation. Among the myriad things, all are responsive to Heaven's transformations. The transformation of Heaven and Earth

---

5. "Emotions" translates *xīn* 心, which in other contexts is rendered "mind."

6. Reading *tiān* 天 as *yāo* 夭.

7. See the Selections on *Yin* and *Yang,* in Part I, Selection 7.

resembles the operation of the four seasons: When the wind of approval arises, it takes the form of warm *qi* and gives fertility to the people. When the wind of disapproval arises, it takes the form of chilly *qi* and sows death among the people. When the wind of joy arises, it takes the form of hot *qi* and has the impact of nourishment and cultivation. When the wind of anger arises, it takes the form of cold *qi* and has the impact of blocking and stopping up [proper circulation]. The human ruler transforms conventional behaviors by means of approval and disapproval, joy and anger. Heaven stirs transformations in grasses and trees by means of warmth, chill, cold, and heat. When joy and anger are timely and proper, the harvest is excellent; when it is untimely and capricious, the harvest is poor. Heaven, Earth, and the human ruler are one.

Thus, the likes and dislikes, joy and anger, of the human ruler, correspond to the warmth, chill, cold, and heat of Heaven. It is not acceptable to issue them forth without carefully considering the proper situation. To have cold when heat is proper, to have heat when cold is proper, would inevitably result in a bad harvest. For the ruler of humankind, to manifest anger when joy is proper, to manifest joy when anger is proper, would inevitably result in a disordered age. For this reason, the great duty of the human ruler is to prudently hold back and yet avoid keeping it inside: to have likes and dislikes, joy and anger, and yet manifest them only when appropriate—like having warmth, chill, cold, and heat issued forth only when timely. A human ruler who holds fast to this principle and does not lose it, who has likes and dislikes, joy and anger, yet never misses the mark—just like spring, autumn, winter, and summer never miss their proper time—can be said to be matching Heaven. One who deeply treasures these four and does not manifest them capriciously can be called Heaven.

7. Selections on *Yin* and *Yang*

Originally, yáng 陽 referred to the sunny side of a hill, while yīn 陰 referred to the shady side. From there, the terms came to be extended to a potentially infinite list of complementary aspects of a thing or situation. For example, bright, rising, dominant, and active are yang characteristics, while dark, falling, submissive, and passive are yin characteristics. Yin and yang are mutually dependent. There cannot be one without the other, and the proper functioning of anything depends upon maintaining the appropriate balance between them. Below are two brief selections from the Luxuriant Dew of the Spring and Autumn Annals, *attributed to Dong Zhongshu, and an excerpt from* The Classic of Sunü.[8] *They illustrate how yin and yang can be*

---

8. For an introduction to Dong Zhongshu and *the Luxuriant Dew of the Spring and Autumn Annals,* see Part I, Selection 1.

applied in a wide variety of contexts, including cosmology, political philosophy, medicine, and even human sexuality.[9]*—Eds.*

Dong Zhongshu, *Luxuriant Dew of
the Spring and Autumn Annals*
translation by Mark Csikszentmihalyi[10]

Dong Zhongshu believed that the natural and proper relationship between yin *and* yang *is continually revealed to human beings through the behaviors and relationships between objects in the natural world. In the* Luxuriant Dew of the Spring and Autumn Annals, yin *and* yang *are likened to the sun and moon and Heaven and Earth. In turn, "the model of man and woman takes as its prototype* yin *and* yang" *(Chapter 76). For Dong,* yin *and* yang *are neither equal and complementary nor opposite and of radically different value. At times,* yin *is associated with what is clearly the negative pole of a contrast: the greedy part of human nature, as opposed to the benevolent* yang *side. In the same vein, it is the threat of* yin *overwhelming* yang *that is the subject of more discussion in the text. In this sense, it is clear that* yang *is more generally associated with positive characteristics. At the same time,* yin *and* yang *are associated with oppositions in which both sides are necessary. As a result, although* yang *receives precedence, the model of the natural world clearly dictates that both* yang *and* yin *have their own proper place and function.* —Tr.

53: "The Foundation of Righteousness"

In all cases, things necessarily are complementary. Complementary means that there necessarily is a top and a bottom, a left and a right, a front and a back, an exterior and an interior. If there is beauty there must be ugliness; if there is agreement there must be opposition; if there is happiness there must be anger; if there is cold then there must be heat; if there is day then there must be night. They are all complements. *Yin* is *yang*'s complement, a wife is a husband's complement, a son is a father's complement, and a subject is a ruler's complement. Everything in the world has a complement, and each instance of complementarity has *yin* and *yang*. *Yin* is connected with *yang* and *yang* is connected with *yin*; a husband is connected with a wife as a wife is connected with a husband; a father is

---

9. See also the selections from the *Changes,* in Part I, Selections 9 and 10.

10. Translation and translator's introduction reprinted with modifications from Robin R. Wang, ed., *Images of Women in Chinese Thought and Culture* (Indianapolis: Hackett Publishing, 2003), p. 168.

connected with a son as a son is connected with a father; a ruler is connected with a subject as a subject is connected with a ruler. The obligations of a ruler and subject, father and son, husband and wife, all are taken from the Way of *yin* and *yang*. The ruler is *yang* and the subject is *yin*; the father is *yang* and the son is *yin*; the husband is *yang*, and the wife is *yin*.

The Way of *yin* is devoid of anything that acts on its own. Neither at its beginning is it able to arise on its own, nor at its end is it able to achieve something separate—which is the meaning of being connected to something. This is why the minister's achievement is connected to the ruler, the son's achievement is connected to the father, the wife's achievement is connected to the husband, and the Earth's achievement is connected to Heaven.

43: "*Yang* Is Exalted, *Yin* Is Humble"

. . . Heaven takes *yin* as the exception as *yang* as the norm. *Yang* emerges and flows south, while *yin* emerges and flows north. The norm is used when a thing is flourishing, while the exception is used when it is ending. Looking at things from this perspective, Heaven makes norms obvious while hiding exceptions; Virtue is first and only later comes punishment. This is why it is said: "*Yang* is the Virtue of Heaven, and *yin* the punishment of Heaven."

Yang qi is warm while *yin qi* is cold; *yang qi* gives while *yin qi* takes away; *yang qi* is benevolent while *yin qi* is criminal; *yang qi* is lenient while *yin qi* is severe; *yang qi* is caring while *yin qi* is hateful; *yang qi* gives life while *yin qi* kills. That is why *yang qi* always dwells in meaningful positions and acts when a thing is flourishing, while *yin qi* dwells in empty positions and acts when a thing is ending.[11]

Classic of Sunü
translation by Ellen Zhang[12]

Sunü was a female advisor to the sagacious Yellow Emperor. The Classic of Sunü *is essentially a sex manual, but one that sees sex as both part of a healthy life and also a manifestation of the underlying* yin/yang *structure of the universe. According to Sunü, the most fundamental sexual technique a man should practice to achieve long life is to "control his emissions": avoid ejaculating, in order to conserve his precious* yang *essence. —Eds.*

---

11. See the Selections on *Qi* in Part I, Selection 6.

12. Translation reprinted with modifications from Robin R. Wang, ed., *Images of Women in Chinese Thought and Culture* (Indianapolis: Hackett Publishing, 2003), p. 192.

The Yellow Emperor asks Sunü, "I am feeling a lack of energy and a disharmony in my body. I am sad and apprehensive. What shall I do about this?"

Sunü replied, "Men are likely to make a mistake during lovemaking. Women conquer men as water conquers fire. Those who know the art of lovemaking are like those who know how to mix the five flavors in a cooking pot to produce a good meal, and like those who know the way of *yin* and *yang* and enjoy the five pleasures. Those who are ignorant of this art die young, without enjoying the pleasure of life. . . . A man must know how to control his emissions and also take medicine. He cannot enjoy life if he is ignorant of the art of love. Men and women are like Heaven and Earth, whose eternal nature lies in their unity. . . . Those who understand the principle of *yin* and *yang* will experience immortality."

The Yellow Emperor asks, "What will happen if one abstains from sex?"

Sunü replies, "That is absolutely out of the question. *Yin* and *yang* have their alterations, as does everything in nature. Human beings should follow the rhythms of *yin* and *yang* just as they follow the changes of the season."

The Yellow Emperor asks, "What are the essential elements that bring about a harmonious union of *yin* and *yang*?"

Sunü replies, "For a man, the essential element is to avoid weakening his strength; for a woman, what is important is orgasm. Those who do not follow this method will decline into weakness."

8. Selections on the Five Phases

The Five Phases (wǔ xíng 五行) are Metal, Wood, Water, Fire, and Earth. "Five Phases" is sometimes translated as "Five Elements," but this is very misleading. In Aristotelian science, earth, water, fire, and air were regarded as the four elements, the underlying constituents that composed everything in the everyday world. In contrast, the Five Phases of the Chinese tradition are categories, not substances. One of the functions of these categories is to correlate phenomena. Following is a sample of some of the many correspondence categories of the Five Phases:

Wood	Jupiter	Blue-green	Spleen	Sour	East	Spring
Fire	Mars	Red	Lungs	Bitter	South	Summer
Earth	Saturn	Yellow	Heart	Sweet	Center	
Metal	Venus	White	Kidney	Spicy	West	Autumn
Water	Mercury	Black	Liver	Salty	North	Winter

As the examples of the compass directions and the seasons illustrate, when the Five Phases are correlated with four items, Earth is treated as an intermediary between the other items.

The Five Phases also identify stages in a process. Sometimes what is relevant is the generating sequence: Wood produces Fire, Fire produces Earth, Earth produces Metal, Metal produces Water, and Water produces Wood. Other times, what is relevant is the overcoming sequence: Wood is conquered by Metal, Metal is conquered by Fire, Fire is conquered by Water, Water is conquered by Earth, and Earth is conquered by Wood.

The following selections illustrate more concretely how the Five Phases are used to categorize and explain. —Eds.

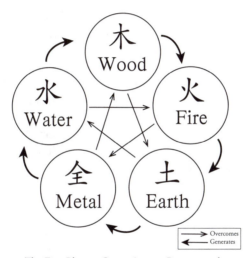

The Five Phases: Outer Arrows Represent the Generation Sequence, while Inner Arrows Represent the Overcoming Sequence.

"Resonating with Things of the Same Kind"
From *Spring and Autumn Annals of Lü Buwei* 13.2
translation by Bryan W. Van Norden

The following selection illustrates the role of the Five Phases both in correlating phenomena and in explaining sequences of change. Each of four legendary sage rulers is associated with one of the Five Phases. For example, the correlation of the sage-king Yu, founder of the Xia dynasty, with Wood explains why the appropriate omens for his reign were grasses and trees that did not wither or lose their leaves, and why it was fitting for his royal color to be green. In addition, the conquest sequence of the phases explains why, when the Xia dynasty decayed, it was defeated by Tang, whose dynasty was associated with the Metal phase. This selection was written before the founding of the Han dynasty, so it does not identify what the successor to the Zhou dynasty will be, but it is confident that it will be a dynasty associated with the Water phase, since the Zhou dynasty is correlated with Fire, and Water overcomes Fire. — Tr.

Whenever a new emperor or king is about to arise, Heaven will invariably make omens appear to the people below. When it was time for the Yellow Emperor, Heaven first made huge earthworms and mole crickets appear. The Yellow Emperor announced, "The *qi* of Earth is ascendant."[13] Because the *qi* of Earth was ascendant, yellow was his royal color, and his activities were those that corresponded to Earth.[14] When it came to be time for Yu, Heaven first caused to appear grasses and trees that did not wither or lose their leaves in the autumn or the winter. Yu announced, "The *qi* of Wood is ascendant." Because the *qi* of Wood was ascendant, green was his imperial color, and his activities were those that corresponded to Wood. When it came to be time for Tang, Heaven first made metal swords appear from the water. Tang announced, "The *qi* of Metal is ascendant." Because the *qi* of Metal was ascendant, white was his imperial color, and his activities were those that correspond to Metal. When it came to be time for King Wen, Heaven first made fire appear, and a red bird holding a crimson scroll alighted upon the altar of the Zhou people. King Wen announced, "The *qi* of Fire is ascendant." Because the *qi* of Fire was ascendant, red was his imperial color, and his activities were those that corresponded to Fire. To attack Fire, one must use Water. Consequently, Heaven will first manifest the ascendancy of the *qi* of Water. When the *qi* of Water is ascendant, the royal color will be black, and the activities will be those that correspond to Water. When the *qi* of Water has unconsciously completed its time and its years are complete, it will shift to Earth again. "Heaven makes the season, but does not help those below to farm."

Things of the same kind summon each other. *Qi* of the same kind harmonize, and notes respond to one another. Thus, if you pluck the C string on one zither, the C string on another zither will start to vibrate, while if you pluck the F string

---

13. See Selections on *Qi,* in Part I, Selection 6.

14. Because of the broad range of correlations associated with the Five Phases, the "activities" relevant to a particular phase could range over the kinds of food the emperor ate, the kinds of music he listened to, what sorts of governmental activities his rule emphasized (e.g., agricultural, military, criminal, public works, government reform), and so on.

on one zither, the F string on another zither will start to vibrate.[15] If you pour Water on level ground, it will flow to where it is already moist, while if you apply Fire to two equal pieces of wood, it will go to the one that is drier.

Attributed to Dong Zhongshu, "The Meaning of the Five Phases" From *Luxuriant Dew of the Spring and Autumn Annals* 42 translation by Mark Csikszentmihalyi[16]

"The Meaning of the Five Phases" has two different goals: to argue for Earth as the supreme phase, and to argue for the behavior of the Five Phases as a model for the behavior in the human realm. The former goal is consistent with the late second- and first-century BCE identification of the Han with the Earth phase (prior to 104 BCE it aligned itself with Water, and after 26 CE, with Fire).[17] The latter goal justifies filial piety and loyalty as "natural" and uses the sequence of the Five Phases to justify hierarchies among officials. This essay is attributed to Dong Zhongshu, but it was probably actually written in the first century BCE. — Tr.

Nature has Five Phases. The first is called "Wood," the second "Fire," the third "Earth," the fourth "Metal," and the fifth "Water." Wood is the beginning of the Five Phases, Water is the end, and Earth is the center. This is their naturally arranged sequence. Wood produces Fire, Fire produces earth, Earth produces Metal, Metal produces Water, and Water produces Wood. This is their "parent–child relationship." Wood resides on the left, Metal on the right, Fire in front, Water in back, and Earth in the center. This is the sequence of their "parent–child relationships," according to which they sustain one another and so they are distributed in this way. This is the reason that Wood sustains Water, Fire sustains Wood, Metal sustains Earth, and Water sustains Metal.

What bestows anything is always called the "parent," what accepts it is always called the "child." Constantly relying on the parent to direct the child is the Way of Heaven. This is the reason that once Wood is born, Fire nourishes it. Once

---

15. This is an authentic phenomenon that is familiar to contemporary musicians. It is relevant to the Five Phases because, in the pentatonic (five-note) scale of traditional Chinese music, the note *gong* (C) corresponds to Earth, and the note *jue* (F) corresponds to Wood.

16. Translation and introduction reprinted with modifications from Mark Csikszentmihalyi, trans., *Readings in Han Chinese Thought* (Indianapolis: Hackett Publishing, 2006), pp. 175–79.

17. Compare the selections from "Resonating with Things of the Same Kind," above.

Metal dies, Water collects it. Fire takes pleasure in Wood and so nourishes it with *yang;* Water defeats Metal and so attends to its funeral with *yin;* and Earth serves Fire with the utmost loyalty.[18] Therefore, the Five Phases are actually the actions of the filial child and the loyal minister.[19]

Is what people routinely called the "Five Phases" the same as the "Five Kinds of Action"? This is exactly the reason that they got that name.

The sages understood this. Therefore, they [established the imperatives that parents should] intensify their caring and diminish their strictness, and [children should] generously nourish them in life and attend to their funerals after death as "natural regulations." If as a child one's approach to one's elders is to nourish them like Fire taking pleasure in Wood, if one attends to one's parent's funeral like Water defeating Metal, and if one serves the ruler like Earth reveres Heaven, then one may be called "a person of action."

The Five Phases move each according to its place in the sequence. The Five Phases take office, each giving play to its own abilities. Therefore, Wood has its place in the east, and authority over spring *qi.* Fire has its place in the south, and authority over the summer *qi.* Metal has its place in the west, and authority over autumn *qi.* Water has its place in the north, and authority over winter *qi.* This is the reason that Wood has authority over life, Metal has authority over death, Fire has authority over heat, and Water has authority over cold. Human beings have no choice but to go by their sequence, and officials have no choice but to go by their abilities. For such are "Heaven's procedures."

Earth has its place in the center and is called "Heaven's moistening." Earth is Heaven's "right hand,"[20] and its virtue is verdant and beautiful. It cannot be assigned a name restricting it to the events of a single season. Therefore, among the Five Phases and four seasons, it is Earth that is universal. Metal, Wood, Water, and Fire each have their own duties, but if they did not depend on Earth they could not establish their direction, just as sour, salty, spicy, and bitter would not be able to become tastes if they did not rely on sweet. Sweet is the basis for the five tastes, just as Earth is the ruler of the Five Phases. That the Five Phases are ruled by the *qi* of Earth is like the five tastes' having the sweet: without it they could not come about. This is the reason that none of the sage's actions are as valuable as loyalty, and [loyalty] is called the "virtue of Earth."

---

18. See Selections on *Yin* and *Yang*, in Part I, Selection 7.

19. In this sentence, "phases" and "action" are the same word in Chinese. Whereas *xíng* 行 is conventionally translated as "phase" in the context of "Five Phases," as a noun in this sentence it means "conduct" or "action." Indeed, the term "Five Phases" was also applied to Confucian virtues and so might be translated as "Five Kinds of Action." In the Han, the latter sense of "Five Phases" was changed to "Five Virtues (*wǔdé* 五德, sometimes translated as "Five Powers"), which is the sense in which the phase "Virtue of Earth" (*tǔdé* 土德) is used later in the essay to refer to loyalty.

20. *Gǔgōng* 股肱 literally means "thigh and upper arm" but here connotes a vital assistant.

For the greatest offices in the human realm, the duties are not named. The [office of] chancellor is an example of this. For the greatest offices in the Heavenly realm, what they produce is not named. Earth is an example of this.

"Great Plan"
From *Documents, Documents of Zhou*
translation by James Legge[21]

The "Great Plan" presents the nine basic principles of government that Heaven gave to King Yu, the founder of the first Chinese dynasty, the Xia. The text includes an influential explanation of the Five Phases, which are implicitly correlated with other sets of five phenomena, including the five flavors of traditional Chinese cooking, the five virtues of a ruler, the five "dividers of time," the five sources of happiness, and the five causes of suffering. —Eds.

The first is called "the Five Phases"; the second, "reverent attention to the five [personal] matters"; the third, "earnest devotion to the eight [goals of] government"; the fourth, "the harmonious use of the five dividers of time"; the fifth, "the establishment and use of royal perfection"; the sixth, "the discriminating use of the three virtues"; the seventh, "the intelligent use of [the means for] the examination of doubts"; the eighth, "the thoughtful use of the various omens"; the ninth, "the hortatory use of the five [sources of] happiness, and the awing use of the six [occasions of] suffering."

1. Of the Five Phases, the first is Water; the second is Fire; the third, Wood; the fourth, Metal; and the fifth, Earth. [The nature of] Water is to soak and descend; of Fire, to blaze and ascend; of Wood, to be crooked and straight; of Metal, to yield and change; while [that of] Earth is seen in sowing seeds and in gathering. That which soaks and descends becomes salty; that which blazes and ascends becomes bitter; that which is crooked and straight becomes sour; that which yields and changes becomes spicy; and from sowing seeds and gathering comes sweetness.

2. Of the five [personal] matters, the first is the bodily demeanor; the second, speech; the third, seeing; the fourth, hearing; the fifth, thinking.[22] [The virtue of] the bodily appearance is respectfulness; of speech, accordance [with

---

21. Reprinted with modifications from James Legge, *The Chinese Classics,* Volume 3, *The Shoo King* (London: Trübner, 1865).

22. These five "matters" are represented as being in the human person what the five *xing* (phases) are in nature. Demeanor is the human correspondence of water, speech that of fire, etc.

the Way]; of seeing, clearness; of hearing distinctness; of thinking, perspicaciousness. The respectfulness becomes manifest in dignity; accordance [with the
Way], in orderliness; the clearness, in wisdom; the dignity, in deliberation; and
the perspicaciousness, in sagacity.

3. Of the eight [goals of] government, the first is food; the second, wealth
and articles of convenience; the third, sacrifices; the fourth, the responsibilities
of the Minister of Works; the fifth, that of the Minister of Instruction; the sixth,
that of the Minister of Crime; the seventh, the observances to be paid to guests;
the eighth, the army.

4. Of the five dividers of time, the first is the year; the second, the moon; the
third, the sun; the fourth, the stars and planets, and the zodiacal spaces; and the
fifth, the calendric calculations.[23]

5. Of royal perfection, the sovereign, having established in himself the highest degree and pattern of excellence, concentrates in his own person the five
[sources of] happiness, and proceeds to diffuse them, and give them to the
multitudes of the people.[24] Then they, on their part, embodying your perfection,
will give it back to you, and secure the preservation of it. . . .

6. Of the three virtues [of government], the first is correctness and straightforwardness; the second, strong rule; and the third, mild rule. In peace and
tranquility, correctness and straightforwardness; in violence and disorder, strong
rule; in harmony and order, mild rule. . . .

7. Of the examination of doubts, officers having been chosen and appointed
for divining by the tortoise-shell and the stalks of the milfoil plant, they are to
be charged to execute their duties. . . .[25]

When you have doubts about any great matter, consult with your own mind;
consult with your high ministers and officers; consult with the common people;
consult the tortoise-shell and divining stalks. If you, the shell, the stalks, the
ministers and officers, and the common people all agree about a course, this is
what is called a great concord, and the result will be the welfare of your person
and good fortune to your descendants. . . .[26]

8. Of the various omens, they are rain, sunshine, heat, cold, wind, and sea-
sonableness. When the five come, all complete, and each in its proper order,

---

23. This division of the Great Plan is substantially the same as Yao's instructions to his as-
tronomers.

24. See item 9 below on the five sources of happiness.—Eds.

25. As Legge observes in his note on this passage, "The practice of divination for the satisfaction of doubts was thus used in China from the earliest times." Although the use of tortoise
shells as "oracle bones" was no longer practiced by the Han dynasty, the stalks of the milfoil
plant continued to be used to correlate a situation with a hexagram from the *Changes*. See the
Changes, in Part I, Selections 9 and 10.—Eds.

26. The text goes on to discuss what the consequences will be if there is disagreement among
these constituencies.—Eds.

[even] the various plants will be richly luxuriant. Should any one of them be either excessively abundant or excessively deficient, there will be evil.

There are the favorable omens: dignity is signified by seasonable rain; orderliness is signified by seasonable sunshine; wisdom is signified by seasonable heat; deliberation is signified by seasonable cold; and sagacity is signified by seasonable wind. There are also unfavorable omens: recklessness is signified by constant rain; presumptuousness is signified by constant sunshine; indolence is signified by constant heat; hastiness is signified by constant cold; and stupidity is signified by constant wind. . . .

9. Of the five [sources of] happiness, the first is long life; the second, riches; the third, soundness of body and serenity of mind; the fourth, the love of virtue; and the fifth, fulfilling to the end the will [of Heaven]. Of the six extreme evils, the first is misfortune shortening the life; the second, sickness; the third, anxiousness of mind; the fourth, poverty; the fifth, wickedness; the sixth, weakness [in following the will of Heaven].

The Eight Trigrams Arranged around the
Yin-Yang Symbol.

9. "Great Appendix"

From the *Changes,* attributed to Kongzi
translation by Jesse Chapman

The origins of the Changes *(Yìjīng 易經) are shrouded in myth. The core
is a manual for divination consisting of sixty-four hexagrams, each of which
is composed of six broken or solid lines (for example, ☷ or ☰). Broken
lines correspond to the cosmological force of* yin, *while unbroken lines correspond to* yang.[1] *Each hexagram (guà 卦) has a name and is associated
with a general "judgment" (tuàn 彖) of it as a whole, in addition to a "line
statement" (yáocí 爻辭) associated with each particular line.[2] By the early*

---

1. See Selections on *Yin* and *Yang,* in Part I, Selection 7.

2. For divination purposes, one performs a procedure to "randomly" determine the number
of the hexagram that is relevant to the situation under discussion. The classic method requires
randomly dividing and subdividing a set of fifty stalks of the yarrow (milfoil) plant, while
an easier alternative method involves throwing a set of three coins, once for each line of the
hexagram. For descriptions of the methods (and an excellent complete translation), see Richard John Lynn, trans., *The Classic of Changes* (New York: Columbia University Press, 1994),
pp. 19–22. For an intriguing contemporary interpretation of the *Changes,* see Carl Gustav

Han dynasty, a series of supporting commentaries, attributed to Kongzi and known as the "Ten Wings" (Shíyì 十翼), circulated along with the earlier text and commentaries of the Changes.[3] *The "Appended Statements" (Xìcí 繫辭), also known as the "Great Appendix" (Dàzhuàn 大傳), became the most influential of these.*

The "Great Appendix" contends that the sages produced the Changes *to mirror the fundamental order of the cosmos in a textual form that makes that order knowable to human beings. Ethically cultivated gentlemen who contemplated the words and images of the* Changes *would not only better understand the underlying order of the cosmos, but would better know when and how to act in the world of human affairs. The "Great Appendix" describes a process that is at once the creation of the* Changes *and the creation of the cosmos. It praises the power of the text as a tool for making ethical or pragmatic decisions, and cites the interpretations of specific lines attributed to Kongzi himself.*

Reading the "Great Appendix" is made easier by familiarizing oneself with certain basic terms of art including alternation (biàn 變), unobstructed flow (tōng 通), and images (xiàng 象). "Alternation" refers to the change of a line in the Changes *from yin to yang, or vice versa, as well as the corresponding process in the cosmos itself. The continual process of alternation leads to "unobstructed flow." It is the ability of the "spirit-like objects," which may refer to the yarrow stalks used for divination or the hexagrams of the* Changes *itself, to respond to the unobstructed flow of the cosmos and the events in the human realm that makes those objects effective instruments for divination. "Images" are the symbols used in the text itself, including the yin and yang lines, prognostic statements, and the hexagrams, and, at the same time, the Patterns inherent in the cosmos, including but not limited to celestial bodies.*

To better understand the context of the entire tradition of reading the Changes, *this translation begins with the first hexagram in the original text of the* Changes *itself, Qián 乾, which consists of all yang lines, ☰, and corresponds to Heaven. (Kūn 坤, the hexagram that consists of all yin lines, ☷, corresponds to Earth. Together Qian and Kun are sometimes conceived of as the primal forces of the universe.) The first selection includes the "judgment" for the hexagram as a whole, its line statements, and the relevant sections of two other commentaries from the "Ten Wings": "Commentary on*

Jung, Foreword to Richard Wilhelm and Cary F. Baynes, trans., *The I Ching* (Princeton: Princeton University Press, 1967).—Eds.

3. According to tradition, Fu Xi discovered the trigrams, the groups of three lines that are the basis of the hexagrams (for example, the hexagram ䷗ is composed of the trigrams ☷ and ☳), King Wen discovered the hexagrams and composed the judgments on them, while the Duke of Zhou composed the line statements.—Eds.

the Judgments" and "Commentary on the Images." The remaining selections are drawn from the "Great Appendix," and illustrate its heterogeneous yet coherent structure. — Tr.

QIÁN 乾

Judgment

Qian is the primal unobstructed flow, beneficial and upright.[4]

Line Statements

First yang line: The dragon is submerged; there is nothing to be done.

Second yang line: The dragon appears in the fields; it is beneficial to meet a great man.

Third yang line: The gentleman does his utmost until the end of the day, and at dusk, he is full of worry. There is danger, but there is no misfortune.

Fourth yang line: It hesitates and leaps about in the deep pool; there is no misfortune.

Fifth yang line: The flying dragon is in the Heavens; it is beneficial to meet a great man.

Sixth yang line: The dragon flies too high; there is cause for regret.

Completely yang lines:[5] A group of headless dragons appears; good fortune.

The "Commentary on the Judgments" says, "Great indeed is the primacy of *Qian*. The myriad things depend upon it for their very beginnings, and Heaven belongs to it. Clouds travel and rain falls; all manner of creatures move about and take form. As the sun moves from dawn to dusk, the six lines of the hexagrams each take form at the right time. At the right time, each of the six dragons ascend to the Heavens. From the alternations and nourishment of the Way of *Qian*, all things obtain their lives and their basic natures. *Qian* protects them and fosters a grand state of harmony, so it says 'it is beneficial and upright.' From the beginning it causes the mass of creatures to emerge, so that the myriad domains are at peace."

The "Commentary on the Images" says, "Heaven moves with robust vigor. The gentleman works to strengthen himself without ceasing. Where it says 'the dragon is submerged; there is nothing to be done,' this means *yang* is at its nadir.

---

4. Interpretations of the meanings of the opening formulas to hexagrams in the *Changes* varied greatly over time.

5. This type of line statement appears with only the *Qian* hexagram, and applies only in cases where a divination has produced all "old" yang lines. (See Gao Heng 高亨, *Zhouyi dazhuan jinzhu* 周易大傳今注 [A Modern Commentary to the Changes and the Great Tradition] [Shandong: Qi Lu shushe, 1979], pp. 59–60.)

Where it says, 'the dragon appears in the fields,' this means its Virtue is put into action and expanded. Where it says that 'he does his utmost until the end of the day,' this means he returns to the Way. Where it says that 'it hesitates and leaps about in the deep pool' this means that it is advancing and that there is 'no misfortune.' Where it says, 'the flying dragon is in the Heavens,' this means that the 'great man' takes action. And where it says 'the dragon flies too high; there is cause for regret' this means that something that is pushed to its limit cannot be maintained for long. The 'completely *yang*' line statement means that nothing can stand above the Heaven's Virtue."

"Great Appendix," Part I

I.1.[6] Heaven is high and Earth is low, and so [the hexagrams] *Qian* and *Kun* were clearly differentiated. Once the low and the high have been made obvious, then the noble and the base take their positions. The movement of Heaven and the stillness of Earth are constant, and so the firmness of *yang* and the suppleness of *yin* can be clearly determined. The four quarters gather together things of the same kind, creatures divide themselves in groups, and good fortune and ill-fortune are born. Images form in Heaven, and contours form on Earth, so that alternations and transformations are made visible. For this reason, the firm and the supple scrape against one another, and the Eight Trigrams jostle one another, drumming one another forth with thunder and lightning and moistening one another with wind and rain, as the sun and moon revolve along their circuits, one cold, the other one hot. The Way of *Qian* forms the male, and the Way of *Kun* forms the female. *Qian* knows the Great Beginning, and *Kun* stirred the formation of things. Through ease, *Qian* understands; through simplicity, *Kun* gains ability. Those who attain the ease of *Qian* are easy to understand. Those who attain the simplicity of *Kun* are easy to follow. Those who are easy to understand win the favor of adherents. Those who are easy to follow achieve success. Those who win the favor of adherents long endure. Those who achieve success are great. To long endure is the Virtue of the worthy. To be great is the legacy of the worthy. Those who attain ease and simplicity grasp the Pattern of Heaven and Earth. And it is the person who grasps the Pattern of the entire world who can take a place at its center.[7]

I.2. The sages established the hexagrams by examining the images and appended statements to them so as to illuminate good and ill-fortune. The firm

---

6. With a single exception noted below, the divisions of the text presented here follow Zhu Xi 朱熹 (1130–1200) *Zhōu Yì běn yì* 周易本義 (*The Fundamental Meaning of the* Zhou *Changes*).

7. "Pattern" (*li* 理), a term referring to the underlying structure of the universe, will become central to later Buddhist and Neo-Confucian thought. See "Explanation of the Trigrams," in Part I, Selection 10; Fazang, "Essay on the Golden Lion," in Part II, Selection 15; and Zhu Xi, *Categorized Conversations*, in Part III, Selection 32.—Eds.

yang lines and supple *yin* lines push against one another and produce alternations and transformations. Thus, good and ill-fortune are images of one's loss
and gain. Regret and difficulty are images of one's worry and apprehension.
Alternations and transformations in the hexagrams are images of advance and
regression. The firm and the soft lines are images of day and night. The movements of the six lines encompass the Ways of the three ultimates [of Heaven,
Earth, and humans]. So the gentleman abides and finds security in the order
of the *Changes*, and takes pleasure in contemplating the statements for each of
its lines. For this reason, when the gentleman abides, that person observes its
images and contemplates its words, and when the gentleman acts, that person
observes its alternations and recites its prognostic statements. And so it says that
person "receives the help of Heaven. Auspicious. There is nothing that is not
beneficial."[8]

I.4. The *Changes* perfectly corresponds to Heaven and Earth, and so it encompasses the entirety of the Way of Heaven and Earth. In it, we may look
above and observe the patterns of the Heavens, and look below to clearly perceive the contours of the Earth. By doing so, we are able to know things that
are readily apparent and those that are hidden. By tracing things back to their
beginnings, and in turn pursuing them forward to their ultimate conclusions,
we may understand the explanations of life and death. Concentrated *qi* produces creatures, and dispersed souls produce alternations, and thus, we may
know the true condition of ghosts and spirits.[9] The *Changes* has the same appearance as Heaven and Earth, and so does not run counter to them. Its wisdom
encompasses the myriad things, and its Way is sufficient to save the world, and
so it does not err. We exercise power but do not become licentious, take joy in
Heaven and understand the mandate, and so need not worry. We are secure in
our territory and sincere in our benevolence, and so able to cherish the world.
The *Changes* emulates the encompassing manner in which Heaven and Earth
nourish things, and so is never excessive. By circuitous routes it develops the
myriad things into maturity, leaving none behind. It knows how to maintain a
state of unobstructed flow with the Way of night and day. And so the spiritual
has no definitive place, and the *Changes* has no definitive form.[10]

I.5. The alternation of *yin* and *yang* is called the "Way."[11] That which ensues
from it is goodness,[12] and that which realizes it completely is human nature.

---

8. Upper *yang* line statement to hexagram 14, "Great Abundance" (Dàyǒu 大有).

9. See Selections on *Qi,* in Part I, Selection 6.

10. Here, as in several other parts of the "Great Appendix," it is unclear whether "changes"
refers to the book, the cosmic process of change revealed by the book, or both. Consequently,
a possible alternative translation of the second phrase is, "and the changes (of the world) have
no definitive form."—Eds.

11. More literally, "a single *yin* and a single *yang* are called 'the Way.'"—Eds.

12. Alternatively, "Goodness sets it on its course."—Eds.

When those who are benevolent see it, they call it "benevolence." And when those who are wise see it, they call it "wisdom." The common people use it every day and yet do not understand it, and so the Way of the gentleman is rare indeed! The manifest aspect of that Way is its benevolence, and its hidden aspect is its Function. It drums forth the myriad things, yet it does not share in the worries of the sage, and so the full measure of its Virtue and its great legacy are maximized. Those who have it in abundance call it "the great legacy" and those who daily renew it call it "the full measure of Virtue." When it generates life, it is called "change";[13] when it brings signs to maturity, it is called "*Qian*," and when it reproduces the images, it is called "*Kun*." When it exhausts the permutations so that what is to come may be known, it is called "prognostication"; when it is in a state of flux and alternation it is called "cause," and when it is unfathomable even by *yin* and *yang* it is called "spirit-like."

I.7. Kongzi said: "The *Changes* is perfect indeed!" It is through the *Changes* that the sages exalted their power and broadened their legacies. In their wisdom they were exalted, but when performing the rituals they were humble. In their exalted wisdom they modeled themselves on Heaven, and in their humble rituals they modeled themselves on Earth. Heaven and Earth take their places and between them the *Changes* is put into practice. When the completed nature is preserved attentively, this is the gate to the righteousness of the Way.

I.10. Kongzi said, "If you understand the Way of alternation and transformation, then you will understand the actions of the spirits![14] There are four aspects of the Way of the sages in the *Changes*: In using it for speech, they held its language in high esteem. In using it for action, they held the alternations of its lines in high esteem. When using it to create concrete things,[15] they held its images in high esteem. And when using it for divination, they held its prognostication statements in high esteem." This is why when the gentleman is about to act, or about to set forth on a course of action, that person consults it by means of words, and receives its command as if it were an echo. It does not matter whether they are close or distant, obscure or buried in the depths, the *Changes* knows of those things that are yet to come. If it is not the most perfected essence of the world, then what could be?

Alternating in threes and fives, its permutations crisscross and combine.[16] Its

---

13. The phrase that is translated as "generates life" (*shēng shēng* 生生) came to play an important role in justifying post-Buddhist Confucian thought. In that context it can be read in a variety of ways, with one influential interpretation suggesting *mutual* life production (translated as "unending generation of life" or "life producing life").—Eds.

14. Zhu Xi places this line at the end of I.9. Following Gao Heng (531), I include it in section 10.

15. "Concrete things" translates *qì* 器. An alternative translation is "implements."

16. According to Zhu Xi, this line refers to the process of counting off numbers using yarrow stalks. *Zhou yi ben yi* 3.11.

alternations flow unobstructed, reproducing the patterns of Heaven and Earth. Its permutations approach the limit, bringing clear distinction to the images of the world. If this is not the perfection of the alternations of the world, then what could be? The *Changes* has no thoughts, and takes no action. Still and unmoved, when stimulated it penetrates all of the events that occur in the world. If this is not the most spirit-like thing in the world, then what could be? It is through the *Changes* that the sages exhausted the depths and peered into the smallest of things. Because it is profound, it is capable of maintaining a state of unobstructed flux with the will of the world. Because it reflects the smallest of things, it is capable of bringing the tasks of the world to completion. Because it is spirit-like, it is quick without being rushed, and arrives at its destination without taking a single step. When Kongzi said, "There are four aspects of the Way of sages in the *Changes*," this is what he meant.

I.11 Kongzi said, "What is it that the *Changes* does? It helps to explain things and accomplish undertakings.[17] It includes within it all the Ways of the world. It is that way, and that's all there is to it." Thus, the sage uses it to penetrate the will of the world, to clearly distinguish the legacy of the world, and to render clear judgments regarding the uncertainties of the world. This is why the Virtue of the yarrow stalks is round and spirit-like, and the Virtue of the hexagrams is square and wise. The significance of the six lines is to inform through their changes. The sages used the *Changes* to guide their minds. They withdrew and remembered it well, and shared in the good and ill-fortune of the people. Because they were spirit-like, they knew what was to come. Because they were wise, they remembered what had already happened. Who could reach such a level of perfection? Only those in ancient days of such profound hearing and sight, astuteness and wisdom, and spirit-like martial power that they did not need to engage in killing.

Thus, fully understanding the Way of Heaven, and clearly perceiving the events that occurred among the people, the sages gave the people these spirit-like things for their use.[18] The sages used them in a reverent and solemn manner, and employed their spirits to illuminate their power. Thus, when the gate is shut it is called "*Kun*," when the gate is open it is called "*Qian*," and the alternation of opening and closing is called "alternation." When this goes on and on without end it is called "unobstructed flux." When it appears it is called an "image." When it takes form it is called a "concrete thing." When it is produced and put into use it is called a "model." When it is beneficial and useful in a variety of circumstances, so that all of the people employ it, it is called "spirit-like." Thus,

---

17. Alternatively, "reveals the true nature of things and shows you how to bring your tasks to completion."—Eds.

18. According to Zhu Xi (3.13a) "these spirit-like things" refers to the yarrow stalks used in divination. Gao Heng suggests that the spirit-like objects are the *Changes* itself (536).

in the changes, there is the Great Ultimate.[19] It generates the two Modes, and the two Modes generate the four Images. The four Images generate the eight Trigrams,[20] and the eight Trigrams clearly distinguish good and ill-fortune. And clear distinction between good and ill-fortune gives rise to the great legacy.

Thus, there is nothing greater in modeling the images than Heaven and Earth; there is nothing greater in alternating in unobstructed flux than the four seasons, and of the images that extend down from Heaven, there are none that blaze brighter than the sun and the moon. There is nothing greater in lofty esteem than wealth and honor. And there is no one greater in gathering things together and making them useful, and in doing deeds of merit and producing concrete things for the benefit of the world, than the sage. In fathoming the profound and searching the hidden, in plumbing the depths and arriving at the distant, so as to fix the good and ill-fortune of the world, and in bringing the strivings of the world to fruition, there is nothing greater than the yarrow stalks and the tortoise shells.[21] Thus, Heaven produced these spirit-like things, and the sage made them into a standard. Heaven and Earth alternate and transform, and the sage emulated them [in the sixty-four hexagrams]. Heaven manifests the images, and made apparent good and ill-fortune, and the sage made images of them. The Yellow River gave forth the Chart, and the Luo River gave forth the Diagram,[22] and the sage made them into a standard. The *Changes* has its four Images and these are how it reveals its meaning. Statements are appended to its lines and these are the means by which it speaks. It distinguishes good fortune from ill so as to render clear judgments.

I.12. The *Changes* says: "He receives the help of Heaven. It is auspicious, and he benefits from it all."[23] The Master said, "Help means aid. He who submits

---

19. This is another sentence in which it is unclear whether "changes" refers to the book, the cosmic process of change revealed by the book, or both.—Eds.

20. This is one of the most important and much discussed sections in the "Great Appendix." In his commentary, Zhu Xi holds that two Modes refer to the dual possibilities of a single line (— and – –), while the four Images refer to the four possible configurations of two lines (═, ══, ══, and ══), and with three lines we arrive at the eight Trigrams (ZYBY 3.13b). (See also "Explanation of the Trigrams," in Part I, Selection 10.) Gao Heng adopts the explanation that the two Modes refer to Heaven and Earth while the four Images refer to the four seasons (538). See also Zhou Dunyi, "Explanation of the Diagram of the Great Ultimate," in Part III, Selection 24.

21. The bottom piece of a tortoise shell, called the plastron, was used as part of a divination ritual prior to the *Changes*.—Eds.

22. Tradition has it that the Yellow River Chart is the source of the Eight Trigrams, while the Luo River Diagram is the source of the schema underlying the "Great Plan" chapter of the *Documents*. (For a translation of the "Great Plan," see Selections on the Five Phases, in Part I, Selection 8.)

23. Upper yang line statement to hexagram 14 "Great Abundance."

gets aid from Heaven; he who is trustworthy receives the aid of other people. To tread the path of trustworthiness and to focus one's thoughts on being yielding is to esteem the worthy. And so such a person receives the aid of Heaven. It is auspicious and he does not fail to benefit."

Kongzi said, "Writing does not give full expression to language, and language does not give full expression to intent. Since this is true, does it follow that we can no longer access the intent of the sages?" Kongzi said, "The sages established the images to give full expression to their intent, and set forth the hexagrams to give full expression to genuine feelings and artifice, and they appended statements to them so as to give full expression to its language. Alternating and flowing along with it, one may fully realize all that is beneficial; dancing and drumming along with it, one may give full expression to its spirit-like qualities."

Are *Qian* and *Kun* the profound source of the *Changes*? Once *Qian* and *Kun* had both been laid out, the *Changes* established itself in their midst. If *Qian* and *Kun* had been destroyed, then there would have been no way for the *Changes* to appear. If the *Changes* did not appear, then *Qian* and *Kun* would have been on the verge of extinction. Therefore, what is above with respect to form is called the "Way," and what are below with respect to form are called "concrete things."[24] When it transforms and is controlled, it is called "alternation," and when it is propelled forward it is called "unobstructed flow." Those who raise it up and give it to the people of the world call it their "work" and their "legacy."

Thus, through the images, the sages had the capacity to perceive the mysteries of the world and to reproduce their forms. They represented the images in a manner appropriate to the objects themselves, and thus these representations were themselves called "images." The sages had the means to see the movements of the world, and to observe the coming together of the flows. They put it into practice in canons and rituals, and they appended statements to it to render clear judgments regarding good and ill-fortune, and they called these "the lines." The full expression of the mysteries of the world lies in the hexagrams. That which drums forth the movements of the world lies in the words of the line statements. That which transforms and commands them lies in the alternations. That which propels them forward and makes them proceed lies in the unobstructed flow. To be spirit-like and clearly perceive it lies in the person. To be silent yet bring it to completion, and to be trustworthy without speaking a word, lies in Virtuous conduct.

Part II

II.5. The *Changes* says, "If you waver and are irresolute, only friends will follow your thoughts."[25] Kongzi said, "What is it that the world thinks of, and that it

---

24. This is one of the most important and much-discussed lines from the "Great Appendix." See Lu Xiangshan, "Correspondence on the Great Ultimate," in Part III, Selection 37.

25. Fourth yang line statement to hexagram 31, "Stirring" (*Xián* 咸).

worries over? All the world returns to the same place, yet along many different paths. Everything arrives at a single destination, yet there are a hundred different worries on the way. What is it that the world thinks of, and that it worries over? The sun goes off and the moon comes. The moon goes off and the sun comes. The sun and moon propel one another forward and give rise to illumination. Cold goes off and the heat comes. Heat goes off and the cold comes. Cold and heat propel one another forward and bring the year to completion. To go off is to contract, and to come is to extend. Contraction and extension stir one another and produce benefit. The inchworm contracts so that it might extend itself. Dragons and snakes hibernate so that they might preserve their bodies. Perfect the righteousness of your spirit, so that you can be put to use. By being put to beneficial use, and by protecting your body, you can esteem your Virtue. I do not know more beyond this point. If you press your spirit to the limit, and understand transformation, that is the full measure of Virtue."

The *Changes* says, "He is trapped under a rock. He is caught in the brambles. Entering his palace, he does not see his wife. Ill-fortune."[26] Kongzi explained, "When you are trapped where you should not be trapped, your reputation will be sullied. And when you are caught where you should not be caught, your body will be in danger. Once you are sullied and in danger, the day of your death draws nigh. How then could you get to see your wife?"

The *Changes* says, "The Duke shoots a hawk upon the high wall and captures it. He does not fail to benefit."[27] Kongzi explained, "The hawk is a bird. The bow and arrow are a set of implements. The archer is a person. The gentleman carries implements on his person, awaits the opportune moment, and acts. How could this be anything but beneficial? He moves without hesitation, so that whenever he goes out hunting he captures something. It means that he acts once he has perfected his implements." Kongzi said, "A petty person is not ashamed of failing to be benevolent, and is not afraid of failing to be righteous. If he does not see a potential for benefit, he exerts no effort, and if he is not subjected to stern authority, he pays it no heed. But if he is presented with a minor warning, he falls in line at once. This is the saving grace of the petty person. This is what is meant when the *Changes* says, 'He wears fetters and his foot is cut off. There is no misfortune.'[28] If you don't pile up your good deeds, then they won't be enough to make your reputation, and if you don't pile up misdeeds, then they won't be enough to destroy your body. A petty person thinks that doing a small good deed is of no benefit, so such a person doesn't do small good deeds. He thinks that doing a small misdeed is of no harm, and so he does not avoid doing small misdeeds. And so his misdeeds pile up to the point where they can no longer be hidden from view, and his culpability becomes so great that he cannot

---

26. Third yin line statement to hexagram 47, "Dire Straights" (*Kùn* 困).
27. Upper yin line statement to hexagram 40, "Escape" (*Jiě* 解).
28. First yang line statement to hexagram 21, "Biting" (*Shìhé* 噬嗑).

escape from it. And so the *Changes* says, 'He wears fetters and his ear is cut off. Ill-fortune.'"[29]

Kongzi said, "Those who are now in danger were once secure in their positions. That which is lost was once possessed and protected. That which is in chaos was once set in order. This is why, when the gentleman is secure, he does not forget what it is like to be in danger. It is why, when he possesses something, he does not forget the possibility of losing it. It is why, when his domain is set in order, he does not forget the possibility that chaos might come. For this reason, he himself is secure, and both his domain and his household can be protected. As the *Changes* says, 'On the verge of loss, on the verge of loss, on the mulberry bush, tie it off.'"[30]

Kongzi said, "Among those whose Virtue is lacking but whose position is exalted, those whose knowledge is limited but whose schemes are great, and those whose strength is little but whose burden is heavy, there are few who do not meet with disaster. As the *Changes* says, 'The leg of the tripod breaks, and the Duke's stew is overturned, and spilled on the ground. Ill-fortune.'[31] This refers to those who cannot bear their responsibilities."

Kongzi said, "One who understands the smallest of things is spirit-like. The gentleman does not flatter those above him, nor does he condescend toward those below him. In this he can be said to understand the smallest of things, for the smallest of things are subtle beginnings of movement. They come before good fortune and ill. When the gentleman notices the smallest of things, he takes immediate action. He does not wait even until the end of the day. As the *Changes* says, 'He is as steadfast as stone, and does not wait until the end of the day. Being upright brings good fortune.'[32] Since he is steadfast as stone, why would he wait until the end of the day? His resolution is clearly recognizable. The gentleman understands both the subtle and manifest aspects of things, and knows when to be supple and when to be firm. And so he is admired by the mass of men."

Kongzi said, "Yan Hui nearly reached perfection![33] If ever he did anything wrong, he always came to understand it was wrong; once he understood, he never acted that way again.[34] As the *Changes* says, 'He returns without having gone too far. There is no great cause for regret. Prime good fortune.'"[35]

---

29. Upper yang line statement to hexagram 21, "Biting" (*Shìhé* 噬嗑).

30. Fifth yang line statement to hexagram 12, "Obstruction" (*Pì* 否).

31. Fourth yang line statement to hexagram 50, "Tripod" (*Dǐng* 鼎).

32. Second yin line statement to hexagram 16, "Joy" (*Yù* 豫).

33. Kongzi's most talented disciple, who died at an early age. See Yang Xiong, "Putting Learning into Practice," in Part I, Selection 4, and Cheng Yi, "What Kind of Learning Was It that Yanzi Loved?" in Part III, Selection 28.

34. Cf. *Analects* 6.3.

35. First yang line statement to hexagram 24, "Return" (*Fù* 復).

10. "Explanation of the Trigrams"

From the *Changes,* attributed to Kongzi
translation by Scot Brackenridge

The trigrams, which were supposedly first discovered by the ancient sage Fu Xi, are sets of three lines, each of which may be either broken or unbroken. Each of the hexagrams of the Changes *is composed of two trigrams. (For example, the hexagram* ䷇ *is composed of the trigrams* ☵ *and* ☷*.) The "Explanation of the Trigrams" (Shuō Guà 說卦) is a section of the "Ten Wings" that discusses the method of naming, and the reasons behind the names, of each of the eight trigrams: Zhèn 震 (Thunder)* ☳*, Xùn 巽 (Wind)* ☴*, Kǎn 坎 (Water)* ☵*, Lí 離 (Fire)* ☲*, Gèn 艮 (Mountain)* ☶*, Duì 兌 (Marsh)* ☱*, Qián 乾 (Heaven)* ☰*, and Kūn 坤 (Earth)* ☷*. It begins by setting the context for the creation of the* Changes *as a method of divination. This is followed by several sequences relating the trigrams through various associations with nature, animals, body parts, family members, and other characteristics. While the overarching tension between binary pairs like yin/yang, soft/hard, past/future, male/female, etc., can be felt throughout, the several enumerations of the eight trigrams also probe deeply into relationships that characterize the* Changes *as a whole. In offering several groupings and arrangements, this commentary derives from a source that transcends simplistic labels, and yet manages to be accessible through the familiar patterns of daily life. The rhythm and repetition of the "Explanation of the Trigrams" would have served as a memory aid in the oral transmission of the text, and, combined with the imagery uniting the human and natural realms, it reproduces the power of an invocation. The following translation is a selection from the complete "Explanation of the Trigrams."—Tr.*

1. Formerly, the sages made the *Changes* in the following manner: invisibly aided by spiritual enlightenment, they grew milfoil plants, and, regarding Heaven as three and Earth as two, they established a system of numbers. By examining the transformations between *yin* and *yang*, they established the trigrams. Bringing out the alternation between hard and soft produced the various individual lines. They were harmoniously in accord with the Way and Virtue, and matched their Patterns with righteousness. They exhaustively investigated the Pattern and fathomed the nature [of things] until they reached the mandate.[36]

2. Formerly, the sages made the *Changes* in the following manner: They wanted to be in accord with the Pattern of the nature [of things] and the

---

36. This is one of the lines most frequently quoted by later Neo-Confucians.—Eds.

mandate. For this reason, they established the Way of Heaven, which they called *yin* and *yang;* they established the Way of Earth, which they called soft and hard; and they established the Way of humans, which they called benevolence and righteousness. Combining the capacities of these three led to a doubling [of their number], and therefore there are six lines in each hexagram. They were divided into *yin* and *yang,* and alternately used soft and hard; and this resulted in the patterns in the six positions of the *Changes.*

3. Heaven [≡] and Earth [≡≡] have their fixed positions, *qi* flows between mountains [☶] and marshes [☱], thunder [☳] and wind [☴] stimulate each other, while water [☵] and fire [☲] work together. In these ways, the eight trigrams mutually interlock. Figuring out the past requires inferring [events], while understanding the future requires anticipating [events]. Therefore, in using the *Changes,* one proceeds by anticipating through numbers.

Thunder is for moving things, Wind is for scattering things, Rain [i.e., Water] is for moistening things, Sun [i.e., Fire] is for drying things, Mountain is for stopping things, Marsh is for making things happy,[37] Heaven is for ruling things, and Earth is for storing things.

---

37. The name of the trigram "Marsh" can also be read "Joy."

Women and Gender

11. Ban Zhao, *Lessons for Women*

translation by Nancy Lee Swann[1]

Ban Zhao.

Lessons for Women *(Nǔ jiè* 女誡*) was written by Bān Zhāo (*班昭*, 45–114 CE), the first female historian and perhaps the greatest female scholar in Chinese history. She completed the* Book of Han, *a history that covers twelve emperors whose reigns span three hundred years of the Han dynasty, when the work was left unfinished after the death of her father and brother. On her own she also wrote narrative poems, commemorations, inscriptions, eulogies, argumentations, commentaries, elegies, essays, and other works.*

Ban Zhao was married at age fourteen to Cao Shishu (Ts'ao Shih-shu). After the early death of her husband, Ban Zhao refused to remarry, in observance of the tradition that widows must practice the virtue of chastity. Emperor He of the Eastern Han summoned her to his palace to give instructions in proper conduct to the empress and the imperial concubines. Here she became well respected for her literary talent as well as her moral integrity.

Lessons for Women *consists of seven short chapters, all of which are included here, and is the earliest text exclusively intended for the education of Chinese women. Ban Zhao addressed it to her "daughters"; that is, to all the younger women in her family, in order to provide them with guidance for achieving domestic*

1. The following translation is reproduced, without any alterations, from Nancy Lee Swann, *Pan Chao: Foremost Woman Scholar of China* (New York: Russell and Russell, 1968 [1932]), and is reprinted by permission of the East Asian Library and the Best Collection, Princeton University. The Editors' Introduction to this translation is taken, with some modifications, from Robin R. Wang, ed., *Images of Women in Chinese Thought and Culture* (Indianapolis: Hackett Publishing, 2003), pp. 177–78.

*harmony and for leading a better life. While her vision of the good life for
women does not differ substantially from the traditional view previously
advanced by male sages and scholars, she does break new ground in arguing
that an education in the Chinese Classics is necessary so that both women
and men can fulfill their familial roles more effectively. Just as the husband
will never be able to guide his wife and family if he remains ignorant about
the teachings of the Chinese Classics, so, too, a wife will never be able to
serve her husband and family if she is kept from being instructed in the
same texts. Although women in pre-modern China never enjoyed the same
opportunities as men, Ban Zhao's insight helped encourage education for
upper-class women.* Lessons for Women *was placed first among the* Four
Books for Women, *along with the* Analects for Women *by the Tang dynasty female scholar Song Ruoxi, the* Instructions for the Inner Court, *by
the Ming dynasty Empress Ren Xiao, and the* Short Record of Models for
Women, *by the Ming dynasty female scholar Liu Shi.* —Eds.

Introduction

I, the unworthy writer, am unsophisticated, unenlightened, and by nature un-
intelligent, but I am fortunate both to have received not a little favor from my
scholarly father, and to have had a (cultured) mother and instructresses upon
whom to rely for a literary education as well as for training in good manners.
More than forty years have passed since at the age of fourteen I took up the
dustpan and broom[2] in the Cao family. During this time with trembling heart
I feared constantly that I might disgrace my parents, and, that I might multiply
difficulties for both the women and the men (of my husband's family). Day and
night I was distressed in heart, (but) I labored without confessing weariness.
Now and hereafter, however, I know how to escape (from such fears).

Being careless, and by nature stupid, I taught and trained (my children)
without system. Consequently I fear that my son Gu may bring disgrace upon
the Imperial dynasty by whose Holy Grace he has unprecedentedly received the
extraordinary privilege of wearing the Gold and the Purple, a privilege for the
attainment of which (by my son, I) a humble subject never even hoped. Nevertheless, now that he is a man and able to plan his own life, I need not again have
concern for him. But I do grieve that you, my daughters,[3] just now at the age
for marriage, have not at this time had gradual training and advice; that you still
have not learned the proper customs for married women. I fear that by failure in
good manners in other families you will humiliate both your ancestors and your
clan. I am now seriously ill; life is uncertain. As I have thought of you all in so
untrained a state, I have been uneasy many a time for you. At hours of leisure I

---

2. An expression for the marriage of the young woman.

3. Not necessarily only Ban Zhao's own daughters, but also the girls of her family.

have composed these seven chapters of instructions under the title, "Lessons for Women." In order that you may have something wherewith to benefit your persons, I wish every one of you, my daughters, each to write out a copy for yourself.

From this time on, every one of you should strive to practice these (lessons).

Chapter One: Humility

On the third day after the birth of a girl the ancients[4] observed three customs: (first) to place the baby below[5] the bed; (second) to give her a potsherd with which to play;[6] and (third) to announce her birth to her ancestors by an offering. Now to lay the baby below the bed plainly indicated that she is lowly and weak, and should regard it as her primary duty to humble herself before others. To give her potsherds with which to play indubitably signified that she should practice labor and consider it her primary duty to be industrious. To announce her birth before her ancestors clearly meant that she ought to esteem as her primary duty the continuation of the observance of worship[7] in the home.

These three ancient customs epitomize a woman's ordinary way of life and the teachings of the traditional ceremonial rites and regulations. Let a woman modestly yield to others; let her respect others; let her put others first, herself last. Should she do something good, let her not mention it; should she do something bad, let her not deny it. Let her bear disgrace; let her even endure[8] when others speak or do evil to her. Always let her seem to tremble and fear. (When a woman follows such maxims as these,) then she may be said to humble herself before others.

Let a woman retire late to bed, but rise early to duties; let her not dread tasks by day or by night. Let her not refuse to perform domestic duties whether easy or difficult. That which must be done, let her finish completely, tidily, and systematically. (When a woman follows such rules as these,) then she may be said to be industrious.

Let a woman be correct in manner and upright in character in order to serve her husband. Let her live in purity and quietness (of spirit), and attend to her own affairs. Let her love not gossip and silly laughter. Let her cleanse and purify and arrange in order the wine and the food for the offerings to the ancestors.[9]

---

4. Ban Zhao does not indicate that any such custom existed in her time; it was the custom of ancients—people who were "ancient," or who lived more than eighteen hundred years ago.

5. That is, on the floor, or the ground.

6. The potsherd was an honorable symbol of domesticity; in ancient times it was used as a weight for the spindle.

7. The worship and obedience due to parents and ancestors.

8. Literally, "Let her hold filth in her mouth, let her swallow insult."

9. The wife had special duties to perform in the periodical sacrifices. It was her duty to prepare the sacrificial cakes, the rice, the millet, and the fruits, and to see to it that they were served in the proper vessels.

(When a woman observes such principles as these,) then she may be said to continue ancestral worship.

No woman who observes these three (fundamentals of life) has ever had a bad reputation or has fallen into disgrace. If a woman fails to observe them, how can her name be honored; how can she but bring disgrace upon herself?

Chapter Two: Husband and Wife

The Way of husband and wife is intimately connected with *yin* and *yang*,[10] and relates the individual to gods and ancestors. Truly it is the great principle of Heaven and Earth, and the great basis of human relationships.[11] Therefore *The Record of Rites* honor union of man and woman; and in *The Book of Odes* the First Ode manifests the principle of marriage. For these reasons the relationship cannot but be an important one.

If a husband be unworthy, then he possesses nothing by which to control his wife. If a wife be unworthy, then she possesses nothing with which to serve her husband. If a husband does not control his wife, then the rules of conduct manifesting his authority are abandoned and broken. If a wife does not serve her husband, then the proper relationship (between men and women) and the natural order of things are neglected and destroyed. As a matter of fact the purpose of these two (the controlling of women by men, and the serving of men by women) is the same.

Now examine the gentlemen of the present age. They only know that wives must be controlled, and that the husband's rules of conduct manifesting his authority must be established. They therefore teach their boys to read books and (study) histories. But they do not in the least understand that husbands and masters must (also) be served, and that the proper relationship and the rites should be maintained.

Yet only to teach men and not to teach women—is that not ignoring the essential relation between them? According to *The Record of Rites,* it is the rule to begin to teach children to read at the age of eight years, and by the age of fifteen years they ought then to be ready for cultural training. Only why should it not be (that girls' education as well as boys' be) according to this principle?

---

10. The fundamental basis of the Chinese conception of nature lies in the revolution of the seasons, in the alternation of heat and cold, of darkness and light. The two antithetic principles were later named *yin* and *yang.*

11. The Chinese have always considered marriage to be the most solemn and important act of life.

Chapter Three: Respect and Caution

As *yin* and *yang* are not of the same nature, so man and woman have different characteristics. The distinctive quality of *yang* is rigidity; the function of *yin* is yielding. A man is honored for strength; a woman is beautiful on account of her gentleness. Hence there arose a common saying: "A man though born like a wolf may, it is feared, become a weak monstrosity; a woman though born like a mouse may, it is feared, become a tiger."

Now for self-culture[12] nothing equals respect for others. To counteract firmness nothing equals compliance. Consequently it can be said that the Way of respect and acquiescence is woman's most important principle of conduct. So respect may be defined as nothing other than holding on to that which is permanent; and acquiescence nothing other than being liberal and generous. Those who are steadfast in devotion know that they should stay in their proper places; those who are liberal and generous esteem others, and honor and serve (them).

If husband and wife have the habit of staying together, never leaving one another, and following each other around within the limited space of their own rooms, then they will lust after and take liberties with one another. From such action improper language will arise between the two. This kind of discussion may lead to licentiousness. Out of licentiousness will be born a heart of disrespect to the husband. Such a result comes from not knowing that one should stay in one's proper place.

Furthermore, affairs may be either crooked or straight; words may be either right or wrong. Straightforwardness cannot but lead to quarreling; crookedness cannot but lead to accusation. If there are really accusations and quarrels, then undoubtedly there will be angry affairs. Such a result comes from not esteeming others, and not honoring and serving (them).

(If wives) do not suppress contempt for husbands, then it follows (that such wives) rebuke and scold (their husbands). (If husbands) do not stop short of anger, then they are certain to beat (their wives). The correct relationship between husband and wife is based upon harmony and intimacy, and (conjugal) love is grounded in proper union. Should actual blows be dealt, how could matrimonial relationship be preserved? Should sharp words be spoken, how could (conjugal) love exist? If love and proper relationship both be destroyed, then husband and wife are divided.

Chapter Four: Womanly Qualifications

A woman (ought to) have four qualifications: (1) womanly virtue; (2) womanly words; (3) womanly bearing; and (4) womanly work. Now what is called womanly virtue need not be brilliant ability, exceptionally different from oth-

---

12. The self-cultivation of the person was of the utmost importance.

ers. Womanly words need be neither clever in debate nor keen in conversation. Womanly appearance requires neither a pretty nor a perfect face and form. Womanly work need not be work done more skillfully than that of others.

To guard carefully her chastity; to control circumspectly her behavior; in every motion to exhibit modesty; and to model each act on the best usage, this is womanly virtue.

To choose her words with care; to avoid vulgar language; to speak at appropriate times; and not to weary others (with much conversation), may be called characteristics of womanly words.

To wash and scrub filth away; to keep clothes and ornaments fresh and clean; to wash the head and bathe the body regularly; and to keep the person free from disgraceful filth, may be called the characteristics of womanly bearing.

With whole-hearted devotion to sew and to weave; to love not gossip and silly laughter; in cleanliness and order (to prepare) the wine and food for serving guests, may be called the characteristics of womanly work.

These four qualifications characterize the greatest virtue of a woman. No woman can afford to be without them. In fact they are very easy to possess if a woman only treasure them in her heart. The ancients had a saying: "Is love afar? If I desire love, then love is at hand!" So can it be said of these qualifications.

Chapter Five: Whole-Hearted Devotion

Now in *The Record of Rites* is written the principle that a husband may marry again, but there is no Canon that authorizes a woman to be married the second time. Therefore it is said of husbands as of Heaven, that as certainly as people cannot run away from Heaven, so surely a wife cannot leave[13] (a husband's home).

If people in action or character disobey the spirits of Heaven and of Earth,[14] then Heaven punishes them. Likewise, if a woman errs in the rites and proper mode of conduct, then her husband esteems her lightly. The ancient book *A Pattern for Women (Nüxian)*[15] says: "To obtain the love of one man is the crown of a woman's life; to lose the love of one man is to miss the aim in woman's life:"[16] For these reasons a woman cannot but seek to win her husband's heart. Nevertheless, the beseeching wife need not use flattery, coaxing words, and cheap methods to gain intimacy.

Decidedly nothing is better (to gain the heart of a husband) than whole-hearted devotion and correct manners. In accordance with the rites and the

---

13. Even following a husband's death, the worthy wife does not leave her husband's home.

14. The belief in the personal intervention of the gods in human affairs was deeply implanted in Chinese faith.

15. Thought to be the title of a long-lost book.

16. The full translation is: "To become of like mind with one man may be said to be the final end; to fail to become of like mind with one man may be said to be the eternal end."

proper mode of conduct, (let a woman) live a pure life. Let her have ears that hear not licentiousness, and eyes that see not depravity. When she goes outside her own home, let her not be conspicuous in dress and manners. When at home let her not neglect her dress. Women should not assemble in groups, nor gather together (for gossip and silly laughter). They should not stand watching in the gateways. (If a woman follows) these rules, she may be said to have whole-hearted devotion and correct manners.

If, in all her actions, she is frivolous, she sees and hears (only) that which pleases herself. At home her hair is disheveled and her dress is slovenly. Outside the home she emphasizes her femininity to attract attention; she says what ought not to be said; and she looks at what ought not to be seen. (If a woman does such as) these, (she may be) said to be without whole-hearted devotion and correct manners.

Chapter Six: Implicit Obedience

Now "to win the love of one man is the crown of a woman's life; to lose the love of one man is her eternal disgrace." This saying advises a fixed will and a whole-hearted devotion for a woman. Ought she then to lose the hearts of her father- and mother-in-law?[17]

There are times when love may lead to differences of opinion (between individuals); there are times when duty may lead to disagreement. Even should the husband say that he loves something, when the parents-in-law say "no," this is called a case of duty leading to disagreement. This being so, then what about the hearts of the parents-in-law? Nothing is better than an obedience that sacrifices personal opinion.

Whenever the mother-in-law says, "Do not do that"; and if what she says is right, unquestionably the daughter-in-law obeys. Whenever the mother-in-law says, "Do that," even if what she says is wrong, still the daughter-in-law submits unfailingly to the command.

Let a woman not act contrary to the wishes and the opinions of parents-in-law about right and wrong; let her not dispute with them what is straight[18] and what is crooked. Such (docility) may be called obedience that sacrifices personal opinion. Therefore the ancient book, *A Pattern for Women*, says: "If a daughter-in-law (who follows the wishes of her parents-in-law) is like an echo and a shadow, how could she not be praised?"

---

17. In the Chinese family system, children, even mature sons and their wives, were morally bound to dwell under the same parental roof. This often resulted in conflicts between the mother-in-law and the daughter-in-law, as well as between a wife and the wives of her husband's brothers, a wife and the unmarried daughters of the family, or the widows of deceased sons, or the young children of the family. There were many opportunities for friction.

18. Proper.

Chapter Seven: Harmony with the Younger Brothers- and Sisters-in-Law

In order for a wife to gain the love of her husband, she must win for herself the love of her parents-in-law. To win for herself the love of her parents-in-law, she must secure for herself the good will of her younger brothers- and sisters-in-law. For these reasons the right and the wrong, the praise and the blame of a woman alike depend upon the younger brothers- and sisters-in-law. Consequently it will not do for a woman to lose their affection.

They are stupid both who know not that they must not lose (the hearts of) younger brothers- and sisters-in-law, and who cannot be in harmony with them in order to be intimate with them. Excepting only the Holy Men, few are able to be faultless. Now Yanzi's[19] greatest virtue was that he was able to reform. Confucius praised him (for not committing a misdeed) the second time. (In comparison with him) a woman is more likely (to make mistakes).

Although a woman possess a worthy woman's qualifications, and is wise and discerning by nature, is she able to be perfect? Yet if a woman lives in harmony with her immediate family, unfavorable criticism will be silenced (within the home. But) if a man and woman disagree, then this evil will be noised abroad. Such consequences are inevitable. *The Classic of Changes* says:

> Should two hearts harmonize,
> The united strength can cut gold.
> Words from hearts which agree,
> Give forth fragrance like the orchid.[20]

This saying may be applied to (harmony in the home).

Though a daughter-in-law and her younger sisters-in-law are equal in rank, nevertheless (they should) respect (each other); though love (between them may be) sparse, their proper relationship should be intimate. Only the virtuous, the beautiful, the modest, and the respectful (young women) can accordingly rely upon the sense of duty to make their affection sincere, and magnify love to bind their relationships firmly.

Then the excellence and the beauty of such a daughter-in-law becomes generally known. Moreover, any flaws and mistakes are hidden and unrevealed. Parents-in-law boast of her good deeds; her husband is satisfied with her.[21] Praise of her radiates, making her illustrious in district and in neighborhood; and her brightness reaches to her own father and mother.

But a stupid and foolish person as an elder sister-in-law uses her rank[22] to exalt herself; as a younger sister-in-law, because of parents' favor, she becomes

---

19. A favorite disciple of Confucius.

20. In loving unity there is strength and beauty as the two (or the group) meet life's responsibilities.

21. Literally, "praises the beauty of her character."

22. The eldest daughter-in-law had control over the other sons' wives.

filled with arrogance. If arrogant, how can a woman live in harmony with others? If love and proper relationships be perverted, how can praise be secured? In such instances the wife's good is hidden, and her faults are declared. The mother-in-law will be angry, and the husband will be indignant. Blame will reverberate and spread in and outside the home. Disgrace will gather upon the daughter-in-law's person, on the one hand to add humiliation to her own father and mother, and on the other to increase the difficulties of her husband.

Such then is the basis for both honor and disgrace, the foundation for reputation or for ill-repute. Can a woman be too cautious? Consequently, to seek the hearts of young brothers- and sisters-in-law decidedly nothing can be esteemed better than modesty and acquiescence.

Modesty is virtue's handle; acquiescence is the wife's (most refined) characteristic. All who possess these two have sufficient [virtues] for harmony with others. In *The Book of Odes* it is written that "here is no evil; there is no dart." So it may be said of (these two, modesty and acquiescence).

12. Liu Xiang, "Mengzi's Mother"

From *Biographies of Women* 11
translation by Pauline C. Lee[23]

The Biographies of Women *(Liènǚzhuàn 列女傳) was compiled by the famous Confucian scholar Liú Xiàng 劉向 (79–8 BCE). Primarily composed of selections from earlier texts, the work is the first extant book in China devoted solely to the subject of women. It consists of 125 biographies of virtuous or vicious women divided into seven categories: matronly deportment, sagacious clarity, benevolent wisdom, chaste obedience, pure righteousness, rhetorical competence, and depraved favoritism. This book was likely intended for the emperor, as a warning against employing vicious women, and for women, as a means to cultivate their virtue.*

The following selection, literally "The Mother of Meng Ke of Zou," is perhaps the most famous in the collection, and tells the story of the mother of Mengzi. Mengzi was a leading Confucian of the Warring States Period (403–221 BCE), and came to be regarded by the Neo-Confucians of later

---

23. The following translation is taken, with some modifications, from Robin R. Wang, ed., *Images of Women in Chinese Thought and Culture* (Indianapolis: Hackett Publishing, 2003), pp. 150–51 and 154–55.

dynasties as a central figure in the transmission of orthodox Confucianism.[24]
The story of Mengzi's mother therefore became a paradigmatic account of
maternal virtue. Mengzi's father died when he was young, so the task of rais-
ing him fell solely on her shoulders. —Tr.

The mother of Meng Ke of Zou was known as Mother Meng.[25] She lived near
a cemetery when Mengzi was young. There, he played at imitating the tasks
performed in a cemetery. With great enthusiasm, he built tombs and performed
burials. Meng's mother said, "This is not the place for me to reside and bring
up my son." Thereupon she departed and took up residence beside a marketplace. Mengzi pretended to perform the job of a peddler pushing goods. Meng's
mother again said, "This is not the place for me to reside and bring up my son."
Again they moved and lived next to a school. Mengzi then played by setting up
sacrificial utensils, and performing the rituals of a guest bowing, giving way,
entering, and departing. Meng's mother said, "Truly I can reside with my son
here." And so they lived there.

When Mengzi had matured, he learned the Six Arts.[26] By the time of his
death he had attained the fame of a great scholar. The gentleman says, "Meng's
mother possessed the gift for slowly transforming people."[27] In the *Odes* it says,

> That admirable person,
> What was he given?[28]

This saying describes this situation.

*

When Mengzi was young, one day he returned home as soon as he arrived at
school. Meng's mother was spinning thread and asked, "How has your learning
progressed?" Mengzi responded, "The same as before." Meng's mother took a
knife and cut her weaving. Mengzi was frightened and asked her the reason for
doing this. Meng's mother said, "My son has given up on learning, much as I
have cut this weaving. A gentleman learns in order to establish a name for himself. He inquires and so attains extensive knowledge. Because of his knowledge,
in repose he is free from worry and, when he takes action, he is able to avoid
harm. Now that you are neglecting your studies, you will not be able to avoid

---

24. See, for example, Han Yu, "On Reading Xunzi," in Part III, Selection 21, and Zhu Xi,
Collected Commentaries on the Mengzi, in Part III, Selection 35.—Eds.

25. "Meng Ke" is the full name of Mengzi. "-zi" is a suffix meaning Master. Zou is the state
in which Mengzi was born and raised.—Eds.

26. The six arts are those of ritual, music, archery, charioteering, writing, and mathematics.

27. The voice of the "gentleman" is employed throughout the *Biographies of Women* as a mode
for evaluating the vices and virtues of the characters.

28. *Odes* 53.

working as a servant, and you will not be able to avoid disaster and misfortunes. In what way does what you are doing differ from spinning thread and weaving in order to provide food? If in mid-course one abandons one's work, how will one be able to clothe one's husband and continuously provide food? A woman who neglects the work that provides food is like a man who falls short in cultivating his Virtue. If he does not become a thief, then he will become a servant!"

Mengzi became frightened. Morning and night he learned diligently and without stopping. He took Zisi as his teacher.[29] Consequently he became known throughout the world as a famous scholar. The gentleman says, "Mother Meng knew the Way of being a person's mother." The *Odes* says,

> That admirable person,
> What was he told?[30]

This saying describes the situation.

*

After Mengzi had married, one day as he was about to enter the private chambers, he saw his wife half dressed in her room. Mengzi was displeased and left without entering. His wife went to bid farewell to Meng's mother and asked permission to leave saying, "I have heard that the Way between a husband and wife does not include the sharing of their private chambers. Now, in a moment of laziness, I was in my room, half dressed and the master saw me. All at once he was displeased. This is treating me as a guest. The proper conduct of a wife does not permit her to stay as a guest overnight. I ask that I may return to mother and father's."

Thereupon Meng's mother summoned Mengzi and said to him, "According to ritual, when one is about to enter through a door, ask who is there. In this way one practices proper respectfulness. When one is about to enter a hallway, you should raise your voice in order to warn others that you are coming. When you are about to enter a room, your gaze should be fixed downwards, as you fear seeing others' shortcomings. Now you have not examined your own practice of ritual, but instead censor the rituals of others. Are you not indeed far from practicing proper ritual?"

Mengzi confessed his faults, and then asked his wife to stay. The gentleman says, "Mother Meng understood proper ritual, and was insightful about the Way of the mother-in-law."

---

29. According to tradition, Zisi, the grandson of Kongzi (Confucius), was Mengzi's teacher.
30. *Odes* 53.

*

Mengzi was residing in the state of Qi and had an air of sadness about him. Mother Meng saw him and said, "You seem to have an air of sadness about you. Why is that?" Mengzi said, "That is not the case." On a different day he was at leisure, leaning against a pillar, and sighed. Mother Meng saw him and said, "Earlier, I saw you had a look of sadness. You said 'That is not the case.' Now you are leaning against a pillar and sighing. Why is this?" Mengzi responded, "I have heard that a gentleman first cultivates himself, and then takes up an official position. He does not employ illicit means in order to receive rewards. He is not greedy for honors and emoluments. If the feudal lords do not listen to his words, he does not try to gain access to their superior. If they listen but do not implement his ideas, the gentleman does not set foot in their court. Now the Way is not practiced in Qi. I desire to leave but my mother is elderly. Because of this I am sad."

Meng's mother said, "The proper ritual conduct of a woman is to prepare the five grains for food, ferment the wine, care for one's mother- and father-in-law, mend clothes, and that is all. Therefore, a woman is cultivated to care for affairs within the home, but does not have the ambition to care for affairs outside. The *Changes* says,

> At home she provides sustenance,
> She cannot be careless in her duties.[31]

The *Odes* says,

> No condemnation, no disputation,
> Her only thoughts are of wine and food.[32]

That is to say, a woman should not determine affairs for herself, but instead has a Way with three 'followings': When young, she follows her father and mother; when she enters into marriage, she follows her husband; when her husband passes away, she follows her son. This is proper ritual. Now my son has grown into a man, and I am elderly. My son should follow his duty. I shall follow my ritual standards."

The gentleman says, "Mother Meng understood the Way of a woman." The *Odes* says,

> Looking pleasant and smiling,
> Never impatient in her teaching.[33]

This saying describes this situation.

---

31. Paraphrasing *Changes,* second line statement to hexagram 37, Jiaren.—Eds.

32. *Odes* 189.

33. *Odes* 299.

*

The eulogy says, "Mengzi's mother taught and transformed step by step. In finding a place for them to live, she considered the abilities he would be able to cultivate. And so, he cultivated an understanding of the human relations. When her son's learning did not progress, she cut the web of her loom in order to chastise him. Her son then fully developed his Virtue, and became the most honored of his time."

Huineng: The Sixth Patriarch of Chan Buddhism.

PART II: CHINESE BUDDHISM

The first Buddhist missionaries arrived in China some time around the first century CE, but Buddhism only gained wide support among intellectuals and the common people after the fall of the Han dynasty (202 BCE–220 CE). When the Han collapsed, China entered the Six Dynasties period (220–581), an era of disunity and warfare. In a situation reminiscent of the earlier Warring States period (403–221 BCE), China was again divided into states competing for supremacy, with rival claimants to the throne. Without a centralized power to maintain intellectual conformity, "unorthodox" teachings like Buddhism had a chance to flourish. In addition, the central message of Buddhism, escape from the suffering of the world, was appealing in this chaotic era. By the time centralized rule was reestablished under the Sui (581–618) and Tang (618–906) dynasties, Buddhism was the de facto state religion, heavily patronized by most emperors.

Buddhism was founded in South Asia by Siddhartha Gautama (possibly fl. 500 BCE, but his dates are disputed). Siddhartha is commonly referred to by the titles "Buddha" (Enlightened One) or sometimes "Shakyamuni" (Sage of the Shakya Tribe). He taught that human suffering, including the cycle of reincarnation, is caused by attachment to the illusion of a permanent self. Because I suffer from the illusion that you and I are distinct, permanent individuals, I will jealously crave any goods that you might get, and angrily fight you for their possession. This leads to stealing, murder, theft, dishonesty, and other forms of cruelty. However, the universe follows a causal law ("*dharma*" in Sanskrit) according to which intentional actions ("*karma*") have morally appropriate consequences. If I harm others, I will suffer similar harms myself, either in my current life, or in a future life into which I will be reincarnated. On this view, good people who inexplicably suffer bad fortune, or bad people who unjustly live well, are receiving the karmic reward for actions in previous lives. They will, likewise, reap the rewards or punishments for their current actions in a future life. Furthermore, even the happiest of ordinary lives is still marked by a particular kind of suffering due to the futile craving for permanent, individual possession of goods. The only way to escape the cycle of suffering and reincarnation is to achieve enlightenment. Enlightenment is to comprehend fully and without reservation the truth of no-self ("*anātman*"): neither the "I" that craves nor the objects of my craving are permanent, independent individuals. All things are "empty" of selves. Although "emptiness" might seem to have negative connotations, Buddhists are quick to point out that emptiness is what makes change, and life itself, possible. To be empty of a permanent self is to be open to transformation, including enlightenment. Those who achieve enlightenment into the emptiness of reality become Buddhas themselves and enter nirvāna (literally, the "extinguishing" of craving), a state of bliss that is beyond description in words.[1]

Buddhism eventually broke into two major sects, Theravāda and Mahāyāna. "Mahāyāna" means Greater Vehicle, and Mahāyāna Buddhists use the denigrating term "Hīnayāna" (Lesser Vehicle) to describe Theravāda Buddhists. According to Mahāyāna, so-called Hīnayāna teaches the less benevolent ideal of the arhat, one who seeks nirvana for himself, while Mahāyāna advocates the ideal of the bodhisattva, who works to alleviate the suffering of everyone. Mahāyāna Buddhists also emphasize the broader scope of the doctrine of emptiness. Full enlightenment requires that one recognize the emptiness of all things, not just the emptiness of the self, but the emptiness of all concrete things, like trees and wagons, as well as abstract things, like time or evil. Theravāda spread to Sri Lanka and Southeast Asia, while Mahāyāna spread to East Asia.

Both Mahāyāna and Theravāda developed subtle philosophical traditions, as they attempted to justify their views and answer objections to them. For example, how is reincarnation possible if there are no selves to be reincarnated? A classic answer is articulated in *The Questions of King Milinda,* a dialogue between the Buddhist monk Nāgasena and a Bactrian king:

> King Milinda said: "Reverend Nāgasena, is it the case that one does not transmigrate and yet is reborn?"
>
> "Yes, sire, one does not transmigrate and yet is reborn."
>
> "How, reverend Nāgasena, is it that one does not transmigrate and yet is reborn? Make a simile."
>
> "Suppose, sire, some man were to light a lamp from another lamp. Did one lamp pass over to the other?"
>
> "No, reverend sir."
>
> "In the same way, sire, one does not transmigrate and yet is reborn."
>
> "Make a further simile."
>
> "Do you remember, sire, when you were a boy learning some verse from a teacher?"
>
> "Yes, reverend sir."
>
> "But, sir, did that verse pass over from the teacher?"
>
> "No, reverend sir."
>
> "In the same way, sire, one does not transmigrate and yet is reborn."
>
> "You are dexterous, reverend Nāgasena."[2]

---

1. Two excellent philosophical introductions to Buddhism are Mark Siderits, *Buddhism as Philosophy* (Indianapolis: Hackett Publishing, 2007), and Walpola Rahula, *What the Buddha Taught* (New York: Grove Press, 1974).

2. N. K. G. Mendis, ed., *The Questions of King Milinda,* trans. I. B. Horner (Sri Lanka: Buddhist Publication Society, 1993), pp. 58–59.

In other words, no self is transmitted through reincarnation; however, intentional actions (*karma*) have consequences for future states, in accordance with the causal structure of the universe (*dharma*). A modern analogy would be that children of parents with substance abuse problems are statistically more likely to develop substance abuse themselves. Genetic and environmental factors cause the substance abuse to be "reborn" in later generations. Of course, parents can break the cycle by recognizing and facing the problem (something analogous to achieving enlightenment), and choosing to raise their own children in a healthy environment.

Buddhists also offer philosophical justifications for the doctrine of no-self. Theravāda Buddhists often argue that all that exists are momentary manifestations of the Five Aggregates (*skandhas*): material form and four kinds of mental states (sensation, perception, volition, and consciousness).[3] Each instance of any one of these is constantly changing, and none of them can plausibly be identified as a persistent "self." For example, if my "self" is my body, then I do not have the same self now that I had a year ago, since most of the cells in my body have died and been replaced since then. Similarly, if my "self" is my memories, I am different every time I remember something new, or forget something I used to remember.[4]

The previous argument for no-self emphasizes *impermanence*. Another line of argument, which was to become particularly influential in Chinese Mahāyāna, stresses *interdependence*. Consider your mental reaction to the argument in the previous paragraph. Was it agreement? Disagreement? Puzzlement? Frustration? Enjoyment? Even if it was transitory, this mental state is certainly part of your identity. But this particular mental state only exists because of this introductory chapter. This chapter only exists because of its editors. Its editors would only have written this introduction because of Siddhartha Gautama. Consequently, your mental state is dependent on not only two contemporary scholars whom you probably have never met, but on an individual who lived more than two millennia ago on the other side of the world. We could draw even more detailed causal connections between you, the editors' parents, their parents' parents, etc.; eventually, we would see that everything that exists is part of a web of relationships. Some Buddhists would argue that this web of relationships is really what defines any one element in it. On this view, there *is* an eternal self; however, it is

---

3. See Zongmi, *On Humanity*, in Part II, Selection 17, for an explanation of the Five Aggregates and a version of the argument for no-self.

4. Buddhists have also examined versions of the Cartesian hypothesis that the self is an immaterial soul that is the subject of our experiences. However, as critics of Descartes have noted in the West, a self-soul would need to meet four challenging requirements: (1) has mental states, but (2) is not identical with those states, yet (3) has a persistent individual identity, and (4) controls a physical body that is metaphysically distinct from it. It is not clear that any entity could meet those criteria.

not an individual self. My self is identical with the rest of the universe, because I exist only as a part of it: "One is all, and all is one."[5] Two of the most influential forms of Chinese Buddhism, Huayan and Chan (the latter better known in the West by its Japanese name, "Zen") both understand "emptiness" in terms of interdependence.

Because Buddhism traces the origin of human wrongdoing to attachment to an illusory self, it views the cardinal vice as selfishness and the cardinal virtue as benevolence. Benevolence has long been an important virtue in Chinese thought, at least as far back as the Warring States Period. However, there have been importantly different conceptions of what benevolence entails. At the most general, a benevolent person is saddened by the suffering of others, takes joy in the happiness of others, and acts appropriately on these feelings in assisting those others. Confucians have stressed that sages have such abundant benevolence that they share the joys and sorrows of everyone in the kingdom. However, they also claim that benevolence has its roots in the affection of children for their parents. As a result (they argue), genuine benevolence must encompass filial piety. In other words, we ought to have greater compassion for and stronger obligations to our parents, friends, teachers, and ruler than we do for complete strangers. In contrast, the Buddhist view is that, since there are no selves, a fully enlightened person will love everyone equally. For this reason, Buddhist monks and nuns in most cultures leave their families behind and remain celibate. Ideally, this encourages them to treat everyone as their brothers and sisters, but from the introduction of Buddhism to China, Confucians have been concerned with this teaching that, in their eyes, undermines the filial piety that is the core of humanity and the root of social relations.[6] Nonetheless, Buddhism had an enduring influence on how Confucians thought about benevolence themselves. The doctrine that everything is interrelated provides a clear justification for benevolence. If you and I are just parts of a greater whole, then my caring about your well-being is justified in the same way that my caring about my own well-being in the future is justified. Over centuries of Buddhist philosophical dominance, this view of benevolence seeped into Confucian thinking, leaving Confucians with the problem of how to reconcile it with filial piety.[7]

One of the reasons that Buddhism has had wide appeal despite the subtlety of its philosophy is its use of "expedient means" (*upāya*). "Expedient means" is a technique of instruction based on the recognition that humans have different levels of understanding of the truth of no-self. In the *Lotus Sutra,* the Buddha

---

5. See Fazang, "The Rafter Dialogue" and "Essay on the Golden Lion," in Part II, Selections 14 and 15.

6. Huiyuan's *On Why Buddhist Monks Do Not Bow Down before Kings,* in Part II, Selection 13, is an effort to address this concern.

7. The Neo-Confucian Cheng Yi wrestles with this problem in his "Reply to Yang Shi's Letter on 'The Western Inscription,'" in Part III, Selection 30.

explains the rationale for expedient means with an elaborate metaphor. Suppose that a fire broke out in the huge mansion of a wealthy man with many young children. The father shouts to the children that they must flee the mansion, but the children do not understand why fire is dangerous and are engrossed in their games, so they ignore their father's warning. The father realizes that he must use an "expedient means" to get his children to flee the fire, so this time he shouts:

> The kind of playthings you like are rare and hard to find. If you do not take them when you can, you will surely regret it later. For example, things like these goat-carts, deer-carts, and ox-carts. They are outside the gate now where you can play with them. So you must come out of this burning house at once. Then whatever ones you want, I will give them all to you!

The Buddha explains that,

> . . . when the sons heard their father telling them about these rare playthings, because such things were just what they had wanted, each felt emboldened in heart and, pushing and shoving one another, they all came wildly dashing out of the burning house.[8]

Even though there were no toys outside the house, what the father said was justified because it led the children to salvation. Similarly, the teachings of Buddhism must be adapted to the level of understanding of one's audience. For those with a low level of understanding, the Buddha is worshipped as a god, and the goal of Buddhism is for one's soul to be reborn in Heaven, with Hell as the alternative for those who do evil. Those with a higher level of understanding, who have a more rarefied grasp of the doctrine of no-self and karmic consequences, recognize that concepts like "Heaven," "Hell," and a personal "soul" are merely expedient means.[9]

When Buddhism reached the peak of its prestige and influence in the Tang dynasty (618–906), it became subject to the institutional corruption that seems to occur within every major spiritual or social movement. Buddhist monasteries were tax-exempt, and often became extremely wealthy through donations from the faithful, and by running their own businesses. Some monks practiced extreme and unhealthy forms of mortification of the flesh, while others were criminals using the monastic life simply as a way of hiding from prosecution. Furthermore, some Buddhists were very strident in their criticisms of Confucianism and Daoism; one even described Confucian and Daoist teachings as nothing but "piss and shit" in comparison with the fine cream of Buddhist

---

8. Burton Watson, trans., *The Lotus Sutra* (New York: Columbia University Press, 1993), p. 57.

9. Mahāyāna Buddhists argue that, while the teachings of "Hīnayāna" might seem to be older (and hence more authentic), the Buddha was simply using expedient means when he taught the lower doctrine of "Hīnayāna" to his less insightful disciples, saving the deeper doctrines of Mahāyāna for his better disciples, who would reveal them in later eras.

teachings.[10] These problems eventually led to rising anti-Buddhist sentiments, and, in the late Tang dynasty, the anti-Buddhist essays of Han Yu (768–824) were seminal in starting the movement eventually known in English as "Neo-Confucianism."[11] Daoists also became increasingly critical of Buddhism, and Emperor Wuzong, a devoted Daoist, instituted an anti-Buddhist policy of seizing monastic property and forcing many monks and nuns to return to the laity (845 CE). Wuzong died soon after this and the policy was reversed under his successor, but Buddhism (while still an important factor in Chinese culture) never recovered its social and intellectual predominance.

The readings in Part II are arranged in chronological order. Huiyuan's *On Why Buddhist Monks Do Not Bow Down before Kings*, is an effort to defend the practices of Buddhist monks that were objectionable to the Confucian sensibilities of many Chinese, such as renouncing one's family and refusing to ritually defer to one's ruler. After reading this work, you may wish to next read Zongmi's *On Humanity,* which was intended as an accessible introduction to Buddhist philosophy. The readings from the great Huayan philosopher Fazang illustrate the subtle metaphysics underlying Chinese Buddhism, while the *Platform Sutra* and the Kōan Selections explain, in different ways, the nature of Buddhist practice.

---

10. Chengguan, *Yanyi chao*, Taisho 36.106a7–12 (cited in Peter N. Gregory, trans., *Inquiry into the Origin of Humanity* [Honolulu: University of Hawaii Press, 1995], pp. 82–83). Obviously, most Buddhist monks and nuns were sincere, and Siddhartha Gautama would have been dismayed by the corruption of Buddhist institutions. (The same could be said about other religious traditions including Christianity, Judaism, Hinduism, and Islam, all of which have sometimes been appropriated in ways contrary to their real meaning.)

11. For selections from Neo-Confucian philosophers, including Han Yu, see Part III.

13. Huiyuan, *On Why Buddhist Monks Do Not Bow Down before Kings*

translation by Justin Tiwald

We move now from the Han dynasty to the Six Dynasties Period that closely followed it, an era that was marked by civil war and political instability. Huìyuǎn 慧遠 (334–416) was an influential Buddhist monk and teacher in this period, and a prominent early spokesperson for what many Chinese saw as an imported religion reflecting foreign values. Among the Buddhist views that sat uneasily with the indigenous Chinese culture, two in particular were flashpoints in public discourse: the requirement that Buddhist monks leave their families, and the notion that monks were not political subjects of their rulers in the same strict sense as ordinary citizens. Both views ran strongly counter to largely Confucian values of loyalty and filial piety that had become thoroughly interwoven with Chinese culture by the time that Buddhism began to attract large numbers of followers.

On Why Buddhist Monks Do Not Bow Down before Kings is Huiyuan's attempt to justify the special political status of Buddhist monks, symbolically expressed in their refusal to bow or show proper reverence (jìng 敬) to their rulers. By the time that Huiyuan wrote this treatise, the issue had been a source of contention for several decades, and numerous public figures had weighed in on the issue, but Huiyuan described himself as dissatisfied with the views expressed by each side, thinking them too emotionally charged to capture the underlying justification for exempting Buddhists from normal civil courtesies. The main line of Huiyuan's argument was that the chief good provided by a ruler to his subjects, translated here as "life" (shēng 生), has little value for a monk, for a monk finds life and all of existence in the cycle of life and death (saṃsāra) an object of unhealthy attachment and the chief source of suffering. Huiyuan builds on this argument to construct a complex and controversial framework for thinking about the special political and social position of the Buddhist monk. — Tr.

1. Buddhist laypersons

Looking into the basis for the main points elucidated by Buddhist teachings, we distinguish [Buddhist practitioners] according to whether or not they have left their families. . . .[1] Those who honor the dharma but stay in their families [i.e.,

---

1. The expression "leave the family" refers to the act of becoming a Buddhist monk or nun, leaving one's natural family in the interest of freeing oneself of the entanglements and attachments that arise from family life. In this section, Huiyuan describes people who have

Buddhist laypersons] are subjects who comply with the transformations of the temporal world.[2] Their basic feelings remain conventional and their outward behavior conforms with what's within the bounds of the temporal world. Thus they have love for those to whom they are related by birth and deferential rituals for honoring their superiors. . . . Complying with the transformations of the temporal world becomes the common practice and they do not strip away what comes naturally to them. Why? Because in emphasizing the value of the body and preserving life they become burdened by hindrances, and when these become deeply and firmly rooted they cannot forget the notion of the persisting self. They make an enclosed garden of their feelings and desires, and make sights and sounds the promenade.[3] When thoroughly immersed in worldly delights they aren't able to rally themselves to leave. For these reasons the teachings [meant for Buddhist laypersons] are restrained, taking these [ethical guidelines] as their outer limit without clarifying what lies beyond. So long as what lies beyond isn't clear to them their behavior will largely be in compliance with the transformations of the temporal world.

Therefore they cannot withhold proper ritual deference [for a ruler] while receiving the benefits of his virtue, nor can they discard due reverence for him while soaking up the benefits of his kindness. For this reason, those who delight in the customs of the Buddha always first honor their parents and revere their lords. Those who would change their conventions and cast off their hairpins [in order to become monks] must always await their [parents and ruler's] sanction and act accordingly. If their parents or lord have doubts, then they retire from pursuing the aim [of becoming a monk] and wait for [the parents and ruler] to become similarly enlightened about the matter. This, then, is why Buddhist doctrine stresses the importance of supporting life and, in matters of governing, lending aid to the king's role in the transformations of the temporal world.

2. Buddhists who leave the family

Those who have left the family are guests beyond the temporal world. In their outward behavior they are cut off from external things. Their doctrine leads them to understand that the reason they are burdened by suffering is because they have a body, and that they can put an end to their suffering by not preserving the body. They understand that generating life[4] depends on being subject

---

committed to Buddhism without going so far as to become monks or nuns, and choose to remain in their families.

2. Literally, "comply with the transformations," but throughout this essay, "the transformations" refers to the world in which transformations take place.

3. Literally, "sounds and colors," a phrase commonly used to refer to the sorts of external enticements that elicit desires and attachment.

4. "Generating life" (in Chinese, *shēng shēng* 生生) is an oft-quoted phrase in the "Great Appendix" to the *Changes,* I.5 (see Part I, Selection 9). Later Confucians insisted that life and life-generativity are sources of value for everyone.

to the transformations of the temporal world, and by refraining from following the transformations they seek out the great ancestral source of the world.[5] Because seeking out the great ancestral source doesn't depend on following the transformations of the temporal world, they do not value the resources required for participation in the cyclical changes.[6] Because putting an end to their suffering doesn't depend on preserving the body, they do not value the benefits of life.

The Pattern [that they adhere to] is contrary to the needs of the physical body, and their Way is opposed to common practice.[7] People such as these commence with their vows by casting off their hairpins [so that they can shave their heads]. They commit themselves [to monastic life] and give form to it by changing their clothes [adopting monastic robes in place of secular clothing]. For this reason, generally those who have left their families pursue their commitments by fleeing the world, and achieve their Way by changing from ordinary customs. Because they change from ordinary customs, their clothing and insignia of rank cannot conform to the same ritual standards specified by secular codes. Because they flee the world, they must raise their outward behavior to a higher level.[8] In this way they are able to rescue ordinary people from drowning in the flow of the temporal world and pull out the hidden roots from many eons [of past lives].[9]

---

5. "Ancestral source of the world" is my translation of *zōng* 宗, sometimes translated more ambiguously as "the First Principle." The term is Daoist in origin but was adopted by early Chinese Buddhists to describe the universal ground or source of all things, the understanding of which gives rise to enlightenment and ultimately to salvation.

6. I follow Anthony C. Yu in reading this line as an attempt to distance the Buddhist monk's goals from the Daoist's, insofar as the Daoist aims to accord with regular changes and the Buddhist seeks to transcend them altogether (*State and Religion in China* [Chicago: Open Court, 2005], p. 109).

7. "Pattern" (*lǐ* 理, sometimes translated as "Principle") is an important term that accounts for the ultimate nature of things, understanding of which gives us general guidelines or aims. The term takes on an increasingly central role in the metaphysics of later Buddhists and Neo-Confucians. For more extensive discussion and analysis of Pattern see Fazang, "Essay on the Golden Lion," in Part II, Selection 15, and Zhu Xi, *Categorized Conversations*, in Part III, Selection 32.

8. "Outward behavior" is my translation of *jì* 跡, rendered more literally as "footprint" but often used to refer to the external and practical manifestations of one's inner beliefs and states of mind.

9. Huiyuan here invokes the Buddhist view that people's worldly fetters are the result of their doings in past lives, in this case an unfathomable number of lives. A more imagistic rendering of the line might be, "pull the hidden roots out from many layers of eons." As a visual metaphor this line is quite suggestive, as the Chinese for "eon" (or "kalpa") suggests a wave of water (*jiébō* 劫波). Seeing "many layers of eons" would be akin to seeing many rows of waves stretching back toward the horizon. If someone is to be in a position to pull them out, he or she must have very strong footing on higher ground (see the previous note on "footprints"), thus justifying a monk's dramatic departure from the normal flow of worldly events and concerns.

They convey themselves a great distance across the ford of the Three Vehicles, opening a path between Heaven and humankind.[10] If they cause just one person to develop complete virtue then the Way will permeate through that person's family and that person's beneficence will flow to all under Heaven.[11] Although they don't occupy the positions of kings or nobles they are truly in harmony with the ultimate [standards of] august rulership, giving life to the people through non-interference and leniency.[12] Therefore, within the family they deviate from the [normal tendency to] attach great importance to natural relationships, but do this without violating their filial responsibilities. Outside the family they refrain from honoring their lord, but do this without losing their reverence for him. Seeing it in this way, one will understand that when someone transcends the transformations of the temporal world in order to seek out the great ancestral source of the world, then the Pattern [that moves him] is profound and his righteous conduct is sincere. . . .

3. Seeking the ancestral source without complying with the transformations[13]

Question: If we inquire into the meaning of Laozi's writings, we find that for him Heaven and Earth become great by attaining a state of oneness [by together forming an integrated system or harmonious whole]. Kings and other lords become worthy of veneration by embodying compliance [with the transformations of the temporal world]. Because [Heaven and Earth] attain a state of oneness, they serve as the foundation for transformation in its myriad forms. Because [kings and other lords] embody compliance, they acquire the meritorious abilities of participation in cyclical changes [which thus makes them worthy of veneration]. So a clear grasp of the ancestral source of the world requires that one fully embody the ultimate state [of the transformations], and fully embodying the ultimate state requires that one comply with the transformations. This is why the ancients found this teaching so appealing, and something from which popular opinion cannot differ. When a view differs [so dramatically] from popu-

---

10. The "Three Vehicles" represent three paths to Buddhist enlightenment, those of the arhat, the pratyekabuddha, and the bodhisattva. (On the arhat and bodhisattva, see the Introduction to Part II. A pratyekabuddha is someone who achieves enlightenment as an individual, neither learning from teachers nor teaching others.) By completing these three paths one will be better positioned to help others be reborn as Heavenly deities or at least human beings, rather than creatures of a lower order.

11. "Family" is my shorthand for "the Six Close Family Relations," which are one's father, mother, older siblings, younger siblings, spouse, and children.

12. In this last clause, Huiyuan quotes *Zhuangzi* 11. My translation is a slight modification from Erik Zürcher, *The Buddhist Conquest of China: The Spread and Adaptation of Buddhism in Early China* (Leiden: Brill, 2007), p. 263.

13. In this section, Huiyuan contrasts the Buddhist and Daoist ways of seeking enlightenment through the great ancestral source (*zong*), arguing that the paths are distinct but nevertheless compatible.

lar opinion there will be no moral implications worth accepting, and yet you speak about not complying with the transformations. Why?

Answer: In general, those who reside within the bounds of the temporal world receive life from the grand process of transformation. Although the great mass of things is of 10,000 varieties, and the refinement and coarseness of them are of different threads, taken as a whole their ultimate differences just lie in the distinction between sentience and insentience. Those with sentience have feelings about the transformations [of things in the world]. Those without sentience have no feelings about the transformations. When something has no feelings about the transformations of the world, its life is exhausted once its process of transformation ends. Such a life does not arise from its feelings, so its physical form decays once its transformations are extinguished. When something does have feelings about the transformations then it can be moved to act by external things. Activity necessarily accords with its feelings, so its life [as a product of action] is not cut off [by death]. Since its life is not cut off [by death] then its transformations develop a wider reach and the bodily forms [of its many lives] pile up in still greater numbers. In this way, its feelings become ever more burdensome and its hindrances become ever more profound. Words cannot describe suffering such as this. . . .

Life is shackled by one's bodily form but depends on the transformations to exist. When the transformations cause the feelings to respond, the mental capacities obstruct one's fundamental state, and so the intelligence dimly perceives the illumination [of its fundamental state].[14] When [such obstructions] form a shell-like enclosure then the only thing preserved over time is the self, and the only thing one traverses is the world of activity.[15] Thus one's sentience loses the driver that would otherwise rein it in and the road to rebirth is opened day after day. How could one be subjected to this problem just once when one has been pursuing covetous desires and affections over the long flow [of time]? For these reasons, those who return to their fundamental state and seek out the ancestral source do not hinder their mental faculties with life. Those who transcend this sinking and filthy enclosure do not hinder their life with feelings. As they do not hinder their life with feelings, their lives can be extinguished. As they do not hinder their mental faculties with life, their mental capacities can reach a state of profundity. As their mental capacities reach a profound state they can break

---

14. "Fundamental state" is my translation of *bĕn* 本, also translated as "root," "origin" or "foundation." Many Buddhists of Huiyuan's era characterized one's original state as a fully formed capacity for Buddhahood—one's "Buddha-nature." Buddha-nature, in their view, is already enlightened, and the obvious fact that we aren't fully enlightened ourselves is because we don't have full access to our own Buddha-nature. Here Huiyuan gives his account of how this unfortunate condition comes about.

15. More literally, "the only thing forded is activity." The self remains stuck in the currents of change and the suffering that they bring about.

the boundaries of the temporal world. This is what's called nirvana. How could "nirvana" be an empty term?

Permit me to extend and flesh out this position. While Heaven and Earth regard the generation of life as their greatest work, they cannot keep a living being from transforming [that is, they cannot stop living things from dying]. And while kings and other lords might regard the preservation of existence as a most meritorious achievement, they cannot stop existing things from suffering. This is why we said earlier that [Buddhists who leave the family] "understand that the reason they are burdened by suffering is because they have a body, and that they can put an end to their suffering by not preserving the body. They understand that generating life depends on being subject to the transformations of the temporal world, and by refraining from following the transformations they seek out the great ancestral source of the world."[16] The significance [of those words] lies herein. . . . It is for this reason that monks reject the practice of paying obeisance to the emperor and raise their service to a higher level. . . .

14. Fazang, "The Rafter Dialogue"

From *Paragraphs on the Doctrine of Difference and Identity of the One Vehicle of Huayan* translation by David Elstein[17]

Huáyán was a form of Mahayana Buddhism that developed in China based on the Flower Garland Sutra *(Huáyán jīng 華嚴經), which came to prominence during the Tang dynasty. Fǎzàng (法藏, 643–712) is traditionally considered the third patriarch of Huayan. He was a prolific writer, authoring commentaries on a number of important Buddhist texts in addition to works that specifically elucidated Huayan teachings. Like his "Essay on the Golden Lion" (Part II, Selection 15), the excerpt below is one of his efforts to explain core Huayan teachings through an extended metaphor, in this case the relation between a part (a rafter) and a whole (a building). This illustrates the Huayan idea of interpenetration, or absence of obstruction between all phenomena. According to the doctrine of emptiness, all phenomena lack an essence that defines what they are, independently of other things. All distinctions between phenomena are conventional, and any attempt at defining a particular phenomenon involves relating it to other phenomena. Huayan philosophy then understands these relations as mutu-*

---

16. See the first paragraph in section 2 of this essay.

17. This translation is based on the text of the *Taishō Tripitika* no. 1866.

ally constituting, so everything defines everything else. This is true of both discrete phenomena and the universe considered as a whole. From a certain perspective, everything is identical because each phenomenon relates to and thus defines every other phenomenon, and so in a sense contains its identity conditions. Yet each phenomenon is also distinct, because if it did not have its particular function it could not relate to other phenomena in the specific way it does, and we would have a different universe from the one we actually have. As Fazang says in the text, each part is identical (in making the whole and in allowing each part to be what it is), and they are identical because they are different.

In this extended metaphor, the building (the whole) can represent the entire universe, while the rafter (a part) can represent any particular phenomenon. Fazang describes six characteristics or different ways of understanding the relation between part and whole as well as the relations between the different parts. 1) Wholeness—the identity of part and whole; 2) Particularity—the distinction between the parts and the whole; 3) Identity—the mutual identity between each part, by virtue of the fact that they together form a whole; 4) Difference—the distinct functions of each part that allow them to form the whole; 5) Integration—how the distinct parts unite as conditions for the whole; 6) Disintegration—the fact that each part maintains its particularity while constituting the whole. This is not a sequence or attempt to explain how the parts actually assemble into the whole, but rather a number of different ways of looking at these relationships, any of which is available at any time, much as we can see a tree as an individual or part of the largest forest at the same time.

In explaining the "six characteristics," Fazang repeatedly tells his interlocutor to avoid the twin errors of "annihilationism" and "eternalism." "Annihilationism" is a kind of nihilism that denies the existence of the phenomenon in question. "Eternalism" is positing something that exists without a cause, and any such thing (according to Buddhists and most Indian philosophers) would be eternal. Metaphysically, Buddhism is a "Middle Way" between annihilationism and eternalism, since it acknowledges the conditional existence of phenomena, yet denies uncaused, independent, or eternal entities.

For clarity, I have added numbers to indicate which characteristic is under discussion. The text is in the form of a dialogue between an imagined interlocutor and Fazang. I have marked the imagined interlocutor's objections and Fazang's responses.—Tr.

Excerpt: "Commentary on the Complete Interpenetration of the Six Characteristics"

The third explanation [of the six characteristics] is in the form of a dialogue. Dependently originated dharmas all interpenetrate.[18] Now let us discuss this in regard to the conditions that constitute a building.

1. Wholeness

Question: What is the characteristic of wholeness? *Answer:* It is the building.

Objection: That is just the various conditions, including the rafter. What is the building? *Reply:* The rafter is the building. What is the reason? Because it is the rafter by itself that makes the building. Apart from the rafter, there can be no building. When there is a rafter, then there is a building.

Objection: If the rafter by itself constitutes the building, then when there are no roof tiles, etc., it should still be able to make the building. *Reply:* When there are no roof tiles, etc. it is not a rafter, and that is why it cannot make the building. It is not that it is a rafter but cannot make the building. Now when speaking of what can make the building, it is just the rafter that can do it, not a non-rafter. Why? Because the rafter is acting as a cause. When it has not made the building it is not acting as a cause, and so it is not a condition. If it is a rafter, it totally forms the building. If it does not totally form the building, it is not called a rafter.

Objection: What is the error [in thinking that] the rafter and other various conditions each contribute a small part of the power to form the building together (rather than each entirely forming the building)? *Reply:* The errors of annihilationism and eternalism. If each condition does not entirely form the building but instead just contributes part of the power to form the building, this is just many small parts. Because they do not constitute a whole building, there is the error of annihilationism. The various conditions all have partial power and cannot constitute the whole. Then if you assert that there is a whole building, it exists without conditions. This is the error of eternalism. If they do not wholly form the building, then when the rafter is removed the whole building should remain, but since the building does not remain whole we know that it is not formed by the joining of several partial powers.

Question: Without one rafter, isn't it [still] a building? *Answer:* It is just a ruined building, not a functional building. That is how we know the functional building entirely depends on the rafter. Because it entirely depends on the rafter, we know the rafter is the building.

---

18. "Dharma" (fǎ 法) is an important but systematically ambiguous term in Buddhism. Here, it refers to the transient and causally conditioned phenomena of the world.

Objection: Since the building is the rafter, then the planks, roof tiles, etc., should also be the rafter. *Reply:* They all are the rafter. Why? Because without the rafter there is no building. If there is no rafter, the building is wrecked. Since the building is wrecked, they are not called planks, roof tiles, etc. This is why the planks, roof tiles, etc. are the rafter. If they were not the rafter, the building could not be constructed. The rafter, tiles, etc. could not exist. Now, since they all exist, we know their characteristics are identical. They are identical with the rafter. And this applies to the other conditions as well in similar fashion.

Thus, whenever all dependently originated dharmas are not complete, they all cease. If they are completed, then their characteristics are identical. Fused and melded together without impediment, they are perfectly free, difficult to conceive and surpassing measure. The nature of dharmas is dependent origination, which can be universally understood through this example.

2. Particularity

There is the characteristic of particularity. The rafter and other conditions for the building are different from the whole. If they were not different, the whole could not exist. *Question:* What does it mean that when there are no parts, there is no whole? *Answer:* Fundamentally, the whole is composed of parts. If there were no parts the whole could not be formed. Thus, they are different. So it is the whole that makes them parts.

Objection: If the whole is identical with the parts, they should not constitute a whole. *Reply:* It is because there is a whole that there are parts. This is why they can constitute a whole. Just as the rafter's being identical with the building is called the characteristic of wholeness, the rafter's [still] being the rafter is called the characteristic of particularity. If it were not identical with the building, it would not be a rafter. If [the building] were not identical with the rafter, it would not be a building. The whole and the parts are identical with each other. This is how you can think of it.

Objection: If their characteristics are identical, then why speak of particularity? *Reply:* It is only because they are identical that they can be particular. If they were not identical, the whole would exist separately from the parts and would not be a whole. The parts would exist separately from the whole and would not be parts. If you think about it, it will become clear.

Objection: What is the error [in thinking that the rafter and the other conditions] are not parts? *Reply:* The errors of annihilationism and eternalism. If there are no parts, there is no distinct rafter, roof tiles, etc. If there are no distinct rafter or roof tiles, then the whole building does not exist, and this is annihilationism. Or, if there are no distinct rafters, roof tiles, etc. and yet the whole building exists, this is to have a building without causes. This is eternalism.

3. Identity

There is the characteristic of identity. The rafter and other conditions join together to create the building. There is no separation between them, so they are all called conditions of the building. This is called the characteristic of identity because they do not make some other thing.

Objection: How is this different from the characteristic of wholeness? *Reply:* The characteristic of wholeness is just from the perspective of looking at the whole building. Now, the characteristic of identity comprises the rafter and other conditions. Although their shapes are different they are the same in having the power to make [the building], and so this is called the characteristic of identity.

Objection: What is the error [in thinking that the rafter and the other conditions] are not identical? *Reply:* If they are not identical, then there are the errors of annihilationism and eternalism. Why? If they were not identical the rafter and other materials would oppose each other and could not combine to create the building. The building would not exist, and this would be annihilationism. If they oppose each other and do not create the building, and yet the building is still held to exist, this building would have no cause. This is eternalism.

4. Difference

There is the characteristic of difference. The rafter and other conditions appear different from each other according to their distinct shapes.

Objection: If they are different, they should not be identical. *Reply:* They are identical only because they are different. If they were not different, then since the rafters are eight feet long, the roof tiles would be as well. This would destroy their character of being fundamental conditions for the building. The identity mentioned above as comprising the building would be gone. Since the building is complete and they are identically called conditions, one should understand their differences.

Objection: How is this different from the characteristic of particularity? *Reply:* The characteristic of particularity explained above was just that the rafter and other conditions were parts of the one building, and so this was explained as the characteristic of particularity. Now, the characteristic of difference is that when looking from the rafter to the other conditions, each has the characteristic of being different from the others.

Objection: What is the error [in thinking that the rafter and the other conditions] are not different? *Reply:* There are the errors of annihilationism and eternalism. Why? Because if they are not different, the roof tiles are identical with the eight-foot-long rafters. This is to destroy their character as fundamental conditions [for the building] and make it impossible for them to construct the building together. This is annihilationism. If the destroyed conditions cannot make the building and yet the building is still held to exist, this building would have no cause. This is eternalism.

5. Integration

There is the characteristic of integration. This is how the building is formed by means of the various conditions. The rafter, etc. are called conditions because they form the building. If this were not so, neither of the two [the building or the conditions] would be. Because they are formed, one knows that each completes the other.

Objection: When we see the rafter and other conditions, each has its own character and does not form the building. Through what cause does the building come to be? *Reply:* It is just because the rafter and other conditions do not create the building that the building comes to be. The reason for this is that if the rafter created the building and lost [its own character], it would lose its fundamental character of rafterness and the building would not be formed. Now, because they do not create the building, the rafter and other conditions appear before us. Because they appear before us, the building is created. Furthermore, if they did not form the building, the rafter and other conditions would not be called "the various conditions." Because they are called conditions, we clearly know they definitely create the building.

Objection: What is the error [in thinking that the rafter and the other conditions] do not become integrated? *Reply:* There are the errors of annihilationism and eternalism. Why? The building itself depends on the integration of the rafter and other conditions. So if they do not integrate, there would be no building. This is annihilationism. Fundamentally, it is because it is a condition for making the building that the rafter is called a rafter. Now if it does not make the building there is no rafter, and this is also annihilationism. If the rafters do not make the building and yet the building exists with no cause, this is eternalism. Furthermore, if the rafter is called a rafter without forming a building, this is also eternalism.

6. Disintegration

There is the characteristic of disintegration. The rafter and other conditions each maintains its own character and do not constitute the building.

Objection: We directly perceive that the rafter and other conditions constitute the building, so how can you say they have not constructed the building? *Reply:* The character of the building is complete because they do not make the building. If they did not maintain their own character in making the building, the building would not come to be. Why? Because if they lost their own character in constructing the building, the building could not come to be. Since the building is complete, we clearly know [the conditions] did not produce it.

Objection: What is the error [in thinking that the rafter and the other conditions] create the building? *Reply:* There are the errors of annihilationism and eternalism. If you say the rafter creates the building, then it loses its character as a rafter. Since it has lost its rafter character, the building has no rafters and cannot exist. This is annihilationism. If the rafter has lost its rafterness and yet the building exists, then there is a building without rafters, and this is eternalism.

To recap, wholeness is the building; particularity is the conditions. Identity is [building and conditions] not opposing each other. Difference is each condition considered separately. Integration is the result of the various conditions. Disintegration is each maintaining its own character. Alternatively, put in verse:

> That the one is identical with the many is called wholeness.
> That the many are not the same as the one is called particularity.
> The various kinds are identical in constituting the whole.
> Each has its particular difference manifested in the identity.
> The wondrous integration is the Pattern of the dependent origination of one and many.
> Disintegration is that each resides in its own character and does not create the whole.
> This belongs to the sphere of wisdom, not discriminatory consciousness.
> Through this expedient device one understands the one vehicle [of Huayan].

15. Fazang, "Essay on the Golden Lion"

translation by Bryan W. Van Norden[19]

China's only empress, Wu Zetian, was particularly fond of Buddhism, so she invited the monk Fǎzàng (法藏) to the palace to explain Huayan Buddhist teachings (704 CE). The empress was having difficulty understanding, until Fazang used a nearby statue of a golden lion as a metaphor. According to Huayan, all that exists are momentary mental and physical events that are connected by causal relationships.[20] The connections among these events are

---

19. The "Essay on the Golden Lion" may be found in the *Taishō Shinshū Daizōkyō*, text 1881, vol. 45, p. 668. However, a much more reader-friendly version of the text (with selections from various commentaries and notes on textual variants) is 方立天,《華嚴金師子章校釋》(北京:中華書局, 1983).

20. The term translated as "cause" in this selection is the same word rendered "condition" in the "Rafter Dialogue." "Condition" is a more accurate translation of the Buddhist technical term; however, I have used "cause" here for greater readability.

referred to as the "Pattern" (lì 理). Because any event exists simply as an aspect of the Pattern, there are no distinct, independent individuals. When someone realizes this, he will escape selfishness and be led to universal compassion for all suffering.

The gold of the statue is a metaphor for the unified, underlying Pattern of relationships, while the appearance of the statue as a lion is a metaphor for our illusory perception of things as independent individuals. We must recognize that the only thing that ultimately exists is the Pattern of relationships among momentary events. (There is really only gold; there is no lion.) However, we must also acknowledge that it is useful and appropriate to continue to speak as if there were independent, persistent individuals. (The gold really does appear to be a lion.)—Tr.

1. Explaining Dependent Arising

This means that the gold lacks any individual nature. It is only due to the causation of the craftsman that the characteristic of the lion arises.[21] The arising is dependent on causation. This is the doctrine of "dependent arising."

2. Explaining the Emptiness of Appearances

This means that the characteristic of the lion is empty. There is really only gold. There is no lion present. The Substance of the gold is never absent.[22] This is the doctrine of "the emptiness of appearances." Nonetheless, the emptiness has no characteristic of its own. It requires the appearance in order to become apparent. This does not prevent appearances from having an illusory existence, which is called "the emptiness of appearances."

3. Delineating the Three Natures

(i) The lion exists because of our feelings; this is called the nature of "pure imagination." (ii) The lion seems to exist; this referred to as the nature of "dependence on others." (iii) The nature of the gold does not change; this is called the nature of "perfection."[23]

---

21. "Characteristic" (*xiàng* 相) is a technical term in Buddhism, referring to the appearance of something, often contrasted with its actual nature. See also §8, below, and the explanation of the term in the introduction to the "Rafter Dialogue," in Part II, Selection 14.

22. "Substance" (*tǐ* 體) is a technical term in Chinese philosophy, and is often contrasted with Function (*yòng* 用): water is Substance, a wave is Function; a lamp is Substance, its light is Function. In this case, gold is Substance, the lion is Function. For more examples, see later in this selection, §6.v, and also Huineng, *Platform Sutra*, in Part II, Selection 16.

23. Some commentators use the metaphor of the rope (originally from Indian Vedanta) to explain the three natures. If one sees a rope coiled on the ground, one might mistakenly think that it is a snake (imagination). The rope exists only because of the minute fibers that make it up (dependence). In reality, it is merely these fibers, and is not a snake (perfection).

4. Making Evident the Non-existence of Characteristics

This means that the gold encompasses the lion completely. Beyond the gold there is no further characteristic of the lion to be found. This is the doctrine of "the non-existence of characteristics."

5. Explaining the Non-existence of Generation

This means that when we correctly view the generation of the lion, it is only gold that is generating. Beyond the gold there is no further thing. Although there is generation or extinction of the lion, the Substance of the gold fundamentally neither increases nor decreases. This is called the doctrine of "the non-existence of generation."

6. Categorizing the Five Teachings[24]

(i) Although the dharma of the lion is generated and extinguished moment by moment due to cause and effect, in actuality there is no characteristic of the lion to be found.[25] This is called "the ignorant dharma of those who merely heard the teachings" [i.e., Hinayana].

(ii) All dharmas, since they generate due to causation, each lack an individual nature, so ultimately there is only emptiness. This is called "the initial teaching of Mahayana" [i.e., the Consciousness-Only School].

(iii) Although ultimately there is only emptiness, this does not prevent there being an illusory existence that is manifested. Because of the conditional existence due to causal generation, dualistic characteristics are preserved.[26] This is called "the final teaching of Mahayana" [i.e., the Tiantai School].

(iv) These dualistic characteristics cease to exist, feelings and falsehood are no longer preserved and neither has any power. Both emptiness and existence are submerged. This is called "the cutting off of doctrines, the mind losing its lodging place, the sudden teaching of Mayahana" [i.e., Chan/Zen enlightenment].

(v) The feelings are extinguished, and the dharmas that are manifestations of Substance become blended into one. All activities and Functions are manifestations of the genuine reality. The myriad appearances burst forth, blended but without confusion. All is one, because all are the same in lacking an individual nature; one is all, because cause and effect follow one another endlessly. Capacity and Function encompass each other, and whether folded into one or

---

24. This section employs a common Buddhist technique of acknowledging the value of other teachings, but identifying them as lower steps on a path to the highest understanding.

25. The Sanskrit term "dharma" is an important but ambiguous term in Buddhism. It can refer to at least two different things: (1) a momentarily existing aspect of existence (e.g., the statue of the lion), or (2) the teachings of Buddhism.

26. The "dualistic characteristics" include the dualisms of "lion" and "gold," "appearance" and "genuine Substance," etc.

unfolded into many, each is in its place. This is called "the all-encompassing Mahayana teaching of oneness" [i.e., Huayan].

7. Mastering the Ten Mysteries

(i) The gold and the lion are simultaneously established, so that both are totally complete. This is called "the teaching of simultaneous completeness and mutual influence."

(ii) If the eye of the lion encompasses the lion completely, then all is nothing but the eye.[27] If the ear of the lion encompasses the lion completely, then all is nothing but the ear. Each of the parts simultaneously encompasses the others so that all are complete. So each one is mixed with the others yet each one is also pure, making a complete Storehouse. This is called the teaching of "the complete Virtue of the pure and mixed Storehouses."[28]

(iii) Although the gold and the lion embrace one another in being established, this does not prevent them from being one and many. In the midst of the Pattern, each event is different.[29] Whether one or many, each occupies its own place. This is called "the doctrine of the mutual embrace and difference of the one and the many."

(iv) All the parts of the lion, each and every hair, by means of the gold, encompass the whole lion completely. Each and every part is completely the eye of the lion. The eye is the ear, the ear is the nose, the nose is the tongue, the tongue is the body. Nonetheless, this does not prevent each of them being in its place and completely established. This is called "the doctrine of all dharma and characteristics being in their places."

(v) If we focus on the lion, there is only the lion and no gold. In this case the lion is manifest and the gold is hidden. If we focus on the gold, there is only the gold and no lion. In this case the gold is manifest and the lion is hidden. If we focus on both aspects, they are both hidden and manifest. In being hidden they are secret, in being manifest they are evident. This is called "the doctrine of the completion of the secret and the evident."

(vi) The gold and the lion, whether hidden or manifest, whether one or many, are both pure and mixed, having capacity and lacking it, both this and that. Leader and follower trade the glory. The Pattern and events are equally

---

27. The eye of the lion is gold, and the whole lion is nothing but gold, so the eye encompasses all there is to the whole lion.

28. The Storehouse (or "Storehouse Consciousness") refers to the shared human potential for either ignorance or enlightenment. See also the discussion of this concept in Zongmi, *On Humanity*, in Part II, Selection 17.

29. In Huayan, we find a complementary pairing of "Pattern" and "events." In Neo-Confucianism, we will see an analogous pairing of Pattern and *qi*. (See Zhu Xi, *Categorized Conversations*, in Part III, Selection 32.)

apparent, and embrace one another without any obstacle to their firm establishment, even in their most minute details. This is called "the doctrine of the mutual embrace and firm establishment of even the most minute."

A Representation of Indra's Web.

(vii) In every one of the lion's eyes, ears, limbs, and joints, and in each and every hair, there is a golden lion. Furthermore, the golden lion in each and every hair simultaneously enters into any one hair. Consequently, in each and every hair, there are a limitless number of lions. Moreover, each and every hair, which carries this limitless number of lions, also enters into any one hair. In this manner it is repeated inexhaustibly, like the jewels in Lord Indra's Net. This is referred to as "the doctrine of the realm of Lord Indra's Net."[30]

(viii) We discuss the lion in order to point out ignorance. We discuss the Substance of the gold to make manifest its genuine nature. We discuss the Pattern and events as well as the Storehouse Consciousness in order to engender correct discernment.[31] This is called "the doctrine of relying on events to make manifest the dharma and engender discernment."

(ix) The lion is a created dharma that is generated and destroyed every moment. Each of these instants of time is divided into three divisions: the past, the present, and the future. And each of these divisions has its own past, present, and future. So there are three times three locations, establishing the "nine periods," which are bound together into one gateway to the teachings of the Buddha.[32] So although there are nine periods, each with its own borders, they are established because of one another. They thereby interfuse, without obstacle, to become one moment. This is called "the doctrine of the distinct formations of the ten periods of different dharmas."[33]

---

30. Indra, a Hindu god, has a net with a jewel at the intersection of every two strands that is so bright it reflects every other jewel in the net. This becomes a Huayan metaphor for the Pattern, in which every aspect of existence (every "event" or "dharma") is connected to, defined by, and reflects every other.

31. See §7.ii above and note 28 for more on the Storehouse Consciousness.

32. The phrase "gateway to the teachings of the Buddha" (literally, "gateway to the *dharma*") may be intended to suggest that everything, no matter how transient or minute, presents a potential opportunity to achieve enlightenment.

33. The "tenth realm" is the complete moment composed of the other nine moments described earlier. The point of this passage is to undermine our attachment to any one moment in time, by calling into question our ability to differentiate one moment from another.

(x) The gold and the lion, whether hidden or manifest, whether one or many, lack any individual natures. It is only due to the machinations of the mind that we discuss events or the Pattern, that there is completion and establishment. This is called "the doctrine of completion due only to the machinations of the mind."

8. Embracing the Six Characteristics

(i) The lion is the characteristic of wholeness. (ii) The distinct parts of the lion are the characteristic of particularity. (iii) That they all originated from one cause is the characteristic of identity. (iv) That the eyes, ears, and other parts do not merge into one another is the characteristic of difference. (v) That all the parts together make up the lion is the characteristic of integration. (vi) That each part occupies its own place is the characteristic of disintegration.[34]

9. Achieving Bodhi

"Bodhi" refers to the Way, to enlightenment. It means that when one sees the lion, one sees that all created dharmas, even before they decay, are already in a state of calm extinction. Following the path that leaves behind both attachment and renunciation, so that we enter the Ocean of Omniscience, is called the "Way." To comprehend that throughout endless time all tribulations are fundamentally lacking in reality is called "enlightenment." When this ultimately embraces all forms of wisdom, it is called "achieving Bodhi."

10. Entering Nirvana

Both the characteristic of the lion and that of the gold are extinguished, without engendering any perturbations. Though the beautiful and the disgusting are present, our heart is as calm as the sea. Deluded thoughts are extinguished and there are no more cravings. One flees all bonds, escapes all limitations, and forever abandons the fount of bitterness. This is called "entering nirvana."

16. Huineng, *Platform Sutra*

translation by Philip J. Ivanhoe

The Platform Sutra of the Sixth Patriarch *(Liùzǔ Tánjīng* 六祖壇經*) is one of the classics of Chinese Buddhism. It purports to be a written transcription of the lectures of Huinéng* 惠能 *(638–713), the "Sixth Patriarch" of the text's title. Huineng is widely regarded as the founder of the Southern School of Chan Buddhism, better known in the modern West by its Japanese*

---

34. This section corresponds to the six "characteristics" discussed in Fazang, "Rafter Dialogue," in Part II, Selection 14.

*name, Zen. Perhaps more than any other spiritual leader, Huineng put
a distinctively Chinese stamp on the Buddhist tradition, combining Chinese and especially Daoist views about agency and mental discipline with
originally Indian Buddhist ideas about enlightenment and salvation. The
sūtra begins with a brief description of Huineng's rise from menial laborer to
standard-bearer for the Chan tradition, describing how he won his predeces-
sor's approval by answering a call to put Buddhist enlightenment in verse.
Huineng then proceeds to elucidate several of the views that characterized his
understanding of Buddhist wisdom and practice. The following translation
draws from both the biographical and the more expositional portions of the
sūtra, with the translator's commentary, in brackets and italics, following
some sections.[35]—Eds.*

4

One day, suddenly and quite unexpectedly, the Fifth Patriarch asked that all
his disciples come to him. When they had gathered together, he said, "I say
to you that birth and death are great affairs for the people of the world.[36] You
disciples practice self-cultivation all day long, but all you seek is [rebirth in]
blessed realms. You do not seek to escape from the bitter sea of birth and death.
Your self-nature deludes you regarding the gateway to blessings; how can it possibly save you? All of you ponder this; return to your rooms and look within
yourselves. Those with understanding and insight will grasp for themselves the
prajñā-wisdom of their fundamental nature.[37] Each of you, write a poem for me.
I will look at your compositions, and if there is one among you who is enlightened regarding the great insight,[38] I will grant him the robe and the *dharma*[39]
and make him the Sixth Patriarch. Quickly now, make haste!"

---

35. This translation is based on the Dunhuang version of the *Platform Sutra*, and was
originally published in Philip J. Ivanhoe, trans., *Readings from the Lu-Wang School of Neo-
Confucianism* (Indianapolis: Hackett Publishing, 2009). It has been abridged and slightly
modified to match the translation conventions of this volume. For a more complete translation of the received text of the *Platform Sutra*, see Stephen Addiss, Stanley Lombardo,
and Judith Roitman, eds., *Zen Sourcebook* (Indianapolis: Hackett Publishing, 2008),
pp. 19–30.

36. Compare Lu Xiangshan's discussion of this idea in his "Letter to Wang Shunbo," in
Part III, Selection 42.

37. *Prajñā* is the Sanskrit term for the liberating wisdom that fully recognizes that all things
ultimately are "empty" of permanent, independent selves.

38. The "great insight" is the truth of emptiness, which constitutes enlightenment.

39. *Dharma* is a Sanskrit word that refers to Buddhist teachings or the Way in general, but its
more technical senses include an object of consciousness or consciousness itself.

6

. . . That evening, at the third watch [midnight], without anyone's knowledge, the head monk, Shenxiu, took up a candle and by its light wrote a poem on the middle of the wall in the south corridor. His poem read:

The body is the tree of insight (*prajñā*);
The mind is like a clear mirror.
Always clean and polish it;
Never allow dirt or dust!

[The head monk Shenxiu writes his verse anonymously, thereby showing admirable humility. His poem offers a good description *of the Buddhist view of things, but it does not* manifest *the highest form of understanding. The illiterate monk Huineng asks someone to read Shenxiu's verse to him; he admires it, pays homage to it, but also sees its limitation. Huineng describes what happened next. — Tr.]*

8

. . . I, Huineng, also composed a poem and asked someone who was literate to write it down for me on the wall of the west corridor as a manifestation of my fundamental mind.[40] Unless one recognizes one's fundamental mind, studying the *dharma* will result in no benefit. If one recognizes one's mind and sees one's nature, one will be enlightened regarding the great insight. My poem went:

Insight fundamentally has no tree;
The bright mirror has no stand.
Buddha-nature is always pure and clean;
How could there ever be dirt or dust?

Another verse went:

The mind is the tree of insight;
The body is the bright mirror's stand.
The bright mirror fundamentally is pure and clean;
How could it be stained by dirt and dust?[41]

[The Platform Sutra *makes clear and often repeats the fact that Huineng was uneducated and illiterate. On the one hand, this offers a polemic against*

---

40. The phrase "fundamental mind" finds one of its earliest uses in *Mengzi* 6A10, where it refers to one's innate, nascent moral sensibilities. It was taken up and used extensively by Neo-Confucians. Here it refers to an innate and perfect Buddha-mind or Buddha-nature.

41. The mind-as-mirror metaphor originally comes from the *Zhuangzi*, and is adopted by many Neo-Confucian texts. A mirror is "calm" and "unattached"; it accurately reflects the world without retaining images of what it reflects, which then would distort its future "functioning." But mirrors do not act. An enlightened Buddhist's "reflections" of the world entail acting in and responding to it in appropriate ways.

the more entrenched and well-educated monastic elite, but its philosophical point is to affirm that insight is wholly innate, not acquired through learning. Huineng's verses correct and complete Shenxiu's earlier verse and attest to his higher spiritual state. The passage concludes by noting that the other students were amazed by Huineng's verses and that the Fifth Patriarch secretly confirmed him as the rightful heir to the dharma. — *Tr.]*

12

. . . Good and learned friends, perfect understanding and insight are inherently within every person. But because of the delusion of their [conditioned] minds, they are unable to attain their own enlightenment. They must seek out a great and learned friend who will show them the way and help them see their true nature. Good and learned friends, enlightenment *is* the completion of wisdom.

13

Good and learned friends, this teaching of mine takes stability and insight as its basis. Never be deluded into saying that insight and stability are separate. Stability and insight are one Substance—not two. Stability is the Substance of insight; insight is the Function of stability. Where there is insight, stability is within the insight. Where there is stability, insight is within the stability. Good and learned friends, this is the principle of the identity of stability and insight.[42]

Students of the Way take heed! Do not say that stability precedes and gives rise to insight or that insight precedes and gives rise to stability. This is to regard stability and insight as separate. Those who embrace such a view profess a dualistic teaching. If what one says is good but one's mind is not good, there is no identity of insight and stability. If one's mind and what one says both are good, then internal and external are one, and there is identity of stability and insight. The practice of enlightening oneself does not lie in verbal arguments. If one argues about which comes first [stability or insight] one will never settle the matter. Instead, one will generate [false notions] of things and the self and will never escape the Four States.[43]

---

42. The concepts of Substance and Function, which originated with the Neo-Daoist thinker Wang Bi (third century CE), are used to make a number of points in the *Platform Sutra,* and they became central terms of art among Neo-Confucians. In §15, below, the *Platform Sutra* claims that a lighted lamp and its light form an inseparable unity. While one can logically conceive of a lighted lamp and its light as separate, they never actually occur apart from each other. Equally important is the normative dimension of these ideas: each and every Substance has a characteristic Function, and it will only fail at that Function when deprived of its natural state (like a broken lamp).

43. The Four States are birth, sickness, old age, and death. The central issue in this section is the relationship between "stability" and "insight." This is an important debate within Buddhist thought and practice. Some Buddhists tend to describe the goal of their practice as

14

Universal stability is to act with a straightforward mind at all times: in motion or at rest, sitting or lying down. The *Vimalakīrti Sūtra* says, "A straightforward mind is the field of the Way. A straightforward mind is the Pure Land." Do not falsely flatter the true Way by paying lip service to straightforwardness. One who talks about universal stability but does not act with a straightforward mind is not a disciple of the Buddha. Only the practice of a straightforward mind—not clinging to any attachment—can be called universal stability.

Deluded individuals are attached to phenomena.[44] They cling to universal stability and to the notion that having a straightforward mind is a matter of sitting motionless, eliminating delusions and not allowing thoughts to arise. They think this is universal stability. But if one follows this kind of practice, one becomes like an insentient thing. In fact, this kind of practice is an impediment to the Way. The Way must be allowed to flow freely. Why would one impede it? As long as the mind does not abide in phenomena, the Way flows freely. If the mind abides, then it is fettered. If sitting motionless [constitutes right practice] it would have been wrong for Vimalakīrti to scold Shariputra for sitting in the forest.[45]

Good and learned friends, I have seen those who teach people to sit viewing the mind and viewing purity, to remain motionless and to not allow thoughts to arise. Exerting themselves in this manner, deluded individuals fail to become enlightened, and clinging to this [method] can even cause them to go insane. There have been several hundred cases in which this has happened. Therefore to teach in this way is a grave mistake.

15

Good and learned friends, in what way do stability and insight form an identity? [They form an identity] in the same way that a lamp and its light [form an identity]. Where there is a lamp, there is light. Without the lamp there is no light. The lamp is the Substance of the light; the light is the Function of the

---

attaining and maintaining complete meditative "stability" or calm. Critics of such a view argue that this can become a selfish desire in its own right and can lead to insentience or even death (see the warnings about "cutting off thoughts" in §17). Instead, these critics advocate cultivating a saving "insight" into the true nature of self and world, as the path to liberation. The *Platform Sutra* insists that these are simply two aspects of the enlightened mind.

44. "Phenomena" here is the same word rendered "characteristic" in Fazang, "The Rafter Dialogue," and "Essay on the Golden Lion," in Part II, Selections 14 and 15.—Eds.

45. This refers to an incident described in the *Vimalakīrti Sūtra,* which is the single most important text for understanding the *Platform Sutra.* [The *Vimalakīrti Sūtra* is an Indian text in which the layman Vimalakīrti teaches the Buddha's chief disciple, Shariputra, that enlightenment should be manifested in everyday activities, and not just when sitting in meditation.—Eds.]

lamp. Though there are two names [i.e., "lamp" and "light"], there are not two Substances.[46] Stability and insight are like this.

16

Good and learned friends, in the *dharma* there is no such thing as sudden or gradual. [However,] among people there are those with sharp and those with dull spiritual capacity. Deluded individuals pursue the gradual [method]. Enlightened individuals follow sudden cultivation.[47] To realize one's fundamental mind is to see one's fundamental nature. Those who are enlightened realize that from the very start there is not the slightest difference.[48] Those who are unenlightened remain forever in the cycle of transmigration.

17

Good and learned friends, this teaching of mine has been handed down from long ago and all [who have taught it] have taken no-thought as its cardinal doctrine, no-phenomena as its Substance, and non-abiding as its foundation. [What do we mean by these?] No-phenomena is to be among phenomena yet separate from them. No-thought is to have thoughts yet not think them. Non-abiding is the fundamental nature of human beings.

Successive thoughts should not abide. Past, present, and future thoughts should succeed one another without being cut off. If a single thought is cut off, the Dharma Body separates from the physical body.[49] As successive thoughts arise, they should not abide in any *dharma*. If a single thought abides, then successive thoughts will abide. This is called being fettered. If succeeding thoughts do not abide in any *dharma* then there will be no fettering. This is to take non-abiding as the foundation.

Good and learned friends, [no-phenomena means] to separate from all phe-

---

46. Literally, "although they have two names, their Substance is fundamentally one and the same."—Eds.

47. "Sharp" and "dull" refer to the different spiritual states individuals are in as a result of past karmic inheritance. The *sūtra* says that the only kind of practice one should engage in is the practice of enlightenment, i.e., being enlightened. One should not simply practice becoming enlightened, for this would be like taking as one's goal studying rather than mastering a discipline (e.g., to aim at continually practicing but never performing on the violin). However, because people have different karmic inheritances, their individual practice must be tailored to their particular capacities. (This is one of the primary reasons for the central role of the teacher in Chan.)

48. That is, no difference between the fundamental mind and fundamental nature of those who follow the sudden method and those who follow the gradual method.

49. The separation of the Dharma Body from the physical body is an oblique reference to death. These two "bodies" are two aspects of the Buddha. Given our form as human beings, the only way we can manifest Buddha-hood is to realize both these aspects of the Buddha together.

nomena. Just be able to separate from all phenomena and the Substance of your nature [will remain] clean and pure. This is why we take no-phenomena as the Substance.

To remain unstained in every [sensory] environment is called "no-thought." In one's thoughts, one should separate from every environment and not give rise to thoughts of any *dharma*. If one stops thinking about everything, one will eliminate all thoughts. [But] if even a single thought is cut off, one will die and be reborn somewhere else. Followers of the Way take heed! Do not be obsessed with thoughts of the *dharma*. It is bad enough if you yourself go astray, [but] to lead others into delusion, unaware of one's own delusion, is to slander the *sūtras* and the *dharma*. This is why no-thought is the cardinal doctrine [of our teaching]. Deluded individuals have thoughts about their environment, and based upon these thoughts, they generate false views. All feelings and erroneous thoughts arise in this way. This is why no-thought is taught as the cardinal doctrine of this teaching.

People of the world! Separate yourselves from phenomena and do not generate thoughts. If one is without [such] thoughts then even [the thought of] no-thought will not be established. What [thoughts] should one be without? What are [true] thoughts? To be [without] thoughts is to be separate from all the feelings of dualism. Thusness is the Substance of thought and thought is the Function of Thusness.[50] If thoughts arise from one's true nature, then one's seeing, hearing, and sensing will be unstained in every environment and one's [true] self will always be present. The *Vimalakīrti Sūtra* says, "Externally, skillfully distinguishing the phenomena of various *dharmas*. Internally, remaining unmoved within the first principle."[51]

18

Good and learned friends, in this teaching, sitting in meditation has never involved viewing the mind or viewing purity, nor should one remain motionless. Suppose one advocates viewing the mind. [Such a] mind is, from the very start, a delusion. And since delusions are illusory, there is really nothing to view. Suppose one advocates viewing purity. [But] one's nature, in itself, is pure. Only because of deluded thoughts is Thusness covered over and obscured. Apart from deluded thoughts, one's nature is pure. If one does not see the fundamental purity of one's own nature and instead stirs up one's mind to view purity, this will

---

50. "Thusness" is another name for the Buddha-nature. On Substance and Function, see footnote 42, above.

51. In this paragraph, the *Platform Sutra*, like the *Vimalakīrti Sūtra*, is saying that one must be *in* the world but not *of* the world. To try to flee the world is simply to indulge a futile, selfish, and karma-generating desire. Instead, one is to allow one's inherent, pure Buddha-nature to function spontaneously, regardless of where one is, including in everyday chores, such as "carrying water and hauling firewood" (as the Tang dynasty Buddhist Pang Yun put it).

only generate delusions of purity. This delusion is without a basis [in reality]; therefore we know that those who view it are viewing a delusion. Purity lacks a phenomenal form, yet some establish a phenomenal form of purity and call this [right] practice. Those who do this obstruct their own fundamental nature and end up being fettered by purity.

If one is [genuinely] motionless, one does not take note of the errors and faults of others. This is the nature [of being] motionless. Deluded individuals keep their physical bodies motionless, but as soon as they open their mouths, they speak of the right and wrong others have done. [This is to] stray from and turn one's back on the Way. Viewing the mind and viewing purity are in fact great obstructions to the Way.

19

Now that we know this to be the case, what do we, who follow this teaching, call "sitting meditation"? In our teaching, [sitting meditation] is to be completely without obstructions. Externally, not to allow thoughts to go out to any environment is "to sit." [Internally], to see one's fundamental nature and maintain one's composure is "to meditate." What do we call meditative stability? Externally, to separate from phenomena is meditation. Internally, to maintain one's composure is stability. If externally there is some phenomenon, internally one's nature remains composed.

Fundamentally, one is pure and stable. One's composure is upset only if one is affected by the environment. If one separates from phenomena and maintains one's composure, then there is stability. Externally, to separate from phenomena is meditation. When internally [and externally] one maintains one's composure, there is stability. What we call "meditative stability" is to be externally meditating and internally stable. The *Vimalakīrti Sūtra* says, "Suddenly and completely, one regains one's fundamental mind." The *Discipline of the Bodhisattva* says, "Fundamentally, one's nature is clean and pure." Good and learned friends, see your own nature and your own purity. Cultivate and practice your own nature. If you put into practice the Dharma Body and you yourself carry out the practice of the Buddha, then you yourself will perfect the Buddhist Way.

17. Zongmi, *On Humanity*

translation by Bryan W. Van Norden

At the peak of Buddhist influence and popularity, the monk Guīfēng Zōngmì 圭峰宗密 (780–841) wrote On Humanity *as an introduction to Buddhism for the general reader. This is also a polemical work, in which Zongmi argues for the superiority of his brand of Buddhism over Confucianism, Daoism, and Buddhist sects other than his own. (The title may even be an indication that this work is intended as a rebuttal to the anti-Buddhist essays of the Confucian Han Yu, including "On the Way."*[52]*) Using a common Buddhist argumentative strategy, Zongmi acknowledges that Confucianism and Daoism both have some value; however, he argues that each really contains only partial truths whose value is limited to particular contexts. Zongmi similarly argues that, while "Hinayana" is far superior to either Confucianism or Daoism, its truth is not as comprehensive as that of Mahayana. ("Hinayana" is the derogatory term that Mahayana Buddhists use for Theravada Buddhists.) Furthermore, within Mahayana Buddhism, the teachings of the Huayan and Chan sects are the highest truths, because they offer the most comprehensive explanations for the ultimate origin of the universe, humanity, suffering, and the potential for nirvana.*

Following is a translation of excerpts from On Humanity. *In addition to leaving out some sections, particularly Zongmi's critiques of the Consciousness-only and the Three Treatise schools of Mahayana, I have also added section headings, and made some small rearrangements of the text for readability. Parenthetical comments are by Zongmi himself, while glosses in brackets are by the translator.*[53]*—Tr.*

Confucianism and Daoism

Those who practice Confucianism and Daoism only know the following. In the short term, they receive their bodily form via a continuous transmission from their "ancestors and forefathers."[54] In the long term, the one *qi* of the primordial chaos divides into two, *yin* and *yang;* these two generate three, Heaven, Earth, and humans; these three generate the myriad things. So the myriad things and humans have *qi* as their foundation.[55] Those who practice Buddhism add the following. In the short term, they get this bodily form as recompense for the karmic consequences they created in previous lives.[56] In the long term, karmic consequences develop from delusion, and bodily form ultimately has the

---

52. See Han Yu, "On the Way," in Part III, Selection 20.

53. For an excellent complete translation (from which I have learned much), see Peter N. Gregory, trans., *Inquiry into the Origin of Humanity* (Honolulu: University of Hawaii Press, 1995).

54. *Documents, Documents of Shang,* "Pan Geng 1."

55. Cf. "Lesson on the Configuration of Heaven," from Selections on *Qi,* in Part I, Selection 6.

56. "Karma" refers to intentional actions (e.g., giving charity to the poor or stealing). "Karmic consequences" are the rewards or retributions for these actions, either in this life or in future lives.

Storehouse Consciousness as its foundation.[57] All of them say that their under-standing is comprehensive, but in reality it is not.

However, Kongzi, Laozi, and Shakyamuni were all perfect sages, who es-tablished their teachings along different paths in accordance with their eras and the circumstances they responded to. Their esoteric and exoteric teachings complement one another and benefit the masses of people. But although each of them is a sage, there are distinctions between those that gave full explanations and those that gave conditional explanations. This is particularly so in regard to encouraging proper action, illuminating the beginning and end of cause and effect, investigating the myriad *dharmas*, and clarifying birth and arising from their roots to their branches.[58] The other two teachings are merely conditional, while Buddhism includes both conditional and full explanations. By encourag-ing good action, discouraging bad action, and promoting goodness, all these teachings contribute to good order, so all three can be followed. But when it comes to inferring from the myriad *dharmas*, exhaustively investigating the Pat-tern and fathoming the nature to the origin, only the teachings of Buddhism are definitive.[59] Nonetheless, scholars nowadays each cling to a single school of thought. Even many of those who take the Buddha as their teacher are still mistaken about the true meaning of Buddhism, and hence are unable to seek out the ultimate origin of Heaven, Earth, humans, and other things.

According to the explanations of Confucianism and Daoism, humans, ani-mals, and other things were all generated and reared by "vacuity" or the "Great Way." They say that "the Way models itself on spontaneity," and generates the primordial *qi*. The primordial *qi* generated Heaven and Earth, and Heaven and Earth generated the myriad things.[60] Therefore, ignorance and wisdom, prestige and lowliness, poverty and wealth, suffering and happiness are all endowed by Heaven, according to fate. Furthermore, after death one goes back to Heaven and Earth, returning to vacuity.

Now I shall briefly critique these teachings. Based on their claim that the myriad things are all generated by "vacuity" and the "Great Way," the Great

---

57. The Storehouse Consciousness is explained below, in the subsection on "The One Vehicle."

58. "*Dharma*" can refer to (1) any of the momentarily existing aspects of existence (e.g., an instant of thought or a transitory configuration of body), (2) the teachings of the Buddha, or (3) the causal laws governing such things as karma.

59. The phrase "exhaustively investigated the Pattern and fathomed the nature" is originally from the *Changes,* "Explanation of the Trigrams," 1, and was frequently quoted by Buddhists but then adopted by Neo-Confucians. See "Explanation of the Trigrams," in Part I, Selec-tion 10.

60. "Spontaneous" is usually translated as "natural" in this anthology. However, in Zongmi's work, he emphasizes the connotation the word has of being "so-of-itself" (i.e., without ex-ternal cause). The expression "the Way models itself on spontaneity" and many of the other concepts in this paragraph are from the *Daodejing,* attributed to Laozi. However, many Con-fucians of Zongmi's era would also accept them.

Way is the foundation of the generation of life and death, worthiness and ignorance; it is the basis of good and bad fortune, prosperity and disaster. Since this foundation always exists, one cannot get rid of disaster, chaos, misfortune, and ignorance. Similarly, one cannot increase prosperity, blessings, worthiness, or goodness. But then of what use are the teachings of Laozi and Zhuangzi? Moreover, since the Way rears tigers and wolves, gave birth to Tyrant Jie and Tyrant Zhou, cut short the lives of Kongzi's disciples Yan Hui and Boniu, and brought disaster upon the loyal Bo Yi and Shu Qi, why should we honor it?[61]

Another problem is that, based on their claim that the myriad things are spontaneously generated and transformed, it should be the case that everything is generated and transformed without any causes or conditions. This would mean that rocks should sometimes generate grass, grass should sometimes generate humans, humans should sometimes generate animals, and so on. Moreover, things should generate and arise without regard to temporal sequence. No one would require any potions to become a Daoist immortal. Universal peace would not require the worthy and the good. Benevolence and righteousness would not require education and practice. But then why did Laozi, Zhuangzi, the Duke of Zhou, and Kongzi establish their teachings as standards for others?

Another problem is that, based on their claim that everything is generated and takes form from the primal *qi*, how is it that the spirit of a baby, at the instant of birth, before it has been conditioned or engaged in any reflection, is already capable of having preferences and being willful? If they reply that, because it exists spontaneously, it has the capacity to develop preferences as its follows its own thoughts, then it should also be the case that it has the capacity to understand the Five Virtues [benevolence, righteousness, wisdom, propriety, and faithfulness] and the Six Arts [ritual, music, calligraphy, arithmetic, charioteering, and archery] simply by following its own thoughts. What need is there to await learning and practice to cause this understanding?[62] Moreover, the *qi* of Heaven and Earth is fundamentally lacking in awareness. If humans are endowed with *qi* that lacks awareness, how can awareness suddenly arise? Grass and trees are endowed with the same *qi*, so why do they not have awareness?

Another problem concerns their claim that poverty and wealth, prestige and lowliness, worthiness and ignorance, goodness and badness, good fortune and bad fortune, calamities and prosperity all are fated by Heaven. If this is the case, then why does Heaven, in assigning fates, give so many poverty and so few wealth, so many lowliness and so few prestige? Why, in general, do so many face

---

61. Yan Hui and Boniu were Kongzi's most virtuous and talented disciples. Bo Yi and Shu Qi were brothers from a ruling family and lived in the Shang dynasty. Both repeatedly sacrificed power and wealth in the interest of protesting wrong and maintaining concord, and both eventually died of starvation.

62. I have left out a section in which Zongmi discusses the testimony of those who claim to remember their former lives.

calamity and so few enjoy prosperity? If the allotments are up to Heaven, why is Heaven so unfair? Moreover, there are those who do wrong but get prestige, those who do right but are impoverished, those who lack Virtue but are wealthy, those who have Virtue but are poor. The unruly have good fortune while the righteous have bad fortune. The benevolent are short-lived while the cruel are long-lived. In general, those who follow the Way are taken down, while those who abandon the Way rise up. Since this is all due to Heaven, Heaven must raise up those who abandon the Way and pull down those who have the Way. Is there no way in which the good and humble are rewarded with prosperity, or the licentious and arrogant are punished with calamity? Moreover, since calamity, chaos, and recalcitrance all are fated by Heaven, then the sages were wrong when, in their teachings, they claimed that one should "hold humans responsible, not Heaven," and "lay the blame on things, not on fate."[63] Nonetheless, the *Odes* castigates bad government; the *Documents* praises the Way of true Kings; the *Rites* advocates compliance with authority; the *Music* advocates improving the people's customs. How could all this be consistent with venerating the intentions of Heaven, and complying with the mind of the Creator of Things?

From the preceding, we know that those who hold only to these teachings still have not reached the origin of humanity.

Hinayana

According to the teaching of Hinayana, due to the power of causes and conditions, the forms of the body and the thoughts of the mind are born and perish every instant, in a never-ending succession, without any beginning. They are like the flowing of a stream or the flickering of a lamp. Bodily form and mind contingently combine, seeming to be a unity and seeming to be constant. The ignorant unconsciously cling to them as the "I."

Valuing this "I" is what gives rise to the three poisons of craving, anger, and delusion. (Craving is craving for fame and profit to glorify this "I." Anger is anger at what is contrary to the feelings, fearing that they will injure this "I." Delusion is succumbing to fantasies that are contrary to the Pattern.) The three poisons stir up thoughts and instigate actions and speech that create all karmic consequences. Once karmic consequences have been created they are difficult to escape. Because of them, one obtains a life of happiness or sadness in one of the Five Destinies [being reborn in Heaven, as a human, as a hungry ghost, as an animal, or in Hell], and lives in one of the Three Realms [of the formless, the formed, and the desirous]. In the life that one receives, one clings to this "I," and this gives rise to the cravings and so forth that create karmic consequences and incur retribution for them.

---

63. Compare *Mengzi* 2B13: "The gentleman is not bitter toward Heaven and does not blame others."

Bodies are born, grow old, become sick, and die. There is death but then birth once again. Likewise, in the universe, there is formation, continuation, destruction, and emptiness. There is emptiness but then formation once again. . . . Eon after eon, coming into existence again and again, the cycle never ends. Like a spinning waterwheel, it has neither beginning nor end. This [cycle] is caused by the failure to understand that this body is fundamentally not an "I." "Is not an 'I'" means that this body fundamentally only becomes a phenomenon due to the causal circumstance of bodily form and mind coming together.[64] (The teachings of Daoism only know about the era of emptiness when this universe had not yet been formed. They refer to the "emptiness," "chaos," "the one *qi*," and so forth, calling it the "primal beginning." They do not know that prior to the emptiness of this world it had already gone through countless millions of sequences of formation, continuation, destruction, and emptiness, ending and then beginning once again. Hence, we know that even Hinayana, the most shallow teaching in Buddhism, already surpasses the deepest explanation of other doctrines.)

Now, if we extend our analysis, there are Four Elements of bodily form—earth, water, fire, and wind—and Four Aggregates of mind—sensation, perception, volition, and consciousness. (Sensation is the capacity for liking or disliking. Perception is the capacity for having mental representations. Volition is the capacity to create actions. Consciousness is the capacity to distinguish between things.) If each of these were the "I," there would be eight selves.[65] Moreover, even within the element of earth there are many more: there are 360 bones, each distinct from the others, along with skin, hair, muscles, liver, heart, spleen, and kidneys, each one different from the others. Likewise, the activities of the mind are not the same: seeing is not hearing, delight is not anger, and so on. From here we can go on to the 84,000 defilements of the body. The number of things is this vast! How can we know for certain which one to take as the "I"? If all of them are "I," then "I" am a million different things. In one bodily form, these things alternate taking control in a chaotic fashion.[66]

There are no other entities beyond these [that could be the "I"]. No matter how much one reflects and reasons about it, the "I" cannot be found. Only then does one come to the insight that this body is simply a phenomenon that results from the contingent coming together [of the Four Elements of bodily form and the Four Aggregates of mind]. Ultimately, there is no "I."

So then on whose account do we crave things or get angry? On whose

---

64. "Phenomenon" here is the word rendered "characteristic" in Fazang's "The Rafter Dialogue," and "Essay on the Golden Lion," Part II, Selections 14 and 15.

65. We could legitimately identify the self with any of the Four Elements of the body or any of the Four Aggregates of the mind, resulting in a total of eight possible identities for the self.

66. Cf. *Zhuangzi*, Chapter 2, in Philip J. Ivanhoe and Bryan W. Van Norden, eds., *Readings in Classical Chinese Philosophy*, 2nd ed. (Indianapolis: Hackett Publishing, 2005), p. 211.

account do we murder and steal? Or on whose account do we give to charity or abstain from wrongdoing? So when one does not obstruct the mind, and does not allow it to have either good or bad effects in any of the Three Realms, but rather cultivates the awareness of no-self in order to cut off craving and the other attachments, one ceases to produce any karmic consequences. This is to realize the true reality of the emptiness of the "I," and to become an arhat: one's body becomes ashes, awareness is extinguished, and one finally cuts off all suffering.[67] According to this school of thought, the *dharmas* of form and mind—along with craving, anger, and delusion—are the roots of the sensory body and the physical world. There is no other *dharma*, whether past or future, that is the root.

Now I shall critique this view. The foundation of bodies over repeated lifetimes and countless universes must in its own Substance be uninterrupted. However, the Five Sense Experiences do not arise without causes; there are times when consciousness is not active (in unconsciousness, sleep, extinction, and in some forms of meditation); and even the Four Elements are not necessary for the beings in the formless realm of Heaven. How is it that these bodies are supported, time after time, without interruption?

From the preceding, we know that those who hold only to this teaching still have not reached the origin of the bodily form.

The One Vehicle

According to the Teaching of the One Vehicle that Reveals the Nature, everything that has feelings has a fundamentally conscious true mind. Without any beginning, it has always remained pure, shining without shadow, always completely knowing. It is also called the "Buddha nature," or the "Storehouse of the Thus-Come." But throughout time, misguided thoughts have covered it, so that people are not conscious of it themselves, but only recognize the qualities of the everyday world, so they become entangled in karmic consequences and endure the bitterness of birth and death. The Buddha took pity on them and explained that everything is empty [of a separate self]. Moreover, he revealed that the conscious true mind of purity is one with all the Buddhas. Therefore, the *Huayan Sutra* says, "O sons of the Buddha, there is not a single one of all those born that does not possess the wisdom of the Thus-come.[68] But because of misguided thoughts and clinging they do not recognize it. If they leave these reckless thoughts, all wisdom, spontaneous wisdom, unobstructed wisdom, will be manifest before them."

The true mind, which is neither generated nor extinguished, is combined with deluded thoughts, which generate and are extinguished, in a manner such

---

67. See the Introduction to Part II on the Mahayana critique of the ideal of the arhat.
68. "Thus-come" refers to the ineffable absolute reality, and the Buddha.

that they are neither one nor distinct. This combination is called the Storehouse Consciousness. This consciousness has the twin significance of awareness and non-awareness. When thoughts are first stimulated because of non-awareness, it is referred to as phenomenal activity. Next, because of the lack of awareness that these thoughts fundamentally have no basis [in reality], they transform into the consciousness that perceives and the objects of perception. After that, because of the lack of awareness that these objects are manifestations of one's own misguided mind, one clings to them as if they definitely existed. This is called "clinging to things." Because one clings to such things, one sees a distinction between oneself and other things, and from this is formed the clinging to the "I." Because of the phenomenon of clinging to the "I," one craves and covets the objects that accord with one's feelings, desiring to satisfy the "I." Similarly, one hates what goes against one's feelings, fearing that it will injure oneself. From this point, ignorant feelings transform and get worse and worse.

Because of being reverent or disrespectful of [the Way] in a previous life, one suffers the consequences of being honored or lowly, with the benevolent being long-lived and the murderous short-lived, the generous being wealthy and the stingy poor, and various other rewards too numerous to mention. Consequently, we may find that this particular bodily self is unfortunate without having done any wrongs, fortunate without having done anything good, long-lived while lacking in benevolence, short-lived without having killed anyone, and so on. These are all determined by the detailed karmic consequences of actions in previous lives. This is what accounts for the differences between what happens "spontaneously" in one's current lifetime. Scholars of other schools do not know about previous existences, but only rely on what is currently visible to them, so they advocate only spontaneity.[69]

The *qi* with which we are endowed, when we infer all the way back to its foundation, is the primordial *qi* of the undifferentiated chaos [referred to by the Confucians and Daoists]. The mind that arises, when we investigate it thoroughly to its source, is the spiritual mind of genuine unity. To put it most precisely, there is nothing outside the mind. Even the primordial *qi* is a transformation of the mind. It belongs to the transformation of consciousness into the objects of perception, which is part of the phenomenal aspect of the Storehouse Consciousness.

How pathetic are petty scholars for the various mistaken views they cling to! Listen, all you who follow the Way: if you desire to become a Buddha, you must illuminate the coarse and the subtle, the roots and the branches. Only then will

---

69. In his critique of Confucians and Daoists, Zongmi claimed that they could not account for why the good sometimes suffer and the bad sometimes flourish. In this paragraph, he argues that Buddhists *can* explain this phenomenon, so the Buddhist explanation is more comprehensive. See the excerpt from *The Questions of King Milinda*, in the Introduction to Part II, on how Buddhists reconcile reincarnation with the doctrine of no-self.

you be able to discard the branches and return to the root, turning to shine light upon the origin of the mind!

18. Selected Kōans[70]

translations by Stephen Addiss and James Green

Many of the readings in Part II have focused on the theoretical and doctrinal aspects of Buddhism. However, Chan Buddhism emphasizes the practical basis of enlightenment over the theoretical. According to Chan ("Zen," in Japanese), everyday activities like cooking or cleaning, if performed with mental focus and reverence, can both facilitate and express enlightenment. Furthermore, two of the activities most commonly associated with Chan are practical techniques: meditation and the gōng'àn 公案 *("kōan" in Japanese). The* Platform Sutra *(Part II, Selection 16) explains that "seated meditation" is simply one aspect of meditation, and that true enlightenment involves maintaining insight and stability in all situations. Below, we present selections from three anthologies of famous kōans. At its most basic, a kōan is a violation of conventional rationality or customs that is used by a master to try to shock a disciple into seeing for himself the underlying unity of reality. Kōans also illustrate the major themes of Chan Buddhism: the transience and insubstantiality of everything individual (even the Buddha and his teachings), achieving enlightenment through actions in the everyday world, the unity underlying the apparent multiplicity of the world, and the need to follow the Way unselfconsciously. The most famous kōan today is probably the riddle, "What is the sound of one hand (clapping)?" formulated by the Japanese Zen master Hakuin (1686–1768). But as the examples below illustrate, a kōan can just as easily be an action, like giving someone an unexpected blow with a stick. The iconoclastic and hyperbolic nature of many kōans is part of what led Confucians (and even more conventional Buddhists) to worry that Chan had slipped into ethical nihilism. (See, for example,* Record of Linji, *section 4,* Recorded Sayings of Zhaozhou, *section 14, and* Gateless Barrier, *section 2.)*

Most of the kōans below involve four of the great Chan masters of the Tang dynasty: Mǎzǔ 馬祖 *(709–788), his disciple Nánquán* 南泉 *(died*

---

70. Translations reprinted with modifications from Stephen Addiss, Stanley Lombardo, and Judith Roitman, eds., *Zen Sourcebook* (Indianapolis: Hackett Publishing, 2008). The Introduction and all footnotes are by the editors of the current volume.

c. 835 CE), his disciple Zhàozhōu 趙州 *(778–897), and Línjì* 臨濟 *(died 866 CE).* —Eds.

Record of Linji

translation by Stephen Addiss

1. Master Linji taught, "Monks, don't be afraid of giving up your bodies and sacrificing your lives for the sake of Buddhism. Twenty years ago when I was at Master Huangpo's place, I asked him about the essence of Buddhism three times, and three times he was kind enough to hit me with his stick. But it was as though he had touched me lightly with a branch of mugwort.[71] Remembering this, I would like the favor of the stick again—is there anyone who can give me a good smack?"

One of the monks stepped forward and said, "I can do it!"

Linji held out his stick to him, but as the monk was getting ready to grasp it, Linji whacked him.

2. Master Linji asked his followers, "Do you want to know Buddhas and Patriarchs? They are standing before me listening to this lecture. You don't have confidence in yourselves, so you run around searching. But even if you find something, it will be nothing but words and phrases, not the living spirit of the Patriarchs.

"Followers of the Way, in my understanding we are no different from Shakyamuni.[72] In everything you do each day, is there anything you are missing? Followers of the Way, if you want to be the same as Buddhas and the Patriarchs, then don't seek outside yourself."

3. Master Linji said, "Followers of the Way, simply follow circumstances and fulfill your karma. When it's time to put on your robe, put it on; when you need to travel, walk onward; when you wish to sit down, just sit; and never have a single thought of entering Buddha-hood. Followers of the Way, Buddhism requires no special efforts. You have only to lead your everyday life without seeking anything more—piss and shit, get dressed, eat your rice, and lie down when you are tired."

4. Master Linji said, "Followers of the Way, if you want to understand the dharma, do not be fooled by others. Whether you turn inward or outward, whatever you encounter, kill it! If you meet a Buddha, kill the Buddha; if you meet a Patriarch, kill the Patriarch; if you meet an enlightened being, kill the enlightened being; if you meet your parents, kill your parents; if you meet your

---

71. Mugwort is a medicinal herb.

72. "Shakyamuni" is another name for Siddhartha Gautama, the Buddha.

relatives, kill your relatives. Only then will you find emancipation, and by not clinging to anything, you will be free wherever you go."

Recorded Sayings of Zhaozhou

translation by James Green[73]

1. Zhaozhou asked Master Nanquan, "What is the Way?"
   Nanquan said, "Ordinary mind is the Way."
   Zhaozhou said, "Then may I direct myself toward it or not?
   Nanquan said, "To seek is to deviate."
   Zhaozhou said, "If I do not seek, how can I know about the Way?"
   Nanquan said, "The Way does not belong to knowing or not knowing. To know is to have a concept; to not know is to be ignorant. If you truly realize the Way of no doubt, it is just like the sky: wide open vast emptiness. How can you say 'yes' or 'no' to it?"
   At these words Zhaozhou had sudden enlightenment. His mind became clear like the moon.

2. A monk asked, "What is my self?"
   Master Zhaozhou said, "Well, do you see the oak tree in the front garden?"

3. Master Zhaozhou instructed the assembly, saying, "I will teach you how to speak. If there is a time when someone questions you, just say, 'I've come from Zhaozhou.' If he asks, 'What does Zhaozhou say about the dharma?' just say to him 'When it's cold, he says it's cold; when it's hot, he says it's hot.' If he further asks, 'I wasn't asking about that kind of thing,' just say to him, 'What kind of thing were you asking about?' If again he says, 'What does Zhaozhou say about the dharma?' just say, 'When I left the Master, he did not give me any message to pass on to you. If you must know about Zhaozhou's affairs, go ask him yourself.'"

4. A monk asked, "What is 'Buddha-mind'?"
   Master Zhaozhou said, "You are mind; I am Buddha. Whether to attend upon me or not, you must see for yourself."
   The monk asked, "You are not lacking it, so shouldn't you be attended upon?"
   Zhaozhou said, "You teach me."

5. A monk asked, "What is multiplicity?"
   Master Zhaozhou said, "One, two, three, four, five."

---

73. From James Green, trans., *The Recorded Sayings of Zen Master Joshu* (Boston: Shambhala Publications, 1998). Reprinted by permission of Rowman & Littlefield.

The monk asked, "What is the reality of non-multiplicity?"

Zhaozhou said, "One, two, three, four, five."[74]

6. A monk asked, "What sort of person is it that goes beyond Buddha?"

Master Zhaozhou said, "Anyone who is leading an ox and ploughing the fields."

7. A monk asked, "What is Buddha?"

Master Zhaozhou said, "Are you not Buddha?"

8. A monk asked, "What is my self?"

Master Zhaozhou said, "Have you eaten breakfast or not?"

The monk said, "I have eaten."

Zhaozhou said, "Then wash out your bowls."

9. A monk asked, "I ask you to say something about that which is immediately at hand."

Master Zhaozhou said, "Pissing is an easy matter; I can do it by myself."

10. A monk asked, "What is the teacher of the seven Buddhas?"

Master Zhaozhou said, "Sleeping when it's time to sleep, waking when it's time to wake."

11. A monk asked, "What is the fact that goes beyond Buddha?"

Master Zhaozhou clapped his hands and laughed.

12. A monk asked, "Please point out the state of 'true ease.'"

Master Zhaozhou said, "Pointing it out makes it uneasy."

13. Master Zhaozhou questioned two new arrivals. Zhaozhou asked the first one, "Have you been here before?"

The novice monk said, "No, I haven't."

Zhaozhou said, "Then go have some tea."

Zhaozhou asked the other monk, "Have you been here before?"

The novice monk said, "Yes, I have."

Zhaozhou said, "Then go have some tea."

The head monk asked, "Why did you tell both the one who had never been here before and the one who had been here before to go have some tea?"

Zhaozhou said, "Head monk!"

The head monk said, "Yes?"

Zhaozhou said, "Go have some tea."[75]

14. Master Zhaozhou was leaving the main hall when he saw a monk bowing to him.

Zhaozhou struck him with his stick.

The monk said, "But bowing is a good thing!"

Zhaozhou said, "A good thing is not as good as nothing."

---

74. Translation modified from Green.

75. Translation modified from Green.

The Gateless Barrier
translation by Stephen Addiss

1. Master Zhaozhou was asked by a monk, "Does a dog have the Buddha-nature or does it not have it?"

Zhaozhou said, "It has nothing."[76]

2. When the monks of the Western and Eastern Halls were quarreling over a cat, Master Nanquan held it up and said, "If you are able to speak, I will spare it; if you cannot speak, I will kill it." No one could answer, so Nanquan proceeded to kill the cat.

That evening Zhaozhou returned from afar, and Nanquan told him what had happened. Zhaozhou took off one sandal, put it on his head, and left.

Nanquan said, "If you had been there, you would have saved the cat."

3. Master Dongshan was asked by a monk, "What is Buddha?"

Dongshan said, "Three pounds of flax."[77]

4. A monk asked, "What is Buddha?"

Master Yunmen replied, "A dried shit-stick."[78]

5. A monk asked Master Mazu, "What is Buddha?"

Mazu answered, "Mind is Buddha."

6. A monk asked Master Mazu, "What is Buddha?"

Mazu replied, "Without mind, without Buddha."

7. A monk asked Master Zhaozhou, "What is the meaning of the First Patriarch coming from the West?"

Zhaozhou answered, "Oak tree in the front garden."[79]

8. The First Patriarch sat facing the wall [in meditation, and would not accept Huike as a disciple]. Huike stood all night in the snow, and then cut off his own arm [as an offering, to prove his dedication. The First Patriarch then

---

76. This is traditionally the first kōan assigned to a novice monk. There is wordplay in the original Chinese of Zhaozhou's reply that is difficult to reproduce in English. It could mean, "It does not have it" but could also mean simply, "Emptiness." The former reading is the most natural, but the possibility of the second reading invites the disciple to think past the more naïve interpretation to see a deeper point (namely, that everything is characterized by "emptiness," not having an independent self). (Translation modified from Addiss.)

77. Flax is a common plant used to make linen textiles.

78. A "shit-stick" is used the way toilet paper was later used. (Toilet paper was first invented in China during the Tang dynasty, but was first used only by the very wealthy.)

79. The First Patriarch was Bodhidharma (died c. 532 CE), an Indian monk who supposedly brought Chan to China from "the West" (i.e., South Asia).

allowed him to ask a question]. Huike said, "Your disciple's mind is not at rest. I beg you, Master, give it peace."

The First Patriarch replied, "Bring me your mind and I will give it peace."[80] Huike said, "I have searched for my mind, but I cannot find it."

The First Patriarch answered, "Then I have given peace to your mind."[81]

---

80. The Neo-Confucian Wang Yangming would later echo this kōan when he challenged one of his disciples, "Give me your selfish desires. I shall overcome them for you" (*A Record for Practice,* section 122).

81. Huike went on to become the Second Patriarch. (Translation of this kōan modified from Addiss.)

Illustration for the *Classic of Filial Piety*, attributed to Ma Hezhi.

PART III: NEO-CONFUCIANISM

The Buddhist (and Daoist) Background to Neo-Confucianism

After almost four centuries of Buddhist intellectual, social, and political dominance, Buddhist concepts, terminology, and ways of conceiving the world pervaded most aspects of Chinese life. Daoist notions had widely permeated as well, and Daoism itself had come to be regarded as the third major source of philosophical and religious insight in China. In spite of their dominance, however, some ideas and values that had been more closely associated with Confucianism continued to have a strong grip on China. Foremost among these was the Confucian view about the priority of the family and the importance of filial piety. The most devoted practitioners of Buddhism, the Buddhist monks and nuns, were required to "leave the family" (*chū jiā* 出家) in order to join the religious community, in large part because they saw special attachments as obstacles to salvation and enlightenment. Buddhist beliefs also complicated the longstanding way of thinking about political authority and social hierarchy.[1] For these reasons and others, Buddhism, in spite of its long reign, remained an awkward fit for traditional Chinese culture.

The featured thinkers of this section, the "Neo-Confucians," demonstrate the power that a popular religion and philosophical worldview can have even over its strongest critics. The movement that we now call Neo-Confucianism (in Chinese, *Dàoxué* 道學 or "The Learning of the Way") was in many ways an attempt to take China back from the grips of Buddhism and Daoism, yet most experts now agree that it had nevertheless adopted—in many cases unknowingly—some Buddhist and Daoist views in its articulation of the tradition. Ostensibly, the Neo-Confucians saw themselves as continuous with the great classical Confucian philosophers, especially Kongzi (Confucius) and Mengzi (Mencius). But, in fact, several elements of Neo-Confucianism stand out as traceable to Buddhism or Daoism.[2]

Chief among these views was the notion that, in some profound sense, all things are unified into a single whole, as though different parts or appendages

---

1. For more on this see Huiyuan's *On Why Buddhist Monks Do Not Bow Down before Kings* in Part II, Selection 13. See also the introduction to Part II for a general discussion of Buddhism and its development in China.

2. For an excellent discussion of the evolution of Confucianism, see Philip J. Ivanhoe, *Confucian Moral Self Cultivation,* 2nd ed. (Indianapolis: Hackett Publishing, 2000).

of the same body—a way of conceiving one's relationship to the whole that was commonplace in Buddhism but rarely seen in classical Confucianism. The Neo-Confucians used a special philosophical term that was also popularized by Buddhism to explain this unity, "Pattern" (*li* 理, also frequently translated as "Principle"). Among the Neo-Confucians, one very widespread (but not universal) way of understanding this unity was as follows: there is something that explains or accounts for the fact that all things contribute to a grand, harmonious process of life generation. Moreover, there is something within each individual thing that explains why it is naturally predisposed to harmonize, which the Neo-Confucians conceived as its own "manifestation" or "instantiation" of Pattern. This too was a characteristically Buddhist way of thinking, uniting the Buddhist notion of an all-encompassing "Buddha-body" with the widespread belief that within each thing there is a "Buddha-nature." The Neo-Confucians also believed that our own particular manifestations of Pattern give us a kind of intuitive access to these larger processes of life generation. This echoed a popular belief among Daoists and Buddhists, although the Buddhists did not generally appeal to life and life-generation as a source of unity or value.[3]

The Major Neo-Confucian Philosophers in Historical Context

Neo-Confucianism came to intellectual maturity during the Song dynasty (960–1279). This period was in many ways a time of vibrant economic and technological development marked by the "growth of cities, increased agricultural production, technological innovation, and population growth. . . . Printing, gunpowder, the mariner's compass, the use of sophisticated techniques and machinery in the large-scale production of iron, silk, and porcelain all point to the wealth and (by some definitions) modernity of the Song."[4] However, many Chinese intellectuals were far from sanguine:

> To them, the Chinese empire, the Chinese way of life, was under threat. The Tang (618–907) empire had collapsed only recently, leaving a once unified realm in a state of fragmentation [during the Five Dynasties period (907–959)]. The Song, to be sure, had begun the task of rebuilding, but since the founding of the dynasty the Chinese state had been repeatedly invaded and occupied by "barbarian" neighbors to the north and northwest. . . . The weakness of the Chinese political and social order thus appeared very real to

---

3. One way that mainstream Neo-Confucians often expressed this point was by saying that the Pattern is "complete" in each individual, so that each individual's particular manifestation of Pattern contains all other manifestations. This strong sense of interlocking unity is reminiscent of the Buddhist metaphor of Indra's Net, described in Fazang's "Essay on the Golden Lion," in Part III, Selection 15.
4. Harold M. Tanner, *China: A History* (Indianapolis: Hackett Publishing, 2009), p. 220.

statesmen and thinkers of the day, who came to trust that a return to right principles, institutions, techniques of governing, and rites—transmitted in all the writings of the sages—would bring renewed strength to the empire and revitalize the Chinese way of life.[5]

These Confucian thinkers laid part of the blame for China's woes on Buddhism. As a result, many Song thinkers took inspiration from the Tang dynasty Confucian Hán Yù 韓愈 (768–824 CE). Han Yu lived during what might be called the heyday of Buddhism, but he argued for a return to the ways of the ancient Confucian sages, and regarded Buddhism as a major threat to traditional social structures. He also helped to define the canon that would eventually be regarded as essential and foundational for all later Confucian scholars.[6] To some extent, the opposition to Buddhism by Han Yu and other Confucians reflected cultural chauvinism against the "foreign" teaching of Buddhism. However, it also expressed legitimate concerns about the problems connected with Buddhism as a social institution.[7]

A further factor leading to the characteristic traits of Neo-Confucianism was

> a growing perception among statesmen and thinkers alike that despite the most earnest attempts during the eleventh century by activist statesmen such as Fàn Zhòngyān 范仲淹 and Wáng Ānshí 王安石 to introduce specific political and social reforms, to advance practical measures intended to address the most pressing political, military, and economic problems facing the dynasty, the empire was nonetheless still in danger. In the late eleventh century and the early twelfth century, the barbarian menace to the north continued to loom large, now in the form of the Jurchen tribespeople. The country's economy remained weak and overburdened, and the Chinese bureaucracy was embroiled in a bitter, paralyzing factionalism. Looking at the failed practical attempts at social and political reform, thinkers concluded that too little attention had been paid by men like Fan and Wang to the inner sphere, to matters of personal morality. . . . These thinkers believed that progress in political and social affairs depended on prior progress in the inner sphere or moral self-cultivation.[8]

There is some dispute about when Neo-Confucianism began, and over which philosophers to count as Neo-Confucians. However, many scholars and adherents of Neo-Confucianism identify two eleventh-century philosophers as the first to recover the Confucian tradition since the end of the classical era, clarifying and elaborating upon it so that it could compete with its Buddhist rival.

---

5. Daniel K. Gardner, trans., *The Four Books* (Indianapolis: Hackett Publishing, 2007), pp. xix–xxi.

6. See especially Han Yu, "Memorandum on a Bone of the Buddha," in Part III, Selection 19.

7. See the discussion in the Introduction to Part II.

8. Gardner, *The Four Books,* pp. xxii–xxiii.

These were Zhōu Dūnyí 周敦頤 (1017–1073) and Zhāng Zǎi 張載 (1020–1077). Drawing extensively from the *Changes* (which he believed to have been composed by sages such as Kongzi), Zhou spelled out many of the basic metaphysical notions and terms that would eventually become standard for mainstream Neo-Confucian philosophers, focusing in particular on what he called the "Great Ultimate," which describes Pattern at its most basic—as the source of *yin* and *yang*.[9] In contrast, Zhang Zai was less influential as a metaphysician, but he was later hailed as the first in the post-classical era to discuss our unity with the world as "one body," which he used to explain the fundamental goodness of human nature and our capacity for profound benevolence or care for others.[10]

Two of the most dynamic teachers and philosophers after Zhou and Zhang were brothers, Chéng Hào 程顥 (1032–1085) and Chéng Yí 程頤 (1033–1107). The two studied under Zhou Dunyi, and were relatives of Zhang Zai. Like Zhang, they were opponents of the new policies of Wang Anshi. According to many mainstream Neo-Confucians, the Cheng brothers were, philosophically speaking, generally on the same page, holding very similar views about metaphysics, ethics, and the shortcomings of rival schools. In fact, some Confucians thought their views so continuous that they often did not bother to distinguish between them, citing or quoting them as "Master Cheng" in their writings. Nevertheless, they did disagree about some significant issues. For example, earlier we explained that Pattern was conceived by mainstream thinkers as the thing that accounts for (the "source" or "basis" for) all other things, including the unified life-giving processes that they so esteemed. That seems to have been the younger brother Cheng Yi's view. Cheng Hao thought that Pattern was the unified life-giving processes themselves, for which there was no separate basis. Cheng Yi also had less confidence than his brother that we could come to understand the world through our own nature, which led him to put greater emphasis on outwardly directed inquiry and study.[11] Cheng Yi outlived his brother by nearly three decades, leaving behind many more students and a greater collection of recorded lessons and writings. This might help to explain why he tended to loom larger in the thought and scholarship of later Confucians.[12]

The four philosophers described above are all Neo-Confucians of the North-

---

9. See Zhou Dunyi, "Explanation of the Diagram of the Great Ultimate," in Part III, Selection 24. See also Selections on *Yin* and *Yang*, in Part I, Selection 7.

10. See Zhang Zai, "The Western Inscription," in Part III, Selection 23.

11. This difference in emphasis was rooted in distinctive understandings of the relationship between our nature and the rest of the cosmos. For elaboration see the introduction to Cheng Hao's "On Understanding Benevolence," in Part III, Selection 25.

12. See the various selections from Cheng Yi and Cheng Hao, in Part III, Selections 25 through 31. The classic study of the philosophy of the Cheng brothers is A. C. Graham, *Two Chinese Philosophers* (Chicago: Open Court Publishing, 1992). See also Mark Berkson, "Review of *Two Chinese Philosophers*," *Philosophy East and West* (February 1995): 292–97.

ern Song dynasty (906–1126), having lived before the Han Chinese rulers were driven out of the North and forced to relocate their capital to Hangzhou, in southern China. The loss of northern China to "barbarian" invaders only intensified the Confucians' sense that their civilization faced a spiritual crisis, and their urgency to find a solution. The Southern Song dynasty (1127–1279) witnessed the rise of the philosopher who would come to be the most important and influential Neo-Confucian in history, Zhū Xī 朱熹 (1130–1200). Zhu is sometimes described as the "great systematizer" of the tradition, because he drew from a vast array of sources to develop one elaborate, multifaceted and remarkably coherent philosophical vision. He was a wide-ranging scholar and prolific writer who produced commentaries on most of the major canonical Confucian texts, and together with Lǔ Zǔqiān 吕祖謙 (1137–1181), he pulled pivotal passages from the works of the four aforementioned Northern Song Confucians to produce the definitive anthology for Neo-Confucian thought, the *Reflections on Things at Hand* (*Jìnsīlù* 近思綠), used by students of Confucianism for several centuries.[13] He also established the curriculum that would eventually be adopted by schools that trained aspiring scholar-officials. Building on Cheng Yi, Zhu developed a nuanced metaphysics that divided the work of explaining reality between two aspects—Pattern and *qi*, the latter being a kind of energetic matter from which things are formed.[14] He developed theories about the major Confucian virtues and showed how they could all fit together, explaining how complex traits like wisdom and righteousness could be understood as functions of the more basic virtue of benevolence. He also developed and defended the view that the natures of all things, including human beings, can be viewed from two perspectives, as the Pattern in itself, or as the Pattern as manifested in the *qi*. The sum total of his writings, commentaries, and lessons take up several thousands of pages in Chinese. There are a few thousand pages of recorded lessons alone, in which Zhu fields questions about everything from history to the finer points of philosophical exegesis, in addition to most of the topics of interest to philosophers the world over. By most measures, Zhu is among the most influential philosophers that China has seen.

Not everyone agreed with Zhu Xi, though. Zhu's leading contemporary opponent was Lù Xiàngshān 陸象山 (1139–1193). Lu defended a model of moral cultivation that relied less on mastering the Confucian classics and more on spontaneously acting in accordance with one's own innate virtuous inclinations. Lu's approach was defended by the next giant among Neo-Confucian philosophers, Wáng Yángmíng 王陽明 (1472–1529), who lived in the much later Ming dynasty (1368–1644). By this time, Zhu Xi's interpretation of Confucianism had become orthodoxy, used as the basis for formulating questions

13. See Wing-tsit Chan, trans., *Reflections on Things at Hand* (New York: Columbia University Press, 1967).

14. See Selections on *Qi*, in Part I, Selection 6.

and grading answers on the civil service examinations, which were the primary route to a government position, and with it wealth and power. Wang thought that Zhu Xi's interpretation, which emphasized study of the classic texts, had profoundly distorted Confucianism, and had produced generations of pedantic bookworms, rather than people who would actively manifest Virtue. Wang defended a model of moral cultivation that relied less on mastering the Confucian classics and more on a combination of spontaneity and careful monitoring of one's own thoughts and inclinations. Among the many ideas that Wang contributed to Neo-Confucian thought and discourse, one of the most widely known is his theory of the "unity of knowing and acting" (*zhī xíng hé yī* 知行合一): that genuine knowledge inherently motivates a person to act appropriately. Another is his view that everyone has access to a special moral faculty called "pure knowing" (*liáng zhī* 良知), sometimes rendered as "innate knowing" or "conscience." Because Wang agreed with many aspects of Lu Xiangshan's critique of Zhu Xi, many people see Neo-Confucianism as having two distinct philosophical lineages: one that begins with Cheng Yi and continues through Zhu Xi (the "Cheng-Zhu School") and another that begins with Lu Xiangshan and continues through Wang Yangming (the "Lu-Wang School"). The Cheng-Zhu School is sometimes also known as the "School of Pattern," due to its emphasis on recovering our innate knowledge of the Pattern through its manifestations in classic texts and external activities, while the Lu-Wang School is sometimes referred to as the "School of Mind," because it emphasizes that we only need to look within our own minds to find the Pattern and thereby be motivated to act in accordance with it.

Neo-Confucianism dominated the Chinese philosophical scene after Zhu Xi, perhaps ending its predominance as an indigenous tradition only in the late nineteenth or early twentieth century, when many Chinese philosophers took an interest in Western thought. Given its stature and durability, we can only bring to light a sliver of the less prominent philosophers affiliated with the tradition. In this part of the volume we highlight two: Luó Rǔfāng 羅汝芳 (1515–1588) and Lǐ Zhì 李贄 (1527–1602). Both philosophers were more unconventional thinkers, taking some of their views and inspiration from Wang Yangming but developing them in surprising new directions. Luo and Li stand out as philosophers who wanted to expand traditional notions about virtue and human relationships to include women. Li is also admired for his views about the importance of living genuinely or authentically, such that we are true to what he called our "child-like minds."

Key Texts

Much as Christian philosophers and theologians appeal to the Bible to support their core religious views, the Neo-Confucians had a set of foundational texts to which they appealed as well. To use contemporary jargon, the Neo-Confucians had their own "canon" of authoritative texts. What made them authoritative was not that they were products of divine revelation, but rather they were either recorded or inspired by the sages. Those teachings and practices of the sages were considered reliable because, as most Neo-Confucians saw it, they had been put to the test and passed. Their tradition held that the ancient sages were very successful at moral cultivation, family management, and the ruling of states. To be sure, the Neo-Confucians sometimes cautioned against naïve confidence in the canon. Some worried that it interfered with a deep and more personal understanding of important truths, and some even speculated that portions were fabricated or corrupted through the passage of time. But generally speaking, if a Neo-Confucian philosopher had a view about something important in ethics, politics, metaphysics, or moral psychology, he found it useful to show that the view was either indicated by—or at least consistent with—their canon. For this reason, they frequently offered their views as interpretations of one or more of the Confucian classics, and much of their philosophical terminology was drawn therefrom.

The rise of Neo-Confucianism marks a transition between an old and a new conception of the Confucian canon. Up through the Tang, Confucians saw the Five Classics as forming the heart of the canon: the *Documents, Odes, Spring and Autumn Annals, Changes,* and *Rites.*[15] Neo-Confucians of the Song and later dynasties continued to regard these works as authoritative, but the focus of study and debate gradually shifted to what came to be known as the Four Books: the *Great Learning, Analects, Mengzi,* and *Mean.*

The *Great Learning* sets forth a framework and set of instructions for moral cultivation, beginning with the much disputed recommendation to "get a handle on things" (*géwù* 格物), which many Neo-Confucians understood as getting a deeper understanding of the Pattern that underlies things. The *Great Learning* identifies a total of eight steps that can bring a person to have a sagely effect on the character of others, but the first three are perhaps the most heavily disputed, and are most widely discussed in this volume: getting a handle on things, extending knowledge, and making thoughts Sincere.[16]

The second and third of the Four Books are the *Analects* and the *Mengzi.* According to the tradition, both are records of the lives and lessons of the Confucian tradition's great founding figures: Kongzi (also known as Confucius, whose disciples supposedly recorded the *Analects*) and Mengzi (also known as Mencius). According to almost all of the Neo-Confucian philosophers, Mengzi's

---

15. See the Introduction to Part I on the Five Classics. Confucians would sometimes use the expression "Six Classics," referring to the preceding texts along with the *Music,* a classic that supposedly existed in the time of Kongzi, but was lost before the Han dynasty.

16. "Sincerity" is a technical term in Neo-Confucianism, referring to genuineness, wholeness of mind, and unity with the cosmos. For more on this important term see the Glossary.

philosophical views were wholly consistent with Kongzi's. The Neo-Confucians regularly discussed a great deal of both texts, but a few passages tend to arise more often than others. Some of Kongzi's remarks to students suggest that "sympathetic understanding" (*shù* 恕) is a fundamental and unifying part of his Way, which many Neo-Confucians took to have profound implications for sagehood and the virtue of benevolence (see *Analects* 4.15, 5.12, and 6.30). Kongzi also famously defines the virtue of benevolence as "overcoming the self" and "turning to ritual" (*Analects* 12.1), which is another set of remarks that are often discussed. The Neo-Confucians were particularly interested in Mengzi for his thesis that human nature is good (e.g., *Mengzi* 6A6), for his brief but suggestive references to "extension" as the technique of ethical cultivation (e.g., *Mengzi* 1A7), and for his discussion of the mysterious "floodlike *qi*" that underlies the courage of worthies and sages (2A2).

The last of the Four Books is the *Mean,* prized for its subtle description of the interconnections among human nature, human psychology, and the cosmos. The Neo-Confucians were particularly interested in the *Mean* for its description of "Sincerity" (*chéng* 誠), which they saw as a kind of metaphysical wholeness required for virtue of any kind. Many also took their views about feelings and the taming of feelings from this text.

It was Zhu Xi who definitively argued for the centrality of the Four Books to Confucian education, and after his death the Four Books became the basis of the civil service examinations. Consequently, for many centuries in China, most students first became acquainted with Neo-Confucianism not by reading the primary writings of the Neo-Confucians themselves (that came later in their education), but by reading the Four Books in conjunction with Zhu Xi's commentaries on them. In the interest of representing that experience, we have provided precisely that in Part III, Selections 33–36. These sections offer snippets of the most interesting and discussed passages from these books along with Zhu Xi's interlinear commentaries, enabling us to approach the deepest insights of the sages as countless millions of Chinese scholars once did.

Key Concepts

Many of the ethical and cosmological concepts of Confucianism were already explained in the Introduction to Part I, including "Heaven," "mandate," "Virtue," and "Way." Above, we discussed several of the terms that became most central to the Confucianism of the Tang and later dynasties, including "Pattern" and "*qi*." Many additional concepts are best understood by exploring how specific thinkers use them in particular texts. However, it will be useful to have a basic grasp of the meaning of some terms that Neo-Confucians took for granted as part of their philosophical worldview. Following Mengzi, Confucians from Han Yu onward regarded four virtues as central to following the Way. Benevolence, the most important of the virtues, is manifested in one's compassion for the suffering of others. It is closely associated with "sympathetic understanding." Righteousness is apparent in one's disdain to do what is dishonorable or ethically shameful. For example, a righteous person would disdain as beneath him accepting a bribe to violate his duties. Wisdom is our capacity to distinguish right from wrong. This is not a purely intellectual knowledge, for a deep (or genuine) knowledge of what is right is the same as approving of the right, while understanding what is wrong involves disapproving of it. The fourth virtue, propriety, involves expressing "respect" or "deference" to others, especially insofar as this is done through "ritual." Consequently, propriety is closely connected with ritual; indeed, both are referred to by the same character: *lǐ* 禮.

"Ritual" originally referred to religious ceremonies, especially sacrificial offerings of food and drink to the spirits of one's ancestors. However, many centuries before the Neo-Confucians (as far back as the time of Kongzi) "ritual" had taken on a wider scope, referring also to matters of etiquette, such as the proper manner in which to greet a guest, or address a subordinate. Eventually, "ritual" became almost synonymous with appropriate behavior in general. Neo-Confucians interpreted ritual, in this broad sense, and human culture in general as manifestations of the Pattern:

> To do nothing contrary to the Pattern whether looking, listening, speaking, or moving—this is ritual. Ritual is the Pattern. Whatever is not the Heavenly Pattern is a selfish desire: even though a person may intend to do good, it will violate ritual. When one lacks human desires everything will be the Heavenly Pattern. (Cheng Yi)[17]

> "Ritual" is Pattern, and it is culture. The Pattern is the substance, and it is the root. Culture is the flower, and it is the branches. (Cheng Hao)[18]

> The word "ritual" refers to the same thing as the word "Pattern." [Those aspects of] Pattern that are manifested and can be seen are called "culture." [Those aspects of] culture that are hidden and cannot be seen are called "Pattern." (Wang Yangming)[19]

Ritual may thus be thought of as the social manifestations of the fundamental Pattern of the universe.

Neo-Confucians often mention a fifth virtue, "faithfulness" (*xìn* 信). This was already an important term for Kongzi. However, for early Confucians faithfulness was primarily trustworthiness, in the sense of honesty, particularly between friends and colleagues. Buddhists later appropriated the term to refer to a firm and unwavering belief in the teachings of "emptiness" and the underlying

---

17. *Er cheng ji*, p. 144.
18. *Er cheng ji*, p. 125.
19. Wang, *A Record for Practice*, §9, in Part III, Selection 43.

identity of everything.[20] Neo-Confucians referred to this general concept—a wholehearted intellectual and motivational commitment to the Way—using several related terms, with varying emphases: "faithfulness" (*xìn* 信) as a personal virtue, "Sincerity" (*chéng* 誠) as the metaphysical state of being faithful to one's true nature, and "actual" (*shí* 實) or "genuine" (*zhēn* 真) as what is ultimately real in contrast with what is "empty" (*kōng* 空) or "artificial" (*wěi* 偽).[21]

The Neo-Confucian emphasis on faithfulness and Sincerity is not solely the result of Buddhist influence, because it reflects a deep concern in Confucianism that one not merely behave in accordance with the Virtues, but act out of the right motivations. From Kongzi himself to Wang Yangming and beyond, the goal of ethical cultivation is not simply to act respectfully toward one's elders, but to be respectful of them, in both feelings and behavior. This is what Mengzi is expressing in two otherwise enigmatic aphorisms: he praised sage-king Shun by saying "He acted out of benevolence and righteousness; he did not act out benevolence and righteousness" (4B19), and he warned those aspiring to follow the Way that "A great person will not engage in 'propriety' that is not propriety, or 'righteousness' that is not righteousness" (4B6).

---

20. See the Introduction to Part II for these doctrines.

21. Because Neo-Confucians came to attach such great importance to "faithfulness," they were sometimes driven to ingenious interpretive moves to explain why "faithfulness" was *not* mentioned in certain contexts. See, for example, Zhu Xi's commentary on *Mengzi* 2A6 in his *Collected Commentaries on the* Mengzi, in Part III, Selection 35.

Han Yu

19. "A Memorandum on a Bone of the Buddha"

translation by Bryan W. Van Norden

Hán Yù 韓愈 *(768–824) is often regarded as the first distinctively Neo-Confucian philosopher. Although his view of human nature is quite different from what later became Confucian orthodoxy, he is seminal for his strident criticisms of Buddhism, his praise of Mengzi as the most "pure" of the followers of Kongzi, and his treatment of the* Great Learning *as a canonical Confucian text. He is also widely admired for his clear, elegant prose style.*

In 819, Han Yu wrote the following "memorandum" (also called a "memorial," an official communication to the Emperor). The Fengxiang Temple had a finger bone that was supposedly from the Buddha himself. This religious relic was going to be taken out of the temple and venerated by faithful Buddhists in a long procession that would culminate in the bone being taken to the royal palace. In this memorandum, Han Yu opposes the Emperor's participation in the veneration. Han Yu was almost executed for his outspoken views on this topic, but his polemical denunciation of Buddhism inspired many Confucians. —Tr.

Han Yu.

I, your servant Han Yu, offer the following opinion: I submit that Buddhism is simply a barbarian teaching.

From the Later Han Dynasty it has infiltrated China. It never existed in high antiquity. Formerly, the Yellow Emperor was on the throne for 100 years, and lived to be 110 years old.[1] His son, Shao Hao, was on the throne for 80 years, and

---

1. The rulers mentioned in this paragraph have all been revered by Confucians for their righteous and benevolent government. See the Introduction to Part I for more on early Chinese sage-rulers.

lived to be 100 years old. *His* son, Zhuan Xu, was on the throne for 79 years, and lived to be 98 years old. *His* son, Emperor Ku, was on the throne for 70 years, and lived to be 105 years old. *His* son, Emperor Yao, was on the throne for 98 years, and lived to be 118 years. The next two emperors, Shun and Yu, both lived to be 100 years old. These were periods of great tranquility. The commoners were at peace, happy and long-lived. Yet China did not yet have Buddhism. Afterwards, in the Shang dynasty, King Tang also lived to be 100 years old. Tang's descendent Tai Wu was on the throne for 75 years. His descendent Wu Ding was on the throne for 59 years. The histories do not state how long they lived, but we can deduce that it was probably no less than 100 years. In the Zhou Dynasty, King Wen lived to be 97 years old, King Wu lived to be 93 years old, and King Mu was on the throne for 100 years. During this period, Buddhist teachings had still not entered China, so it was not because they served Buddhism that they reached such longevities.

It was in the time of Emperor Ming of the Han dynasty that there began to be Buddhist teachings [in China]. Emperor Ming was on the throne a mere 18 years. After him periods of chaos and destruction succeeded one another, and reigns were not long. Since the Six Dynasties, the service to Buddhism has gradually become more strict, yet dynasties succeed one another more rapidly. The only exception was Emperor Wu of the Liang dynasty, who was on the throne for 48 years. He thrice offered to resign and become a Buddhist monk [and was only dissuaded by his sons and ministers]. In the sacrifices to his ancestors, he did not use sacrificial animals [as required by Confucian ritual], and only ate one meal a day, consisting of merely fruits and vegetables. In the end, he was besieged by the rebel Hou Jing, and starved to death in the Tai palace. Soon after that the entire state collapsed. People serve the Buddha seeking good fortune, but they just get more misfortune. If we look at it from this perspective, we can understand that the Buddha is unworthy to be served.

When Emperor Gaozu [the founder of the current dynasty, the Tang] first accepted the resignation of the Sui dynasty, he consulted his advisors about eliminating [Buddhism and Daoism]. At that time, the talent and understanding of the assorted ministers was not profound. They were unable to deeply understand the Way of the Former Kings, what was appropriate in past and present, and express the Emperor's sagacious insight in order to relieve the bane of the era. Consequently, the policy was eventually stopped. I, your servant, have always regretted this.

I submit that Your Most Royal Majesty's courage and sagacity is incomparable among rulers of the last thousand years. At the beginning of your reign, you did not allow people to abandon their homes to become Buddhist monks and nuns or Daoist priests, nor did you allow the establishment of Daoist temples and Buddhist monasteries. I, your servant, have always thought that the intention of Gaozu would certainly be carried out in the hands of Your Majesty. Could it be that not only will this not be carried out, but Buddhism and Daoism will even be encouraged to spread unrestrained?!

Now I hear that Your Majesty has ordered a group of monks to greet a bone of the Buddha at Fengxiang, and that Your Highness will observe from a stand as it is brought into the royal palace. And further, I hear that you have ordered all temples in turn to pay homage to it. Although I am quite ignorant, I certainly understand that Your Majesty is not so deluded regarding the Buddha that you pay this respect for the sake of good fortune. It is simply that the people are happy about the abundant harvest, and in accordance with people's feelings you are preparing a novel spectacle for the gentlemen and commoners of the capital, a simple contrivance for amusing them. After all, how could someone as sagaciously enlightened as you are believe in this kind of thing? However, commoners are foolish and benighted. They are easily confused and have difficulty understanding. Should they see Your Majesty acting like this, they will begin to say that you serve the Buddha with genuine feelings. They shall all say, "The Son of Heaven is greatly sagacious, and furthermore reverently faithful with his whole mind. Who are we commoners that we should begrudge [serving the Buddha] with our lives?" Singeing their heads and burning their fingers, in groups of hundreds, they will rend their clothes and give away their money, from morning till night, floundering around in imitation of one another, fearing only that they will be left behind, old and young running to and fro, abandoning their tasks. If this is not immediately suppressed, and [the bone] passes from temple to temple, there will definitely be those who mortify their own flesh in the name of paying homage to it. Corrupting public morals and making ourselves ridiculous to the world like this are not insignificant matters.

Now, the Buddha was fundamentally a barbarian. He did not understand Chinese; his clothes were in a different style; his mouth did not speak the doctrines of the Former Kings; his body did not wear the clothes of the Former Kings; he did not know of righteousness between ruler and minister, or of the feelings between father and son. If he were still alive today and came on a diplomatic mission to our court, Your Majesty would accept him, but do nothing more than grant him an audience in the reception hall, give him a banquet, present him with a [proper] set of clothes, and have him escorted to the border, not allowing him to confuse the masses. And now that he has been dead for a long time, how could it be proper to let this decayed bone, this vile refuse, enter the royal palace?

Kongzi said, "Revere ghosts and spirits but keep them at a distance."[2] When the assorted lords of ancient times conducted mourning in their states, they first ordered the shamans to "sweep away" bad fortune using a peach-tree branch, and only then would they mourn. Now, without reason, we take a filthy object and view it ourselves, without the shamans going first, and not using a peach-tree branch. Yet the assembled ministers do not express their disapproval, and the Censorate does not point out the error. I, your servant, am genuinely ashamed of it. I plead with you to hand over this bone to an official, to be tossed

---

2. *Analects* 6.22.

into water or fire, and be completely destroyed. Put a stop to the doubts of the world. Head off any confusion on the part of later generations. Make the people of the world recognize that what a great sage like yourself does stands out from the commonplace. Would this not be glorious?! Would this not be joyful?! And if the Buddha really has a soul that can cause misfortune, let any calamities fall upon me, your servant. With Heaven as my witness, I would not regret it.

With unlimited gratitude and the highest sincerity, this memorandum is respectfully submitted for your attention,

with awe and trepidation,
by your servant,
Han Yu

20. "On the Way"

translation by Bryan W. Van Norden

This brief essay gives a challenging philosophy of history that attempts to justify Confucianism and explain why Daoism and Buddhism may seem plausible, yet are actually dangerous to society. It has influenced many, including Zongmi, who wrote a Buddhist rebuttal to it, and Zhang Xuecheng, who used some of its ideas for his own interpretation of Confucianism.[3] —Tr.

To love broadly is what is meant by "benevolence." To act appropriately is what is meant by "righteousness." To follow and move toward these is what is meant by the "Way." To be sufficient in oneself without relying on the external is what is meant by "Virtue." "Benevolence" and "righteousness" are fixed terms. The "Way" and "Virtue" are open concepts. Hence, there is the Way of the gentleman and of the petty person, and there is the Virtue that is unfortunate and that which is auspicious.[4]

When Laozi treated benevolence and righteousness as petty, it was not that he was slandering them. It was that his perspective was petty. If someone sitting in a well looks up at the Heavens and says, "Heaven is tiny," it is not Heaven that is tiny. Laozi regarded trivial kindness as benevolence, and petty carefulness as righteousness. It is appropriate that he would treat these things as petty. But what he meant by the Way, and what he treated as the Way, is not what I mean

---

3. See Zongmi, *On Humanity*, in Part II, Selection 17, and Zhang Xuecheng, "On the Way," in Part IV, Selection 52.

4. The Chinese *dé* 德 is like the English "virtue" in that it usually refers to a stable disposition toward morality, but can also have the sense of the distinctive disposition of something, whether good or bad (e.g., "arsenic kills in virtue of being a poison").

by the Way. What he meant by Virtue, and what he treated as Virtue, is not what I mean by Virtue. In general, what I mean by the Way and Virtue is what is harmonious with benevolence and righteousness. This is the common doctrine of the world. What Laozi meant by the Way and Virtue abandoned benevolence and righteousness. This is the private doctrine of a single person.

The Way of the Zhou Dynasty declined. Kongzi passed away. There was the Qin dynasty burning of books. There was the Huang-Lao Daoism of the Han dynasty.[5] There was Buddhism during the Six Dynasties period and the Sui dynasty. When doctrines regarding the Way, Virtue, benevolence, and righteousness did not tend toward Yangism, then they tended toward Mohism; or if they did not tend toward Daoism, then they tended toward Buddhism.[6] If they entered into the one, they would always come out into the other. Entering, they treated it as their master; leaving, they treated it as their slave. Entering, they sided with it; leaving, they slandered it. Alas! If later people desired to hear an explanation of benevolence, righteousness, the Way, and Virtue, whom could they follow to listen to? The Daoists say, "Kongzi was actually a disciple of our teacher." The Buddhists say, "Kongzi was actually a disciple of our teacher."[7] Those who favored Confucianism, when they heard their theories, delighted in their novelty and regarded themselves as petty. Then they too said, "Our teacher actually did once treat them as his teachers." They not only expressed this with their mouths but wrote this in their books. Alas! Even if later people desired to hear an explanation of benevolence, righteousness, the Way, and Virtue, whom could they follow to seek for it? What a great fondness people have for whatever is unusual! They do not seek out the sprouts or follow them to the tips, but only wish to hear of what is unusual.

In ancient times, the people were composed of four groups [i.e., scholars, farmers, craftsmen, and merchants]. Nowadays, the people are composed of six groups [Daoist priests and Buddhist monks in addition to the original four]. So in ancient times, those who taught occupied one of the groups; nowadays, those who teach occupy three of the groups. For one farming household there are six households that eat its grain; for one craftsman household there are six households that use its implements; for one merchant household there are six households that get goods from it. How could the people not be impoverished and resort to stealing?

---

5. On the Qin dynasty burning of books and Huang-Lao Daoism, see the Introduction to Part I.

6. This is a reference to *Mengzi* 3B9 (in Part III, Selection 35), which identifies Mohism and Yangism as the two major opponents of Confucianism during the Warring States Period (403–221 BCE). Like many later Confucians, Han Yu suggests that the Buddhism and Daoism of his own era are analogous to the Mohism and Yangism of Mengzi's era.

7. It was an often-heard myth that Kongzi was originally a disciple of either Laozi or the Buddha. (There is no historical basis for either claim.)

In ancient times, people were harmed in many ways. Only when there were sages in place were people taught the Way of nurturing one another. The sages made rulers for the people, made teachers for them, drove off vermin, snakes, and wild animals, and made them dwellings in the central plains. They were cold, and so the sages taught them to make clothing. They were hungry, and so the sages taught them to make food. When they lived in trees they fell, and when they lived in caves they became ill, so the sages taught them to make houses. The sages instituted craftsmen to supply tools for the people's use. The sages instituted merchants, in order for the people to exchange what some had and others lacked. The sages instituted doctors and medicines, in order to save the people from accidents and death. The sages instituted funerals and rituals in order to expand the people's love and kindness. The sages instituted rituals in order to put in sequence first and last. The sages instituted music, in order to express the people's pent-up feelings. The sages instituted government, in order to curb the people's laziness. The sages instituted punishments, in order to weed out the brutal. When the people cheated one another, the sages instituted tallies, official measures, and scales, in order for people to have faithfulness again. When the people stole from one another, the sages instituted city walls, armor, and swords, in order to protect them. In general, whenever anything harmful came, the sages instituted preparations against it; whenever problems developed, the sages instituted defenses against them. Yet nowadays there is the doctrine, "If sages do not die, great thievery will not stop. . . . Cut up the official measure and break the scales and the people will cease to fight."[8] Alas! They simply have not reflected upon this. If there had been no sages in ancient times, humans would long ago have perished. Why? We have no feathers or fur, scales or shells in order to endure the cold and heat [of the winter and summer]; we have no claws or fangs in order to compete for food [with other animals].

For this reason, rulers are the ones who issue orders, and ministers are the ones who put the ruler's orders into effect and govern the people. The people produce grain, hemp, and silk; they make tools and vessels; they exchange goods in order to serve those who are above them. If rulers do not issue orders, they lose that by which they are rulers. If ministers do not put into effect the orders of the rulers and govern the people, and if the people do not produce grain, hemp, and silk, make tools and vessels, and exchange goods in order to serve those above, then they deserve to be punished. Yet nowadays there is the Buddhist teaching that says, "One must cast aside ruler and minister, do away with father and son, forbid the Way of mutual nurturing," in order to seek their so-called "purity" and "nirvana." Alas! On the one hand, Buddhists and Daoists are fortunate that they did not come *during* the Three Dynasties, so that they were not eliminated by Yu, Tang, Wen, Wu, the Duke of Zhou, and Kongzi; on the other hand, they are unfortunate that they did not come *before* the Three Dynasties, so that they were not corrected by Yu, Tang, Wen, Wu, the Duke of Zhou, and Kongzi.

---

8. *Zhuangzi* 10.

An emperor and a king differ in their names, but that by which they are sages is one. In the summer one wears light clothes, in the winter one wears heavy clothes; when thirsty one drinks, and when hungry one eats. The activities differ, but that by which they are wise is one. Yet nowadays there is the saying, "Why not practice the no-activity of high antiquity?"[9] This is like challenging those who wear heavy clothes in winter, saying, "Why not wear light clothes; they're easier to wear?" Or like challenging those who eat when they are hungry, saying, "Why not drink; it's easier?"

The *Great Learning* says, "The ancients who desired to enlighten the enlightened Virtue of the world would first put their states in order. Those who desired to put their states in order would first regulate their families. Those who desired to regulate their families would first cultivate their selves. Those who desired to cultivate their selves would first correct their minds. Those who desired to correct their minds would first make their thoughts have Sincerity."[10] Thus, what the ancients meant by correcting their minds and making their thoughts have Sincerity resulted in action [not nonaction]. Nowadays, people desire to correct their minds but treat as external the world and the state, extinguishing Heaven-given universals. Someone is a son, but he does not treat his father as a father; someone is a minister, but he does not treat his ruler as a ruler; someone is one of the common people, but he does not treat his duties as duties.

When Kongzi composed the *Spring and Autumn Annals*, if any of the assorted lords used barbarian rituals, he treated them as barbarians, while those who adopted Chinese culture he treated as Chinese. The *Analects* says, "Barbarians with rulers are not as good as Chinese without them." The *Odes* says, "The Rong and Di barbarians, these he chastised; / the Jing and the Shu barbarians, these he punished."[11] Nowadays, people take up the barbarian teachings [of Buddhism] and put them above the teachings of the Former Kings. Have they not completely become barbarians themselves?!

Now, what is meant by the "teachings of the Former Kings"? Loving broadly is what they meant by "benevolence." To act in an appropriate way is what they meant by "righteousness." To follow and go toward these is what they meant by the "Way." To sufficiently have it in oneself that one need not rely upon anything external is what they meant by "Virtue." Their literature was the *Odes, Documents, Changes,* and *Spring and Autumn Annals.* Their methods were ritual, music, punishments, and government. Their peoples were the scholars, farmers, craftsmen, and merchants [and not monks and priests]. Their roles were ruler and minister, father and son, teacher and friend, guest and host, elder and younger brother, and husband and wife. Their clothes were of hemp or silk. Their dwellings were homes and palaces [not Daoist temples and Buddhist monasteries]. Their foods were grains and rice, fruits and vegetables, fish

---

9. Cf. *Daodejing* 57.

10. *Great Learning,* Classic 4, in Part III, Selection 33.

11. *Analects* 3:5 and *Odes* 300.

and meat [so they were not vegetarians like the Buddhists]. The Way they made was easy to understand and the teachings they made were easy to practice. For this reason, if one shapes oneself in accordance with them, one will be agreeable and fortunate. If one shapes others in accordance with them, they will be loving and public-spirited. If one shapes one's mind in accordance with them, it will be harmonious and peaceful. If one shapes the world and the state with them, there will be no place that is not as it should be. For this reason, the feelings of the living are satisfied, and the rituals for the dead are fully carried out. When the shrine sacrifices are performed, the spirits of Heaven alight; when the temple sacrifices are performed, the ghosts of humans enjoy them.

Someone may ask: "This Way: what Way is it?"

I reply: "This Way of which I speak is not what the Daoists and Buddhists refer to as the Way. Instead, this Way was transmitted by Yao to Shun; it was transmitted by Shun to Yu; it was transmitted by Yu to Tang; it was transmitted by Tang to Wen, Wu and the Duke of Zhou. Wen, Wu, and the Duke of Zhou transmitted it to Kongzi. It was transmitted by Kongzi to Mengzi. When Mengzi died, it did not succeed in being transmitted. Xunzi and Yang Xiong grasped parts of it but not its essence; they spoke of it but not in detail.[12] Up to the Duke of Zhou, [these sages] were rulers. Hence, their actions were put into effect. After the Duke of Zhou, they were ministers. Hence, they offered more developed explanations.

This being the case, how should things be dealt with? I say, "If *they* are not blocked, the Way will not flow. If *they* are not stopped, the Way will not be practiced. Treat their people as people [rather than as monks and priests]. Burn their books. Convert their temples into houses. Illuminate the Way of the Former Kings in order to guide them. Let widows, widowers, orphans, the bereft, the abandoned, and the sick be nurtured. Couldn't this be done?"

21. "On Reading Xunzi"

translation by Bryan W. Van Norden

Although the title of this essay is "On Reading Xunzi," what is perhaps most important about it is that it establishes Mengzi as the most orthodox (the most "pure") of the followers of Kongzi. This is very significant, because while Mengzi had always been considered an important Confucian thinker, it is only with the Neo-Confucians that he attains the status of the orthodox inheritor and expositor of the Way of the sages. — Tr.

---

12. For Han Yu's views on Xunzi and Yang Xiong in relation to Mengzi, see his "On Reading Xunzi," in Part III, Selection 21.

It was only when I first read the *Mengzi* that I finally understood that the Way of Kongzi is worthy of veneration, that the Way of the sages is easy to practice, that it is easy for a king to act like a king, and it is easy for a usurper to act like a usurper. In my opinion, after the immediate disciples of Kongzi passed away, the only one who really venerated the sages was Mengzi. I only got to read the writings of Yang Xiong much later, and this made me venerate and have faith in Mengzi even more. If the writings of Yang Xiong lead one to venerate Mengzi even more, is Yang Xiong not then also a disciple of the sages?![13]

The Way of the sages was not transmitted down through the generations. As the Zhou dynasty decayed, those who liked to meddle in affairs each sought the patronage of rulers with their own theory. In droves they created chaos together. The Six Classics [*Odes, Documents, Changes, Spring and Autumn Annals, Rites,* and *Music*] and the theories of the Hundred Schools of philosophers got lumped together. Nonetheless, old masters and great Confucians still existed. However, after the burning of books during the Qin Dynasty and the Huang-Lao Daoism of the Han Dynasty, [it seemed that] the only pure ones whose works survived were Mengzi and Yang Xiong.[14] But I obtained the writings of Xunzi and then realized that there was Xunzi too. When I examined his words, they at times seemed unorthodox, but if one seeks for their basis, their differences from Kongzi are slight. Would he not be between Mengzi and Yang Xiong [in his orthodoxy]?

Kongzi edited the *Odes* and *Documents*; he wrote and corrected the *Spring and Autumn Annals*. What was consistent with the Way he preserved; what deviated from the Way he expunged. Hence, the *Odes, Documents,* and *Spring and Autumn Annals* have no imperfections. I want to edit out what in Xunzi is inconsistent [with the Way of the sages], and add it to the corpus of the sages. Would this not be what Kongzi would have wanted?

Mengzi was the purest of the pure. Xunzi and Yang Xiong were largely pure, but with small imperfections.

22. "On Human Nature"

translation by Bryan W. Van Norden

In this essay, Han Yu takes a stand on the issue of whether human nature is good, bad, or a mixture of both. His position on this topic is quite different

---

13. Yang Xiong (53 BCE–18 CE), in addition to praising Mengzi, criticized the dominant trends in Han dynasty Confucianism, which he saw as both heterodox and overly scholastic. See Yang Xiong, "Putting Learning into Practice," in Part I, Selection 4.

14. On the Qin dynasty burning of the books and Huang-Lao Daoism, see the Introduction to Part I.

*from that of Buddhists like Zongmi, who regarded the "fundamental nature"
of all humans as identical and perfectly good. Ironically, the views of later
Neo-Confucians such as Zhu Xi and Wang Yangming are closer to that of
Zongmi than to that of Han Yu. —Tr.*

"Nature" is that which is completely created at birth. "Feelings" are generated
when one encounters other things. There are three grades of human nature, and
what constitutes the nature are five things. There are three grades of feeling, and
what constitutes the feelings are seven things. Someone may ask: "What are
these?" I reply: "The grades of human nature are the higher, the middle, and the
lower. The higher among them has goodness in it and nothing else. The middle
among them can be led higher or lower. The lower among them has badness
in it and nothing else." As for the five things that constitute the nature, I say
that they are benevolence, propriety, faithfulness, righteousness, and wisdom.
In relation to these five, the higher nature is dominated by one and puts it into
practice with the other four. The middle nature, in relation to these five, does
not completely have any one, so it sometimes acts against it, and in relation
to the other four it is confused. The lower nature, in relation to these five, acts
against the one and is perversely opposed to the other four.[15] The grades of human nature follow the grades of the feelings. The grades of the feelings are the
higher, the middle, and the lower. I say that the seven things that constitute
the feelings are happiness, anger, sadness, fear, love, dislike, and desire.[16] In the
higher kind of feelings, each of these seven, when it is active, finds the mean. In
the middle kind of feelings, these seven are sometimes excessive and sometimes
lacking, but nonetheless they seek to accord with the mean. In the lower kind of
feelings, one acts in accordance with the feelings regardless of whether they are
lacking or excessive. The grades of the feelings follow the grades of the natures.

Mengzi's doctrine of the nature was, "Human nature is good." Xunzi's doctrine of the nature was, "Human nature is bad." Yang Xiong's doctrine of the
nature was, "Goodness and badness are mixed in human nature." Now, to say
that one begins good but can become bad, or that one begins bad but can become good, or that one begins mixed but becomes good or bad—these all hold
up one point and leave aside the other extremes, grasping one and losing the
other two. When Shu Yu was born, his mother looked at him and knew that

---

15. Han Yu's account of the different grades of nature is variously interpreted. I think he
means that all the other virtues depend upon the extent to which a person is committed to
benevolence. In the most noble people, benevolence dominates and the other four virtues
follow from it; in middling people, benevolence dominates inconsistently, so the other virtues manifest unpredictably; in bad people, benevolence is rejected, so the other virtues are
routinely ignored.

16. This complete list of seven feelings comes from the *Rites*, "Li Yun." But it is also suggested
in the *Mean* 1.iv, in Part III, Selection 36.

he would definitely die as a result of bribery. When Yang Siwo was born, Shu Xiang's mother heard his cry and knew that he would definitely destroy his own clan some day. When Ziyue Jiao was born, his elder brother Ziwen regarded it as very sad, because he knew that the ghosts of the Ruo Ao clan would no longer eat [because the ancestral sacrifices would end when the clan was wiped out]. Is human nature actually good then?[17]

When Hou Ji was born, his mother was in no pain. By the time he began to crawl, he already had understanding and knowledge. When King Wen was in his mother, his mother had an easy pregnancy. After he was born, his caretakers did not have any difficulties with him. After he began his studies, his teachers had no troubles with him. Is human nature actually bad then?

Yao's son Dan Zhu, Shun's son Shang Jun, King Wen's sons Guanshu Xian and Caishu Du—it is not that the habits they were raised in were not good, but in the end they became licentious.[18] Shun's father, the Blind Man, and Yu's father, Gun [were both notoriously bad fathers]—it was not that the habits they raised their sons with were not bad, but in the end their sons became sages. Is human nature actually a mixture of good and bad? Hence, I say that when those three Masters [Mengzi, Xunzi, and Yang Xiong] discussed the nature, they held up one kind but set aside the other extremes, grasping one but losing the other two.

Someone may ask: "That being the case, can those whose natures are of the highest or lowest grade not ultimately change?" I reply: "Those of the highest grade can learn and thereby become more enlightened. Those of the lowest grade can be in fear of the august and thereby seldom do wrong. For these reasons, those of the highest grade can be taught and those of the lowest grade can be regulated. But as for their quality, Kongzi said that it could not be changed."[19]

Someone may ask: "Why is it that those who discuss the nature nowadays differ from this?" I reply: "Those who discuss it nowadays do so by mixing in Buddhism and Daoism. If one discusses it mixing in Buddhism and Daoism, how could their teachings not be different from this?"

---

17. You do not need to know the details of the lives of the individuals mentioned in this paragraph. The important point is that it was (supposedly) evident to others at the moment of their births that they would go on to do great evil. The next paragraph gives examples of people whose Virtue was evident at their birth, and the paragraph after that gives examples of individuals who turned out badly, despite having Virtuous families, or turned out Virtuously, despite having vicious parents.

18. Because of their sons' bad characters, the sage-kings Yao and Shun passed them over for the succession to the throne. Later, after the founding of the Zhou dynasty, Guanshu and Caishu plotted against their brother, the Duke of Zhou.

19. *Analects* 17.3, in Part III, Selection 34.

The Philosophical Foundations

Cheng Hao and Cheng Yi.

23. Zhang Zai, "The Western Inscription"

translation by Bryan W. Van Norden and Justin Tiwald

The "Western Inscription" is a brief statement that the philosopher Zhāng Zǎi 張載 (1020–1077) wrote and posted on the western wall of his study (hence its title). This inspiring work became one of the fundamental expressions of the ethical views of the Confucian revival of the Song dynasty. After you have read it, ask yourself: In what ways is the ethics of "The Western Inscription" similar to that of Buddhists, and in what ways is it different?[1]—Eds.

---

1. This is a question that concerned later Confucian philosophers. See, for example, Cheng Yi's "Reply to Yang Shi's Letter on 'The Western Inscription,'" in Part III, Selection 30.

Heaven is the father; Earth is the mother.[2] And I, this tiny thing, dwell enfolded in Them. Hence, what fills Heaven and Earth is my body, and what rules Heaven and Earth is my nature. The people are my siblings, and all living things are my companions. My ruler is the eldest son of my parents, and his ministers are his retainers. To respect those great in years is the way to "treat your elders as elders." To be kind to the orphaned and the weak is the way to "treat your young ones as young ones."[3] The sage harmonizes with Their Virtue; the worthy receive what is most excellent from Them.

All under Heaven who are tired, crippled, exhausted, sick, brotherless, childless, widows or widowers—all are my siblings who are helpless and have no one else to appeal to. To care for them at such times is the practice of a good son. To be delighted and without care, because trusting Them, is the purest filial piety. To defy Them is to rebel against Virtue. To do harm to benevolence is to be a thief [of people's virtue].[4] One who aids the bad is an unworthy child, while one who makes proper use of his body is an exemplary one.[5] By understanding the transformations of things, one will ably carry on Their affairs. By thoroughly grasping the spirit, one will ably continue Their plans. Be free of shame by doing nothing against one's conscience even in the most private corners of one's home. Maintain personal discipline by preserving the mind and nourishing the nature.

The sage Yu disliked strong alcohol and looked after his parents.[6] Ying Kaoshu nurtured fine character in others [by serving as an exemplar of filial piety].[7] Shun's merit lay in working tirelessly to please his parents.[8] Shen Sheng's respect was such that he never tried to escape the death sentence [that his father unjustly decreed for him].[9] Zengzi preserved the body that he received from his

---

2. Literally, "*Qian* is the father; *kun* is the mother," where *qian* is the purely *yang* hexagram, and *kun* is the purely *yin* hexagram of the *Changes.* See the *Changes,* "Great Appendix," I.1, in Part I, Selection 9.

3. The quoted phrases are from *Mengzi* 1A7, in Part III, Selection 35. The meaning is that one treats the elderly and young ones as the elderly and young ones *should be treated.*

4. A reference to *Mengzi* 1B8.

5. See *Mengzi* 7A38: "The body and its desires are part of our Heaven-given nature. But only a sage can make proper use of this body."

6. *Mengzi* 4B20 says that sage-king Yu "disliked strong alcohol but was fond of good teachings." For Yu in the context of ancient Chinese history, see the Introduction to Part I.

7. This refers to Yǐng Kǎoshū 潁考叔, apparently a border warden in the Eastern Zhou period. The *Zuozhuan* recounts a story in which Ying Kaoshu is treated to a fine dinner by a powerful duke but sets aside a piece for his absent mother. This simple act of filial love moves the duke to make amends with his own mother (*Zuozhuan,* Duke Yin, year 1).

8. For more on Shun's extraordinary filial piety, see *Mengzi* 4A2, 5A2, and 7A35.

9. See the *Rites,* "Tan Gong," part 1.

parents and returned it intact.[10] Yin Boqi was wonderous in his steadfast obedience to his father's orders.[11]

Riches, honor, good fortune, and abundance shall enrich my life. Poverty, humble station, distress, and sorrow shall lovingly guide me to completion. Living, I serve Them compliantly; dead, I shall be at peace.

24. Zhou Dunyi, "Explanation of the Diagram of the Great Ultimate"

translation by Bryan W. Van Norden and Justin Tiwald

Most of the Neo-Confucians shared a common understanding of the nature and structure of the cosmos. This is due in large part to Zhōu Dūnyí 周敦頤 (1017–1073), whose "Explanation of the Diagram of the Great Ultimate" was treated as a foundational text in cosmology and metaphysics. Zhou offers this short treatise as a way of explaining the various components illustrated in the Diagram of the Great Ultimate (below).[12] Zhou's interpretation takes many of its cues from the "Great Appendix" to the Changes, *which states: "Thus, in the changes, there is the Great Ultimate. It generates the two Modes,[13] and the two Modes generate the four Images. The four Images generate the eight Trigrams."[14] This presents a picture of the universe as having its source in a primordial unity (the Great Ultimate), which bifurcates into two complementary aspects (yin and yang). In the Diagram, the open circle at the top corresponds to the Great Ultimate, and the second circle from the top, with its semicircular bands of black and white, symbolizes the alternation and mixing of yin and yang. The third level down in the Diagram shows the Five Phases. This seems to deviate from the account in the "Great Appendix," which states that the "two Modes" generate the "four Images,"*

---

10. Zengzi was one of Kongzi's most accomplished disciples and purportedly the author of the Commentary section of the *Great Learning* (see Part III, Selection 33) and the *Classic of Filial Piety* (*Xiàojīng* 孝經). Zhang is alluding to the following passage: "Every hair and bit of skin in our bodies is received from our parents, and one dare not injure or ruin them. This is the beginning of filial piety" (*Xiaojing,* "Kaizong Mingyi," part 1).

11. Yin Boqi stood aside and let a younger stepbrother assume the throne that was rightfully his. See *Han Shi Waizhuan* 韓詩外傳, vol. 7, section 15.

12. The origin of the Diagram itself is disputed. Lu Xiangshan charged that it came from Daoism (see Lu Xiangshan, "Correspondence on the Great Ultimate," in Part III, Selection 37).

13. The two Modes are generally taken to be *yin* (represented by the – – line) and *yang* (represented by the —— line).

14. *Changes,* "Great Appendix," I.11, in Part I, Selection 9.

consisting of greater yang, *lesser* yang, *greater* yin, *and lesser* yin. *However, the capacity of Earth to act as an unnamed intermediary between the other phases can be used to arrive at a correlation between the Five Phases and four Images:*

Phase	*Fire*	*Water*	*Earth*	*Wood*	*Metal*
Image	*Greater Yang* ⚌	*Greater Yin* ⚏		*Lesser Yang* ⚎	*Lesser Yin* ⚍

Now we come to the fourth level from the top in the Diagram, which represents the generation of male and female genders. The passage from the "Great Appendix" states that the four Images generate the eight trigrams, and Zhou refers to the masculine and feminine aspects of reality as Qián 乾 *and* Kūn 坤, *terms which refer to the purely* yang *and purely* yin *trigrams,* ☰ *and* ☷.[15] *Finally, the bottom level of the Diagram represents the genera-tion of the "myriad things," all the concrete entities that make up the world. Although the myriad things are diverse, they are represented as an open circle to emphasize their interdependence.*

Traditionally, the Diagram can be read in two ways: when read from top to bottom, as we have been doing, it describes how the myriad individual things come into existence from the fundamental unity of the universe. When read from bottom to top, by contrast, the diagram shows us how we can align ourselves with (and participate in) these cosmic processes. Thus, the top to bottom reading presents a cosmology, while the bottom to top reading provides us with an ethical framework.

That Zhou became the acclaimed pioneering theorist of Neo-Confucian metaphysics is due largely to the advocacy of Zhū Xī 朱熹 *(1130–1200), who came to define orthodox Neo-Confucianism in the twelfth century and thereafter.[16] But this does not mean that Zhu (or other later Neo-Confucians) correctly understood Zhou's metaphysics. It seems likely that, for Zhou, the Diagram depicts the origin of things in time, with the "Great Ul-timate" referring to a primordial, undifferentiated* qi *that differentiates into* yin *and* yang *and eventually transforms into the myriad individual things.[17] In contrast, Zhu Xi understood the Diagram as representing a conceptual*

---

15. In most contexts, "*qian*" and "*kun*" would refer to the pure *yang* and pure *yin* hexagrams, ䷀ and ䷁, and it is possible that they have that sense here. See also "Explanation of the Tri-grams," in Part I, Selection 10.

16. See Zhu Xi, *Categorized Conversations,* in Part III, Selection 32.

17. Try reading Zhou's "Explanation of the Diagram of the Great Ultimate" in the light of the cosmogony in "Lesson on the Configuration of Heaven," in Selections on *Qi,* in Part I, Selection 6.

relationship between the complete Pattern of the universe (the Great Ultimate), and its various manifestations in qi, *including the transformations of* yin *and* yang, *the Five Phases, and the generation of specific creatures out of male and female.*[18]—Eds.

The ultimateless yet also the Great Ultimate!

The Great Ultimate moves and creates *yang*. Its movement reaches the ultimate and then it is still. It is still and creates *yin*. The ultimate of stillness returns to moving.[19] Moving and stillness in alternation are the basis for one another. When divided into *yin* and *yang*, the two Modes are established. *Yang* transforms and *yin* harmonizes, and it creates Water, Fire, Wood, Metal, and Earth. When the *qi* of these Five [Phases] spread out in accordance with the natural flow, the four seasons are enacted through them. The Five Phases are unified as one system of *yin* and *yang*. *Yin* and *yang* are unified as the Great Ultimate. The Great Ultimate is fundamentally the ultimateless. At birth, each of the Five Phases has its own nature.

The reality of the ultimateless, the essence of *yin* and *yang*, and the essence of the Five Phases coalesce in a process of mysterious conjunction. The Way of *qian* brings masculinity to completion; the Way of *kun* brings femininity to completion. These two *qi* influence one another and transformatively create the myriad things. The myriad things generate life, and their transformations are limitless.[20] But it is only humans who obtain

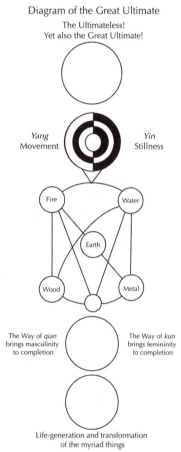

Diagram of the Great Ultimate.

---

18. This is related to the issue over how to interpret the line "what is above with respect to form is called the Way, and what are below with respect to form are called concrete things" (*Changes*, "Great Appendix," I.12, in Part I, Selection 9). For a critique of Zhu Xi's view, see Lu Xiangshan, "Correspondence on the Great Ultimate," in Part III, Selection 37.

19. "Stillness" translates the character *jìng* 靜. In some other selections in Part III, *jing* is translated as "tranquility."

20. "Generate life" translates the same phrase that is translated elsewhere as "life generation" and "life producing life" (*shēng shēng* 生生). The phrase is taken from the *Changes*, "Great Appendix" I.5, which states, "[when the Way] generates life, it is called 'change'" (see Part I,

what is excellent and most perspicacious. For as soon as their form is alive their spirit manifests intelligence. The five [Virtues] in their nature are stimulated to act.[21] Good and bad are distinguished and the myriad affairs occur.

The sage settles these affairs by using the mean, correctness, benevolence, and righteousness. (The way of the sage is nothing more than benevolence, righteousness, the mean, and correctness.)[22] He makes stillness his guiding principle. (Having no desires, he is therefore still.) He establishes the ultimate standard for humanity. Thus, for the sage, "his Virtue matches Heaven and Earth, his illumination matches the Sun and Moon, the sequence [of his activities] matches the four seasons, his good and bad fortunes match up with the ghosts and spirits."[23] The gentleman's cultivation is good fortune; the petty person's recalcitrance is bad fortune.

It is therefore said: "[the sages] established the Way of Heaven, which they called *yin* and *yang;* they established the Way of Earth, which they called soft and hard; and they established the Way of humans, which they called benevolence and righteousness."[24] And it is also said: "tracing things back to their beginnings, and in turn pursuing them forward to their ultimate conclusions, we may understand the explanations of life and death": herein lies the perfection of the great *Changes*![25]

Selection 9). Some Buddhists explicitly disavowed that there is ultimate value in life or life-production (see Huiyuan, *On Why Buddhist Monks Do Not Bow Down before Kings,* in Part II, Selection 13). Neo-Confucians rallied around the phrase as a way of distinguishing their view from the Buddhist one, arguing on the basis of the *Changes* that the universe as we find it has ultimate value after all.

21. These five Virtues are benevolence, righteousness, wisdom, propriety, and faithfulness.

22. Zhou's mention of "the mean" refers to the appropriate middle point between extremes. For more on this notion see Zhu Xi's "Collected Commentaries on the *Mean,*" in Part III, Selection 36.

23. Here Zhou quotes from the "Wenyan" commentary (one of the "Ten Wings") to the first hexagram (*Qián* 乾) in the *Changes*.

24. *Changes*, "Explanations of the Trigrams," Section 2, in Part I, Selection 10.

25. *Changes*, "Great Appendix," 1.4, in Part I, Selection 9.

25. Cheng Hao, "On Understanding Benevolence"

translation by Philip J. Ivanhoe[26]

Cheng Hao (1032–1085) and his brother Cheng Yi (1033–1107) are the two figures most responsible for what became the mature Neo-Confucian synthesis of ethics, metaphysics, and textual interpretation. All three subjects are evident in the following brief but pregnant essay. Cheng Hao suggests that all the cardinal virtues of the Confucian tradition are manifestations of benevolence. Benevolence itself is grounded in the fact that the underlying nature of everything, its Substance, is one and the same, even though the manifestations of that Substance, its Functions, are varied. The key to ethical cultivation is to "get" (to grasp intellectually and motivationally) the Pattern that interconnects everything, and focus on it through a kind of reverential attention. To do so effectively is to achieve Sincerity, the state of integrity with one's fundamental nature, which results in spontaneously virtuous action. Cheng Hao justifies this interpretation by citing a range of canonical Confucian texts.

The subtle differences between Cheng Hao and Cheng Yi are also evident in this essay. To a greater extent than his brother, Cheng Hao emphasized the underlying unity between one's own nature and the rest of the universe. Because of this extreme monism, Cheng Hao placed less importance than did Cheng Yi on scholarly "inquiry and investigation," holding that they were not essential, so long as we maintain a reverential focus on the fundamental nature we share with everything else. The points of agreement between Cheng Hao and Cheng Yi were shared by almost all later Confucians, while their differences became the basis for the later split between the followers of Zhu Xi and the followers of Lu Xiangshan and Wang Yangming. —Eds.

Those engaged in learning must first understand benevolence. Benevolence is to be completely and thoroughly one Substance with all things. Righteousness, propriety, wisdom, and faithfulness all are manifestations of benevolence. Once you get this Pattern, all that remains is to preserve it through Sincerity and reverential attention.[27] There is no need for caution or restraint, no need for inquiry

---

26. All translations from Cheng Hao and Cheng Yi based on *Collected Works of the Two Chengs* (*Er Cheng ji* 二程集), Vol. 1 (Beijing: Zhonghua shuju, 2004). The present work, "On Understanding Benevolence," appears on pp. 16–17 of this edition. [We have edited these translations to ensure consistency of terminology and citation across this anthology. The translator is not responsible for any infelicities or errors that we have introduced.—Eds.]

27. "Reverential attention" is a special term in Neo-Confucian discourse, referring to the combination of concentration and respect characteristic of someone performing an important ritual.—Eds.

or investigation. If one becomes lax, then there is a need to be on guard. If one is not lax, why would one need to be on guard? While one has yet to grasp this Pattern, there is a need for inquiry and investigation. If one has preserved benevolence for a long time, one naturally will understand; why would one need inquiry and investigation?

This Way is not opposed to any thing. The word "great" is inadequate to describe it.[28] The Functions of everything within Heaven and Earth are my Functions. Mengzi said, "The myriad things are all complete within us." I must examine myself and discover Sincerity, then I will experience the greatest of joys.[29] If I look within and find a lack of Sincerity, it will be as if there is something standing in opposition to me. If I try to bring myself and what opposes me together, in the end I will fail; how could I possibly experience joy?[30]

The point of [Zhang Zai's] "The Western Inscription" is to provide a thorough account of the Substance of benevolence.[31] If one preserves benevolence in this way, then what else is there to do? Mengzi said, "One must work at it, but do not aim at it directly. Let the mind not forget, but do not 'help' it grow."[32] Never exerting even the slightest effort—this was his way of preserving [benevolence]. If one preserves it, one will bring the self together with [all the things of the world]. Pure knowing and pure capability are never lost; nevertheless, if old habits of mind have not been eliminated one must preserve and exercise "this mind."[33] After some time, one then will succeed in casting out old habits. This Pattern is concise and simple; the only worry is that one will not be able to hold on to it.[34] Once, though, one succeeds in embodying benevolence and experiencing its joy, one no longer will worry about being unable to hold on to it.

---

28. Compare chapter 25 of the *Daodejing*, which says of the Way, "I do not know its proper name. . . . Forced to give it a proper name, I would call it 'Great.'"

29. Paraphrasing *Mengzi* 7A4, in Part III, Selection 35.

30. The thought is that the attempt to join with something opposed to oneself carries with it the idea that it is something other than the self. The ideal is to see all things as the self.

31. See Zhang Zai, "The Western Inscription," in Part III, Selection 23.

32. *Mengzi* 2A2.6, in Part III, Selection 35.

33. For the phrases "pure knowing" (*liáng zhī* 良知) and "pure capability" (*liáng néng* 良能), see *Mengzi* 7A15, in Part III, Selection 35. The phrase "this mind" (*cǐ xīn* 此心) is found in a different passage, *Mengzi* 1A7, but was adopted by many Neo-Confucians to refer to the pure and perfect innate moral mind. See Part III, Selection 35 for both passages.

34. This and the following line allude to *Analects* 15.33, in Part III, Selection 34.

26. Cheng Hao, "Letter on Calming the Nature"

translation by Philip J. Ivanhoe[35]

I have benefitted from your letter in which you discuss the idea that in calming the nature one can never be wholly unmoved since one still is disturbed by things outside the self.[36] This idea has been thoroughly discussed by worthy scholars such as yourself; what could you possibly learn from me? Nevertheless, I have thought the matter through and make bold to share my ideas.

What is called calmness is to remain calm whether in movement or at rest; there is no going after things, no welcoming things, no inside, no outside. If one regards exterior things as outside the self, and sees them dragging one away and one following after them, this is to regard one's own nature as having an inside and an outside. Moreover, if one's nature can follow after things, roaming outside the self, then while it is outside, what remains inside? This is to try cutting off outside temptations without understanding that one's nature is without inside and outside. Once one regards inside and outside as separate roots [of one's nature], how can one possibly talk about being calm?

The constant Pattern of Heaven and Earth is that their mind is within all the myriad things and so they have no mind of their own. The constant Pattern of sages is that their feelings appropriately accord with the myriad affairs and so they are without feelings of their own. And so, in the learning of cultivated individuals, nothing is more important than being broad and impartial and to respond appropriately to things as they arrive. The *Changes* says, "If you are steadfastly correct, there will be good fortune and you will have no regrets. If you waver and are irresolute, only friends will follow your thoughts."[37] If one is unsettled by the need to eliminate outside temptations, then as you wipe them out in the east they will spring up in the west! It is not just that time is insufficient but since their source is inexhaustible, there is no way one ever could possibly eliminate them.

Each of the feelings of human beings has its own deluding obsession, and so none can fully accord with the Way. The main sources of difficulty are self-centeredness and relying on cleverness. If one is self-centered, one cannot regard action as natural. If one relies on cleverness, one cannot regard enlightenment

---

35. *Collected Works of the Two Chengs,* pp. 460–61.

36. "Calming the nature" (*dìng xìng* 定性), or "calming the mind" (*dìng xīn* 定心) are the standard ways of translating the Buddhist term *samādhi,* the state of mind attained through the practice of meditation. (See Huineng, *Platform Sutra,* in Part II, Selection 16.) Neo-Confucians also advocated cultivating a calm state of mind but sought to distinguish their practice and goal from the Buddhist ideal.

37. *Changes,* fourth line-statement to hexagram 31, Xian. [Also quoted in the "Great Appendix," II.5, in Part I, Selection 9.—Eds.]

as spontaneous. Now to seek to reflect a realm devoid of things with a mind that hates external things is like looking for one's reflection in the back of a mirror. The *Changes* says, "Resting on one's back, one loses a sense of oneself. Walking through one's courtyard, one fails to see others."[38] Mengzi also says, "What I so dislike about clever people is their tendency to bore through to their conclusions."[39] Better than rejecting what is outside and affirming what is within is to forget both outside and inside. If you forget both, you will be placid and relaxed. Relaxed, you will become calm. Calm, you will become enlightened. Enlightened, how could you be troubled by the need to respond to things?

The joy of sages is the joy that is appropriate in response to things. The anger of sages is the anger that is appropriate in response to things. This is why the joy and anger of sages is not tied to their minds but to things. In light of this, how could a sage ever fail to respond to things? How could one reject following after what is outside and approve of seeking what is within? Now, do we not see that there is a great difference between self-centered or clever joy and anger and the correct and proper joy and anger of sages?

Among human feelings, the one most easily aroused and most difficult to control is anger. But if when roused to anger one can, for a moment, forget one's anger and look at what is right and wrong according to the Pattern, one will see that outside temptations are not worth one's concern, and one will be halfway to attaining the Way.

I am unable to talk about the most subtle ideas; add to that the fact that my writing is crude and awkward. Moreover, I have been busy with my official duties and so have not been able to think these things through carefully. I look forward to your reply to know what I have gotten right and wrong. I believe, though, that in regard to the main issues, I am close to being correct. The ancients thought it wrong to seek afar when the Way is near at hand. Only someone with your intelligence and insight can decide these issues!

27. Cheng Hao, Selected Sayings

translation by Philip J. Ivanhoe[40]

1. If you believe recklessness and delusion are the result of having a bad nature, please go find a good nature and exchange it for this bad nature! The Way is one's nature. If you seek for the Way outside of the nature or the nature outside of the

---

38. *Changes,* judgment on hexagram 52, Gen.

39. *Mengzi* 4B26.

40. All translations from Cheng Hao and Cheng Yi based on *Collected Works of the Two Chengs* (*Er Cheng ji* 二程集), Vol. 1 (Beijing: Zhonghua shuju, 2004); page numbers of that edition are listed in brackets at the end of the relevant passage.

Way, this is wrong. When the sages and worthies discussed natural virtue, they said that from the start the self is perfect, complete, and sufficient. If one is without stain or fault, then simply put this self into action. If one has incurred some stain or fault, then correct this through reverential attention and return to your earlier state. What enables you to return to your earlier state is that the self is fundamentally perfect, complete, and sufficient. If it is appropriate to cultivate and correct the self, and you cultivate and correct the self, this is righteousness. If there is no need to cultivate and correct the self, and you do not cultivate and correct the self, this too is righteousness. And so, in every case, [the Confucian Way] is simple, clear, and easy to carry out. In contrast, Chan Buddhists always advance the most extreme and unusual views, for example, their teaching about how the mountains, rivers, and broad expanse of Earth before one all are manifestations of one's "mysterious true mind." [41] What do such mountains, rivers, and broad expanses of Earth have to do with you?

In the case of Kongzi, even though the Way was as clear as the sun or stars above, still he was worried that there were things about it that his disciples were unable to grasp. And so, he said, "I would rather not speak." Yanzi understood what he meant in silence, but the others could not avoid harboring doubts, and so Zigong asked, "What are we, your disciples, going to record?" To this Kongzi replied, "Does Heaven speak? And yet the four seasons pass along and the various creatures are born"; this makes things perfectly clear. [42] If you are able to penetrate through to the meaning of these words, this is like the insight found in meditation; there is nothing more to understand, because there is no further explanation that can be given. Fundamentally, this Pattern admits of no duality. [p. 1]

2. No creature between Heaven and Earth is lacking in the Pattern. I have often thought about how many of the rulers and ministers, fathers and sons, elder and younger brothers, and husbands and wives in the world simply fail to fulfill their proper social obligations. [p. 2]

3. Between Heaven and Earth, it is not human beings alone who possess the upmost intelligence. Your mind is none other than the mind of grass, trees, birds, and beasts. The only difference is that human beings are endowed with the proper mean of Heaven and Earth. [p. 4]

---

41. Compare the discussion of the Storehouse Consciousness in Zongmi, *On Humanity*, in Part II, Selection 17. For one of the Indian sources of this view, see the *Laṅkāvatāra Sūtra* (Guṇabhadra edition), Chapter 2.

42. *Analects* 17.19. Yanzi (Yan Hui) was Kongzi's most promising disciple. Kongzi initially thought he was stupid, because he never asked any questions, but then he realized that Yan Hui understood everything without needing to ask any questions (*Analects* 2.9). For more on Yanzi, see Cheng Yi, "What Kind of Learning Was It that Yanzi Loved?" in Part III, Selection 28, and *Analects* 6.11 and 12.1, in Part III, Selection 34.

4. [Gaozi, arguing against Mengzi, claimed that] "What is inborn is called the nature."[43] The nature is *qi; qi* is the nature; this is what we are born with. In the endowment of *qi* that people receive at birth, as a matter of Pattern, there is good and bad. This, though, does not mean that from the start people are born with these two things opposing each other within their nature. There are some who are good from an early age and some who are bad from an early age. These are results of differing endowments of *qi*. For example, Hou Ji had a majestic and eminent appearance when just a baby, and when Ziyue Jiao was born, people could tell that he would wipe out Ruo Ao's clan.[44] The good certainly is the nature, but we cannot say that the bad cannot be called the nature as well.

"What is inborn is called the nature." The state prior to the "tranquility that people are born with" cannot be described.[45] As soon as we can talk about the nature, it is no longer the nature [in its unadulterated form]. Whenever people talk about the nature, they only are talking about "that which ensues from it is goodness."[46] Mengzi's claim that human nature is good is one example. "That which ensues from it is goodness" is like water's propensity to flow downward.

All water is water. Some flows all the way to the sea without ever becoming tainted. In such cases, what need is there to apply human effort? Some water, before it has flowed very far, becomes increasingly turbid. Some becomes turbid only after it has flowed over a great distance. Some water is extremely turbid, some only slightly so. Although clear and turbid water surely are different, it is unacceptable to say that turbid water is not water. If there is turbidity, then people must put forth effort in order to cleanse it. If their efforts are swift and bold the water will clear quickly; if their efforts are slow and remiss the water will clear slowly. Once clear, all there will be is the original water that started to flow. It is not that clear water has been brought in to replace the turbid or that the turbid water has been culled out and set off to one side. The clearness of water is like the goodness of the nature. And so, it is not that good and bad are two things opposing each other within the nature, each coming forth from it. This Pattern [i.e., the nature] is the mandate of Heaven. To obey and follow it is the Way. To follow this and cultivate it, so that each person fulfills her or his

---

43. *Mengzi* 6A3.

44. Hou Ji was a minister of Emperor Shun and is said to have displayed such qualities "when he was just able to crawl." See *Odes* 245. The story about Ziyue Jiao is found in the *Zuo Commentary*, Duke Xuan, year four. When he was born, Zi Wen said, "He must be put to death. He has the form of a bear or tiger and the voice of a wolf. If he is not put to death, he will wipe out Ruo Ao's clan." (Cf. Han Yu, "On Human Nature," in Part III, Selection 22.)

45. *Rites*, "Record of Music." The idea is that before the nature manifests itself in phenomenal form, in its pure and perfect state, it has no qualities through which it can be understood.

46. *Changes*, "Great Appendix," I.5, in Part I, Selection 9. The "it" refers to the Way, which is the interplay of *yin* and *yang*.

proper social obligations, is education.[47] If starting from the mandate of Heaven and following it out to education, I neither add to nor detract from it, this is like the way Shun possessed the empire as if it meant nothing to him.[48] [p. 10–11]

5. The good and bad throughout the world are all according to the Pattern. What is called bad is not fundamentally bad. It is just that in some cases there is excess and in others a falling short. Cases like Yang Zhu and Mozi offer good examples.[49] [p. 14]

6. Learners must perfectly embody "this mind." Even if one's learning is not complete, whenever a thing or affair comes along, one must respond to it. One's response will be decided by one's endowment and limitations, and though one may not precisely hit the mark, one will not be far off. [p. 14]

7. Learners must preserve "this mind" through the practice of reverential attention. It will not do if they feel anxious or oppressed. They should deeply and earnestly tend and nurture it and wholly immerse themselves in it. Only then will they "get it for themselves."[50] If one pursues it feeling anxious and oppressed, this only manifests self-centeredness. In the end, this will prove insufficient as a means to attain the Way. [p. 14]

8. The sage is Heaven and Earth. What is Heaven and Earth missing? How could Heaven and Earth ever have a mind to select and separate good from bad? Heaven and Earth welcome all things, accommodate all things, cover over all things, and bear up all things, but they always deal with things according to the Way. If one draws near to good things but keeps distant from bad things, then you will have no dealings with many things. How could you ever be Heaven and Earth if you did that? And so sages aim at "comforting the aged, trusting their friends, and cherishing the young."[51] [p. 17]

9. In my mind, I know clearly and without doubt that the origin and cause of life and death, preservation and loss is nothing other than the Pattern. When Kongzi said, "Since you do not understand [how to serve] the living, why ask about [how to serve] the dead?" he was speaking very loosely.[52] Serving the dead is part of life; there is no other Pattern. [p. 17]

---

47. On the progression beginning with the mandate of Heaven and moving through Pattern (the nature), the Way, and on to education, see the *Mean* 1.i, in Part III, Selection 36.

48. This description of Shun references *Analects* 8.18.

49. Yang Zhu and Mozi were contemporaries of Mengzi who supposedly advocated egoism and impartial caring, respectively. See *Mengzi* 3B9, in Part III, Selection 35. Cheng Hao is suggesting that Yang Zhu "fell short" by advocating insufficient concern for others and too much concern with himself, while Mozi was "excessive" in insisting we care for all things impartially.

50. *Mengzi* 4B14; cf. 3A4.

51. This description of the sages is taken from *Analects* 5.26.

52. *Analects* 11.12. Cheng Hao is suggesting that Kongzi said this only because he was addressing his impetuous disciple Zilu, who needed to hear this particular piece of advice on that occasion.

10. Mengzi said, "For cultivating the mind, nothing is better than having few desires."[53] If one's desires are few, the mind naturally will gain complete Sincerity. Xunzi said, "For nurturing the mind, nothing is better than complete Sincerity."[54] But if there is complete Sincerity, what need is there for nurturing? This not only shows that he did not understand complete Sincerity but also that he did not understand how to nurture it. [p. 18]

11. Mengzi was a person endowed with exceptional talent; he does not offer helpful examples from which to learn. Learners should study Yanzi. He was close to becoming a sage and offers good examples of how to apply oneself.[55] [p. 19]

12. "The unending generation of life is called 'change.'"[56] This is what Heaven employs in order to propagate the Way. Heaven takes life and nothing other than life as the Way. What ensues from this Pattern of life is goodness. Goodness carries the connotation of origination. "Origination is at the forefront of goodness."[57] The myriad things all possess the sense of spring [i.e., the spirit and inclination to grow]; this is what is meant by "That which ensues from it is goodness, and that which realizes it completely is human nature."[58] Completion, though, requires that each of the myriad things completes its nature in its own way. [p. 29]

13. Gaozi's claim that "What is inborn is called the nature" is acceptable.[59] We can say this is the nature of all living things produced between Heaven and Earth. While we can say this is the nature of all living things, still we must distinguish the nature of an ox from the nature of a horse. Gaozi [mistakenly] referred to these as all the same. If, along with the Buddhists, one claims that every living thing has spirit and all possess Buddha-nature, this cannot be accepted. "'Nature' means what is mandated by Heaven. The 'Way' means following one's nature,"[60] refers to what Heaven endows [to each thing] below. "When the myriad things take on their physical forms . . . [so that] each attains its proper nature as decreed,"[61] this is what is called the nature. To accord with one's nature without losing it is called the Way. All of these statements apply equally to human beings and other creatures. To accord with one's nature means that horses follow the nature of horses and not the nature of oxen. Oxen follow

---

53. *Mengzi* 7B35, in Part III, Selection 35.

54. *Xunzi* 3. On the status of Xunzi among Neo-Confucians, see Han Yu, "On Reading Xunzi," in Part III, Selection 21.

55. On Yanzi, see above, note 42.

56. *Changes,* "Great Appendix," I.5, translated slightly differently in Part I, Selection 9.

57. *Changes,* "Wenyan," commentary on the hexagram Qian.

58. *Changes,* "Great Appendix," I.5, in Part I, Selection 9.

59. *Mengzi* 6A3.

60. *Mean* 1.i, in Part III, Selection 36.

61. *Changes,* "Commentary on the Judgments" on the hexagram Qian.

that nature of oxen and not the nature of horses. This is what is called "following the nature." Now human beings are within Heaven and Earth and flow in the same stream as the myriad creatures;[62] when has Heaven ever taken the time to distinguish that this is a human being and this a creature? "'Education' means cultivating the Way";[63] this is something that is the exclusive affair of human beings. If they lose their fundamental nature, they must engage in cultivation in order to recover it, and so they enter onto the path of learning. If from the start they do not lose it, what cultivation would they undertake? They would simply "act out of benevolence and righteousness."[64] Once the fundamental nature has been lost, one must cultivate it. "When the completed nature is preserved attentively, this is the gate to the righteousness of the Way."[65] This implies that each of the myriad things carefully preserves its completed nature; this is also the idea of "the unending generation of life." Heaven takes life and nothing other than life as the Way.[66] [pp. 29–30]

14. Taking someone's pulse is one of the best ways to experience benevolence.[67] [p. 59]

15. Contemplate the baby chicks. (This is a way to contemplate benevolence.) [p. 59]

16. [One should not] practice memorization and recitation or pursue broad erudition, for "to trifle with things dissipates the will."[68] [p. 60]

17. Zhou Dunyi would not remove the grass growing in front of his window. When asked about this he would say, "I think of it as myself." [p. 60]

18. When I practice calligraphy I maintain deep reverential attention. It is not because I want the characters to be done well but because this is an opportunity for learning. [p. 60]

19. The manner in which Zhuangzi describes the Substance of the Way is truly excellent in many respects. Laozi's chapter, "The Spirit of the Valley Never Dies," is absolutely extraordinary.[69] [p. 64]

---

62. Cf. *Mengzi* 7A13.

63. *Mean* 1.i, in Part III, Selection 36.

64. Cf. *Mengzi* 4B19.

65. *Changes*, "Great Appendix," I.7, in Part I, Selection 9.

66. "Unending generation of life" is taken from *Changes*, "Great Appendix," I.5, translated slightly differently in Part I, Selection 9.

67. The word translated "experience" (*ti* 體) here is elsewhere translated "Substance." The idea is that to understand any virtue in the full sense requires that one experience it for oneself, that one embody it.

68. The quotation is taken from *Documents, Documents of Zhou*, "Hounds of Lü."

69. The text of Laozi's chapter is as follows: "The spirit of the valley never dies; / She is called the 'Enigmatic Female.' / The portal of the Enigmatic Female / Is called the root of heaven and earth. / An unbroken, gossamer thread, / It seems to be there, / But use will not unsettle it." (*Daodejing* 6, in Philip J. Ivanhoe and Bryan W. Van Norden, eds., *Readings in Classical*

20. The Chan Buddhist doctrine of "leaving the world" is like closing one's eyes so that one does not see one's nose—but the nose is still where it belongs. [p. 64]

21. Sages don't memorize things and so they keep things in memory. People today forget things because they memorize things. If one cannot keep things in memory, one cannot handle affairs well; such problems arise from weakness in cultivation. [p. 64]

22. One day, when Cheng Hao was in Shan Zhou, he was helping with the repair of a bridge. They needed a long beam and searched far and wide among the people, looking to find one. Later, when he would go out or return from his residence, whenever he saw a fine tree in the nearby woods he would start estimating its length. He brought this incident up to his students as a warning that "nothing should be retained in the mind." [p. 65]

23. In general, it is because human beings have separate bodies that they have self-centered desires. This is why it is difficult for them to form a unity with the Way. [p. 66]

24. There are no things apart from the Way and no Way apart from things. This is why there is nowhere within Heaven and Earth you can go and not encounter the Way. If we turn to the relationship between father and son, it is found in the familial love between them. If we turn to the relationship between ruler and minister, it is found in the seriousness between them. The same is true if we turn to the relationships between husband and wife, elder and younger, or friend and friend; there is nowhere one can turn and not find the Way.[70] This is why "the Way is something that one cannot depart from for even a moment."[71] Nevertheless, those who ruin proper relationships between people and turn away from the Four Elements stray far from the Way.[72] This is why, "Cultivated people are not absolutely for or absolutely against anything; they judge all by the standard of what is right."[73] If one is absolutely for or absolutely against something, then one creates distance between oneself and the Way and loses the complete perfection of Heaven and Earth. [For example] the learning of Buddhists contains "reverential attention to straighten the inner aspects of life,"

Chinese Philosophy, 2nd ed. [Indianapolis: Hackett Publishing, 2005], pp. 165–66.) Laozi and Zhuangzi were regarded as the ancient founders of Daoism, so it is striking that Cheng Hao would praise one of them in this manner.

70. Collectively, these are known as the "Five Relationships." They are first described in *Mengzi* 3A4.

71. *Mean* 1.ii, in Part III, Selection 36.

72. According to Buddhist teachings, these are the four constituent elements of the phenomenal world: earth, water, fire, and wind. Here they are being used to represent the physical, everyday world. (These are not the same as the Five Phases of traditional Chinese cosmology.) See the discussion in Zongmi, *On Humanity,* in Part II, Selection 17.

73. *Analects* 4.10.

but they lack "righteousness to square the outer aspects of life."[74] And so, those who strictly adhere to their teachings become like withered, dried out wood and those who loosely follow them end up reckless and disorderly. This is why the teachings of Buddhism are too narrow and limited. Our Way is different: it is simply "following one's nature."[75] This Pattern is perfectly described by Kongzi in the "Great Appendix" to the *Changes*.[76] [pp. 73–74]

25. There is unity between the Pattern and the mind but human beings are not able to join them into a unity. [p. 76]

26. There has never been any duality between Heaven and human beings. There is no need to talk about bringing them together. [p. 81]

27. To discuss the nature without discussing *qi* would be incomplete. To discuss *qi* without discussing the nature would be unenlightened. [p. 81]

28. After one has become still, observe the myriad creatures as they are of themselves; all possess the sense of spring. [p. 84]

29. "Reverential attention to straighten the inner aspects of life; righteousness to square the outer aspects of life. When reverential attention and righteousness are established, Virtue will never be alone."[77] Virtue will never be alone: because one regards oneself as the same as other things, one can never be alone. [p. 117]

30. The Way has but one root.[78] Some say, "To embrace Sincerity with the mind is not as good as embracing the mind with Sincerity. To form a triad with Heaven and Earth through the utmost Sincerity is not as good as forming one body with human beings and things through the utmost Sincerity."[79] Such a view assumes that there are two roots [for the Way]. Know that there are not two roots; then you will have the Way that "brings peace to the world through earnestness and respect."[80] [pp. 117–18]

31. [The *Changes* states,] "What is above with respect to form is called the Way, and what are below with respect to form are called concrete things."[81] If, as some have claimed, one says that what is "purely tenuous and absolutely great" is the Way of Heaven, one is talking about physical things and not the Way.[82] [p. 118]

32. [The *Changes* states,] "Reverential attention to straighten the inner aspects of life; righteousness to square the outer aspects of life."[83] This is the Way

---

74. *Changes*, "Wenyan," commentary on the hexagram Kun.

75. *Mean* 1.i, in Part III, Selection 36.

76. For the final reference see *Changes*, "Great Appendix," in Part I, Selection 9.

77. *Changes*, "Wenyan," commentary on the hexagram Kun.

78. Referring to *Mengzi* 3A5, which criticizes those who mistakenly identify "two roots" to ethical cultivation.

79. Cheng Hao discreetly fails to identify the author of this saying as Zhang Zai.

80. *Mean* 33.

81. *Changes*, "Great Appendix," I.12, in Part I, Selection 9.

82. A reference to the kind of view held by Zhang Zai in regard to the "Greatly Tenuous" (*tàixū* 太虛).

83. *Changes*, "Wenyan," commentary on the hexagram Kun.

that brings together inside and outside.[84] In contrast, the Buddhist account of inside and outside is incomplete.[85] [p. 118]

33. Reverential attention overcomes every depravity. [p. 119]

34. Each of the myriad things has its correlate. For every case of *yin* there is *yang;* for every instance of good there is bad. When *yang* grows, *yin* diminishes; when good increases, bad decreases. This is all the Pattern. Can one not extend this far and wide? Human beings simply must understand this. [p. 123]

35. It is because they delight in Heaven that "the benevolent are not anxious."[86] [p. 125]

36. To hitch up oxen and ride horses are things decided according to their respective natures. Why not ride oxen and hitch up horses? It is not in accord with the Pattern. [p. 127]

37. In cases such as Yanzi being fated to have too short a life, if we look at it from the perspective of the one individual involved, we could say that it was unfortunate, but if we look at it from a larger perspective nothing was added to or taken away from the world, nothing was advanced or withdrawn.[87] It's like the case of a single household with five sons, three of whom become rich and honored, two of whom end up poor and lowly. From the perspective of the two sons, there is deficiency; from the perspective of the father and mother and entire family, there is abundance. Had someone like Kongzi, who was perfectly Virtuous, received an esteemed position, this would have been a perfect turn of events.[88] If we take the individual perspective of Kongzi or Yanzi, we could say there was deficiency in regard to their lives, but if we speak from the perspective of the assembled sages—Yao, Shun, Yu, Tang, Wen, Wu, and the Duke Zhou— then there is abundance in the world. [p. 131]

38. If someone does not advance in learning, this shows a lack of courage. [p. 141]

39. [Kongzi said, "If one hears the Way in the morning, one could die in the evening without regret."][89] To "hear the Way in the morning" is to know how to be a human being. To "die in the evening without regret" means not to have lived a vain or hollow life. [p. 361]

40. Sages are the complete perfection of the Virtue of benevolence. The way in which benevolence makes the sage can be compared to carving a dragon out of wood. The wood is benevolence and the dragon is the sage. Can one say that the wood makes the dragon? And so, to "bestow bounty upon the people" and "save the masses" are the proper affairs of the sage; singling out benevolence

---

84. Cf. the *Mean* 25, in Part III, Selection 36.

85. Cf. §24, above.

86. *Analects* 9.29, in Part III, Selection 34.

87. On Yanzi, see above, note 42.

88. Of course, Kongzi never did find a ruler who appreciated and employed him in such a position.

89. *Analects* 4.8.

for comment, the passage describes it as "the ability to take what is near as an analogy."⁹⁰ [p. 362]

41. Kongzi said that a cultivated person "does not grumble against Heaven or complain about other people."⁹¹ This is how things should be according to Pattern. [p. 362]

42. The way that wind sways bamboo illustrates the way in which one can have "no mind" in the course of stimulus and response. If someone makes me angry, I do not let it linger in my mind. It must be like the way the wind moves the bamboo.⁹² [p. 393]

43. Cheng Yi's disciple, Chen Jingzheng, said to Cheng Hao, "As far as I am concerned, what fills up the space between Heaven and Earth is all my nature; moreover, I no longer feel that my body is my own."

Smiling, Cheng Hao replied, "When others have eaten their fill are you no longer hungry?" [p. 413]

28. Cheng Yi, "What Kind of Learning Was It that Yanzi Loved?"

translation by Philip J. Ivanhoe⁹³

Three thousand disciples studied inside Kongzi's gate but he only praised Yanzi as loving learning.⁹⁴ There was not one among his three thousand disciples who did not study and thoroughly comprehend the *Odes*, the *Documents*, or the Six Arts.⁹⁵ In light of this, what kind of learning was it that Yanzi alone loved? It was the learning that leads to the Way of the sage.

Can one learn to be a sage?

I say yes!

What is the Way of such learning? Of the available essences within heaven and earth, human beings receive the most elegant and refined of the Five Phases.⁹⁶

---

90. *Analects* 6.30, in Part III, Selection 34.

91. *Analects* 14.35.

92. On the doctrine of "no mind," see Huineng, *Platform Sutra,* in Part II, Selection 16.

93. Translation of this and the following selections from Cheng Yi are based on *Collected Works of the Two Chengs* (*Er Cheng ji* 二程集), Vol. 1 (Beijing: Zhonghua shuju, 2004); page numbers of that edition are listed in brackets at the end of the relevant passage.

94. Kongzi regarded Yanzi (Yan Hui) as his most promising disciple, and deeply mourned the fact that Yanzi died young. When asked which of his disciples was "fond of learning," Kongzi mentioned only Yanzi (*Analects* 6.3). See also *Analects* 6.11 and 12.1, in Part III, Selection 34.

95. The Six Arts are ritual, music, archery, charioteering, writing, and mathematics.

96. See Selections on the Five Phases, in Part I, Selection 8.

The fundamental [nature] of human beings is pure and tranquil, and before they manifest this outwardly its five characteristic aspects all are present within; these are called benevolence, righteousness, propriety, wisdom, and faithfulness. When human beings take on physical form at birth, things in the outside world impact upon their physical form and disturb the mean within them. When the mean within them is disturbed, this produces the seven feelings; these are called happiness, anger, sorrow, joy, love, hate, and desire. As feelings gain in strength and become more dissolute, they chip away at the [fundamental] nature. This is why those who are morally aware restrain their feelings so that they accord with the mean within them. They correct their minds and nurture their natures; this is called transforming feelings into [fundamental] nature. The foolish do not know to control their feelings; they give rein to their feelings and end up depraved and perverted. They fetter their [fundamental] nature and destroy it; this is called transforming [fundamental] nature into feelings.

The Way of all learning is simply to correct the mind and nurture the nature. When the mean within is correct and in a state of complete Sincerity, one is a sage. For the learning of the superior person the first imperative is enlightening one's mind: understanding what to nurture. After that, one earnestly proceeds, aiming to arrive at one's destination. This is what [the *Mean*] refers to as "becoming enlightened by having Sincerity."[97] And so, those engaged in learning must fully fathom their minds. "To fathom one's mind is to know one's nature."[98] If they understand their nature, return to it, and ensure its complete Sincerity, they will be sages. And so the *Documents* says, "[The virtue of] thinking is perspicaciousness . . . perspicaciousness [becomes manifest] in sagacity."[99] The way to complete Sincerity is to have faith in the Way. If one has faith in the Way, one will practice it with determination. When one practices it with determination, one will hold on to it securely. Then one's mind shall never be separated from benevolence, righteousness, conscientiousness, and faithfulness: "When pressed and hurried, one always turns to these; in difficulty and trial, one always turns to these."[100] Whether in public or at home, in speech and silence, one always turns to these. If after considerable time has passed one still holds on to these, one will reside at ease in them. Then wherever one may go, "every turn of one's movements and expressions will precisely accord with ritual,"[101] and the mind of depravity or perversity will never arise.

In all that Yanzi did, he would "not look in violation of the rituals . . . not listen in violation of the rituals . . . not speak in violation of the rituals . . .

---

97. *Mean* 21, in Part III, Selection 36.

98. *Mengzi* 7A1, in Part III, Selection 35.

99. *Documents, Documents of Zhou,* "Great Plan," translated in Selections on the Five Phases, in Part I, Selection 8.

100. *Analects* 4.5.

101. *Mengzi* 7B33.

not move in violation of the rituals."[102] Kongzi praised him by saying, "If he achieved one good thing, he would clasp it to his breast and never let it go."[103] Kongzi also said of him, "He did not transfer his anger or make the same mistake twice"[104] and "if ever he did anything wrong, he always came to understand it was wrong; once he understood, he never acted that way again."[105] This is how Yanzi sincerely loved and learned [the Way].

In all he looked at, listened to, talked about, or did, Yanzi always followed ritual. That wherein he differed from the sages is that sages "get it without reflection," "hit the mean without effort," and "perfectly hit the Way,"[106] whereas Yanzi had to reflect first and only then got it, make an effort and only then attain the mean. This is why Kongzi said that there was still the slightest of difference between Yanzi and the sage.[107]

Mengzi said, "Those who have filled out the core [aspects of Virtue] and radiate its glory are called great. Those who are great and have been fully transformed are called sagely. Those who are sagely but beyond common understanding are called spiritual."[108] We can say that Yanzi's Virtue was "filled out" and "radiated its glory." What he had not yet attained was that while able to hold on to [Virtue] he still was not fully transformed by it.[109] Since he loved to learn, had he been granted a few more years of life, he soon would have been fully transformed. This is why Kongzi said, "What a great misfortune that his allotted life was so short!"[110] Kongzi was aggrieved that Yanzi had not attained sagehood. What is called "being fully transformed" is to enter the state of the spiritual and remain spontaneously so, the state in which one does not have to think in order to get things right and does not have to make an effort in order to attain the mean. This is what Kongzi was referring to when he said, "At seventy, I could follow my mind's desires without ever overstepping the bounds."[111]

Someone asked, "Sages are those who are born with moral understanding. Now you say people can attain sagehood through learning. Is there any textual basis for this claim?"

Cheng Yi replied, "Yes, there is. Mengzi said, 'Yao and Shun had it by nature;

---

102. *Analects* 12.1, in Part III, Selection 34.

103. *Mean* 8.

104. *Analects* 6.2.

105. *Changes,* "Great Appendix," II.5, in Part I, Selection 9.

106. *Mean* 20.xii, in Part III, Selection 36.

107. Paraphrasing *Changes,* "Great Appendix," II.5, in Part I, Selection 9.

108. *Mengzi* 7B25.

109. Cf. *Analects* 15.33, in Part III, Selection 34.

110. *Analects* 6.2. Kongzi is bemoaning and Cheng Yi referring to the fact that Yanzi died young, at thirty-two years of age.

111. *Analects* 2.4, in Part III, Selection 34.

Tang and Wu returned to it.'[112] To 'have it by nature' is to be born with moral understanding; to 'return to it' is to come to moral understanding through learning. Moreover, Kongzi was one who was born with moral understanding, while Mengzi was one who came to moral understanding through learning. People of later ages failed to understand this, saying sagehood requires one to be born with moral understanding and is not something one can attain through learning. As a result, the Way of learning was lost. People stopped looking for it within themselves and instead sought for it outside themselves. They came to devote themselves to extensive learning, forced memorization, clever writing, and elegant rhetoric, working to make their words elaborate and flowery. As a consequence, few have attained the Way. The learning of today is very different from the learning that Yanzi loved." [pp. 577–78]

29. Cheng Yi, "Remembrance of Taking Care of Fish"

translation by Philip J. Ivanhoe

Outside, in front of my studio, there was a large stone basin. Some of our family members had bought some baby fish to feed to the cat, but when I saw them [out of the water] blowing bubbles and gasping for air, I could not bear the sight and saved more than a hundred, putting them in the stone basin and taking care of them. The large ones were as thick as a finger, the thin ones as thin as a chopstick. Cradling my cheeks with my hands, I watched them throughout the day. When I first released them in the water, I felt satisfied and elated that the fish were in their element. In the end, watching them, I felt moved by compassion, touched deeply.

Reading the works of the ancient sages and surveying their official regulations, I found they "did not allow fine-meshed nets into the ponds and lakes" nor did they "allow fish less than one foot in length to be killed; such fish could not be sold in the market place and people were not allowed to eat them."[113] This is what the benevolence of sages, which seeks to take care of living creatures and avoid harming them, is like. If we hunt creatures in this way, we can delight in them being alive and following their natures; what is more proper than this!

O fish! O fish! I am not able to protect you from every sharp hook and fine-meshed net, but I can help you avoid being roasted and fried, sucked and chewed! I know the great expanses of the rivers and seas afford you the chance to follow your nature. I have thought about releasing you into them but have

---

112. *Mengzi* 7B33.

113. Quoting *Mengzi* 1A3, and paraphrasing *Rites*, "Regulations of a King," respectively.

not yet taken that route. I am only able to prolong your life by providing a few dippers full of water. Helping you is what I truly want, and many of you have been able to live on, but how should I feel about the myriad of other types of creatures between heaven and earth?

O fish! O fish! You have moved my heart to compassion! How, though, can this end with just fish? And so, I have written this remembrance of taking care of fish.

Addendum

It has been almost thirty years since I wrote my "Remembrance of Taking Care of Fish."[114] I came across it stuck between some old rush mats and seeing it made me heave a sigh. In my youth I had such lofty ambitions. I could not endure doing harm to creatures. Comparing what I knew then with how I am today, I feel ashamed to have turned my back on my initial aspirations. Am I not close to being one of "those who throw themselves away?"[115] I offer this to young people today; they should take me as a warning! [pp. 578–79]

30. Cheng Yi, "Reply to Yang Shi's Letter on 'The Western Inscription'"

translation by Philip J. Ivanhoe

Cheng Yi's disciple Yang Shi criticized Zhang Zai's "The Western Inscription,"[116] stating that its doctrines were the same as those of Mozi, the ancient opponent of Confucianism who advocated "impartial caring." Neo-Confucians saw Mozi's doctrine as anticipating the undifferentiated compassion of Buddhism, both of which they regarded as antithetical to filial piety. In the following letter, Cheng Yi defends Zhang Zai against Yang Shi's criticisms. The discussion is phrased in terms of Mengzi's famous, but enigmatic, critique of Mohism: "Heaven, in giving birth to things, causes them to have one root," while Mozi mistakenly "gives them two roots" (Mengzi 3A5). Although the argument of this letter is dense and subtle, it is helpful in illustrating how Neo-Confucians attempted to reconcile the monistic metaphysics that they inherited from Buddhism with traditional Confucian filial piety. —Eds.

---

114. Cheng Yi wrote the original essay when he was twenty-one years old.

115. For this idea, see *Mengzi* 4A10, in Part III, Selection 35.

116. See Part III, Selection 23.

The ideas expressed in your ten-chapter-long *On History*, which you sent to me, are perfectly correct. As soon as I had the chance to look at this work, someone borrowed it from me, so I will have to wait for the chance to read it through more carefully. I can't say as much for your discussion of "The Western Inscription." While it is true that Zhang Zai at times is mistaken in what he says (for example, in places in his *Correcting Youthful Ignorance*), as a work, "The Western Inscription" explains how to extend Pattern to preserve righteousness, and in this respect expands upon themes earlier sages had yet to address. It is equal in merit to Mengzi's discussions of the goodness of human nature and how to cultivate one's *qi*.[117] (These two also are themes earlier sages had yet to address.) How can you equate it with the writings of Mozi? "The Western Inscription" clearly explains that Pattern is one but its manifestations are many. Mozi's doctrine is that there are two roots but no distinctions in manifestation. ([Mengzi's statement that we should] treat the elders of our family as elders should be treated and treat our young ones as young ones should be treated and then extend such treatment to the elders and young ones of others expresses the idea that the Pattern is one.[118] [Mozi's] love without distinction or degree expresses the idea of having two roots.[119]) A confusion that can occur when making distinctions of degree [in one's affection] is that they can lead to selfishness winning out and thereby failing to attain benevolence, but the error in having no distinctions in the manifestations is that one will practice impartial care and thereby lack righteousness. To clearly establish distinct manifestations and to extend the unity of the Pattern, in order to prevent the tendency to let selfishness win out, is the method of benevolence.[120] To be without distinctions and be misled by impartial care, to the point of where one will "have no father," is to do violence to righteousness.[121] For you to equate these things is quite a mistake! Moreover, you say that it only talks about the Substance of [benevolence] and never touches on its Function, but since the aim of "The Western Inscription" is

---

117. See *Mengzi* 3A1 and 6A6, on human nature, and 2A2.3–5, on *qi*, in Part III, Selection 35.

118. Paraphrasing *Mengzi* 1A7, in Part III, Selection 35.

119. It is not obvious what the "two roots" are that Mengzi refers to in his criticism of the Mohists. However, Neo-Confucians often accuse Buddhists of a mistaken dualism that distinguishes the illusory everyday world from a pure internal world, and leads them to flee commitments to the family for a selfish escape. Consider Zhang Zai's comment that Buddhists "regard human life as a delusion. How could they be said to understand humanity? Heaven and humans are one thing, but they accept the former and reject the latter. How could they be said to understand Heaven?" (*Zheng meng* 17)—Eds.

120. Kongzi describes "the ability to take what is near as an analogy" as "the method of benevolence," in *Analects* 6.30, in Part III, Selection 34.

121. *Mengzi* 3B9, in Part III, Selection 35, where Mengzi criticizes Mozi's philosophy as having this consequence.

to get people to extend and carry it out, it is fundamentally about the Function [of benevolence]. Isn't it strange for you to say it never touches on this! [p. 609]

31. Cheng Yi, Selected Sayings

translation by Philip J. Ivanhoe[122]

1. Cheng Yi said, "Buddhists simply seek to frighten people with their teachings about life and death. It is odd that in the course of the past two thousand years no one has realized this, which only goes to show how successfully they have frightened people. The sages and worthies regarded life and death as fundamentally different affairs; they saw nothing to fear about them and so did not discuss life and death.[123] Buddhists are afraid of life and death and so all they can do is talk about them incessantly. The most common sorts of people fear many things and are easily motivated by self-interest. As for Chan Buddhists, though they say they are not like this, in its essence, their teaching comes down to the same idea: in everything they desire gain."

His disciple Yu asked, "I do not know whether their teachings about life and death were something that originally developed out of an open spirit of inquiry and only later came under the spell of this obsession [i.e., with personal gain] or were they something that from the start was the result of a desire for gain?"

Cheng Yi replied, "From the start these were the result of a desire for gain. And so, those who study them believe these teachings out of a desire for gain. Zhuangzi's saying, 'Don't disturb the process of transformation,'[124] expresses the same idea. The harms done by the teachings of Yang Zhu and Mozi no longer remain in the present age.[125] The harm done by Daoist teachings, in the end,

---

122. Translation of this and the following selections from Cheng Yi are based on *Collected Works of the Two Chengs* (*Er Cheng ji* 二程集), Vol. 1 (Beijing: Zhonghua shuju, 2004); page numbers of that edition are listed in brackets at the end of the relevant passage.

123. I take Cheng Yi's point to be that Confucians deny that there is an interconnected *cycle* of life and death while Buddhists believe in such and so live in fear. In *Analects* 11.12 the disciple Zilu asked Kongzi about death; Kongzi replied, "While you do not yet understand life, how can you understand death?" Cheng Yi explained Kongzi's reply by saying, "When you understand the Way of life, you will understand the Way of death." (Quoted by Zhu Xi, *Lunyu jizhu,* not in this volume.)

124. Zhuangzi was an ancient Daoist philosopher. The "process of transformation" refers to death. (See *Zhuangzi* 6.)

125. Yang Zhu and Mozi were contemporaries of Mengzi. Yang Zhu supposedly advocated egoism, which undermined one's obligation to one's ruler, and Mozi advocated impartial caring, which undermined filial piety. (See *Mengzi* 3B9, in Part III, Selection 35.) Later Confucians likened the Daoists to Yang Zhu and the Buddhists to Mozi.

is minor. It is only Buddhism that in the present age is discussed by everyone, overflowing and flooding up to the heavens. The harm it does is without bounds!" [p. 3]

2. The mind of any person is the mind of heaven and earth. The Pattern of any thing is the Pattern of the myriad things. The course of any day is the course of any year. [p. 13]

3. Those engaged in learning must understand the age in which they live; those who do not cannot be said to have learning. Yanzi was able to be happy even when living in a poor and narrow lane because Kongzi lived during the same age.[126] In the time of Mengzi, there were no others of noble character; how could he not take the burden of preserving the Way upon his own shoulders? [p. 15]

4. Genuine knowledge is different from common knowledge. I once met a farmer who had been mauled by a tiger. Someone reported that a tiger had just mauled someone in the area and everyone present expressed alarm. But the countenance and behavior of the farmer was different from everyone else. Even small children know that tigers can maul people and yet this is not genuine knowledge. It is only genuine knowledge if it is like that of the farmer. And so, there are people who know it is wrong to do something and yet they still do it; this is not genuine knowledge. If it were genuine knowledge, they definitely would not do it. [p. 16]

5. Pattern should be exhaustively investigated; our nature should be fathomed, but we cannot talk about exhaustively investigating or fathoming the mandate of Heaven.[127] The mandate is something we can only arrive at. Zhang Zai once compared the mandate to a spring, and likened exhaustively investigating Pattern and fathoming our nature to digging a trench in order to draw the spring along. This analogy, though, presents the trench and the spring as two separate things. Later, I felt the need to correct this account. [p. 27]

6. [The *Changes* states,] "Still and unmoved, when stimulated it penetrates [all of the events that occur in the world]."[128] Heavenly Patterns already are completely present, they have never been lacking in the slightest. They were not preserved by Emperor Yao; they were not destroyed by Tyrant Jie. The constant Patterns between father and son, minister and ruler do not change. How could they ever be moved? Because they are unmoved they are called "still." Although they are unmoved, when stimulated they penetrate [all phenomena in the world]. Stimulation does not extend beyond the self. [p. 43]

---

126. *Analects* 6.11, in Part III, Selection 34.

127. The first chapter of the "Explanation of the Trigrams" (in Part I, Selection 10) says, "[The sages] exhaustively investigated the Pattern and fathomed the nature [of things] until they reached the mandate [of Heaven]."

128. *Changes*, "Great Appendix," I.10, in Part I, Selection 9.

7. If one is benevolent one will be unified; if one is not benevolent one will feel duality.[129] [p. 63]

8. It is difficult to put a name on the Way of benevolence. The only thing that comes close is disinterestedness, but disinterestedness does not ensure that one is benevolent. [p. 63]

9. One cannot talk about the nature in terms of inside and outside. [p. 64]

10. After one forgets reverential attention, one always will be reverently attentive. [p. 66]

11. The mind of the sage never resides anywhere, but there is nowhere it does not reside. In general, the Way of the sage is to bring together inside and outside and embody the myriad things. [p. 66]

12. One cannot say the dead possess consciousness; one cannot say they are without consciousness. [p. 66]

13. [The *Changes* states,] "The alternation of *yin* and *yang* is called the 'Way,'" but the Way is not the alternation of *yin* and *yang*; the Way is that by which there is the alternation of *yin* and *yang*. It is like the way in which "the alternation of opening and closing [a door] is called 'alternation.'"[130] [p. 67]

14. Those good at describing how to govern the world are not distressed that laws and regulations are not established but that people have failed to complete or perfect themselves. Those who are good at cultivating the self are not distressed that the quality of people's initial talents is not fine but that teachers and students are not enlightened. If peoples' initial talents are not completed or perfected, even if there are excellent laws and fine thoughts, who will carry them out? If teachers and students are not enlightened, even if one is endowed with great talent, who will be able to complete or perfect it? [p. 69]

15. Laozi talked about "non-intentional action" and also talked about how "through non-intentional action, nothing is left undone."[131] He was saying that whenever one intends to act one is to act in a non-intentional way; this itself, though, is to act in an intentional way. When Kongzi wrote the ["Great Appendix" to the] *Changes*, he never taught about "non-intentional action"; he only talked about "no thoughts" and "no action."[132] This was a warning not to force action. Nevertheless right after saying this, he added "Still and unmoved, when stimulated it penetrates [all of the events that occur in the world]."[133] This, the Pattern of movement and stillness, has never been a one-sided doctrine. [p. 76]

---

129. The words translated "unity" and "duality" are literally "one" and "two," respectively. The idea is that the person of benevolence feels one with all things. Those lacking benevolence feel a duality between themselves and the rest of the world; they experience the world as other and opposed to themselves.

130. *Changes,* "Great Appendix," I.5 and I.11.

131. *Daodejing,* chapters 37, 48. (Laozi is traditionally identified as the founder of Daoism.)

132. *Changes,* "Great Appendix," I.10, in Part I, Selection 9.

133. *Changes,* "Great Appendix," I.10, in Part I, Selection 9.

16. The source of learning is reflection. [p. 80]

17. Those who are "great and have been fully transformed" have unified themselves with Pattern.[134] Because they are unified, they are without self. [p. 143]

18. If one possesses a governing principle one will be tenuous;[135] if one is without a governing principle one will be stuffed solid. This is something one must attend to. [p. 144]

19. If people are impartial they will possess unity; if they are selfish they will display diversity. Complete appropriateness returns to unity; perfect righteousness allows no duality. The differences between "human minds" are like the differences between human faces; these are nothing but manifestations of a selfish mind.[136] [p. 144]

20. All things have their roots and their branch tips; one cannot sever the branch tips from the roots and regard them as two distinct affairs.[137] "Keeping the dust down by sprinkling water and sweeping it up, answering when called and responding to questions" these are things that are as they are, but there is that which makes them what they are.[138] [p. 148]

21. The Way spontaneously produces the myriad things. If we consider a season of birth and growth, it is the Way that produces birth and the Way that produces growth. It is not that the Way uses the *qi* that already has produced birth to later produce growth. The Way is the spontaneous, "unending generation of life."[139] [p. 149]

22. Those who guard against depravity of course possess unity. But if one takes unity as one's governing principle there will be no reason to talk about guarding against depravity. What can one say to those who regard unity as difficult to realize and do not apply themselves to spiritual practice? What is unity? There is nothing to it: simply be upright and reverent and the mind will possess unity. With unity there naturally will be nothing wrong or wicked. If one just cultivates oneself with this in mind the heavenly Patterns will spontaneously become clear. [p. 150]

---

134. *Mengzi* 7B25.

135. Tenuousness is a desirable quality as it connotes openness and receptivity. Its contrasting vice is to have a fixed and predetermined mind, which does not allow one to receive and adapt to things as they are.

136. The two characters translated here as "human minds" (*rénxīn* 人心) also connote the "human mind," which is the fallible, phenomenal correlate of the "mind of the Way" (*dàoxīn* 道心).

137. The metaphor of root and branch tip represents the idea that all Patterns (roots) have corresponding phenomenal manifestations (branch tips). It also connotes that the former are not visible but originate and sustain what is visible, and that there is a vital, organic unity between these ontologically different aspects of the universe.

138. *Analects* 19.12.

139. *Changes*, "Great Appendix," I.5, translated slightly differently in Part I, Selection 9.

23. [When the *Great Learning* discusses] "getting a handle on things" in order to exhaustively investigate the Pattern, this does not imply the need to exhaustively investigate the Pattern of each thing in the world.[140] If you exhaustively investigate the Pattern in just one case, you can infer the remaining Patterns. Take filial piety as an example; one must understand what makes something a case of filial piety. If one can't exhaustively investigate the Pattern of one case, then try another. Whether one starts with an easy or more difficult case should be decided in light of one's abilities. It is like the fact that there are thousands of streets and roads that lead to the capital; you only need to follow one of them in order to get there. The reason such an approach will enable you to exhaustively investigate the Pattern is that all the myriad things share this Pattern. All things or affairs, however small or trivial, possess this Pattern. [p. 157]

24. Someone asked, "What is the first step in advancing in cultivation?"

Cheng Yi replied, "Nothing comes before 'correcting one's mind' and 'making one's thoughts have Sincerity.'[141] Making one's thoughts Sincere lies in 'extending knowledge,' and 'extending knowledge lies in getting a handle on things. . . . Every thing has a Pattern. What is needed is to fully investigate their Patterns. Investigating Patterns can start in many ways. Some will read books, illuminating the Pattern of righteousness through discussion. Others will evaluate people and things of the past and present, distinguishing what is right and wrong. Still others will respond to the situations and things they encounter and deal with the appropriately. These are all investigating the Pattern."

Someone asked, "In getting a handle on things must one get a handle on each and every thing, or can one simply get a handle on one thing and come to know the myriad Patterns?"

He replied, "How would one understand like that? To try to understand the myriad Patterns through getting a handle on one thing—even someone like Yanzi would not dare to follow such a method! What is necessary is to get a handle on one situation today, and then get a handle on another situation tomorrow. When one has build up a lot of knowledge, only then will one come to a comprehensive understanding."[142] [p. 188]

25. Self-restraint requires reverential attention; to advance in learning depends on the extension of knowledge. [p. 188]

26. All things in the world can be understood through Pattern. [As the *Odes* state,] "If there is a thing, there is a norm."[143] Each thing must have a Pattern. [p. 193]

---

140. *Great Learning,* Classic 4–5, in Part III, Selection 33.

141. Cheng Yi bases his theory of ethical cultivation on the steps in the *Great Learning*. His view is the basis of Zhu Xi's later interpretation. See *Great Learning,* Classic 4, and Commentary 5, in Part III, Selection 38.

142. Translation of this passage by Bryan W. Van Norden.

143. Paraphrasing *Odes* 260, which is also cited in *Mengzi* 6A6, in Part III, Selection 35.

27. Someone asked, "Do joy and anger emerge from the nature?"

Cheng Yi replied, "They certainly do. As soon as there is conscious life, there is the nature, and as soon as there is the nature, there are feelings. If there were no nature, how could there be feelings?"

It was further asked, "What about the idea that joy and anger emerge from outside [the self]?"

Cheng Yi replied, "They do not emerge from outside; when stimulated by things outside, they are aroused within."

It was asked, "Is it that the nature can have joy and anger in the way that water can have waves?"

Cheng Yi replied, "Yes. It is the nature of water to be clear, level, and still, like the surface of a mirror, but when it flows over pebbles or down slopes it becomes agitated and roiled, or when wind blows across its surface, it can form into dashing waves. How, though, can this be regarded as the nature of water? In the nature of human beings there are only the 'four beginnings.'[144] How could the many bad acts that people commit be part of the nature of human beings? Nevertheless, without water, how could there be waves? Without the nature, how could there be feelings?" [p. 204]

28. Those who do not yet understand the Way are like drunks. While drunk, there is nothing they will not do, but once they sober up they are ashamed about what they did. Those who have not yet made progress in learning think of themselves as without faults, but once they begin to understand, whenever they think back upon what they did in former days, they are frightened and afraid. [p. 221]

29. Someone asked, "Does writing literary compositions harm one's pursuit of the Way?"[145]

Cheng Yi replied, "Yes, it harms one's pursuit of the Way. Whenever one works at writing a literary composition, if one does not concentrate on what one is doing the results will not be elegant. If one concentrates on what one is doing, one's will is constrained by this activity. If one does this, how could one achieve the greatness of Heaven and Earth? The *Documents* says, 'To trifle with things dissipates the will.'[146] To work at writing literary compositions is to trifle with things. My disciple Lü Yushu wrote a poem that reads:

---

144. The "four beginnings" are the feelings of compassion, disdain, deference, and approval/disapproval. See *Mengzi* 2A6, in Part III, Selection 35.

145. Cheng Yi criticizes the kind of polished literary style that was revered both as an aesthetic ideal and as a way to excel in the official examinations. In this passage, he plays on the many senses of the character *wén* 文, the basic meaning of which is "pattern" or "composition" (in the most general senses). Cheng Yi thinks it good to observe and pass on records of the normative patterns in or composition of Nature and society that lead to good order, but condemns the cultivation of artificial patterns (i.e., a flowery style of literary composition) that serve to distract one from the Way.

146. *Documents, Documents of Zhou,* "Hounds of Lü."

If one studies as Yuan Kai did, one will become an addict,[147]
If one writes like Xiangru, one will be seen as an entertainer.[148]
Independent, we stand at Kongzi's gate, with no purpose,
Other than honoring Yanzi's success at fasting the mind.[149]

What a fine poem! When the ancients pursued learning, they only worked at cultivating the authentic feelings of their nature; they did not pursue other types of learning. Today, those who work at literary composition are devoted to phraseology and structure in order to please people's ears and eyes. Since they work at pleasing people, what are they if not entertainers?"

Someone asked, "Did the ancients learn to produce compositions?"

Cheng Yi replied, "People look at the Six Classics and on this basis say that Kongzi wrote literary compositions.[150] They do not understand that he just took what had accumulated in his heart and naturally formed these into compositions; this simply illustrates the point that 'those with Virtue will surely have something to say.'"[151]

Someone asked, "Why did Kongzi praise Ziyou and Zixia for being learned in regard to composition?"[152]

Cheng Yi replied, "When did Ziyou and Zixia ever pick up a brush and work at developing a polished literary style? Moreover, how can forms of composition found in such things as 'contemplating the composition of the heavens' in order to understand the changing of the seasons, and 'contemplating the composition of human society in order to transform and perfect the world'[153] be confused with the compositions of polished literary style?"[154] [p. 239]

30. Someone asked, "When we 'get a handle on things,' are the things outside the self or within the nature?"

Cheng Yi replied, "It doesn't matter. Whatever is before one's eyes is a thing

---

147. Du Yuankai (222–284 CE) was a former military commander who was so enamored with the *Zuozhuan* that he wrote a commentary on it that stretched to more than one hundred thousand characters.

148. Sima Xiangru (179–127 BCE) was a famous Western Han dynasty writer and master of the rhapsody or poetic exposition style of poetry.

149. In *Zhuangzi* 4, there is a famous story of how, with the help of Kongzi, Yanzi succeeded in the task of fasting the mind, making it so still that the Way gathered within it.

150. The *Six Classics* are the *Odes, Documents, Rites, Changes, Spring and Autumn Annals,* and the *Music.* Kongzi supposedly was involved in writing or editing these works.

151. *Analects* 14.4. The passage continues, "but those who have something to say do not necessarily possess Virtue."

152. *Analects* 11.3. These were disciples of Kongzi.

153. *Changes,* "Commentary on the Judgments" on hexagram 8, Bi.

154. Cf. the discussion of writing in this selection to Wang, *A Record for Practice,* §11, in Part III, Selection 43.

and each and every thing has the Pattern. From that which makes fire hot and water cold to the proper relationship between ruler and minister or father and son, all these are Pattern."

It was further asked, "If one exhaustively investigates the Pattern of one thing, does one only see the Pattern of that one thing or does one see all the various Patterns?"

Cheng Yi replied, "One must seek to understand everything, but even Yanzi only could understand ten things when he heard of one.[155] Later, when one gains a comprehensive understanding of Pattern, one can understand even hundreds of millions of things." [p. 247]

31. Learning was easier in ancient times; learning today is difficult. The ancients began the learning for children at the age of eight and the learning for adults at the age of fifteen.[156] They had literature to nurture their eyes, music to nurture their ears, rituals to nurture their four limbs, singing and dancing to nurture the *qi* of their blood, and righteousness and Pattern to nurture their minds. Now, almost all of this is lost; all we have are righteousness and Pattern to nurture our minds. Can one be lax in one's efforts? [p. 268]

32. There are two types of "unperturbed mind."[157] One can be unperturbed as a result of having attained the Way or one can be unperturbed because one controls one's mind with the standard of righteousness.[158] This is righteous; this is not righteous. I should choose what is righteous; I should reject what is not righteous. This is what it means to control one's mind with the standard of righteousness. If righteousness is within me and I act out of righteousness,[159] I am at ease and naturally accord with the Way;[160] there is nothing to control. This is a distinctive sense of being unperturbed. [p. 273]

33. [The *Analects* and the *Mean* both discuss conscientiousness and sympathetic understanding.] Conscientiousness refers to being without improper behavior. Conscientiousness is the Way of Heaven. Sympathetic understanding is a human affair. Conscientiousness is the Substance; sympathetic understanding is its Function.[161] The conscientiousness and sympathetic understanding referred

---

155. *Analects* 5.9.

156. Zhu Xi follows Cheng Yi's age guidelines (see his preface to the *Great Learning* in Part III, Selection 33).

157. See *Mengzi* 2A2, in Part III, Selection 35.

158. The distinction Cheng Yi draws here is remarkably like what Aristotle draws between the fully virtuous and the continent.

159. Cf. *Mengzi* 4B19.

160. Paraphrasing *Mean* 20.xii, in Part III, Selection 36.

161. "Substance" and "Function," two key terms in Neo-Confucian metaphysics, are best understood via examples. A lamp is Substance, its light is its Function. An eye is Substance, seeing is its Function. Water is Substance, a wave is Function.

to in the line [from the *Mean*], "Conscientiousness and sympathetic understanding are not far from the Way,"[162] are not the same as the conscientiousness and sympathetic understanding referred to in the line [from the *Analects*], "My Way is bound together with one thing."[163] [p. 274]

34. [The *Documents* states,] "The human mind is precarious; the mind of the Way is subtle."[164] The mind is wherever the Way is; what is subtle is the Substance of the Way. The mind and the Way are comingled together in unity. In contrast with those who have lost their pure mind, we call it the mind of the Way.[165] Those who have lost their pure mind are precarious. To be "refined and unified"[166] is the way to put into practice the Way. [p. 276]

35. Cheng Yi's disciple Meng Dunfu asked, "What do you think about Zhuangzi's "Discussion of Making Things Equal"?[167]

Cheng Yi replied, "Was Zhuangzi's aim to make equal the Patterns of things? The Patterns of things have always been equal. Why would they have to wait for Zhuangzi in order to be equal? If he sought to make the physical forms of things equal, the physical forms of things have never been equal. How could one equalize them?[168] This shows that Zhuangzi had only a shallow grasp of the Way. He did not understand in his heart and so subsequently produced such a view." [p. 289]

36. Dogs, oxen, and human beings all know what to approach and what to avoid; their natures are fundamentally the same. These other animals, though, are limited by their physical forms and so cannot change. It is like light shining through a hole in the wall: what comes through does not change, but is square or round, depending on the shape of the hole. The light that shines through, though, is all the same. It is only because of their physical endowments that things are different. And so, in regard to the claim that "what is inborn is called the nature," Gaozi thought all creatures were alike while Mengzi regarded this as wrong.[169] [p. 312]

37. Conscientiousness is the great and impartial Way for all the world.

---

162. See the *Mean* 13, in Part III, Selection 36.

163. Kongzi's disciple Zengzi explains the "one thing" Kongzi referred to in terms of conscientiousness and sympathetic understanding. See *Analects* 4.15, in Part III, Selection 34.

164. *Documents, Documents of Yu,* "Counsels of the Great Yu."

165. The phrase "pure mind" is inspired by "pure knowing" and "pure capability" in *Mengzi* 7A15, in Part III, Selection 35.

166. *Documents, Documents of Yu,* "Counsels of the Great Yu."

167. *Zhuangzi* 2.

168. Cheng Yi surely had in mind a line from the *Mengzi* that says, "It is in the very nature of things to be unequal." See *Mengzi* 3A4.

169. The quoted phrase is attributed to the rival philosopher Gaozi in *Mengzi* 6A3. Cheng Yi's interpretation is that, while Gaozi is correct that the ultimate nature of animals and humans is the same, their physically embodied natures are different.

Sympathetic understanding is the means to practice it. Conscientiousness refers to the Substance of the Way. Sympathetic understanding is its Function; it is the Way of human beings. [p. 360]

38. [Kongzi said, "Knowing it is not as good as being fond of it; being fond of it is not as good as taking joy in it."][170] As for those who "know it," it lies in another but they know it. As for those who are "fond of it," they are earnest but still cannot possess it. As for those who "take joy in it," it is something they have within themselves. [p. 361]

39. The "human mind" is human desire; the "mind of the Way" is Heavenly Pattern. [p. 364]

40. When their Patterns have been corrected, all the myriad things are a unity. This is [what the *Analects* means by] "bound together with one thing."[171] [p. 365]

41. Someone mentioned having "no mind." Cheng Yi said, "It is not correct to talk about having no mind; rather, one should say 'no selfish mind.'"[172] [p. 440]

---

170. *Analects* 6.20, in Part III, Selection 34. The "it" that is known, liked, and enjoyed is the Way.

171. Cheng Yi is relating the notion of "unity" to the "one thread" that Kongzi claimed runs through his Way. See *Analects* 4.15, in Part III, Selection 34.

172. For the phrase "no mind," see Huineng, *Platform Sutra*, in Part II, Selection 16.

Zhu Xi

———

32. *Categorized Conversations*

translation by Bryan W. Van Norden

Zhū Xī 朱熹 *(1130–1200) is the figure most responsible for what became orthodox Neo-Confucianism. The son of an outspoken government official,*
Zhu studied the Confucian classics
as a youth, and had already passed
the highest level of the civil service
examinations by the age of 19. He
held a handful of government posi-
tions during his lifetime, and acquit-
ted himself well in each. However,
his long-term historical influence
is due to his roles as a teacher and
scholar. Zhu acknowledged that he
was initially attracted to Buddhism
and Daoism, but he later became a
passionate advocate of the Confucian
tradition.

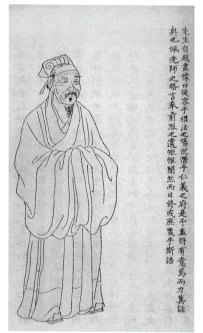

Zhu Xi.

    Zhu Xi shifted the focus of Confu-
cian education from the Five Classics
to the Four Books. The Five Classics
were the Documents, Odes, Spring
and Autumn Annals, Rites, *and*
Changes. *These works have an an-*
cient association with Confucianism,
and were canonized early in the Han
dynasty (202 BCE–220 CE). However, they have several disadvantages
when used for ethical cultivation and inspiration: they are long, often writ-
ten in archaic language, and sometimes obscure in their ethical implications.
Consequently, Zhu Xi proposed focusing on the shorter, more accessible, and
ethically relevant Four Books: the Great Learning, Analects, Mengzi, *and*
Mean. *In order to help students understand the Four Books, Zhu Xi wrote*
commentaries on each of them, frequently citing what he regarded as some

of the best earlier interpretations. Zhu Xi interprets each of the Four Books in terms of a detailed metaphysical view that is never stated explicitly in any of these works. According to this view, everything that exists has two aspects: qi *(the underlying "stuff" out of which things are condensed) and the Pattern (the abstract structure of the universe). Cheng Yi and Cheng Hao originally formulated this metaphysics (explained in more detail below), but Zhu Xi systematized, clarified, and disseminated it. As a result, this version of Neo-Confucianism is often referred to as the Cheng-Zhu School, or as the School of Pattern.*[1]

Zhu Xi apparently shared his father's penchant for fearless denunciations of official corruption and incompetence, and it made him powerful enemies. As a result, a few years before Zhu Xi's death the government declared the Cheng-Zhu School of Confucianism heretical. However, a little more than a century later, Zhu Xi's Collected Commentaries on the Four Books *became the basis of the civil service examinations and remained so as long as the exams continued to exist (1313–1905).*[2] *The Four Books as interpreted by Zhu Xi continue to exert enormous influence on how Confucianism is understood; even today, many scholars assume that Zhu Xi's readings are correct.*

Because of Zhu Xi's importance, we have included several sections on his views. The current selection is intended as a general introduction to Zhu Xi's philosophy. It includes excerpts from the Categorized Conversations of Master Zhu *(a topically organized anthology of Zhu Xi's sayings and dialogues with his disciples), interspersed with explanatory comments by the translator of this section. In this selection, the original Chinese text is indented as "block quotes" and the translator's commentary is not.*

After this introduction to Zhu's thought through his Categorized Conversations, *we will provide four selections on his reading of the* Great Learning, Analects, Mengzi, *and* Mean. *These consist of excerpts from Zhu Xi's* Collected Commentaries on the Four Books, *perhaps the most widely read and influential philosophical work of Zhu's. In those excerpts, the original text of the Four Books is in boldface, while Zhu Xi's commentary is in brackets in regular font. — Tr.*

---

1. See the selections from Cheng Hao and from Cheng Yi, in Part III, Selections 25 through 31.

2. The civil service examinations were an important route to power, prestige, and wealth. Although reformers sometimes attempted to shift the focus away from the teachings of Zhu Xi, they were never able to do so in a fundamental way. See Benjamin A. Elman, *A Cultural History of Civil Examinations in Late Imperial China* (Berkeley: University of California Press, 2000). For an entertaining satire of the exams, see Wu Jingzi, *Rulin waishi,* available in English as Wu Ching-tzu, *The Scholars,* trans. C. T. Hsia (New York: Columbia University Press, 1993).

Categorized Conversations

[Only the numbered quotations below are from the Categorized Conversations *of Master Zhu. All other text is explanation and commentary by the translator of this section.[3]]*

Metaphysics

By the time the Cheng-Zhu School of Confucianism developed, the Buddhist notion of the Pattern (*lǐ* 理) had become an entrenched part of the Chinese philosophical vocabulary. It seemed almost obvious that everything is part of a web of interconnections, and that this web is present in everything that exists. (Compare the notion of Indra's Web.[4]) The Buddhists embraced the ethical implication of this metaphysics: individuality is an illusion, so we should show universal compassion for everyone. But this is inconsistent with Confucian ethics, which requires differentiated concern between different specific individuals. For example, filial piety demands that *I* have greater affection and respect for *my* father than I do for yours, while *you* have greater affection and respect for *your* father than for mine. The challenge facing the Confucians was to justify filial piety in terms of the conceptual framework they had inherited. The solution offered by the Cheng-Zhu School was that everything that exists has two aspects: the Pattern (the structure of the universe, which is shared by and connects everything) and *qi* (the spatial "stuff" that constitutes concrete individuals).

Qi 氣 is a term with deep roots in Chinese thought, but by the Han dynasty it had come to refer to the fundamental stuff out of which the physical universe condenses.[5] *Qi* has the following attributes:

- *Qi* exists in space and time.
- *Qi* is self-generating and self-moving.
- *Qi* exists in qualitatively different forms, which can be described as *yin* and *yang*, "dark" and "bright," "turbid" and "clear," "coarse" and "refined," or as corresponding to the Five Phases.[6]

---

3. Unless otherwise indicated, translations are based on Zhu Xi, *Zhuzi yulei*, vol. 1, reprint (Beijing: Zhonghua shuju, 1986). Parenthetical numbers following a translation indicate the page number and the column number from this edition. An outstanding translation of other selections from the *Zhuzi yulei* is Daniel Gardner, *Learning to Be a Sage* (Berkeley: University of California Press, 1990).

4. See Fazang, "Essay on the Golden Lion," and "The Rafter Dialogue," in Part II, Selections 14 and 15.

5. See Selections on *Qi,* in Part I, Selection 6.

6. See Selections on *Yin* and *Yang* and Selections on the Five Phases, in Part I, Selections 7 and 8.

Qi has been variously translated as "psychophysical stuff," "material force," and "ether," but none of these is adequate, because we really do not have a corresponding concept in Western thought. Consequently, we will leave it untranslated.[7]

According to Neo-Confucian metaphysics, *qi* and the Pattern are the two aspects of everything that exists. As Zhu Xi explains,

1. In the world there has never been *qi* without the Pattern, and there has never been the Pattern without *qi*. (2:5)

While *qi* is the physical "stuff" that constitutes individuals, it is Pattern that determines both the descriptive and the normative structure of the universe:

2. It is certain that everything in the world has a reason why it is as it is, and a standard to which it should conform. This is the Pattern.[8]

When one of Zhu Xi's disciples asked for help in understanding this distinction, he replied:

3. For example, in serving your parents you ought to be filial, and in obeying your elder brothers you ought to be fraternal: these kinds of things are standards to which you should conform. However, *why* you must be filial in serving your parents, and *why* you must be fraternal in obeying your elder brother these are the reasons why it is as it is. (vol. 2, 414:8)

Zhu Xi gives a number of examples that illustrate the role of the Pattern in explaining the descriptive regularities of the world:

4. Someone asked, "How does the Pattern manifest itself in the *qi*?"
Zhu Xi replied, "It is due to Pattern that the complex interrelationships between *yin* and *yang* and the Five Phases do not lose their order. But if *qi* had not condensed, Pattern would have nothing to adhere to." (3:8)

5. Someone asked, "You say that Pattern is something that people and other things equally receive from Heaven. But do even insentient objects have the Pattern?"
Zhu Xi replied, "They certainly do have the Pattern. For example, a boat can only travel on water, and a cart can only travel on land." (61:14)

But the Pattern also determines the ethical facts:

---

7. *Qi* is unlike matter as conceived of by classical physics in that it is self-generating and self-moving; *qi* is also unlike the mass-energy of contemporary physics in that the Neo-Confucians did not conceptualize it as numerically quantified. As Benjamin Schwartz noted, the closest Western equivalent is perhaps the *apeiron*, the "boundless," referred to by the pre-Socratic philosopher Anaximander (Schwartz, *The World of Thought in Ancient China* [Cambridge, MA: Harvard University Press, 1985], p. 183).

8. Zhu Xi, *Daxue huowen* 15a:3 in *Hui'an Xiansheng Zhu Wen'gong Wenji* (SBCK ed.). Translation modified from Gardner, *Learning to Be a Sage*, p. 90.

6. A person is created by the coming together of Pattern and *qi*. The Heavenly Pattern is inherently vast and inexhaustible. Nonetheless, were it not for the *qi,* there would be nowhere for this Pattern to adhere to. Hence, the *yin* and *yang qi* must interact, congealing and coming together, and only then can this Pattern have a place to affix itself. The ability of all people to speak, move, think, and act is due to the *qi*. But filial piety, brotherly respect, conscientiousness, faithfulness, benevolence, righteousness, propriety, and wisdom are all manifestations of the Pattern. (65:12)

Contemporary Western readers may have difficulty understanding how the Pattern is both prescriptive and descriptive, since it has become almost a dogma that there is a sharp dichotomy between "ought" and "is." Intuitively, though, there is often an intimate connection between matters of fact and judgments of value. For example, the Pattern accounts for the following pairs of descriptive and prescriptive facts:

- A human will lose concentration if she does not get enough sleep in a twenty-four-hour period.
- A surgeon should get enough sleep prior to going into the operating room.

Similarly,

- A human baby cannot care for itself.
- Parents should love and nurture their offspring.

While the Pattern accounts for the normative and descriptive structure of the universe, *qi* is necessary to give the Pattern physical form:

7. *Qi* is capable of condensing to create things, but Pattern has no thoughts, no cogitation, and no creation. But in the place where the *qi* condenses, Pattern is there. When it comes to the generation of the people, things, plants and animals of Heaven and Earth, each has its seed. There definitely cannot be the generation of a thing out of barren soil without a seed. This is all due to *qi*. Pattern is a realm of emptiness and purity, lacking form. But it cannot create. *Qi* is capable of fermenting and condensing to generate things. But whenever the *qi* is there, Pattern is in it. (3:13)

Zhu Xi is similar to Buddhists in holding that the Pattern is the same in everything:

8. When people and things are created, Heaven endows them with the Pattern, and it is always the same Pattern. (58:14)

9. Heaven and Earth, *yin* and *yang,* life and death, day and night, ghosts and spirits—these are just the one Pattern. (vol. 2, 618:8)

Since the Pattern is the same in everything, we see corresponding structures among a range of different phenomena:

10. Living things also have the Pattern. It is like a precious jewel that has fallen to the very bottom of the muck. Nonetheless, there are some spots where it shines through its endowment [of *qi*] and it is not obscured. For example, tigers and wolves have fathers and sons, bees have rulers and ministers, jackals and otters [leave food behind to] give thanks, geese and swans mark social distinctions. This is why we refer to them as "benevolent beasts" or "righteous beasts." (73:5)

11. Someone asked, "Do withered things have the Pattern or not?"

Master Zhu replied, "As soon as there is a thing, there is the Pattern. Heaven does not create a writing brush: people take rabbit hairs and use them to make a brush. But as soon as the brush exists, there is the Pattern."

There was a further question: "Then how are benevolence and righteousness manifested in the writing brush?"

Master Zhu replied, "Subtly, in minute aspects, benevolence and righteousness are manifested." (61:12)

Zhu Xi sometimes uses the distinction between Substance and Function to explain the relationship between the underlying Pattern and its various manifestations:

12. The myriad things all have the Pattern, and their Patterns all come from one source. However, the roles that they occupy are different, so the Functions of their Patterns are not one. As a ruler, one must be benevolent; as a minister, one must be reverent; as a child, one must be filial; as a father, one must be kind. Each thing fully has the Pattern. And though each thing is different in its Function, everything is a manifestation of the one Pattern. (vol. 2, 398:9)

Zhu Xi's illustrations of the Substance/Function distinction are very similar to those that had been given by the Buddhists:

13. It's like how water sometimes flows, sometimes collects, and sometimes is stirred up into waves: these are Function. That the body of the water can flow, can collect, and can be stirred up into waves is Substance. Or it's like how a body is Substance, while the eyes seeing, the ears hearing, the hands and feet moving are Function. Or it's like how this hand is Substance, and the fingers moving and picking something up are Function. (101:8)[9]

Since the Pattern is ultimately one and the same in everything, it is *qi* that accounts for the fact that there are different things in the world. Zhu Xi uses various metaphors to explain the relationship between the one Pattern and the *qi* that determines its manifestations:

---

9. Recall Huineng's use of the simile of the lamp and its light from the *Platform Sutra*, in Part II, Selection 16, and Fazang's metaphor of the gold and the lion, in Part II, Selection 15.

14. People and things have natures that are fundamentally the same; it is simply that their endowments of *qi* differ. It's like water. It never fails to be clear, but if you put it in a white bowl, it is all white; if you put it in a black bowl, it is all black; if you put it in a blue bowl, it is all blue. Nature is particularly difficult to explain. It is fine to say that it is the same, but also fine to say that it differs. It's like the Sun shining through a crack. The length and size of the cracks are not the same, but it is still the same Sun shining through them. (58:11)

15. The Pattern is in the *qi* like a bright jewel is in water. Pattern in clear *qi* is like a jewel in clear water: its brightness is fully visible. Pattern in turbid *qi* is like a jewel in turbid water: you cannot see its brightness outside. (73:8)

It is tempting to assimilate the relationship between the Pattern and *qi* to the relationship between Aristotle's form and matter. However, this comparison is deeply misleading, because there are distinct Aristotelian forms for distinct kinds of things: the form of a human, the form of a dog, etc. In contrast, there is only one Pattern, but it manifests itself differently in different endowments of *qi*.

In the technical language of metaphysics, we can say that *qi* is responsible for *speciation* and *individuation*. In other words, Pattern is one and the same in everything, so *qi* accounts for the fact that there are different kinds of things, and for the fact that there are numerically distinct individuals:

16. It's like this piece of wood: it only has one Pattern, but this grain runs this way and that grain runs that way. Or it's like a house: it only has one Pattern, but there is a kitchen and a reception hall. Or it's like plants and trees: they only have one Pattern, but there are peaches and plums. Or it's like this crowd of people: they only have one Pattern, but there is the third son of the Zhang family and the fourth son of the Li family; the fourth son of the Li family cannot become the third son of the Zhang family, and the third son of the Zhang family cannot become the fourth son of the Li family. It's all like *yin* and *yang,* or like what the "Western Inscription" means by Pattern is one but its manifestations are diverse.[10] (102:8)

In the following passage Zhu Xi explains in more detail the role of *qi* in speciation:

17. If we simply discuss it in terms of *qi*, then people and things all are created by getting *qi*. But if we discuss it in terms of refined and coarse, then people get *qi* that is correct and penetrating, while things get *qi* that is partial and constricted. Because people get what is correct, this Pattern is penetrating and not constricted. Because things get what is partial, this Pattern is

---

10. Cheng Yi attributed the slogan "Pattern is one but its manifestations are diverse" to Zhang Zai, and claims that it is the fundamental message of Zhang's "The Western Inscription." See Cheng Yi, "Reply to Yang Shi's Letter on 'The Western Inscription,'" in Part III, Selection 30, and Zhang Zai, "The Western Inscription," in Part III, Selection 23. Interestingly, the phrase does not actually occur in "The Western Inscription."

constricted and lacks knowledge. . . . Because people receive the most correct *qi* of Heaven and Earth, they are able to understand the overarching Pattern, and have awareness. Things receive the partial *qi* of Heaven and Earth. . . . There are some things that have knowledge, but they only understand one small path. For example, birds know to have filial piety, otters know to perform ritual sacrifices, dogs are able to guard palaces, and oxen are able to plough.[11] People, in contrast, can have knowledge of and do anything. (65:14)

In addition to its roles in speciation and individuation, a third role of *qi* is *ethical qualification.* Although we humans all have *qi* that is similar enough to make us members of the same species, some of us are ethically superior to others because our *qi* is more "bright" and "clear":

> 18. If we talk about it in terms of [the *qi*] humans are endowed with, there are differences of dark and bright, clear and turbid. Hence, those who are the most lofty of the wise and are born knowing it have *qi* that is purely clear and bright, without the least darkness and turbidity.[12] This is why those who are born knowing it and put it into action effortlessly, like Yao and Shun, are capable of it without learning. Next are those who are just below being born knowing it. They can only know after they have learned it, can reach it only after they have practiced it. Next after that are those whose endowment is partial and have some obscurations, so they must painfully make an effort. "If others only need to do one, you must do a hundred; if others only need to do ten, you must do a thousand."[13] Only then will you be able to reach the second level below those born knowing it. But if you approach it without stopping, what you achieve will be identical with what they achieve. (66:2)

In other words, one's innate disposition may make it easier or more difficult to be virtuous. However, it is possible for anyone to become a sage, so one cannot evade one's responsibility for striving to become a better person. This view that, despite our differences in aptitude, we all have a responsibility to strive for our ethical improvement has deep roots in Confucianism. For example, Kongzi contemptuously dismissed the excuse of a disciple who whined that his "strength is insufficient" to follow the Way.[14] Similarly, Mengzi stated that those who falsely claim they are incapable of virtue "throw themselves away."[15]

---

11. Zhu Xi believes that the tendency of birds to return to their parents' nest is a manifestation of the Pattern of filial piety, while the tendency of otters to drop some of the shellfish they open is a manifestation of the Pattern of ritual sacrifices.

12. The phrase "most lofty of the wise" is from *Analects* 17.3, in Part III, Selection 34. The phrases "born knowing it" and (in the next sentence) "put it into action effortlessly" are from *Mean* 20.viii, in Part III, Selection 36.

13. *Mean* 20.xiv, in Part III, Selection 36.

14. *Analects* 6.12, in Part III, Selection 34.

15. *Mengzi* 4A10, in Part III, Selection 35.

The Pattern/*qi* framework is remarkably flexible and powerful, and the Cheng-Zhu School uses it to explain all the key terms used in the ancient Confucian classics, including "Way," "Heaven," "nature," "mind," and "mandate." One of their interpretive techniques is to suggest that different terms often refer to the same underlying reality, but stress different aspects or manifestations of that reality:

> 19. A disciple asked, "'Heaven' is used when discussing it in terms of being natural. 'Mandate' is used when discussing it in terms of its manifestations or what things are endowed with. 'Nature' is used when discussing its complete Substance or what the myriad things get in order to be alive. 'Pattern' is used when discussing it as the standard of each things and activity. But if we discuss them together, Heaven *is* the Pattern, the mandate *is* the nature, and the nature *is* the Pattern. Is this right?"
>
> Master Zhu replied, "It is. However, people nowadays often talk as if Heaven is not also the 'great blue expanse above.' I personally think we cannot do without this 'great blue expanse.'" (82:4)

> 20. Someone asked, "What is the difference between the Way and the Pattern?"
>
> Master Zhu replied, "The Way is the path; the Pattern is the differentiations."
>
> The questioner continued, "Is it like the grain in wood?"
>
> Master Zhu replied, "It is."
>
> The questioner said, "In that case they seem to be the same."
>
> Master Zhu replied, "The word 'Way' is the overarching term, while 'Pattern' is the many differentiations within the Way." (99:9)

Some of the most subtle but intriguing applications of this metaphysics are in the area of philosophical psychology:

> 21. There were questions about the nature, feelings, mind, and benevolence. Master Zhu replied, "Zhang Zai explained it very well. He said, 'the mind is what connects the nature and the feelings.' And when Mengzi said, 'the mind of compassion is the beginning of benevolence, the mind of disdain is the beginning of righteousness' he explained the nature, feelings, and mind extremely well.[16] The nature never fails to be good. The feelings are the expressions of the mind, and sometimes fail to be good. So we cannot say that what is not good is *not* the mind. However, the fundamental Substance of the mind never fails to be good. When what flows from it is not good, this is because the feelings are misled by things. Now, 'nature' is a general term for the Pattern, while 'benevolence,' 'righteousness,' 'propriety,' and 'wisdom' are all names for individual Patterns within the nature. 'Compassion,' 'disdain,' 'deference,' and 'approval and disapproval' are all names for expressions of the feelings when the feelings come from the nature and are all good. (92:10)

---

16. *Mengzi* 2A6, in Part III, Selection 35.

Zhu Xi uses these distinctions to give a metaphysical interpretation to the ancient Confucian Mengzi's claim that human nature is good, and to explain why people do bad things, despite having a good nature:

> 22. There is only one overarching Pattern within Heaven and Earth. Human nature is just the Pattern. The reason that there are good people and bad people is simply due to the clear or turbid embodied disposition with which each is endowed.[17] (68:2)

> 23. Nature may be compared to water. It is fundamentally always clear. But if you collect it in a clean vessel, it will be clear; if you collect it in a vessel that is not clean, then it will be dirty; if you collect it in a vessel that is filthy, then it will be turbid. However, its fundamental clarity is always there. Once it is turbid, it is difficult to make it clear. Hence, only after using the utmost effort will one be able to get it. Then "even if you are foolish, you will become enlightened; even if you are weak, you will become strong."[18] (72:12)

> 24. The nature is like water, and the embodied nature is like adding a little oil and salt, so that it all has a certain flavor. (68:5)

> 25. Nature is like water: if it flows through a clear channel it is clear; if it flows through a dirty channel it is turbid. If the embodiment is clear and correct, one gets [the nature] completely and is a human; if the embodiment is turbid and partial, one gets it in a darkened manner and is a bird or beast. *Qi* can be clear or turbid. Humans get clear *qi*, while birds and beasts get turbid *qi*. The great Substance of humans is fundamentally clear, hence we differ from animals. However, there are also those with turbid *qi*, who are not too far from being birds or beasts. (73:1)

> 26. You have such-and-such a Pattern and only then do you have such-and-such a *qi*. If you have such-and-such a *qi*, then you must have such-and-such a Pattern. When the endowment of *qi* is clear, you get a sage or a worthy. It's like a precious jewel in clear, cold water. When the endowment of *qi* is turbid, you get the ignorant and the worthless. It's like the jewel is in turbid water. What is referred to as "enlightening one's enlightened Virtue" is taking this jewel out of the turbid water and cleaning it off.[19] (73:4)

Ethics and Cultivation of the Self

Zhu Xi uses the metaphysics of Pattern and *qi* to provide a framework for his views on learning and education as tools of personal cultivation. One of the most distinctive aspects of Zhu Xi's philosophy is his emphasis on book learning and formal education as tools for ethical development:

---

17. "Embodied disposition" is literally "materialized *qi*," 氣質, *qì zhì*.

18. *Mean* 20.xv, in Part III, Selection 36.

19. *Great Learning*, Classic 1, in Part III, Selection 33.

27. When humans are born the overarching Pattern is already complete in them. The reason that they have to read books is simply that they have not understood much through their own experience. The sages *did* understand much through their own experience, so they wrote it down in books to let others understand. What is important for those who read books today is to understand the overarching Pattern. But when they understand the Pattern, it will be something that they already had originally, not something added from outside. (161:4)

Zhu Xi has a subtle and multifaceted theory of ethical cultivation, but two of the most important aspects of it are (1) coming to know the Pattern and (2) focusing on that knowledge so that it is always reflected in one's emotions and actions. He uses phrases taken from the ancient classics to describe these two steps, referring to the former as (1) "extending knowledge," "getting a handle on things," and "exhaustively investigating,"[20] and the latter as (2) "maintaining reverence" and "focusing on one thing":

28. The spiritual task of the learner consists simply of two activities: maintaining reverence and exhaustively investigating. These two activities are mutually reinforcing. If you are able to exhaustively investigate, then you will daily advance in the task of maintaining reverence. If you can maintain reverence, then you will daily advance in the task of exhaustively investigating. It is like a person's feet. When the right foot steps, the left foot pauses; when the left foot steps, the right foot pauses. (150:9)

29. One must first "extend knowledge" and only then engage in cultivation. (152:6)

30. Someone asked, "Which is first, exhaustive investigation or accumulating righteousness?"

Zhu Xi replied, "Exhaustive investigation is first. However, there is not a clear dividing line between first and later." (152:8)

Extending knowledge is primarily a matter of book learning:

31. Read books in order to observe the intentions of sages and worthies. Follow the intentions of sages and worthies to observe the natural Pattern. (162:8)

32. All the words of the sages are the natural and Heavenly Pattern. (179:8)

Because reading is primarily a matter of ethical cultivation, it is a demanding process:

33. The words of sages have layer upon layer of meaning. You must enter deeply into them. If you only get to the surface, you will make mistakes. Only if you submerge yourself in them will you get it. (162:12)

---

20. On these phrases, see Zhu Xi's Commentary on the *Great Learning*, Commentary 5, in Part III, Selection 33.

34. When people read words, they only look at the first layer of meaning, and fail to seek for the second layer. (162:13)

Reverence, the second step or aspect of ethical cultivation, is a kind of mental focus on whatever one is doing:

35. Do not look upon reverence as a distinct activity. It is simply to collect one's spirit and focus it on one thing. (215:16)

36. Someone asked, "Regardless of whether you are seated in meditation or responding to affairs, you must maintain focus. Is that right?"

Master Zhu replied, "Your meditation should not be like that of Chan Buddhists, who 'enter into stability,' cutting off all thoughts. Simply gather your mind and don't let your thoughts run wild. Your mind will then calmly maintain focus without any effort. When an affair arises, you will respond to it; when the affair has passed, you will return to being calm." (217:5)[21]

37. You must remain focused whether you are practicing poetry, music, dance, or recitation. If you are practicing archery but your mind isn't there, how can you hit the target? If you are practicing charioteering but your mind isn't there, how can you steer the horses? Calligraphy and mathematics are the same. (217:8)

When selfish thoughts intrude upon one's extension of knowledge and reverence, one must overcome them by a sheer act of will:

38. Reverence is like plowing and irrigating the fields; "overcoming the self" is like getting rid of weeds. (214:5)[22]

39. "Extending knowledge," reverence, and "overcoming the self" may be compared to the activities of a household. Reverence is guarding the door. Overcoming the self is fending off robbers. Extending knowledge is investigating the internal and external affairs of the household. (151:12)

Disagreements with Other Confucians

Many aspects of Zhu Xi's view would be shared by other Confucians in his era. In particular, most later Confucians throughout Chinese history would agree with the following claims:

- human nature is good
- concepts like "mind" and "human nature" should be interpreted in terms of an overarching Pattern that is somehow shared by everything
- "selfish desires" are the primary impediments to Virtue.[23]

---

21. Ironically, this is similar to the advice the Chan Buddhist Huineng gives in the *Platform Sutra*, in Part II, Selection 16.

22. "Overcoming the self" is a phrase from *Analects* 12.1, in Part III, Selection 34.

23. For notable exceptions to this consensus on the second and third views, see the selections from Dai Zhen and Zhang Xuecheng, in Part IV, Selections 51 and 52.

However, the details of Zhu Xi's view were controversial even during his own lifetime. The disputes centered on two related issues: (1) the relationship between knowledge and action, and (2) the precise metaphysics of Pattern (especially the proper understanding of the Great Ultimate and the mind).[24]

Knowledge and Action

Because the Pattern determines the ethical facts, and because the Pattern is fully present within each person's mind, "extending knowledge" is a matter of self-discovery. Consequently, some Confucians argued that book-learning was superfluous. However, Zhu Xi thinks that most of us have endowments of *qi* that are too "turbid" for us to have unmediated, intuitive knowledge of the Pattern:

> 40. A disciple said, "When I was in Hunan, I met a master who taught people to simply act."
>
> Zhu Xi replied, "If one is not enlightened about the Pattern of righteousness, how can one act?"
>
> The disciple said, "He said 'when you do it, then you will see it.'"
>
> Zhu Xi replied, "This is like walking down a road: if you cannot see, how can you walk? Nowadays, many people teach others to simply act, setting themselves up as an authority to teach others. There is naturally a kind of person whose disposition is good, who does not need to exhaustively investigate, get a handle on things, or extend knowledge. But the sages made the *Great Learning* to let others enter the realm of sages and worthies. Once people are enlightened about the Pattern of the Way, they will naturally always be filial in serving their relatives, be fraternal in serving their elder brothers, and faithful in interacting with friends." (152:14)
>
> 41. When people study, of course they want to get it from their own mind, and embody it in their self. But if they do not read books, they will not know what getting it from their own mind is. (176:4)
>
> 42. It is only because people have selfish thoughts that sages and worthies left behind myriad sayings in order to sweep aside people's selfish thoughts and allow them to make whole their minds of compassion and disdain.[25] (188:6)

Most of Zhu Xi's comments on knowledge suggest that it is possible to know the Pattern yet not act in accordance with it.[26] (This is why extending knowledge has to be supplemented with reverence and overcoming the self.)

> 43. Knowledge and action always need each other. It's like how eyes cannot walk without feet, but feet cannot see without eyes. If we discuss them in

---

24. See Lu Xiangshan, "Correspondence on the Great Ultimate," and Wang Yangming, *A Record for Practice,* in Part III, Selections 37 and 43.

25. See *Mengzi* 2A6, in Part III, Selection 35.

26. In Western philosophy, the phenomenon of doing what one knows to be wrong is called weakness of will (or *akrasia* in Classical Greek).

terms of their sequence, knowledge comes first. But if we discuss them in terms of importance, action is what is important. (148:1)

44. When people know something but their actions don't accord with it, their knowledge is still shallow. But once they have personally experienced it, their knowledge is more enlightened, and does not have the same significance it had before. (148:2)

Among the most notable critics of Zhu Xi's two-step understanding of the relationship between knowledge and action is Wang Yangming, who defended "the unity of knowing and acting."[27]

The Great Ultimate

One of the most subtle issues debated by the Neo-Confucians was the meaning of the term "Great Ultimate," which first appears in the "Great Appendix" to the *Changes*. The phrase is also used in Zhou Dunyi's "Explanation of the Diagram of the Great Ultimate," which opens, "The ultimateless yet also the Great Ultimate!"[28] Zhu Xi's basic view is that "Great Ultimate" is another name for the Pattern, and that Zhou Dunyi described it as "the ultimateless" in order to make clear that Pattern in itself has no concrete form; it requires *qi* for embodiment:

45. "Great Ultimate" is just another term for Pattern. (2:3)

46. Someone asked, "The Great Ultimate is not some undifferentiated thing that existed before Heaven and Earth; instead, it is a name for the sum total of the Pattern of the myriad things. Is this correct?"

Master Zhu replied, "The Great Ultimate is simply the Pattern of the myriad things of Heaven and Earth. If one discusses it in terms of Heaven and Earth, the Great Ultimate exists in Heaven and Earth; if one discusses it in terms of the myriad things, the Great Ultimate exists in each of the myriad things. It actually is the case that, before Heaven and Earth existed, this Pattern existed. '[It] moves and creates *yang*' is just the Pattern, and 'It is still and creates *yin*' is also just the Pattern."[29] (1:1)

47. Someone asked, "Since each and every thing possesses the one Great Ultimate, is the Pattern complete in all of them?"

Master Zhu replied, "You can say that it is complete, or you can say that it is partial. If one discusses it in terms of the Pattern, then it is complete in all of them. If one discusses it in terms of the *qi,* then it cannot fail to be partial." (57:16)

---

27. See especially Wang Yangming, *A Record for Practice,* in Part III, Selection 43.

28. See Zhou Dunyi, "Explanation of the Diagram of the Great Ultimate," in Part III, Selection 24. For the original occurrence of the phrase, see the "Great Appendix," I.11, in Part I, Selection 9.

29. The quoted phrases are from Zhou Dunyi's "Explanation of the Diagram of the Great Ultimate," in Part III, Selection 24.

These seemingly innocuous claims led to great controversy. In order to see why, we need to understand how they relate to Zhu Xi's doctrines on the relationship between knowledge and action. According to Zhu Xi, we must engage in book-learning and formal education to overcome our selfish desires, purify our endowment of *qi,* and rediscover the Pattern that constitutes our nature. The words of the sages as recorded in the Four Books can help us do this because they convey generalizations or abstractions of the Pattern, which we can then later apply to concrete situations. Therefore, there is a sense in which the Pattern is conceptually prior to its embodiments in *qi.* In other words, we can know what it is to be a good parent, child, ruler, or subjects in general, before we know anything about particular individuals who are parents, children, rulers, or subjects. In the following passages, Zhu Xi tries to explain to his disciples the sense in which the Pattern (i.e., the Great Ultimate) is prior to its manifestations. To borrow Western metaphysical terminology, we might say that the Great Ultimate is conceptually prior, but not temporally prior, to its embodiments in *qi:*

48. Someone asked, "Did Pattern exist first or did *qi* exist first?"

Master Zhu replied, "Pattern has never been separated from *qi.* However, the Pattern is 'above with respect to form,' while *qi* is 'below with respect to form.'[30] If one discusses it in terms of being above or below with respect to form, how can there not be before and after? Pattern has no form, while *qi* is coarse and has impurities." [3:3]

49. Someone asked, "What does it mean that there must first exist such-and-such a Pattern and only then exist such-and-such a *qi*?"

Master Zhu replied, "Fundamentally one cannot talk about them in terms of first and later. Nonetheless, if one is forced to extend back to where they come from, then one must say that there first exists the Pattern. However, the Pattern is not a distinct thing; it simply exists within the *qi.* If there were no *qi,* the Pattern would have no place to adhere to. *Qi* is metal, wood, water, and fire; Pattern is benevolence, righteousness, propriety, and wisdom."[31] (3:5)

50. Someone asked about the claim that Pattern is first and *qi* is later.

Master Zhu replied, "Fundamentally there is no first and later. However, if we extend back in time, it *seems* as if Pattern is first and *qi* is later."

51. Someone asked for an explanation of how Pattern exists first and then *qi* exists later.

Master Zhu said, "This is not a good way to put it. Whether Pattern existed first and *qi* existed later, or Pattern existed first and *qi* existed later—

---

30. *Changes,* "Great Appendix," I.12, in Part I, Selection 9. One of the major disputes among Neo-Confucians is over how to interpret these key phrases.

31. On the correspondence between these four virtues and the Five Phases, see Zhu Xi's commentary on *Mengzi* 2A6, in Part III, Selection 35. See also Selections on the Five Phases, in Part I, Selection 8.

these are things that we cannot infer from today. Nonetheless, if one judges it by our ideas, then one suspects that the *qi* is dependent on the Pattern to flow. Whenever the *qi* congeals, Pattern is present." (3:12)

52. Someone asked, "If it is the case that 'if the Pattern exists then the *qi* exists,' then doesn't it seem that one should not distinguish them as first and later?"

Master Zhu said, "If forced to pick one, it is Pattern that exists first. It is simply that one should not say, 'today the Pattern exists, tomorrow the *qi* exists.' But there must be a first and later, and if somehow all the mountains, rivers, and the earth itself should vanish, Pattern would still be here." (4:1)

53. Someone asked, "Yesterday you said that it actually is the case that, before Heaven and Earth existed, Pattern existed. What does this mean?"

Master Zhu replied, "There actually was simply the Pattern before Heaven and Earth existed. Because there is the Pattern, there is Heaven and Earth. If the Pattern did not exist, then there would be no Heaven and Earth, no humans, no things—there would be none of these things that carry the Pattern. There is the Pattern, hence there is the flowing *qi*, and it nurtures the myriad things."

Someone asked, "By 'it nurtures them' do you mean that the Pattern is what nurtures them?"

Master Zhu replied, "There is the Pattern, hence there is the *qi* that flows and nurtures. The Pattern has no concrete form." (1:8)

Zhu Xi's interpretation of the Great Ultimate would be passionately criticized by his contemporary, Lu Xiangshan, who thought that it encouraged learners to focus on an abstract realm that would distract them from the concrete task of ethical action in this world.[32]

When you read Zhu Xi's *Collected Commentaries on the Four Books* (in Part III, Selections 33 through 36), keep an eye out for how the metaphysical and ethical issues discussed above guide Zhu Xi's interpretations of the texts.

Miscellaneous Sayings

I shall close this section with a few of Zhu Xi's most memorable quotations from the *Categorized Conversations:*

54. With each blow, a scar! With each punch, a fistful of blood! When you read the words of others, you should approach it the same way. Don't be lazy! (164:1)

55. The problem with people is that they only know how to doubt the views of others but don't know how to doubt their own views. If they tried to critique themselves like they critique others, they would come close to seeing their own strengths and weaknesses. (187:2)

---

32. See Lu Xiangshan, "Correspondence on the Great Ultimate," in Part III, Selection 37.

56. Sages do not know that they are sages. (232:5)

57. Kindness and generosity are what we need as the foundation. As for courage and determination, we can't do without them, but they have to be kept in place. (239:6)

58. There is a certain sort of talk among the current generation that encourages laziness. People say things like, "I would not dare to carelessly criticize my elders!" or "I would not dare to assert my own uninformed opinions!" These are simply expressions of laziness! Certainly one shouldn't unthinkingly criticize one's elders, but what harm is there in discussing what is right or wrong with their actions? And certainly one shouldn't insist on one's own opinions, but when we read books, we will have doubts and have insights. Naturally we will have opinions. Those who don't have opinions simply have not read carefully enough to have any doubts! (190:11)

33. *Collected Commentaries on the* Great Learning

translation by Bryan W. Van Norden[33]

It is Zhu Xi who is responsible for making the Four Books central to the Confucian canon: Great Learning, Analects, Mengzi, *and* Mean. *In addition, Zhu Xi's* Collected Commentaries on the Four Books *became the orthodox interpretation for the civil service examinations, and continues to have an immense influence even today. Three points are especially noteworthy about Zhu Xi's interpretations. First, he believes that the Four Books express a unified view of the Way (even though they were written by different authors over several generations). Consequently, he frequently interprets passages in one text in the light of passages from other texts. See, for example, how his interpretation of the* Great Learning, *Chapter 5 influences his understanding of* Analects 4.15, *and vice versa. The second point to notice is that Zhu Xi interprets each of the Four Books in terms of the metaphysics of the Pattern, the abstract structure of the universe, and* qi, *the underlying "stuff" out of which things are condensed. Thus, Zhu Xi appeals to the metaphysics of Pattern and* qi *to explain why Mengzi's statement that human nature is always good (*Mengzi 6A6) *is consistent with Kongzi's claim that human natures are merely similar to one another (*Analects 17.2). *(See Zhu Xi's* Categorized Conversations, *Part III, Selection 32, for an introduc-*

33. This translation is based on the *Sibu beiyao* edition of Zhu Xi, *Daxue jizhu*. My translation is very abridged, leaving out passages that will be opaque or uninteresting to contemporary readers. For a complete translation, see Ian Johnston and Wang Ping, trans., *Daxue and Zhongyong* (Hong Kong: Chinese University Press, 2012).

tion to the metaphysics of Pattern and qi.*) Finally, as Zhu Xi himself would stress, what is most important in reading the classics and commentaries is that we be open to the important ethical lessons they try to impart. Generations of the greatest minds and most noble leaders of China, Japan, and Korea have found inspiration in these texts; we can too.*

Zhu Xi recommended that students begin their study of the Four Books with the Great Learning. *The* Great Learning *is an ancient text that was originally just a chapter in a longer work, the* Rites. *However, it began to circulate as an independent text, and became increasingly important among Neo-Confucians, beginning with Han Yu.*[34] *Zhu Xi believed that the text of the* Great Learning *had been miscopied by careless scribes who did not understand its deep meaning. Consequently, he extensively rearranged the text. Zhu Xi is also responsible for what became the standard view that the* Great Learning *consists of two parts: a "Classic" section, which had been written by Kongzi, and a "Commentary" on the Classic, which had been written by Kongzi's disciple Zēngzǐ* 曾子. *In addition to rearranging the text, Zhu Xi added his own commentary on the* Great Learning, *which became the orthodox interpretation, although it was challenged by Wang Yangming in his "Questions on the* Great Learning*" (in Part III, Selection 38). In this translation, the original text of Kongzi's "Classic" and Zengzi's "Commentary" is given in* **boldface**, *while Zhu Xi's commentary on each is given in* Roman font, *set off from the boldface text by square brackets. All footnotes and all sentences in italics are by the translator.* — *Tr.*

Zhu Xi's Preface

[The book, the *Great Learning*, is the method by which the ancient school of Great Learning educated people. From the time Heaven gave birth to the people, it gave everyone a nature with benevolence, righteousness, propriety, and wisdom. Nonetheless, the embodied dispositions with which they are endowed are sometimes unequal.[35] Consequently, some are unable to know what is within their natures, and to bring their natures to completion. As soon as those who were intelligent and wise enough to be able to fathom their natures stood out among them, Heaven mandated that they become the rulers and teachers of countless millions, and made them bring order to and educate others, so that they could revive their natures. This is the manner in which (the sagely sovereigns and emperors) Fu Xi, Shen Nong, the Yellow Emperor, Yao, and Shun

---

34. See Han Yu, "On the Way," in Part III, Selection 20.

35. Although Zhu Xi insists that all people are born with the same original nature, he allows that people are born with different qualities of *qi*. Some people's *qi* is innately prone to intelligence and enlightenment, while other people's *qi* is ignorant and darkened. However, everyone can, through effort, become good. For more on this point, see Zhu Xi's commentary on *Analects* 17.2, in Part III, Selection 34.

carried on for Heaven and achieved perfection. The position of the Minister of Education and the office of the Director of Music were then established. Thus, the standard provided by the glory of the Three Dynasties (the Xia, Shang, and Zhou) gradually became complete.

[Everywhere, from the King's palace, to the capitals of the states, on down to the smallest villages there were schools. Eight years after birth, sons and younger brothers, from those of the King and dukes on down to those of the commoners, entered the school of Lesser Learning, where they were educated about the etiquette of "sweeping and cleaning, responding and replying, entering and exiting," as well as the adornments of (the Six Arts of) ritual, music, archery, charioteering, calligraphy and arithmetic.[36]

[When they were fifteen, then from the heir apparent of the Son of Heaven and his other sons, on to the heirs of dukes, ministers, chief counselors, high officials, along with all who were outstanding among the people—all entered the school of Great Learning, where they were educated about the Way of exhaustively investigating the Pattern, correcting the mind, cultivating oneself, and bringing order to others.[37] This was how the education of the schools, and the division between greater and lesser was distinguished.

[So schools were widely established in this way, and the details of the sequence and techniques of education were like this. The manner in which they educated people was always rooted in the personal practice of the people's ruler and the abundant understanding of his own mind. It did not demand anything beyond the people's daily lives and relationships. Consequently, at that time, everyone learned, and what they learned was nothing other than knowing what their natures have inherently, and what they should do according to their personal responsibilities. Each strived to exert his utmost effort at this. This is the manner in which, during the time of the ancient summit of civilization, there was glorious rule above, and fine customs below. And this is what later ages have been unable to attain.

[When the Zhou dynasty declined, no more rulers arose who were sages or worthies, the government schools were no longer maintained, education decayed, customs deteriorated, and soon even a sage like Kongzi could not get the position of advisor to a ruler in order to put into effect his government by education. Thereupon, Kongzi alone recited and transmitted the model provided by the Former Kings as a call to later generations. The Classic section of the following work makes clear the enlightened method of Great Learning for those who have already completed the Lesser Learning. Kongzi's three thousand disciples all heard his explanation of it, but it was Zengzi and his lineage alone that grasped the essence, so he made a Commentary in order to express its meaning.

---

36. *Analects* 19.12.

37. On Zhu Xi's claim that students began the Great Learning at the age of fifteen, see *Analects* 2.4, in Part III, Selection 34.

But after Mengzi passed away, the transmission ceased, and although the book still existed, few were those who understood it.

[From that time forth, shallow Confucians practiced memorizing and reciting texts, and writing ornate essays. Their effort was twice that required for the Lesser Learning, but had no benefits. The unorthodox teachings about "nothingness" (of the Daoists) and about "Nirvana" (of the Buddhists) seemed more "lofty" than the Great Learning but lacked substance. Other techniques and schemes—all designed only to achieve success and fame—and the various techniques of the Hundred Schools, sprouted up in throngs: all confusing the world, bewitching the people, and choking off benevolence and righteousness. The unfortunate result was that rulers could not hear the basics of the great Way, and commoners could not enjoy the benefits of good order.

[Yet the Heavens are ever-turning; wherever things go, they always come back. Now, in the Song dynasty, Virtue has again flourished. Good order and education have been cultivated. Thus, Cheng Yi and Cheng Hao emerged and were able to continue the tradition of Mengzi. They began to genuinely revere the *Great Learning* and publicize it. Although I myself am not quick-witted, I was fortunate to have learned from them indirectly. Seeing that the text of the *Great Learning* has been corrupted, I have, despite my own lack of sophistication, edited it, interspersed my own humble opinions, and supplied some missing pieces of text—until later gentlemen come along to do a better job.

[My (Zhu Xi's) masters the Cheng brothers said, "The *Great Learning* is a surviving book of the lineage of Kongzi. It is the gateway by which those starting their learning enter into Virtue. It is only because of the survival of this book— along with the *Analects* and *Mengzi*—that we see the program of learning that the ancients engaged in. Learners must start with this. Then they will come close to not making any mistakes."]

Classic Section by Kongzi
(with commentary by Zhu Xi)

1. The Way of Great Learning lies in enlightening one's enlightened Virtue. It lies in renewing the people. It lies in resting in the ultimate good.[38]
["Great Learning" is the learning of an adult. "Enlightened Virtue" is something people get from Heaven. It is receptive, spiritual, and unclouded. It contains the entire Pattern so that it can respond to the myriad kinds of situations. However, it is sometimes darkened, due to the restrictions caused by our endowments of

---

38. The first phrase could be rendered freely but accurately as "The goals of higher education are. . . ." ("Great Learning" has become the standard expression in contemporary Chinese for a university.) The phrase that Zhu reads as "renewing the people" (*xīnmín* 新民) is actually an emendation of the original text, which reads "loving the people" (*qīnmín* 親民). Zhu Xi adopts this emendation from Cheng Yi, but Wang Yangming argues against it in his "Questions on the *Great Learning*," in Part III, Selection 38.

qi and the obscurations of human desires. Nonetheless, the enlightenment of its fundamental Substance is never extinguished. Hence, learners should follow its manifestations and thereupon enlighten it in order to return to its beginning (before it was embodied in *qi*).

["Renewing" means stripping away what is old. This part means that, having already enlightened one's own enlightened Virtue, one should then extend it to reach others, making it so that they too have the wherewithal to get rid of impurities from their old contaminations.

["Resting" has the meaning that one must arrive at this and not wander away. "Ultimate good" is the highest point of what should be so according to the Pattern of situations. This part means that "enlightening one's enlightened Virtue" and "renewing the people" should both rest in the point of ultimate goodness and not wander away. In general, one must have the wherewithal to fully fathom this Heavenly Pattern up to its highest point, and not deviate so much as the breadth of a hair due the selfishness of human desires. These three (enlightening, renewing, and resting) are the main themes of the Great Learning.]

2. When one knows the place to rest, only then is one settled. When one is settled, only then is one able to be tranquil. When one is tranquil, only then is one able to be at peace. When one is at peace, only then is one able to ponder. When one ponders, only then is one able to get it. ["The place to rest" is where one ought to stop, which is just where the "ultimate good" lies. One "knows" it and then one's will has a "settled" direction. "Tranquil" means that one's mind does not move recklessly. "Peace" means that one is at peace where one dwells.[39] "Ponder" means to meticulously examine the situations one deals with. "To get it" means to get the place where one rests (which is the highest good).]

3. Things have their roots and their branches. Situations have their endings and their beginnings. To know what to put first and last is to come close to the Way. [Enlightened Virtue is the root. Renewing the people is the branches. Knowing the place to rest is the beginning. To be able to get it is the end. The root and the beginning are what to put first; the branches and the end are what to put last. This summarizes the meaning of the two previous verses.]

4. The ancients who desired (i) to enlighten the enlightened Virtue of the world would first (ii) put their states in order. Those who desired to put their states in order would first (iii) regulate their families. Those who desired to regulate their families would first (iv) cultivate their selves. Those who desired to cultivate their selves would first (v) correct their minds. Those who desired to correct their minds would first (vi) make their thoughts have Sincerity. Those who desired to make their thoughts have Sincerity would first (vii) extend their knowledge. Extending knowledge lies in (viii) getting

---

39. Cf. *Analects* 4.2: "Those who are not benevolent cannot long dwell in difficulty, nor can they long dwell in delight. But the benevolent are at peace in benevolence, and the wise crave benevolence."

a handle on things.[40] [(i) "To enlighten the enlightened Virtue of the world" is to arrange it so that the people of the world have the means to enlighten their enlightened Virtue. (v) The "mind" is the master of the self. (vi) "Thoughts" are the expressions of the mind. To make the expressions of one's mind have "Sincerity" is to desire that one is never conflicted and does not deceive oneself.[41] (vii) To "extend" one's knowledge is to desire that one has completely fathomed what one knows.[42] (viii) "Getting a handle on" is reaching. "Things" means situations in general. To completely reach the Pattern of things and affairs is to desire that there is nowhere in their farthest reaches one does not get to. These eight (enlightening the enlightened Virtue of the world, putting the state in order, regulating one's family, cultivating one's self, correcting one mind, making one's thoughts have Sincerity, extending knowledge, and getting a handle on things) are the steps of the Great Learning.]

5. Only after (viii) one gets a handle on things (vii) does knowledge reach the ultimate. Only after knowledge has reached the ultimate (vi) do thoughts have Sincerity. Only after thoughts have Sincerity (v) is the mind correct. Only after the mind is correct (iv) is the self cultivated. Only after the self is cultivated (iii) is the family regulated. Only after the family is regulated (ii) is the state ordered. Only after the state is ordered (i) is the world at peace. [(viii) "One gets a handle on things" when there is nowhere one fails to get to, even in the farthest reaches of the Pattern of things. (vii) "Knowledge has reached the ultimate" when one has completely fathomed what one's mind knows. (vi) After knowledge has been fathomed, then one's thoughts can succeed in having Sincerity. (v) After one's thoughts have Sincerity, then one's mind can succeed in becoming correct.

[Cultivating one's self and the steps leading up to it (cultivating one's self, correcting one's mind, making one's thoughts have Sincerity, extending one's

---

40. "Getting a handle on things" is vague in English, but the Chinese *gé wù* 格物 is equally vague. Many contemporary translators render it "investigating things," following Zhu Xi's interpretation (see Commentary 5, below). However, Wang Yangming said that it meant "to rectify things," meaning to correct things, including one's own thoughts (see Wang, "Questions on the *Great Learning*," in Part III, Selection 38). Our translation of "getting a handle on things" aims to be neutral between the competing interpretations.

41. Following the Song dynasty text of 祝氏 which reads 欲其必自慊而無自欺 rather than the Yuan dynasty text of 倪氏 which reads 欲其一於善而無自欺.

42. "Extend" is one of several technical terms used by Zhu Xi to refer to the process by which one comes to recognize that ethically relevant similarities between situations. Zhu Xi adopts this concept from Mengzi, who says, for example, that nobles know that being addressed disrespectfully is shameful. However, if they "fill out" this "mind," they will recognize that failing to remonstrate with a ruler who plans on doing something foolish or unethical is the same "category" of action (*Mengzi* 7B31, in Part III, Selection 35). In addition, Zhu Xi explains that "sympathetic understanding" is a matter of self-consciously "extending" from one's own desires and preferences to those of others (see his commentary on *Analects* 6.30, in Part III, Selection 34).

knowledge, and getting a handle on things) are the activities of "enlightening one's enlightened Virtue." Regulating one's family and the steps that follow it (regulating one's family, putting the state in order, bringing peace to the world) are the activities of "renewing the people." To get a handle on things and to reach the ultimate of knowledge is to "know the place to rest." Making one's thoughts Sincere and the steps that follow it (making one's thoughts Sincere, correcting one's mind, cultivating one's self, regulating one's family, bringing order to the state, and bringing peace to the world) are the steps in getting to the place where one rests.]

6. From the Son of Heaven on down to the common people, all regarded cultivating one's self as the root. [Correcting one's mind and the steps that precede it (getting a handle on things, extending knowledge, making one's thoughts have Sincerity, correcting one's mind) are the manner in which one cultivates one's self. Regulating one's family and the steps that follow it (regulating one's family, ordering one's state, bringing peace to the world) is taking this and applying it.]

7. A tree with gnarled roots never has straight branches. What you treat as significant will never become insignificant, and what you treat as insignificant will never become significant. [The "roots" means one's self. What is "significant" means the family. These two verses (6, 7) summarize the meaning of the preceding two verses (4, 5).

[The preceding Classic, in one chapter, is a teaching by Kongzi that was passed down by his disciple Zengzi. The following Commentary, in ten chapters, is the interpretation of his disciple Zengzi, recorded by Zengzi's disciples. The old edition (as found in the *Rites*) has many errors and omissions. In the present version, I have followed what was established by Cheng Yi, as well as further investigation into the text, to divide it into the sequence that follows.]

[In general, the text of the Commentary comments on the Classic in a selective way that seems to lack any coherence. But the Pattern of the text is linked and interconnected like blood vessels. The deep and the shallow, the beginnings and the endings are subtle in the extreme. If one reads it to familiarity and savors it, one should eventually see this, yet never completely fathom its significance.]

Commentary Section by Zengzi
[with subcommentary by Zhu Xi]

[The "Classic" section of the Great Learning, *above, is attributed to Kongzi. The following sections of the* Great Learning *are supposedly the "Commentary" on the Classic by Kongzi's disciple, Zengzi. In addition, Zhu Xi wrote his own commentary (technically called a "subcommentary") on Zengzi's "Commentary." Zengzi's "Commentary" is in* **boldface**, *while Zhu Xi's subcommentary is in* Roman font *enclosed in brackets. All sentences in italics and footnotes are by the translator.*

[Chapters 1 through 4 of Zengzi's "Commentary" cite various Confucian classics (mostly the Documents *and* Odes*) to illustrate verses 1–3 of the "Classic" section above. These chapters have been left out of this translation. — Tr.]*

Chapter 5

This is what is meant by the ultimate of knowledge. [There was additional text preceding this verse that is now lost. This is only the summarizing phrase of the section.

[The fifth chapter of the Commentary, which presumably explained the meanings of "getting a handle on things" and "extending knowledge," is now lost. I (Zhu Xi) have taken the liberty of using the interpretation of Master Cheng to supply it. He said that what is meant by "extending knowledge lies in getting a handle on things" is that desiring to extend my knowledge lies in encountering things and exhaustively investigating their Pattern. In general, the human mind is sentient and never fails to have knowledge, while the things of the world never fail to have the Pattern. It is only because the Pattern is not yet exhaustively investigated that knowledge is not fully fathomed. Consequently, at the beginning of education in the Great Learning, the learner must be made to encounter the things of the world, and never fail to follow the Pattern that one already knows and further exhaust it, seeking to arrive at the farthest points. When one has exerted effort for a long time, one day, like something suddenly cracking open, one will know in a manner that binds it all together. Then there will be nothing one fails to get to, whether inner or outer, refined or coarse, and the complete Substance and great Function of our mind will never fail to be enlightened.[43] This is what is called "getting a handle on things." This is what is meant by "the ultimate of knowledge."]

Chapter 6

1. What is meant by "making thoughts have Sincerity" is to let there be no self-deception. It is like hating a hateful odor, or loving a lovely sight.[44] This is called not being conflicted. Hence, the gentleman must be careful

---

43. As Zhu Xi explains in his commentary on the *Mean* 1.iv, the Pattern is Substance, while acting in accordance with it is Function. For an example of Zengzi achieving the sort of sudden understanding that Zhu Xi has in mind, see *Analects* 4.15, in Part III, Selection 34. On "Substance" and "Function" in general, see Zhu Xi, *Categorized Conversations,* in Part III, Selection 32.

44. The phrase "a lovely sight" has the connotation of something sexually attractive. Xie Liangzuo, whom Zhu Xi quotes with approval in his commentary on *Analects* 9.17, explains, "Loving a lovely sight (*hào hǎo sè* 好好色) and hating a hateful odor are Sincerity. Loving Virtue like one loves sex (*hào sè* 好色)—this is to Sincerely love Virtue. However, people are seldom able to do this."

even when alone. ["Making thoughts have Sincerity" is the chief step in self-cultivation. "Self deception" is when one knows to do good in order to avoid the bad, yet the expressions of one's mind are not completely genuine. "Not conflicted" is being happy and content. "Alone" is a place where others do not perceive you, and you alone perceive. This verse means that those who desire to cultivate themselves, when they know to do good in order to avoid the bad, must then genuinely make an effort and forbid self-deception, making their hatred of the (ethically) hateful be like their hating a hateful odor, and their loving what is good like their loving a lovely sight. In these cases their concentration is very decisive, and they must get what they are seeking in order to be happy and contented within themselves. They may not just act recklessly, and follow along with what is external to impress others. But their being genuine or not is, generally, something that others cannot perceive. They themselves alone perceive it. Hence, they must be attentive in regard to this in order to examine the most minute tendencies (toward genuineness or artificiality).]

2. **The petty person, when he is alone and does what is not good, has nothing he will not do. Only when he sees a gentleman is he evasive, hiding what is not good, and emphasizing his good points. But others look at him like they can see his insides. So of what benefit is this? This is what is meant by "What is Sincerely inside will take form outside." Hence, the gentleman must be careful even when alone.** [This means that the petty person does what is not good in darkness, but in the light wishes to hide it. This is not a matter of not knowing that one ought to do good and ought to avoid the bad. It is just that one is unable to genuinely make an effort to reach this. But although he desires to hide what is bad, in the end he is unable to hide it. He desires to feign doing good, but in the end he is unable to feign it. Of what benefit is this? This is why the gentleman seriously guards against it, and why he must be careful even when alone.]

3. **Zengzi said, "What is seen by ten eyes, what is pointed at by ten hands—is it not important?"** [The text cites this in order to illuminate the meaning of the previous verse. It means that, even if one is in the midst of dark solitude, one cannot hide one's goodness or badness. How frightening!]

4. **If one is wealthy, one's rooms will be beautiful. If one is Virtuous, one's self will beautiful. If one's mind is relaxed, one's body is comfortable. Hence, a gentleman must make his thoughts have Sincerity.** [This means that, if one is rich, then one is able to have beautiful rooms. If one has Virtue, then one is able to have a beautiful self. Hence, if one's mind has nothing to be ashamed about, then it will be relaxed and at peace, and one's body will always be at ease. This is what it is like for Virtue to make the self beautiful. In general, goodness being genuine inside and taking form outside is like this. Hence, he says this again in order to summarize it.

[The Classic section says, "Those who desired to make their thoughts have Sincerity would first extend their knowledge." But it also says, "Only after knowledge has reached the ultimate do thoughts have Sincerity." Suppose one has not fully fathomed the enlightenment of the mind's Substance. In this case, there will be some expressions of the mind on which one is incapable of genuinely making an effort, so that one is reckless and deceives oneself. Nonetheless, one may already be enlightened, but not be attentive to it. Then one does not fully possess one's own enlightenment, and one lacks the foundation for advancing in Virtue. Hence, the point of this chapter can be understood only as a continuation of the previous chapter. Only then will one be able to see the beginning and ending of making an effort. As this section explains, the sequence may not be disordered, and no steps can be skipped.][45]

Chapter 7

1. What is meant by the claim that cultivating one's self lies in correcting one's mind is that, if the mind is angry about something, one will not be able to make it correct; if one is frightened of something, then one will not be able to make it correct; if one is fond of something, then one will not be able to make it correct; if one is anxious about something, then one will not be able to make it correct. [These four are all the Functions of the mind that everyone has. But if one has them but fails to examine them, then desires are stimulated, the feelings are overwhelming, and the Functions will not be correctly performed.]

2. If the mind is not present, one looks but does not see, one listens but does not hear, one eats but does not appreciate the taste. [To the extent that the mind is not preserved, one lacks the capacity to examine one's self. Consequently, a gentleman must examine and pay reverential attention to the mind in order to make it upright. Only then will "this mind" constantly be preserved and there will be no respect in which one's character is not cultivated.[46]]

---

45. Zhu Xi identifies two separate steps in the process of self-cultivation. There is coming to understand the Pattern in things, and then there is having Sincerity in regard to this understanding. In other words, one must understand what is good and what is bad (this is a matter of "getting a handle on things" and "extending understanding"), and *then* come to dislike what is bad as much as one dislikes a bad stench, and like what is good as much as one likes an appealing sight (this is a matter of "making one's thoughts have Sincerity"). ("Sincerity" is a key concept in Zhu Xi's thought. For more on it, see the *Mean* 20, in Part III, Selection 36.) Wang Yangming would later strongly object to Zhu Xi's two-step cultivation process on the grounds that it introduces a dangerous division in the process of self-cultivation. There are not two steps, Wang insists. Instead, there is a "unity of knowing and acting" (*zhī xíng hé yī* 知行合一). See Wang, *A Record for Practice,* especially § 5, in Part III, Selection 43.

46. "This mind" is a technical term among Neo-Confucians, for whom it refers to our pure, innate, moral sensibility. It is contrasted with the mind insofar as it is obscured by selfish thoughts and desires. The original source of the expression is *Mengzi* 1A7, in Part III, Selection 35.

3. This is what is meant by the claim that cultivating one's self lies in correcting one's mind.

[This continues the previous chapter in order to set up the following chapters.

[When thoughts have Sincerity, then one truly lacks badness and genuinely has goodness. This is the manner in which one is able to preserve "this mind" in order to examine one's self. Nonetheless, if one only knows to make the thoughts have Sincerity, but is unable to minutely examine whether "this mind" has been preserved or not, then one will lack the wherewithal to make what is within oneself upright and cultivate one's self.][47]

> [Chapters 8 through 10 have been left out of this translation. They respectively discuss "cultivating one's self" in connection with "regulating one's family," "regulating one's family" in connection with "putting one's state in order," and "putting one's state in order" in connection with "bringing peace to the world."—Tr.]

34. *Collected Commentaries on the* Analects

translation by Bryan W. Van Norden[48]

The Analects *is the collected sayings and dialogues of Kongzi (Confucius, 551–479 BCE) and some of his disciples. It is composed of 20 "books" (which are really the length of chapters), divided into "chapters" (each of which ranges in length from one sentence to at most a few paragraphs). In choosing which passages to include, I have focused on those most discussed by the Neo-Confucians, even though this leaves out many sections of great intrinsic interest. "The Master," in this text, always refers to Kongzi himself. Kongzi's interlocutors in the selections below are his disciples. Text in* **boldface** *is the original text of the* Analects. *Text in* Roman font *is Zhu Xi's commentary. The people whom Zhu Xi cites in his commentary are earlier commentators on the* Analects. *Sentences in italics and all footnotes are by the translator.—Tr.*

---

47. "Reverence" or "reverential attention" (*jìng* 敬) is a technical term for Zhu Xi, referring to inner mental focus on the mind, one's innate moral sense. If one lacks reverence, passions such as anger, fear, and desire will obscure one's moral knowledge and lead one to do wrong. With reverence, one can "preserve the mind" (存心), so that one follows the Way. Consequently, reverence connects moral knowledge with moral action.

48. This translation is based on the *Sibu beiyao* ed. The chapter divisions follow Edward Slingerland, trans., *Confucius: Analects: With Selections from Traditional Commentaries* (Indianapolis: Hackett Publishing, 2003).

Zhu Xi's Preface

[Master Cheng said, "The *Analects* was completed by the disciples of Youzi and Zengzi, because they are the only two disciples who are referred to with the title 'Master' (i.e., the '–zi' suffix)." Master Cheng also said, "Of those who read the *Analects*, there are some who read it completely and it has no effect. There are some who read it and find one or two phrases that they like. There are some who read it and know enough to be fond of it. And then there are some who read it and find that 'unconsciously, one's hands are moving to its rhythms, one's feet are dancing to its tunes.'"[49] Master Cheng also said, "People today do not know how to read (with understanding). For example, if someone reads the *Analects*, before reading it he is a certain sort of person, and after reading it he is still the same sort of person. This is (how we know they are) not capable of reading." Cheng Yi also said, "I read the *Analects* when I was 17 or 18, and at that time I already understood the meanings of the individual words. But it was only after I had read it for much longer that I finally appreciated its deep meaning and significance."]

1.1 The Master said, "To learn and continually practice it—is this not a pleasure? ["To learn" means to emulate. Human natures are all good, but there are those who come to awareness of it first, and those who come to awareness of it later. Those who come to awareness of it later must emulate what those who come to awareness of it earlier do. Only then can they become enlightened about their goodness and return to their source.] **To draw friends from afar—is this not a joy?** ["Friends" are those who are the same kind of person as oneself. Cheng Yi said, "If one extends goodness to others, one will have masses of faithful followers."] **To not become bitter when others fail to appreciate oneself—is this not a gentleman?"** ["Gentleman" is a term for one of complete Virtue. Yin Tun said, "Learning lies in oneself. Being appreciated or not lies in others. Why should one be bitter?"]

1.2 Youzi said, "A person who is filial and respectful is seldom fond of rebelling against superiors. And it is never the case that one who is not fond of rebelling against superiors likes to create chaos. [Youzi was one of Kongzi's disciples. To serve one's parents well is being "filial"; to serve one's elder siblings and other elders well is being "respectful."] **A gentleman focuses on what is fundamental. When what is fundamental is established, the Way grows. May we not say that filiality and respect are what is fundamental to the practice of benevolence?"** ["Fundamental" is literally root. Benevolence is the Pattern of love, and the Virtue of the mind. Cheng Yi said, "One practices being filial and respectful in the family, and only then extends benevolent love to other things. This is what Mengzi meant by 'treat one's kin as kin and then be benevolent to the people.'[50] Hence, being filial and respectful is what

---

49. *Mengzi* 4A27, in Part III, Selection 35.

50. *Mengzi* 7A45.

is fundamental to practicing benevolence. But if one discusses it in terms of the nature, then benevolence is what is fundamental to filiality and respect." Someone asked Cheng Yi, "Does 'filiality and respect are what is fundamental to the practice of benevolence' mean that from being filial and respectful one can extend to benevolence?" Cheng Yi replied, "No. Practicing benevolence begins from filiality and respect. Being filial or respectful is one activity of benevolence. It's fine to say that they are what is fundamental to *practicing* benevolence, but it is not acceptable to say that they are what is fundamental to benevolence itself. You see, benevolence is the nature. Filialty and respect are Functions of it. In the nature there is only benevolence, righteousness, propriety, and wisdom—these four. How could filialty and respect come from that alone? However, benevolence is primarily a matter of love, and no love is greater than love for one's kin. Hence, it says that filiality and respect are what is fundamental to the practice of benevolence."]

1.4 Zengzi said, "I examine myself daily on three counts. Have I failed to be conscientious in anything I have taken on for others? In my interactions with friends, have I failed to be faithful? Have I failed to practice what was handed down to me?"[51] [Zengzi was one of Kongzi's disciples. To fully fathom one's self is what is meant by "conscientious." To make it genuine is what is meant by "faithfulness." "What was handed down" means what one receives from one's teachers. "Practice" means to do it until one is fully familiar with it. Xie Liangzuo said, "The learning of all the various disciples came from the sage, Kongzi. Yet afterwards, their teachings became increasingly farther from his and they increasingly lost what was genuine in it. The learning of Zengzi alone focused on using one's mind on what was internal. Hence, what he passed on had no obscurations. This can be seen in his student, Zisi, and his student's student, Mengzi."]

2.4 The Master said, "At fifteen, I set my mind upon learning. [What "learning" means here is the Way of Great Learning. To set one's mind on it is to have one's every thought be on it without ever growing tired.] **At thirty, I was firmly established.** [When one has the ability to firmly establish oneself, one can preserve it so firmly that effort is no longer required to keep one's mind on it.] **At forty, I was no longer confused.** [When one no longer has any doubts about the way that things and activities should be, then one's knowledge is enlightened and effort is no longer required to preserve it.] **At fifty, I understood the mandate of Heaven.** [The "mandate of Heaven" is the activity of the Way of Heaven, and is what is endowed in each thing. It is the reason why things and activities should be as they are. When one knows this, one's knowledge has become completely pure, and "no longer confused" is inadequate to describe

---

51. The last phrase is the origin of the title of Wang Yangming's work, *A Record for Practice*, in Part III, Selection 43.

it.] **At sixty, my ear was attuned.** [When one understands what one has heard without any reservations, one's knowledge has reached the ultimate. One gets it without reflecting upon it.] **At seventy, I could follow my mind's desires without ever overstepping the bounds."** [This means to "put it into action effortlessly," and to "hit the mean without effort."[52]

[Cheng Yi said, "Kongzi was 'born knowing it.'[53] He discusses getting there through learning only in order to encourage later people to improve through their efforts. . . . To 'understand the mandate of Heaven' is 'to fully investigate the Pattern' and 'fathom one's nature.'"[54] In my (Zhu Xi's) humble opinion, the sage is one of those "born knowing it" who "puts it into action effortlessly."[55] He definitely does not need to build it up gradually. However, in his own mind he never says of himself that he has reached the ultimate point. In all of a person's daily activities, there must be cases in which he alone is aware of his improvement, while others cannot know of it. Thus, describing himself based on others, he wants learners to take this description as a model and encourage themselves to work at it. It is not the case that in his mind he actually regards himself as a sage, and merely feigns (humility) for this purpose. All the later cases (where Kongzi uses) self-deprecating language have the same significance.]

2.15 The Master said, "If one learns but does not reflect, one will be lost. If one reflects but does not learn, one will be in danger." [Those who do not seek for it in themselves are benighted and do not get it. Those who do not put the activities into action are in a precarious state and not at ease with it. Cheng Yi said, "'broadly learning about it, intently asking about it, carefully reflecting upon it, insightfully distinguishing it, and earnestly putting it into action'—if you cast aside any one of these five, it is not learning."[56]]

4.15 The Master said, "Shen! My Way is bound together with one thing!" Zengzi said, "Of course!" ["Shen!" is Kongzi shouting Zengzi's personal name to tell him something. "Of course!" is Zengzi answering Kongzi immediately and without any doubt. The mind of a sage is one undifferentiated Pattern; it responds universally and is appropriate in the minutest details; each of its Functions is distinct. Zengzi, in the operations of his own mind, was pretty much already minutely examining and putting it into practice energetically. However, he did not yet realize that its Substance is one. The Master recognized that he had truly piled up effort for a long time, and must have grasped some part of it. Hence, Kongzi shouted at Zengzi in order to tell him. Zengzi was in

---

52. *Mean* 20.viii and 20.xii, in Part III, Selection 36.

53. For the phrase, see *Mean* 20.viii, in Part III, Selection 36. But contrast *Analects* 7.19, where Kongzi denies being this sort of person.

54. *Great Learning*, Commentary 5, and *Mean* 22, in Part III, Selection 33 and Selection 36.

55. *Mean* 20.viii, in Part III, Selection 36.

56. *Mean* 20.xiii, in Part III, Selection 36.

fact able to silently know his meaning. This is precisely why he responded immediately and without doubt.[57]]

The Master left, and the other disciples asked Zengzi, "What did he mean?"

Zengzi replied, "The Way of the Master is conscientiousness and sympathetic understanding, and that is all."[58] [Fully fathoming oneself is what is meant by "conscientiousness." To extend oneself (to others) is what is meant by "sympathetic understanding." The Master's one Pattern being undifferentiated, responding universally and being appropriate in the minutest detail may be compared to Heaven and Earth's having "ultimate Sincerity without rest," so that the myriad things each obtains its proper place.[59] There is no further method beyond this, and there is no need for further extension. Zengzi apprehended this, but it is difficult to express this in words. Hence, in order to make it clear so that others could understand it, he borrowed the notion that the learner's technique is to fully fathom oneself and extend oneself to others.[60]

[Now, to have "the utmost Sincerity without rest" is the Substance of the Way. It is that by which there is one foundation beneath the myriad manifestations. For the myriad things to each obtain its proper place is the Function of the Way. It is that by which there are myriad manifestations of the one foundation. If one looks at it like this, one can understand the significance of saying it "is bound together with one thing."

[Hence, some say, "One's inner mind (中心) is conscientiousness (忠). A mind congruent with (如心) the feelings of others is sympathetic understanding (恕)." This expresses the same basic idea.]

---

57. Zengzi is a particularly important disciple, because he supposedly wrote the Commentary section of the *Great Learning*. In this passage, we see the moment when he grasps the essence of the Confucian Way. *Analects* 4.15 is thus a concrete illustration of the moment when one has a breakthrough in understanding the Pattern, as described in Zhu Xi's commentary on the *Great Learning*, Commentary 5 (in Part III, Selection 33). Notice also how much the interaction between Kongzi and Zengzi is like a kōan exchange between a Zen Buddhist Master and disciple. The Master catches the disciple off-guard with a cryptic comment. The disciple, prepared by his previous meditation and study, achieves enlightenment. (See Selected Kōans, in Part III, Selection 18.)

58. The parallels with a kōan exchange continue. Having achieved enlightenment, the disciple is now himself a Master ("-zi" in Chinese). When the other disciples rush up to ask him for an explanation, he cannot put into words the insight into the "one" that he now shares with the Master, so instead he mentions *two* things, thereby using "expedient means" in teaching. (See the Introduction to Part II on the Buddhist technique of "expedient means.")

59. *Mean* 26.

60. This is a reference to the *Mean* 13, which Zhu Xi takes to mean that to be conscientious and sympathetic is not identical with fully following the Way; however, one who is on the path to the Way would do well to strive for them. For more on the contrast between sympathy and benevolence, see *Analects* 5.12, 6.30, and 15.24, below.

5.12 Zigong said, "What I do not desire others to do to me I also desire not to do to others."

Kongzi replied, "Ah, Zigong! That is not something you have reached!" [What Zigong is talking about is the practice of a benevolent person: someone who does not need to force himself to be that way. This is why the Master thinks it is something Zigong has not "reached." Cheng Yi said, "'What I do not desire others to do to me I also desire not to do to others' describes benevolence. 'That which you do not desire, do not inflict upon others' is sympathetic understanding.[61] Sympathetic understanding is something that Zigong could sometimes force himself to do, but benevolence is something he had not reached." In my (Zhu Xi's) humble opinion, "I do not" indicates something that has become natural, while "Do not" expresses an imperative. This is the distinction between benevolence and sympathetic understanding.[62]]

5.13 Zigong said, "The Master's cultural brilliance is something one can get to hear of, but one cannot get to hear his teachings on one's nature and the Way of Heaven." ["Cultural brilliance" is the external manifestations of his Virtue. These are things like his august bearing and eloquence. "Nature" is the Heavenly Pattern with which people are endowed. The "Way of Heaven" is the fundamental Substance of what is natural according to the Heavenly Pattern. They are in actuality one and the same Pattern. The passage means that the Master's "cultural brilliance" was manifested externally every day, so it was definitely something that those learning from him could all hear of. But when it came to "nature" and the "Way of Heaven," the Master "seldom spoke of them,"[63] so there were those learning from him who could not hear of them. In general, the teaching of sages does not skip any steps. In this passage, Zigong is just beginning to hear about (nature and the Way of Heaven), so he sighs at how exquisite they are.[64]]

6.11 The Master said, "How worthy was Yan Hui! With just a single basket of grain and a single bowl of soup, living in a humble alley, others would be inconsolably sad. Yet this would not alter the sort of joy Yan Hui had. How worthy was Yan Hui!" [Cheng Yi said, "It was not that Yan Hui de-

---

61. *Analects* 15.24, below.

62. On the distinction between sympathetic understanding and genuine benevolence, see also *Analects* 4.15, above, *Analects* 6.30, below, and *Mean* 13.

63. *Analects* 9.1.

64. On the surface, 5.13 seems to say that Kongzi did not talk about "nature" and the "Way of Heaven" at all. And this seems supported by the text of the *Analects*, in which these topics seldom come up. However, Zhu Xi argues that Kongzi had esoteric teachings on these topics that he revealed to students only when they were ready to hear them. Zhu would say that the others of the Four Books and the "Great Appendix" to the *Changes* reveal these teachings. See also the discussion of this passage in Zhang Xuecheng, "On the Way," in Part IV, Selection 52.

lighted in only having a basket of food, a bowl of soup, and living in a humble alley. It was that he did not allow his poverty to burden his mind and alter his joy. Hence, the Master praised him as worthy." Cheng Hao said, "When I was learning from Zhou Dunyi, he would often encourage me to 'seek what Kongzi and Yan Hui took joy in. What activity was it that gave them joy?'" In my humble opinion, Cheng Hao quoted this without explaining it because he wanted learners to deeply reflect upon it and get it for themselves. We likewise do not dare presume to explain it. Learners should simply practice becoming "broadly cultured" yet "restrained by the rituals," until they "cannot stop," and fully exert their abilities.[65] Only then will they come close to understanding it for themselves.]

6.12 Ran Qiu said, "It is not that I do not delight in your Way, Master. It is that my strength is insufficient."

The Master said, "Those whose strength is insufficient collapse in the middle of the Way. In this case, you draw a line." [Hu Yin said, "Ran Qiu said this because he had just heard the Master praise Yan Hui for the fact that (even his poverty) had not altered his joy. However, if Ran Qiu had Sincerely delighted in the Way of the Master like one's mouth delights in the taste of fine meat, then he would definitely have exhausted his strength in seeking it. How could he have been concerned that his strength was insufficient? Those who do not advance because they 'draw a line' simply move backwards day by day."]

6.20 The Master said, "Knowing it is not as good as being fond of it; being fond of it is not as good as taking joy in it." [Yin Dun said, "'Knowing it' is knowing that *this Way* exists. 'Being fond of it' is being fond but not yet getting it. 'Taking joy in it' is taking joy in it because one has started to get it.'" Zhang Jingfu said, "This describes how those who learned in ancient times would spur themselves on without tire."]

6.30 Zigong asked, "If someone were to bestow bounty upon the people and were able to save the masses, how would you regard him? Could he be called benevolent?"

The Master said, "What difficulty would there be in regarding him as benevolent? Would he not be a sage? Even [the sage-kings] Yao or Shun would have trouble achieving that. Benevolent people, desiring to establish themselves, establish others; desiring success for themselves, help others succeed. [To have reached others with one's own self is to have a benevolent mind. If we look at it like this, we can see how the Heavenly Pattern flows through everything without a gap. No description of the Substance of benevolence is more incisive than this.] **The ability to take what is near as an analogy can merely be called the method of benevolence."** [Taking what is near, in oneself, is to take what one desires for oneself and use it as an analogy with others, know-

---

65. *Analects* 9.11, in which Yan Hui describes his own experience learning with the Master. Cf. *Analects* 6.27.

ing that what they desire is also like this. Only then can one extend what one desires to reach to others. This is the activity of sympathetic understanding and merely the *method* of benevolence. If one makes an effort at this, one will be able to overcome the selfishness of one's human desires and make complete the Heavenly Pattern that we have in common.[66]

[Cheng Hao said, "A medical text describes numbness of the hands and feet as being 'unfeeling.'[67] This expression describes it perfectly. Benevolent people regard Heaven, Earth, and the myriad things as one Substance. Nothing is not oneself. If you recognize something as yourself, there are no limits to how far (your compassion) will go. But if you do not identify something as part of yourself, you will have nothing to do with it. This is like how, when hands and feet are 'unfeeling,' the *qi* does not properly flow and one does not identify them as part of oneself. And so, to 'bestow bounty upon the people' and 'save the masses' are the actions of a sage, but benevolence itself is exceedingly difficult to describe, so Kongzi simply said, 'desiring to establish themselves, they establish others; desiring success for themselves, they help others succeed.'[68] He wanted to lead us to regard benevolence in this way so that we grasp the Substance of benevolence."[69]]

9.29 The Master said, "The wise are not confused. The benevolent are not anxious. The courageous have no fear." [When one's enlightenment is sufficient to illuminate the Pattern, one is "not confused." When one's Pattern is sufficient to overcome selfishness, one is not anxious. When one's *qi* is sufficient to "harmonize with righteousness and the Way," one is "not afraid." This is the sequence of learning.[70]]

12.1 Yan Hui asked about benevolence. The Master said, "To overcome the self and turn to ritual is the practice of benevolence. If for one day one could overcome the self and turn to ritual, the whole world would turn to benevolence. Practicing benevolence comes from the self. How could it come from others?" ["Benevolence" is the complete Virtue of one's

---

66. Zhu Xi here draws a precise distinction between sympathetic understanding, a mere approximation of benevolence, and benevolence itself. The genuinely benevolent person is spontaneously compassionate and intuitively shares the joys and sorrows of others; the merely sympathetic person has not reached this stage, and still must force himself to engage in the reflective process of putting himself in the place of another. See also *Analects* 4.15 and 5.12, above, *Analects* 15.24, below, and *Mean* 13, in Part III, Selection 36.

67. "Unfeeling" is literally "not benevolent" (*bù rén* 不仁).

68. The quoted phrases are from *Analects* 6.30. The former is part of a question asked by the disciple Zigong, while the latter is part of Kongzi's response.

69. I was greatly assisted in rendering this passage by an unpublished translation by Philip J. Ivanhoe.

70. The descriptions of these three virtues make subtle references, respectively, to *Great Learning*, Classic 1 (in Part III, Selection 33), *Analects* 12.1, below, and *Mengzi* 2A2.4 (in Part III, Selection 35).

fundamental mind. "Self" here refers to selfish desires. "Ritual" is the adorn-ments of the Heavenly Pattern. "Practicing benevolence" is the means by which one makes complete the Virtue of one's mind. Now, the Virtue of the mind is simply the Heavenly Pattern, but it is invariably ruined by human desires. Hence, those who practice benevolence must be able to overcome selfish desires and turn toward ritual. Then all their activities will be the Heavenly Pattern and the Virtue of their fundamental mind will be restored completely within them.]

Yan Hui then asked, "May I ask about the steps to achieve this?"

The Master replied, "Do not look in violation of the rituals. Do not listen in violation of the rituals. Do not speak in violation of the rituals. Do not move in violation of the rituals."

Yan Hui said, "Although I am not clever, I shall try to follow this saying." [What is "in violation of the rituals" is one's selfishness. When selfishness is over-come, then "every turn of one's movements and expressions precisely accords with ritual,"[71] and in one's daily life everything will be the activity of the Heav-enly Pattern. Yan Hui silently understood the Pattern and realized for himself that he had the strength to overcome (selfishness). Hence, he immediately took it as his personal responsibility without any doubts.]

14.24 The Master said, "Those who learned in ancient times did it to improve themselves. Those who learn today do it to impress others." [In my humble opinion, sages and worthies have given many explanations of the distinction between "getting it" and "losing" it, when one engages one's mind. However, nothing is as incisive and indispensible as this saying. If one can in-sightfully distinguish these and daily examine oneself, then one will come close to never being benighted about the teachings one follows.[72]]

15.24 Zigong asked, "Is there one teaching that one can practice through-out one's life?"

Kongzi replied, "Would it not be sympathetic understanding? That which you do not desire, do not inflict upon others." [Extending oneself to other things is inexhaustible in its application. Hence it can be practiced throughout one's life. Yin Tun said, "What is crucial in learning is recogniz-ing what is essential. Zigong's question can be said to recognize what is es-sential. Kongzi only told him about 'the method of benevolence.'[73] But if one were to extend it until it reached the ultimate, even the selflessness of a sage would not exceed it.[74] Is it not appropriate that one practice it throughout one's life?"]

---

71. *Mengzi* 7B33.

72. Implicitly referring to *Mean* 20.xiii (in Part III, Selection 36) and *Analects* 1.4, above.

73. On the distinction between the "method of benevolence" and benevolence itself, see *Analects* 6.30, above.

74. "Selflessness" is *wú wǒ* 無我, which is also the technical term for the Buddhist doctrine of "no-self." (See the Introduction to Part II.)

15.33 The Master said, "If one's wisdom reaches it, but one's benevolence cannot preserve it, then even if one gets it, one will necessarily lose it. [If one's wisdom is sufficient to know the Pattern of something, but one's selfish desires separate one from it, then one's self will be unable to possess it.] **If one's wisdom reaches it, and one's benevolence is able to preserve it, yet one is not dignified in supervising the people, they will not respect him.** [If "one is not dignified," it is generally that one's bad habits are well established internally, and one is not restrained externally. Consequently, the people do not see one as awe-inspiring and are careless.] **If one's wisdom reaches it, and one's benevolence is able to preserve it, and one is dignified in supervising the people, yet one does not accord with ritual in directing them, one is still not yet good."** ["Ritual" is the ornamentation of the Pattern of righteousness. In my humble opinion, when one has achieved benevolence through learning, then one has goodness within oneself and the great foundation has been established. If one is "not dignified in supervising the people" or "does not accord with ritual in directing them," these are small imperfections in one's endowment of *qi* or learning. Nonetheless, one with these imperfections has still not fully fathomed the Way of goodness. Hence, the Master talks about them in order (of importance), so that people will know that as one's Virtue becomes more complete, one's responsibilities become more comprehensive. One cannot regard these things as insignificant details and be careless about them.]

17.2 The Master said, "Natures are close to one another, but by practice they become far apart from one another." [When this passage refers to "natures," it is discussing them in terms of embodied dispositions. Embodied natures certainly have some differences between the fine and the bad. Nonetheless, at the beginning, they are not very far from each other. But if one's practices are good, one becomes good, and if one's practices are bad, one becomes bad. Thereupon, they begin to be far from one another.

[Cheng Yi said, "This passage is discussing embodied natures; it is not discussing the fundamental nature. If one discusses what is fundamental, the nature is simply the Pattern. The Pattern never fails to be good. This is what Mengzi meant by 'human nature is good.' How could they merely be 'close to one another'"?]

17.3 The Master said, "Only the most lofty of the wise and the most lowly of the ignorant do not change." [This continues the discussion of the previous chapter. Despite the closeness of people's embodied dispositions, there is still a settled distinction between those that are fine and those that are bad. This is not something that is a result of practice.

[Cheng Yi said, "Human nature is fundamentally good. So how could there be those who cannot be changed? If one talks about their natures, they are all good. But if one talks about their capacity, then there are 'the most lowly of the ignorant' who 'do not change.' There are two kinds who are meant by 'the most lowly of the ignorant': 'those who are destroying themselves' and 'those who throw themselves away.'[75] If people merely bring order to themselves with goodness, then none cannot be changed. Even if one is in the most extreme ignorance, all can gradually advance by grinding away at it.[76] It is only those who destroy themselves—who refuse it by not having faithfulness [in benevolence and righteousness]—and those who throw themselves away—who cut themselves off from it by not acting—who could not be transformed and enter into it even if they lived among sages. This is whom Kongzi meant by 'the most lowly of the ignorant.' Nonetheless, it is not that their embodiment necessitates being benighted and ignorant. For example, Tyrant Zhou had talent that exceeded that of others, yet he repeatedly acted perversely. Because he cut himself off from the good, sages would describe him as 'the most lowly of the ignorant.' But it is because of what he turns toward that one judges him to be genuinely ignorant."]

35. *Collected Commentaries on the* Mengzi

translation by Bryan W. Van Norden[77]

Mengzi was a Confucian of the fourth century BCE, most famous for his claim that human nature is good. He argued for this with the famous thought experiment of someone suddenly seeing a child about to fall into a well (2A6). Anyone in such a situation, Mengzi suggested, would have a feeling of "alarm and compassion," which is evidence of our innate virtue. However, this virtue has not been fully "extended" in most of us, so ethical cultivation is required. Although classical texts and wise masters have important roles to play in this cultivation, the process is ultimately "internal," in that our ethical development must always grow out of our innate ethical feelings, and never be forced.

Mengzi was criticized by the Confucian Xunzi, who claimed that human nature is bad and that Mengzi failed to acknowledge the extent to which humans must be reshaped by education and ritual practice in order to become virtuous. Xunzi's dour emphasis on forcefully reshaping human nature is closer to what became the dominant view among Han Confucians such as Dong Zhongshu.[78] However, when Neo-Confucians reacted against

75. *Mengzi* 4A10, in Part III, Selection 35.

76. The notion of ethical cultivation as like "grinding" is suggested by *Analects* 1.15.

77. This translation is based upon the *Sibu beiyao* edition of the *Mengzi jizhu*. Section numbering follows Bryan W. Van Norden, trans., *Mengzi: With Selections from Traditional Commentaries* (Indianapolis: Hackett Publishing, 2008).

78. See Dong Zhongshu, "An In-Depth Investigation into Names and Designations," in Part I, Selection 1.

Buddhism, they took their inspiration from Mengzi, whom they labeled the "Second Sage," after Kongzi himself. Mengzi's claim that human nature is good seemed plausible to an audience that was already familiar with the concept of a pure Buddha-nature that we all share. In addition, Mengzi stated that his goal was to oppose the teachings of Yang Zhu and Mozi (3B9). Yang Zhu claimed that it is natural for humans to be purely self-interested, and that Confucian virtues are artificial deformations of human nature. Mozi was an impartial consequentialist, who argued that genuine benevolence requires us to promote the well-being of everyone, regardless of whether they are a stranger or our own kin. Although both of them had ceased to be influential by the Han dynasty, the Neo-Confucians saw an important parallel between contemporary Daoists and Yang Zhu, and between Buddhists and Mozi. Just as Mozi advocated "impartial caring," which Mengzi saw as undermining filial piety, so did Buddhists advocate universal compassion, which led Buddhist monks and nuns to leave their families behind. And just as Yang Zhu advocated being "for oneself," so did contemporary Daoists selfishly (in the view of the Neo-Confucians) seek their own individual immortality through meditative practices, magic, and alchemy.

Following are selections from the Mengzi, *the eponymous collection of his sayings, his dialogues with rulers and disciples, and his debates with rival philosophers. The text of the* Mengzi *is in* **bold font**, *with Zhu Xi's commentary in* Roman font *within brackets. The people whom Zhu Xi cites in his commentary are earlier commentators on the* Mengzi. *Sentences in italics and all footnotes are by the translator.—Tr.*

Zhu Xi's Preface

[Master Cheng said, "Mengzi's contributions to followers of the sages is greater than can be described in words! Kongzi spoke only of 'benevolence.' Mengzi opened his mouth and spoke of 'benevolence and righteousness' together. Kongzi only spoke of 'setting one's mind on it.' Mengzi spoke of so many aspects of 'cultivating *qi*.' With these two words alone he made a great contribution!" Master Cheng also said, "Mengzi made a great contribution to later generations with his teaching that 'human nature is good.'" Master Cheng also said, "Mengzi's doctrines about the goodness of human nature and cultivating the *qi* are both things that former sages had not yet expressed.'"[79]]

---

79. It is important to understand that the Cheng brothers and Zhu Xi are *not* claiming that Mengzi invented or discovered any of these doctrines. It is a fundamental commitment of Neo-Confucians that there is one Way and that it was transmitted in an unbroken line from the ancient sage kings (like Yao, Shun, and Yu) to Kongzi, to his disciple Zengzi, to Zengzi's disciple (and Kongzi's grandson) Zisi, and then to Zisi's disciple Mengzi. The point made in Zhu Xi's Preface is that Mengzi put into words what the former sages "had not yet *expressed*" (because it was not necessary to state it explicitly in *their* historical contexts).

[In the following passage (1A7), Mengzi asks King Xuan of Qi whether it is true that he has spared an ox being led to slaughter because he "could not bear its frightened appearance, like an innocent person going to the execution ground." When the king confirms the story, Mengzi tells him that the benevolence he showed in sparing the ox demonstrates that he can become a great king, like the ancient sages. — Tr.]

1A7 The king was pleased and said, "The *Odes* say, 'It was the mind of another person / But I took the measure of it.'[80] **This describes you. I was the one who did it, but when I reflected and sought it out, I did not understand my mind. Yet when you spoke there was again a feeling of compassion in my mind. In what way does this mind accord with being a king?"**[81] [Because of Mengzi's words, the king's mind from the previous day sprouts up again, so he understands that "this mind" is not something one gets externally. However, he still does not understand how to reflect upon its foundation and extend it.]

Mengzi said, "Suppose there were someone who reported the following to Your Majesty: 'My strength is sufficient to lift five hundred pounds, but not sufficient to lift one feather. My eyesight is sufficient to examine the tip of the finest hair, but I cannot see a wagon of firewood.' Would Your Majesty accept that?"

The king replied, "No."

Mengzi continued, "In the present case, your kindness is sufficient to reach animals, but the benefits do not reach the commoners. Why is this case alone different? Hence, not lifting one feather is due to not using one's strength. Not seeing a wagon of firewood is due to not using one's eyesight. The commoners not receiving care is due to not using one's kindness. Hence, Your Majesty's not being a genuine king is due to not acting; it is not due to not being able. . . . [Among all the natures in the world, human nature is the most precious. Hence, humans are of the same kind as one another and are affectionate to one another. As a result, the manifestations of "compassion" are intense in relation to the people but weaker in relation to other animals. In the technique of extending benevolence, being benevolent to the people is easy while being sparing of animals is more difficult. In the present case, since the king is already able to extend "this heart" to animals, his caring for the people and thereby becoming a genuine king "is not due to not being able," but is simply that he is unwilling to act.] **Treat your elders as elders, and extend it to the elders of others; treat your young ones as young ones, and extend it to the young ones of others. Then you can turn the whole world in the palm**

---

80. *Odes* 198.

81. The phrase "this mind" becomes a key term in Neo-Confucianism, where it is taken to refer to the Pattern of one's mind.

of your hand. The *Odes* say, 'He set an example for his wife, / It extended to his brothers, / And so he controlled his family and his state.'[82] This means that he simply took this mind and applied it to that. Hence, if one extends one's kindness, it will be sufficient to care for all within the Four Seas. If one does not extend one's kindness, one will lack the wherewithal to care for one's own wife and children. That in which the ancients greatly surpassed others was nothing else than this: they were simply good at extending what they did." ["To treat as elders" is to serve them in the manner that elders should be served. "Your elders" is your own father and elder brothers. The "elders of others" are the fathers and elders brothers of other people. "To treat as young ones" is to nurture them as one should nurture young ones. "Your young ones" means your own children and younger brothers. The "young ones of others" means the children and younger brothers of other people. If one is unable to extend one's kindness, the masses will rebel and one's family will be dispersed. Hence, one will lack the wherewithal to care for one's own wife and children. In general, relatives of the same flesh and blood fundamentally have one and the same *qi,* and are not merely, like other humans, of the same kind as us. Hence, the ancients needed to first extend from being kind to their kin, and only then reach to being benevolent to the people. Only when they had a surplus (of compassion) to extend would they reach to being sparing of animals. In all cases, one extends from what is near to what is far, one extends from what is easy to what is difficult. In the present case, the king has reversed this.] . . .

2A2 1. [Mengzi's disciple] Gongsun Chou asked, "Suppose that you were to be appointed to the position of high noble or prime minister in Qi and were given an opportunity to put the Way into practice there. If you could do that, it would not be surprising if the ruler of Qi were to become a hegemon, or even a genuine king. Would having this opportunity perturb your mind?"

Mengzi replied, "It would not. My mind has been unperturbed since I was forty."

Gongsun Chou said, "In that case, Master, you have far surpassed Meng Ben!"

Mengzi replied, "That is not difficult. Even Gaozi had an unperturbed mind before I did." [Meng Ben was a courageous warrior. He had courage that comes simply from the *qi* of one's blood. Gongsun Chou uses him to praise Mengzi for achieving something as difficult as an unperturbed mind. Mengzi explains that, even though he did not know the Way, Gaozi was able to achieve an unperturbed mind before Mengzi did. Hence, this cannot be considered something difficult.[83]] . . .

---

82. *Odes* 240.

83. Gaozi is a rival philosopher who regarded righteousness as "external" to human nature. He is discussed later in 2A2 and in 6A6 (below).

2. Gongsun Chou said, "Then may I ask in what ways you excel others, Master?"

Mengzi replied, "I have knowledge of words, and I am good at cultivating my floodlike *qi*."[84] [Gongsun Chou is asking how Mengzi's unperturbed mind differs from that of Gaozi.]

3. Gongsun Chou asked, "May I ask what you mean by 'floodlike *qi*'"?

Mengzi replied, "It is difficult to put into words. It is *qi* that is supremely great and supremely unyielding. If one cultivates it with uprightness and does not harm it, it will fill up the space between Heaven and Earth. [Cheng Yi said, "Heaven and humans are one. There is no distinction. The 'floodlike *qi*' is simply my *qi*. If one cultivates it and does not harm it, then it will fill up Heaven and Earth. But as soon as there is the obscuration of a single selfish thought, then it sinks and is starved, becoming exceedingly small."]

4. "It is *qi* that harmonizes with righteousness and the Way. Without these, it starves. ["Righteousness" refers to the judgments of the mind. "Way" refers to what is natural according to the Heavenly Pattern. "Starve" means that it is depleted and does not fill the body. What the passage means overall is that if one can fully cultivate this *qi,* then one's *qi* will harmonize with and be assisted by (the Way and righteousness), so that one will be courageous and resolute in one's actions, without any doubts. Without this *qi,* then even though what one does at any moment will not necessarily deviate from the Way and righteousness, one will unavoidably have doubts and fears, and because one's body has not been filled by (this *qi*), one will not always have the means to act.]

5. "It is produced by accumulated righteousness. It cannot be obtained by a seizure of righteousness. If some of one's actions leave one's mind unsatisfied, it will starve. Hence, I say that Gaozi never understood righteousness, because he regarded it as external. [This means that, although the *qi* can harmonize with the Way and righteousness, the beginning of nurturing it is for one's every activity to harmonize with righteousness. If one examines oneself and is always upright, one will have no misgivings, and this *qi* will naturally develop within oneself. It is not as if one can perform one act that happens to harmonize with righteousness and then seize it from outside oneself. But Gaozi did not understand this Pattern. Hence he said, "benevolence is internal, but righteousness is external," and moreover did not take becoming righteous as a (personal) task.[85] Hence, he was unable to accumulate righteousness in order to produce the floodlike *qi*.]

6. "One must work at it, but do not aim at it directly. Let the mind not forget, but do not 'help' it grow. Do not be like the man from Song. Among the people of the state of Song there was one who, concerned that his grain

---

84. Intuitively, the "floodlike *qi*" is the strength of motivation that allows one to persevere in the face of dangers and obstacles. See also Selections on *Qi*, in Part I, Selection 6.

85. *Mengzi* 6A4.

might not be growing, pulled on it. Unaware of what he had actually done, he returned home, and said to his family, 'I am worn out from helping the grain to grow today.' His son rushed out and looked at it: the grain had withered. Those in the world who do not 'help' the grain to grow are few. Those who abandon it, thinking it will not make any difference, are those who do not weed their grain. Those who 'help' it grow are those who pull on the grain. Not only does this not help, but it even harms it." [This means that those who cultivate their *qi* must take "accumulating righteousness" as their task, but not anticipate the results. Sometimes one will not be filled (with the *qi*). In that case, one must simply not forget the task one has, and cannot act artificially to help it grow. These are the steps in "accumulating righteousness" and "cultivating the *qi*." (In the story of the farmer from Song) to "abandon" and "not weed" the grain corresponds to forgetting one's task. To "pull on" and "'help' the grain to grow" corresponds to not getting anything from one's efforts, and then recklessly acting in an artificial way. If one does "not weed," then one will simply fail to nurture it. However, if one "pulls" on it, one will actually injure it. If one can avoid these two things, the *qi* will be cultivated and unharmed. Someone like Gaozi, who is unable to accumulate righteousness and wants to forcefully regulate his mind, will never be able to avoid the defect of directly "helping." He not only is not good at nurturing (his *qi*), but he even harms it.]

7. Gongsun Chou asked, "What do you mean by 'having knowledge of words'?"

Mengzi replied, "If someone's expressions are one-sided, I know what is deluding him. If someone's expressions are excessive, I know what entangles him. If someone's expressions are heretical, I know what separates him from the Way. If someone's expressions are evasive, I know what exhausts him. And when these states grow in the mind, they are harmful in governing. When they are manifested in governing, they are harmful in one's activities. When sages arise again, they will certainly not disagree with this."...

2A6 1. Mengzi said, "Humans all have minds that are not unfeeling toward others. [The mind of Heaven and Earth is to give life to things, so each thing that they give life to gets this same mind of Heaven and Earth as its mind. Therefore, humans all have a mind that is not unfeeling toward others.]

2. "The Former Kings had minds that were not unfeeling toward others, so they had governments that were not unfeeling toward others. If one puts into practice a government that is not unfeeling toward others by means of a mind that is not unfeeling toward others, bringing order to the whole world is in the palm of your hand. [This means that, although the masses have a mind that is not unfeeling toward others, material desires injure it, and little survives. Hence, they are incapable of investigating and extending it into governmental affairs. Only sages keep the Substance of this mind whole, both when being stimulated and in their responses. Hence, they always put into effect a government that is not unfeeling toward others.]

3. "The reason why I say that humans all have minds that are not unfeeling toward others is this. Suppose someone suddenly saw a child about to fall into a well: anyone would have a mind of alarm and compassion—not because one sought to get in good with the child's parents, not because one sought fame among their neighbors and friends, and not because one would dislike having a bad reputation. ["Compassion" is intense hurt and deep pain. This is precisely what is meant by "minds that are not unfeeling toward others." This verse means that at the time one suddenly sees, one has "this mind."[86] When it is expressed after seeing this, it is not from those three things [getting in good with the child's parents, seeking fame, and disliking a bad reputation]. Cheng Hao said, "One's bosom is filled with the mind of compassion." Xie Liangzuo said, "What people must do is to recognize their true mind. When they 'suddenly see a child about to fall into a well,' their mind is 'alarmed,' and this is just their true mind. They get it without reflection; they hit the mark without having to work at it. This is due to the naturalness of the Heavenly Pattern." 'Getting in good,' 'seeking fame,' and 'disliking a bad reputation' are simply the selfishness of human desires.]

4. "From this we can see that if one is without the mind of compassion, one is not a human. If one is without the mind of disdain, one is not a human. If one is without the mind of deference, one is not a human. If one is without the mind of approval and disapproval, one is not a human. ["Disdain" is being ashamed of one's own failure to be good, and hating what is not good in others. "Deference" is to decline being relieved of a responsibility, and to grant things to others. "Approval" is when you know that something is good and regard it as right. "Disapproval" is when you know that something is bad and regard it as wrong. What makes up a person's mind does not go beyond these four. Hence, he enumerated all of them after discussing compassion.[87] The verse means that if a person lacks these, then he is not worth being called a "human," and by means of this it makes clear that one must have them.]

5. The mind of compassion is the beginning of benevolence. The mind of disdain is the beginning of righteousness. The mind of deference is the beginning of propriety. The mind of approval and disapproval is the beginning of wisdom.[88] ["Compassion," "disdain," "deference," and "approval and disapproval" are feelings. Benevolence, righteousness, propriety, and wisdom are the nature. The mind is what links the nature and feelings. "Beginning" means the tip. By following the expression of the feelings, one can succeed in seeing the

---

86. *Mengzi* 1A7, above.

87. Zhu Xi makes clear in his commentary on *Mengzi* 2A7 that he thinks righteousness, wisdom, and propriety are all ultimately manifestations of benevolence. (In Western terms, Zhu Xi believes in "the unity of the virtues.")

88. These are the four "cardinal virtues" of the Neo-Confucian tradition: the virtues that ultimately encompass all lesser good traits and dispositions.

fundamental state of the nature. It is like when there is a thing inside something but the tip is visible outside.]

6. "People having these four beginnings is like their having four limbs. To have these four beginnings but to say of oneself that one is unable [to be virtuous] is to steal from oneself. To say that one's ruler is unable is to steal from one's ruler. [Four limbs are something that people must have. If one says of oneself that one is incapable, this is simply material desire obscuring it.]

7. "In general, having these four beginnings within oneself, if one knows to fill them all out, it will be like a fire starting up, a spring breaking through! If one can merely fill them out, they will be sufficient to care for all within the Four Seas. If one merely fails to fill them out, they will be insufficient to serve one's parents." [The four beginnings lie in oneself, and can be discovered everywhere. If one knows to extend these, and fill out this fundamental capacity one has, then one's being "daily renewed, and again renewed" will naturally be unstoppable.[89] If one can follow this and fill it out, then although the Four Seas are distant, they will be within one's capacity, and there will be no difficulty in caring for everyone. If one is unable to fill them out, then even if the responsibility is quite personal, one will be incapable of it.

[What this chapter discusses is that human nature and feelings, and the Substance and Function of the mind are at root complete and well ordered like this. If learners reflect and seek to silently understand this and fill it out, then they will be able to completely fathom what Heaven has given us. Cheng Yi said, "People all have this mind, but only the gentleman is capable of expanding and filling it out. Those who are incapable of this all 'throw themselves away.'[90] But whether we fill it out or not lies in ourselves alone." He also said, "The four beginnings do not discuss 'faithfulness,' because if one already has a mind that is Sincere about the four beginnings, faithfulness is in their midst." In my humble opinion, faithfulness in relation to the four beginnings is like Earth in relation to the Five Phases. It has no definite place; it has no established role; it has no special *qi*. Yet Water, Fire, Metal, and Wood all rely upon this to be born. Hence, Earth never fails to be among the other Four Phases. It is entrusted with being king of the four seasons. Its Pattern is like this.][91]

3A1 1. When Duke Wen of Teng was still only Heir Apparent, he had to go

---

89. Paraphrasing *Great Learning*, Commentary 2.

90. *Mengzi* 4A10, below.

91. Zhu Xi thinks it calls for comment that Mengzi does not mention faithfulness in his catalogue of Virtues in 2A6. (On the importance of faithfulness and Sincerity in Neo-Confucian thought, see the Introduction to Part III.) The explanation offered by Cheng Yi and Zhu Xi is that faithfulness is simply the state of having the other Virtues with firm conviction. Zhu Xi explains that we see the same Pattern with faithfulness in relation to the other four virtues, and Earth in relation to the rest of the Five Phases. (See Selections on the Five Phases, in Part I, Selection 8.)

on a mission to Chu. Passing through Song, he met Mengzi. 2. Mengzi told him the Way of the goodness of the nature, and in his discussions always praised Yao and Shun. [The "nature" is the Pattern that humans are endowed with at birth by Heaven. It is the ultimate of pure goodness. It never has any badness. At their start, people have not the least difference from Yao and Shun. But the multitude of people sink into selfish desires and lose it. Yao and Shun simply lacked the obscuration of selfish desires and were capable of filling out their nature. Hence, whenever Mengzi had a discussion with the Heir Apparent, he told him each time the Way of the goodness of the nature, and always praised Yao and Shun to give it substance. He wanted him to know that one does not seek to borrow benevolence and righteousness from outside. Sages can learn and attain the ultimate, and do not spare any effort. Disciples, in contrast, are incapable of understanding all of their expressions, so one plucks out the main meaning like this. Cheng Yi said, "The nature is precisely the Pattern. If one traces the source of the Patterns of the world to what they come from, they never fail to be good. 'When happiness, anger, sadness and joy have not yet been expressed,' how could anything not be good? 'When they are expressed but all hit the right points,' there is nowhere one goes where one is not good.[92] When the expressions do not hit the mark, only then does one fail to become good. Hence, in general, when discussing good and bad, it is always good first and only then bad. In discussing good luck and bad luck, it is always good luck first and only then bad luck. In discussing right and wrong, it is always right first and only then wrong."]

3. The Heir Apparent of Teng returned from Chu, and again met with Mengzi. Mengzi said, "Do you doubt my teachings, your lordship? The Way is one, and only one. [People of that time did not know the fundamental goodness of the nature, and regarded being a sage or worthy as something one could not aspire to. Hence, the Heir Apparent could not help but have doubts about Mengzi's teachings, so he came again and sought to meet him. Perhaps he thought there might be some other account, one that was less exalted and less demanding. Mengzi realized this. Hence, he simply stated it like this, in order to illuminate the fact that, whether in ancient times or today, both sages and the ignorant fundamentally have one and the same nature. His former teaching had already fathomed the matter. There was no other account.]

4. "Cheng Jian said to Duke Jing of Qi, 'If they are men and I am a man, why should I be awed by them?' Yan Hui said, 'What sort of person was Shun? What sort of person am I? Those who are able to act are just like this.' Gongming Yi said, 'In saying, "King Wen is my teacher," how could the Duke of Zhou mislead me?'[93] ["They" (in the phrase "if they are men") means

---

92. *Mean* 1.iv, in Part III, Selection 36.

93. On Yan Hui (Yanzi), see *Analects* 6.11, in Part III, Selection 34, and Cheng Yi, "What Kind of Learning Was It that Yanzi Loved?" in Part III, Selection 28. On Shun, King Wen, and the Duke of Zhou, see the Introduction to Part I.

sages and worthies. "Those who are able to act are just like this" means that people who are capable of acting (the right way) are all like Shun. Gongming Yi was a worthy from Lu. "King Wen is my teacher" is a saying of the Duke of Zhou. Gongming Yi also regarded King Wen as someone who could be his teacher. Hence, he recited the saying of the Duke of Zhou, and sighed, "He would not deceive me." Mengzi had already informed the Heir Apparent that the Way does not have two paths. He then cites these three sayings to illuminate this, desiring the Heir Apparent to have firm faithfulness and apply effort, so as to take sages and worthies as his teachers, and not turn and seek other accounts.]

5. "Now, Teng is, if one evens out its shape, fifty leagues square. But it still can become a good state. The *Documents* says, 'If the medicine does not make you dizzy, it will not cure your illness.'[94] [This means that, although Teng is a small state, it still can be well-ruled. But he fears that, if he is comfortable with what is less exalted, he will not be able to "overcome the self."[95] Then he will not be able to dispense with what is bad and do what is good.

[In my humble opinion, Mengzi's teaching that the nature is good is first seen here, and is found in detail in Book 6; however, if one silently thinks it over and draws the inferences, then there is nowhere in the seven books (of the *Mengzi*) that is not this Pattern. Master Cheng is correct in saying that (Mengzi) develops what was not expressed by previous sages and makes a contribution to all followers of the sages.]

3B9 Gongduzi said, "Outsiders all say that you are fond of arguing with others, Master. May I ask why?"

Mengzi replied, "How could I be fond of arguing with others? I simply have no choice. . . . The doctrines of Yang Zhu and Mozi fill the world.[96] **The doctrines that do not tend toward Yang Zhu tend toward Mozi. Yang Zhu is 'for oneself.' This is to have no ruler. Mozi is 'impartial caring.' This is to have no father. To have no father and have no ruler is to be an animal. As Gongming Yi said, 'In the kitchens there is fat meat, and in the stables there are fat horses. Yet the people look gaunt, and in the wilds are the bodies of those dead of starvation. This is to lead animals to devour people.' If the Ways of Yang Zhu and Mozi do not cease, and the Way of Kongzi is not made evident, then evil doctrines will dupe the people, and obstruct benevolence and righteousness. If benevolence and righteousness are obstructed, that leads animals to devour people. I am afraid that people will begin to devour one another!** [Yang Zhu only understood loving oneself, and did not understand the righteousness of extending the self. Hence, he "had no ruler." Mozi's love had no differentiations, so he looked upon his closest kin as no different from the masses. Hence, he "had no father." "To have no father and

---

94. *Documents, Documents of Shang,* "Charge to Yue, Part I."

95. *Analects* 12.1, in Part III, Selection 34.

96. See the Translator's Introduction to this selection for more on Yang Zhu and Mozi.

have no ruler" is for the human Way to perish, and to simply be an animal.] **Out of fear of the preceding, I defend the Way of the former sages, fend off Yang Zhu and Mozi, and get rid of specious words, so that evil doctrines will be unable to arise. If they arise in one's minds, they are harmful in one's activities. If they arise in one's activities, they are harmful in governing. When sages arise again, they will certainly not disagree with this.** [Cheng Hao said, "The harm caused by Yang Zhu and Mozi is worse than the harm caused by the doctrines of Shen Buhai and Hanfeizi.[97] But the harm caused by Buddhism (in our own era) is even worse than the harm caused by Yang Zhu and Mozi. Yang Zhu's 'for oneself' causes uncertainty about righteousness. Mozi's 'impartial caring' causes uncertainty about benevolence. In contrast, it is easy to see the shallowness and vulgarity of the doctrines of Shen Buhai and Hanfeizi. Hence, Mengzi regards fending off the doctrines of Yang Zhu and Mozi as the most urgent task in his confused era. The doctrines of Buddhism are close to the Pattern, so the harm that they do is incomparably greater than that of Yang Zhu and Mozi."]

". . . How could I be fond of arguing with others? I simply have no choice. Anyone who can use words to fend off Yang Zhu and Mozi is a disciple of the sages."

4A10 1. Mengzi said, "One cannot have a discussion with those who are destroying themselves. One cannot work with those who throw themselves away. Those whose words slander propriety and righteousness are those whom I mean by 'those who are destroying themselves.' Those who say, 'I myself am unable to dwell in benevolence and follow righteousness' are those whom I mean by 'those who throw themselves away.' [Those who are destroying themselves do not know that propriety and righteousness are fine things, so they slander them. Even if one has a discussion with them, they will never have faithfulness. Those who throw themselves away know that benevolence and righteousness are fine things, but they sink into sloth. They say of themselves that they are definitely unable to act. If one takes action with them, one will definitely be unable to encourage them to strive. Cheng Yi said, "If people simply govern themselves with goodness, there are none who cannot change. Even though they may be the most abysmally benighted and ignorant, all can gradually hone themselves and advance. It is only 'those who destroy themselves' who separate themselves from it by not having faithfulness, and 'those who throw themselves away' who cut themselves off from it by 'not acting.'[98] Even if a sage lived with them, they would be unable to transform and

---

97. Shen Buhai and Hanfeizi were "Legalists," who argued that government must use explicit laws and clear bureaucratic rules that are enforced by lavish rewards for compliance and strict punishments for disobedience. Confucians regarded their approach to government as cruel and rigid.

98. *Mengzi* 1A7, above.

enter into (the Way). This is what is meant by 'the most lowly of the ignorant do not change.'"[99] **2. Benevolence is people's peaceful abode. Righteousness is people's proper path. 3. How sad it is when people vacate their peaceful abode and do not dwell in it, or set aside their proper path and do not follow it."**

4A27 Mengzi said, "The core of benevolence is serving one's parents. The core of righteousness is obeying one's elder brother. The core of wisdom is knowing these two and not abandoning them. The core of ritual propriety is adorning these two. The core of music is to delight in these two.

"If one delights in them, then they grow. If they grow, how can they be stopped? If they cannot be stopped, then soon, unconsciously, one's hands are moving to their rhythms, one's feet are dancing to their tunes."

4B12 Mengzi said, "Great people are those who do not lose their child-like mind." [The mind of great people penetrates the myriad transformations. The mind of a child is pure unity without artificiality. What makes people into great people is just that they are not tempted by things and have the ability to complete the purity and lack of artificiality of their fundamental state. When they "fill them out" like this, then there is nothing that they do not know and nothing that they are not capable of.[100] This is the ultimate of greatness.]

6A6 1. [Mengzi's disciple] Gongduzi said, "According to Gaozi, 'Human nature is neither good nor not good.' [In recent times, the doctrines of Su Shih and Hu Hong have been like this.[101]] **2. Some say, 'Human nature can become good and it can become not good. Therefore, when Sage Kings Wen and Wu arose, the people were fond of goodness. When Tyrants You and Li arose, the people were fond of destructiveness.' 3. Some say, 'There are natures that are good, and there are natures that are not good. Therefore, with Sage King Yao as a ruler, the sage Shun had an evil brother, Xiang. With the Blind Man as a father, there was the sage Shun. And with Tyrant Zhou as their nephew, and as their ruler besides, there were Viscount Qi of Wei and Prince Bigan.'** [Han Yu's doctrine of the three grades of human nature was like this.[102]] **4. Now, you say that human nature is good. Are all those others, then, wrong?"**

---

99. *Analects* 17.3, in Part III, Selection 34.

100. *Mengzi* 2A6, above.

101. Su Shi (1037–1101) was a famous poet, essayist, painter, and statesman of the generation before Zhu Xi. Hu Hong (1106–1161) was a leading figure in the Hunan School of Neo-Confucianism, which was an alternative to the Cheng-Zhu School. Zhu Xi objected strongly to Hu's view (which he believed was shared by Su Shi) that "human desires" (including desires for food and sex) are simply the Function of human nature. For an excellent discussion, see Conrad Schirokauer, "Chu Hsi and Hu Hong," in Wing-tsit Chan, ed., *Chu Hsi and Neo-Confucianism* (Honolulu: University of Hawaii Press, 1986), pp. 480–502.

102. See Han Yu, "On Human Nature," in Part III, Selection 22.

5. Mengzi said, "Their innate feelings can only become good. This is what I mean by calling their natures good. [The feelings are the activity of the nature. In terms of what is fundamental, human feelings can only become good and cannot become bad. From this we can see that human nature is fundamentally good.] **6. As for their becoming not good, this is not the fault of their potential.** [Since human nature is good, our potential is also good. When people fail to become good, it is due to the fact that they sink into material desires, rather than the fault of their potential.]

7. "Humans all have the mind of compassion. Humans all have the mind of disdain. Humans all have the mind of respect. Humans all have the mind of approval and disapproval. The mind of compassion is benevolence. The mind of disdain is righteousness. The mind of respect is propriety. The mind of approval and disapproval is wisdom. Benevolence, righteousness, propriety, and wisdom are not welded to us externally. We inherently have them. It is simply that we do not reflect upon them. Hence, it is said, 'Seek it and you will get it. Abandon it and you will lose it.' Some differ from others by two, five, or countless times—this is because they cannot fathom their potentials.

8. "The *Odes* says,

> **Heaven gives birth to the teeming people.**
> **If there is a thing, there is a norm.**
> **This is the constant that people cleave to.**
> **They are fond of this beautiful Virtue.**[103]

Kongzi said, 'The one who composed this ode understood the Way!' Hence, if there is a thing, there must be a norm. It is this that is the constant people cleave to. Hence, they are fond of this beautiful Virtue." [Cheng Yi said, "The 'nature' is simply the Pattern. The nature is one and the same from the sages Yao and Shun to the person in the street. Our 'capacity' is endowed by the *qi*. *Qi* can be clear or turbid. Those endowed with clear *qi* are worthy, while those endowed with turbid *qi* are ignorant. However, if one 'knows it through learning,' then whether the *qi* was clear or turbid, one can achieve goodness and return to the fundamental nature.[104] This is what is meant by 'The sages Tang and Wu made it into their selves.'[105] And when Kongzi said that 'the most lowly of the ignorant do not change,' he simply meant those who 'destroy themselves' or 'throw themselves away.'"[106]

[In my humble opinion, Cheng Yi's explanation of "capacity" is slightly different from that in Mengzi. Mengzi is discussing it with a focus on what emanates from the nature. Hence, he regards the "capacity" as only good. Master

---

103. *Odes* 260.

104. *Mean* 20.viii, in Part III, Selection 36.

105. *Mengzi* 7A30.

106. *Analects* 17.3, in Part III, Selection 34, and *Mengzi* 4A10, above.

Cheng is discussing it with a focus on the endowment of *qi*. In this sense, "capacity" certainly has differences of enlightened and benighted, strong and weak.]

6A15 Gongduzi asked, "We are all people, yet some become great people and some become petty people. Why is this?"

Mengzi replied, "Those who follow the greater part of themselves become great people, while those who follow the petty part of themselves become petty people." [The "greater part" is the mind. The petty part is things like one's eyes and ears.]

Gongduzi said, "We are all people, so why do some follow the greater part of themselves and some follow the petty part of themselves?"

Mengzi replied, "It is not the purpose of the ears and eyes to reflect, so they are misled by things. Things interact with things and simply lead them along. But the purpose of the mind is to reflect. If it reflects, then it will get it. If it does not reflect, then it will not get it. This is something Heaven has given us. If one first takes one's stand on what is greater, what is lesser will not be able to snatch it away. This is how to become a great person." [The purpose of the ear is to listen. The purpose of the eye is to see. Each has its own purpose, and is unable to reflect. For this reason, each is misled by external things. Since they are unable to think and are misled by external things, they too are nothing other than "things." Consequently, there is no difficulty in seeing that, when external things interact with these things, they are simply led along by them.[107] The mind, in contrast, can reflect; reflecting is its purpose. Whenever something comes up, if the mind succeeds in its purpose, then it gets the Pattern of that thing, and cannot be misled by it. However, if the mind fails in its purpose, it will not get the Pattern of the thing, and it will be misled by it. Ears, eyes, and the mind are all things that Heaven has given us, but the mind is the greatest. If we are able to take our stand on the mind, then we will never fail to reflect upon whatever comes up, and the desires of our ears and eyes will be unable to steal it. This is the way to become a great person.]

7A1 Mengzi said, "To fathom one's mind is to know one's nature. To know one's nature is to know Heaven. [The mind is the human awareness, equipped with the complete Pattern, which responds to the myriad situations. The nature is the Pattern that the mind is equipped with, and Heaven is what the Pattern comes from and expresses. Humans, having this mind, never fail to have the complete Substance. Nonetheless, if they do not exhaustively investigate the Pattern, there will be respects in which they are obscured and will

---

107. In Western philosophy, we tend to think of the eyes and ears primarily as sensory organs. As such, their characteristic errors are generally cognitive (e.g., Descartes' example of how an oar in water can appear broken when it is not). However, in Chinese philosophy, "ears and eyes" is generally metonymy for the *desires* of the ears and eyes (e.g., for attractive sights and pleasing sounds). Thus conceived, their characteristic errors are excessive or inappropriate desires or feelings.

be unable to fathom the capacity of this mind. Hence, if one is able to extend the complete Substance of one's mind to the ultimate, not failing to fathom a single aspect, one will have exhaustively investigated the Pattern and there will be nothing that one fails to know. Once one knows the Pattern, what one follows and expresses will never overstep it. To put it in the terms of the *Great Learning*: "To know one's nature" is what is meant by "getting a handle on things"; "to fathom one's mind" is what is meant by "knowledge reaching the ultimate."[108]] **To preserve one's mind and nourish one's nature is the way to serve Heaven. To not become conflicted over the length of one's life but to cultivate oneself and await one's fate is the way to take one's stand on fate."** [Cheng Yi said, "The mind, the nature, and Heaven are all one Pattern. However, if one discusses it from the perspective of the Pattern, one calls it 'Heaven.' If one discusses it from the perspective of the endowment that we receive, one calls it our 'nature.' If one discusses it from the perspective of what is preserved in a person, one calls it the 'mind.'"]

7A4 Mengzi said, "The myriad things are all complete within us. [This is talking about the fundamental state of the Pattern. At its greatest, it involves the relations between ruler and minister, father and son. At its smallest, it involves the most insignificant of things and affairs. The nature that we are endowed with does not lack a single aspect of the Pattern that one ought to follow.] **There is no greater joy than to examine oneself and discover Sincerity.** [Sincerity is genuineness. This means that if one examines one's self and the complete Pattern is all actually "like hating a hateful odor, like loving a lovely sight,"[109] then one's actions will never have to be forced and one will always do what one craves. No joy is greater than this.] **3. If one must seek benevolence, nothing is better than to force oneself to act out of sympathetic understanding."** [If one examines oneself and has Sincerity, one is already benevolent. But if one does not have Sincerity, there are still selfish thoughts interfering, and the Pattern is not pure. Hence, in all activities one should force oneself to extend to others. When one is close to the shared Pattern, benevolence is not far away.[110]]

7A15 Mengzi said, "That which people are capable of without learning is their pure capability. That which they know without pondering is their pure knowing. ["Pure" refers to the fundamental goodness. Cheng Yi said, "'Pure knowing' and 'pure capability' come from Heaven, and have no other source. They are not dependent upon others."] **Among babes in arms there are none that do not know to love their parents. When they grow older, there are none that do not know to revere their elder brothers.** ["Babes in arms" refers to when they are two or three years old, know how to smile, and can be carried in one's arms. "Loving their parents" and "revering their elder brothers" are what is meant by "pure knowing" and "pure capability."] **Treating one's parents as**

---

108. *Great Learning,* Classic 5, in Part III, Selection 33.

109. *Great Learning,* Commentary 6, in Part III, Selection 33.

110. Cf. *Analects* 6.30, in Part III, Selection 34.

parents is benevolence. Revering one's elders is righteousness. There is nothing else to do but extend these to the world." [This means that although
loving one's parents and revering one's elder brothers are the private matters of
a single person, the way to become benevolent and righteous is to extend them
in the same way to everyone in the world.]

7A17 Mengzi said, "Do not do that which you would not do; do not
desire that which you would not desire. Simply be like this." [Li Yu said,
"People all have a mind that will not do certain things and does not desire certain things. But as soon as a selfish thought sprouts, if one is unable to regulate
it with ritual and righteousness, then one will frequently do what one 'would
not do' and desire what one 'would not desire.' To examine that mind is what is
meant by 'filling out' one's 'mind of disdain.'[111] If this happens, one's righteousness will be inexhaustible. Hence, he says, 'Simply be like this.'"]

7B31 Mengzi said, "People all have things that they will not bear. To extend this reaction to that which they will bear is benevolence. People all have
things that they will not do. To extend this reaction to that which they will
do is righteousness. [People all have the minds of compassion and disdain.[112]
Hence, no one fails to have things that he will not bear or will not do. These
are the beginnings of benevolence and righteousness. Nonetheless, because of
the partiality of their *qi* and the obscuration of their material desires, there are
sometimes other cases in which people are unable to have these reactions. But if
they extend what they are able to do so that they reach to what they are unable
to do, then there will be nothing in which they are not benevolent and righteous.] If people can fill out the mind that does not desire to harm others,
their benevolence will be inexhaustible. If people can fill out the mind that
will not trespass, their righteousness will be inexhaustible. If people can fill
out the core reaction of refusing to be addressed disrespectfully, there will be
nowhere they go where they do not do what is righteous. If a noble speaks
when he may not speak, this is tricking someone with speech. If one does
not speak when he should, this is tricking someone with silence. These are
both in the category of trespassing." [When someone is being glib or secre-
tive, the intention is to defraud someone. This is in the category of trespassing,
but since it is more subtle, people easily overlook it. Hence, he particularly
holds it up as an example to clarify that one must extend the mind that will not
trespass so that it reaches to and avoids this. Only then will one be able to fill
out the mind that will not trespass.]

7B35 Mengzi said, "For cultivating the mind, nothing is better than having few desires. If someone has few desires, although there will be times
when he does not preserve [his mind], they will be few. If someone has many
desires, although there will be times when he does preserve it, they will be
few." ["Desires" are things like the desires of the mouth, nose, ears, eyes, and

---

111. *Mengzi* 2A6, above.

112. *Mengzi* 2A6 and 6A6, above.

four limbs. If these are many and unregulated, then even though one never lacks the capacity to preserve it, one will invariably lose one's fundamental mind. This is something that learners must be deeply on guard about. Cheng Yi said, "One need not be overwhelmed for it to be a desire. So long as one has a preference for something, that is a desire."]

36. *Collected Commentaries on the* Mean

translation by Bryan W. Van Norden[113]

Like the Great Learning, *the* Mean *was originally a chapter in the* Rites *that came to be treated as a separate work. Its authorship is traditionally attributed to Zǐsī* 子思, *the grandson of Kongzi. It is conventional to refer to this work as the* Mean *or* Doctrine of the Mean. *However, the Chinese title is* Zhong yong, *which Zhu Xi interprets as hitting the mean between extremes: literally, the "center" (zhōng* 中*), as determined by the common (yōng* 庸*) Pattern that structures the world. Zhu Xi recommended that one study it only after the* Great Learning, Analects, *and* Mengzi, *because it is the most esoteric and challenging of the Four Books. The people whom Zhu Xi cites in his commentary are earlier commentators on the* Mean. *All footnotes are by the translator. —Tr.*

Zhu Xi's Preface

[My (Zhu Xi's) masters the Cheng brothers said, "What does not deviate is called the 'mean.' What does not vary is called 'common.' The mean is the correct Way of the world; what is common is the established Pattern of the world."

[This work is the method for training the mind that was passed down by the disciples of Kongzi. Zisi, Kongzi's grandson, feared that mistakes would develop about it over time. Hence, he wrote it as a book and entrusted it to his disciple Mengzi. The beginning of this book (Chapter 1) explains the one Pattern; the middle (Chapters 2–20) lays out how it applies to the myriad things; the end (Chapters 21–33) returns to harmonize it as one Pattern. If you spread out this one Pattern, it will fill up all six directions; if you roll it up, it will be hidden in what is most secret. You can savor it endlessly, and everything one learns from it is genuine. Good readers will benefit from investigating it, and even if one applies it to the end of one's life one will not be able to exhaust it.]

---

113. This translation is based on the *Sibu beiyao* ed. of Zhu Xi, *Zhongyong jizhu*. My translation is selective and leaves out many phrases and sections that will be opaque or of less interest to most contemporary readers. For a complete translation, see Ian Johnston and Wang Ping, trans., *Daxue and Zhongyong* (Hong Kong: Chinese University Press, 2012).

Chapter 1

(i) "Nature" means what is mandated by Heaven. The "Way" means following one's nature. "Education" means cultivating the Way. [Nature is simply the Pattern. Heaven generates the myriad things in accordance with *yin, yang,* and the Five Phases, and gives them form with *qi.* It also endows them with the Pattern, which is the same as mandating them (to be a certain way). So when humans and things are generated, they each receive an endowment of the Pattern, which constitutes the Five Virtues (of benevolence, righteousness, wisdom, propriety, and faithfulness). This is what is meant by the "nature." The Way is the path. When each human and thing follows what is natural for its nature, then, in its daily activities, each has the path that it ought to follow. This is what is meant by the "Way." Although each person's nature and Way is the same, there are sometimes differences in the endowment of *qi,* so there cannot help being differences between those who go too far and those who don't reach to it. The sages cultivated people and things, based on what they ought to do, making a standard for the world. This is what is meant by "education." This refers to things like rituals and music, or punishment and government. In general, what makes people people, what makes the Way the Way, and what makes the education of the sages—if you seek out its source, each has what is fundamental to it in Heaven and is complete in ourselves. If learners realize this, they will know that they must exert effort in their learning and never stop. Hence, readers should deeply embody and silently understand what Zisi explains in this opening.]

(ii) The Way is something that one cannot depart from for even a moment. If one could depart from it, it would not be the Way. For this reason, the gentleman is careful even before he sees anything; he is concerned even before he hears anything.[114] [The mind of the gentleman always preserves reverence. Even though one has not yet seen or heard anything, he does not dare to be careless. This is the means by which one preserves the fundamental state of the Heavenly Pattern, and does not allow oneself to depart from it for even a moment.]

(iii) Nothing is more evident than what is hidden; nothing is more manifest than what is subtle. Hence, the gentleman is careful even when alone.[115] [This means that even in darkness or in the most trifling of affairs, when the signs of something have not yet taken concrete form, there is already incipient

---

114. Zhu Xi explains that this verse "is not about closing one's eyes and covering one's ears; it is about the point 'when happiness, anger, sadness, and joy have not yet been expressed' [verse iv]" (*Zhuzi yulei,* vol. 4, p. 1499, ln. 6).

115. Earlier commentators have taken verses (ii) and (iii) as describing the same issue, but Zhu Xi argues that there is a distinction: "The former verse explains preserving the original state of the Heavenly Pattern; the latter verse explains restraining human desires when they are about to sprout" (*Zhuzi yulei,* vol. 4, p. 1503, ln. 3).

activity. . . . For this reason, a gentleman is constantly on guard and devotes special effort to nipping his human desires in the bud, not allowing them to grow in private, lest he end up far from the Way.]

(iv) When happiness, anger, sadness and joy have not yet been expressed, it is called the "mean." When they are expressed but all hit the right points, it is called "harmony." The mean is the great foundation of the world. Harmony is the universal Way of the world. [Happiness, anger, sadness, and joy are feelings. When they have not yet been expressed, this is in the nature. Because they have not deviated at all, we call this the "mean." For them to be expressed but all hit the right points is for the feelings to be correct. Because there is no respect in which they are aberrant, we call this state "harmony." The "great foundation" is the nature that is mandated by Heaven. The Patterns of the world all flow from this. It is the Substance of the Way. The "universal Way" refers to following this nature. It is what the whole world, past and present, follows in common. It is the Function of the Way. This section explains the Virtue of nature and feelings in order to explain what it means that "one cannot depart from it for even a moment."]

(v) If one achieves the mean and harmony, Heaven and Earth will find their places, and the myriad things will be nurtured.

[The myriad things of the world and I are fundamentally one Substance, so if my mind is correct, the mind of the world will also be correct; if my *qi* is harmonious, the *qi* of the world will also be harmonious. Hence, its efficacy can be this great. These ultimate achievements of learning and inquiry, these activities that sages are capable of—from the very start do not depend on anything external, and the education that cultivates the Way is also within oneself. And although there is a distinction of activity and tranquility between Substance and Function, and there must first be the establishment of the Substance and only then the Function to put it into effect, nonetheless there are not in actuality two separate activities. Hence, in this last verse, he talks about them together in order to summarize the meaning of the previous verses.

[In the preceding Chapter, Zisi transmitted the meaning that had been handed down in order to safeguard this teaching. In the opening (i), he explains that the basis of the Way issues from Heaven and cannot be changed. Its Substance is complete in us and we cannot depart from it. Next (ii–iv), he explains the essentials of cultivating and examining it. Finally (v), he explains the ultimate of the transformative effects of sages and spirituality.

[Through the preceding, he hoped students would examine and seek for it in themselves in order to get it for themselves. By this means, they will get rid of the selfishness that pursues external temptations, and instead fill out their fundamental goodness. Yang Shi referred to this section as the "essential points" of the whole work. The following ten or so chapters are Zisi citing the words of the Master, Kongzi, in order to draw out the conclusions of this chapter.]

Chapter 4

The Master said, "I realize that the Way is not put into practice: the wise overshoot it; the foolish do not come up to it. I realize that the Way is not understood: the worthy overshoot it; the unworthy do not come up to it. There are no people who do not eat and drink, but few are those who are able to appreciate the flavors!"

Chapter 6

The Master said, "Was not Sage King Shun greatly wise! Shun was fond of asking questions and fond of examining even seemingly simple-minded views. He minimized what was bad in them and held up what was good. He grasped both sides of things and then applied the mean in dealing with the people. Was it not these things that made him Shun?"

Chapter 10

(i) Zilu asked about strength of character.[116] [Zilu is Kongzi's disciple. Zilu was fond of courage, hence he asks about strength.] **(ii) The Master said, "Do you mean the strength of southerners, the strength of northerners, or your own strength? (iii) To be broad and gentle in educating, to not take vengeance on those who fail to follow the Way—this is strength for southerners. The gentleman dwells in this. (iv) To sleep with a weapon by one's side, to not mind dying—this is strength for northerners. The merely strong dwell in this. (v) Hence, a gentleman is harmonious but not pandering: how great is his strength! He takes an unwavering stand on the mean: how great is his strength! When the state has the Way, he does not change his former practices: how great is his strength! When the state lacks the Way, he does not change even if it leads to his death: how great is his strength!"** [The Master tells Zilu these things in order to restrain his inflexible *qi* and encourage him to have the courage of Virtue and righteousness.]

Chapter 13

The Master said, **"The Way is not far from people. People who practice a Way that is far from themselves are not practicing *the* Way.** [The "Way" is simply "following one's nature." Consequently, it is something that the masses are able to know and able to practice. Thus, it is never far from people. If those who practice the Way disdain what is commonplace and nearby, regarding it as unworthy of practice, and instead become intent upon lofty, distant, and difficult to practice activities, it will not be the means to genuinely practice the

---

116. Here and later in the *Mean* "strength" refers not to physical power but to strength of character or fortitude.

Way.[117]] **The *Odes* say, 'Carve the hatchet, carve the hatchet / Not too far is the pattern to match it.' One grasps a hatchet to carve a hatchet handle. Only because of perspective do they seem far from each other. Similarly, the gentleman governs people in accordance with people, and stops once he has reformed them.** [This means that, when one grasps a hatchet to cut the handle of a hatchet out of some wood, the standard for the length of *that* handle one is cutting lies in *this* handle that one is holding. Nonetheless, there is a distinction between *that* and *this*, so when one looks at them while cutting, they will seem far from each other. Similarly, when one "governs people in accordance with people," the Way of being a person lies in each person's self. Initially, there is no distinction of *that* and *this*. Hence, when a gentleman governs people, he governs the people's selves by means of the people's own Way. When he has been able to reform them, he stops, and does not direct them further. In general, he demands of them only what they are able to know and able to do. He does not want them to regard anything far from people as the Way. This is what Zhang Zai meant by, "If one's hopes for people are in accordance with the masses, they will follow easily."]

"Conscientiousness and sympathetic understanding are not far from the Way. 'Do not inflict upon others what you would be unwilling to accept if it were inflicted upon yourself.' [To fathom one's own mind is conscientiousness. To extend oneself to others is sympathetic understanding. . . . If one gauges the minds of others by means of one's own mind, one will never find them to be different. From this we can see that the Way is not far from people. Consequently, 'do not inflict upon others what you yourself do not want' is not far from people. And this is the practice of the Way. What Zhang Zai referred to as "loving others with the mind that loves oneself" is fathoming benevolence like this.] **There are four aspects to the Way of a gentleman, and I, Kong, have been unable to attain even one. 'Serve one's father with what one seeks from his own son'—I have been unable to do this. 'Serve one's ruler with what one seeks from one's own ministers'—I have been unable to do this. 'Serve one's elder brother with what one seeks from one's younger brother'—I have been unable to do this. 'First do for one's friends what one seeks from them'—I have been unable to do this.**

"If there is anything inadequate in your everyday practice of Virtue, or your everyday care in speech, do not dare to be lax about it. If you have any remaining strength, do not dare to leave it unexhausted. Let one's words look to one's actions, and one's actions look to one's words. How can a gentleman fail to be earnest?" [The Way is not far from people. In general,

---

117. Although he never says so explicitly, Zhu Xi reads this section of the *Mean* as a criticism of doctrines like Buddhism and Daoism that demand of people practices that are supposedly "lofty," but difficult, uncommon, and unnatural, like celibacy, asceticism, and a form of compassion that dissolves filial piety.

what you yourself demand of *others* is precisely what it ought to be according to the Way. Hence, reflect upon this and demand it of *yourself* in order to cultivate yourself. . . . This is all there is to regarding the Way as something that is not far from people. This is what Zhang Zai meant by "To have a mind that demands of oneself what one demands of others is to fathom the Way."]

Chapter 20

[The following chapter (20) is the first to discuss Sincerity in detail. However, what is called "Sincerity" is the crux of this whole book.]

(i) **Duke Ai asked about governing. (ii) The Master said, "The government of Sage Kings Wen and Wu has been recorded. If the people flourish, their government becomes legendary. If the people die, their government perishes. (iii) The Way for people depends upon zeal in governing, just as the Way for soil depends upon zeal in planting. Governing is like growing vines. (iv) Hence, governing depends on people, one gets people through one's character, one cultivates one's character with the Way, and one cultivates the Way with benevolence.**

(v) **"Benevolence is being a human, and its greatest form is being kind to one's kin. Righteousness is appropriateness, and its greatest form is respecting the worthy. Ritual grows out of the differences in being kind to one's kin, and the gradations in respecting the worthy. (vi) Hence, a gentleman cannot fail to cultivate his self. Thinking to cultivate his self, he cannot fail to serve his kin. Thinking to serve his kin, he cannot fail to know people. Thinking to know people, he cannot fail to know Heaven.**

(vii) **"The universal Way of the world has five aspects, and there are three things by means of which one puts it into action. The five aspects are the relationships between ruler and minister, father and son, husband and wife, elder and younger brothers, and friends. These five make up the universal Way of the world. Wisdom, benevolence and courage—these three things— are the universal Virtues of the world. But that by means of which one puts them into action is one.** [The "universal Way" is the path that the world follows in both the past and the present. It is the same as what the *Documents* refers to as the "Five Paradigms," and is what Mengzi is referring to when he says, "Between father and son there is affection, between ruler and minister there is righteousness, between husband and wife there is distinction, between older and younger there is precedence, and between friends there is faithfulness."[118] Wisdom is that by means of which one knows this [Way]. Benevolence is that by means of which one embodies this. Courage is that by means of which one is firm in this. These three are referred to as the "universal Virtues" because they are the Pattern that the world receives in both the past and the present. The "one"

---

118. See *Documents, Documents of Yu,* "Canon of Shun," and *Mengzi* 3A4, respectively.

refers to Sincerity. Although everyone follows the universal Way, without these three Virtues, they will lack the ability to follow it. Although everyone receives the universal Virtues, as soon as one lacks Sincerity, human desires intrude, and "Virtue" is no longer Virtue. As Master Cheng said, "What is referred to as Sincerity is nothing beyond making these three have genuineness and Sincerity. There is no Sincerity that goes beyond these three."[119]]

(viii) "Some are born knowing it; some know it through learning; some know it only after difficulty. But what they come to know is one thing. Some put it into action effortlessly; some put it into action to profit from it; some put it into action only after exertion. But what they achieve is one thing." [What one knows and what one practices is the universal Way. If one discusses it in terms of its manifestations, the means by which ones knows it is wisdom; that by means of which one puts it into practice is benevolence; that by means of which one reaches the accomplishment of knowledge and achieves unity is courage. If one discusses it in terms of its gradations, then to be born knowing or putting it into action effortlessly is due to wisdom; to know it through learning or put it into action in order to profit from it is due to benevolence; to know it only after difficulty or put it into action only after exertion is due to courage. In general, although human nature never fails to be good, due to differences in endowments of *qi*, there are those who hear the Way early and those who hear it late; there are those who find the Way easy to practice and those who find the Way difficult to practice it. Nonetheless, if people are able to be strong without giving up, then what they achieve will be one and the same. As Lü Dalin said, "Although the paths that people start on are different, the place that they arrive will be the same: this is what makes it the mean. The reason that the Way is not known or put into practice is that people fret about whether they have the capacity to be born with knowledge or put it into action effortlessly, and they denigrate knowing with difficulty and putting it into action after exertion."]

(ix) The Duke said, "Your teachings, Master, are the height of nobility! But I am genuinely recalcitrant and unable to live up to them."

The Master replied, "To be fond of learning is close to wisdom; to put effort into one's actions is close to benevolence; to know what is shameful is close to courage. [As Lü Dalin said, "The ignorant think they are right and do not seek further; the selfish are bound by human desires and forget to reflect; the weak are content to be inferior to others, yet still do not defer to them. Hence, being fond of learning is not wisdom, but it is sufficient to overcome ignorance; putting effort into one's actions is not benevolence, but it is sufficient to forget selfishness; to know what is shameful is not courage, but it is sufficient to rouse one from weakness."] **(x) If one knows these three things, one will know how to cultivate one's self. If one knows how to cultivate one's self, one knows**

---

119. For more on "Sincerity," a key concept in Zhu Xi's thought, see *Great Learning*, Commentary 6, in Part III, Selection 33.

how to govern others. If one knows how to govern others, one knows how to govern the states of the world. . . .

(xi) "The people cannot be governed when those in subordinate positions are not captivated by those above. There is a Way for those above to captivate them: if there is not faithfulness between friends, they will not captivate them. There is a Way of faithfulness between friends: if there is not compliance between kin, there will not be faithfulness between friends. There is a Way of compliance between kin: if one examines one's self and does not have Sincerity, there will not be compliance between kin. There is a Way of Sincerity of self: if one is not enlightened about goodness, one's self will not have Sincerity. ["If one examines one's self and does not have Sincerity" means that, when one examines and seeks for it in what is preserved and expressed in one's self, one is not yet able to be genuine and avoid obliviousness. "If one is not enlightened about goodness" means that one is not yet able to examine the fundamental state of the Heavenly mandate in the human mind, and to genuinely know where the highest good is.] (xii) Sincerity is the Way of Heaven. To make it have Sincerity is the Way of humans. Those who have Sincerity hit the mean without effort; they get it without reflection; they perfectly hit the Way: they are sages! To make it have Sincerity is to grasp what is good and firmly hold onto it. ["Sincerity" refers to what is authentic and avoids obliviousness. It is the fundamental state of the Heavenly Pattern. "To make it have Sincerity" refers to when one is not yet able to be authentic and avoid obliviousness, but desires to be authentic and avoid obliviousness. This is what humans ought to do. The Virtue of sages is undifferentiated Heavenly Pattern, authentic and without obliviousness. It does not need to make an effort in order to hit the Way exactly. It is simply the Way of Heaven. If one has not yet achieved sagehood, one cannot fail to have the selfishness of human desires, and one's Virtue cannot be completely authentic. Hence, if one is not yet able to get it without reflection, then one must *choose* goodness, and only then can one be enlightened about the good. If one is not yet able to hit the mean without effort, then one must firmly hold onto it, and only then can one make one's self have Sincerity. This is what is referred to as the human Way. To get it without reflecting is to be born knowing it. To hit the mean without effort is to effortlessly put it into practice. To *choose* the good is an activity inferior to knowing through learning; to firmly hold onto it is an activity inferior to putting it into practice to profit from it.]

(xiii) "One must *broadly* learn about it, *intently* ask about it, *carefully* reflect upon it, *insightfully* distinguish it, and *earnestly* put it into action. (xiv) This means that it is not learning if one 'learns' but is still incapable of applying it. It is not asking if one 'asks' but still does not know. It is not reflecting if one 'reflects' but still does not get it. It is not distinguishing if one 'distinguishes' but still does not see it clearly. It is not putting it into 'action,' if one acts but is not earnest in doing it.

"If others only need to do one, you must do a hundred; if others only need to do ten, you must do a thousand. (xv) Then you will be able to follow this Way. Even if you are foolish, you will become enlightened; even if you are weak, you will become strong." [Lü Dalin said, "The gentleman learns simply in order to transform his innate disposition and that is all. If Virtue overcomes innate disposition, then the ignorant can achieve enlightenment, and the weak can achieve strength. If it cannot overcome it, then although one has 'set one's mind upon learning,' one will not be able, if ignorant, to achieve enlightenment, or, if weak, to 'be firmly established.'[120] That is all there is to it. In general, our natures are all equally good without any evil. This is the respect in which humans are the same. Our innate capacities are benighted or enlightened, weak or strong. This is the respect in which humans are different. 'Making it have Sincerity' is the means by which we reflect upon what is common and transform what is different. Now, if you seek to transform a disposition that is not noble into one that is noble, but you do not make a hundredfold effort, it will be inadequate to achieve it. Suppose people try to transform their dispositions that are not noble into ones that are noble, but are careless in their learning, making an effort one moment and being lazy the next, and when they are ultimately unable to transform, say, 'When one's Heaven-given disposition is not noble, learning cannot transform it.' This is to end up 'throwing oneself away.'[121] This is the height of lacking benevolence!"]

Chapter 21

[The following chapter is Zisi presenting a teaching based on the Master's thoughts about the Way of Heaven and the Way of humans in the previous chapter (20.xii). The twelve chapters following it (22–33) are all the teachings of Zisi, reflecting upon, extending and clarifying the meaning of this chapter.]

If one becomes enlightened by having Sincerity, this is said to be by "nature." If one achieves Sincerity by being enlightened, this is said to be by "education." If one has Sincerity, then one will be enlightened; if one is enlightened, then one will have Sincerity. [When one's Virtue never fails to be genuine and one's enlightenment leaves nothing unilluminated, one has the Virtue of the sages. This is when one has it because one treats it as one's nature.[122] This is the Way of Heaven. When one first becomes enlightened about goodness, and only then actualizes one's goodness, this is the learning of a worthy person. This is when one enters into it from education. This is the Way of humans. If one has Sincerity, one will not fail to be enlightened about anything. If one is enlightened, then one can attain Sincerity.]

---

120. *Analects* 2.4, in Part III, Selection 34.

121. *Mengzi* 4A10, in Part III, Selection 35.

122. Compare *Mengzi* 7A30: "The sage-kings Yao and Shun treated it as their natures; the sage-kings Tang and Wu treated it as their selves."

Chapter 22

[This chapter discusses the Way of Heaven.]

Only those of the utmost Sincerity in the world are able to fathom their natures. Those who are able to fathom their natures are able to fathom the natures of others. Those who are able to fathom the natures of others are able to fathom the natures of things. Those who are able to fathom the natures of things can assist the transformations of Heaven and Earth. Those who can assist the transformations of Heaven and Earth can form a triad with Heaven and Earth. ["The utmost Sincerity in the world" refers to the genuineness of the Virtue of sages. No one in the world can add anything to it. Those who "fathom their natures" have a Virtue that never fails to be genuine. Hence, they lack the selfishness of human desires; they examine and follow the mandate of Heaven that is within us all, in both the great and the small, the refined and the crude, never failing to fathom any of it by so much as a hair's breadth. The nature of other people and things is also my nature. However, the endowments of *qi* that give us form are not the same, so there are differences among us. . . . This is the activity of one who "becomes enlightened by having Sincerity" (Chapter 21).]

Chapter 23

[This chapter discusses the Way of humans.]

The next level is those who extend from a partial knowledge. Those with a partial knowledge are able to have Sincerity. When one has Sincerity, it takes form. When it takes form, it becomes evident. When it becomes evident, then it enlightens. When it enlightens, then there is action. When there is action, then there is transformation. When there is transformation, there is metamorphosis. Only those of the highest Sincerity are able to engage in metamorphosis. [In general, human natures are never different, but there are differences in *qi*. Hence, only sages are able to fathom the complete Substance of their natures. Those at the next level must extend all of the partial manifestations of goodness that sprout, until each reaches its ultimate. If everything that is partial is fully extended, then one's Virtue will never fail to be genuine, and the inevitable results will be taking form, becoming evident, acting and transforming. If one accumulates this to the point that one is able to metamorphosize, then the subtlety of one's Sincerity will be no different from that of sages.]

Chapter 25

Sincerity is to make oneself complete, and the Way is to guide oneself. [One discusses "Sincerity" when talking about the mind, because it is what is fundamental. One discusses the "Way" when talking about the Pattern, because it is the Function.] **Sincerity is the beginning of things, and it is their end. Without Sincerity, there are no things. For this reason, making things have**

Sincerity is what the gentleman regards as most precious. [The things of the world are all made by the genuine Pattern. Hence, only when it gets this Pattern will there be this thing. When one has fathomed the Pattern that a thing gets, then one has fathomed the thing; there is nothing beyond this. Hence, as soon as a human's mind fails to be genuine, then although he acts, it amounts to nothing. So a gentleman must regard Sincerity as most precious. In general, if the human mind is able to always be genuine, then it creates the means to complete oneself, and one will never fail to follow the Way that is within us all.] **Sincerity is not simply making oneself complete. It is also the means by which one brings things to completion. To make oneself complete is benevolence; to make things complete is wisdom. Sincerity is the Virtue of one's nature; it is the Way that harmonizes external and internal. Hence, it is appropriate in every circumstance.** [Although Sincerity is the means by which one brings oneself to completion, when one has the means to complete oneself, it will naturally extend to things, and the Way will be practiced regarding them too. Benevolence is the preservation of the Substance, and wisdom is the manifestation of the Function. These are all things that our nature inherently has. There is no distinction here between the internal and the external. When one has gotten it oneself, then it will become manifest in activities. If you practice it at all times, everything will be appropriate.]

Critics of Zhu Xi

37. Lu Xiangshan, "Correspondence on the Great Ultimate"

translation by Philip J. Ivanhoe[1]

Letters to Zhu Xi

Lù Xiàngshān 陸象山 *(1139–1193) was a contemporary of Zhu Xi, as well as an influential philosophical rival. Lu offered a competing vision of*

Confucian Scholar.

*Confucianism whereby the transformative insights of the tradition were more immediately accessible to human experience, without presupposing prior mastery of the textual tradition or a grasp of what he saw as esoteric points of ethics and metaphysics. Although their disagreements were many, they were perhaps made most explicit in a well-known exchange of letters written in the late twelfth century. The primary subject of these letters was Zhu Xi's interpretation of the Great Ultimate (*tàijí 太極*) and the Ultimateless (*wújí 無極*). The phrase "Great Ultimate" originally comes from the "Great Appendix" to the* Changes. *This work is attributed to Kongzi, so Zhu and Lu agree about the orthodoxy of this notion. However, Zhu Xi also followed Zhou Dunyi's "Explanation of the Diagram of the Great Ultimate," which seems to equate the* "Great Ultimate" *with the "Ultimateless." Zhu Xi thought that Zhou Dunyi used this language to express the insight that the Great Ultimate was the*

---

1. This translation is based on that in Philip J. Ivanhoe, trans., *Readings from the Lu-Wang School of Neo-Confucianism* (Indianapolis: Hackett Publishing, 2009). It has been abridged and slightly modified to match the translation conventions of this volume. We are responsible for any infelicities or errors that result.—Eds.

Pattern in itself, prior to its embodiment in concrete things.[2] *Lu Xiangshan objects to using the phrase "Ultimateless" to interpret the teachings of Kongzi. Some of his arguments are textual (e.g., the absence of the expression "Ultimateless" from the* Changes*); other arguments are about orthodoxy (e.g., his claim that the concept of the "Ultimateless" seems Daoist in origin). Underlying this debate, though, is a fundamental disagreement over the nature of ethical cultivation. For Zhu Xi, those learning the Way should first attempt to grasp the Pattern in the abstract, especially through book learning. "Great Ultimate" is a name for this Pattern, and the term "Ultimateless" helps clarify that it is something that transcends its concrete manifestations. For Lu Xiangshan, all humans are already capable of following the Way, prior to learning from the classics. Consequently, the "Great Ultimate" must be grasped in its specific manifestations, not in the abstract. Below are excerpts from Lu's two letters to Zhu Xi on the subject.* —Eds.

First Letter to Zhu Xi

. . . The sages and worthies of ancient times only looked to Pattern to determine what is right. Yao and Shun were sages but they "consulted the hay bearers and firewood carriers."[3] Zengzi had his son change the mat beneath him, but this [inappropriate mat] was noticed by a young servant boy who was holding a candle.[4] The commentary on the hexagram *Meng* in the *Changes* says, "Accepting the advice of a woman will lead to good fortune."[5] So, even the words of women and young boys should not be disregarded. Mengzi said, "It would be better to be without the *Documents* than to trust in them completely. In the 'Completion of War' chapter of the *Documents* I accept only two or three strips [of characters]."[6] If words do not accord with Pattern, even though they come from some ancient text, one must not presume to trust them completely. Even the wise can make one mistake in a thousand; even the ignorant can have one insight in a thousand. How can one be lax in one's view of what people say?

[In his letter to you] my elder brother, Suoshan, said,

---

2. See *Changes,* "Great Appendix," I.11, in Part I, Selection 9; Zhou Dunyi, "Explanation of the Diagram of the Great Ultimate," in Part III, Selection 24; Zhu Xi, *Categorized Conversations,* in Part III, Selection 32.

3. *Odes* 254.

4. *Rites,* "Tan Gong." The sons of Zengzi (one of Kongzi's disciples, and the author of the Commentary section of the *Great Learning*) had used a fine mat for their ill father to lie upon. When its quality was noted by a young lad bearing a candle, Zengzi insisted that it be replaced with a mat appropriate to his station.

5. *Changes,* second line statement on hexagram 4, *Meng:* "Showing forbearance toward the ignorant will lead to good fortune. Accepting the advice of a woman will lead to good fortune. . . ."

6. *Mengzi* 7B3. "Strips" refers to the strips of bamboo upon which the text was written.

[Zhou Dunyi's] "Explanation of the Diagram of the Great Ultimate" is different in kind from his *Comprehending the* Changes, and I doubt that the former is really the work of Zhou Dunyi. If this is wrong [and it really is Zhou's work], then perhaps it was written at a time when his learning had not matured. Or perhaps it represents the work of some other thinker and people in later ages have failed to see [that Zhou is not the author]. The "Pattern, Human Nature, and the Mandate" chapter of *Comprehending the* Changes, says, "Abide in the mean. The two *qi* and Five Phases transform and generate the myriad things. The Five Phases produce their diverse forms, while the two *qi* provide their substance or material. The two *qi* at their root are one." When this text talks about "one" or the "mean" this is the Great Ultimate. It never adds Ultimateless on top of the Great Ultimate. In the "Activity and Tranquility" chapter, it talks about the Five Phases, *yin* and *yang*, and the Great Ultimate, but again, there is no use of the term "Ultimateless." Regardless of whether the "Explanation of the Diagram of the Great Ultimate" is really someone else's work, [which Zhou Dunyi] passed on, or a work that he himself composed when he was young, we know that by the time he wrote *Comprehending the* Changes he never mentioned "Ultimateless." From this we can surmise that by this time he realized that this idea was wrong.

We must carefully and seriously consider Suoshan's view on this topic. . . .

In your letter to Suoshan you say, "If one does not talk about the Ultimateless, then the Great Ultimate will be equated with some thing and prove inadequate as the source and basis for the myriad transformations. If one does not talk about the Great Ultimate, then the Ultimateless will fade into emptiness and stillness and prove inadequate as the source and basis for the myriad transformations."

Without a doubt, the Great Ultimate is how things are in the Pattern and this is why Kongzi explained this idea clearly. He did not rely upon unsubstantiated theories to establish his view, which simply would have encouraged later people to spread idle and misleading gossip through speech and writing. That the Great Ultimate is the source and basis of the myriad transformations is simply what it always has been. How could the questions of whether or not it can prove adequate to this task or capable of fulfilling this role be settled by whether or not people *talk* about it?

The "Great Appendix" to the *Changes* says, "In the changes is the Great Ultimate."[7] Kongzi talked about what is or what exists; now you talk about what is not or what does not exist. Why? When Kongzi composed the "Great

---

7. *Changes*, "Great Appendix," I.11, in Part I, Selection 9. [There is ambiguity here about whether "changes" refers to the book, to the cosmic process of change the book reveals, or to both. This passage goes on to say of the Great Ultimate, "It generates the two Modes, and the two Modes generate the four Images. The four Images generate the eight Trigrams, and the eight Trigrams clearly distinguish good and ill-fortune."—Eds.]

Appendix," he did not talk about the Ultimateless. As a result, has the Great Ultimate been equated with some thing and proven inadequate as the source and basis for the myriad transformations? . . .

In your second letter [to my brother Suoshan] you went on to say, "the Ultimateless is what is without form and the Great Ultimate is what has Pattern" and "Zhou Dunyi feared that students would mistakenly think that the Great Ultimate was a distinct material thing and so he employed the two characters 'Ultimate-less' [literally, 'lacking an ultimate'] in order to make this clear."[8] But the "Great Appendix" to the *Changes* says, "What is above with respect to form is called the 'Way.'"[9] It also says, "The alternation of *yin* and *yang* is called the 'Way.'"[10] If the alternation of the *yin* and *yang* already marks the state of being above with respect to form, how much more clear is it that this must be true of the Great Ultimate![11] Everyone who understands the meaning of the text knows that this is true. I never have heard of anyone, since the "Great Appendix" first came into being down to contemporary times, who mistakenly thought that the Great Ultimate was a distinct material thing. If there are some who are so dull that they make this kind of mistake, why shouldn't we just treat them as people who lack the ability to "come back with the other three corners" [when given the first]?[12] Why would such a possibility worry old Zhou Dunyi to the point where he would make the special effort of adding the two characters "Ultimateless" on top of "Great Ultimate" in order to explain what it means?

Furthermore, one can't use words about things with specific forms to explain what the word "ultimate" means. Now, in general, the "great" is the middle or mean.[13] So, to say 'Ultimateless' [literally "lacking an ultimate"] would be like saying "lacking a middle." How could this ever do? If one is worried that students will get mired in [an excessive concern with] material things and wants to offer further explanation, then it would be appropriate to say something like

---

8. See *Da Lu Zijing Er* 答陸子靜二 in *Zhuzi Wenji* 朱子文集 vol. 4 (Taibei: Defu wenjiao jijinhui 德富文教基金會, 2000): 1434–35.

9. *Changes,* "Great Appendix," I.12, in Part I, Selection 9.

10. *Changes,* "Great Appendix," I.5, in Part I, Selection 9.

11. Lu Xiangshan interprets the obscure phrase from the "Great Appendix" "above with respect to form" as meaning that the Way is within physical form, but superior with respect to other forms. Zhu Xi, in contrast, interprets the same line as meaning that the Way metaphysically transcends things that have physical form.—Eds.

12. *Analects* 7.8, "The Master said, 'I do not open up the Way to those who lack ardor; I do not offer explanations to those who are not trying to explain things for themselves. If I hold up one corner [of the square] and they cannot come back with the other three, I do not repeat the lesson.'" Lu's point is that even Kongzi did not worry about or even continue to teach people who were so dull that they would make the kind of mistake Zhu Xi thinks *most* students would be likely to make.

13. The idea is that this balanced state, in which there are no distinct and separate forms, is the source of all particular things.

what one finds in the *Odes* when it talks about "the workings of high Heaven" and elaborates on this by saying, they "are without sound or scent."[14] How could one ever see fit to add Ultimateless on top of the Great Ultimate?[15]

The two words "Ultimate-less" are from the chapter 28 in the *Daodejing*; it does not appear anywhere in the writings of our sage [Kongzi]. The opening chapter of the *Daodejing* says, "The nameless is the beginning of Heaven and Earth; the named is the mother of the myriad creatures." And yet, at the end [of the chapter] he [Laozi] equates them [i.e., the nameless and named].[16] This is Laozi's guiding doctrine, and yet [the opening lines of the "Explanation of the Diagram of the Great Ultimate"]—"The Ultimateless yet also the Great Ultimate"—expresses the very same idea!

Laozi's philosophy is incorrect because he did not clearly comprehend the Pattern. This is what beclouded his understanding. You have exerted great effort in following this teaching [regarding the Ultimateless and Great Ultimate] and practiced it for a long time; why have you never been able to discern what is wrong with it? It is absolutely clear that the teaching about "residing in the mean" found in *Comprehending the* Changes is not the same in kind; why have you not distinguished between them?

The two words, "Ultimate-less," appear in the opening line of the "Explanation of the Diagram of the Great Ultimate" and yet are not found anywhere in *Comprehending the* Changes. The sayings and writings of the two Cheng brothers are quite extensive, but they too never once mention the expression "Ultimateless." Even if we grant that Zhou Dunyi really did have the diagram [of the Great Ultimate] from the start, when we consider that he never mentions the term "Ultimateless" in his later works, we can see that his philosophy had advanced and that he no longer endorsed such a view.

Second Letter to Zhu Xi

. . . We all "lack a regular teacher."[17] Wandering through the muddled mass of teachings, we search and look, both high and low. Although one may claim one understands the Pattern, how can one be sure that this is not just a private opinion or deluded view? One clap of thunder follows another; one person sings and hundreds join in harmony—we cannot know if we are right or wrong. We must exercise extreme caution in this regard!

It is fortunate that people doubt one another and do not agree. In the midst of those who share a common aspiration, it is naturally appropriate that all fully

---

14. *Odes* 235.

15. In the next paragraph, not included here, Lu cites evidence that the "Diagram of the Great Ultimate" may itself be Daoist in origin, rather than Confucian.—Eds.

16. The *Daodejing*, attributed to Laozi, is the foundational text of Daoism.

17. Compare *Analects* 19.22, which describes how Kongzi "lacked a regular teacher" but endeavored to study the ancients and learn from whomever he could.

express their sincere thoughts and apply themselves to "grinding and polishing" one another in an effort to reach agreement about what is right and true.[18] The respect in which "great Shun was great was in agreeing with others. He delighted in adopting the ideas of others in order to help him do what is good."[19] [When he was living in rustic conditions and among crude people,] "whenever he heard a single good word or saw a single good act, he was like a mighty river overflowing its banks. Flooding forth, none could stand in his way."[20]

The primary focus of your last letter is the term "Ultimateless," but your account relies upon an explication of "Pattern." Your most important point is, "Through this [i.e., the Ultimateless] we are able to have a luminous and veridical apprehension of the genuine Substance of the Great Ultimate."[21] But in my humble opinion, you, my dear friend, have not experienced a veridical apprehension of the Great Ultimate. If you had really, accurately apprehended the Great Ultimate, you would not have preceded [your discussion of the Great Ultimate] with talk about the Ultimateless or followed it by appending the expression "the genuine Substance [of the Great Ultimate]." To begin your discussion with talk about the "Ultimateless" is precisely [as you yourself have said] "to stack a bed on top of one's bed." To follow the discussion by adding the expression "the genuine Substance [of the Great Ultimate]" is precisely [as you yourself have said] "to build a house underneath one's house."[22] The claims made by an insubstantial view certainly are inherently unlike those made by a substantial view.

Concerning the Great Ultimate, you have said, "It is precisely because it is the absolute and extreme ultimate for which no name can be named that we distinguish it by calling it 'the Great Ultimate.' . . . We refer to it as we do because it is the most extreme ultimate in all the world and nothing more can be said about it than this."[23] Why then is there any need to add the term "Ultimateless?" If you want to talk about the fact that it [i.e., the Great Ultimate] exists in no definite place and has no distinctive form, then, as I urged you to do in my earlier letter, it would be appropriate to say something like what one finds in the *Odes* when it talks about "the workings of high Heaven" and elaborates on this by saying, [they] "are without sound or scent."[24] Why do you think it is best to add the term "Ultimateless" on top of "Great Ultimate"? The "Great Appendix" to the *Changes* says, "The spiritual [efficacy of the sage] has no definite

---

18. *Odes* 55, which is cited in *Analects* 1.15.

19. *Mengzi* 2A8.

20. *Mengzi* 7A16.

21. Quoting an earlier letter, the fifth Zhu wrote to Lu, in which Zhu Xi responds to a prior letter from Lu. See *Da Lu Zijing Wu* 答陸子靜五 in *Zhuzi wenji*, p. 1440.

22. Ibid., p. 1441.

23. Ibid., p. 1441.

24. *Odes* 235.

place." How could anyone talk about the spiritual not existing at all? It goes on to say, "the changes [of the world] have no definitive form."[25] How could anyone talk about the changes not existing at all? Laozi taught that, "What does not exist is the beginning of Heaven and Earth; what exists is the mother of the myriad creatures." He also said that, "By cleaving always to what does not exist, one can contemplate their mystery; by cleaving always to what exists, one can contemplate their manifestations."[26] Simply by placing the character "not existing" before "ultimate," you have the philosophy of Laozi.[27] How can you deny this? It is only because Daoists are beclouded in this way [i.e., in believing in the primacy of what does not exist] that they have drifted into relying upon prognostication and magic in an attempt to ward off fear and superstition.

This Pattern, though, always has existed in the universe. How could anyone say that it does not? If there were no Pattern, then "rulers would not be rulers, ministers would not be ministers, fathers would not be fathers, and sons would not be sons."[28] Yang Zhu never espoused doing without a ruler, but Mengzi understood him as supporting this idea. Mozi never espoused doing without a father, but Mengzi understood him as supporting this idea.[29] This shows why Mengzi was one who "has knowledge of words."[30] The ultimate is none other than this Pattern. . . .

As for your explicit claim that *yin* and *yang* are forms and material things and cannot be regarded as the Way—this is even more difficult to accept![31] The *Changes* teaches that the Way is "the alternation of the *yin* and *yang*" and that is all.[32] As for preceding and following, beginning and ending, movement and stillness, darkness and light, above and below, advancing and retreating, going and coming, closing and opening, filling and emptying, waxing and waning,

---

25. *Changes,* "Great Appendix," I.4, in Part I, Selection 9.

26. *Daodejing* 1.

27. "Ultimateless" (*wújí* 無極) is literally a combination of "not existing/lacking" (*wú* 無) and "ultimate" (*jí* 極).

28. *Analects* 12.11. Lu's point is that without Pattern to serve as the ultimate moral standard, there could be no firm basis for such normative distinctions. The implication is that Zhu sides with the Daoists (and Buddhists) in seeing some conception of nothingness or emptiness as the ultimate ground of the phenomenal world. Lu correctly sees this as a dire threat to the foundations of Confucian ethics, as understood in his time.

29. On Yang Zhu and Mozi, see *Mengzi* 3B9, in Part III, Selection 35.

30. *Mengzi* 2A2.7, in Part III, Selection 35. [Lu's point is that, because Yang Zhu and Mozi failed to grasp the Pattern of righteousness and benevolence, their views were ultimately ungrounded, and hence equivalent to these extreme formulations.—Eds.]

31. Lu offers the gist of what Zhu Xi says in the letter that he has referred to throughout. See *Zhuzi wenji,* p. 1441. See above, note 11, on the difference between Zhu Xi's and Lu Xiang-shan's interpretation of the phrase "above with respect to form" from the "Great Append[i]" to the *Changes.*

32. *Changes,* "Great Appendix," I.5, in Part III, Selection 9.

honor and lowliness, nobility and baseness, exterior and interior, hidden and manifest, attracting and repelling, agreeing and opposing, preservation and annihilation, gaining and losing, going out and coming in, carrying things out and storing them away—how could these be anything other than the alternation of the *yin* and *yang*? . . .

The "Explanation of the Trigrams" says:

> Formerly, the sages made the *Changes* in the following manner: They wanted to be in accord with the Pattern of the nature [of things] and the mandate. For this reason, they established the Way of Heaven, which they called *yin* and *yang;* they established the Way of Earth, which they called soft and hard; and they established the Way of humans, which they called benevolence and righteousness.[33]

Part II of the "Great Appendix" elaborates further, saying:

> The *Changes* is broad, great, detailed, and comprehensive. In it, one finds the Way of Heaven. In it, one finds the Way of human beings. In it, one finds the Way of Earth. It embraces these three powers and doubles them, yielding six [lines in each hexagram]. The six lines are nothing other than the Way of the three powers.[34]

But your view is that the *yin* and the *yang* are not the Way, and you explicitly refer to them as "forms" and "material things." How can you lack such insight regarding the difference between the Way and material things? . . .

38. Wang Yangming, "Questions on the *Great Learning*"

translation by Philip J. Ivanhoe[35]

Wang Yangming (1472–1529) is one of the most fascinating Neo-Confucians. He was not only a very successful general and provincial governor, but also a philosophical "master," whose devoted disciples clung to his every word. Today, he is best remembered as one of the most brilliant and influential criti-   Zhu Xi, counted along with Lu Xiangshan as one of the founders of   ng School, or School of Mind.

ation of the Trigrams," 2, in Part I, Selection 9.

ppendix," II.10. Cf. "Explanation of the Trigrams," 2, in Part I, Selec-

Philip J. Ivanhoe, trans., *Readings from the Lu-Wang School of Neo-*
lis: Hackett Publishings, 2009). We have modified the original
sistency across selections in this volume. We are solely responsible
or errors.—Eds.

In his youth, Wang's intellectual loyalties were torn between Daoism and the Cheng-Zhu School of Confucianism. However, he movingly describes how he became disillusioned with Zhu Xi's approach. Wang and his friend Qian were debating the merits of thoroughly investigating the Pattern in everything as a tool for ethical cultivation, and Wang challenged his friend to investigate the Pattern of some bamboo in front of the nearby pavilion:

> *Day and night Qian went ahead trying to investigate to the utmost the Pattern in the bamboos. He exhausted his mind and thoughts and on the third day he was tired out and took sick. At first I said that it was because his energy and strength were insufficient. Therefore I myself went to try to investigate to the utmost. From morning till night, I was unable to find the Pattern of the bamboos. On the seventh day I also became sick because I thought too hard. In consequence we sighed to each other and said that it was impossible to be a sage or a worthy, for we do not have the tremendous energy to investigate things that they have.*[36]

Despite his uncertainties, Wang became active in public affairs and developed a distinguished reputation. However, he encountered a stunning reversal when he challenged the actions of a powerful court eunuch, who retaliated by having Wang publicly beaten (a punishment both humiliating and life-threatening) and assigning him to a menial position in a distant and primitive region. Facing deprivation and hardship, and isolated from intellectuals, Wang suddenly had an epiphany that revealed to him why he was never satisfied with the teachings of Zhu Xi. He later described his insight in a poem he wrote for his students:

> *Everyone has within an unerring compass;*
> *The root and source of the myriad transformations lies in the mind.*
> *I laugh when I think that, earlier, I saw things the other way around;*
> *Following branches and leaves, I searched outside!*[37]

Although Wang would become Zhu Xi's greatest critic, the two share many basic views. They both believe that human nature is fundamentally identical with the Pattern, that this Pattern links everything together into a potentially harmonious whole, and that human wrongdoing is the result of selfish thoughts and desires interfering with the proper functioning of the Pattern. Arguably, Wang's various criticisms of Zhu are ultimately grounded in two fundamental disagreements:

(1) Zhu Xi believed that it was possible to know the good but to fail to be properly motivated by it. As a result, he held that ethical cultivation is a

---

36. *Chuanxilu* 319. Translation modified from Wing-tsit Chan, trans., *Instructions for Practical Living and other Neo-Confucian Writings by Wang Yangming* (New York: Columbia University Press, 1962), p. 249.

37. Wang, "Four Verses on Pure Knowing Written for My Students," from Ivanhoe, *Readings from the Lu-Wang School of Neo-Confucianism,* p. 181.

*multi-step process that involves, first, coming to know the Pattern of things in the world, and then becoming practically motivated by that knowledge through achieving Sincerity. In contrast, according to Wang, there is a "unity of knowing and acting" (*zhī xíng hé yī 知行合一*). To know the good is to be motivated to act in accordance with it, and those who do not behave virtuously lack ethical knowledge. (2) Zhu Xi and Wang agree that humans are born with complete ethical knowledge. However, according to Zhu Xi, the* qi *of most people is so "turbid" that we are incapable of recognizing most of the Pattern on our own. We only catch fleeting glimpses of it, and must carefully study the classic texts, written by the sages, and follow the guidance of wise teachers to help us recover our underlying knowledge. Wang criticizes Zhu Xi's approach as overly scholastic, and likely to produce pedantic bookworms rather than active moral agents. Extensive study is unnecessary, Wang insists, because each human has the capacity at every moment to pierce the veil of selfishness and express their true moral nature. He adopts the phrase "pure knowing" from Mengzi to describe this capacity.*[38]* Consequently, Wang encourages learners to look for the answers in themselves, rather than relying on anything external. As he would dramatically put it in another of his poems: "The thousand sages are all passing shadows, / Pure knowing is my teacher!"*[39]

The following essay, "Questions on the Great Learning," *is an excellent introduction to Wang's thought. However, it can best be understood after reading Zhu's* Collected Commentaries *on the* Great Learning, *which is often the target of Wang's criticisms. Wang disagreed with Zhu over many aspects of the* Great Learning, *but especially over two key phrases: "getting a handle on things" and "extending knowledge." Zhu Xi held that the key to ethical cultivation is to "get a handle on things" in the sense of grasping the Pattern as manifested in the various texts, situations, and objects that one encounters. Grasping more and more of the Pattern, inferring from what one knows to what one does not know, is called "extending knowledge." In contrast, Wang argued that "getting a handle on things" is more like handling situations properly, "correcting" our own thoughts and the situations that those thoughts are about.*[40]* And because he believes that all humans have unmediated access to "pure knowing," Wang holds that "extending knowledge" is*

---

38. *Mengzi* 7A15, in Part III, Selection 35.

39. Wang, "On Longevity," from Ivanhoe, *Readings from the Lu-Wang School of Neo-Confucianism,* p. 184.

40. "Getting a handle on things" is *gé wù* (格物), which is more commonly translated "investigating things." However, the latter translation is biased in favor of Zhu Xi's interpretation. Consequently, in this volume we have used "getting a handle on things" to try to reflect the ambiguity in the original Chinese, which can be used to support either Zhu's or Wang's interpretation.—Eds.

more like extending one's arm (exercising a capacity one has) than it is like extending one's vocabulary.[41]

The text below is organized in terms of questions from a hypothetical interlocutor followed by Wang's answers. The questions proceed almost line-by-line through the Classic section and Commentary, chapter 6, of the Great Learning.[42]*—Eds.*

Introduction by Qian Dehong

Whenever my teacher accepted a new student, he would always rely upon the first chapters of the *Great Learning* and the *Mean* to show him the complete task of sagely learning and acquaint him with its proper path. I received and recorded the "Questions on the *Great Learning*" the night before the master set off to suppress a rebellion occurring in the area of Si'en and Tianzhou.[43]

* * *

1. [Question:] "A former scholar considered the *Great Learning* to be the learning appropriate for a great person. May I ask, how is it that the learning of such a great person lies in 'enlightening one's enlightened Virtue'?"[44]

[Master Yangming replied]: "Great people regard Heaven, Earth, and the myriad creatures as their own bodies.[45] They look upon the world as one family and China as one person within it. Those who, because of the space between their own physical form and those of others, regard themselves as separate [from Heaven, Earth, and the myriad creatures] are petty persons. The ability great people have to form one body with Heaven, Earth, and the myriad creatures is not something they intentionally strive to do; the benevolence of their minds is fundamentally like this. How could it be that only the minds of great people are one with Heaven, Earth, and the myriad creatures? Even the minds of petty people are like this. It is only the way in which such people look at things that makes them petty. This is why, when they see a child [about to] fall into a well,

---

41. I borrow this simile from David S. Nivison, "The Philosophy of Wang Yangming," in *The Ways of Confucianism* (Chicago: Open Court Publishing, 1996), p. 225.

42. Wang follows the original version of the *Great Learning* from the *Rites,* rather than Zhu Xi's rearranged and emended version, but we shall provide references to Zhu Xi's version for ease of cross-reference.

43. Si'en and Tianzhou were two prefectures in present-day Guangxi Province.

44. *Great Learning,* Classic, Verse 1, in Part III, Selection 33. [Wang and his questioner are here siding with the Han dynasty commentator Zheng Xuan (127–200) over Zhu Xi on the proper way to understand the word "great" in the phrase "Great Learning."—Eds.]

45. Literally, "Great people regard Heaven, Earth, and the myriad creatures as one Substance." Here and below, "body" is the word translated "Substance" elsewhere in this volume. On the Substance/Function distinction, see Zhu Xi, *Categorized Conversations,* in Part III, Selection 32.—Eds.

they cannot avoid having a mind of alarm and compassion for the child.[46] This is because their benevolence forms one body with the child. Someone might object that this response is because the child belongs to the same species. But when they hear the anguished cries or see the frightened appearance of birds or beasts, they cannot avoid a sense of being unable to bear it.[47] This is because their benevolence forms one body with birds and beasts. Someone might object that this response is because birds and beasts are sentient creatures. But when they see grass or trees uprooted and torn apart, they cannot avoid feeling a sense of sympathy and distress. This is because their benevolence forms one body with grass and trees.[48] Someone might object that this response is because grass and trees have life and vitality. But when they see tiles and stones broken and destroyed, they cannot avoid feeling a sense of concern and regret. This is because their benevolence forms one body with tiles and stones.

"This shows that the benevolence that forms one body [with Heaven, Earth, and the myriad creatures] is something that even the minds of petty people possess. Such a mind is rooted in the nature mandated by Heaven and is naturally luminous, shining, and not beclouded.[49] This is why it is called 'enlightened Virtue.' The minds of petty people have become cut off and constricted, and yet the benevolence that forms one body [with Heaven, Earth, and the myriad creatures] is able to be as unclouded as what Heaven originally endowed. This occurs in those times when they have not yet been moved by desires or obscured by selfishness. Once they have been moved by desires or obscured by selfishness, beset by thoughts of benefit and harm and stirred by feelings of indignation and anger, they will then attack other creatures, injure their own kind, and stop at nothing. At the extreme, they will even murder their own kin and wholly lose the benevolence that forms one body [with Heaven, Earth, and the myriad creatures]. And so, if only they are without the obscuration of selfish desires, even the minds of petty people will have the same benevolence that forms one body [with Heaven, Earth, and the myriad creatures] that great people possess. As soon as there is obscuration by selfish desires, then even the minds of great people will become cut off and constricted, just like those of petty people. This is why the learning of the great person indeed lies only in getting rid of the obscuration of selfish desires, thereby enlightening one's enlightened Virtue and

---

46. Paraphrasing the example of the child at the well from *Mengzi* 2A6, in Part III, Selection 35.

47. *Mengzi* 1A7 offers the example of King Xuan being "unable to bear" the anguished cries and frightened appearance of an ox being led to slaughter. Mengzi goes on to infer a general aversion to seeing any animal suffer. See Part III, Selection 35.

48. Cheng Hao reports that, "Zhou Dunyi would not remove the grass growing in front of his window. When asked about this he would say, 'I think of it as myself.'" *Er Cheng ji* 二程集, Vol. 1 (Beijing: Zhonghua shuju, 2004), p. 60.—Eds.

49. Paraphrasing *Mean* 1, in Part III, Selection 36.

知行合一

restoring the fundamental state of forming one body [with Heaven, Earth, and the myriad creatures]. It is not anything that can be added to this fundamental body."

2. [Question:] "In that case, why [does the learning of the great person] 'lie in loving the people'?"[50]

[Master Yangming] replied: "Enlightening one's enlightened Virtue is the Substance of forming one body with Heaven, Earth, and the myriad things. Loving the people universally extends the Function of forming one body with Heaven, Earth, and the myriad things.[51] And so, enlightening one's enlightened Virtue must find expression in loving the people, and loving the people simply is the way one enlightens one's enlightened Virtue. This is why it is only when I love my father, the fathers of other people, and the fathers of everyone in the world that my benevolence truly forms one body with my father, the fathers of other people, and the fathers of everyone in the world. It is only when I truly form one body with them that the enlightened Virtue of filial piety begins to be enlightened. It is only when I love my elder brother, the elder brothers of other people, and the elder brothers of everyone in the world that my benevolence truly forms one body with my elder brother, the elder brothers of other people, and the elder brothers of everyone in the world. It is only when I truly form one body with them that the enlightened Virtue of brotherly love begins to be enlightened. It is the same in regard to rulers and ministers, husbands and wives, and friends; it is the same in regard to mountains and rivers, ghosts and spirits, birds and beasts, and grass and trees. (It is only when I truly love them all and universally extend my benevolence that forms one body with them that my enlightened Virtue will be enlightened in every respect, and I can really form one body with Heaven, Earth, and the myriad things. This is what it means to 'enlighten the enlightened Virtue of the world.' This is what it means to regulate one's family, put one's state in order, and bring peace to the world. This is what it means to 'fathom one's nature.'"[52])

3. [Question:] "In that case, why [does the learning of the great person] 'lie in resting in the ultimate good'?"[53]

[Master Yangming] replied: "The ultimate good is the highest standard for enlightening one's enlightened Virtue and loving the people. The nature mandated by Heaven is the ultimate good in its purest state. To be luminous,

---

50. Wang and his interlocutor here follow the original phrasing of the *Great Learning* from the *Rites,* not Zhu Xi's emendation of this line. Contrast *Great Learning,* Classic, Verse 1, in Part III, Selection 33.

51. The point is that enlightening one's enlightened Virtue is the goal of moral cultivation itself—its body or Substance—while loving the people is the natural operation or Function of such a virtuous state.

52. *Great Learning,* Classic, Verses 4–5; *Mean* 22, in Part III, Selections 33 and 36.

53. *Great Learning,* Classic, Verse 1, in Part III, Selection 33.

shining, and not beclouded are manifestations of the ultimate good. This is the fundamental state of enlightened Virtue or what is called 'pure knowing.' When the ultimate good is manifested, whatever is good will appear as good and whatever is bad will appear as bad. We will respond to the weighty or the light, the substantial or the insubstantial as these affect us. Our changing postures and various actions will stick to no fixed principle, and yet none will fail to attain its Heavenly mean. This is the ultimate of what is 'constant' for human beings and the 'norm' for things.'[54] It admits neither the slightest deliberation or doubt nor the most miniscule addition or subtraction. If there is even the slightest deliberation or doubt or the most miniscule addition or subtraction, then this constitutes the petty cunning of selfish thought and is no longer the ultimate good. But of course, if one has not mastered being 'careful even when alone' and is not 'refined and unified,' then how could one have attained such a state?[55]

"It is only because the people of later ages don't understand that the ultimate good is within their own minds and instead use their selfish cunning to grope and search for it outside their own minds that they mistakenly believe that 'each affair and every thing has its own fixed Pattern.'[56] In this way, the proper standard for right and wrong becomes obscured; they [become preoccupied with] disconnected fragments and isolated shards, human desires run amok, and Heavenly Pattern is lost.[57] As a consequence, the learning of enlightening one's enlightened Virtue and loving the people is thrown into confusion and turmoil throughout the world. Now, in the past, there certainly were those who wanted to enlighten their enlightened Virtue throughout the world. Nevertheless, simply because they did not understand what it is to rest in the ultimate good and instead exerted their selfish minds toward the achievement of excessively lofty goals, they were lost in vagaries, illusions, emptiness, and stillness and had nothing to do with the family, state, or world. The followers of the Buddha and Laozi are like this. Now, in the past, there certainly were those who wanted to love the people. Nevertheless, simply because they did not understand what it is to rest in the ultimate good and instead dissipated their selfish minds in what is base and trifling, they were lost in calculation, scheming, cleverness, and techniques and had nothing to do with the Sincere expression of benevolence

---

54. Paraphrasing *Odes* 260, which in turn is quoted in *Mengzi* 6A6, in Part III, Selection 35.

55. Quoting *Great Learning,* Commentary 6, in Part III, Selection 33, and *Documents, Documents of Yu,* "Counsels of the Great Yu." The latter describes the difference between the wayward "human mind" and the ideal "mind of the Way."

56. Quoting Zhu Xi. See Zhu Xi, *Daxue huowen,* in *Zhuzi quanshu* (Shanghai: Shanghai guji chubanshe, 2002), vol. 6, p. 510.

57. Wang is here criticizing an encyclopedic, scholastic form of scholarship like that of Zhu Xi, arguing that it is not adequate for moral knowledge. For a discussion, see Philip J. Ivanhoe, *Ethics in the Confucian Tradition,* 2nd ed. (Indianapolis: Hackett Publishing, 2002), pp. 77–80.

or compassion. The followers of the Five Despots and those who pursue worldly success are like this.[58] All of these mistakes arise from failing to understand what it is to rest in the ultimate good. And so, resting in the ultimate good is related to enlightening one's enlightened Virtue and loving the people as the compass and square are related to what is round and square, as ruler and tape are related to long and short, and scale and balance are related to light and heavy. If what is round or square does not accord with the compass and square, it will deviate from its standard. If what is long or short does not accord with the ruler and tape, it will miss its measure. If what is light or heavy does not accord with the scale and balance, it will lose its balance. Those who [attempt to] enlighten their enlightened Virtue or love the people without resting in the ultimate good will lose the root. And so, resting in the ultimate good in order to enlighten one's enlightened Virtue and love the people—this is called the learning of the great person."

4. [Question:] "'When one knows the place to rest, only then is one settled. When one is settled, only then is one able to be tranquil. When one is tranquil, only then is one able to be at peace. When one is at peace, only then is one able to ponder. When one ponders, only then is one able to get it.'[59] What about these lines?"

[Master Yangming] replied: "It is only because people don't understand that the ultimate good is within their own minds that they search for it on the outside. They mistakenly believe that 'each affair and every thing has its own fixed Pattern,'[60] and so they search for the ultimate good within each affair and every thing. This is why they [become preoccupied with] disconnected fragments and isolated shards; confused and disheveled, they have no stable orientation. Now, once one understands that the ultimate good lies within one's own mind and does not depend upon anything outside, then one's intentions will have a 'settled' orientation and one no longer will suffer the misfortunes of being [preoccupied with] disconnected fragments and isolated shards and being confused and disheveled. Once one no longer suffers the misfortunes of being [preoccupied with] disconnected fragments and isolated shards and is no longer confused and disheveled, then one's mind will not engage in wanton activity and one will be able to be 'tranquil.' Once one's mind no longer engages in wanton activity and one is able to be tranquil, then one's mind will be relaxed and leisurely in its daily operation, and one will be able to be 'at peace.' Once one is able to be at peace, then whenever a thought arises or an affair affects one, one's 'pure knowing' will spontaneously inquire and explore as to whether or not this is the

---

58. The Five Despots were five particularly bad rulers from the *Spring and Autumn Period* (722–481 BCE). See *Mengzi* 6B7. Those who pursue "worldly success" want to achieve status and profit by any means. These two form a natural group of self-interested miscreants.

59. *Great Learning*, Classic, Verse 2, in Part III, Selection 33.

60. Quoting Zhu Xi; see the citation above, note 56.

ultimate good, and so, one will be able to 'ponder.' If one is able to ponder, then all one's decisions will be precise, all one's responses will be appropriate, and one can thereby 'get' the ultimate good."

5. [Question:] "'Things have their roots and their branches.'[61] A former scholar took 'enlightened Virtue' as the 'root' and 'renewing the people' as the 'branches'—seeing these as two separate things opposing each other as inner and outer. 'Situations have their endings and their beginnings.' The same former scholar took 'knowing the place to rest [i.e., the ultimate good]' as the 'beginning' and 'being able to get [the ultimate good]' as the 'ending'—seeing these as a single affair connected like head and tail. If we follow your explanation [of the text] and read 'renewing the people' as 'loving the people,' then isn't there a problem with this explanation of roots and branches?"[62]

[Master Yangming] replied: "This explanation of roots and branches in general is correct. If we read 'renewing the people' as 'loving the people' and say that 'enlightening one's enlightened Virtue' is the 'root' and 'loving the people' is the 'branch,' this explanation cannot be considered wrong. But we simply must not separate branch and root and regard them as two separate things. Now, the trunk of a tree can be regarded as its 'root' while the tips of the limbs can be regarded as its 'branches.' But it is only because the tree is a single thing that these can be called its 'roots' and 'branches.' If you say that the trunk and the tips of the limbs are separate things altogether, then how can you talk about these purportedly separate things as [related] 'roots' and 'branches?' The meaning of the phrase 'renewing the people' is different from the meaning of 'loving the people,' and so the work of enlightening one's enlightened Virtue naturally is seen as something distinct from 'renewing the people.' [But] if one understands that enlightening one's enlightened Virtue is loving the people and that loving the people is how one enlightens one's enlightened Virtue, then how could one separate enlightening one's enlightened Virtue and loving the people and regard them as two separate things? The real problem with this former scholar's explanation is that he did not understand that enlightening one's enlightened Virtue and loving the people are fundamentally a single affair, and so he came to regard them as two separate things. This is why, even though he understood that roots and branches should be seen as one thing, he could not avoid separating them into two things."

6. [Question:] "I see how the section of text that begins with 'The ancients who desired to enlighten the enlightened Virtue of the world . . .' and that runs through 'would first cultivate their selves' can be understood on your explana-

---

61. *Great Learning*, Classic, Verse 3, in Part III, Selection 33.

62. "A former scholar" here is a discreet way of referring to Zhu Xi. The original text of the *Great Learning*, Classic, Verse 1 has the phrase "loving the people" (*qīn mín* 親民), but Zhu Xi (following Cheng Yi) emends it to "renewing the people" (*xīn mín* 新民). Wang rejects this emendation.

tion of enlightening one's enlightened Virtue and loving the people. But may I ask about the sequence of spiritual training and manner in which one should put forth effort that is described in the section beginning with 'Those who desired to cultivate their selves' and that runs through 'extending knowledge lies in getting a handle on things?'"[63]

[Master Yangming] replied: "This section of the text offers a complete and detailed description of the effort needed to enlighten one's enlightened Virtue, love the people, and rest in the ultimate good. Now, we can say that 'self,' 'mind,' 'thoughts,' 'knowledge,' and 'things' describe the sequence of spiritual training. While each has its own place, in reality they are but a single thing. We can say that 'getting a handle,' 'extending,' 'making Sincere,' 'correcting,' and 'cultivating' describe the spiritual training used in the course of this sequence. While each has its own name, in reality they are but a single affair. What do we mean by 'self'? It is the way we refer to the physical operation of the mind. What do we mean by 'mind'? It is the way we refer to the luminous and intelligent master of the person. What do we mean by 'cultivating the self'? It is the way we refer to doing what is good and getting rid of what is bad. Is the physical self, on its own, able to do what is good and get rid of what is bad, or must the luminous and intelligent master of the person first want to do so and only then will one physically start to do what is good and get rid of what is bad? And so, those who want to cultivate themselves must first correct their minds.

"Now, the mind in its fundamental Substance is the nature. Since the nature is only good, the mind in its fundamental Substance is wholly correct. Why, then, must one make an effort to correct it? Since, as noted above, the fundamental Substance of the mind is wholly correct, it is only when thoughts and ideas begin to stir that there is that which is not correct. And so, those who wish to correct their minds must correct their thoughts and ideas. Whenever they have a good thought, they must really love it, 'like loving a lovely sight.' Whenever they have a bad thought, they must really hate it, 'like hating a hateful odor.'[64] Then, all of their thoughts will be Sincere and their minds can be rectified.

"However, one's thoughts give rise to what is bad as well as to what is good. If one does not have a way to make clear the difference between these two, the true and the deviant will become confused with each other and mixed together. Then, even those who wish to make their thoughts Sincere will be unable to do so. And so, those who wish to make their thoughts Sincere must 'extend their

---

63. *Great Learning*, Classic, Verse 4, in Part III, Selection 33. [In Ivanhoe's original translation, "getting a handle on things" is "rectifying one's thoughts (about things)." For more on this phase see the introduction to this selection. See Ivanhoe, *Ethics in the Confucian Tradition*, pp. 97–99, for a discussion of the different interpretations of Zhu Xi and Wang Yangming.—Eds.]

64. *Great Learning*, Commentary 6, in Part III, Selection 33.

knowledge.' To 'extend one's knowledge' (*zhi* 致) means to reach to the ultimate (*zhi* 至), like in the phrase, 'Mourning reaches to (*zhi* 致) the full extent (*zhi* 致) of grief.'[65] The *Changes* says, 'Reach to (*zhi* 至) the full extent (*zhi* 至) of what one knows.'[66] [In the latter passage,] 'the full extent of what one knows' is a matter of knowing. 'Reaching to the full extent' is extending to the ultimate. To fully extend one's knowledge is not like the so-called 'filling out' of what one knows that later scholars talk about.[67] It is simply to extend fully the 'pure knowing' of my own mind. Pure knowing is what Mengzi was talking about when he said that humans all have 'the mind of approval and disapproval.' The mind of approval and disapproval 'knows without pondering' and is 'capable without learning.'[68] This is why it is called 'pure knowing.' This is the nature mandated by Heaven, my mind in its fundamental Substance, which spontaneously is pure knowing, enlightened, and aware.

"Whenever a thought or idea arises, on its own, my pure knowing knows. Is it good? Only my pure knowing knows. Is it not good? Only my pure knowing knows. It never has a need to rely on other people's opinions. This is why even a petty person who has done bad things and would stop at nothing, still, 'when he sees a gentleman, he is evasive, hiding what is not good, and emphasizing his good points.'[69] This shows the degree to which their pure knowing will not allow people to hide from themselves. Those who want to distinguish the good from the bad in order to make their thoughts Sincere can only do so by extending to the ultimate the knowledge of pure knowing. Why is this? If, as a thought or idea arises, my pure knowing knows it is good, but I am not able to Sincerely love it, and I later turn my back upon it and cast it aside, then I take what is good as bad and obscure my own pure knowing, which knows the good. If, as a thought or idea arises, my pure knowing knows it is not good, but I am not able to Sincerely hate it, and I later follow and act upon it, then I take what is bad as good and obscure my own pure knowing, which knows what is bad. In such cases, though one says one knows, one still does not know. [Under such circumstances,] can one's thoughts be made Sincere? Now, if one Sincerely loves and hates what pure knowing [knows to be] good or bad, then one will not be deceiving one's own pure knowing, and one's thoughts can be made Sincere.

"Now, does the desire to extend one's pure knowing refer to something

---

65. Quoting *Analects* 19.14.

66. *Changes*, "Wenyan," commentary on the hexagram *Qian*. Here and with the prior quotation Wang attempts to bolster his interpretation by supplying glosses on key terms supported by passages from the classics. The words *zhi* 至 and *zhi* 致 are closely related, so he glosses them in terms of one another.

67. *Mengzi* 2A6, in Part III, Selection 35. Here, Wang is criticizing Zhu and his followers, who argued that one must augment and enlarge one's moral knowledge.

68. *Mengzi* 7A15, in Part III, Selection 35.

69. *Great Learning*, Commentary 6, in Part III, Selection 33.

shadowy and vague; does it imply remaining suspended in what is empty and incorporeal? [No!] It requires one to always be working at some concrete task or affair.[70] And so, extending one's knowledge must lie in getting a handle on things. A 'thing' is a task or affair. A thought always arises in regard to some affair or other. The affair that is the object of a thought is called a thing. To 'get a handle on' is to correct. It refers to correcting whatever is not correct and returning to what is correct. Correcting whatever is not correct means to get rid of what is bad. Returning to what is correct means to do what is good. This is what it means to 'get a handle on' something. For example, the *Documents* says, '[The good qualities of Emperor Yao] got a handle on [i.e., reached to] [Heaven] above and [Earth] below,' '[Emperor Shun's Virtue] got a handle on [i.e., reached to] the temple of the illustrious ancestors,' and '[The king's ministers] got a handle on [i.e., rectified] his errant mind.'[71] 'Got a handle on' in the expression 'getting a handle on things' combines these two meanings [i.e., 'to reach' and 'to rectify'].[72]

"Even though one Sincerely wishes to love the good known by pure knowing, if one doesn't actually do the good in regard to the thing about which one is thinking, then one has not yet gotten a handle on some aspect of this thing and the thought of loving it is not yet Sincere. Even though one Sincerely wishes to hate the bad known by pure knowing, if one doesn't actually get rid of the bad in regard to the thing about which one is thinking, then one has not yet gotten a handle on some aspect of this thing; the thought of hating it is not yet Sincere. Now, concerning the good that is known by one's pure knowing, if one actually does the good in regard to the thing about which one is thinking to the very utmost of one's ability and, concerning the bad that is known by one's pure knowing, if one actually gets rid of the bad in regard to the thing about which one is thinking to the very utmost of one's ability, then one will fully get a handle on things and what is known by one's pure knowing will not be diminished or obstructed in any way. [This knowledge] then can reach its ultimate extension. As a result, one's mind will be pleased with itself, happy and without any lingering regrets; the thoughts that arise in one's mind at last will be without a trace of self-deception and can be called Sincere. This is why it is said that 'only after one gets a handle on things does knowledge reach the ultimate.

---

70. Wang here alludes to a teaching first seen in *Mengzi* 2A2.6 (in Part III, Selection 35) but which Wang interprets in his own distinctive way. For a discussion of this issue, see Ivanhoe, *Ethics in the Confucian Tradition*, pp. 92–94, 100–101, 107–8.

71. Quoting, respectively, *Documents, Documents of Yu,* "Canon of Yao"; *Documents of Yu,* "Canon of Shun"; and *Documents of Zhou,* "Charge of Jiong." For the contexts, see Legge, *The Shoo King*, pp. 15, 41, and 585.

72. Wang wants to combine these two meanings in order to make clear that the thoughts of the mind that are to be rectified have objects outside the mind; the process is not simply inward-looking but is directed out to events and affairs in the world.

Only after knowledge has reached the ultimate do thoughts have Sincerity. Only after thoughts have Sincerity is the mind correct. Only after the mind is correct is the self cultivated.'[73]

"While one can say that there is an ordering of first and last in this sequence of spiritual training, the training itself is a unified whole that cannot be divided into any ordering of first and last. While this sequence of spiritual training cannot be divided into any ordering of first and last, only when every aspect of its practice is highly refined can one be sure that it will not be deficient in the slightest degree. This explanation of getting a handle, extending, making Sincere, and correcting helps us to understand the orthodox tradition of [the sage emperors] Yao and Shun and is the mental seal of Kongzi's approval."[74]

---

73. *Great Learning*, Classic, Verse 5, in Part III, Selection 33.

74. The language of this last line invokes terms and ideas of the Chan School, as seen in texts such as the *Platform Sutra* (Part II, Selection 16). The "orthodox tradition" of the Chan school was a mind-to-mind transmission "that does not lie in writing or words." It was affirmed through receipt of a "mental seal" between patriarchs, which in essence was the mind of the Buddha. Wang is saying that the true Confucian tradition is likewise a transmission of the mind.

Lu Xiangshan

39. Short Meditations and Poetry

translation by Philip J. Ivanhoe[1]

Lu Xiangshan offered a very different vision of Confucian ethical cultivation from that of Zhu Xi.[2] Whereas Zhu Xi emphasized the importance of

Lu Xiangshan.

intense scholarly effort to discover the Pattern of things, especially as revealed in the Four Books, Lu argued that humans have an innate ability to know right and wrong, and simply must decide to exercise this ability in order to become Virtuous. This approach led Lu to deemphasize the importance of the written word. He famously said, "The Six Classics are all one's footnotes!" Consequently, he would no doubt be immensely pleased that we have included only a handful of his brief reflections, sayings, correspondence, and poetry in this anthology. He would invite us, though, to honestly seek the right Way to live in our own minds, and follow the answer we find there. —Eds.

1. Reflect and Get It[3]

Righteousness and Pattern are in the minds of human beings. As a matter of fact, these are what Heaven has endowed us with, and

---

1. This and all later translations from Lu Xiangshan are based on Philip J. Ivanhoe, trans., *Readings from the Lu-Wang School of Neo-Confucianism* (Indianapolis: Hackett Publishing, 2009). We have modified the translation to match the conventions of this volume. We are solely responsible for any resulting errors or infelicities.—Eds.

2. See the Editors' Introduction to Lu Xiangshan, "Correspondence on the Great Ultimate," in Part III, Selection 37, for an overview of Lu and his differences from Zhu Xi.—Eds.

3. This is a meditation on *Mengzi* 6A15 (in Part III, Selection 35): "The purpose of the mind is to reflect. If it reflects, then it will get it." (The "it" is the Pattern in one's mind.)—Eds.

they can never be effaced or eliminated [from our minds]. If one becomes obsessed with [desires for] things and reaches the point where one violates Pattern and transgresses righteousness, usually this is simply because one fails to reflect upon these things [i.e., the righteousness and Pattern that lie within one]. If one truly is able to turn back and reflect upon these things, then what is right and wrong and what one should cleave to and what one should subtly reject will begin to stir, separate, become clear, and leave one resolute and without doubts.

2. Seek It and You Will Get It[4]

Pure knowing lies within human beings;[5] although some people become mired in dissolution, pure knowing still remains undiminished and enduring [within them]. Such [dissolution] is what leads the most foolish and undistinguished people to cut themselves off from contact with the benevolent and cultivated and in extreme cases to "throw themselves away" and fail to seek after it.[6] Truly, if they can turn back and seek after it, then, without needing to make a concerted effort, what is right and wrong, what is fine and foul, will become exceedingly clear, and they will decide for themselves what to like and dislike, what to pursue and what to abandon. They will turn away from the things that the foolish and undistinguished do and turn toward the affairs of the benevolent and cultivated "like a mighty river overflowing its banks and flooding forth to the sea. Who could stand in their way?"[7] This requires nothing more [than to turn back and seek within]; what one seeks is within oneself; there has never been anyone who sought for it but failed to get it. "Seek it and you will get it"—this is Mengzi's teaching.

3. Written at Goose Lake to Rhyme with My Brother's Verse[8]

Old graves inspire grief, ancestral temples reverence.
This is the human mind, never effaced throughout the ages.
Water flowing from a brook accumulates into a vast sea;

---

4. This is a meditation on lines that Mengzi quotes in *Mengzi* 6A6 (in Part III, Selection 35) and 7A3: "Seek it and you will get it. Abandon it and you will lose it." (What is to be sought and gotten is the Pattern in the mind.)

5. Pure knowing (*liáng zhī* 良知) is a term of art, taken from *Mengzi* 7A15, in Part III, Selection 35. It refers to an innate, fully formed, and perfect moral faculty, an unerring sense of right and wrong, which when sincerely followed comes with sufficient motivation to propel one to action. This is a critical term in Wang Yangming's philosophy as well.

6. "Throw themselves away" is an expression from *Mengzi* 4A10, in Part III, Selection 35. The "it" they fail to seek is the mind, which is the source of pure knowing.

7. *Mengzi* 7A16. In the original, the quotation was used to describe Emperor Shun.

8. This poem was written on the occasion of the famous meeting Lu and his brother had with Zhu Xi, and is intended as a critique of Zhu Xi's method of cultivation. The poem subtly makes reference to several Confucian classics, including the *Analects, Changes,* and *Mean.*

Fist-sized stones form into the towering peaks of Mount Tai and Hua.
Easy and simple spiritual practice, in the end, proves great and long lasting.
Fragmented and disconnected endeavors leave one drifting and bobbing
   aimlessly.
You want to know how to rise from the lower to the higher realms?
First you must—this very moment—distinguish true from false!

40. Recorded Sayings

translation by Philip J. Ivanhoe

1. "There is no affair outside the Way; there is no Way outside affairs." The master often spoke these lines.

2. The Pattern of the Way simply is right in front of your eyes. Even those who perceive the Pattern of the Way and dwell in the realm of the sages see only the Pattern of the Way that is right in front of your eyes.

3. The *Analects* contains many passages for which we lack the full context, so it is hard to get a handle on them. For example, there are passages such as "if one's wisdom reaches it, and one's benevolence is able to preserve it . . ."[9] We don't know what it is that wisdom reaches and benevolence preserves. Or, for example, in the passage, "To learn and continually practice it," we don't know what it is that we are supposed to continually practice.[10] If one's study lacks a fundamental root or basis, then such passages are not easy to read. If one's study has a fundamental root or basis, then one will know that what "wisdom reaches" is *this*, what "benevolence preserves" is *this*, what one is to "continually practice" is *this*, what one delights in is *this*, and what one takes joy in is *this* [fundamental root or basis]. Like water pouring off a high roof: if one understands the fundamental root or basis, the Six Classics are all one's footnotes![11]

4. The teaching about the [distinction between] "Heavenly Pattern" and "human desires" obviously is not the most elevated of views. If Pattern is the Heavenly and desires are the human, then this denies the identity of the Heavenly and the human. For the most part, this teaching can be traced to Laozi. The "Record of Music" chapter of the *Rites* says:

> Human beings are still and quiet at birth; this is their Heavenly nature. When influenced by things, they begin to stir; these movements are the desires of [our] nature. When we come into contact with things, our consciousness becomes aware of them; as a result, likes and dislikes take shape. . . . When

---

9. *Analects* 15.33, in Part III, Selection 34.

10. *Analects* 1.1, in Part III, Selection 34.

11. The line about water off a high roof is taken from the *Documents, Documents of Yu,* "Yi and Ji."

[this process reaches the point where] one is unable to reflect upon oneself, Heavenly nature is obliterated.

For the most part, the teaching about the "Heavenly Pattern" and "human desires" is derived from this passage, and these words in the "Record of Music" are rooted in Laozi's teachings.

Furthermore, to claim that stillness alone is Heavenly nature—does this imply that movement is *not* an expression of Heavenly nature? The *Documents* says, "The human mind is precarious. The mind of the Way is subtle."[12] Many commentators understand the "human mind" to mean human desires and the "mind of the Way" to mean Heavenly Pattern.[13] But this is wrong. There is only one mind. How could human beings have two minds? If one speaks from the perspective of human beings, then one says that it is "precarious." If one speaks from the perspective of the Way, then one says that it is "subtle." A lack of reflection leads to wildness; an ability for careful reflection leads to sagehood. Is this not precarious! It is without sound or scent, without form or embodiment.[14] Is this not subtle! If we draw upon the *Zhuangzi*, we find, "Minute and insignificant, they join in with human beings! Immense and great, alone they roam within Heaven!"[15] The *Zhuangzi* also says, "The Way of Heaven and the Way of human beings are far apart from one another!"[16] This clearly is to split and divide the Heavenly and the human into two separate things.

41. "Letter to Zeng Zhaizhi"[17]

translation by Philip J. Ivanhoe

. . . Your affliction, my friend, is simply that you do not understand this Pattern; you have no master within. So whenever you encounter some frivolous theory or vague view, your only recourse is to rely on some idea you picked up from someone else to serve as your master. [In doing so,] the endowment that Heaven has granted to you becomes a guest and the positions of master and guest are inverted. You become lost and cannot find your way back, confused and unable to sort things out. These simple and clear Patterns can be taught to women and young children, but they are lost on and confound dedicated scholars who devise and in turn become wrapped up within their own irrelevant theories. They

---

12. *Documents*, *Documents of Yu*, "Counsels of the Great Yu."

13. This is a criticism of the views of Zhu Xi and his followers.

14. *Odes* 235.

15. Paraphrasing *Zhuangzi* 5.

16. Paraphrasing *Zhuangzi* 11.

17. Zeng Zhaizhi was a disciple of Zhu Xi, but one who also studied with Lu Xiangshan.

spend their years and end their days without ever attaining any grand insight. Are they not profoundly pathetic?

Had you been born in the orderly and flourishing age of antiquity and received the nurturing influence of the former sage-kings, you certainly would not suffer from this affliction. Even dedicated scholars will suffer from this kind of misfortune and harm if born in a later age, when true learning is cut off, the Way has declined, and [the world] is filled and overflowing with heterodox doctrines and perverse theories, which spread and block up [the Way]. They will sink into the same depraved state as ordinary men who indulge their feelings and follow every desire. Is this not using the pursuit of learning to slaughter the world?

Those in later ages who talk about the *Changes* take its teachings to be supremely mysterious and profound. Students dare not speak lightly about what it says. And yet, when Kongzi commented upon the *Changes*, he said:

> Through ease, *Qian* understands; through simplicity, *Kun* gains ability.[18] Those who attain the ease of *Qian* are easy to understand. Those who attain the simplicity of *Kun* are easy to follow. Those who are easy to understand win the favor of adherents. Those who are easy to follow achieve success. Those who win the favor of adherents long endure. Those who achieve success are great. To long endure is the Virtue of the worthy. To be great is the legacy of the worthy. Those who attain ease and simplicity grasp the Pattern of Heaven and Earth.[19]

Mengzi said, "The great Way is like a wide road. Is it difficult to understand?"[20] Kongzi said, "Is benevolence far away? If I desire benevolence, *this alone* will bring benevolence."[21] Kongzi also said, "To overcome the self and turn to ritual is the practice of benevolence. If for one day one could overcome the self and turn to ritual, the whole world would turn to benevolence."[22] He also said, "He was not thinking of her; [had he thought of her,] what distance would there have been between them?"[23] Mengzi once said, "The Way is nearby but is sought in things far away; one's task lies in what is simple but is sought in what is difficult."[24] He also said:

---

18. *Qian* and *Kun* are the first two of the sixty-four hexagrams. *Qian* represents pure *yang,* while *Kun* represents pure *yin,* and thus they are often treated as the fundamental forces of the cosmos.

19. *Changes,* "Great Appendix," I.1, in Part I, Selection 9.

20. *Mengzi* 6B2.

21. *Analects* 7.30.

22. *Analects* 12.1, in Part III, Selection 34.

23. *Analects* 9.30. Kongzi here is commenting on the male and female subjects of a line of poetry.

24. *Mengzi* 4A12.

The Way of Yao and Shun is nothing more than filial piety and respect for elder brothers. To walk sedately behind one's elders shows respect for elder brothers; to walk in an agitated fashion preceding one's elders fails to show such respect. Is walking sedately something people *cannot* do? No, it is something they simply *do not* do.[25]

He also said, "If people can fill out the mind that does not desire to harm others, their benevolence will be inexhaustible. If people can fill out the mind that will not trespass, their righteousness will be inexhaustible."[26] He also said, "To have these four beginnings [of Virtue] but to say of oneself that one is unable [to be virtuous] is to steal from oneself. To say that one's ruler is unable is to steal from one's ruler."[27] Mengzi also said, "Those who say, 'I myself am unable to dwell in benevolence and follow righteousness' are those whom I mean by 'those who throw themselves away.'"[28] For the most part, the words of the ancient sages and worthies all tally and accord with one another.

In general, the mind is one and Pattern is one. "In the final analysis these form a unity; in their essence, they are one."[29] This mind and this Pattern actually do not admit any duality. This is why Kongzi said, "My Way is bound together with one thing."[30] Mengzi said, "The Way is one, and only one."[31] He also said, "There are only two Ways: benevolence and lack of benevolence."[32] "Benevolence" is none other than this mind and this Pattern. When Mengzi says, "seek it and you will get it,"[33] what you "will get" is this Pattern. When he talks about "those who are first to understand," what they "understand" is this mind. When he talks about "those who are first to awaken," what they awaken to is this Pattern.[34] When he talks about how all young children "know to love their parents," it is this Pattern.[35] When he talks about how, as they grow, they all know "know to revere their elder brothers," it is this Pattern. When he claims that if "someone suddenly saw a child about to fall into a well, anyone would

---

25. *Mengzi* 6B2. Lu moves the last line of the original to the front of the passage, as it appears here.

26. *Mengzi* 7B31, in Part III, Selection 35.

27. *Mengzi* 2A6, in Part III, Selection 35.

28. *Mengzi* 4A10, in Part III, Selection 35.

29. Lu is quoting the Tang dynasty emperor Xuan Zong's (r. 712–56) preface to the *Classic of Filial Piety*.

30. *Analects* 4.15, in Part III, Selection 34.

31. *Mengzi* 3A1, in Part III, Selection 35.

32. *Mengzi* 4A2.

33. *Mengzi* 6A6, in Part III, Selection 35, and 7A3.

34. *Mengzi* 5A7.

35. This and the following sentence are quoting *Mengzi* 7A15, in Part III, Selection 35.

have a mind of alarm and compassion," it is this Pattern.[36] The reason that we are ashamed of shameful things and despise what is despicable is this Pattern. The reason we approve of what is right and disapprove of what is wrong is this Pattern. The reason we yield when it is proper to yield and defer when it is proper to defer is this Pattern. Reverence is this Pattern; righteousness also is this Pattern. What is inside is this Pattern; what is outside also is this Pattern.[37] This is why the *Changes* says, "Being straight and square, he is great. Then without practice, he attains advantage everywhere."[38] Mengzi says, "That which people are capable of without learning is their pure capability. That which they know without pondering is their pure knowing."[39] "This is something Heaven has given us."[40] "We inherently have them"; they "are not welded to us externally."[41] This is why he said, "The myriad things are all complete within us. There is no greater joy than to examine oneself and discover Sincerity!"[42] This is our "fundamental mind."[43] This is what he calls our "peaceful abode" and "proper path."[44] This is what he calls our "spacious residence," "proper place," and "great path."[45] The ancients personally attained this [mind and Pattern] and so possessed the real thing itself.[46] When they spoke about Pattern it was Pattern in itself. When they talked about affairs it was actual affairs. Their Virtue was substantial virtue; their actions were concrete acts. . . .

42. "Letter to Wang Shunbo"

translation by Philip J. Ivanhoe

Lu Xiangshan offers an extended Neo-Confucian critique of Buddhism in this important correspondence with Wáng Shùnbó 王順伯. Major themes

---

36. *Mengzi* 2A6, in Part III, Selection 35.

37. The references to "reverence," "righteousness," "what is inside," and "what is outside" in the previous lines draw upon the *Changes,* "Wenyan," commentary on the hexagram Kun.

38. *Changes,* second line statement on hexagram 2, Kun.

39. *Mengzi* 7A15, in Part III, Selection 35.

40. *Mengzi* 6A15, in Part III, Selection 35.

41. *Mengzi* 6A6, in Part III, Selection 35.

42. *Mengzi* 7A4, in Part III, Selection 35.

43. *Mengzi* 6A10.

44. *Mengzi* 4A10, in Part III, Selection 35.

45. All three terms are found in *Mengzi* 3B2.

46. The idea is that the ancients were not dealing with speculative theories, hypothetical accounts, or semblances of principles. They dealt exclusively in real events and robust virtues.

that emerge include (1) his proposal that Buddhists practitioners are essentially motivated by self-interest or personal profit, insofar as their ultimate concern is personal salvation, and (2) his contention that Buddhist teachings require practitioners to deny their humanity, which is for most people a hopeless task. —Eds.

Generally speaking, within schools of learning there are teachings and there are the actual forms of life. . . . In the past, those who had a teaching were grounded in the corresponding form of life. In later times, those who sought the form of life had to depend on the corresponding teaching. And so, whenever students seek some form of life, they must first practice the corresponding teaching. But even once people have begun to practice a teaching, there are some who succeed and some who do not. Some succeed in living the actual form of life and some succeed only in getting the teaching and fail to live the actual form of life. Within a given teaching, there are distinctions between what is shallow and profound, subtle and crude, partial and complete, and pure and adulterated. Such distinctions also are found within the actual practice of a form of life. All of the differences described above are found within every school and noted by those within the schools themselves. If we consider the mutual criticisms that members of the three schools level at one another concerning their differences and similarities—what they grasp and what they miss, what they are right about and what they are wrong about—and if we explore the distinctions between what is shallow and profound, subtle and crude, partial and complete, and pure and adulterated in regard to what each school succeeds or fails at in terms of both their teaching and actual form of life, we cannot determine whether every school does equally well or if any one is the best.

In your last two letters to my elder brother, your overall point was that Confucianism and Buddhism were the same, and that if we compare them point by point, we will find that they are, as they say, "equal in every regard." But I have used the two words "righteousness" and "profit" to differentiate Confucianism from Buddhism. I have also used the words "public-mindedness" and "selfishness," but what I really have in mind is righteousness and profit.

When Confucians consider the life that human beings live between Heaven and Earth, they say that we are the most intelligent and valuable of all the myriad creatures and along with Heaven and Earth are one of the "three ultimates."[47] For Heaven, there is the Way of Heaven; for Earth, there is the Way of Earth; for human beings, there is the Way of humanity. If humans fail to fully instantiate the Way of humanity, then they cannot stand together alongside Heaven and Earth. Humans have five senses and each has its particular task. From these arise the distinctions between right and wrong, success and failure. From these arise teaching and learning. This is the foundation upon which Confucian

---

47. *Changes,* "Great Appendix," I.2, in Part I, Selection 9.

teachings have been established, and why I say they concern what is righteous and public-minded.

When Buddhists consider the life human beings live between Heaven and Earth, they say that there is a [cycle of] birth and death, transmigration and rebirth, and suffering and affliction. They regard life as extremely painful and seek a way to avoid it. According to them, those who have attained the Way and achieved enlightenment realize that fundamentally there is no birth and death, transmigration and rebirth, or suffering and affliction. This is why their teachings claim [the cycle of] "birth and death is a great affair." The so-called resolution to become a bodhisattva, to which you refer, only concerns this one great affair.[48] This is the foundation upon which Buddhist teachings have been established, and why I say they concern what is profitable and selfish.

Because [Confucians] are concerned only with righteousness and the public [good], they seek to put the world into good order. Because [Buddhists] are concerned only with profit and selfish [good], they seek to flee the world [completely].[49] Although Confucian [teachings] talk about "what is without sound or scent" and has "no definitive place" and "no definitive form," their guiding aim always is to put the world into good order.[50] Although Buddhist [teachings] talk about saving all sentient creatures, even those yet to be born, their guiding aim always is to flee the world [completely].

Now those who practice the Way of the Buddha are all human beings. Since they are human beings, how can they completely cast off the benevolence and righteousness that we Confucians [advocate]? Even though they leave their families, they still advocate practicing the four kindnesses.[51] In their everyday lives, Pattern remains rooted in their minds and cannot be eradicated or erased. They clearly preserve it, at least in certain respects. Nevertheless, their teachings were not developed with the aim of preserving it. And so, whether or not it is preserved is of no importance to those who are far advanced in the earnest practice of their Way.

As for us Confucians, we say, "That whereby human beings are distinguished from [other] animals is subtle and minute. The common people abandon it, while the cultivated person preserves it."[52] Buddhists are concerned with not yet being free from transmigration and rebirth and the endless cycle of birth

---

48. On the "great affair," see the *Platform Sutra*, §4, in Part II, Selection 16. On the notion of a bodhisattva, see the Introduction to Part II.

49. That is to say, they seek a path that leads out of cyclic existence altogether.

50. *Odes* 235; *Changes*, "Great Appendix," I.4, in Part I, Selection 9.

51. To "leave one's family" is to take up the religious life as a monk or nun. The four kindnesses are good acts that all laymen should practice toward their fathers and mothers, their rulers, all sentient creatures, and the "three treasures"—the Buddha, the *dharma*, and the *sangha* (the community of monks and nuns).

52. *Mengzi* 4B19.

and death, which they call "floating and sinking in the sea of birth and death." But how could our sages and worthies remain "floating and sinking in the sea of birth and death?" Our sages and worthies do not suffer from what the Buddhists are concerned about. As a result, their teachings were not developed with the goal of avoiding such things, and these topics are not the guiding aim of what they say.

And so, our sages and worthies do not suffer from what the Buddhists are concerned about, but the sages and worthies of Buddhism do suffer from what we Confucians are worried about [i.e., not working to put the world into good order]. If one were to hold Buddhist sages and worthies to the standard one finds in the *Spring and Autumn Annals,* even children know they could not avoid blame. If one looks at them in terms of what their teachings were developed to address, then the difference between Confucianism and Buddhism is the difference between the public-minded and selfish and between righteousness and profit, respectively. They are distinct from each other and mutually exclusive; one cannot say they are the same. . . .

Wang Yangming

43. *A Record for Practice*

translation by Philip J. Ivanhoe[1]

A Record for Practice, an anthology of Wang's sayings and dialogues with his disciples, is a fascinating and wide-ranging work.[2] It is particularly  *helpful in illuminating his most famous and influential teaching, the unity of knowing and acting (zhī xíng hé yī 知行合一),[3] and pointing toward his ultimate ideal of regarding Heaven, earth, and the myriad creatures as one body (tiān dì wàn wù wéi yì tǐ 天地萬物為一體).[4] Wang believed that all human beings are endowed with a complete repertoire of the Pattern, which enables them to understand how things are and should be in the world. The mind of human beings is Pattern in its knowing, conscious mode, and by bringing the Pattern of the mind into play we can understand the world around us as well as our proper place within it. However, human beings are embodied creatures, and the various types of* qi *that constitute our physical forms interfere with the Pattern of our minds and lead us to mistakenly see ourselves as separate and cut off from the myriad Patterns that inform, structure, and give meaning to the rest of the world. This inclines us to*

Wang Yangming.

---

1. Translation based on Philip J. Ivanhoe, trans., *Readings from the Lu-Wang School of Neo-Confucianism* (Indianapolis: Hackett Publishing, 2009). We have modified the original translation to conform to the translation conventions of this volume. Any resulting infelicities or errors are our responsibility. The section numbers below correspond to those in ͻriginal version, for those who would like to compare the two.—Eds.

2. For a brief overview of Wang's life and philosophy, see the introductioᴰ ming, "Questions on the *Great Learning*," in Part III, Selection 38.

3. Since Wang often describes knowledge and action in terms of the (and acting, I translate his doctrine as "the unity of knowing and acting" common "unity of knowledge and action." For a discussion, see Ivanͻ *cian Tradition*, 2nd ed. (Indianapolis: Hackett Publishing, 2002),

4. "Body" here is the same word rendered "Substance" elsewheͻ

be overly self-centered, which generates selfish desires; these mislead us into acting badly, thereby reinforcing and intensifying our sense of isolation and alienation. In order to overcome these pernicious tendencies, we must learn to "rectify our minds" by "extending pure knowing" as we interact with and act in the world each day. Rather than thinking about ethics, *we are to* think ethically *about everything we do. Wang thought that even hardened criminals could hear and heed the guidance of pure knowing; the challenge was to pay attention and to cultivate a vigilant awareness of the promptings of one's own mind. "Even robbers and thieves know that they should not steal. When they steal, they still feel shame within them."*[5]

Once we begin to cultivate the required awareness and attentiveness, our pure knowing will start to inform and guide us. This process will move us from what Wang called "ordinary knowledge" (cháng zhī 常知) *to "real knowledge"* (zhēn zhī 真知). *Roughly speaking, we will move from knowing about ethics to ethical knowledge. The latter is substantially constituted by a strong disposition to attend and respond affectively to ethical situations and act properly and without hesitation. This is the crux of Wang's teaching of the "unity of knowing and acting." There is no real moral knowledge that does not lead one to act; one cannot really possess moral knowledge if one has not properly engaged in moral activity.*

Wang deployed his teaching about the unity of knowing and acting to make a variety of different points, and this wide and varied use of a doctrine to effect moral improvement in students is a clear example of Wang's emphasis on therapy over theory. Wang's ultimate goal—one might say his ideal of spiritual health—was overcoming the sense of isolation and alienation, which is the shadow of a self-centered view of one's relationship to the world. The unity of knowing and acting played a subtle but vital role in effecting a cure for the malady of an excessive concern for the self. The more readily and regularly one's actions flowed spontaneously out of pure knowing, the less distance and separation one felt between the self and the world. The operation of pure knowing leads to hooking oneself up with the world; one responds to it in a seamless process of perception, weighing, judging, willing, and acting. In the course of this process, one comes to see that the Patterns of one's mind are the Patterns that one encounters everywhere in the world. One comes to realize the truth of what Lu Xiangshan said: "The universe is my mind. My mind is the universe."

Wang, though, expressed Lu's earlier idea in his own distinctive fashion, proclaiming that we should "regard Heaven, earth, and the myriad creatures

---

[5]. The quotation (my translation) is from a portion of *A Record for Practice* not in this volume. ...are Wing-tsit Chan, *Instructions for Practical Living* (New York: Columbia University ...p. 194.

as our own bodies."[6] *Here again, it is easy to misconstrue what Wang is saying. He is not claiming that we are physically coextensive with all the things of the world. Rather, he is invoking the notion that there is a deep and undeniable connection between each of us and every aspect of reality. We are "one" in the sense of sharing a common Pattern, which links us and leads us to care, in varying ways and degrees, about the world. It is not that the world would not exist without the human mind, but rather that it would not be what it is without the shared interaction between it and human beings.*

For Wang, the teaching that we are one body with the myriad creatures was not just true but of ultimate significance; realizing this state defined and constituted the goal of his spiritual practice. Those who really understand, who themselves embody this fact about the world, will feel and act accordingly. Knowing and acting will form a unity and lead them to care in the right ways, to the right degree, and for the right reasons for everything in the universe. — Tr.

Xu Ai's Preface

Among the disciples was one who, on his own, had written down Master Wang's teachings. Hearing of this, the Master said, "Sages and worthies teach in the same way that physicians prescribe medicine.[7] They always match the treatment to the ailment, taking into consideration the various symptoms and, whenever appropriate, adjusting the dosage. Their sole aim is to eliminate the ailment. They have no predetermined course of action. Were they indiscriminately to stick to a single course [of treatment], rarely would they avoid killing their patients. Now, with you gentlemen, I do nothing more than diagnose and polish away each of your particular prejudices or obsessions. As soon as you manage to make these changes, my words become nothing but useless tumors. If, subsequently, you preserve my words and regard them as dogma, you will one day mislead yourselves and others. Could I ever atone for such an offense?"

Since I had carefully written down some of the Master's teachings, one of my fellow students remonstrated with me. I then said to him, "In taking your position, you are indiscriminately sticking to a single course and have lost the Master's meaning. Kongzi once said to Zigong, 'I prefer not talking.'[8] Yet on another day, he said, 'I have talked with Yan Hui all day long.'[9] Now, why wasn't he consistent in what he said? Since Zigong sought sageliness only in words, Kongzi used 'not talking' as a warning to him, to help him feel for it with

---

6. See Wang Yangming, "Questions on the *Great Learning*," in Part III, Selection 38. For a discussion of this teaching, see Ivanhoe, *Ethics in the Confucian Tradition*, pp. 27–30.

7. Compare the example of this metaphor in Wang Yangming, Miscellaneous Writings, "Letter to Liu Yuandao," in Part III, Selection 44.

8. *Analects* 17.17.

9. *Analects* 2.9.

his mind and seek a personal attainment. Yan Hui listened in silence to what Kongzi said, and in his mind he understood.[10] In him, there was nothing lacking. Therefore, Kongzi talked to him all day long—like a river bursting its banks and rushing to the sea. Thus, Kongzi's not talking to Zigong was not [speaking] too little, and his talking to Yan Hui all day long was not [speaking] too much. Each received what was appropriate to him." In our present situation, writing down what the Master says, as I have done, is surely contrary to his wishes. Since we disciples continue to enjoy his company, what possible purpose could this serve? However, on some occasions we must be away from the Master's side, and at some point we all must live apart from the group. At such times, the Master's inspiring example is far away, and we are unable to receive his admonitions. If one of limited abilities, such as I, did not receive the Master's teachings and was unable, regularly, to receive his admonitions and instructions, it would be rare indeed if one were not overcome [by the task] and lost.

Regarding the Master's teachings, if we disciples only let them "enter our ears and pass out our mouths"[11] and do not ourselves personally embody these teachings, then in writing them down I have indeed committed a crime against our teacher. However, if from this record we can grasp the general idea of his teachings and Sincerely realize them in concrete action, then this record is truly the mind of the Master, which can "talk [to us] all day long."[12] Can one do without any part of it? Having completed my record, I wrote this down as a preface to the first section in order to make [my intention] clear to my fellow students.[13]

3. I asked, "If one seeks for the ultimate good only in the mind, I fear that one will not fully grasp the Patterns of all the world's affairs."

The Master said, "The mind *is* Pattern. Is there any affair outside the mind? Is there any Pattern outside the mind?"

I said, "For example, in the filial piety with which one serves one's parents, the conscientiousness with which one serves one's ruler, the faithfulness with which one interacts with one's friends, or the benevolence with which one governs the people—in each of these [activities], there are many Patterns. I fear that all of them must be carefully investigated."

The Master sighed and said, "This way of explaining things has impeded understanding for a long, long time. How can I bring forth enlightenment with just a single word? Suppose, though, that I talk about it along the lines of the

---

10. *Analects* 7.2.

11. *Xunzi* 1. See Eric Hutton, trans., *Xunzi*, "An Exhortation to Learning," in Philip J. Ivanhoe and Bryan W. Van Norden, eds., *Readings in Classical Chinese Philosophy*, 2nd ed. (Indianapolis: Hackett Publishing, 2005), p. 257.

12. *Analects* 2.9.

13. This concludes Xu Ai's preface to *A Record for Practice*. What follows are excerpts from the *Record* itself, beginning with section 3 of the complete text.—Eds.

question you asked. For example, in serving one's parents, it will not do to go and seek the Pattern of filial piety in one's parents. In serving one's ruler, it will not do to go and seek the Pattern of conscientiousness in one's ruler. In one's interactions with one's friends or in governing the people, it will not do to seek the Pattern of faithfulness or benevolence in one's friends or in the people. All of these [Patterns] are only found here in 'this mind.'[14] The mind is Pattern. When this mind is kept completely free of the slightest impediment from selfish desire, then it is Heavenly Pattern. There is no need to add anything from outside. When the pure Heavenly Pattern of the mind is applied in serving one's parents, it is filial piety. When it is applied in serving one's lord, it is conscientiousness. When it is applied in interactions with one's friends or in governing the people, it is faithfulness or benevolence, respectively. The only thing one needs to do is to exert oneself to keep this mind free of human desires and preserve Heavenly Pattern."

I said, "Hearing you explain it in this way, I feel that I have gained some understanding, but the old explanation remains coiled up within my breast. I still can't fully cast it out. For example, in serving one's parents, one is to do things such as 'warm their bed in winter and cool it in summer, to adjust everything for their comfort, and to inquire about their health each morning.'[15] There are so many aspects and details; shouldn't these be explored and investigated?"

The Master said, "Why would one not explore and investigate [such things]? One just needs some definite way to proceed. One just needs to explore and investigate them by keeping this mind free of human desires and preserving Heavenly Pattern. For example, when one explores and investigates providing warmth for one's parents in the winter, one simply needs to fully express the filial piety of this mind; one's only fear is that some trace of human desire gets mixed in. When one explores and investigates providing cool comfort to one's parents in the summer, one simply needs to fully express the filial piety of this mind; one's only fear is that some trace of human desire gets mixed in. One just needs to explore and investigate this mind. If this mind is completely free of human desire and is pure Heavenly Pattern, then one has a mind that is Sincere in its filial piety toward one's parents. In winter, it will naturally think about one's parents being cold and explore ways to provide them with warmth; in summer, it will naturally think about one's parents being hot and explore ways to provide them with cool comfort. These are all just the detailed expressions of a Sincere, filial mind. But one first must have this Sincere, filial mind; only then will one have these detailed expressions. If we compare [the expression of filial

---

14. Wang adopts the expression "this mind" (*cǐ xīn* 此心) from the *Mengzi* 1A7 (in Part III, Selection 35) and uses it here and elsewhere as a term of art. For Wang, it refers to the "fundamental mind," or the mind in its pure and unadulterated state.

15. *Rites*, "Summary of the Rites." Compare Legge, *Li Chi*, reprint, volume 1 (New York: University Books, 1967), p. 67.

piety] to a tree, then the Sincere, filial mind corresponds to the roots and the detailed expressions are the branches and leaves. One first must have the roots; only then will one have branches and leaves. One cannot first go looking for branches and leaves and only then plant the roots. The *Rites* says, 'A filial son, cherishing profound love [for his parents], will always have a harmonious air about him. One with a harmonious air about him will always have a pleasant countenance. One with a pleasant countenance will always be compliant and accommodating.'[16] One must have profound love as the root, then naturally one will be like this."

4. Zheng Zhaoshuo asked, "[Aren't there] some cases in which the ultimate good must be sought in things and affairs?"

The Master said, "The ultimate good is simply 'this mind' [in the state where] the purity of Heavenly Patterns is fully attained.[17] Why would one seek [for the ultimate good] in things and affairs? But perhaps you could offer some examples."

Zhaoshuo said, "For example, when serving one's parents, the particular way in which one should provide warmth or cooling comfort to them [as required] or the proper way in which to serve or nurture them—the appropriate methods for such things must be sought and only then can one attain the ultimate good. This is why one must engage in the effort of 'learning,' 'asking,' 'reflecting,' and 'distinguishing.'"[18]

The Master said, "What you describe are simply the various details about how to provide warmth or cool comfort to [one's parents] or the proper way to serve or nurture [them]; such things can be explored and fully understood in a day or two. What need is there for 'learning,' 'asking,' 'reflecting,' and 'distinguishing'? It is just that if one wants this mind to be [in the state where] the purity of Heavenly Patterns is fully attained when one provides warmth or cool comfort [to one's parents] or when one is serving or nurturing [them], one must engage in 'learning,' 'asking,' 'reflecting,' and 'distinguishing' or one will commit a minute error in the beginning that leads to a major mistake in the end. This is why even sages need the teaching about being 'refined and unified.'[19] If the ultimate good only meant getting the details of behavior correct, then an actor who was able to perform correctly the various details of behavior concerning how to provide warmth or cool comfort [to one's parents] or the proper way to serve or nurture [them] could be said to have attained the ultimate good."

This day provided me with greater understanding.

5. I did not understand the Master's teaching about the unity of knowing

---

16. *Rites*, "Meaning of Sacrifices." Compare Legge, *Li Chi*, vol. 2, pp. 215–16.

17. On the phrase "this mind," see above, note 14.

18. *Mean* 20.xiii–xiv, in Part III, Selection 36.

19. *Documents, Documents of Yu*, "Counsels of the Great Yu." The quoted phrase describes how to preserve the "mind of the Way" in the face of the temptations of the "human mind."

and acting. Having debated it back and forth with Huang Zongxian and Gu Weixian without coming to any resolution, I asked the Master about it.

The Master said, "Try offering an example and let us see."

I said, "For example, there are people who despite fully knowing that they should be filial to their parents and respectful to their elder brothers, find that they cannot be filial or respectful. From this it is clear that knowing and acting are two separate things."

The Master said, "They already have been separated by selfish desires; this is not the fundamental Substance of knowing and acting. There never have been people who know but do not act. Those who 'know' but do not act simply do not yet know. Sages and worthies taught people about knowing and acting so that people would return to the fundamental Substance of knowing and acting and not just do what they could and quit. Thus, the *Great Learning* gives us examples of true knowing and acting, saying it is 'like loving a lovely sight' or 'hating a hateful odor.'[20] Seeing a lovely sight is a case of knowing, while loving a lovely sight is a case of acting. As soon as one sees that lovely sight, one naturally loves it. It is not as if you first see it and only then, intentionally, you decide to love it. Smelling a hateful odor is a case of knowing, while hating a hateful odor is a case of acting. As soon as one smells that hateful odor, one naturally hates it. It is not as if you first smell it and only then, intentionally, you decide to hate it. Consider the case of a person with a stuffed-up nose. Even if he sees a malodorous object right in from of him, the smell does not reach him, and so he does not hate it. This is simply not to know the hateful odor.

"The same is true when one says that someone knows filial piety or brotherly respect. That person must already have acted with filial piety or brotherly respect before one can say he knows them. One cannot say he knows filial piety or brotherly respect simply because he knows how to *say* something filial or brotherly. Knowing pain offers another good example. One must have experienced pain oneself in order to know pain. Similarly, one must have experienced cold oneself in order to know cold, and one must have experienced hunger oneself in order to know hunger. How can knowing and acting be separated? This is the fundamental Substance of knowing and acting, before any selfish thoughts have separated them. The sages taught people that this is how things must be in order to have knowledge. If this is not how things are, one simply does not know. This is a critical, practical form of spiritual training. What is the point of earnestly insisting that knowing and acting are two separate things? What is the point of my insisting that they are one? If one does not understand the guiding aim behind these different explanations and just insists on saying they are one or they are two—what is the point?"

I said, "The ancients talked about knowing and acting as two things, and they did so because they wanted people to distinguish them clearly. On the one hand,

---

20. *Great Learning,* Commentary 6, in Part III, Selection 33.

one was to work at knowing; on the other hand, one was to work at acting. In this way, one would have a place to begin one's spiritual training."

The Master said, "This [interpretation] loses the guiding aim of the ancients. I have said that knowing is the intent of acting and that acting is the work of knowing and that knowing is the beginning of acting and acting is the completion of knowing. Once one understands this, then if one only talks about knowing, [the idea of] acting is already present, or if one only talks about acting, [the idea] of knowing is already present. The reason that the ancients first talked about knowing and then talked about acting is only because there is a type of person in the world who foolishly acts upon impulse without engaging in the slightest thought or reflection. Because they always act blindly and recklessly, it is necessary to talk to them about knowing; only then can their actions be made correct. There is also a type of person who is vague and irresolute; they engage in speculation while suspended in a vacuum and are unwilling to apply themselves to any concrete actions. Because they only grope at shadows and grab at echoes, it is necessary to talk to them about acting; only then can their knowing be made real. The ancients could not but talk in this way, in their effort to augment deficiencies and remove obscurations. If one grasps this underlying aim, then talking about either [knowing or acting] will suffice.

"But people today instead separate knowing and acting into two distinct tasks to perform and think that one must first know and only then can one act. They say, 'Now I will perform the task of knowing, by studying and learning. Once I have attained real knowledge, I then will pursue the task of acting.' And so, till the end of their days, they never act, and till the end of their days, they never know. This is not a minor malady, nor did it arrive just yesterday. My current teaching regarding the unity of knowing and acting is a medicine directed precisely at this disease. It is not something I simply conjured up out of thin air; the fundamental Substance of knowing and acting has always been like this. Now if one understands the underlying aim [of this teaching], then there is nothing wrong with saying that they are two, for they are only one. If one says that they are one but fails to understand the underlying aim [of this teaching], then how will that help? One would only be speaking idle words."

6. I asked, "Yesterday when I inquired about the Master's teachings concerning 'resting in the ultimate good,' I felt as though I was making progress on my spiritual task. But when I thought about it in connection with Zhu Xi's view concerning 'getting a handle on things'[21] I could not, in the end, reconcile the two [views]."

The Master said, "Getting a handle on things is the work of resting in the ultimate good. If one understands the ultimate good, one understands getting a handle on things."

---

21. *Great Learning*, Classic 4–5 in Part III, Selection 33. Also see Wang Yangming, "Questions on the *Great Learning*," in Part III, Selection 38.

I said, "Yesterday, when I thought about Zhu Xi's views concerning getting a handle on things in light of your teachings, I seemed to get the general idea. But Zhu Xi's views are supported by the line from the *Documents* about being 'refined and unified,'[22] the line from the *Analects* about 'pursuing an expansive study of culture and restraining oneself with the rituals,'[23] and the line from the *Mengzi* that says 'to fathom one's mind is to know one's nature.'[24] Under the weight of this evidence, I have not been able to break free of Zhu Xi's view."

The Master said, "Zixia had devout faith in Kongzi, while Zengzi turned to look [for the truth] within himself. Devout faith surely is good, but it is not as genuine as turning to look within oneself. Now since you have not 'grasped it with your own mind,' why do you not seek the truth rather than simply remaining habituated to what you have heard in the past?[25] For example, even though Zhu Xi had great respect for and faith in Cheng Yi, when he encountered a point that he could not grasp with his own mind, did he ever just follow him? The teachings concerning being 'refined and unified,' 'pursuing an expansive study of culture and restraining oneself with the rituals,' and 'fathoming one's mind' and 'knowing one's nature' are consistent with my views. The only problem is that you have not reflected sufficiently upon these matters.

"Zhu Xi's views concerning getting a handle on things cannot avoid being forced and contrived and do not represent the original aim of this doctrine. Being 'refined' is the work of being 'focused.' 'Pursuing expansive study' is the work of 'restraining oneself.'[26] Since you already understand my teaching about the unity of knowing and acting, then when either [knowing or acting] is mentioned, you know [that the other is implied]. 'Fathoming one's mind,' 'knowing one's nature,' and 'knowing Heaven'[27] is what those who are 'born knowing it' and 'put it into action effortlessly' do.[28] 'Preserving one's mind and nourishing one's nature to serve Heaven'[29] is what those who 'know it through learning' and 'put it into action to profit from it' do.[30] 'To not become conflicted over the

---

22. *Documents, Documents of Yu*, "Counsels of the Great Yu."

23. *Analects* 6.27.

24. *Mengzi* 7A1, in Part III, Selection 35.

25. This section refers to a part of *Mengzi* 2A2 not included in this anthology, and also quotes part of Zhu Xi's commentary on that passage. In that commentary, Zhu suggests that, while Zixia's faith in Kongzi was admirable, Zengzi's self-reflection, which allowed him to grasp the answer for himself, was superior.

26. Wang is referring to the classical teachings mentioned previously. His point is that these are not distinct tasks but merely different aspects of a single, unified effort: to express the pure Heavenly Patterns within the mind as one encounters things and events in the world.

27. *Mengzi* 7A1, in Part III, Selection 35.

28. *Mean* 20.viii, in Part III, Selection 36.

29. *Mengzi* 7A1, in Part III, Selection 35.

30. *Mean* 20.viii, in Part III, Selection 36.

length of one's life but to cultivate oneself and await one's fate'[31] is what those who 'know it only after difficulty' and 'put it into action only after exertion' do.[32] The mistake in Zhu Xi's teachings about getting a handle on things lies in reversing this hierarchy. He thought that 'fathoming one's mind' and 'knowing one's nature' concern 'getting a handle on things' and 'knowledge reaching the ultimate.'[33] This is to require a beginning student to do what those who are 'born knowing it' and 'put it into action effortlessly' do. How can they possibly do that?"

I asked, "Why is it that 'fathoming one's mind' and 'knowing one's nature' are things that those who are 'born knowing it' and 'put it into action effortlessly' do?"

The Master said, "The nature is the Substance of the mind. Heaven is the source of the nature. To fathom the mind is simply to fathom the nature. 'Only those of the utmost Sincerity in the world are able to fathom their natures,' and thereby understand the transformations of Heaven and Earth.[34] Those who preserve their minds have not fathomed them. To understand Heaven is to understand in the way that those responsible for a district or county understand that the affairs [of their district or county] are *their* affairs. This is to be one with Heaven. To 'serve Heaven' is comparable to how children serve their parents or ministers serve their lords.[35] Only if one fulfills one's service with respect and reverence can one avoid error. Even so, this is to be at one remove from Heaven. Herein lies the difference between sages and worthies.[36]

"As for 'not becoming conflicted over the length of one's life,'[37] this [maxim] is designed to teach students to single-mindedly work at doing good without allowing a concern for failure or success, early death or long life to shake their commitment to do good. Students should just work at 'cultivating oneself and awaiting one's fate,'[38] knowing that failure or success, early death or long life are matters of fate [mandated by Heaven] and that such things need not 'perturb one's mind.'[39] Although those who 'serve Heaven' are at one remove from Heaven, they already see the Heavenly right before them. Those who 'await fate'

---

31. *Mengzi* 7A1, in Part III, Selection 35.

32. *Mean* 20.viii, in Part III, Selection 36.

33. *Mengzi* 7A1 and *Great Learning*, Classic 5, in Part III, Selections 35 and 33.

34. *Mean* 22, in Part III, Selection 36.

35. *Mengzi* 7A1, in Part III, Selection 35.

36. Sages know Heaven and hence, like a good magistrate or prefect, see whatever must be done as their personal responsibility. In this sense they are one with Heaven. Worthies, like children and ministers, make an effort to serve Heaven but are not in full communion with Heaven. The former have fathomed their minds, while the latter merely preserve their minds.

37. *Mengzi* 7A1, in Part III, Selection 35.

38. Paraphrasing *Mengzi* 7A1, in Part III, Selection 35.

39. *Mengzi* 2A2, in Part III, Selection 35.

still have not seen [the Heavenly] before them in this way but are waiting for an experience like this. These are all [tasks] for beginning students and convey a sense of difficulty and diligence. But now what [Zhu Xi teaches] reverses the order [of learning] and leaves students with no place to begin."

I asked, "Yesterday, after listening to your instructions, I could dimly discern that one's spiritual training must be as you describe. Now, hearing your explanation, I no longer can doubt that this is true. Yesterday, it dawned on me that the word 'thing' in the expression 'getting a handle on things' has the same meaning as the word 'undertaking' or 'affair.' Both words refer to the mind."

The Master said, "That is so. The governor of the body is the mind. What the mind puts forth are thoughts. The fundamental nature of thoughts is knowledge. Where there is a thought, there is a thing. If one's thoughts are on serving one's parents, then serving one's parents is a thing. If one's thoughts are on serving one's ruler, then serving one's ruler is a thing. If one's thoughts are on being benevolent to the people or caring for other creatures, then being benevolent to the people or caring for other creatures are things. If one's thoughts are on looking, listening, speaking, or acting, then looking, listening, speaking, or acting are things. This is why I say that there is no Pattern outside the mind and no thing outside the mind. The *Mean*'s teaching that 'without Sincerity, there are no things'[40] and the tasks of 'enlightening one's enlightened virtue' described in the *Great Learning* are nothing other than examples of making one's thoughts Sincere. The task of making one's thoughts Sincere is nothing other than 'getting a handle on things.'"

7. The Master also said, "The expression 'getting a handle' in 'getting a handle on things,'[41] is like 'getting a handle' in the line from the *Mengzi*, which says, '[Only] a great man [is able to] get a handle on [i.e., rectify] the ruler's mind.'[42] It means to eliminate whatever is not correct in order to maintain the correctness of the fundamental Substance of the mind. Wherever there is a thought, one eliminates whatever is not correct in order to maintain what is correct. At all times and in every circumstance, one preserves Heavenly Patterns. This is what it means to fully realize Pattern. Heavenly Patterns are none other than 'enlightened Virtue'; fully realizing Heavenly Patterns is nothing other than 'enlightening one's enlightened Virtue.'"[43]

8. The Master also said, "Knowing is the fundamental Substance of the mind.

40. *Mean* 25, in Part III, Selection 36.

41. *Great Learning,* Classic 4, in Part III, Selection 33.

42. *Mengzi* 4A20. In Ivanhoe's original translation, this sentence reads, "The word *ge* in *gewu* is like the *ge* in the line from the *Mengzi,* which says, '[Only] a great man [is able to] rectify (*ge*) the ruler's mind." We have modified the line to match the convention translations of this volume, but Ivanhoe's translation is more accurate in representing Wang's own interpretation.—Eds.

43. *Great Learning,* Classic 1.

The mind naturally is able to know. When it sees one's parents, it naturally knows to be filial. When it sees one's elder brother, it naturally knows to be respectful. When it sees a child [about to] fall into a well, it naturally knows the mind of compassion.[44] This is none other than pure knowing. There is no need to seek for such [knowledge] outside [the mind]. If the operation of pure knowing is not blocked by selfish thoughts, then, as it is said, 'If people can fill out the mind that does not desire to harm others, their benevolence will be inexhaustible.'[45] Nevertheless, most people are not able to avoid being blocked by selfish thoughts, and so they must engage in the tasks of extending their knowledge and getting a handle on things in order to overcome selfishness and return to Pattern. Once their pure knowing is able to work its way through the obstruction and flow freely, this is extending their knowledge. When their knowledge is extended, their thoughts are made Sincere."

9. I asked, "You, Master, take the 'extensive [study] of culture' to be the spiritual task of 'restraining oneself with ritual.'[46] I have pondered this in depth but have been unable to understand it in the least. Please show me what you mean."

The Master said, "The word 'ritual' refers to the same thing as the word 'Pattern.' [Those aspects of] Pattern that are manifested and can be seen are called 'culture.' [Those aspects of] culture that are hidden and cannot be seen are called 'Pattern.' This involves only one thing. Restraining oneself with ritual is simply to want 'this mind' to remain pure Heavenly Pattern.[47] If one wants this mind to remain pure Heavenly Pattern, one must apply effort wherever Pattern is manifested. If it is manifested while serving one's parents, then one must study how to preserve Heavenly Pattern while serving one's parents. If it is manifested while serving one's ruler, then one must study how to preserve Heavenly Pattern while serving one's ruler. If it is manifested while living in wealth and honor, or poverty and humble circumstances, then one must study how to preserve Heavenly Pattern while living in wealth and honor, or poverty and humble circumstances. If it is manifested while living in difficulty and deprivation or among barbarians, then one must study how to preserve Heavenly Pattern while living in difficulty and deprivation or among barbarians.[48] The same practice should be followed whether one is active or at rest, speaking or silent; wherever [Pattern] is manifested—right there is where one must learn to preserve Heavenly Pattern. This is what I mean by saying that to engage in 'the extensive study of culture' is the spiritual task of 'restraining oneself with

---

44. *Mengzi* 2A6, in Part III, Selection 35.

45. *Mengzi* 7B31, Part III, Selection 35.

46. *Analects* 6.25. These lines traditionally have been interpreted as referring to two distinct yet complementary types of effort: the extensive study of culture and restraining oneself through ritual practice.

47. On the expression "this mind," see above, note 14.

48. The last two lines draw directly upon *Mean* 14.

ritual.' The extensive study of culture is to be 'refined'; restraining oneself with ritual is to be 'unified.'"[49]

10. I asked, "[Zhu Xi said that] 'the mind of the Way always is the governor of the self and the human mind always obeys it.'[50] Seen in light of your teachings regarding being 'refined and unified,' this claim seems flawed."

The Master said, "That is correct. The mind is one. Before it is mixed with what is human, it is called the mind of the Way. After being mixed with human artifice, it is called the human mind. When the human mind attains its correct state, it is the mind of the Way. When the mind of the Way loses its correct state, it is the human mind. From the very start, there are not two minds. Cheng Yi said, 'The human mind is human desire; the mind of the Way is Heavenly Pattern.'[51] While this way of putting it seems to divide [the mind into two things], it succeeds in conveying the basic idea. Now, to say that the mind of the Way is the governor and the human mind obeys its commands, this is to posit the existence of two minds. Heavenly Pattern and human desires cannot be in play at the same time, and so how could one have Heavenly Pattern as the governor and human desires subsequently obeying its commands?"

11. I asked about Wenzhongzi and Han Yu.[52]

The Master said, "Han Yu was a great literary man but nothing more, while Wenzhongzi was a worthy scholar. Because people of later ages only esteem literary talent, they have glorified Han Yu. But the fact is that Han Yu was vastly inferior to Wenzhongzi."

I asked, "Why then did [Wenzhongzi] commit the mistake of imitating the classics?"

The Master said, "I am afraid that imitating the classics cannot wholly be condemned. Could you explain to me the difference between imitating the classics and the intent behind the writings of scholars in later ages?"

I said, "Scholars writing today are not without the intention of advancing their reputations, but their primary aim is to elucidate the Way. Imitating the classics, though, is purely aimed at [gaining] a reputation."

---

49. *Documents, Documents of Yu,* "Counsels of the Great Yu." On one reading of the passage of the *Documents* referenced here, being "refined" and "unified" is necessary to achieve the subtle powers of discernment associated with "the mind of the Way," as opposed to the weaker powers of the precarious "human mind." For more discussion of this passage and an illustration of its importance to the Neo-Confucians, see §34 of Cheng Yi's "Selected Sayings," in Part III, Selection 31.—Eds.

50. See Zhu's Preface to the *Mean* (not included in this volume). For the "mind of the Way" and the "human mind," see the previous note.—Eds.

51. *Extant Works of the Cheng [Brothers] from Henan,* chap. 19.

52. Wenzhongzi (584–617) was an eminent Confucian of the Sui dynasty. He thought of himself as equal to Kongzi, which has lowered him in the eyes of most Confucians. Among Wenzhongzi's now lost works are various "supplements" to the classics. On Han Yu, see Part III, Selections 19 through 22.

The Master asked, "In elucidating the Way, whom are people emulating?"

I replied, "Kongzi edited and transmitted the Six Classics in order to elucidate the Way."[53]

The Master said, "Then why is imitating the classics not emulating Kongzi?"

I replied, "Writing that [elucidates] reveals something about the Way, while
imitating the classics seems only to imitate what has come down to us. I am
afraid that this does not in any way augment the Way."

The Master said, "By 'elucidating the Way' do you mean to return to simplicity and purity and manifest these in one's actual practice, or do you mean to
dress up and embellish one's words and just wrangle and contend with others?
The great chaos found throughout the world today has arisen because vacuous writing has flourished while actual practice has declined. If the Way were
elucidated throughout the world, there would be no need to transmit the Six
Classics. Editing and transmitting the Six Classics was something that Kongzi
could not but do. From the time when Fuxi first drew the Eight Trigrams to the
age of King Wen and the Duke of Zhou, commentaries on the *Changes,* such as
the *Mountain Ranges* and *Returning to the Treasury*, were written.[54] These came
in every shape and form, varied in content, and no one knows how many were
produced. [As a result,] the Way of the *Changes* was thrown into great chaos.
Kongzi saw that the fashion of indulging in superfluous writing was gaining
strength with each day and the production of such explanations would never
cease. And so, he took the commentaries provided by King Wen and the Duke
of Zhou and added his own exposition to these, insisting that this was the only
way to grasp the true meaning of the *Changes*. As a result, the proliferation of
commentaries ceased and those who talked about the *Changes* began to form a
unified consensus.

"The same is true in the cases of the *Documents, Odes, Rites, Music,* and *Spring
and Autumn Annals*. Following the opening four chapters of the *Documents* and
the first two chapters of the *Odes,* no one knows how many thousands of reams
of works such as the *Nine Hills* and the *Eight Inquiries* as well as various licentious and superfluous verses were written.[55] The names and institutions of rituals and music also were produced in inexhaustible abundance. It was only after
Kongzi edited and eliminated these and transmitted orthodox versions [of these
texts] that such commentaries ceased being produced. When did Kongzi ever

---

53. The Six Classics are the Five Classics transmitted since the Han dynasty (*Odes, Documents,
Changes, Spring and Autumn Annals,* and *Rites*) along with the *Music,* which was already lost
by the Han, but supposedly existed as a classic in the time of Kongzi.—Eds.

54. The commentaries on the *Changes* that are mentioned are now lost. See the Introduction
to Part I on Fu Xi, King Wen, the Duke of Zhou and the other historical figures mentioned
below.—Eds.

55. The *Nine Hills* and the *Eight Inquiries* are now lost historical works.

add a single word to the *Documents, Odes, Rites,* or *Music?* The various teachings in the present *Rites* are all things added by later Confucians; these are not part of Kongzi's original text. As for the *Spring and Autumn Annals,* while it is said that Kongzi 'made' it, in fact it consists of the old text of the official history of the state of Lu.[56] When people describe Kongzi as 'writing' [the classics], they mean he wrote down the old texts. When they talk about him 'editing' [the classics], they mean he eliminated all that was superfluous. He reduced and never added to the classics. When Kongzi transmitted the Six Classics, he feared that superfluous writings would cause chaos throughout the world. He only sought to simplify them so that they would not mislead the people. He worked to get rid of the words so that people could grasp the true meaning. He did not want to teach through words at all.

"After the Spring and Autumn Period [722–481 BCE], superfluous writings grew ever more numerous and the world grew ever more chaotic. What was wrong with the First Emperor's burning of the books was that he did this out of a selfish motivation, and it was improper to burn the Six Classics. If at the time his intent had been to make clear the Way and to burn all the books that opposed the classics and violated the Pattern, then his actions would have been proper and would happen to have conformed to [Kongzi's] ideas about editing and transmitting [the classics].[57] Since the Qin and Han dynasties, writing has grown more numerous with each passing day. One could not possibly get rid of it all. The best that one can do is to take Kongzi as one's model: record what comes close to being correct and make it known. As a consequence, perverse theories will gradually be abandoned. I don't know what Wenzhongzi intended to accomplish when he imitated the classics, but I strongly endorse what he did and feel that if another sage were to arise, he would find nothing wanting [in Wenzhongzi's actions].

"The reason the world is not well ordered is simply because [superfluous] writing has increased so dramatically while actual practice has declined. There are those who set forth their personal opinions and play the novel off against the strange, all in order to seduce the average person and win fame for themselves. They do so only to disorder the understanding of the world and muddy the eyes and ears of the people, so that they will waste their time competing with one another writing flowery compositions in order to win acclaim in their age, and will no longer comprehend conduct that honors what is fundamental, esteems what is real, reverts to simplicity, and returns to purity. This all began with those who practiced writing."

I replied, "But some writing seems indispensable. For example, in the case of

---

56. For the tradition that Kongzi composed the *Spring and Autumn Annals,* see the Introduction to Part I.—Eds.

57. On the Qin burning of books, see the Introduction to Part I.—Eds.

the classic *Spring and Autumn Annals*, were it not for the *Zuozhuan* [the classic] would probably be difficult to comprehend."[58]

The Master said, "To say that we must have the *Zuozhuan* before we can understand the *Spring and Autumn Annals* is to regard [the classic] as if it were a partially quoted phrase. Why would Kongzi exert such an effort to produce writing that is so difficult and obscure? Most of the *Zuozhuan* is simply the old text of the official history of the state of Lu. If we must read it before we can understand the *Spring and Autumn Annals*, why would Kongzi have felt a need to edit [the classic]?"

I replied, "Cheng Yi said that, 'The commentary to the *Spring and Autumn Annals* presents cases; the classic presents judgments.'[59] For example, the *Spring and Autumn Annals* says that a certain king was murdered or a certain state attacked. If these affairs are not described clearly, it would likely be difficult to reach a judgment."

The Master said, "In saying this, Cheng Yi probably was just according with the views of contemporary scholars; this does not reflect Kongzi's intention in composing the classics. For example, if the *Spring and Autumn Annals* says that a certain king was murdered, since we know that the murder of a king is a crime, what need is there to inquire about the details of the murder?

"Similarly, only the king can launch an attack of rectification.[60] If the *Spring and Autumn Annals* says that a certain state was attacked, since we know that attacking a state is a crime, what need is there to inquire about the details of the attack? Kongzi's sole intention in transmitting the classics was to rectify people's minds, preserve Heavenly Pattern, and eliminate human desires. If some affair concerned the preservation of Heavenly Pattern or the elimination of human desires, then Kongzi often would speak about it, or if someone asked a specific question, he would explain things according to that person's ability to understand. But even in such cases, he would not go on at length, because he feared that people would only seek [the truth] within words. This is why he said, 'I would prefer not to speak.'[61] How could he allow himself to offer detailed descriptions of all those affairs that give rein to human desires and annihilate Heavenly Pattern? This is to aid chaos and abet villainy. This is why Mengzi said, 'No one in Kongzi's school talked about the affairs of Duke Huan or Duke Wen,

---

58. The *Zuozhuan* is the *Commentary of Zuo*, attributed to Zuo Qiuming. It provides a wealth of historical detail about events in the original text of the *Spring and Autumn Annals*.

59. This line is found in the *Extant Works of the Cheng [Brothers] from Henan*, chap. 16, and the "Extension of Knowledge" ("Zhì zhī 致知") chapter of *A Record for Reflection*.

60. An "attack of rectification" was a punitive assault led by the legitimate king to subdue an unruly vassal state. Any military action involving one vassal state attacking another was *ipso facto* illegitimate.

61. *Analects* 17.19.

and so these things have not been handed down to later ages.'[62] This approach is characteristic of the Confucian School. Contemporary scholars, though, talk only about the learning suited to a despot. And so, they want to know many subtle plans and crafty schemes. What they know is all aimed at gaining some profit or advantage, which is diametrically opposed to Kongzi's intention in composing the classics. How can such people understand?"

Thereupon, the Master sighed and said, "It is not easy to talk about this with those who are not 'advanced in Heavenly Virtue.'"[63]

He continued, saying, "Kongzi said, 'Even in my time, historians leave some things out of their accounts.'[64] Mengzi said, 'It would be better to be without books than to trust in them completely. In the "Completion of the War" in the *Documents*, I accept only two or three strips [of characters].'[65] When Kongzi edited the *Documents*, he covered the four to five hundred years of the Yao, Shun, and Xia dynasty periods in several chapters. Why did he not record at least one more affair [from this period]? Through this we can understand Kongzi's intention. His only aim was to eliminate superfluous writing. Scholars of later ages have worked to the contrary and only aim at adding more."

I said, "Kongzi's sole intention in transmitting the classics was to eliminate human desires and preserve Heavenly Pattern. This offers a perfect explanation for why he did not want to describe in detail the affairs in the period of the Five Despots and the time that followed.[66] But why did he not offer more details about the time before the reigns of Yao and Shun?"

The Master said, "In the age of Fuxi and the Yellow Emperor, affairs were few and far between; only in rare cases have they been handed down [to later generations]. This can help us to imagine how pure, graceful, modest, and simple their age was and how free it was of any air of ornamentation or embellishment. This was the method of governing practiced in high antiquity, something later ages are incapable of attaining."

---

62. Paraphrasing a portion of *Mengzi* 1A7 not included in this anthology.

63. *Mean* 32.

64. *Analects* 15.25. The idea is that even in the decadent age in which Kongzi lived, some historians would still do the right thing by leaving irrelevant or immoral details out of their accounts.

65. *Mengzi* 7B3. The "Completion of the War" (*Documents, Documents of Zhou*) purportedly describes the triumph of King Wu over Tyrant Zhou. Mengzi could not accept its gory descriptions of this campaign. In his mind, an enlightened conqueror could never wreak such carnage. Compare Lu's reference to Mengzi's comment in his "First Letter to Zhu Xi," in Part III, Selection 37.

66. The Five Despots were five particularly bad rulers from the Spring and Autumn Period; see *Mengzi* 6B7. [On Yao, Shun, and the historical figures and events of the following paragraphs, see the Introduction to Part I.—Eds.]

I said, "There were records of the Three Sovereigns that were handed down to later ages. Why did Kongzi edit them out?"

The Master said, "Even if such records did indeed exist, because of changes that arose over the course of generations, they would gradually have become inappropriate. As customs began to change [over the ages], ornamentation and embellishment became more and more dominant. Even by the end of the Zhou dynasty, one could no longer substitute the customs of the Shang or Xia dynasties, even if one wanted to, not to mention [the customs of] Yao or Shun—much less Fuxi or the Yellow Emperor! Nevertheless, while their methods of governing were different, they followed the same Way. Kongzi reverently passed down the ways of Yao and Shun and made clear the methods of Wen and Wu. But the methods of Wen and Wu are the Way of Yao and Shun. Because they adjusted their methods of governing in accordance with the times, their institutions, programs, policies, and laws naturally were not the same. Certain aspects of the administration of the Shang and Xia were inappropriate when handed down to the Zhou. This is why 'the Duke of Zhou aspired to combine the best of the Three Sovereigns . . . whenever he encountered something inappropriate [for his time], he would gaze toward the heavens and reflect until day passed into night.'[67] How much more difficult is it to appropriate the methods of government used in high antiquity! This certainly is why Kongzi endorsed reducing the records [of such times] to an absolute minimum."

He continued, saying, "To maintain a policy of 'non-action' and prove incapable of adjusting one's methods of governing in accordance with the times, as the Three Sovereigns did, but instead insist on implementing the customs of high antiquity is the approach and method of Buddhists and Daoists. To adjust one's methods of governing in accordance with the times but prove incapable of rooting all one's practices in the Way, as the Three Sovereigns did, and instead to act with your mind on profit and advantage is the policy of despots and those who follow them. Scholars in later ages have talked up and down and back and forth but all they ever talk about is the method and approach of despots."

13. I said, "When former scholars discussed the Six Classics, they regarded the *Spring and Autumn Annals* as a work of history. But since works of history are only records of affairs, I am concerned that in the end this means that to some degree it differs in nature from the other five classics."

The Master replied, "If you talk about it in terms of affairs, it is a work of history; if you talk about it in terms of the Way, it is a classic. But affairs are the Way and the Way is affairs. The *Spring and Autumn Annals* is also a classic; the [other] five classics are also histories.[68] The *Changes* is a history of Fuxi. The *Documents* is a history of the times of Yao, Shun, and those who followed them.

---

67. *Mengzi* 4B20.

68. Wang's idea in this section, that the classics can be understood as histories, influenced and was developed by the Qing dynasty Confucian Zhang Xuecheng. See Part IV, Selection 52.

The *Rites* and the *Music* are histories of the Three Dynasties. They concern the same affairs; they concern the same Way. Where lies their alleged difference?"

44. Miscellaneous Writings

translation by Philip J. Ivanhoe

This section consists of eight brief selections on a variety of topics. The first two, "Correcting Errors" and "Encouraging Goodness through Reproof" are part of a longer work, "Essential Instructions for Students at Longchang." The other selections are letters Wang wrote to his friends, students, and relatives. —Eds.

1. Correcting Errors

Even great worthies cannot avoid committing some errors; nevertheless, this in no way detracts from their being great worthies, because they are able to correct their errors. And so, what we esteem is not being without errors but being able to correct one's errors. You gentlemen think about this for yourselves; in the course of your normal day, are there occasions when in your conduct you have been deficient in regard to humility, modesty, conscientiousness, or faithfulness? Have you been inadequate in terms of filial piety or friendship or succumbed to fraudulent, deceitful, mean, or stingy habits? I doubt that any of you have reached such a state, but if unfortunately any of you have, it will be because you unknowingly have walked down the path of error and earlier did not have the benefit of talking and practicing with teachers and friends and receiving their guidance and encouragement. I ask you gentlemen to turn and reflect upon yourselves. If there is the rare one among you who is tending in this direction, you absolutely must bitterly regret your mistake. Nevertheless, you should not become dissatisfied with yourself over this and allow it to weaken your resolve to correct your errors and follow what is good. If one day, people can completely wash away their old stains, even if they were bandits or thieves in the past, this in no way detracts from their being gentlemen today. However, should you say, "I used to be like that in the past, but today, even though I have corrected my errors and follow the good, no one trusts me," but you have not atoned for your former errors and instead shrink back in shame and willingly remain in a polluted state, I have absolutely no hope for you!

2. Encouraging Goodness through Reproof

To encourage goodness through reproof is the way of friends, but you must present such reproofs conscientiously and lead others well. You must be exceedingly conscientious and loving and as accommodating and flexible as you can be, so that you get others to listen and follow, to understand and reform. If you move them without inciting anger, you are doing well. If you begin by suddenly and thoroughly exposing their errors and wickedness, disparaging and reviling them in ways they cannot endure, you will only succeed in eliciting feelings of deep shame and heated resentment. Even though they may desire to comply and follow along with you, under such circumstances, they will be unable to do so. You will only stir them up and lead them to do what is bad. And so, whenever someone points out another's shortcomings or attacks their hidden weaknesses only to make a display of their own personal uprightness, this should never be called encouraging goodness through reproof. Nevertheless, while correcting faults is something I should not do to others, it is something others can do to me, for all those who attack my failings are my teachers. How could I not receive such admonitions joyfully and take them to heart?

I have yet to attain any real insight into the Way, and my study of it remains crude and inept. You gentlemen have made a mistake following me up to this point. When I think of this throughout the course of each night, I realize that I have yet to reach the point where I avoid doing what is *truly* bad—much less the point where I merely avoid making simple errors! People say that the proper way to serve a teacher is to "neither oppose your teacher nor cover up your teacher's faults."[69] But they go on to say that you should not admonish your teacher, and this is wrong! The way to admonish your teacher is to be upright without reaching the point of opposition and to be accommodating without reaching the point of covering up faults. If I am right about something, such an approach will make clear what is right; if I am wrong about something, it will allow me to eliminate what is wrong. This shows how "teaching and learning support each other."[70] You gentlemen should begin your practice of *encouraging goodness through reproof* with me!

3. Reply to Huang Zongxian and Ying Yuanzheng

I feel that last night I talked too much, but on the occasion of meeting you two gentlemen, I could not but talk too much! Since I am not very advanced in the course of my learning, some of what I said was highly unpolished. Nevertheless, it concerned part of the real spiritual effort that we share in common. If at first what I said does not make sense to you, please do not dismiss it lightly, for you surely will see pieces that suddenly fall into place.

The mind of a sage does not contain even the slightest obscuration, and so there is no need to eliminate or polish away anything. But the mind of the

---

69. *Rites,* "Tan Gong."
70. *Rites,* "Record of Learning."

ordinary person is like a dirty and stained mirror.[71] One needs to make a concerted effort at cutting away and polishing in order to completely eliminate the various defilements covering it. After such an effort, even the smallest speck of dust will easily be seen [upon the mirror's surface], and brushing it off will require little effort. At such a stage, one already has realized the Substance of benevolence. Even before defilements are eliminated, there naturally will be small spots of clarity [on the mirror's surface]. If dust or dirt falls upon such places, they certainly will be seen and easily can be brushed away. But when defilements are piled upon such dirt and dust, there comes a point when they no longer can be seen. Here lies the difference between those who "know it through learning" and "put it into action to profit from it" and those who "know it only after difficulty" and "put it into action only after exertion."[72]

I hope that you will not doubt what I say simply because these ideas are so difficult and challenging. Human beings are disposed to delight in ease and dislike difficulty; many also labor under layers of obscuration because of selfish thoughts and accumulated [bad] habits. However, once one sees through these impediments, naturally the task will no longer seem difficult. Among the ancients, some risked their lives ten thousand times and were happy to do so in order to attain this realization. Earlier, we did not grasp the idea that we had to direct our attention inward, and so naturally we had no way of talking about this kind of spiritual effort. Now that we have reached this stage of understanding, we must be on guard not to allow our delight in ease and dislike of difficulty to lead us to slide into Chan Buddhism. Eighty to ninety percent of what we discussed yesterday, concerning the differences between Confucianism and Buddhism, was explained by Cheng Hao when he said that Buddhists exert "reverential attention to straighten out the inner life" but lack "righteousness to rectify the exterior life," and so in the end they fail in their efforts to use "reverential attention to straighten out the inner life."[73]

4. To My Younger Brothers

I have received a number of your letters and all of them show that you are aware of and contrite about your shortcomings and possess an abundance of enthusiasm. This gives me boundless delight and comfort! And yet, I do not know whether your words express a Sincere heart or are said simply to provide a nice impression.

The enlightenment of our fundamental mind is as brilliant as the noonday

---

71. Cf. Huineng, *Platform Sutra*, §6 and §8, in Part II, Selection 16.

72. Paraphrasing *Mean* 20.viii, in Part III, Selection 36. The idea is that those who make an initial effort to clean their spiritual mirror—a metaphor for the mind—have an easier time than those who let defilements pile up.

73. See Cheng Hao, "Selected Sayings," in Part III, Selection 27, §24.

sun. There are none who have done wrong who fail to know that they are wrong; the only problem is that they are unable to correct themselves. The moment there is a single thought to correct [oneself], the fundamental mind is attained.

Who is without fault? "The important thing is to correct [ourselves]."[74] Ju Boyu was a great worthy, and yet he said he "wished to correct his faults but had been unable to do so."[75] King Tang and Kongzi were great sages and yet the former said, "I willingly correct my faults," while the latter said, "I wish to be without major faults."[76] People all say, "If one is not a Yao or a Shun, how can one be without faults?" Even though this is a saying that has been handed down through time, it does not help us understand the mind of Yao or Shun. Had Yao or Shun thought or felt that they were completely free of faults, they would have lacked the very thing needed to be a sage. The maxim that they shared between them was, "The human mind is precarious. The mind of the Way is subtle. Be ever refined and unified in order to hold fast to the mean!"[77] Since they thought that the human mind was precarious, this shows their minds were the same as other human beings'. To be "precarious" is to be [prone to commit] faults. Only because they remained "cautious and apprehensive"[78] and worked to be "refined" and "unified" were they able to "hold fast to the mean" and avoid faults.

The sages and worthies of ancient times always saw their own faults and corrected them. This is how they were able to be without faults. It was not that their minds really were different from other human beings'. To be "careful even before seeing anything, concerned even before hearing anything" is the spiritual effort of always being able to see one's own faults.[79] Recently, I have seen places in my own life where I need to exert this kind of effort, but because the bad habits I picked up every day have accumulated to the point where they are now deep-seated flaws, I lack the courage to rectify these faults. And so, I am eager to inform you early on, my younger brothers, about this. Do not be like me and allow bad habits to accumulate to the point where they become deep-seated and are difficult to rectify.

When young, people have the energy and spirit to rally to a cause and the obligations of family life do not yet weigh upon their minds. Therefore, it is very easy for them to apply themselves. As they mature, their worldly obligations grow more onerous and their energy and spirit gradually diminish with each passing day. Nevertheless, if they earnestly make an effort and commit themselves to learning, they still can achieve something of note. When they reach the

---

74. *Analects* 9.23.

75. *Analects* 14.26.

76. *Documents, Documents of Shang,* "The Announcement of Zhonghui"; *Analects* 7.16.

77. *Documents, Documents of Yu,* "Counsels of the Great Yu."

78. *Documents, Documents of Yu,* "Counsels of Gao Yao."

79. *Mean* 1.ii, in Part III, Selection 36.

age of forty or fifty years old, they are like the sun setting behind the hills; they gradually fade and are extinguished, and nothing can bring them back. This is why Kongzi said, "If someone reaches the age of forty or fifty years old and you have not heard of him, then there is no need to hold him in awe."[80] He also said, "When one is old and the *qi* of his blood has declined, he guards against acquisitiveness."[81] I recently have observed this infirmity in my own life. And so, I am eager to inform you early on, my younger brothers, about this. Take advantage of this time in your lives to exert yourselves! Do not let this time pass and leave you with only regrets.

5. Letter to Liu Yuandao

In your last letter you said, "I want to enter into sitting meditation on some desolate mountain in order to cut myself off from the affairs of the world, shield myself from thoughts and feelings, and cultivate my spiritual awareness. I must examine myself until I can maintain a comprehensive understanding, day and night, without cease; then, I can respond to the world [untainted] by feelings." You also said, "I want to pursue this goal through stillness, as it seems to be the shortest and most direct route, but I cannot slide into an empty lassitude." These aspirations suffice to show your remarkable commitment to the Way and your uncommon resolve.[82] The other things you said in your letter reveal that you are a person of insight. This is wonderful, wonderful indeed!

Now, the way that good doctors cure an illness is to match the treatment to the ailment, taking into consideration the various symptoms and, whenever appropriate, adjusting or augmenting the treatment. The sole aim is to eliminate the disease. They do not start out with a fixed prescription, which they apply to every patient without asking about the particular symptoms.[83] Why should a gentleman's learning differ in any way from this? Yuandao, you can assess the severity of your own illness, ascertain your own symptoms, and in light of these determine your own treatment. In this way, you will avoid harming yourself. I fear that your single-minded desire to cut yourself off from the affairs of the world, shield yourself from thoughts and feelings, and incline to an amorphous stillness already has led you to develop a nature of empty lassitude. Even though you desire to avoid sliding into empty lassitude, this is something you cannot avoid.

At the end of the day, though there is no fixed prescription for curing illness, the principle of getting rid of the illness does constitute a fixed approach.

---

80. *Analects* 9.22.

81. *Analects* 16.7, in Selections on *Qi,* in Part I, Selection 6.

82. Compare *Analects* 8.7.

83. This metaphor of the good doctor is picked up by Wang's disciple Xu Ai in his Preface to *A Record for Practice,* in Part III, Selection 43.

If you only understand the idea of applying medicine according to the disease and do not understand that the application of certain medicines can itself *cause* disease, your loss will be equally grave. When you have time, you should familiarize yourself with Cheng Hao's "Letter on Calming the Nature."[84] When you do, your views will change.

I am sorry that I have not gone into greater detail on the topic of illness and just dashed this singularly poor response off in a hurry.

6. Reply to Inquiries Made by a Friend[85]

In your letter, you asked, "Up until now, former scholars all took 'learning,' 'asking,' 'reflecting,' and 'distinguishing' as pertaining to knowing while 'earnestly putting it into action' pertained to acting.[86] They clearly distinguished between these two things [i.e., knowing and acting]. Now, though, you alone say that knowing and acting form a unity. I cannot but have doubts about this."

My answer is as follows: "I have spoken about this on many occasions. Everything that is referred to as 'acting' is simply the actual performance of some affair. If one actually engages in the effort of learning, asking, reflecting, and distinguishing, then learning, asking, reflecting, and distinguishing are examples of acting. Learning is learning some affair; asking is asking about some affair; reflecting and discriminating are reflecting upon and discriminating in regard to some affair. And so, acting is learning, asking, reflecting, and distinguishing. If you say that you first learn, ask, reflect, and distinguish in regard to some affair and afterward you go on to act, how do you carry out this learning, asking, reflecting, and distinguishing while suspended in a vacuum? When it is time to act, how can you carry out learning, asking, reflecting, and distinguishing? The enlightened, conscious, refined, and discerning aspects of acting are knowing. The authentic, direct, earnest, and genuine aspects of knowing are acting. If in acting, one is incapable of being refined, discerning, enlightened, and conscious, then one acts wantonly. This illustrates why 'if one learns but does not reflect, one will be lost';[87] one must then go on to talk about the need for knowing. If in knowing, one is incapable of being authentic, direct, earnest, and genuine, then one's thinking is reckless. This illustrates why 'if one reflects but does not learn, one will be in danger'; one must then go on to talk about the need for acting. From the beginning, there has only been a single spiritual task. Whenever the ancients talked about knowing and acting, it was always with the aim of correcting or explaining some problem in regard to this single spiritual task; they never split off and separated them into two different affairs, as people do today. My

---

84. Included in this volume, in Part III, Selection 26.

85. The friend is not identified by Wang.

86. *Mean* 20.xiii, in Part III, Selection 36.

87. For this and the following quotation, see *Analects* 2.15, in Part III, Selection 34.

theory of the unity of knowing and acting, on the one hand, is simply a theory aimed at correcting and explaining a contemporary problem; on the other hand, this is how knowing and acting are and always have been in both Substance and structure. My friend, you simply must experience this for yourself in reference to some actual affair, and in that moment you will grasp the truth. Now, instead, you only look for understanding from the meaning of words, and so you are pulled this way and that, wandering in every direction, and the more you talk, the more confused you become. This is precisely a failure resulting from an inability to maintain the unity of knowing and acting."

You also said, "Lu Xiangshan's discussions of learning share both many similarities and many differences with those of Zhu Xi. You [Wang Yangming] have said, 'Xiangshan saw directly and clearly where to begin one's learning.' But when I look at Xiangshan's writings, I find he says that learning consists of clear explanation and concrete practice and that 'extending knowledge' and 'getting a handle on things' pertain to clear explanation.[88] Given this, I see no difference between Xiangshan's views and Zhu Xi's, but, on the contrary, see dissimilarity between his views and your theory about the unity of knowing and acting."

My answer is as follows: "In regard to learning, the gentleman pays no mind to similarities or differences but only to what is correct. The similarities between my views and those of Lu Xiangshan are not the result of a lack of independence on my part or a desire to agree with him. The places where we disagree, I do not try to cover up. The differences between my views and those of Zhu Xi are not the result of a desire on my part to differ with him. The fact that we agree about some points takes nothing away from our agreement. Suppose Bo Yi, Liuxia Hui, Kongzi, and Mengzi were to gather together in some hall; just because their views would in some respects be partial and in others complete, and their deliberations, discussions, and opinions would not in every respect be alike would not take anything away from the fact that they all are equally sages and worthies.[89] When scholars in later ages discuss learning, they always agree with whatever their faction advocates and attack whatever is different; this is the result of their selfish dispositions and frivolous feelings. In behaving like this, they treat the work of sages and worthies as if it were some child's game."

You also asked, "The theory of the unity of knowing and acting is the most commanding feature of your view about learning. Since in this respect you differ from Lu Xiangshan, may I please ask in what respects your views are alike?"

My answer is as follows: "'Knowing' and 'acting' in fact are two words referring to a single spiritual task. This spiritual task requires words in order to be explained perfectly and completely, without omission or flaw. If one sees clearly and precisely where to begin—that in fact there is only one place to

---

88. On the debate over how to interpret these phrases, see *Great Learning*, Commentary 5, and Wang Yangming, "Questions on the *Great Learning*," in Part III, Selections 33 and 38.

89. Bo Yi and Liuxia Hui were famous worthies. See *Mengzi* 5B1.

begin—then even though knowing and acting are separated and explained as if they were two different things, in the end they always will be in the service of the one spiritual task. If at first the two are not well integrated and brought together, in the end, as they say, 'a hundred thoughts will come to the same conclusion.' Those who do not see clearly and precisely where to begin and in fact treat knowing and acting as two separate things, even if they take up the theory of the unity of knowing and acting, I am afraid they will never find a way to bring them together. Moreover, since they work at them as two separate things, then from start to finish they will be unable to find a place to set to work."

You also asked, "The theory of the extension of pure knowing truly is a teaching one could hold, 'waiting a hundred generations for a sage to appear [and confirm it] without being misled.'[90] Since Xiangshan saw clearly and precisely where to begin, how is it that his views on this topic differ [from yours]?"

My response is as follows: "Over time, Confucians have handed down this kind of interpretation about 'extending knowledge' and 'getting a handle on things.' Xiangshan received these teachings and did not scrutinize or doubt them in any way. As a result, these are places where his views are not wholly refined, which is something that should not be covered up."

I would add, "Knowing that is authentic, direct, earnest, and genuine is acting. Acting that is refined, discerning, enlightened, and conscious is knowing. If in moments of knowing, one's mind is unable to be authentic, direct, earnest, and genuine, one's knowing will be incapable of being enlightened, conscious, refined, and discerning. But it is not that in periods of knowing one only aims at being enlightened, conscious, refined, and discerning and not authentic, direct, earnest, and genuine. If in moments of acting, one's mind is unable to be enlightened, conscious, refined, and discerning, one's actions will be incapable of being authentic, direct, earnest, and genuine. But it is not that in moments of acting, one aims only at being authentic, direct, earnest, and genuine and does not want to be enlightened, conscious, refined, and discerning. The Substance of the mind always knows 'the transformations of Heaven and earth.'[91] 'Heaven knows the great beginning,'[92] and so does the Substance of the mind."

7. Reply to Wei Shiyue

Shi Yi arrived and provided me with an account of your efforts at "daily renovation,"[93] and I also received your letter. Your commitment and earnestness are a source of boundless joy and comfort for me. In your letter, when you talk

90. *Mean* 29.

91. *Mean* 22, in Part III, Selection 36.

92. Literally, "*Qian* knows the great beginning." See *Changes*, "Great Appendix," I.1, in Part I, Selection 9.

93. *Great Learning*, Commentary 2.

about those who claim that they are acting on pure knowing, but instead rely on personal feelings or thoughts, take these to be pure knowing, and act upon these feelings or thoughts rather than their innately endowed pure knowing—this shows that you already have recognized and explored this shortcoming.[94] Thoughts should clearly be distinguished from pure knowing. Whenever an idea arises in response to any thing or affair, this is called a "thought." Thoughts can be either correct or incorrect. That which is able to know which thoughts are correct and which incorrect is called pure knowing. If one relies upon pure knowing, then one will never act incorrectly. Your doubts in regard to being in the grip of a desire for fame, swayed by circumstances, and so on all concern cases in which the intention to extend pure knowing is not yet wholly Sincere and perfect. If it were wholly Sincere and perfect, there naturally would be no such problems. Those who find it difficult to begin a task or who suffer from being negligent or compromising do so because their intention to extend pure knowing is not yet Sincere and perfect and their perception of pure knowing is not yet penetrating and complete. If their perception of pure knowing were penetrating and complete, then in their encounters with fame or circumstances there would be nothing but the marvelous operation of pure knowing. Since apart from fame or circumstances there is no pure knowing, how could one possibly be constricted by fame or swayed by circumstances?[95] This can occur only if one is moved by selfish thoughts and fails to accord with the fundamental state of pure knowing.

Those who share our aims in the present age, although they all know that pure knowing operates everywhere, as soon as they enter the realm of social relationships and interactions, they immediately separate human feelings and the Patterns of things from pure knowing and regard them as two separate affairs. This is something that one absolutely must examine.

8. To Huang Zongxian

Engaging in the spiritual task [of self-cultivation] is ten times more difficult when one holds an official position than when one retires to the mountains and forest glens. If someone in office is without good friends to admonish and correct him on a regular basis, his normal, everyday aspirations can only rarely avoid silently shifting and secretly being carried off; as his determination weakens, it deteriorates and dissipates with each passing day. Recently, I said

---

94. The word "thought" is a term of art for Wang. As is clear further on, it refers to one's response to some thing or event—real or imagined—and can be either in accord with pure knowing and hence correct or aligned with personal preference and hence selfish.

95. Pure knowing only operates *in response to* actual things and affairs such as the fame and circumstances described by Wei. It responds to such things as a mirror "reflects" the objects that come before it, "illuminating" the ethical features of these things and events. Once these pass, there is nothing left behind.

to Huang Chengfu that since neither of you have many friends in Beijing, the two of you should agree between yourselves that whenever one sees the other unsettled in any way, he will uphold the need to extend pure knowing; in this way, you can keep each other on course and in line.

Only the most courageous people can resolve to remain silent just as their speech waxes most eloquent, can tightly collect and restrain themselves as their passions are on the brink of bursting forth, or can quietly dissipate their anger and desire just as these are about to boil over. Nevertheless, when one has a direct and intimate understanding of pure knowing, such tasks naturally are not difficult. If we look for the source of these various shortcomings [i.e., in regard to speech, feelings, and anger and desire], it does not lie in the foundation of pure knowing; they only arise when pure knowing has become obscured and blocked up. When pure knowing arises, it is like the sun shining forth; all ghosts and demons dissolve and disappear [in its light]. When the *Mean* says, "to know what is shameful is close to courage," what is meant by "knowing what is shameful" is simply the shame one feels when one is unable to extend one's pure knowing.[96] Many people today feel ashamed when they are unable to force others to accept what they say, when they are unable to overwhelm others with their passions, or when they are unable to give full rein to their anger and desires. They do not understand that these various shortcomings all are things that obscure and block up their pure knowing and are precisely the kind of thing about which a gentleman should be most ashamed. And so, contrary to what is right, people today take it as shameful that they are unable to obscure and block up their pure knowing. This is precisely to be ashamed of something that is not shameful and to have no shame about what is truly shameful. Is this not lamentable indeed?

You two gentlemen are my intimate friends, and nothing is more important to me than helping you in some way. My wish is that you both become like the so-called great ministers of ancient times. Those in ancient times who were known as great ministers were renowned, not because of their intelligence and resourcefulness, but only because they were "plain and unaffected, lacking other abilities, mild and straightforward, with a generous spirit."[97] In terms of intelligence and resourcefulness, you gentlemen are exceptional and far surpass the vast majority of people. The only reason you lack confidence in yourselves is that you are not yet able to extend your pure knowing and have not yet attained the state of being "plain and unaffected," "mild and straightforward."

The present state of the world may be compared to a person suffering numerous grave maladies. The only real hope of bringing the dead back to life in this case lies with you gentlemen. But how can you treat the ills of the world before curing yourselves? In the depths of my heart, I have an idea that I feel compelled

---

96. *Mean* 20.ix, in Part III, Selection 36.

97. *Documents, Documents of Zhou,* "Declaration of the Duke of Qin."

to share with you in every detail. Whenever the two of you meet, I hope you secretly will invoke this thought to help keep each other on course and in line. You must conquer and expel every vestige of selfishness, really form one body with Heaven, Earth, and the myriad creatures, truly "pacify and save"[98] the world, and return it to the ideal state of rule that existed during the Three Dynasties.[99] Then, you will prove yourselves worthy of our sagely and enlightened emperor, repay the favor he has shown you, and by contributing to this great enterprise not waste your time on earth.

I lie here on my sickbed among the mountains and forest glens and can only prepare medicines and drugs in an effort to prolong my life. But I am in profound sympathy with you gentlemen out there [serving as officials], and so, before realizing what was happening, I find that I have gone into such extensive detail. I hope you will make allowances for my excessive show of feeling.

---

98. *Documents, Documents of Zhou,* "The Charge to Zhong of Cai."
99. The golden age of the Xia, Shang, and Zhou dynasties.

Women and Gender

"Admonitions of the Court Instructress," attributed to Gu Kaizhi.

45. Cheng Yi, "Biographies of My Parents"

From *Reflections on Things at Hand*
translation by Wing-tsit Chan[1]

Cheng Yi's brief biographical accounts of his parents are from the section on "The Way to Regulate the Family" from Reflections on Things at Hand, *a highly influential anthology of Neo-Confucian writings, compiled by Zhu Xi and Lǔ Zǔqiān 呂祖謙 (1137–1181). Cheng Yi's account gives a highly representative description of what an ideal father and mother were like, according to orthodox Confucianism. —Eds.*

My late father[2] was a chief officer of the first rank.[3] His private name was Xiang and his courtesy name was Bowen [1006–1090]. Over the years he obtained

---

1. From "The Way to Regulate the Family," chapter 6 of *Jinsìlù* 近思錄. Translation taken, with modifications, from Wing-tsit Chan, *Reflections on Things at Hand* (New York: Columbia University Press, 1967), pp. 179–81. Reprinted with permission of the publisher. In the original Chinese, these biographies have no title, but we have supplied one for ease of reference. All footnotes are by the translator unless otherwise indicated. —Eds.

2. In this biography, Cheng Yi called his father "sir" or "the gentleman" and his mother "madame." I have used "father" and "mother" instead.

3. During the Song dynasty, this was an honorary position with a salary but no official duties. Previously the duty of a chief officer had been to deliberate on state matters.

five hereditary positions due an official's son and gave them to descendants of his brothers. When he gave orphaned girls in the community in marriage, he always did his best. He gave away his official remuneration to support poor relatives. His brother's wife, whose maiden name was Liu, became a widow, and he supported and took care of her wholeheartedly. When her son-in-law died, he welcomed my cousin, supported and provided her son with an education, and treated him like his own son and nephew. Later, when my cousin's own daughter also became a widow, fearing that my cousin was deeply grieved, he took the widowed daughter home and gave her in marriage. At that time his official position was minor and his remuneration slight. He denied himself in order to be charitable to others. People felt that he did what was difficult for others to do.

Father was kindhearted and sympathetic but at the same time firm and decisive. In his daily associations with the young and the lowly, he was always careful lest he hurt them. But if they violated any moral Pattern, he would not give in. Not a day passed when he did not inquire whether those who served him were adequately fed and clothed.

He married Miss Hou.[4] My mother was known for filial piety and respectfulness in serving her parents-in-law. She and father treated each other with full respect, as guests are treated. Grateful for her help at home, father treated her with even greater reverence. But mother conducted herself with humility and obedience. Even in small matters, she never made decisions alone but always asked my father before she did anything. She was benevolent, sympathetic, liberal, and earnest. She cared for and loved the children of my father's concubines just as she did her own. My father's cousin's son became an orphan when very young, and she regarded him as her own.

She was skillful in ruling the family. She was not stern, but correct. She did not like to beat servants but, instead, looked upon little servants as her own children. If we children should scold them, she would always admonish us, saying, "Although people differ in noble and humble stations, they are people just the same. When you grow up, can you do the same thing?"[5] Whenever father got angry, she always gently explained the matter to him. But if we children were wrong, she would not cover up. She often said, "Children become unworthy if a mother covers up their wrongdoings so the father is unaware of them."

Mother had six sons. Only two are still living.[6] Her love and affection for us were of the highest degree. But in teaching us she would not give in a bit. When we were only several years old, sometimes we stumbled when we walked. People in the family would rush forward to hold us, for fear we might cry. Mother would always scold us with a loud voice and say, "If you had walked gently, would you have stumbled?" Food was always served us by her side. If we

---

4. Daughter of Hou Daoji, a magistrate and a native of Taiyuan Prefecture in modern Shanxi.

5. Which the little sons presumably had accused the servants of failing to do.

6. Cheng Hao and Cheng Yi. The other four died young.

swallowed the sauces, as we often did, she would immediately shout and stop us, saying "If you seek to satisfy your desires when you are young, what will you do when you grow up?" Even when we gave orders to others, we were not allowed to scold in harsh language. Consequently my brother and I are not particular in our food and clothing, and do not scold people in harsh language. It is not that we are this way by nature but that we were taught to be like this. When we quarreled with others, even if we were right, she would not take sides with us. She said, "The trouble is that one cannot bend and not that one cannot stretch out." When we were somewhat older, we were always told to keep company with good teachers and friends. Although we were poor, whenever someone wanted to invite a guest, she would gladly make preparations for it.

When mother was seven or eight, she read an ancient poem, which says,

> Women do not go out of doors at night.
> If they do, they carry a lighted candle.[7]

From then on, she never went outside the gate of her living quarters after dark. As she grew up, she loved literature but did not engage in flowery compositions. She considered it vastly wrong for present-day women to pass around literary compositions, notes, and letters.

46. Zhu Xi, "The Way of the Family"

From *Further Reflections on Things at Hand*
translation by Allen Wittenborn[8]

The following selections come from Further Reflections on Things at Hand. *The selections consist of key remarks pulled from thousands of pages of lessons and dialogues of Zhu Xi. The book was compiled by Zhāng Bóxíng 張伯行 (1651–1725) a great admirer of Zhu and an adherent of Zhu's vision of Confucianism. Students used the book as a kind of primer or introduction to Zhu's thought, allowing them to become acquainted with his teaching without reading through the thousands of pages of his recorded lessons and instructions available at the time. The book is organized into themes that are modeled on Zhu's own* Reflections on Things at Hand, *in which Zhu, together with his coeditor Lǚ Zǔqiān, offered his own primer by selecting from the lessons and writings of his Neo-Confucian predecessors. We selected the following excerpts from the part of the book entitled "The Way of the Family,"*

---

7. Paraphrasing the *Rites*, "Regulations for Domestic Life."

8. Translation modified from Allen Wittenborn, *Further Reflections on Things at Hand: A Reader* (University Press of America, 1991). Reprinted by permission of the publisher and Allen Wittenborn.

for their relevance to the relationships between sons and mothers, fathers and daughters, and husbands and wives (that last of which was considered to be one of the five fundamental human relationships, by Confucian reckoning). Here we see an understanding of women and their ethical obligations confined largely to their role in supporting the family. —Eds.

Preface[9]

This section discusses regulation of the family, which originates with oneself and extends to others. Nothing comes before the family. The daily practice of proper social relations must not for a moment be lost. When you have sincerely achieved self-discipline, you can apply this to the family and the family can be so regulated.

1. Master Zhu said: The Way which pervades the world truly originates with the nature endowed by Heaven's mandate, and is carried out in the relations between ruler and subject, father and son, brother and brother, husband and wife, friend and friend.

2. Master Zhu said: Relations between father and son, and brother and brother are universal relationships, and serve as cornerstones in the triadic relations of the union of individuals. The relation between spouses is the source from which universal relationships are continued. Relations between ruler and subject are what universal relationships depend on for completion. Relations between friends are what universal characteristics depend on for being upright. These, then, comprise the social network in the Way of benevolence, and establish humankind's highest moral standard, and cannot even for a day be neglected.

3. Master Zhu said: The reason why a person has this body is to receive the outer appearance from their mother while their inner disposition comes from their father. Although someone may be extremely violent, they will see a child and feel compassion. On the other hand, a baby infant will see its father and laugh. How can it be otherwise?

4. Master Zhu answered Chen Fuzhong: It is worrying that domestic affairs and various and sundry matters interfere with one's learning. There certainly does not seem to be anything that can be done except to be very diligent, and to recognize that in all things there is the Pattern of the Way. Don't let it easily get away from you. Even more, if you see some everyday illness, you really have to root it out, and then you will be on the proper way to learning. But what more can we do? If an uncaring mind develops, or disinterest arises, then affairs and Patterns will be split in two. Studying books will certainly be of no use.

5. Someone said: Fathers and sons hope for there to be familial love between them. Ruler and subject hope for there to be righteousness between them.

---

9. The Preface is presumably by Zhang Boxing. —Eds.

Master Zhu said: It isn't that they hope for it to be like this. It is just that of itself there is familial love between father and son, and of itself there is righteousness between ruler and subject.

6. Master Zhu said: Admonish frequently but be gradual and cautious. Do not be rash and violent; rather exercise composure.

7. Master Zhu said: The intimacy between a father and son is the acme of Heavenly Pattern and human feelings.

8. Someone asked, the feelings parents have for a child are that of inexhaustible tenderness and love, and a desire that they be intelligent and firmly established. Is this what is called a Sincere mind?

9. Ye Chengzhi asked a question concerning the unfortunate situation wherein a stepmother and half brother are unable to get along.

Master Zhu said: From old it has been this way. You can look at the case of Shun for that.[10] And later on situations were even more numerous. All we can do is hope that the children will be filial.

10. Yu Yin had this to say: Zhongzi's brother was not unkind. Why avoid him? Zhongzi's mother was not without compassion. Why set her apart?[11]

Master Zhu said: The kindness between brothers may be different in form but is the same in spirit. Whether in matters of life and death, of misery and joy, there is no occasion when they are not mutually dependent.

12. Master Zhu said: Brothers may have the misfortune of being contentious and quarrelsome at home, but when there is outside insult only in common accord can they guard against it. Even if you have a very good friend, how can you help him? Fu Chen said: "Though brothers may have minor squabbles, this is not cause to throw away fraternal affection."

13. Someone asked, conscientiousness is simply an honest heart. In the day-to-day exercise of human relations everyone should go by this. Why is it that the word "conscientiousness" is used only in connection with service to a superior?[12]

Master Zhu said: Fathers and sons, brothers and brothers, husbands and wives—all these relations are Heavenly Pattern. There is no one who does not himself understand love and reverence. Even though the ruler-subject rela-

---

10. For one account of Shun's treatment of his parents and half brother see *Mengzi* 5A.1–7; also, 4B26, 28.

11. Yu Yin is likely a reference to the usurper of the throne from his half brother, Guang (Duke Zhuang). The Marquis of Qi, being childless, declared Guang, his niece's eldest son, as a successor. Later, however, Rongzi, his favorite concubine, bore him a child, Zhongzi (probably the one in question in this passage) whom the marquis favored over Guang. The Marquis of Qi unsuccessfully tried to prevent the successions of Guang in favor of Zhongzi. Rongzi eventually was executed and Zhongzi arrested. See *Zuozhuan*, "Duke Xiang Gong," year 19.

12. The character translated here as "conscientiousness" is *zhōng* 忠, which is sometimes used more narrowly to refer to the virtue of loyal service to a superior.—Eds.

tionship is also based on Heavenly Pattern, and thus one of righteousness and harmony, still the average person easily becomes morally lax. Therefore, it is necessary to speak of "conscientiousness," but even this does not sufficiently explain it.

14. Master Zhu answered Hu Bofeng: To live as a man and woman is the most intimate affair, and the exercise of the Way is found therein. This is why the Way of the gentleman is so widespread,[13] and yet secret. It lies within darkness and obscurity, where it cannot be seen atop the sleeping mat [where passions may be aroused],[14] and people may look on it with contempt. But this is not the way of our natural endowment. The Way of the gentleman begins its rise in the confidential moments between husband and wife,[15] but in its furthest extent it reaches from the heights of Heaven to the depths of the Earth. If we fail to understand the personal caution of the gentleman,[16] then how can we ever realize it? . . . The *Understanding Words* says: "The Way exists in matters of food and drink and man and woman, but anyone engulfed in its flow will not understand its essence." It also says: "Through contact [husbands and wives] will know propriety; through intercourse they will know the Way. Only through concentration can we protect it without losing it." This is the meaning.

15. Master Zhu said: [The relationship between] husbands and wives is the most intimate and the most private of all human relations. We may not want to tell something to a father or brother, but it can all be told to one's wife. These are the most intimate of human affairs and the Way is exercised therein.

16. Master Zhu said: The feelings between husband and wife are very intimate, but they can easily become overindulgent. Unless you are especially careful, selfish desires will find you playing on the field of frivolity, and self-deceit will leave you in the arena of ignorance. If you understand the importance of the beginning of things, and the moment of secret subtlety, exercise caution and be in awe. Then moral cultivation will come from within—use it to serve fathers and brothers, and deal with companions and friends. In all of this your efforts will easily be effective.

17. Master Zhu said: The beneficial rain that falls from the mixing of Yin and Yang is like the Way of the home that comes from the harmony between husband and wife. Therefore, those who are husband and wife should endeavor to be united in mind for it is not fit to reach the point of anger.

---

13. For Zhu's exclamation that the Way of the gentleman is widespread, see the *Mean* 12.

14. The parenthetical remarks concerning "darkness and obscurity" and the "conjugal mat" follow the comments of Zhang Boxing.

15. For the "confidential moments between husband and wife," see the *Mean* 12.

16. The "personal caution of the gentleman" refers to Kongzi's dictum that part of the make-up of such a person is to be watchful over himself even when he is alone, that is, to guard against self-deception. See *Great Learning*, Commentary 6, in Part III, Selection 33.

18. Someone asked, a wife is subject to seven grounds for divorce.[17] Nevertheless, is this a proper principle of the Way and not a measure of expediency?

Master Zhu said: It is.

19. Master Zhu said: To do wrong is unbecoming for a wife, and to do good is also unbecoming for a wife. A woman is merely to be obedient to what is proper. If a daughter does nothing wrong, that is enough. If she does good, then likewise, that is neither a favorable nor a desirable thing. Only spirits and food are her concern, and not to occasion sorrow to her parents is all that is called for. The *Changes* says, "Do not give in to presents and gifts; only through firm correctness will there be auspicious things."[18] And Mengzi's mother said, "The proper ritual conduct of a woman is to prepare the five grains for food, ferment the wine, care for one's mother- and father-in-law, mend clothes, and that is all."[19] Therefore, a woman should bear the refinement of the inner chambers and desist from any ulterior motives.

20. Master Zhu said: Of all the human relationships, those between friends are the most important.

21. Master Zhu then talked about poverty: If friends can manage their money with mutual benefit, and without violating the principle of the Way, it is all right to have money. Clearly, if their relationship is in accordance with the Way, and meets with propriety, even Kongzi would accept this. If you do not mutually entrust in the right way, but simply benefit each other with money, that is definitely out of the question.

22. Master Zhu said: When friends are at odds the problem should be cleared up, but cleared up gradually. If there is no outstanding reason, then it isn't necessary to break relations. When there is intimacy do not lose that which makes it intimate; when there is something important do not lose that which makes it important.

25. Master Zhu said: When the groom goes to receive his bride at her home without seeing her parents, this is because she has not yet met her in-laws. If [the bride] enters his home without meeting the in-laws, this is because her proper role as a wife has not yet been completed.

---

17. The seven traditional reasons for which a man could divorce his wife were the following: (1) failure to produce a male heir, (2) adultery, (3) disrespect to the parents-in-law, (4) being contentious and quarrelsome, (5) stealing, (6) jealousy, and (7) incurable disease. The theory was that any of these would result in a ruined household, and to prevent this the wife would be forced to leave the home on any one of the seven grounds.

18. *Changes,* third line statement on hexagram 37, Jiaren.—Eds.

19. See Liu Xiang's "Mengzi's Mother," Part I, Selection 12.

47. Luo Rufang, "Essay on the Hall of Motherly Affection and Chaste Widowhood at Linchuan, Jiangxi"

translation by Yu-Yin Cheng[20]

Due to the tremendous influence of Wang Yangming in the Ming dynasty, a significant body of Neo-Confucian intellectuals began to entertain views quite different from the orthodoxy of Zhu Xi and his philosophical predecessors. One of the more remarkable philosophical movements that arose in this period was associated with the Tàizhōu School 泰州學派, a group of thinkers who took the views of Wang Yangming in a radical new direction. Wang had promoted the notion that people have an innate and fully formed moral faculty that he called liáng zhī 良知, *translated in this volume as "pure knowing."[21] Taizhou thinkers shared Wang's belief in pure knowing, but also stressed—even more than Wang—the universality and accessibility of the faculty. Everyone, regardless of background, gender, or even age, has pure knowing, and one need not be deeply immersed in a classical Confucian education in order to draw or act on it. Building on these presuppositions, some Taizhou thinkers began to argue for greater equality and a more inclusive role for women in public life. Here we will look at an essay by one such thinker, Luó Rǔfāng 羅汝芳 (1515–1588). Luo was deeply convinced that women should have access to and engage in the literary, philosophical, and religious pursuits that were traditionally reserved for men. He argued that women stood to make tremendous contributions to these areas and that they were fully entitled to the benefits of philosophical and religious enlightenment. Luo also pushed for a more inclusive framework with which to understand human relationships, one that takes account of the important role that women play in moral life and moral cultivation. Indeed, as we will see, some of his writings might even suggest that the relationship between mother and child is deeper and more fundamental for moral development than any other. —Eds.*

---

20. The following translation is taken, with some modifications, from Susan Mann and Yu-Yin Cheng, eds., *Under Confucian Eyes: Writings on Gender in Chinese History* (Berkeley and Los Angeles: University of California Press, 2001), pp. 114–15. There it appears under the title "Essay on the Hall of Motherly Nurturance and Chaste Widowhood at Linchuan, Jiangxi," substituting "nurturance" for "affection" as a translation of *ci* 慈 (compassion or care, especially the care of parents for their children).

21. See, for example, Wang Yangming, "Reply to Wei Shiyue," in Part III, Selection 44, §7.

A mother nurtures her child with affection and a child serves his mother with filiality. This is the normal capacity of every human being. Such normal capacities are bestowed by Heaven. They are rooted in the mind and given expression in feelings, and will never stop. A mother's affection, the natural outpouring of her mind's feelings, invokes her child's filiality, and the child repays her affection with filial piety. If we recognize that a mother's affection is "normal," we must also acknowledge that when great hardship befalls her and she must sustain her affection for her child while preserving her fidelity to her husband, her actions have exceeded the norm and become extraordinary.

From ancient times to the present, there has never been a woman who has not reared a child after she becomes a mother. When times are normal, her affection toward her child is easy to sustain. But in extraordinary circumstances, it may prove difficult. In times of hardship a mother may suffer greatly even while she tries to sustain her affection for her child, which will in turn invoke the child's filiality. But by the same token, hardship will make it difficult to behave in a filial manner to repay his mother's affection. A case in point is what happened to the student Chen Shiwei.

Shiwei's father died soon after he was born. At the time his mother, Lady Dong, had just passed her sixteenth year, yet she vowed resolutely to rear her infant son. So desolate was her life that she only had her own form and shadow for consolation. Yet in order to bring glory to her husband's family, she wished her son to grow into a dignified man of spirit and serve as an official with ritual duties. The extraordinary hardship she suffered, as difficult as climbing a ladder to reach Heaven, fills us with admiration and also with sadness. And now His Highness, Prince Yi, has specially composed the following tribute, inscribing the words "Motherly Affection and Chaste Widowhood" on the tablet of the hall in his own hand; and the tablet has been duly presented by Prefect Gu of Jianchang and Magistrate Zhu of Nancheng. This is not simply to praise Madame Dong's virtue, but also to manifest clearly the hardships and difficulties she suffered!

Facing the conditions of her life, Madame Dong exhausted her energies to overcome hardship, remaining faithful and chaste for years, just exactly as it had been recorded in the detailed records of her deeds, which are so unbearably painful to read that one closes the book without finishing. Having passed decades in this manner, she now claims the accolades of the present.

Reflecting on his mother's suffering, her son Shiwei is easily moved within his heart; reading the tablet inscribed in her memory, he also easily expresses his heart outwardly. And isn't this just as it should be, when filial piety responds to parental affection, flowing out naturally from one's Heavenly-bestowed mind, and love is aroused spontaneously, without encumbrance?

Mengzi wrote: "There is a way to please one's parents. If one examines himself and finds that he is not Sincere, he cannot please his parents."[22] Our minds and

---

22. Translation of *Mengzi* 4A12, from Wing-tsit Chan, *A Source Book in Chinese Philosophy* (Princeton: Princeton University Press, 1963), p. 74.

our feelings are innately endowed by Heaven. What we sense and what we touch stimulate them and arouse them spontaneously. Can this happen in the absence of Sincerity? I have never known a person who was Sincere who failed to please his parents; nor have I ever known a child who pleased his parents who failed to be loyal. . . . Shiwei, who has learned about pure knowing under the tutelage of his uncle, Chen Mingshui, is striving to fulfill his ambition to become a sage. Surely he will achieve his aim gradually over time without worries. . . .

In ancient times there was a saying: "Filial piety—extend it to spread over the four seas! Array it to fill Heaven and earth! Continue it day and night from the past into the present!"[23] These are hardly empty words. What is to prevent our Shiwei from achieving everything he is capable of?

---

23. This appears to be a paraphrase of remarks in the *Rites,* "Meaning of Sacrifices."—Eds.

Li Zhi

—

48. "A Letter in Response to the Claim that Women Cannot Understand the Way Because They Are Shortsighted," from *A Book to Burn*

translation by Pauline C. Lee, Rivi Handler-Spitz, and Haun Saussy[1]

*The essay by Luo Rufang (Part III, Selection 47) gave us our first glimpse of some of the philosophy associated with the Taizhou School, notable for arguing that the moral capacity for "pure knowing" (*liang zhi) is both universal and accessible to everyone regardless of background, and for thinking more expansively about the social and moral roles of women and other groups traditionally excluded from public life. Li Zhi 李贄 (1527–1602) was one of the most representative Taizhou philosophers. A public intellectual, historian, and a celebrated commentator on popular literature, Li was something of a contrarian who openly embraced views that deeply offended conservative Confucian sensibilities about sex, love, gender, and classical education in the Confucian*

Li Zhi.

---

1. Translation forthcoming in *A Book to Burn: Banned Writings of a Ming Iconoclast*, by Rivi Handler-Spitz, Pauline C. Lee, and Haun Saussy (New York: Columbia University Press, 2015). Used with permission. This translation is based on *A Book to Burn* (*Fenshu* 焚書), Beijing: Zhonghua shuju, 1961, pp. 98–99.

canon. (Knowing how his views would be received by mainstream literati, he gave the names A Book to Hide *and* A Book to Burn *to his two most significant collections of writings.)²Although he generally considered himself a Confucian, he nevertheless drew liberally from a variety of religious and philosophical traditions. In the following essay, Li argues for a kind of moral equality between women and men. —Eds.*

Yesterday I had the opportunity to hear your esteemed teaching wherein you proclaimed that women, being shortsighted, are incapable of understanding the Way. Indeed this is so! Indeed this is so!

Women live within the inner chambers while men wander throughout the world.³ There exists vision that is shortsighted and vision that is farsighted; this fact need not be discussed. But what is called shortsightedness comes about when one has not seen anything beyond the inner chambers. In contrast, the farsighted deeply investigate the clear, vast, and open fields. The shortsighted perceive only what happens within a hundred year span—what happens within the lifespan of their children and grandchildren or what affects their own bodies. The farsighted see beyond their own physical bodies, transcend the superficial appearances of life and death, and extend into a realm that is immeasurably, incomparably large, larger than what the numbers a hundred, a thousand, a million, a billion, or an eon can measure. The shortsighted hear only the chatter in the streets, the viewpoints of those in the alleys, and the talk of children in the marketplace. The farsighted are able to hold great men in deep awe; they dare not disrespect the words of the sages, and moreover, they are unmoved by the dislikes and prejudices that come from the mouths of commoners.⁴

I humbly propose that those who desire to discourse on shortsightedness and farsightedness should do as I have done. One must not stop at the observation that women's vision is shortsighted. To say that male and female *people* exist is acceptable. But to say that male and female *vision* exist, how can that be acceptable? To say that shortsightedness and farsightedness exist is acceptable. But to say that a man's vision is entirely farsighted and a woman's vision is wholly shortsighted, once again, how can that be acceptable?

---

2. For a complete translation of the latter, see *A Book to Burn: Banned Writings of a Ming Iconoclast,* by Rivi Handler-Spitz, Pauline C. Lee, and Haun Saussy (New York: Columbia University Press, 2015).

3. Alluding to *Rites,* "The Pattern of the Family."

4. Li Zhi quotes from *Analects* 16.8. "The gentleman stands in awe of three things: the Mandate of Heaven, great men, and the teachings of the sages. The petty person does not understand the Mandate of Heaven, and thus does not regard it with awe; he shows disrespect to great men, and ridicules the teachings of the sages." Translation by Edward Slingerland in Philip J. Ivanhoe and Bryan W. Van Norden, eds., *Readings in Classical Chinese Philosophy,* 2nd ed. (Indianapolis: Hackett Publishing, 2005), pp. 47–48.

Suppose there exists a person with a woman's body and a man's vision. Suppose she delights in hearing upright discourse and knows that uncultivated speech is not worth listening to; she delights in learning about the transcendent and understands that the ephemeral world is not worth becoming attached to. If men of today were to see such a woman, I fear that they would all feel shame and remorse, sweat profusely, and be unable to utter a single syllable. This person with a woman's body and a man's vision is perhaps the very sort of person Kongzi wandered the world in search of. He desired to meet her just once but could never find her. In our times we merely see women as shortsighted creatures. Isn't this grievously wrong? However, whether or not these views are wrong, why should women worry over what we think of them? But perhaps a disinterested observer would find this ridiculous.

From our present perspective we can observe the following: Yi Jiang, a woman, "filled in the ranks," being the ninth of King Wu's ministers. Nothing hindered her from being counted as one of the "ten able ministers" alongside Zhou, Shao, and Taigong.[5] Wen Mu, a sagely woman, rectified the customs of the southern regions.[6] Nothing prevented her from being praised along with San Yisheng and Tai Dian as one of the "four friends" [who helped King Wu in his difficulties].[7] These trifling, worldly deeds responded to the needs of the time: the concern [of Kings Wu and Wen] was no more than to establish one era of peace, and yet they dared not link short-sightedness with women and farsightedness with men. Those who study the transcendent Way and desire to be like Shakyamuni and Kongzi—people who, having heard the Way in the morning, could die contentedly in the evening—have even less reason to draw this distinction.[8]

---

5. Yi Jiang was the consort of King Wu, the founder of the Zhou dynasty, and she is sometimes said to have taken part in the council of ministers. In *Analects* 8.20, Kongzi is recorded as saying, "Is not the saying that talents are difficult to find, true? [Though the rulers of remote antiquity had able advisors,] yet there was a woman among them. Thus there were only nine able men [among the ten advisors]" (trans. modified from Legge, *Confucian Analects, Great Learning, and Doctrine of the Mean* [London: Trübner, 1893]). *Documents, Documents of Zhou*, "Lord Shi," refers to the "ten able ministers" of King Wu; see Legge, *The Shoo King* (London: Trübner, 1865), p. 292. Dukes Zhou and Shao were brothers of King Wu who assisted in the founding of the dynasty; Taigong was a disaffected general of the Shang who came over to the Zhou. Li Zhi combines the two passages.

6. Wen Mu is the honorary designation of Tai Si, the consort of King Wen and mother of King Wu. The ancient commentaries to the *Odes* credit her with having given such a standard of virtuous behavior that the customs of the southern regions were "rectified."

7. King Wu was imprisoned by his sovereign, King Zhou of Shang, who was jealous of his subordinate's greater reputation. According to the *Zuozhuan* (Duke Xiang, 31st year), Wu's "four friends" paid a ransom to free him. The four named in the *Documents* were Taigong, Nan Gongshi, San Yisheng, and Hong Yao—all male. Li Zhi may be misremembering the passage, or relying on a different interpretation.

8. Li Zhi quotes from *Analects* 4.8: "He has not lived in vain who, hearing the Way in the morning, dies that very night." Shakyamuni is the historical Buddha.

If a small-minded man in the street were to hear someone talk about farsighted women, he would relentlessly upbraid the speaker for imagining that women could "peek out from behind the doors of the inner chambers,"[9] and in the name of maintaining "female" chastity, consider Wen Mu and Yi Jiang to be criminals. Isn't this grievously wrong? Thus, all gentlemen who consider themselves endowed with farsightedness should neither behave in such a way as to incite the ridicule of their betters, nor strive to gain the approval or affection of small-minded men of the marketplace. If one desires to be admired by small-minded men of the marketplace, then one is just another such small-minded creature. Is this farsightedness, or is this shortsightedness? One needs to decide this for oneself. I say that a farsighted woman who can rectify human relations and serve as a propitious example of excellence is the sort of person who is born only once in several hundred years, and comes as the result of accumulated virtue.

There once was a woman named Xue Tao who came from the city of Chang'an.[10] Yuan Weizhi[11] heard about her and requested a posting in Sichuan so that he could meet Xue Tao. Before Weizhi's departure, Tao wrote a poem "In Praise of Four Friends" to reciprocate his good intentions.[12] Weizhi acknowledged her as his superior by far. Weizhi was an outstanding poet in his day. Was it easy for him to acknowledge anyone as his superior? Ah! A literary talent such as Tao's can attract the admiration of people a thousand miles away. What if there were a woman wandering through this world with an understanding achieved by studying the Buddha's teachings? If one were to meet a woman who transcended this material world, could anyone possibly refuse to greatly admire her? But there has never been such a thing, you say. Have you not heard the story of Layman Pang?[13]

Layman Pang came from the city of Hengyang in the Chu region. He and his wife, Mother Pang, and their daughter, Ling Zhao, revered the Chan master Mazu[14] and made him their teacher. They sought to transcend the material

---

9. *Changes,* second line statement on hexagram 20, Guan.

10. Xue Tao (768–c. 831), honorary title "Lady Collator of Books," was one of the most distinguished women poets of her day and a famous courtesan of the Tang dynasty. Although born in the Tang capital of Chang'an, she spent most of her life in Sichuan. She shared her poetry with eminent poets such as Du Fu, Bai Juyi, and Yuan Zhen.

11. Yuan Zhen, courtesy name Weizhi (779–831), was a poet and the author of the short story "The Story of Yingying," much later adapted as the Yuan drama *The Story of the Western Wing*. In addition to his literary career, Yuan Zhen was also a prominent government official, a person of vision, intent on social as well as literary reform. In 809, he travelled to Sichuan as an investigating censor on an inspection tour and at this time asked to meet Xue Tao.

12. The "Four Friends" in this instance are the four constant companions of the scholar: paper, ink, brush, and inkstone.

13. Pang Yun, often referred to as Pang Gong (c. 740–c. 808), turned in the middle of his life to Chan Buddhism and was said to have attained the ultimate spiritual enlightenment. His poems are found in *The Recorded Sayings of Layman Pang* (*Pang jushi yulu*).

14. Mazu (709–788), a native of Sichuan, is one of the most renowned Chan sages.

world and one day they escaped the cycle of rebirth. By putting aside the things of this world, they gave inspiration for all humanity. I hope, sir, that this man's story can stand as an example of what it is to be a farsighted person. If you tell me, "I must wait to discuss this issue with the likes of a small-minded person from the marketplace," then I am at a loss for words.

49. "On the Child-like Mind"

translation by Pauline C. Lee[15]

The following essay is often regarded as the most definitive statement of Li Zhi's philosophy. In it, he appeals to the notion of the "child-like mind" (tóng xīn 童心), which he takes from Mengzi *4B12: "Great people are those who do not lose their childlike mind." Here, "child-like mind" connotes purity and lack of corruption. Li argues that the spontaneous moral responses, originating in this "child-like mind," are better by virtue of being genuine and closely connected to our innate moral sensibilities. —Eds.*

In the concluding remarks to his preface to the *Western Chamber* the Farmer of Dragon Ravine[16] stated: "Those who understand me shall not say I still possess the child-like mind."[17]

The child-like mind is the genuine mind. If one denies the child-like mind, then he denies the genuine mind. As for the child-like mind, free of all falsehood and entirely genuine, it is the fundamental mind[18] at the very beginning of the

---

15. Translation from *Li Zhi, Confucianism, and the Virtue of Desire* (Albany: SUNY Press, 2012), pp. 123–25. Used with permission. This translation is based on the Chinese text in *A Book to Burn* (*Fenshu* 焚書), Beijing: Zhonghua shuju, 1961, pp. 98–99.

16. The *Western Chamber* 西廂記, a thirteenth-century, Yuan dynasty drama by Wang Shifu 王實甫 (ca. 1250–1300), was often considered a subversive work in traditional China and was banned during the Yuan, Ming, and Qing dynasties. Those who commented on the work sought anonymity through pseudonyms. The Farmer of the Dragon Cave Mountain is an unknown commentator.

17. The Farmer of the Dragon Ravine is the commentator of a 1582 edition of the *Western Chamber*. The quotation is drawn directly from the preface of this edition. Eng Chew Cheang translates the relevant portion of this preface as follows:

> Having leisure at my humble home, I casually punctuate [the text of the Hsi-hsiang chi.] . . . [Often] I hold the text and alone chant [the poems contained in it] during the windy and rainy days, or the beautiful moonlight nights. [In so doing,] I while away the time, and break [the strains] of poverty and sadness. *Those who understand me must not say that I still possess the mind of an infant.* (italics mine)

18. The concept of "fundamental mind" (*běnxīn* 本心) finds its original source in *Mengzi* 6A10.

first thought. Losing the child-like mind is losing the genuine mind. Losing the genuine mind is losing the genuine self. A person who is not genuine will never again regain that with which he began.

A child is the beginning of a person; the child-like mind is the beginning of the mind. As for the beginning of the mind, how can it be lost! How is it possible, suddenly, to lose the child-like mind? From the beginning, aural and visual impressions enter in through the ears and eyes. When one allows them to dominate what is within oneself, then the child-like mind is lost. As one grows older, one hears and sees the "Patterns of the Way" [i.e., moral teachings].[19] When one allows these to dominate what is within oneself, then the child-like mind is lost. As one grows older, the Patterns of the Way that one hears and sees grow more numerous with each day, thus extending the breadth of one's knowledge and perceptions. Thereupon, one realizes that one should covet a good reputation, and endeavor to enhance one's reputation. One then loses one's child-like mind. One realizes that a bad reputation is to be disdained, and endeavors to conceal such a reputation. One then loses one's child-like mind.

The Patterns of the Way that one hears and sees all come from extensive reading and acquaintance with moral Pattern, but did not the sages of antiquity read books? When they did not read books, their child-like mind was secure and preserved; when they studied extensively, they protected their child-like mind and kept themselves from losing it. They are unlike those students for whom the more they read and become acquainted with moral Pattern, the more they obstruct their child-like mind. Now, if by extensively reading and acquainting oneself with moral Pattern students obstruct their child-like mind, then why did the sages so often write books and establish teachings that obstruct what these students do? Since the child-like mind is obstructed, then when one speaks, one's words will not come from one's heart. When one manifests such words by carrying out governmental affairs, then his governing of affairs will have no foundation. When one employs such words in writing compositions, one's compositions will fail to express the truth. If the beauty does not come from within, if the brightness is not born from true sincerity,[20] then even the attempt to create one sentence of virtuous words[21] will fail, in the end. What is the reason for this? Because when the child-like mind is obstructed, the Patterns of the Way that come from outside the self become one's mind.

---

19. What is translated here as "Patterns of the Way" (*Daoli*), is also translated as "Overarching Pattern" (see Part III, Selection 32, §20). In this context, Li Zhi seems to have in mind discrete lessons, reasons, or guidelines regarding moral behavior.—Eds.

20. Li Zhi plays on a passage from *Mengzi* 7B25: "To possess it fully in oneself is called 'beautiful,' but to shine forth with this full possession is called 'great.'" Translation by D.C. Lau, *Mencius* (New York: Penguin Books, 1970).

21. This passage draws on a passage found in the *Analects*, 14.5: "The virtuous will be sure to speak correctly, but those whose speech is good may not always be virtuous." Translation by Legge, *Confucian Analects, Great Learning, and Doctrine of the Mean* (1893).

Now, if the mind is comprised of the Patterns of the Way, which one hears and sees, then what is spoken are all words of the Patterns of the Way; they are not the spontaneous words that come from the child-like mind. Though these words may be artful, what do they have to do with who one is? How could this lead to anything other than phony people speaking phony words, enacting phony actions, and producing phony writings? Once a person is a phony, then everything he does is phony. From this, we can see that if one speaks phony words with a phony person, then the phony person will be pleased. If one speaks of phony affairs with a phony person, then the phony person will be pleased. If one discusses phony literature with a phony person, then the phony person will be pleased. When everything is phony, then nowhere will there be anyone who is displeased. When the entire theater is filled with phonies, how can a short person standing in the middle of the audience discriminate between good and bad?[22]

And so, even the most exquisite writing in the world can be destroyed by phony people and then will not be read by later generations. Is this so rare an occurrence? What is the reason for this? The most exquisite literature in the world all comes from the child-like mind. As long as the child-like mind is constantly preserved, then the Patterns of the Way, which enter in through the eyes and the ears, will not come to dominate what is within oneself. Then no age will lack great literary works and no person will lack literary talent. There will be no structurally or stylistically forced, phony literature!

Why must verse necessarily be in the unregulated style of classical poetry or collections such as the *Literary Selections*?[23] Why must prose necessarily be like that written in the pre-Qin period? Writing evolved through the ages and became the literature of the Six Dynasties, changed and became the new regulated verse of the Tang. These changed again and developed into fantastic tales,[24] changed yet again and became play-scripts[25] which developed into Yuan comedies, which in turn evolved into *The Western Chamber*[26] and *The Water Margin*,[27] and now has become the eight-legged essay[28] of today. All the most exquisite

---

22. The reference to a "short person" is to the common Chinese saying "a short person watching the theater" referring to a short person standing amidst the audience in a theater who applauds or boos with the audience even though he cannot see the play.

23. The *Literary Selections* (*Wenxuan* 文選) by Xiao Tong (501–531) is one of the most influential literary anthologies in Chinese history.

24. "Fantastic tales" emerge in the late Tang period.

25. "Play-scripts" emerge during the early Yuan period.

26. *The Western Chamber* is comprised of five Yuan dynasty comedies.

27. *The Water Margin* differs in form from *The Western Chamber* in that the former is a collection of chapters rather than of discrete plays.

28. The eight-legged essay is a highly structured essay prescribed as the standard form of examination answer from the mid-fifteenth century until the beginning of the twentieth

literature from the past through the present cannot be discussed in terms of the tendencies of the ages that preceded or followed them. Therefore, I am drawn to the spontaneous writings of those with a child-like mind. Why speak of the Six Classics! Why speak of the *Analects* and the *Mengzi*!

Now, the words one finds in the Six Classics, the *Analects*, and the *Mengzi*, either express the excessive praise and reverence of official historians or the inordinate praise of loyal subjects. If they are neither of these, then they are what inexperienced followers and dimwitted disciples have written down of their teachers' sayings. In some cases, what they recorded had an introduction but lacked a conclusion. In other cases, we have a conclusion but are without the introduction. The disciples just wrote down what they happened to see, but scholars of later generations did not critically examine these writings. They declared that these books came from the mouths of sages and established them as classics. Who knows whether or not these writings really are the words of the sages?

Even if these words did come from the sages, they were spoken to address a particular need, much like the case of prescribing a medication for a specific illness. The sages simply attended to specific situations and applied certain methods in order to save this dimwitted disciple or that inexperienced follower. While a particular medicine might cure one particular phony's illness, such prescriptions are difficult to administer [to all patients]. Given this, how could it be fitting to take these writings as the ultimate standard for thousands of generations? And so, the Six Classics, the *Analects*, and the *Mengzi* have become nothing more than a crib sheet for those belonging to the School of Pattern, a fountainhead for the phonies.[29] Certainly these texts cannot shed light on matters by speaking with words that come from the child-like mind. Oh where can I find a genuine great sage who has not lost his child-like mind and have a word with him about literature?[30]

century. Essays had eight prescribed sections. Candidates for civil service examinations were given selected phrases from classical texts and then asked to write a three- to four-hundred-character–long commentary using the eight-legged essay format.

29. The "School of Pattern" (*Lixue* 理學) refers to Neo-Confucians who largely follow Zhu Xi, and of course Zhu Xi himself.—Eds.

30. This sentence plays on a passage from chapter 26 of the *Zhuangzi*: "Where can I find someone who has forgotten words so that I may have a word with him!"

"Village School," by Xu Yang.

PART IV: LATE IMPERIAL CONFUCIANISM

The beginning of the seventeenth century marks a shift away from Neo-Confucianism, both the orthodox form associated with Cheng Yi and Zhu Xi, and the less orthodox forms associated with Wang Yangming and others. None fell entirely out of favor, and in fact Cheng-Zhu thought continued to have a firm grip on the education system, as it was still necessary to memorize Zhu's interpretations of the classics in order to pass the all-important civil service examinations. Nevertheless, China of the late Ming through the mid-Qing dynasties witnessed the rise of a new type of Confucian thinker, one who brought greater historical and philological rigor to his work and, consequently, suspected that Neo-Confucian interpretations of the great sages (especially Kongzi and Mengzi) had been distorted by Daoist and Buddhist ways of thinking. In Part IV, we look at the distinctive and new philosophical ideas and frameworks that emerged from this shift.

Late imperial Confucianism was diverse, reflecting a more expansive sense of curiosity and openness to new ideas, but three trends stand out in this period. The first is the rise of *statecraft* (*jīngshì* 經世). Prior to this period, mainstream Neo-Confucians were more interested in the character of those with political authority than in the finer points of how they wielded their power. As the *Great Learning* proclaimed, rulers must first "correct their minds" and "cultivate their selves" and only then can they "put their states in order."[1] Once the mind was corrected and the self cultivated, specifying the policies to be implemented was no longer necessary, for the sage-like political leader could be counted on to exercise compassion and good judgment in his administration. By the seventeenth century, however, some Chinese philosophers decided that they could no longer wait for sages to appear. The political and military strength of the Ming dynastic rulers had declined, "barbarians" were threatening the territorial integrity of the Han people, and the state bureaucracy was weighed down by corruption. Rather than pin their hope for a better government on the arrival of supremely virtuous administrators and rulers, it was better to reform governmental institutions so that they could work reasonably well for imperfect people. Confucian philosophers in this period thus turned to institution-building and developing new theories of governance.

Two of the great reform-minded Confucians of this era were Gù Yánwǔ 顧炎武 (1613–1682) and Huáng Zōngxī 黃宗羲 (1610–1695). Both were scholars of

---

1. *Great Learning,* Classic, in Part III, Selection 33.

many talents, but they shared a common interest in developing (1) institutional checks and balances, (2) mechanisms for informing the central government about the effects of its policies on localities, and (3) protections to allow representatives of those localities to speak freely. Some modern scholars now describe Gu and Huang as the first serious "constitutionalists" in Chinese history, insofar as they thought there should be certain rules and regulations that constrain even the emperor of China. The first selection in Part IV is Huang's famous defense of this idea, "On Law."

As many feared, the Ming dynasty did collapse and, even more distressingly for the Han Confucians, the dynastic rulers who took their place were "barbarians" from the northeast. These Manchurians, who had previously belonged to a vassal state of China, had now become the rulers of what would be the last imperial dynasty, the Qing (1644–1911). As in past instances of foreign rule, the Han Chinese chafed at the indignity of being forced to adopt the customs and authority of a people that lacked the long heritage of which they were so proud. In point of fact, the ruling Manchurians arguably adopted more of the language and cultural practices of the Han Chinese than vice versa. They even embraced Confucian principles of education and governance, and most of the essential components of Zhu Xi's curriculum lived on in state schools and the imperial examination system. But many Han Confucians continued to resent and openly defy their Manchurian rulers. Both Gu Yanwu and Huang Zongxi joined up with Ming resistance groups, which fought (ultimately without success) to retain Han control over the ever-smaller territory not yet conquered by the Qing. Most of Huang Zongxi's major works—including "On Law"—were written during this period.

What the Chinese called "statecraft" was much broader in scope than one might think. It included almost all of the areas of study seen as necessary for the regulatory functions of the state, including hydraulics (for irrigation and flood control) and astronomy (for the design of calendars). Even history and mathematics were considered important components of statecraft (both Gu and Huang were accomplished historians as well as political thinkers). As statecraft began to flourish, it brought new and more demanding notions of what counted as good evidence or arguments. This explains another major trend in the scholarship of late imperial Confucians: *evidential studies* (*kǎozhèng xué* 考 證學). Confucian practitioners of evidential studies saw themselves as engaged in a more concrete and evidence-based pursuit than their Neo-Confucian predecessors. If one wanted to reconstruct the thought of Kongzi or Mengzi, they reasoned, "empty speculation" would not succeed; instead, what is needed are rigorous methods of textual analysis and historical and linguistic evidence. (Today the Chinese phrase for "evidential studies" is sometimes translated as "philology," using a term that traditionally describes careful, historically and linguistically sophisticated study of old texts.)

A final trend of note is that, for the first time in the history of China, there was a large class of Confucian literati that saw themselves as *professional scholars*. Previously, Confucian scholarship had been linked with civil service. People tended to think the best use of a Confucian education was either to serve in government or train others to do so. (Self-cultivation was important too, of course, but it was supposed to be the kind that prepared someone for the challenges of office, even if never put to use.) But in the late imperial period, the number of official positions made available through the imperial examination system began to shrink, and even as more people were taking the exams, fewer positions were available for the handful that passed. Furthermore, more and more patronage was put toward statecraft and evidential studies, both because they were useful to the political authorities and because they yielded impressive and tangible results.

Thanks to the success of evidential studies, the Chinese literati developed powerful new tools and resources for their research, including such things as reference works on the ancient pronunciation of Chinese characters and gazetteers describing the history and geography of localities in great detail. This period also saw historically unprecedented advances in mathematics and astronomy. As a result, many people who undertook a classical Confucian education—still the most widely available and publically supported education available—made successful careers funded primarily by research and teaching. The most esteemed scholar of evidential studies in the Qing dynasty, Dài Zhèn 戴震 (1724–1777), never held government office until he was given an honorary position near the end of his life. Many of the dynasty's most successful writers and researchers saw themselves as contributing to a field or area of study rather than to public administration.

These thinkers' interest in new fields and methods brought a different character to their philosophy. All had a deep and nuanced understanding of the Chinese language and its history, and this is reflected in their work, which is often attentive to subtle differences in grammar or the changing senses of terms over the nearly two millennia between them and the classical Confucian philosophers. Most of these thinkers were also excellent historians, alert to the ways that concepts and frameworks reflect their historical context, so they were keen on reconstructing the classical Confucian views without the conceptual baggage of Daoism and Buddhism. However, Confucian practitioners of evidential studies still shared some important presuppositions with their Neo-Confucian predecessors: for the most part, the philosophers among them continued to accept the authority of the Four Books (the *Great Learning, Analects, Mengzi,* and *Mean*) and Five Classics (the *Documents, Odes, Spring and Autumn Annals, Rites,* and *Changes*), and moreover they assumed that the views expressed therein were more or less consistent with one another. So, for example, they generally worked from the presupposition that Kongzi and Mengzi were "on the same page," philosophically speaking. Just as the Neo-Confucians had done, they freely used textual evidence from one canonical source to support their interpretations of other works in the canon.

Of the major philosophers of this period, the one with the most lasting impact is Dai Zhen. Although Dai was widely admired for making tremendous contributions to philology, phonology, astronomy, and trigonometry, he was nevertheless deeply committed to understanding the classics on philosophical terms, maintaining that it brought a necessary unity and purpose to all of his studies. In his era, there was a growing tension among scholars between evidential studies and what they called "studies of morality and Pattern" (*Yìlǐ zhī xué* 義理之學). Answering objections that would sound familiar to many philosophically minded scholars today, Dai felt the need to defend his studies of morality and Pattern against the charge that it was empty, too prone to personal whim or bias, and not sufficiently grounded in verifiable evidence. And like many philosophically minded scholars today, Dai responded that his more speculative interests were required for a more holistic and ethical orientation toward life, something that mere historical or linguistic research could not provide.

Dai devoted his final years to revising a philosophical text that, in a sense, he had been working on for nearly half of his lifetime: *An Evidential Commentary on the Meanings of Terms in the* Mengzi. In that text he is concerned most of all with recapturing the original philosophical vision of Mengzi, after centuries of distortion by his Neo-Confucian predecessors. He had two particularly powerful objections to Neo-Confucianism: first, he was convinced that Neo-Confucian theories of moral deliberation did not have any built-in way of tracking the relevant moral facts. He worried that they were over-reliant on deeply felt, "spontaneous" feelings and intuitions, which yielded only "personal opinions" and not judgments informed by the distinctions that we should observe in order to bring about greater order, which was his more down-to-earth interpretation of the term "Pattern."[2] Second, he thought that the Neo-Confucians had too strong a reading of Mengzi's famous claim that human nature is good. In Dai's view, human nature is good in the sense that it predisposes us to *become* good if we have the right education and a healthy environment, not that we are born with a well-formed capacity to behave virtuously from the start, waiting to be recovered after eliminating biases and self-centered desires. (Here he had in mind what Zhu Xi and others called our "fundamental nature.")[3] In the interest of developing a superior alternative grounded in the Confucian classics, Dai built on two general themes that appeared frequently in the Confucian canon. The

---

2. Pattern (*li* 理) is a central notion in the ethics and metaphysics of orthodox Neo-Confucianism. For the orthodox philosopher Zhu Xi's understanding of the term, see Part III, Selection 32.

3. See Zhu's comments on *Mengzi* 6A6 in Part III, Selection 35.

first was empathy or sympathetic understanding (*shù* 恕), and the other was the importance of exercising discretion or "weighing" (*quán* 權) when faced with unusual or complex situations.[4]

No doubt Dai suspected that a long philosophical treatise would not be well received by his colleagues in evidential studies, but he nevertheless clung to the hope that they would recognize his *Evidential Commentary* as providing the real fruits of his widely admired work in philology and other evidential disciplines. In a short letter that he sent to his closest friend and colleague in the last year of his life, suffering from ailments that would ultimate bring it to an untimely end, Dai wrote:

> Of all of the works I have authored in my modest lifetime, the single most important is *An Evidential Commentary on the Meanings of Terms in the* Mengzi, for it contains the essentials for setting people's minds aright. Our contemporaries inflict great harm on the people by falsely regarding their own personal opinions as [expressions of] the Pattern, no matter how correct or perverse they may be. Thus I had no choice but to write my *Evidential Commentary*.[5]

One of the last great philosophers of this period was Zhāng Xuéchéng 章學誠, (1738–1801). Zhang was an outstanding historian, having both a capacious mind for historical details and all of the advantages of someone doing historical research during the heyday of evidential studies. But like Dai, whom he both criticized and greatly admired, he saw his work as necessarily intertwined with philosophy. One of Zhang's driving concerns was how best to refine ethical assessment or judgment. He argued that we must have several "virtues of the historian" in order to determine our moral obligations and the values that we should promote. Seeing the full scope of history gives us a sense of perspective, proportion, and epistemic humility. It also helps us to recognize the distinctive needs of our era, which vary from one age to the next. Finally, a sense of one's historical place provides concrete content to otherwise abstract and ambiguous recommendations featured in more theoretical approaches to ethics.

Neither Dai Zhen nor Zhang Xuecheng had much of an immediate effect on the philosophical discourse of their era. By the time of Dai's death, many evidential scholars had begun to lose interest in philosophy altogether, and some even lamented that he spent (or "wasted") so much his talents on what they saw as a fruitless enterprise. Needless to say, defenders of orthodox Neo-Confucianism were not receptive to Dai's views, and even in recent times

---

4. For remarks on sympathetic understanding in the classical Confucian canon see *Analects* 4.15, 5.12, and 6.30, all translated in Part III, Selection 34. For remarks on weighing or discretion see *Mengzi* 1A7, 4A17, and 7A26.

5. "Letter to Duàn Yùcái, II 與段玉裁二," appendix to Hu Shi's 胡適 *The Philosophy of Dai Zhen* 戴東原的哲學 (Taipei: Taiwan shang wu yin shu guan, 1996), p. 364.

Dai has been dismissed by some more mainstream Confucians as "not really profound."[6] Zhang was well regarded for his views on education but his more philosophical writings had little direct impact. But each philosopher flourished in his "philosopher afterlife," so to speak. Not long after Zhang's death, Chinese philosophers began to take a great deal of interest in Western thought, and with it many of the historicist views that they found in philosophers like Hegel, which stimulated interest in Zhang. Reformist leaders and participants in the May Fourth Movement found in Dai a kind of proto-egalitarian thinker, seeking an ethics that takes account of the powerless and downtrodden even while working within the indigenous Chinese tradition.[7] Dai is now frequently presented as the last great Confucian of the indigenous tradition, and many credit him for showing definitively that the Neo-Confucians read their tradition through Daoist and Buddhist lenses.

---

6. Wing-tsit Chan, trans., *A Source Book in Chinese Philosophy* (Princeton: Princeton University Press, 1963), p. 711.

7. During this period, critics of the Neo-Confucian establishment often invoked Dai's phrase "using Pattern for persecution of others" (*yǐ Lǐ shā rén* 以理殺人), referring to his charge that mainstream Neo-Confucian ethics encouraged the powerful to pass moral judgments based solely on personal opinion, unchecked by sympathetic consideration for the wants and needs of their subordinates. For more on the May Fourth Movement, see the introduction to Part V.

50. Huang Zongxi, "On Law"

From *Waiting for the Dawn*
translation by Justin Tiwald[1]

Huáng Zōngxī 黃宗羲 *(1610–1695) was a prominent Confucian philosopher and a master of "statecraft," the wide array of methods and disciplines considered useful for practical, state-related affairs. He is best known for his work on history and politics. Huang's most productive period of scholarship came after the Ming dynasty was overthrown and replaced by the Manchurian Qing rulers, an event that deeply distressed him. In Huang's view, a major culprit in the Ming collapse was its ineffectual political institutions, which prevented and discouraged emperors from taking account of the public good. Huang was thus among the Confucian political thinkers who was most open-minded about reforms to the dynastic system of government. He was particularly interested in mechanisms for providing the imperial court reliable information and advice, most famously through a system of academies that would serve as a staging ground for criticism and debate. He also advocated for institutional checks on the power of the emperor, proposing that executive functions should be entrusted to a prime minister who is chosen on the basis of merit. Huang pushed for different and seemingly more democratic ways of conceiving the roles and responsibilities of people in government office, arguing that the enlightened rulers of ancient times saw themselves more like guests and their subjects more like masters or hosts. Although Huang's reforms were not well received by scholar-officials in his era, they were enthusiastically embraced by many reform-minded scholar-officials at the end of the Qing dynasty and continue to attract much interest today.*

"On Law" is among the most widely discussed of Huang's political tracts. In it, he argues against two views embedded in traditional Confucian political thought. The first is that laws and institutional regulations are only as good as the people who use them, so that blame for a state's failure (or credit for its success) goes not to the laws and regulations but to the people who use them. This was the view captured in the classical Confucian philosopher Xunzi's popular slogan, "there are people who create order; there are no laws that create order."[2] The second traditional view is that any law is legitimate if sanctioned by a legitimate ruler, so that laws get their legitimacy from

---

1. This translation is based on the text of Huang's *Míng Yí Dài Fǎng Lù* 明夷待訪錄 (Taipei: Zhonghua Shuju, 1965).

2. This appears in the opening lines of the *Xunzi*, ch. 12 ("The Way of the Ruler"). See Eric L. Hutton, trans., *Xunzi: The Complete Text* (Princeton: Princeton University Press, 2014), p. 117, Lines 2–3.

the ruler's authority, not by direct appeal to independent moral standards.
Shockingly for his time, Huang rejected both of these positions. — Tr.

Until the end of the Three Dynasties there were [proper] laws; ever since the Three Dynasties there have been no [proper] laws.[3]

How can I say such a thing? The Two Emperors and the Three Kings[4] understood that the people of the world couldn't be without nourishment and so, for the people's sake, granted them fields for the cultivation of crops. They knew that the people of the world couldn't be without clothing and so, for the people's sake, granted them land on which to plant hemp and mulberry trees. They knew that the people of the world couldn't be without instruction and so, for the people's sake, gave them schools to excite their interest in learning, instituted marriage rituals to guard against licentious behavior, and required military service to guard against social disorder. These were the laws until the end of the Three Dynasties. They were never established solely for the sake of the rulers themselves.

In later times after the rulers of humankind acquired the world, they feared only that their claim to the throne wouldn't last for long, and that their descendants wouldn't be able to keep it. The laws were then made out of the worry that these events might come to pass. That being the case, their so-called "laws" were laws made for the sake of their families and not for the sake of all the people. For this reason, when the Qin overthrew the feudal states and set up administrative regions, they used those administrative regions to provide for their personal interests. The Han rulers enfeoffed the sons of their concubines so that they could maintain control for themselves.[5]

The laws of the Three Dynasties "harbored the world with the people of the world."[6] It wasn't necessary to take all of the profitable goods from every hill and pond, nor were they too suspicious to allow others the authority to reward or punish. Honor did not depend on being involved in court life nor was it lowly to live in the backcountry. In later generations they came to criticize the looseness of such laws, but in the world [of the Three Dynasties] the people didn't

---

3. The Three Dynasties are the Xia, Shang, and Zhou. For an overview of the dynasties and their most enlightened rulers, see the Introduction to Part I.

4. The worthy and virtuous founding figures in the Three Dynasties.

5. Huang Zongxi's point is that the Han emperors tried to maintain control over all of the state by maximizing the number of immediate relatives who held positions of power. Gaozu, the founder of the Han, initially enfeoffed some non-relatives for rendering exceptional service to the throne, but by the end of his life Gaozu came to see such "kings of a different family name" (*yixing wang* 異姓王) as a major threat to his power. The practice of installing non-relatives ended shortly after his death.

6. A different interpretation of the phrase more widely translated as "hiding the world in the world," from the *Dazong shi* 大宗師 chapter of the *Zhuangzi*.

see high status as desirable nor low status as detestable. The looser the laws, the less disorder that was produced. This could be called "lawfulness without laws."[7]

The laws of later generations "harbor the world in the [ruler's personal] treasure chest."[8] They don't want to leave profitable goods to people of low status and they inevitably want to accumulate wealth for those of high status. When they employ a person they suspect him of selfishness and hire yet another person to keep his selfishness in check. When they implement a policy they worry that it will be easy for people to cheat and establish another policy to guard against cheating. All the people of the world know the location of [the ruler's] treasure chest, and so the ruler is constantly preoccupied with worries that it will be taken. Consequently, the laws have to be made tight. The tighter the laws, the more disorder that springs up in their midst. These could be called "unlawful laws."[9]

Commentators maintain that each dynasty has its own laws, and that the descendants adopt the laws of their ancestors as a matter of filial piety. Now former kings created unlawful laws because they couldn't conquer the selfish excesses of their own desires and profit-seeking, and later kings sometimes destroy their ancestral laws because they too can't conquer the selfish excesses in their desires and profit-seeking. While it is true that destroying laws inflicted harm on the world, [one shouldn't assume] that those laws were originally founded with harmless intentions. People always want to get us mixed up in fine-grained debates to win a little extra name recognition for upholding the institutions of the founders. This is a case of vulgar Confucians parroting the arguments [of former times].

According to some pundits, whether the world is in a state of order or disorder has nothing to do with whether [specific] laws are preserved or eliminated. Now among the great regime changes from the past to the present, there have been two that went from top to bottom—one in the Qin and the other in the Yuan. These washed away all of the organization and management brought about by the compassion and love of the ancient sage-kings. So unless we undertake far-reaching reflection and deep reading, tracing back through each and every change so as to reconstruct the [ancient sage-kings'] well-field system, feudal system, schools, and system of military service, then even if there are small reforms, in the end the people's sorrows still won't cease.

Some pundits say, "There are people who create order; there are no laws that create order."[10] To this I say, "Only if there are laws that create order can there be people that create order." Since unlawful laws shackle people's hands and feet,

---

7. Or perhaps "lawful order without specific laws" (*wufa zhi fa* 無法之法).

8. A paraphrase of the *Spring and Autumn Annals of Master Yan* (*Yanzi chunqiu* 6.18).

9. This is one of Huang's best-known expressions, indicating a distinction between the laws that happen to be "on the books" (so to speak) and proper or legitimate laws.

10. A quotation from the *Xunzi*, ch. 12. See the introduction to this essay.

even those that are capable of creating order are unable to overcome the pushing and pulling or the suspicions and doubts that keep them constantly on the lookout. When there is something to be set up or implemented they just finish their own share. They are content to use the most expedient methods and thus unable to achieve anything outside of the sphere [defined by their legal obligations]. If the laws of the former kings still existed, all would have aspirations that go beyond what's just legally required. Where their aspirations were right they would be put into effect, and where their aspirations were wrong [their effects] wouldn't cut so deep or spread so widely as to inflict harm on the world. This is why I say, "Only if there are laws that create order will there be people that create order."

51. Dai Zhen, Selections from *An Evidential Commentary on the Meanings of Terms in the* Mengzi

translation by Justin Tiwald[11]

Dài Zhèn 戴震 *(1724–1777) was one of the most productive and influential scholars during one of China's most fertile periods of scholarship, the mid-Qing dynasty. Dai had humbler origins than most of his peers, coming from a poor merchant family that could not afford the individual tutoring normally required for academic success in his day. But by all accounts he was something of a prodigy, and at a young age his work attracted the attention of prominent philologists. He went on to make tremendous contributions to several fields, including astronomy, phonology, and trigonometry. But he saw his more philosophical projects as his life's work, and devoted his final years to writing and revising his philosophical masterpiece,* An Evidential Commentary on the Meanings of Terms in the *Mengzi.*

In his Evidential Commentary, *Dai offers a comprehensive critique of the views of orthodox Neo-Confucians, whom Dai refers to as "Later Confucians" or "Song Confucians" (because the first widely influential Neo-Confucians lived in the Song dynasty). Among his criticisms were the charges that the Song Confucians were too dismissive of human desires, didn't fully recognize the need for sympathy and deliberation in moral action, and had too metaphysical a reading of "Pattern." Dai attributed many of these errors to their unacknowledged and probably unconscious appropriation of*

---

11. This translation is based on the text of the *Dai Zhen ji* 戴震集 (Shanghai: Shanghai Classics Press, 2009).

Daoist and Buddhist ideas. However, what most attracted the attention of later philosophers was Dai's argument that Song Confucianism made it too easy to ignore the interests of subordinates and members of the underclass, weakening or overlooking the facets of moral judgment and character that help decision-makers take account of others' wants and needs. Although the treatise does not visit this argument at every turn, Dai cited his worries about neglect of the powerless as the main reason for writing the Evidential Commentary,[12] *and it may be that his interest in this issue was rooted in his own struggles as a member of a poor and relatively powerless family. The following selections from Dai's* Evidential Commentary *touch upon the major criticisms described here.* — Tr.

Section 1: Pattern (*Li*)[13]

[Dai Zhen's Evidential Commentary *is organized into several parts, each devoted to a particular philosophical term or phrase. The first and most extensive part focuses on the character* lǐ 理, *translated in this volume as "Pattern." Dai's custom is to begin the discussion of each important term with a special section devoted to philological analysis. Sometimes he does this by giving his readers phrases or binomes in which it appears. Another favorite technique is to show how it was used in selected passages in ancient texts.*

*[In his discussion of the character for "Pattern" (*li*) Dai's main concern is to correct the widespread belief that classical Confucian philosophers regarded Pattern as being a kind of metaphysical entity responsible for perfect powers of moral perception and motivation endowed in us at birth.*[14] *In opposition to the Later Confucians, Dai maintains that classical Confucians used "Pattern" in a variety of important but less mysterious and metaphysical ways. Chief among these is that "Pattern" refers to states of affairs when they are "in good order" or "well ordered," in which each part plays its distinctive role and is easy for moral agents to grasp. In the following selections, Dai sometimes moves between the sense of "li" as a noun meaning "Pattern" and the sense of "li" as a verbal adjective meaning "Well Ordered" or "In Good Order." To remind readers that all of these are just different usages of the same character, I will put these phrases in capital letters.* — Tr.]*

"Pattern" is a term that makes reference to the close examination of things for the subtle and minute characteristics that should be distinguished in order to separate things. This is why it is called "the Pattern for separating things" [*fēnlǐ*

---

12. See the Introduction to Part IV.
13. All section titles are the translator's and not Dai Zhen's.
14. See Zhu Xi's *Categorized Conversations*, Part III, Selection 32.

分理]. When applied to concrete materials, it appears in the expressions "the pattern of the folds in the skin" [*jǐlǐ* 肌理], "the pattern of capillary pores" [*còulǐ* 腠理][15] and "refined patterns" [*wénlǐ* 文理].

When things are successfully separated so that the individual strands [*tiáo* 條] are not intertwined, this is called "Well Ordered" (*tiáolǐ* 條理).[16] Mengzi declared that "Kongzi is [like] a complete orchestra," explaining, "it is the work of wisdom to begin [a concert] in Good Order and is the work of the sage to maintain that Good Order through to the end."[17] To account for the supreme sageliness and wisdom of Kongzi, this description simply holds up his [capacity for] Good Order.

The *Changes* says, "All of the world's Patterns are attained in ease and simplicity."[18] Here it speaks of "ease and simplicity" rather than [their human correlates] "benevolence and wisdom" because it is discussing the hexagrams *qián* 乾 [symbolizing Heaven] and *kūn* 坤 [symbolizing Earth].[19] When a person "understands by what comes easily" his understanding is the same as benevolence, love, fair consideration and sympathy. When a person is "able to accomplish something by means of what's simple," that which he accomplishes

---

15. The network of pores and capillaries by which some *qi* is absorbed through the skin.

16. More literally, "individual cords arranged in a pattern." Dai offers a more complete account of Pattern's function in distinguishing and ordering things in an earlier text, *Remnants of Words* (*Xùyán* 緒言), vol. 1, section 9. There, Dai usefully illustrates both senses of "Pattern" by explaining what it means for parts of a plant to "follow" or "adhere to" (*xún* 循) their Patterns. As he describes it, each of the parts has a unique function that enables them all to mutually nourish one another, as when the roots draw nutrients from the soil and the leaves collect dew and sunlight from above, thereby absorbing and circulating among themselves the different sources of sustenance that both roots and leaves require.

17. *Mengzi* 5B1. In this passage, Mengzi explains that Kongzi harmonizes the admirable characteristics of famous sages that came before him, drawing upon each at its appropriate time rather than relying exclusively on one. In this (Mengzi suggests) he is like a musician who uses the appropriate instrument at its appropriate time, rather than trying to perform an entire concert with one instrument alone. For further discussion of the analogy between Kongzi and a "complete orchestra," see Zhāng Xuéchéng's "On the Way," I.5–7, in Part IV, Selection 52.

18. *Changes*, "Great Appendix" I.1, translated slightly differently in Part I, Selection 9.

19. The *Changes* gives brief accounts of trigrams and hexagrams that many Chinese thinkers saw as representing cosmic forces—forces that they also believed to have correlates in human life. According to the *Changes*, qian represents Heaven and the origin of things and kun represents Earth and the completion of things. (See "Great Appendix," I.1, in Part I, Selection 9.) For Dai, the operations attributed to qian and kun correlate with the workings of benevolence (*rén* 仁) and wisdom (*zhì* 智). Dai suggests that the *Changes* gives us insight into the two virtues but doesn't mention them by name because its most immediate concern is to describe the operations of cosmic forces characterized by qian and kun, from which features of their correlated human virtues can then be inferred. In short, we can discover how benevolence and wisdom create Good Order ("attain Pattern") by seeing how Heaven and Earth create Good Order on a grander scale.

takes no special effort.[20] "If it's easy then one will find it easy to understand; if it's easy to understand then one will be intimately acquainted with it; if one is intimately acquainted with it then one can persevere for a long time; one who can persevere for a long time has the virtuous character of a worthy." A person who fits this description has the virtue of benevolence. "If it's simple then it is easy to follow; if it's easy to follow then one will achieve; if one achieves then one can become great; becoming great is the work of a worthy."[21] A person who fits this description has wisdom. When all states of affairs in the world are distinguished and analyzed into separate strands and then taken up with benevolence and wisdom, how can one mistake any of the subtle and minute characteristics?

The *Mean* says: "With careful examination of the refined Patterns, [the sage] is able to distinguish things from one another."[22] The "Record of Music" says: "Music in the proper sense is able to pervade and connect the Pattern in human relationships [*lúnlǐ* 倫理]."[23] As Zhèng Xuán explains in his commentary on the passage, "to be Well Ordered [*li*] is to be separated into parts [*fen*]."[24] In his preface to the *Explanation of Simple and Compound Characters*, Xǔ Shèn says, "By knowing the pattern for separating things, things can be mutually distinguished."[25]

What the ancients meant by *li* was never at all like what Later Confucians meant by *li*.

Section 2: Heavenly Pattern and Sympathetic Understanding

[In this section, Dai continues to work on giving a less metaphysical account of Pattern. In his era, due largely to the influence of the Song Confucians, many thought Pattern can take the form of a native capacity for moral insight and moral motivation, which is well-formed from the start. When

---

20. In the "Great Appendix" I.1 to the *Changes*, the text says that *qian* (Heaven) "knows through the easy" and that *kun* (Earth) "is able [to accomplish things] through the simple (translated slightly differently in Part I, Selection 9). Dai explains how these distinctive powers operate in human activity as well—namely, by making things easily understood and by effortless action. The phrase I translate as "that which . . . takes no special effort" is a reference to *Mengzi* 4B26, which describes how the ancient sage Yu managed to control floodwaters by channeling rather than resisting their natural flow. Dai says more about this feature of virtuous action in section 11, where he explains why it's important to channel rather than suppress human desires.

21. *Changes*, "Great Appendix," I.1, translated slightly differently in Part I, Selection 9.

22. *Mean* 31.

23. Chapter 19.

24. See Zheng's commentary on the "Record of Music" chapter of the *Rites* (*Sibu beiyao* 11:8a).

25. The *Explanation of Simple and Compound Characters* (*Shuōwén jiězì* 說文解字) is a dictionary of sorts, composed in the first or second century. In short, Dai finds numerous sources that show that Pattern is used to *distinguish* the parts of things, in stark contrast to the Neo-Confucian view that Pattern *unifies* things.

describing Pattern in its role as well-formed moral guide, Neo-Confucians often refer to it as "Heavenly Pattern," suggesting that these moral capacities are endowed by Heaven at birth. Neo-Confucians take the phrase "Heavenly Pattern" from an intriguing passage in the "Record of Music (Yuèjì 樂記)," a chapter of the much more comprehensive classic known as the Rites. *As we will see, the passage is somewhat more compatible than others with the Neo-Confucian interpretation of Pattern as fully formed moral guide, so it is Dai's task to show that we can make sense of the text's use of "Heavenly Pattern" without assuming that interpretation. To this end, Dai argues that the phrase actually refers to a state of one's own feelings and desires when they are appropriately informed by a combination of our natural dispositions and sympathetic concern. —Tr.]*

Question: What did the ancients mean when they spoke of "Heavenly Pattern"?

Answer: Pattern consists of feelings that are not in error. Whenever one grasps the essential feelings one grasps Pattern.[26] So when one has some matter that would affect others, one should turn within oneself and reflect tranquilly [*jìng sī* 靜思], "If someone else were to affect me in this way, would I be able to accept it?" Whenever one imposes some responsibility on others, one should turn within oneself and reflect tranquilly, "If someone else were to impose this responsibility on me, would I be able to fully exert myself to fulfill it?" When one applies the measure of the self to others, Pattern can become clear.

"*Heavenly* Pattern" refers to a *natural* Pattern for differentiating between things.[27] With the natural Pattern for differentiating, one uses one's own essential feelings to measure the feelings of others, such that all get what's right and fair. The "Record of Music" [which is the canonical source of the term "Heavenly Pattern"] says the following:

> That people are tranquil [*jìng*] at birth is due to their Heavenly nature. That people act when stimulated by external things is due to the desires of their nature. Once external things reach them, they develop an understanding of those things, and only then do their feelings of love and hatred take shape. But when the feelings of love and hatred aren't regulated from within and human understanding is led astray by things outside of them, then unless they can turn within themselves [to engage in reflection], their Heavenly Pattern will be extinguished.[28]

---

26. "Essential feelings" translates *qíng* 情, which is often rendered more plainly as "feelings" or "emotion." As will become evident, Dai sometimes uses the term to refer to certain feelings that are both constant and shared in common with other human beings, and discovered through sympathy.

27. My emphasis. Dai's answer carefully distinguishes between the significance of "Pattern" as a general ethical term and "Heavenly Pattern" in the narrower and more technical sense that he finds in the classics.

28. "Record of Music," section 19 of the *Rites*.

The term "extinguished" indicates that it is completely destroyed and disappears. [The "Record of Music"] also says:

> Now the capacity of external things to stimulate people is inexhaustible. And unless people's feelings of love and hatred are regulated [from within] then the more things reach them the more people will be changed into things.[29] For people to change into things is for their Heavenly Pattern to be extinguished while fully indulging their human desires. Thereupon their minds becomes rebellious and deceitful, they do things that are licentious or create disorder, and thus the strong coerce the weak, the many are cruel to the few, those with knowledge swindle the ignorant and the bold impose bitter hardships on the timid. The sick are not cared for. The old, young, orphaned, and childless do not attain their due place. This is the way of great disorder.

If we sincerely turn within ourselves and reflect on the essential feelings of the weak, the few, the ignorant, and the timid as well as the sick, the old, the young, the orphaned, and childless, how could these others really differ from ourselves? In that period of tranquility before being stimulated by external things, our blood-and-*qi* and cognitive faculties are placid and without error. That's why these things are called our "Heavenly nature." When we reach the point when we are stimulated to act, then the desires [that motivate the action] issue from our nature. [At this stage,] one person's desire is the same as the desires of all people under Heaven. That's why they're called "the desires of our nature."

But once the feelings of love and hatred have taken shape, one can satisfy one's own feelings of love and hatred without considering other people's feelings of love and hatred, frequently robbing others in order to indulge one's own desires. Those who "turn within themselves" consider the feelings they would have if they themselves were receiving the treatment of another person indulging his desires. When the essential feelings reach their fair and proper level, this is the regulation of one's feelings of love and hatred, and this is to be in accordance with Heavenly Pattern. What the ancients called Heavenly Pattern was never anything like what later Confucians called Heavenly Pattern.

Section 4: Pattern vs. Personal Opinion

[The next passage begins an account of Dai's moral epistemology. Roughly, Dai thinks there is a distinction between sound moral views, which he characterizes as "Well-Ordered" and "righteous" (lǐyì 理義), and mere "personal opinion" (yìjiàn 意見). The important question here is whether a moral view or conclusion meets the following test: is it the sort of thing that all other people would, in principle, agree with? In the course of developing

---

29. That is, they will lose their Heavenly nature and become more *like* external things, lacking the powers of reflection and self-regulation that make them distinctively human. Here it is useful to bear in mind that plants and non-human animals also count as "things" (*wù* 物).

this idea Dai makes several interesting claims. For example, he implies that there is a kind of publicity condition for moral knowledge, so that all correct moral views and conclusions should be accessible to all human minds (in some sense not fully spelled out here). He also introduces a distinction between two kinds of cognitive activity: grasping moral patterns and applying them in one's actions. Finally, Dai takes this opportunity to introduce the problem of arriving at moral knowledge under conditions where we can't entirely trust our own judgment—an issue that he will take up again in section five. —Tr.]

Question: The *Mengzi* says, "Pattern [*li*] and righteousness [*yi*] are that which all minds prefer in common. The sages were just the first to grasp that which our minds prefer in common."[30] Here again Pattern [and being Well-Ordered] is described in terms of mind. Why is that?

Answer: *Only* if it's what all minds affirm in common can it be called Pattern and righteousness.[31] That which is not yet affirmed in common and still inheres in one's personal opinions is neither Pattern nor righteousness. When one person regards something as so and the myriad generations of people throughout the world would say "this is correct and cannot be changed," this is what is meant by "affirmed in common."

The text refers to Pattern to highlight the mind's ability to make distinctions, and refers to righteousness to highlight the mind's ability to consider and decide a matter. After things have been clearly distinguished so that [we can see how] each has its unchangeable standard, the word for this is "Well-Ordered."[32] If some particular thing is made to fit these [standards], the word for this is "righteous." Therefore, clearly understanding Pattern is a matter of clearly understanding the relevant distinctions, and perfecting righteousness is a matter of perfecting one's consideration and decision [about whether something fits with those distinctions]. If one doesn't clearly understand Pattern then one will often be confined to noticing dubious similarities, which gives rise to confusion and doubt. If one hasn't perfected righteousness, [one's consideration and decision] will often be mixed together with personal bias and harm the true way of the matter. This is to seek Pattern and righteousness while one's wisdom is insufficient for the task. Thus, [what one finds under these unfortunate circumstances] cannot be called a Pattern [of Good Order] or righteousness.

Since we are not sages, it is rare that we are without some blindness, but blindness comes in both profound and slight forms. Among human beings, there are none more dangerous than those who are blind but take themselves to be wise, who trust their personal opinions and insist that they are both [expressions of]

---

30. *Mengzi* 6A7.8. See Van Norden 2008.

31. My emphasis.

32. That is, "Pattern" in its adjectival sense.

Pattern and righteous. My fear is that those who seek Pattern and righteousness will allow personal opinion to take on those roles. Who knows how much harm the masses will ultimately receive from people such as this!

Section 5: Personal Opinion vs. Sympathetic Concern

[In the previous section, Dai proposed that a proper grasp of a Pattern of Good Order is distinguished from personal opinion by the fact that it can pass a kind of publicity test, being accessible and ultimately affirmable by all people in all times. He also noted a danger in alternative accounts of moral knowledge: if it makes it possible for someone to hold views that can't be submitted to the publicity test, then it's hard to see how people could know whether their conclusions about Pattern really are accurate ones. This raises an issue that we might characterize as a problem of "higher-order ignorance," which arises when we are both ignorant about some moral matter—e.g., how much leniency to show our employees—and also ignorant about the very fact that we're ignorant. We saw Dai conclude that the real, large-scale threat to human welfare comes from this higher-order ignorance, which he describes as the more "profound" form of blindness (as opposed to the "slight" form). Now, in Section 5, Dai's interlocutor presses him on the problem of higher-order ignorance. As the interlocutor points out, it seems that only one kind of person could ever really know whether she or he correctly understands Patterns, and that is the sage. Everyone else must admit to having flawed judgment. Isn't this just as true for Dai's view as for his opponents?—Tr.]

Question: In the accounts found in Confucian books from the Song dynasty onward, they regard Pattern as though there were some thing within, obtained from Heaven and endowed in its entirety in the mind. Now in your description of Mengzi's position you say, "When one person regards something as so and the myriad generations of people throughout the world would say 'this is correct and cannot be changed,' this is what is meant by [the Pattern that is] 'affirmed in common.'"[33] You also say "Pattern" refers to that which, in some affair, the clear understanding of the mind sees without error, such that one's feelings neither exceed nor fall short of their mark. This denies the view that Pattern is like a thing endowed in its entirety in the mind. And you hold that "that which is not yet affirmed in common still inheres in one's personal opinions and is neither Pattern nor righteousness."[34]

But the *Mengzi* says that "the sages were the first to grasp what our minds prefer in common."[35] Mengzi certainly never praised people lightly, which suggests

---

33. See *Section 4* of Dai's *Evidential Commentary.*
34. *Ibid.*
35. *Mengzi* 6A7.

that one must indeed be a sage to be capable of grasping Pattern. While that may be so, all people have families, have affairs of state and even matters that pertain to the entire world. Surely they shouldn't have to wait until they achieve sagely wisdom before proceeding to deal with these matters?

Answer: One rarely sees the word "Pattern" in the Six Classics, the words of Kongzi and Mengzi, or even in the biographies and assorted historical documents. But nowadays all people, even the most foolish of people who engage in perversion and self-indulgence, readily invoke Pattern when making managerial decisions or holding another person accountable. Since the Song dynasty certain mutually reinforcing habits have become established custom, so that people now regard Pattern as though there were some thing within, obtained from Heaven and endowed in its entirety in the mind. And accordingly they allow personal opinion to take on the role of Pattern. Consequently, "Pattern" will stretch forward for those who are domineering, exploit their positions, and speak eloquently, and "Pattern" will bend back for those who are weak, intimidated, and tongue-tied. Alas, who could say that it is against Pattern to regulate affairs or control others in this way?

We might even take someone who is honest and self-possessed and whose mind has no private inclinations toward evil, yet when it comes time to make managerial decisions or hold someone accountable, he will rely on his own personal opinions, taking what he himself affirms to be right and what he himself rejects to be wrong. He may believe himself to have a strict disposition, have an upright nature, and despise bad tendencies as though a personal foe, but he will not understand how difficult it is to fully grasp [the Pattern in] affairs, how easy it is for judgments of right and wrong to slip into bias. People will often be harmed by him without his ever becoming aware of it, or he will see it clearly only after the matter has passed and it is too late for regrets. Alas, who could say that it is against Pattern to regulate affairs or control others in this way?

There are few wise people but many fools in the world. When you have someone whose clarity of understanding is greater than most, this may be far from sagehood but everyone still infers that he is wise, for most people certainly do have more blindness when compared with the grasp of Pattern found in those they infer to be wise. But if we compare the grasp of Pattern found in those they infer to be wise with that of the sage, [it is evident that] one is completely free of blindness only after becoming a sage.

The mind responds to everything it encounters with an internal judgment. If we are quick to call this [an expression of] Pattern then it will not be something that the ancient sages and worthies ever regarded as Pattern. Not only would the ancient sages and worthies deny it, so would ordinary people of former days. Unlike people of today, they did not say "Pattern" as soon as they opened their mouths. While people of former times understood that they could not use the name "Pattern" for the personal opinions within themselves, people nowadays use the word lightly. Among those who regard Pattern as though there were some thing within, obtained from Heaven and endowed in its entirety in the mind, all have allowed their personal opinions to take on the role of [Pattern].

Now people err when they defer to their personal opinions, but can achieve a complete grasp when they seek their essential feelings for themselves. [As evidence, consider this from the *Analects*:]

> Zigong asked, "Is there one teaching that one can practice throughout one's life?"
>
> Kongzi replied, "Would it not be sympathetic understanding? That which you do not desire, do not inflict upon others."[36]

In its description of putting states in order and bringing peace to the world, the *Great Learning* says no more than this: "that which you hate in those above you, do not use in directing those below you; that which you hate in those below you, do not use in serving those above you." It uses this to describe proper relations between superiors and subordinates. To describe the proper relations between elders and juniors, it says "that which you hate in those before you, do not use in preceding those after you; that which you hate in those after you, do not use in following those before you." And to describe proper relations between equals it says "that which you hate in those on your right do not use in your interactions with those on your left; that which you hate in those on your left do not use in your interactions with those on your right."[37]

"That which you do not desire" and "that which you hate" refer to nothing more than the ordinary and constant feelings of human beings. The texts do not mention Pattern and yet Pattern is fully expressed in these remarks, for it is just a matter of measuring feelings with one's essential feelings. One does not deal with his affairs by having the mind issue forth a personal opinion. If one were to seek Pattern, and refer to [what one finds] as Pattern without drawing on the essential feelings, this would be nothing but personal opinion. When people give free rein to their opinions it's always the masses that are harmed by it.

Section 11: *Against Eliminating Desires*

[Much of Dai's critique of the Neo-Confucians concerns their understanding of the relationship between moral agency and the elimination of desires. The sticking point, Dai suggests, is the Neo-Confucians' proposal that eliminating desires does most of the work of preparing someone to act rightly and virtuously. Dai offers a few lines of argument against this way of thinking. For example, he argues that some of our moral faculties are developed through education, not just discovered, fully formed, after the bad desires are removed. He also argues that we must have strong and even self-interested desires in order to be able to fully sympathize with others, and we need

---

36. See *Analects* 15.24 in Part III, Selection 34.

37. All three passages are quoted from the *Great Learning*, Commentary 10.

*sympathy in order to have the trait of benevolence (*ren*), the most important of Confucian virtues.*[38] *In this section, Dai introduces one of his most memorable arguments against eliminating desires. He contends that attempting to suppress or eliminate desires has destructive effects on human behavior and character, which can be likened to the destructive effects of attempting to contain floodwaters by damming them. In this succinct sketch of Dai's psychology of desire, he agrees that desires—like floodwaters—shouldn't be left to run unchecked, but he thinks they can be harnessed or conducted in more productive ways, much as good engineering can channel floodwaters into canals. In articulating this view, Dai also weaves in an array of passages in the Confucian classics, showing how they can be pieced together to make a coherent vision of the relationship between desire and what he calls "the way of mutual nourishment and growth."—Tr.]*

Question: The "Record of Music" says that "Heavenly Pattern is extinguished while fully indulging in human desires."[39] This saying seems to treat the distinction between [what comes from] Pattern and [what comes from] desire as a distinction between what's right and what's wrong. How do you deal with this?

Answer: Human nature is analogous to water, while desire is analogous to the water's flow.[40] When we prevent the desires from exceeding their proper bounds, this is to act in accordance with the Heavenly Pattern and the way of mutual nourishment and growth [*sheng* 生], which is analogous to water taking its proper course across the land. [By contrast,] when we indulge our human desires so fully that the mind becomes rebellious and deceitful, and we do things that are licentious or create disorder, this is analogous to cases in which the water overflows its banks and inundates the Central States.[41]

The sages taught people to turn within themselves and consider the feelings they would have if they were treated as they treat others.[42] This is analogous to the sage Yu's methods for guiding the waters [of China's great rivers]: he did not attempt to stop the waters from flowing, fearing the bad effects of flooding; instead he "guided them to places where no special effort was required."[43] To

---

38. See section 21 of Dai's *Evidential Commentary*, below.

39. "Record of Music," section 19 of the *Rites*. For the full passage see section 2 of Dai's *Evidential Commentary* above.

40. Mengzi famously likens human nature to water in *Mengzi* 6A2.

41. Here Dai refers to the outcomes of "fully indulging the desires" described in the "Record of Music," quoted in Section 2 of his *Evidential Commentary*. On a standard Confucian version of history, flooding periodically disrupted the food supply and social stability of early Chinese civilization. For more on this see the Introduction to Part I.

42. For a description of "turning within oneself" see Dai's discussion of the "Record of Music" in section 2 above.

43. Quoting the *Mengzi's* description of Yu's methods of flood control (4B26, Van Norden, trans.). According to the legend, Yu developed his methods after failed attempts to control floods by damming the rivers. When the floods came, damming the rivers only caused the

block the water's flow in fear of flooding is to establish a theory [of flood control] that requires special effort and cuts the water off directly at its source. This is analogous to the [theory] of suppressing or eliminating the desires.

[Mengzi speaks of] "the mouth's relation to flavors, the eyes' relation to appearances, the ears' relation to sounds, the nose's relation to smells, and the four limbs' relation to comfort." Later Confucians saw these as the selfishness of human desire, but Mengzi said they were "of our nature" and added that "a mandate lies in them."[44] "Mandate" in its proper sense is a word that describes restrictions, as in the expression "if mandated to go east then one cannot go west." So Mengzi was saying that the desires of human nature must be regulated. If they are regulated and not excessive, this is in accordance with Heavenly Pattern. But this doesn't assume that Heavenly Pattern is right and human desire is wrong. Heavenly Pattern consists in regulating one's desires so that one doesn't thoroughly indulge the human desires.

For these reasons, while the desires cannot be fully indulged, they cannot be eliminated either. How can we say that it is against Heavenly Pattern when the desires are regulated so that they neither exceed nor fall short of our essential feelings?

Section 13: The Relationship Between What's Natural and What's Necessary

[By this point in Dai's Evidential Commentary, *he has given a number of arguments against the heavy-handed metaphysics of his Song Confucian (Neo-Confucian) predecessors, trying to show how the explanatory work that his predecessors attributed to Pattern can in fact be done without having to posit Pattern as some sort of formless or irreducibly abstract thing. In this section, he turns to examine his predecessors' way of using Pattern to account for ethical imperatives or "what's necessary" (*bìrán 必然*). This gives Dai an opportunity to highlight some of the virtues as well as the defects in his opponents' views on ethical necessity, and also to reveal more about Dai's alternative way of accounting for necessity without appealing to formless entities. —Tr.]*

Question: Ever since the Song dynasty, people have said that Pattern is obtained from Heaven and endowed in its entirety in the mind. And since they think Pattern is something we all receive equally, they trace any differences in our levels of wisdom or foolishness to [differences in] our endowments of *qi*.[45] They

---

waters to spill over into fertile and habitable lands, which is contrary to the "way of mutual nourishment and growth" Dai mentions above. By contrast, Yu was able to channel the floodwaters into irrigation canals, contributing to nourishment and growth. See *Mengzi* 3B9 and 6B1, and James Legge, trans., "The Documents of T'ang," in *The Shoo King*, vol. 3 (Hong Kong: Hong Kong University Press, 1960).

44. *Mengzi* 7B24.

45. For a fuller exposition of this theory see the introductory comments to Zhu Xi's metaphysics in Zhu's *Categorized Conversations*, Part III, Selection 32.

substantiate their theories about the tension between Pattern and desires by using general notions about the differences between reverential attention and careless abandon or between deviance and rectitude. As for Daoist admonitions to
"embrace oneness" and "be without desires" and the Buddhist admonition to "be
constantly alert," these make reference to what the Daoists and Buddhists call
the "true master" and "true emptiness," and Confucians now treat these notions
as the learning of the Confucian sages by substituting "Pattern" for these terms.[46]
Since they regard Pattern as something obtained from Heaven, they then set up
a theory about the relationship between Pattern and *qi* that likens them to two
things blended and merged into one object. They describe Pattern in superlative
terms, calling it "utterly pure and expansive," but this just exchanges the word
"Pattern" for what Laozi, Zhuangzi, and Buddhists refer to as "true master" and
"true emptiness." This is just to transfer the words of Laozi, Zhuangzi, and the
Buddhists [into Confucian discourse], treating them as the words of Six Classics, Kongzi, and Mengzi. How do we now dissect and distinguish between these
two traditions so that they aren't confused with one another?[47]

Answer: With respect to Heaven, Earth, people, things, affairs, and actions,
I have not heard of any that cannot be talked about in terms of its Pattern [of
Good Order]. This is affirmed by the *Odes'* remark that "for every thing there is
a norm."[48] In this remark the term "thing" refers to concrete material items and
concrete affairs, and the term "norm" is a name for the pure and correct form of
these things. To grasp the Pattern of Heaven, Earth, people, things, affairs, and
actions is to restore them to the state that is necessary for them [*bìrán*], without
ever eliminating anything that comes naturally to them [*zìrán*].

Now in regard to the vastness of Heaven and Earth, the profusion of people,
and the convolutions and particular components of affairs, as soon as one grasps
their Pattern then it is much like a straight line fitting exactly to the plumb-line,
a level fitting exactly to the surface of still water, a circle fitting exactly to the
compass or a square shape fitting exactly to a carpenter's square. One can then
use inference to extend this to all the world and the countless generations of
people, making it a standard for all. The *Changes* says, "When [the great person]
precedes Heaven, Heaven does not resist him. When he follows behind Heaven,
he accords respectfully with Heaven's seasons. If Heaven does not resist him,
how much less will the people resist him! How much less will the spirits resist

---

46. The true master (*zhēnzǎi* 真宰) and true emptiness (*zhēnkōng* 真空) are Daoist and Buddhist notions of a guiding force that operates behind the more tangible face of worldly events.

47. In short, given that Song and later Confucians snuck so much Daoist and Buddhist
metaphysics into their own interpretation of the character *li* ("Pattern"), they make it look
as though the great Daoists, Buddhists, and Confucians all had the same sense of the word
in mind. But the interlocutor thinks the original Confucians must have had a different sense
and so invites Dai to identify those differences.

48. *Odes* 260.

him!"[49] The *Mean* says, "[The gentleman] examines his way by comparing it with the way of the three kings, and finds it without a mistake. He sets it up before Heaven and Earth, and finds nothing in it that is contrary to their mode of operation. He presents himself with it before spiritual beings, and has no uncertainty. He can be without doubts as he waits for the rise of a sage a hundred ages after."[50] When something meets all of these qualifications, this is the grasping of Pattern and what all minds affirm in common.

Mengzi says, "The compass and the carpenter's square are perfections of the circle and square, just as [the behavior of the] sage is the perfection of human relations."[51] When we employ refined words to talk about the Pattern of Heaven and Earth, it is just like when we talk about how a sage can serve as a model to be emulated. Were someone to so revere Pattern that he would say Heaven, Earth, and the fundamental forces of *yin* and *yang* are not worthy enough to bear it—this, necessarily, would be inconsistent with its being the Pattern of Heaven, Earth, and the forces of *yin* and *yang*.[52] In this respect Pattern stands to Heaven, Earth, and the forces of *yin* and *yang* as sageliness stands to the sage. Is it really possible to so exalt a person's sageliness that one can say the sagely person is unworthy to bear it? The sagely person is still a person. Because he has so thoroughly manifested the Pattern of persons, people join together in attributing sagely wisdom to him. But thoroughly manifesting the Pattern of persons is nothing other than thoroughly manifesting what's necessary [*biran*] in basic human relationships and everyday life. To infer from this to an ultimate norm that cannot be changed is [to grasp] what's necessary for it. This is just to talk about its state of perfection, not to trace back to its underlying root or origin.[53]

---

49. Quoting the "Wenyan Commentary" (*Wényán zhuàn* 文言傳) of the *Changes,* on the *qian* hexagram. The standard discovered by the person who grasps Pattern can be applied so widely that Heaven itself can live by it.

50. Chapter 30, Legge's translation, substantially altered to reflect Dai's interpretation (James Legge, *The Li Ki,* Kessinger Publishing, 2004). Here again, Dai's major point is that grasping Pattern gives one a standard that applies at all places and times.

51. *Mengzi* 4A2, my translation. This introduces Dai's view that ethical norms can be explained as features or attributes of natural things in their perfected state, rather than as some mysterious and irreducible object-like Pattern.

52. To see Dai's point, consider what would happen if we tried to detach the idea of "greatness" from the types of things to which it is attributed, such as music or food. There can be greatness as a quality of food or music, but it's hard to see how there could be greatness that doesn't modify anything at all—greatness simpliciter. Dai takes his opponents to be engaged in a fool's errand of a similar nature: seeking a Pattern that determines what counts as perfection and Good Order, without specifying what bears the perfection.

53. Having explained that a Pattern is really just an idealized variant of the thing that it's a Pattern *of,* Dai now proceeds to explain how the Song Confucians came to reify Pattern, conceiving of it as like an object that stands apart from the things that bear it.

Later Confucians went searching too far. In their discussions, they simply assume that the ideas, teachings, thought, and principles that were meant to describe a perfected state were like substantial things themselves. They said that these things come into being when they are blended and merged with *qi*. Those who heard this view became accustomed to it and didn't scrutinize it, so that no one knew how much it differed from the doctrines of the Six Classics, Kongzi, and Mengzi.

If we seek what's necessary and can't be changed in all matters concerning Heaven, Earth, people, things, affairs, and actions, then the Pattern will be manifestly clear. But if we proceed to regard it as so exalted and great that we're not content to call it the Pattern of Heaven, Earth, people, things, affairs, and actions, and if we instead say "Pattern is omnipresent" and see it as though a substantial thing, scholars will be utterly at a loss and their hair will turn gray in their search for a thing that can't be found. It's not that the words of the Six Classics, Kongzi, and Mengzi are difficult to understand. It's just that the commentaries that have been passed down to us mutually reinforce one another, so that people become accustomed to them from childhood and give them no further thought.

Section 21: An Alternative to the "Two Natures" Doctrine

[Dai's Neo-Confucian opponents hold that human beings have two natures, one of which is good and well formed (called the "fundamental nature" or "the nature of Heaven and Earth") and the other that usually contains impurities that interfere with the natural functioning of the good nature (called the "embodied" or "material" nature, constituted of qi*). Mainstream Neo-Confucians use the two natures doctrine to explain how, in spite of the fact that we have well-formed moral dispositions, we nevertheless often fail to recognize or do what is right, or fail to act from good motives. As they see it, we often act wrongly because selfish desires and biases in the embodied nature interfere with the more spontaneous reactions of the fundamental nature, distorting what would otherwise be correct moral perception, judgment, and motivation. Although the two-natures doctrine offers a clever way of explaining our moral failures, it's hard to find direct textual evidence that the classical Confucians held such a view. There isn't a single passage in the* Four Books *that mentions two different kinds of nature, nor even one that clearly uses "nature" (*xing 性*) in two distinctive senses. In lieu of direct evidence, mainstream Neo-Confucians instead lean heavily on a particular passage in the* Analects: *"Human beings are similar by nature; by practice they become far apart" (*Analects 17.2*). The Neo-Confucians assumed that Kongzi believed human nature is perfectly good for all people at all times, yet here he seems to say that our natures can vary and change. The natural way to explain this, they contend, is to say that Kongzi thinks we have two natures: the eternally good one that is the same in everyone, and the changeable*

one that differs from individual to individual. In this section, Dai explains what he thinks has gone wrong with this interpretation and then offers his own "one nature" account as a more plausible alternative. In doing so, Dai deploys a number of arguments that have tremendous implications for his philosophical system more generally, making this section one of the most important in the book. Notable points include his view that humans share certain moral predispositions with animals but possess a unique capacity to cultivate or develop them, his proposal that distinctively moral attitudes and dispositions are rooted in the love of life and fear of death, and his histori-cally unusual claim that love of one's own life is no less a component of benevolence or virtuous care than love of the life of others. —Tr.]

Question: The *Analects* says the natures of human beings are nearly alike.[54] The *Mengzi* says human nature is good.[55] Ever since Cheng Yi and Zhu Xi began distinguishing between these two theses—maintaining that each is speaking separately about just one kind of nature—they believed Kongzi's remarks to be compatible with an account of nature that they took from Gàozǐ, which held that "'nature' is what living things have by birth."[56] They created a special term "the embodied nature" [to refer to the nature that's "nearly alike" and "what liv-ing things have by birth"], and the nature that Mengzi called "good" they took to be Pattern, regarding it as the underlying root that gives life to things. [They said that] animals and humans obtain the latter kind of nature alike, and even went so far as to express some doubts about the *Mengzi*.[57]

In this way they said that the ["good"] nature just is Pattern. But if this view can't even be reconciled with the *Mengzi,* how would we be able to reconcile it with the *Changes* or the *Analects?* Upon hearing Gaozi's position that "'nature' is what living things have by birth," Mengzi was moved to criticize him for it. Don't the doctrines of Cheng and Zhu [on human nature] come close to sup-porting Gaozi and criticizing Mengzi?[58]

Answer: The teachings that Cheng Yi and Zhu Xi first pursued were those of

---

54. *Analects* 17.2, in Part III, Selection 34.

55. *Mengzi* 6A6, in Part III, Selection 35.

56. See *Mengzi* 6A3. Gaozi was one of Mengzi's regular opponents in debate, and seemed to think that human nature just refers to dispositions we have by virtue of being living things, thus making it difficult to see what could be distinctive (or distinctively moral) about human beings. Elsewhere in this volume, the phrase "what living things have by birth" is translated as "what is inborn." See Cheng Hao, "Selected Sayings," in Part III, Selection 27, §§4 and 13.

57. The *Categorized Conversations of Master Zhu* records that Zhu thought some of Mengzi's written views on human nature were poorly expressed, either due to textual corruption or, perhaps, a rare slip in the great teacher's otherwise impeccable habit of carefully choosing his words. See Zhu's remarks on *Mengzi* 4B19 and 6A3 in *Categorized Conversations,* vol. 4 (not translated in this volume).

58. For Cheng Hao's qualified endorsement of Gaozi's view, see his "Selected Sayings" §13, in Part III, Selection 27.

Laozi, Zhuangzi, and the Buddhists. Laozi, Zhuangzi, and the Buddhists saw their spirits as having great value but treated their bodily forms as external to themselves, and they expressly turned their backs on the [Confucian] sages and slandered the [Confucian virtues of] benevolence and righteousness. [In contrast to the above Daoists and Buddhists,] Gaozi never distinguished between spirit and form, which is why he said "by nature we want food and sex."[59] And he prized what comes naturally, which is why he said that human nature is "neither good nor not good."[60] Although he never slandered the virtues of benevolence and righteousness, at bottom his intentions were no different from those of Laozi, Zhuangzi, and the Buddhists, for he likened the virtue of righteousness to cups and bowls, suggesting that one can only succeed in making the cups and bowls by ruining the willow tree from which they are carved.[61]

All things that are made of blood and *qi* understand the love of life and fear of death, and accordingly they pursue what's beneficial and avoid what's harmful.[62] Even if some differ in their clarity of understanding, they're the same in that they don't leave the condition of loving life and fearing death. The difference between humans and animals does not lie in this.

Due to the fact that they have limited awareness and understanding, animals know their mothers but not their fathers. But the tendency to love their progenitors and offspring, the mutual love of mates, the fact that members of the same species do not devour one another and that those accustomed to living together do not bite each other—these things advance from their love of life and fear of death. In one case they may care about their private interests, in another case they may extend it to those near and dear to them, but both are in the domain of benevolence. To care about one's private interests is to have benevolent love for one's self, and to extend it to those near and dear is to have benevolent love for one's near and dear. Such are the natural expressions of the mind's faculty of understanding. The difference between humans and animals does not lie here either.

Gaozi took natural tendencies [*ziran*] to be the effects of a thing's nature [*xing*] and believed righteousness does not come naturally. On the contrary, he thought it required the regulation of one's natural tendencies, so that it was the

---

59. *Mengzi* 3A4.

60. *Mengzi* 6A6.

61. *Mengzi* 6A1.

62. In this and the next twelve paragraphs, Dai lays out a kind of philosophical account of the fundamental similarities and differences between human beings and animals. Like many philosophers, a major objective is to identify what's most distinctive about human beings. In reconstructing his view, it is worth remembering that the Chinese character for "life" (*sheng*) refers not just to the state of being alive but also to birth and growth, so if we love our own lives we want not just to survive but also to have children and develop into mature and complete versions of our selves.

effect of forced compliance. This is why he said, "Benevolence is internal, not external, but righteousness is external, not internal."[63] At bottom the aim of this theory is just to preserve what we as living things have by birth.

Lu Xiangshan said, "Just as badness can harm the mind, so too can goodness harm the mind."[64] This saying is actually the main point of Laozi, Zhuangzi, Gaozi, and the Buddhists, prizing what comes naturally for the sake of preserving what we as living things have by birth. They correctly saw that we harm what we as living beings have by birth when we give free rein to our desires and drift into badness, but they thought it would diminish what we as living beings have by birth even when we yearn for benevolence and righteousness, behave in a good manner, labor at our studies, and exhaust our thoughts in contemplation. Their views thereupon became fixed and their minds unperturbed.[65] Such is their theory that "'nature' is what living things have by birth." How could it ever be made compatible with the views of Kongzi?

When the *Changes*, the *Analects*, and the *Mengzi* discuss nature, all are speaking of a nature formed of specific allotments from the forces of *yin*, *yang*, and the Five Phases. After the natures are formed, the individual differences between humans and the hundred creatures are set by differences of degree in their allotments of partiality and completeness, thickness and thinness, clearness and opacity, and understanding or confusion. To speak only of what living things have by birth is to treat human beings as identical to dogs and oxen without taking note of their differences . . .

[Consider how] crows feed their elderly parents in repayment, ospreys observe distinctions between the sexes, bees and ants recognize rulers and subjects, wolves offer their prey as sacrifices, and otters offer fish as sacrifices—these behaviors conform to what human beings call benevolence and righteousness, but each is just formed by nature. On the other hand, human beings can expand and fill out their understanding so that they are able to reach the point of spiritual clarity and complete the virtues of benevolence, righteousness, propriety, and wisdom.[66] Benevolence, righteousness, propriety, and wisdom are nothing else but that in which the mind's powers of clarity have reached their stopping point, where the understanding has reached its fullest measure.

Understanding, awareness, and the powers of movement—these are what [both] humans and animals have by birth as living beings. Why they differ in degrees of understanding, awareness, and powers of movement—this is due to special differences in their natures.

---

63. *Mengzi* 6A4.

64. *Xiangshan Quanji* 象山全集, vol. 35.

65. See *Mengzi* 2A2, in Part III, Selection 35.

66. "Spiritual understanding" (*shén míng*) refers to a state of knowledge so deep and pervasive that it has a profound motivational and transformative effect on the knower. Benevolence, righteousness, (ritual) propriety, and wisdom are Mengzi's four cardinal virtues.

Mengzi said, "Patterns [of Good Order] and righteousness are that which all minds prefer in common. The sages were just the first to grasp that which our minds prefer in common."[67] When Mengzi needed to extend his refutation of Gaozi's thesis that righteousness is external, he said that Pattern and righteousness are made from the nature, not that the nature is made from Pattern. In its proper sense, "the nature" refers to the blood-and-*qi* and the understanding of the mind that originates in the forces of *yin*, *yang*, and the Five Phases, the differences in which can be used to distinguish between any animal and human. In their proper sense, "Well-Ordered and righteous" refer to those activities that are carried out without doubts, when the human mind's understanding is such that it has penetrating insight whenever it gives something due thought.

When Mengzi "told [Duke Wen of Teng] the Way of the goodness of human nature, in his discussions he always praised the sages Yao and Shun."[68] But he didn't mean that all human beings are like Yao and Shun by birth. From Yao and Shun on down there certainly are small differences between each gradation, and their endowments of *qi* certainly aren't equal, so surely there are some differences in their natures. But when applied to human relations and daily activities, the understanding of the human mind will, according to the circumstance, know compassion, know disdain, know deference, and know approval and disapproval. These are the initial clues that we can cite, and this is what's meant by the doctrine that human nature is good.

If one takes that understanding of compassion and then expands and fills it out, one will be in full possession of the virtue of benevolence. If one takes that understanding of disdain and then expands and fills it out, one will be in full possession of the virtue of righteousness. If one takes that understanding of deference and then expands and fills it out, one will be in full possession of the virtue of propriety. If one takes that understanding of approval and disapproval and then expands and fills it out, one will be in full possession of the virtue of wisdom. Benevolence, righteousness, propriety, and wisdom are all specifications of beautiful virtue.

Mengzi said, "Suppose someone saw a child about to fall into a well: anyone in such a situation would have a feeling of alarm and compassion."[69] But what's called compassion and what's called benevolence aren't like things stored in the mind, standing apart from the faculty of understanding. It is because one understands for oneself the love of life and fear of death that one feels alarm about the endangerment of the child and would respond compassionately to the child's death. How could one have a mind that feels alarm and distress if he were without a mind that loves life and fears death?

And the same is true analogously for disdain, deference, and approval and

---

67. *Mengzi* 6A7.

68. *Mengzi* 3A1, in Part III, Selection 35.

69. *Mengzi* 2A6, in Part III, Selection 35.

disapproval. If we were to shed completely the desires for drink, food, sexual intimacy, and every affective reaction to external things, thereby returning to a state of mental tranquility and oneness, wherein could there be disdain, deference, or approval and disapproval? From this it can be understood that benevolence, righteousness, propriety, and wisdom are nothing else. They do not transcend the love of life and fear of death, the desires for drink, food, sexual intimacy, and every affective reaction to external things, thereby returning to a state of mental tranquility and oneness. Moreover, beautiful virtue is constituted by nothing other than that which we are able to carry out without doubts, relying on the powers of understanding that are distinctive of the human mind, those which distinguish us from animals.

The ancient worthies and sages did not seek outside of the desires for what they regarded as benevolence, righteousness, propriety, or wisdom, nor did they separate these virtues from the blood and *qi* or mind's faculties of understanding. But later Confucians regarded them as like a separate object, anchored and attached to [the desires, blood and *qi,* and mind's understanding] to form a [separate] nature. This was because they mixed in the teachings of Laozi, Zhuangzi, and the Buddhists, and in the end this obscured the teachings of Mengzi, Kongzi, and the Six Classics . . .

52. Zhang Xuecheng, "On the Way"

translation by Philip J. Ivanhoe[70]

Zhāng Xuéchéng (章學誠, *1738–1801) is best known today for his slogan, "The classics are all histories."*[71] *Zhang meant by this that works like the* Odes *and* Documents *are not to be understood as making statements about the Way, but rather as illustrations of how the Way was manifested in the concrete historical situations of the ancient sage-kings. Zhang believed that many later Confucians were led by their mistaken understanding of the classics to produce "empty words" (* kōngyán 空言*): writing that is too abstract and intended simply to impress the reader. In contrast, a genuine sage only*

---

70. The following translation is based on Philip J. Ivanhoe, trans., *On Ethics and History: Essays and Letters of Zhang Xuecheng* (Stanford: Stanford University Press, 2009), sections I.1–5, 7, II.1–3, III.3. It follows the Dàliáng 大梁 (1833) edition of this work. We have modified the translation to conform to the conventions of this anthology and we are solely responsible for any resulting errors or infelicities.—Eds.

71. Literally, *liù jīng jiē shǐ* 六經皆史, "the Six Classics are all histories" (see the opening of Zhang's *Yìjiào* 易教, "The Teachings of the *Changes*," for one occurrence of this phrase). The Six Classics were the Five Classics (*Odes, Documents, Rites, Spring and Autumn Annals,* and *Changes*) along with the *Music.*

speaks and acts in response to the concrete needs of his historical era. The following essay, "On the Way," is influenced by Han Yu's work of the same title (in Part III, Selection 20). Like Han Yu, Zhang presents an account of the relationship between the Way and history, and on this basis argues for an interpretation of what the Way really is. Zhang takes issue with earlier scholars who claimed that Kongzi was somehow greater than other sages. Zhang argues that sages do different things, not because some are better than others, but because their unique historical moments call on them to perform in different ways. Kongzi preserved the classics and taught students because (lacking a government position), all he could hope to do was to preserve knowledge of the Way for future generations. The Duke of Zhou was an equally great sage who, because of his own historical situation, was able to put the Way into practice. In short, Zhang challenges Confucians to stop blindly doing what Kongzi did and mindlessly repeating what Kongzi said, and instead do what Kongzi would do, if he were in their concrete historical context. One of the things that makes Zhang's approach particularly interesting for contemporary Confucians is that it provides a justification for deviating from traditional practices and modernizing Confucianism, in light of the fact that our political, economic, and technological context is so different from that of Kongzi. (Zhang himself did not draw such radical conclusions from his own work, though.)—Eds.

Section I

1. Dong Zhongshu said, "The great source of the Way came from Heaven."[72] One might ask, though, did Heaven actually "ordain it explicitly and in detail"?[73] My reply is that I am unable to know anything about how things were before there was Heaven and Earth; when, however, Heaven and Earth produced human beings, the Way existed but had not yet taken shape. As soon as there were three people living together in one house, the Way took shape but was not yet plainly manifested. When there came to be groups of five and ten and these grew to hundreds and thousands, one house could not possibly accommodate them all, and so they split into groups and separated into classes, and the Way became manifest. The concepts of benevolence and righteousness, loyalty and filial piety, and the institutions of penal and administrative laws, ritual, and music were all things that could not but arise thereafter.

2. When human beings came into being, the Way existed. However, because they did not fully understand themselves, it did not yet take shape. When three people were living together in one house, then each morning and evening they had to open and shut the doors and gates, and they had to gather firewood and

---

72. See the biography of Dong Zhongshu in the *History of the Han Dynasty* (*Hànshū* 漢書).
73. *Mengzi* 5A5.

draw water in order to prepare the morning and evening meals. Since they were not just one single person, there had to be a division of responsibilities. Sometimes, each attended to his or her own work; sometimes work was alternated and each took a turn. This indeed was a situation that could not have been otherwise, and there developed the Patterns of equality, peace, structure, and order. Then, fearing that people would quarrel over the delegation of responsibilities, it became necessary to bring forward the one most advanced in years to keep the peace. This too was an inevitable state of affairs, and as a result the distinctions between old and young and between honored and humble took shape. When there came to be groups of five and ten and then hundreds and thousands and these split into groups and separated into classes, it became necessary for each elder to have charge of his own group of five or ten. When these groups accumulated to hundreds and thousands, such a large number of people required management and direction, and so it was necessary to advance the one most outstanding in talent to order the complex relationships among them. The situation became complicated, requiring leadership to employ the people effectively, and so it was necessary to advance the one greatest in Virtue to control the development of things. This too was an inevitable state of affairs; as a result, the idea of setting up a sovereign appeared, along with the ideas of establishing teachers, of marking off fields and dividing the country into provinces, as well as the notions of the well-field system, feudal investiture, and schools.[74] The Way thus is not something the wisdom of a sage can [simply] manufacture; it is in every particular instance gradually given shape and manifested and inevitably develops from the nature of the state of things. Therefore, it is said to be "of Heaven."

3. The *Changes* says, "The alternation of *yin* and *yang* is called the Way."[75] This indicates that the Way already was present before human beings existed. The *Changes* also says, "That which ensues from it is goodness, and that which realizes it completely is human nature."[76] This shows that Heaven is manifested in human beings and that Pattern is attached to *qi*. Therefore, those matters for which one can describe the form or name the name are all the detailed effects of the Way but they are not themselves the Way.[77] For the Way is that by which all things and affairs are as they are [*suǒyǐrán* 所以然]; it is not how they should

---

74. "Feudal investiture" is the system by which the sovereign divided his domain into states, each of which was ruled by a lesser noble (e.g., a duke) who owed support and loyalty to the king. The "well-field system" was the supposed ancient system of land allocation that divided a plot of land into nine squares of equal area (making a pattern similar to that of the Chinese character for "well," *jǐng* 井). Each of eight families was to tend one of the squares on the perimeter as its own and all were to tend the central square together for the state.

75. *Changes*, "Great Appendix," I.5, in Part I, Selection 9.

76. Ibid.

77. Zhang here paraphrases Wáng Bì's 王弼 (226–249) commentary on the opening lines of the first chapter of the *Daodejing*.

be [*dāngrán* 當然]. However, all that human beings are able to see is how things and affairs should be [the *dangran*]. From the beginning of humankind, to groupings of five and ten, on to hundreds and thousands, and up to the creation of sovereigns and teachers and the distinguishing of provinces and the marking off of fields, it appears always that there was first some need and then the meeting of it, first some anxiety and then the expression of it, first some abuse and then the remedying of it. The institutions of the sage-emperors Fuxi, Shennong, the Yellow Emperor, and his grandson Zhuanxu were, in their first conception, merely like this. Their laws accumulated and over time became good and perfect, and with the reigns of Yao and Shun the goodness in them was brought forth fully. The Shang dynasty inherited the Xia's review of this tradition, and by the time of the Eastern Zhou, there was nothing to regret in any detail of it. It was like some water spilled from a goblet that gathers volume little by little and eventually becomes a great and mighty river, or like little mounds of earth that accumulate to form hills and mountains. This was simply due to the nature and logic of the situations these rulers were in. We cannot thereby conclude that the sageliness of Yao and Shun exceeded that of Fuxi and the Yellow Emperor, or that the spirit-like genius of Wen and Wu was superior to that of Yu and Tang. The later sages modeled themselves on the earlier sages, but they did not model the earlier sages themselves; rather, they modeled that about them through which the Way gradually took shape and was manifested. The Three Sovereigns "exerted no effort and the world was transformed of itself."[78] The Five Emperors "explained things and accomplished undertakings."[79] The Three Kings established institutions and transmitted a model to their posterity. The differences in their ways of governing and in their transforming influence, which are apparent to men of later times, are only of this sort: When a sage at any given time created an institution, it was like wearing linen in the summer and fur in the winter. Their institutions are not instances of their giving rein to their fancy, saying, "I must do such-and-such in order to be different from men of former times," or "I must do such-and-such in order that I may make my fame equal to that of the former sages." These things were all necessary results of the alternation and revolution of *yin* and *yang*, but they themselves cannot be considered the Way, which is the alternation of *yin* and *yang* itself. The alternation and revolution of *yin* and *yang* are like the wheels of a cart. The sage's fashioning of institutions, just like the wearing of linen in the summer and fur in the winter, is like the tracks of such wheels.

4. The Way is what it is of itself; sages do what they do of necessity. One might ask, "Are these things the same?" My reply is that they are not. The Way does not act and is so of itself; sages see what they see and cannot but do as they do. Therefore, one may say that sages give Substance to the Way, but one may

---

78. Paraphrasing the *Daodejing*, chapter 57. See also chapter 37.
79. *Changes,* "Great Appendix," I.11, in Part I, Selection 9.

not say that sages and the Way are one in Substance.[80] Sages see what they see and hence they cannot but do as they do. The multitude sees nothing, and so do what they do without being aware of it. One might ask, "Which is closer to the Way?" My reply is that to do as one does without being aware of it is the Way. It is not so much that the multitude sees nothing, but rather that the thing cannot be seen. Doing as they do of necessity is how sages accord with the Way, but it is not the Way itself. Sages seek the Way, but the Way cannot be seen. And so the multitude doing as it does without being aware of it is what sages rely upon to see the Way. Doing as one does without being aware of it is the trace of the alternation of *yin* and *yang*. Worthies learn from sages; superior people learn from worthies, but sages learn from the multitude. This does not mean that they study the multitude itself; rather, it means that the Way must be sought in the traces of the alternation of *yin* and *yang*. In the period of time stretching from the beginning of Heaven and Earth down through the reigns of emperors Tang and Yu and the Xia and the Shang dynasties, these traces were already numerous, and in the course of historical adaptation, Patterns had become complete.[81] The Duke of Zhou, being a sage endowed by Heaven with pure knowing, and happening to live at a time when the accumulated wisdom of antiquity had been transmitted and preserved, and the Way and proper models were complete, was able to sum up, in his Patterns and policies, the "complete orchestra" of all past time.[82] This came to be simply as a result of his position in time; it was not that the Duke of Zhou's sagely wisdom caused this to be so. As I see it, all the sages of remote antiquity studied the unself-conscious nature of the people, but the Duke of Zhou also had a comprehensive view of what the sages since antiquity had done of necessity and he *understood* their actions as well. The Duke of Zhou was of course a sage endowed by Heaven with pure knowing but [his unique accomplishment] was not something that his wisdom could cause to be so. It was caused to be so by his position in time. . . . And so, while various periods of antiquity have been alike in having creative and illustrious sages, the position of summing up the "complete orchestra" of the past is the Duke of Zhou's alone. This was so because his position in time happened to be what it was; not even the Duke of Zhou himself realized that this was the case.

5. Mengzi tells us, "Kongzi may be said to have summed up the 'complete orchestra.'"[83] Now I have said that it was the Duke of Zhou who summed up the

---

80. If the sage and the Way were one in Substance, though we could separate them conceptually, neither could exist apart from the other.

81. Paraphrasing the *Changes*, "Great Appendix," II.2.

82. For "pure knowing," see *Mengzi* 7A15, in Part III, Selection 35. For "complete orchestra" as a description of Kongzi, see *Mengzi* 5B1. This antithesis between the Way and proper models (*fǎ* 法) is another expression of the contrast between *suǒyǐrán* and *dāngrán* (see section 3, above).

83. *Mengzi* 5B1.

"complete orchestra." Does this not seem to contradict Mengzi's claim? Well, the meaning of the expression "to sum up" is to collect together all of a group and unify it. From the beginning of Heaven and Earth down to the emperors Yao and Shun and the Xia and Shang dynasties, sages always had attained the position of emperor; their government and their care of the people derived from the working out of the Way as required by circumstances. The Duke of Zhou, in fulfilling the Virtue of Kings Wen and Wu, happened to live at a time when the work of emperors and kings was complete and when one dynasty had profited from the experience of another to the point where nothing further could be added. And so, he was able to rely on this past accumulation to form his own institutions and to "sum up" in the Way of the Zhou dynasty the "orchestra" of the ancient sages. This in fact is what is meant by "summing up the complete orchestra."

Kongzi had Virtue but lacked position.[84] In other words, there was no one from whom he could acquire the power to create institutions. He could not even take his place as a single instrument, so how could he possibly sum up the complete orchestra? This does not mean that Kongzi's quality as a sage was in any way inferior to that of the Duke of Zhou; it is simply that the time in which he lived caused things to be like this. In saying that Kongzi "summed up the complete orchestra," Mengzi was actually comparing him to Bo Yi, Yi Yin, and Liuxia Hui.[85] Mengzi knew that these three men all were sages, but he feared that his disciples might wonder if Kongzi's status as a sage was the same as theirs. When his disciple Gongsun Chou asked if Kongzi was like these men, Mengzi had no satisfactory way to express Kongzi's complete perfection, which distinguished him from the limited excellence of these three. And so he compared the situation to a musical orchestra. Therefore, the statement about Kongzi and the "complete orchestra" applies only in regard to these three sages; it is not a thorough or adequate description of Kongzi. To take it as a thorough or adequate description of Kongzi would actually belittle Kongzi. Why? Because the Duke of Zhou, in summing up the complete orchestra of Fuxi, the Yellow Emperor, Yao, Shun, et al., had actually studied these successive sages. Had the Way and proper models of these sages not existed, he of course could not have come to be the Duke of Zhou, as he was. Kongzi did not "sum up the complete orchestra" of Bo Yi, Yi Yin, and Liuxia Hui in this way, for he never studied Bo Yi, Yi Yin, and Liuxia Hui. Are we to say that had Bo Yi, Yi Yin, and Liuxia Hui not lived, Kongzi would not have come to be the sage that he was? Mengzi's words make sense only when taken in their proper context. We must not "let language injure meaning."[86] . . .

---

84. *Mean* 28. Compare *Analects* 8.14 and 14.27.

85. Three early sages to whom Kongzi is compared and found superior in *Mengzi* 5B1.

86. That is to say, we should not take the words so literally that we fail to appreciate their intent. This phrase is actually a paraphrase of *Mengzi* 5A4.

7. Suppose that someone were to say, "I grant that Kongzi and the Duke of Zhou share a common Way, but are we to suppose that the Duke of Zhou 'sums up the complete orchestra' while Kongzi does not?" I would reply by saying that Kongzi's "complete orchestra" is not that spoken of by Mengzi. As I see it, Mengzi, like the Duke of Zhou, summed up Fuxi, Shennong, The Yellow Emperor, his grandson Zhuanxu, Yao, Shun, and the Three Dynasties—not Bo Yi, Yi Yin, and Liuxia Hui.

When the functions of ruler and teacher separated and it consequently became impossible to keep government and doctrine united, this was the result of Heavenly decreed destiny. The Duke of Zhou "summed up the orchestra" of the tradition of government, while Kongzi displayed the highest excellence in regard to true teaching. The achievement of each was determined by the nature of things and in neither do we have a case of a sage [intentionally] differing from those who preceded him. This was the result of the Way and proper models deriving from Heaven. Hence, prior to the Song dynasty, in schools, equal reverence was paid to the Duke of Zhou and to Kongzi. The Duke of Zhou was regarded as the foremost sage and Kongzi as the foremost teacher, presumably on the grounds that the fashioning of institutions is something characteristic of sages, while the establishing of teachings is something characteristic of teachers. This is why Mengzi says that the Way of the Duke of Zhou and Kongzi is one and the same.[87]

However, if the Duke of Zhou and Kongzi were able to establish the epitome of government and teaching because of their times and circumstances, is it then to be supposed that the sage is in fact dependent upon time and circumstance? Zaiwo held that Kongzi was more worthy than Yao or Shun. Zigong maintained that since humankind first arose there had never been anyone like Kongzi. Youruo, in comparing Kongzi to the sages of antiquity, said that he stood out above all others.[88] These three philosophers all ignored the Duke of Zhou and paid honor only to Kongzi. This is explained by Zhu Xi's remark that, "sages differ in respect to actions and achievements."[89] Nevertheless, in government there is a display of actual deeds, whereas teachings only pass along empty words. Persons of later times accepted the remarks of the three philosophers and vigorously extolled Kongzi as superior to Yao and Shun and on this basis placed great value on "nature" and "fate" while slighting action and achievement. From that point on, the political achievements of all the sages came to seem inferior to the

---

87. Mengzi does not say this in so many words, but does speak of "the Way of the Duke of Zhou and Kongzi," treating it as one tradition. For example, see his remarks concerning Chen Liang in *Mengzi* 3A4.

88. From a portion of *Mengzi* 2A2 not in this anthology.

89. This is actually a remark made by Cheng Yi which Zhu Xi quotes as part of his commentary on *Mengzi* 2A2 (from a portion of his *Collected Commentaries on the* Mengzi not in this anthology).

academic discussions of Confucian scholars. . . . Now there is no better way to honor Kongzi than to pay close attention to his character as a man. If people do not understand the reality of Kongzi and merely make it their business to revere and worship him, they will talk more and more vaguely and mysteriously about him until the term "sage" becomes simply an expression interchangeable with "divinity" and "Heaven." How will this add to our present understanding?

Therefore, we should not compare the relative merits of Kongzi and the Duke of Zhou. Speaking metaphorically, Zhuangzi said of "spirit-like people" that "from their dust and chaff you could mold the sages Yao and Shun!"[90] Surely Confucian scholars ought not to copy his ideas! Therefore, those who wish to understand the Way must first understand what it is that made the Duke of Zhou and Kongzi what they were.

Section II

1. Han Yu said,

> Up to the Duke of Zhou, [these sages] were rulers. Hence, their actions were put into effect. After the Duke of Zhou, they were ministers. Hence, they offered more developed explanations.[91]

Now, it is by "developing explanations" that the Way is made clear, but it is also in this way that the Way is obscured. Kongzi assimilated the Way of the Duke of Zhou and made his teachings shine forth for all time. However, in doing this, Kongzi never devised theories of his own. He made clear the Six Classics and preserved the old statutes of the Duke of Zhou. This is why he said, "A transmitter and not a creator, I trust in and love antiquity"[92] and "There are, I suppose, those who act without knowledge, but I do not do so."[93] "The things of which the master regularly spoke were the *Odes*, the *Documents*, and the maintenance of rites."[94] This is to "illuminate the Way of the former kings in order to guide [the people]."[95] It was not that Kongzi exalted the former kings in order to humbly cultivate his own character, and therefore did not create anything of his own.[96] Basically, there was nothing that Kongzi could have created. Having Virtue but being without position, Kongzi had no authority to create

---

90. *Zhuangzi* 1, translated in Philip J. Ivanhoe and Bryan W. Van Norden, eds., *Readings in Classical Chinese Philosophy,* 2nd ed. (Indianapolis: Hackett Publishing, 2005), p. 212.

91. Han Yu, "On the Way," in Part III, Selection 20. The "it" that they were able to put into practice is of course the Way.

92. *Analects* 7.1.

93. *Analects* 7.27.

94. *Analects* 7.17.

95. Han Yu, "On the Way," in Part III, Selection 20.

96. The word *zuò* 作 means both "to create" and "to write." Here it means both to devise social and political institutions and to set down one's ideas about them in writing.

institutions, and he couldn't teach others with empty words, for, as it is said, "without demonstration one will not be believed."[97] . . .

Scholars have paid honor to Kongzi in a way that seems to appropriate him as the founding teacher of their own particular group. In doing this they reveal that they actually do not understand Kongzi. Kongzi taught the ultimate perfection of the Way for human beings; he cannot be said to have taught the ultimate perfection of the Way for scholars. When a scholar is someone of great worth who has not encountered an enlightened ruler to serve or secured a position from which he can put the Way into practice, he then will spend his life preserving the Way of the ancient kings for people to study in later ages. This is a necessity imposed upon him by his situation. What the Way for human beings enjoins is broad and great. Surely it is not right for those who have not encountered an opportunity to serve in some official capacity to stick unwaveringly to this course of preserving the ancient way for posterity and avoid having anything further to do with human affairs. The *Changes* developed from the trigrams of Emperor Fuxi, but we need not follow him in wearing straw clothing and living in the wilds.[98] The *Documents* begins with the "Canon of Shun," but we need not weep and cry to Heaven as Shun did.[99] My point is that the domain in which the truth of these classics is to be applied always differs. How then can those who study Kongzi say that they will not attempt any active achievement but will instead set their sights upon passing on the doctrine in an age when the Way is not practiced?[100]

2. The *Changes* says, "what is above with respect to form is called the 'Way,' and what are below with respect to form are called 'concrete things.'"[101] The Way can no more be abstracted from the material world than a shadow can be separated from the shape that casts it. Because those in later ages who accepted Kongzi's teachings obtained them from the Six Classics, they came to regard the Six Classics as books that set forth the Way. However, they failed to realize that the Six Classics all belong to the realm of concrete "things." For example, the *Changes* is a book that explains things and helps people to succeed in their undertakings. In the Zhou court the Grand Diviner was in charge of it. It is therefore clear that its use was the responsibility of a specific office and that it was classed as a government document. Similarly, the *Documents* was the responsibility of the Historian of the Exterior; the *Odes* was part of the charge of the Grand Preceptor; the *Rites* comes from the Master of Ceremonies; for the *Music*

---

97. *Mean* 28.

98. *Changes*, "Great Appendix," II.2.

99. From the *Documents, Documents of Yu*, "Counsels of the Great Yu." Compare *Mengzi* 5A1.

100. Such as was the case in Kongzi's age. See *Analects*, 5.7, 14.36, and 18.7.

101. *Changes*, "Great Appendix," I.12, in Part I, Selection 9. Zhang interprets this line as meaning that "concrete things" (the various phenomena of the physical world) are merely manifestations of the Way—not the Way itself.

there was the Master of the Court Orchestra; and for the *Spring and Autumn Annals* of each state there was a State Recorder.[102] In the three royal dynasties and in earlier times, the *Odes*, *Documents*, and other classical disciplines were taught to everyone. It was not, as in later times, when we find the Six Classics placed on a pedestal, treated as the special subject matter of the Confucian school, and singled out as books which set forth the Way. The reason, as I see it, was that students in ancient times studied only what was in the charge of state officials, the state's doctrines of government, and they simply applied this learning to the ordinary problems of everyday human obligations. They saw what they found in the classics simply as things that had to be as they were. They never saw beyond this any "Way" set forth in these books.

Kongzi transmitted the Six Classics to instruct posterity because he believed that the Way of the ancient sages and kings is something that cannot be seen, while the classics are the "thing" that comes from the Way, which can be seen. He thought that people of later times, who have not themselves seen the ancient kings, ought to use these records concerning actual things and affairs, which they could keep and treasure, in order to grasp in understanding the invisible Way. And so Kongzi made clear the government doctrines of the ancient kings and the documents, which the officials had kept, in order to show them to others. He did not write theories of his own, which would have been to talk about the Way divorced from the real world. When Kongzi explained why he wrote the *Spring and Autumn Annals*, he said, "I could have set forth my principles in empty words, but they would not have been as trenchant and clear as they are when illustrated in [concrete] actions and events."[103] We see clearly then that there is no Way set forth in the classics apart from the documents illustrating political doctrines and the day-to-day functioning of human relationships. . . .

3. The *Changes* says, "When those who are benevolent see it, they call it 'benevolence.' And when those who are wise see it, they call it 'wisdom.' The common people use it every day and yet do not understand it."[104] It is in this manner that the Way becomes hidden. Now of course it is nobler to see it and say what it is, than to use it every day without realizing what it is. Nevertheless, when people do not recognize the Way, the Way is preserved; when it is seen and characterized, it is destroyed. When the great Way becomes hidden, it becomes so not because of ordinary ignorance but because of the confused views of the

---

102. Zhang's point is that the basic classical texts were all official documents and are to be read as materials showing how the Way was *manifested* rather than as books containing statements *about* the Way.

103. A quote attributed to Kongzi but not part of the present text of the *Analects*. See chapter 130 of the *Records of the Grand Historian*.

104. *Changes*, "Great Appendix," I.5, in Part I, Selection 9. The "it" that these people see and use is of course the Way.

worthy and the wise. We may suppose that when the roles of official and teacher, of governing and instructing, were united, all the most intelligent people in the world conformed to one standard. And so, as the Way was found preserved in [actual] "things," people's minds harbored no wayward thoughts. When official and teacher, governing and instructing, separated and intelligent and talented people no longer conformed to a [single] standard, then, because the alternation of *yin* and *yang* produces partiality in one's endowed nature, it was simply inevitable that each person took his own opinion as the inviolable truth.[105] Now if the regulation of rituals and the control of music each has its own special officer in charge, even someone who had both the eyes of Li Lou and the ears of Music Master Kuang could not but conform to the pattern [of ritual] and the scale [of music].[106] However, if, on the grounds that the official traditions have broken off, I say that I will make my teachings shine with the Way and Virtue, then everyone will put forward his own conception of the Way and Virtue. Therefore, Kongzi "transmitted but did not create," and made clear the Six Arts, preserving the old traditions of the Duke of Zhou, not daring to discard actual things and affairs and speak of the Way.[107] However, the [Zhou dynasty] philosophers, in their confusion, talked of "the Way" readily enough. Zhuangzi compares them to the ear, eye, mouth, and nose.[108] Sima Tan distinguished six schools of philosophy, while Liu Xiang classified them into nine traditions.[109] Each school believed that it alone possessed the absolute truth and envisioned reordering the world according to its own "Way." However from an enlightened point of view, these various schools of thought are seen merely as descriptions based upon limited views of the Way. It was hardly the case that the Way had really become what they said it was.

Now, the Way is revealed in the realm of actual things and affairs; it is not

---

105. By "*yin* and *yang*" Zhang means both changing historical conditions and trends (see Section I) and the contrary directions that individual tastes or interests may take (see Section III).

106. Li Lou is the paragon of sharp-sightedness and Music Master Kuang the paragon of keen hearing.

107. Zhang's use of the term "Six Arts" (*liuyi* 六藝) is unusual. It normally refers to the six arts of ceremony, music, archery, charioteering, literature, and mathematics. However, for Zhang, the Six Arts are traditional areas of learning associated with the six ancient classics: the *Documents, Odes, Music, Rites, Changes,* and the *Spring and Autumn Annals.* Following Liu Xin, Zhang believed that these different areas of learning were originally associated with distinct bureaucratic offices.

108. Zhuangzi compares the various schools of philosophy to the different organs of sense, each capable of perceiving only one aspect of reality and incapable of appreciating the others. For a translation, see Burton Watson, *The Complete Works of Chuang Tzu* (New York: Columbia University Press, 1968), p. 364.

109. For Sima Tan's comment, see *Records of the Grand Historian,* chapter 130. For Liu Xiang's comment, see *Hanshu,* chapter 30.

something named by human beings.[110] It was when there were people talking about the Way that the Way began to be labeled differently by different people. This is what is meant by, "The benevolent person sees it and calls it benevolence; the wise person sees it and calls it wisdom." When people followed the Way in their actions, the Way could not be possessed by anyone. Only when people all preached their own conception of the Way and each acted according to his conception of it, did the Way come to be the possession of individuals. And so we speak of "the Way of Mozi," or "the Way of Xuzi."[111] The Way took form as soon as three people lived together and it attained perfect realization with the Duke of Zhou and Kongzi. The sages from age to age never singled it out and called it "the Way" just as the members of a household, when at home, do not use their surname among themselves. However, when the many schools of philosophy sprouted up and talked about "the Way," [Confucian] scholars could not but pay honor to the sources of their own tradition. And so, for example, one speaks of "the Way of Yao and Shun," and another of "the Way of the Duke of Zhou and Kongzi." For this reason, Han Yu said that Way and Virtue are "open concepts."[112] However, when Way and Virtue become open concepts, this is their ruination.

Section III

3. Zigong said, "The Master's cultural brilliance is something one can get to hear of, but one cannot get to hear his teachings on one's nature and the Way of Heaven."[113] Now of course everything the master talked about concerned human nature and the Way of Heaven. And yet he never explicitly indicated what these were by saying, "This is human nature" or "This is the Way of Heaven." That is why Zigong did not say, "One cannot get to hear about one's nature and the Way of Heaven," but instead said, "One cannot get to hear *his teachings on* one's nature and the Way of Heaven." Everything that Kongzi talked about concerned human nature and the Way of Heaven, but he never explicitly said what human nature and the Way of Heaven were because he feared that people

---

110. The idea is, first, that no fixed concept is adequate for the Way and, second, that the truth is not the property of any one tradition. It is therefore not only wrong but also senseless to speak of "the Way of Kongzi" or "the Way of Mozi."

111. Xuzi (not to be confused with "Xunzi") was an anti-Confucian philosopher whose position is discussed and criticized in *Mengzi* 3A4.

112. Han Yu, "On the Way," in Part III, Selection 20. "Open concepts" (literally: "empty positions") are terms with meanings that are not a fixed part of the terms themselves. In the case of such concepts, each thinker or school fills in the meaning in a different way.

113. *Analects* 5.13, in Part III, Selection 34. For a study of this passage, which includes an analysis of Zhang's interpretation, see Ivanhoe, "Whose Confucius? Which *Analects*? Diversity in the Confucian Commentarial Tradition," in Bryan W. Van Norden, ed., *Confucius and the* Analects: *New Essays* (New York: Oxford University Press, 2002), pp. 119–33.

would abandon [actual] "things" in their search for the Way. Kongzi could have talked about the rites of the Xia and the Shang dynasties but said that these were all unsubstantiated and would not be trusted.[114] And so we see that in every case, the master only talked about those things that could be attested in [actual] things. He never vainly employed empty words in order to explain the Way.

Zengzi "truly piled up effort for a long time" and then Kongzi said to him that it "is bound together with one thing."[115] Zigong understood after engaging in extensive study and then Kongzi said to him that he "binds it together with one thing."[116] Had they not "truly piled up effort for a long time" and understood after engaging in extensive study, they would not have had any basis upon which to have it "bound together with one thing."[117] Textual commentaries and philosophical research prepare one to seek the traces of the ancient sages, but excessive memorization and recitation of the classics is simply like piling up wares in the market place [without ever selling any of them]. When one engages in writing, it should be with a desire to make clear the minds of the ancient sages. To indulge oneself in an embellished style of writing is simply to amuse oneself with a kind of game. Heterodox doctrines and improper schools of study each regard their Way as the [true] Way and their Virtue as [true] Virtue, but they can never lead one to a correct understanding of the Way.[118] Learning based upon memorization and recitation of the classics and an elegant style of writing cannot but take the Way as its guiding principle, and yet when taken to the deluded extremes of excessive recitation and self indulgent amusement, its very source is forgotten.

Scholars of the Song dynasty rose up and attacked these tendencies saying that such efforts represented an obsession with "things" in the absence of an understanding of the Way. Now as for those who become obsessed with "things" without having an understanding of the Way, it is proper to illustrate the Way to them in "things." Where the Song scholars went wrong was in trying to get people to abandon "things" and just talk about the Way. Kongzi taught people to "make an extensive study of literature," but scholars of the Song said, "To

---

114. *Mean* 28. Compare *Analects* 3.9.

115. Quoting *Analects* 4.15 and Zhu Xi's commentary on it, in Part III, Selection 34.

116. *Analects* 15.3. [In this passage, Kongzi asks Zigong, "Do you take me to be one who understands after engaging in extensive study?" And when Zigong admits that he does, Kongzi states, "That is not so. I have bound it together with one thing."—Eds.]

117. Zhang here follows Zhu Xi's interpretation of *Analects* 15.3, according to which 4.15 and 15.3 are similar in that each represents a disciple's expression of insight into the Way that Kongzi taught. Zhang also seems to accept Zhu Xi's opinion that 15.3 concerns achieving understanding through *learning,* while the other passage, 4.15, concerns achieving understanding through *action.*

118. Zhang is again referring to the opening lines of Han Yu's "On the Way," where "Way" and "Virtue" are described as "open concepts" (see Part III, Selection 20).

trifle with things dissipates the will."[119] Zengzi taught people, "In one's words stay far from what is improper," but the scholars of the Song said, "To work at literature injures the Way."[120] As for what the Song scholars said, it is an excellent prescription for a desperate situation. However a prescription should only attack the disease that is infecting one's vital organs. The ideas of the Song scholars seem to regard the organs themselves as a disease and want to get rid of them entirely! In their search for "human nature" and "Heaven" they de-emphasized recitation of the classics and suppressed writing. What is there to choose between two such extreme views? Nevertheless, their great finesse in the analysis of Pattern and the sincerity of their practice far exceeded anything found in the scholars of the Han and Tang dynasties. Mengzi said, "The Pattern and righteousness please my mind just as the meat of grass and grain fed animals pleases my palate."[121] Moral Patterns cannot be captured in empty words; they need extensive study to give them reality and literary embellishment to give them expression. When these three are combined together, then one is almost there!

Though the Way of the Duke of Zhou and Kongzi is far away, it is not conveyed merely by labored interpretations [of the classics]. In the present age, teachers of the classics hold deep animosity for one another, literary men have little regard for one another, and the various philosophers of "human nature" and "Heaven" are divided into the competing schools of Zhu Xi and Lu Xiangshan.[122] The followers of Zhu Xi and Lu Xiangshan attack one another, while those who talk about "learning" and "literature" ape whatever fashion is in vogue without ever realizing their error. The present situation is just as Zhuangzi once said: "Each of the hundred schools goes off in its own direction without ever turning back. They can never be reconciled and brought together!"[123] Is it not sad!

---

119. For Kongzi's remark, see *Analects* 6.27, 12.15, etc. Cheng Hao and Cheng Yi are among the "Song scholars" whom Zhang has in mind. See Cheng Hao, Selected Sayings, in Part III, Selection 27, §16, and Cheng Yi, Selected Sayings, in Part III, Selection 31, §29.

120. For Zengzi's comment, see *Analects* 8.4. Cheng Yi said something like the phrase the Zhang attributes to "Song scholars," in Part III, Selection 31, §29.

121. *Mengzi* 6A7.

122. See the selections from Zhu Xi and Lu Xiangshan, in Part III.

123. *Zhuangzi* 33. See Burton Watson, *The Complete Works of Chuang Tzu*, p. 364.

Frame from "The Evil Life of Confucius," Cultural Revolution Propaganda Poster.

PART V: THE TWENTIETH CENTURY

The Fall of the Qing Dynasty

The first part of the Qing dynasty (1644–1911) was a period of tremendous expansion and prosperity, culminating in the reign of the Kangxi emperor (1661–1722), a great statesman, military leader, and patron of culture and scholarship. By the end of his reign, Chinese territory stretched as far as Tibet, Taiwan, and what is now Mongolia. However, within a century after Kangxi's rule, the Qing dynasty was in serious decline, and less than a century after that the Qing, and the imperial system of government, were gone forever. The final section of this anthology covers the rich period of philosophical reflection and soul-searching prompted by the decline of China's last imperial dynasty and the rise of Western influence within its borders.

One of the turning points for the Qing dynasty was the First Opium War of 1839–1842. The West had been importing products from China for years, particularly tea, silk, and porcelain. However, the Chinese had little use for Western products, so a severe trade imbalance developed, in which silver was being drained from the West to pay for Chinese goods. Unscrupulous British traders developed a solution to the problem by exporting opium from India into China. Opium addiction became a serious problem in Chinese society, and in 1839, the Confucian official Lin Zexu received imperial approval to seize and destroy British opium shipments. Lin also wrote an impassioned letter to Queen Victoria, appealing to her conscience and asking her to stop the opium trade. The British responded by sending ships and troops to coerce China to allow opium importation. The Qing government was decisively defeated, and China was forced to accept humiliating terms in the Treaty of Nanjing, including paying an indemnity and ceding control of Hong Kong to Britain.

Two other major disasters followed this humiliating event. The first was the Taiping Rebellion of 1850–1864, instigated by a group of militant, unorthodox Chinese Christians that was led by a man who claimed that he was Jesus' younger brother. The imperial government eventually prevailed in this civil war, but by the time it ended approximately twenty million people had died. Then, as if things could not get any worse, the Second Opium War (1856–1860) broke out during the Taiping Rebellion. This war went as badly for China as the First Opium War, and led to more indemnities and more concessions from the Qing government. By the end of the nineteenth century, foreign powers had begun to talk openly about "carving the Chinese melon," meaning dividing up China into "spheres of influence" that each state could economically exploit. Because of these experiences, China remains, even today, very sensitive about anything it perceives to be foreign interference in Chinese affairs, or efforts to separate anything it regards as part of China. This is true whether we are talking about Tibet, Taiwan, or the Senkaku Islands.

Meanwhile, in Japan, China's neighbor to the East, the traditional social and political structure was overthrown during the Meiji Period (1868–1912). The warrior class of samurai were transformed into or replaced with merchants and other more enterprising members of the upper class, as Japan sent students to the West to learn everything they could about Western science and technology, including railroads, telegraphs, newspapers, rifles, canons, warships, and medicine. The process was so effective that Japan was soon able to force its will on its neighbors as easily as had the Western powers. As a result of the First Sino–Japanese War (1894–1895), China was again forced to pay indemnities and make territorial concessions.

Although there were a handful of modernizers in the Qing court, they were often stymied by entrenched conservative scholars who showed nothing but contempt for Western culture and technology, even when facing the prospect of complete foreign control or internal collapse. The Qing eventually made a few reforms (such as establishing what would become Peking University in 1898 and eliminating the Confucian civil service examinations in 1905), but it was too little too late.[1] The Qing dynasty sputtered and gasped its way to its conclusion in 1911, when Sun Yat-sen founded the Republic of China.[2]

From the Republic of China to the People's Republic of China

China's suffering and exploitation were not over, though, because the Republic of China did not have the power to unify China any more than had the Qing government. China quickly sank into a period of chaos in which many areas were dominated by local warlords. China was also still subject to foreign imperialism, as was illustrated by the events that led to the May Fourth Movement, to which we now turn.

As part of "carving the Chinese melon," Germany had been granted special economic and legal rights in Shandong Province. When World War I broke out, China fought on the Allied side, in exchange for a promise that Shandong

---

1. Traditionally, the Empress Dowager Cixi is blamed for much of the Qing failure to adapt. However, a recent revisionist account argues that Cixi's faction at court was a dynamic force for change and modernization, but was held back by more conservative members of the aristocracy. See Jung Chang, *Empress Dowager Cixi: The Concubine Who Launched Modern China* (New York: Knopf, 2013).

2. The Republic of China (ROC) is not the same as the later People's Republic of China (PRC), discussed below.

would be returned to their rule. Unfortunately, among the many imprudent and unjust aspects of the 1919 Treaty of Versailles was that it simply transferred the German concessions in Shandong to Japan. This sparked widespread protests in China against imperialism and in favor of political reform and modernization. This May Fourth Movement was the most visible event in the broader New Culture Movement that traced its origins to scholars at Peking University and the founding of the seminal journal *New Youth* in 1915. The slogan of the New Culture Movement was that China must "overturn the shop of Kongzi," meaning eliminate the legacy of Confucianism and modernize. One of the major figures of the New Culture Movement was Hú Shì (Hu Shih 胡適, 1891–1962). After going abroad to obtain degrees from Columbia and Cornell, Hu returned to China and became a leading advocate of democracy, natural science, and technological development.[3] While intellectuals such as Hu Shih took inspiration from the Western capitalistic nations, others believed that, after years of imperialistic exploitation by countries such as the United Kingdom and France, China was better off allying itself with the rising Communist movement. The Chinese Communist Party was founded in 1921 by Chén Dúxiù 陳獨秀 (1879–1942), the leftist intellectual who had established the periodical *New Youth,* and Lǐ Dàzhāo 李大釗 (1888–1927), one of the earliest prominent Chinese Marxist philosophers.[4]

In 1926, the Republic of China (now dominated by the Chinese Nationalist Party) launched the Northern Expedition, a military campaign to end the period of "warlordism" and unify China. The campaign ultimately succeeded, but during the conflict the Civil War broke out between the Nationalists and the Chinese Communists. The Nationalists almost wiped out the Communists, who were forced to engage in the infamous retreat known as the "Long March." However, when Japan provoked war with China in 1937, the Nationalists and Communists agreed to suspend their hostilities to fight the Japanese invasion. The Civil War resumed after the Japanese defeat in World War II in 1945, and this time it was the Nationalists who made a desperate retreat, to the island of Taiwan (where the Republic of China continues today). The charismatic peasant turned revolutionary leader Máo Zédōng 毛澤東 (Mao Tse-tung, 1893–1976) emerged as the undisputed leader of the Chinese Communists, and announced the founding of the People's Republic of China (PRC) from atop the Gate of Heavenly Peace to a cheering crowd in Tiananmen Square in 1949.

Mao and the other Chinese Communists were officially dismissive of traditional Chinese philosophy; however, the situation is more complex than the official line may suggest. Some of Mao's own thought betrays traditional influences. For example, his guerrilla strategy of warfare may have been inspired by the *Daodejing,* and one of his major philosophical works, the essay "On

---

3. See Hu Shih, "The Civilizations of the East and the West," in Part V, Selection 54.
4. See Li Dazhao, "Women's Liberation and Democracy," in Part V, Selection 53.

Contradiction," can be seen as reflecting the theory of complementary opposites, *yin* and *yang*, outlined by the *Changes*.[5]

A much more explicit influence of traditional philosophy can be seen in the thought of Liú Shǎoqí 劉少奇 (1898–1969), who became the second president of the PRC. In Liu's *On the Ethical Cultivation of Communist Party Members*, he confronts a theoretical problem that has long bothered Chinese Communists. According to Marx, the beliefs of an individual are determined by his socioeconomic context. Because most Chinese were not born into a communist society, how could they learn to think and act like Communists? Liu's ingenious solution was to develop a communist theory of ethical self-cultivation. This theory was not only inspired by traditional accounts of self-cultivation, but it even cites Confucian classics in order to make its points! Liu brilliantly synthesized Chinese Communism and Confucianism.[6]

Liu had long been a trusted colleague of Mao's. However, when Liu became president, he reversed the more extreme of Mao's economic and social policies, so Mao turned on him during the Great Proletarian Cultural Revolution (1966–1976). This movement was instigated by Mao, supposedly to eliminate "bourgeoise elements," "capitalist roaders," and the last traces of "feudalism" in the Party and society at large. Traditional Chinese philosophy was part of the "feudal" past that this movement aimed to overturn. With all the ruthlessness of the Inquisition and objectivity of the Salem witch hunt, the Red Guards hunted down suspected counterrevolutionaries, publicly humiliating them, beating them, and in some cases simply murdering them. Liu Shaoqi was one of the victims of the Cultural Revolution. He was removed as president and forced to issue a series of "self-criticisms" in which he publicly confessed his "errors," which seemed to largely consist of having the temerity to disagree with Mao.[7] Liu was then arrested and disappeared from public view, dying a few years later in prison.

During this period, interest in and study of traditional Chinese thought continued outside of mainland China (particularly in Hong Kong and Taiwan). One of the most significant intellectual events was the development of "New Confucianism." New Confucianism should not be conflated with Neo-Confucianism; however, the two movements are closely related. This is illustrated by "Manifesto on Behalf of Chinese Culture," a seminal essay published in 1958 by five leading New Confucian scholars.[8] The Manifesto claims that "Chinese culture has enjoyed from its origin a unitary orthodoxy," in contrast with the West, which

---

5. However, Mao suggests that he is following the dialectical materialism of Lenin, and this was certainly an important source of his ideas.

6. See Liu, *On the Ethical Cultivation of Communist Party Members*, in Part V, Selection 55.

7. See Liu Shaoqi, "Self-Criticism," in Part V, Selection 56.

8. See Mou Zongsan et al., "Manifesto on Behalf of Chinese Culture," online at www.hackettpublishing.com/mou_zongsan_manifesto.

is more fragmentary, due to its multiple cultural sources: "Generally speaking, western science and philosophy originated from Greece, the legal system from Rome, and religion from Hebrew sources."⁹ This unitary orthodoxy consists of "the Chinese Learning of the Mind and Nature."¹⁰ The New Confucians follow the Neo-Confucian understanding of Chinese intellectual history: there is really only one Chinese Way; it has been preserved throughout Chinese history; Kongzi passed it on to Mengzi; it was recovered and explicated by the Neo-Confucians of the Song and Ming dynasties, such as Zhu Xi.

The Manifesto is critical of both the May Fourth Movement and the Chinese Communists for dismissing the value of China's "unitary orthodoxy." However, it acknowledges that "historical Chinese culture lacked the modern Western democratic system, Western scientific study, and the current practical skills in technology. As a result, China has been unable to attain real modernization and industrialization."¹¹ Nonetheless, the Manifesto suggests that democracy, science, and technology are not only consistent with Confucianism, but will allow a more complete expression of its tenets.

One of the most noted authors of the New Confucian Manifesto was Móu Zōngsān 牟宗三 (1909–1995), a sophisticated and prolific philosopher who wrote in depth on philosophers as diverse as Zhu Xi, Kant, Hegel, and the Chinese Buddhists. One of Mou's overarching goals was to produce and defend a master narrative about the history of Chinese thought, which he believed would tell a somewhat different story for Confucianism than many had believed. According to Mou, the true inheritor of the tradition of Kongzi and Mengzi was not the orthodox Song Neo-Confucian Zhu Xi but rather the Ming Neo-Confucian Wang Yangming, by way of some lesser-known students of the Cheng brothers. He used this revised account of the proper Confucian lineage to show the inherent ethical and theoretical advantages of Confucianism over Kantianism. Citing and elaborating upon Wang's notion of an innate moral faculty of "pure knowing," Mou argued that Confucianism offered the possibility of a kind of moral autonomy or independence from external forces as Kant did, but that unlike Kant, Confucianism grounded it in a proper moral metaphysics, treating moral norms as real things rather than as practical or necessary presuppositions.

---

9. This is from a portion of the Manifesto not translated in the excerpts available on the book's website. See Carson Chang, Hsieh Yu-wei, Hsu Foo-kwan, Mou Chung-san, and Tang Chun-i, "A Manifesto on the Reappraisal of Chinese Culture," in T'ang Chun-i, *Essays on Chinese Philosophy and Culture* (Taipei, Taiwan: Student Book Company, 1987), p. 504.

10. See Mou Zongsan et al., "Manifesto on Behalf of Chinese Culture," §6.

11. This is from a portion of the Manifesto not included in the excerpts available on this volume's website. See Carson Chang et al., "Manifesto on the Reappraisal of Chinese Culture," in Tang Chun-i, op. cit., pp. 526–27.

China Today and Tomorrow

The Cultural Revolution ended and most of Mao's policies were reversed after his death in 1976. China quickly opened up again to foreign trade (on its own terms, this time), and the economy raced forward once the communist shackles were removed. Although China is not a true democracy and certain sensitive topics may not be discussed in the media, the Chinese people enjoy considerably more intellectual freedom today than they did under Mao. Philosophy in the Chinese academy has expanded to include almost the entire gamut of Western thinkers. Students in Chinese universities now have almost as much access to professors of German phenomenology or Anglo-American analytic philosophy as they do specialists in the "Three Teachings" of Confucianism, Daoism, and Buddhism. But traditional Chinese philosophy indisputably has a strong grip on the popular imagination in China, and this is not likely to change in our lifetimes or the lifetimes of our children.[12] Given the economic and political importance of China in the world today, it behooves all informed people to learn about these doctrines. In addition, those of us who have had the privilege of teaching Chinese philosophy in the West can attest to the fact that students of all backgrounds see the intrinsic interest of this great intellectual tradition. The present volume only gives a glimpse into its depth and diversity. We hope that, despite the limitations of our effort, you will be inspired to learn more, and follow the example of Kongzi's greatest disciple, Yan Hui, who said:

> The more I look up at it, the higher it seems; the more I delve into it, the harder it becomes. Catching a glimpse of it before me, I then find it suddenly at my back. The Master is skilled at leading me on, step by step. He broadens me with culture and restrains me with the rituals, so that even if I wanted to give up I could not.[13]

---

12. One indication of the interest in traditional Chinese thought is the fact that a popular introduction to the wisdom of Kongzi was a surprise best seller in 2007: Yu Dan's *Insights into the* Analects (Yu Dan, *Lunyu xinde* [Taibei: Linking Books, 2007]). There are at least 10 million copies of this book in print.

13. *Analects* 9.11, translation modified from Edward Slingerland, trans., *Confucius: Analects: With Selections from Traditional Commentaries* (Indianapolis: Hackett Publishing, 2003).

53. Li Dazhao, "Women's Liberation and Democracy"

translation by Justin Tiwald[1]

Lǐ Dàzhāo 李大釗 (1888–1927) was an influential philosopher in the early twentieth century, when Chinese intellectuals began to study Western thought in earnest. Although in his youth he was interested in reform-minded Confucians like Huang Zongxi (see Selection 50) and Kāng Yǒuwéi 康有為 (1858–1927), Li eventually rejected Confucianism in favor of Marxism. It is for his work and activism as a Marxist thinker that he is best known. Li eventually took academic and administrative positions at Peking University, which put him at the center of the anti-traditionalist "New Culture Movement" or "May Fourth Movement."[2] He also co-founded the Chinese Communist Party with Chén Dúxiù 陳獨秀 (1879–1942).

Li and other May Fourth thinkers began to take an interest in women's rights in the 1910s, just as movements toward women's suffrage were gaining traction in major Western democracies and more female philosophers began to appear in American and European intellectual circles.[3] In China, by contrast, there were neither durable gains for women's rights nor any high-profile female philosophers. It would be another few decades before women writers began to have an impact on the political thought of China, writers such as the novelist and activist Dīng Líng 丁玲 (1904–1986).[4]

Li Dazhao closely followed Western advances in women's equality and rights, reading the works of major suffragists and feminist socialists. "Women's Liberation and Democracy," published in 1919 and widely discussed by his contemporaries, offers his most succinct case for greater inclusion of women in political and public life. In it, Li spells out a position that might be categorized as a form of "difference feminism," which maintains that there are intrinsic differences between male and female genders, but argues that this is precisely what necessitates the full participation of both

---

1. This translation is based on the original version of the essay, published in *Shàonián Zhōngguó* 少年中國 1.4, (1919): 27–28.

2. For more on these movements see the Introduction to Part V.

3. The United Kingdom made partial concessions to suffragists in 1918, and the United States granted women the right to vote in 1920.

4. Ding Ling was an early feminist activist and proponent of coeducation. In the early 1940s, she wrote powerful and daring criticisms of the behavior of her male counterparts in the Communist Party. An important biographical account of Ding Ling's life appears in Jonathan D. Spence's *The Gate of Heavenly Peace* (New York: The Viking Press, 1981).

genders in all spheres of life, including politics. All footnotes are by the translator. —Eds.

There is a strong relationship between *democracy*[5] and women's liberation. True *democracy* is only realized once women are liberated. If the *democracy* is one in which the women are not liberated then it is decidedly not a true *democracy*. If we seek a true *democracy* then we must necessarily seek women's liberation.

There are two reasons for this.

First, if a society only offers men opportunities to act but, in shutting out the female half of the population, does not permit women to be active in society, then (apart from the fact that this nearly expels them from the life of the society) that society will surely be an autocratic, perverse, brutal, callous, and arid one, and decidedly lacking the spirit of *democracy*.[6] Because the male temperament contains numerous autocratic elements, it depends entirely on the moderate, refined, and loving temperament of the female half in order to balance one another out. Only then can they preserve the naturally egalitarian temperament of the human race, and only then can they express the spirit of *democracy*. We Chinese forbid women from participating at all in the life of society and there are very strict boundaries between men and women, which results in a male autocratic society—not just a society in which men have autocratic control over women, but one with autocracy between men as well.

Where life in its substance is callous, unfeeling, arid, and without flavor, that spirit of moderation, refinement, and love has no opportunity to manifest. If we want to be able to realize true *democracy* in China we must first create a women's liberation movement in order to enable women's spirit of moderation, refinement, and love wherever there are opportunities to correct the autocracy and brutality of men. After a long period of accumulation, habits will form. They can then become imperceptible and effect change on an autocratic society, making it a *democracy*.

Secondly, modern European and American *democracy* is not yet true *democracy*.

---

5. Li sometimes uses English terms that did not yet have widely shared and standardized Chinese equivalents at the time of writing. "Democracy" is one of those terms. Accordingly, "democracy" is italicized in this translation, as are all other phrases originally in English.

6. Sometimes we think of democracy primarily as a political institution, one that regularly permits ordinary citizens to select their leaders through free and fair elections. This is a minimalist conception that Li finds unhelpful, because even in states where leaders are elected democratically it is possible for some groups to dominate others. (This is a common Marxist critique of Western liberal democracy, even today.) This leads him to a more expansive notion, where a state is democratic if it can govern without domination: "The purpose of true democracy is to abolish the relation of rule and subjugation, to break the system that wrongly uses people like objects" (Li Dazhao, "Democracy and Ergatocracy 平民政治与工人政治," in *Li Dazhao wen ji* 李大钊文集, vol. 2, Beijing: *Renmin chu ban she,* 1984), p. 506; originally published in *Xīn qīng nián* 新青年 9.6 (1922).

That is because all of their [political or social] movements, laws, expressed views, and systems of thought all take men as their foundation, completely indifferent to their implications for the well-being of the female half. Even if [these supposedly democratic movements, laws, and views] are "concerned with" the interests of the women on whose behalf they work, they actually are not in the interests [of women], and lack the earnestness of those who act in their own interests. Surely the term "the people" is not monopolized by men alone. The female half of the population is undoubtedly included therein. Brougham Villiers said it well: "*The formula of democracy is not government of the people for the people by the men, but by the people.*"[7] To interpret his general point, *democracy* is not the politics of the people's rights and the people's authority as carried out by men, but the politics of the people's rights and the people's authority as carried out by the people as a whole. Here what's called "the people as a whole" is inclusive of both the male and female sexes.

All classes in society can be changed. The rich can become poor and the poor can become rich. Landlords and capitalists can become workers and workers can turn into landlords and capitalists. When society undergoes suitable transformations these differences of class could vanish. Only the distinction between the two sexes of man and woman exists as a permanent boundary, one that cannot be changed. So there is nothing more critical than having *democracy* between the sexes. And if we want *democracy* between the sexes then there is nothing more critical than the women's movement.

54. Hu Shih, "The Civilizations of the East and West"

Hú Shì (Hu Shih 胡適, 1891–1962) was one of the leading figures in the New Culture and May Fourth movements, which criticized the mainstream Chinese tradition (particularly Confucianism) and called on China to adopt Western science, technology, and democracy. He received his undergraduate degree from Cornell University, and his doctorate from Columbia University, both in philosophy. Under the influence of his teacher John Dewey, one of the leading American philosophers of his era, Hu became an advocate of the American philosophical movement known as Pragmatism after his return to China. He was particularly influential in the movement to write in vernacular Chinese, rather than Literary Chinese (the Chinese equivalent of

---

7. Brougham Villiers was the penname of Frederick John Shaw (1863–1939), an advocate for women's suffrage in Great Britain. The line quoted by Li comes from his *Modern Democracy: A Study in Tendencies* (London: T.F. Unwin, 1912), p. 215. I have corrected some errata to reflect Shaw's original wording and punctuation.

Latin). In the Chinese Civil War, he sided with the Nationalists, and served for several years as the ambassador of the Republic of China to the United States. Hu Shih wrote the following essay in English in response to European and Asian writers who had (in the aftermath of World War I) grown pessimistic about Western civilization, and begun to admire what they saw as the superior civilization of the East.[8]—Eds.

In recent years the despondent mood of a number of European writers has led to the revival of such old myths as the bankruptcy of the material civilization of the West and the superiority of the spiritual civilization of the Oriental nations. When I was in Germany last year, a German savant most solemnly assured me that the civilization of the East was based on spiritual principles. "In the East," said my enthusiastic friend, "even souls are selected on the basis of moral fitness. For does not the doctrine of the transmigration of souls imply the idea of moral selection?" Although these expressions represent nothing more than the pathological mentality of war-stricken Europe, they have already had the unfortunate effect of gratifying the vanity of Oriental apologists and thereby strengthening the hand of reaction in the East. In the West, too, one could see, as I have seen during my recent travels, that such loose thinking was leading not a few people away from a proper understanding of their own civilization which is fast becoming the world civilization. It is in the hope of furnishing a new point of view and a new basis of discussion that I now offer these few reflections on the civilizations of the East and the West.

I

Indeed there is no such thing as a purely material civilization. Every tool of civilization is produced by human intelligence making use of the matter and energy in the natural world for the satisfaction of a want, a desire, an aesthetic feeling, or an intellectual curiosity. A clay pot is no more material than a love lyric; nor is St. Paul's Cathedral less material than the Woolworth Building. Indeed when man first made fire by accidentally drilling wood, the invention was regarded as such a spiritual thing as to be attributed to one of the greatest gods. In the East, all the legendary kings of China were not priest-philosophers, but inventors. Such, for example, were Suìrén [燧人], the discoverer of fire; Yǒucháo [有巢], the first builder of houses; and Shénnóng [神農], the first teacher of agriculture and medicine.

Our forefathers were quite right in deifying the creators of tools. Man is a tool-making animal, and it is tool-making which constitutes civilization. The invention of fire created a new epoch in the history of human civilization;

---

8. First published in Charles Beard, ed., *Whither Mankind* (New York: Longman, Greene and Co., 1928). This version is edited for length, and romanizations have been converted to Pinyin. Footnotes are by Hu Shih unless indicated otherwise.—Eds.

agriculture, another; the invention of writing, a third; printing, a fourth. It was the invention of the telescope and the steam-engine and the discovery of electricity and radioactivity that have made the modern world what it is today. And if the priests of the Medieval Age were justly canonized as saints, Galileo, Watt, Stephenson, Morse, Bell, Edison, and Ford certainly deserve to be honored as gods and enshrined with Prometheus and Cadmus.[9] They represent that which is most divine in man, namely, that creative intelligence which provides implements and makes civilization possible.

The civilization of a race is simply the sum total of its achievement in adjusting itself to its environment. Success or failure in that adjustment depends upon the ability of the race to use intelligence for the invention of necessary and effective tools. The difference between the Eastern and Western civilizations is primarily a difference in the tools used. The West has during the last two hundred years moved far ahead of the East merely because certain Western nations have been able to devise new tools for the conquest of nature and for the multiplication of the power to do work. The East, whence have come a number of the epoch-making tools of ancient civilization, has failed to carry on that great tradition and is left behind in the stage of manual labor while the Western world has long entered the age of steam and electricity. This, then, is the real difference between the Oriental and the Western civilizations. The Oriental civilization is built primarily on human labor as the source of power whereas the modern civilization of the West is built on the basis of the power of machinery.

II

Let all apologists for the spiritual civilization of the East reflect on this. What spirituality is there in a civilization which tolerates such a terrible form of human slavery as the rickshaw coolie?[10] Do we seriously believe that there can be any spiritual life left in those poor human beasts of burden who run and toil and sweat under that peculiar bondage of slavery which knows neither the minimum wage nor any limit of working hours? Do we really believe that the life of a rickshaw coolie is more spiritual or more moral than that of the American workman who rides to and from his work in his own motor-car, who takes his whole family out picnicking on Sundays in distant parks and woods, who listens to the best music of the land on the radio for almost no cost, and whose children are educated in schools equipped with the most modern library and laboratory facilities?

---

9. James Watt (1736–1819) was a Scottish engineer who significantly improved the efficiency of steam engines. George Stephenson (1781–1848) designed the first inter-city railway line. The gods Prometheus and Cadmus were credited with introducing fire and the alphabet to humans, respectively.—Eds.

10. A "coolie" (*kŭlì* 苦力) is someone who does extremely demanding physical labor. The term is often regarded as derogatory today.—Eds.

It is only when one has fully realized what misery and acute suffering the life of rickshaw-pulling entails and what effects it produces on the bodily health of those human beasts of burden—it is only then that one will be truly and religiously moved to bless the Hargreaveses, the Cartwrights, the Watts, the Fultons, the Stephensons, and the Fords who have devised machines to do the work for man and relieve him from much of the brutal suffering to which his Oriental neighbor is still subject.[11]

Herein, therefore, lies the real spirituality of the material civilization, of mechanical progress *per se*. Mechanical progress means the use of human intelligence to devise tools and machines to multiply the working ability and productivity of man so that he may be relieved from the fate of toiling incessantly with his unaided hands, feet, and back without being able to earn a bare subsistence, and so that he may have enough time and energy left to seek and enjoy the higher values which civilization can offer him. Where man has to sweat blood in order to earn the lowest kind of livelihood, there is little *life* left, letting alone civilization. A civilization to be worthy of its name must be built upon the foundation of material progress. As the Chinese statesman Guǎn Zhòng [管仲] (d. 645 BCE) said twenty-six centuries ago, "When food and clothing are sufficiently provided for, honor and disgrace can be distinguished; and when granaries are full, the people will know good manners." This is not to drag in the so-called economic interpretation of history: it is simple commonsense. Picture a civilization where boys and girls and old women with bamboo baskets tied to their backs and with pointed sticks in hand, flock to every dumping place of refuse and search for a possible torn piece of rag or a half-burnt piece of coal. How can we expect a moral and spiritual civilization to grow up in such an atmosphere?

Then people may point to the religious life in those regions where the material civilization is low. What spirituality is there, let us say, in the old beggar-woman who dies in the direst destitution, but who dies while still mumbling, "Namo Amita Buddha!"[12] and in the clear conviction that she will surely enter that blissful paradise presided over by the Amita Buddha? Do we earnestly think it moral or spiritual to inculcate in that beggar-woman a false belief which shall so hypnotize her as to make her willingly live and die in such dire conditions where she ought not to have been had she been born in a different civilization?

No! All those hypnotic religions belong to an age when man had reached

---

11. James Hargreaves (1720–1778) invented the spinning jenny, which allowed workers to produce more yarn in the same amount of time. Edmund Cartwright (1743–1823) invented the power loom, which increased the productivity of weavers. Robert Fulton (1765–1815) developed the first commercially successful steamboat.—Eds.

12. This sentence, meaning "Homage to the Amita Buddha" is daily recited by followers of the Paradise (Pure Land) Sect of Buddhism.

senility and felt himself impotent in coping with the forces of nature. Therefore he gave up the fight in despair and, like the disappointed fox in the ancient fable who declared the grapes sour because he could not reach them, began to console himself and teach the world that wealth and comfort are contemptible and that poverty and misery are something to be proud of. From this it was only a step to the idea that life itself was not worth living and that the only desirable thing was the blissful existence in the world beyond. And when wise men calmly taught these ideas, fanatics went further and practiced self-denial, self-torture, and even suicide. In the West, saints prayed, fasted, slept on pillars, and whipped themselves at regular intervals. In medieval China, monks prayed, fasted, and, feeding themselves daily with fragrant oil and tying their bodies with oiled cloth, gladly burned themselves to death as offerings to some deity of Mahayana Buddhism.[13]

It took over a thousand years for a portion of mankind to emerge from the civilization which glorifies poverty and sanctifies disease, and slowly build up a new civilization which glorifies life and combats poverty as a crime. As we look around today, the religions of the Middle Ages are still there, the churches and cathedrals are still there, the monasteries and nunneries are still there. How is it that the outlook upon life has so radically changed? The change has come because in the last two centuries men have hit upon a few key inventions out of which a vast number of tools and machines have been constructed for the control of the resources and powers in nature. By means of these machines men have been able to save labor and reduce distance, to fly in the air, tunnel the mountains, and sail underneath the deep seas, to enslave lightning to pull our carriages and employ "ether" to deliver our messages throughout the world.[14] Science and machinery seem to meet no resistance from nature. Life has become easier and happier, and man's confidence in his own powers has greatly increased. Man has become the master of himself and of his own destiny. Thus a revolutionary poet sings:

> I fight alone, and win or sink,
> I need no one to make me free;
> I want no Jesus Christ to think
> That he could ever die for me.[15]

Thus the new civilization of the new age has given to men a new religion, the religion of self-reliance as contrasted with the religion of defeatism of the Middle Ages.

---

13. Compare this to Han Yu's criticism of Buddhism in "A Memorandum on a Bone of the Buddha," in Part III, Selection 19.—Eds.

14. Although no longer accepted by contemporary physicists, "ether" was the supposed physical medium through which electromagnetic waves (e.g., radio) were propagated.—Eds.

15. Proem, in *Arrows in the Gale*, by Arturo Giovannitti (1914).

III

I began by pointing out the spirituality of the most material phase of modern Western civilization, namely, its technological phase. Modern technology is highly spiritual because it seeks, through human ingenuity and intelligence, to relieve human energy from the unnecessary hardships of life and provide for it the necessary conditions for the enjoyment of life. Whatever be the use man may make of the resultant comfort and leisure, the relief of suffering and hardship is in itself spiritual.

I shall now try to show the spirituality of the other phases of the Western civilization. I shall leave out art, music, and literature, for it is evident to all that the West has its art and literature which are at least comparable with those found in the East, and its music which is certainly far more advanced than any which the Oriental countries can boast.

Let us begin with Science. Whatever may be our divergent views regarding the exact definition of the life of the spirit, probably no one today will deny that the desire to know is one of the legitimate spiritual demands of mankind. Yet practically all the older civilizations have tried to suppress this intellectual longing of man. According to the Book of Genesis, the Fall of Man was caused, not by Woman, but by the acquisition of Knowledge. Most of the Oriental religions taught such slogans as "No knowledge, no desire"; "Know nothing and follow the plan of God"; "Abandon wisdom and shun sagacity."[16] A great sage of the East, Zhuangzi, declared: "Life is finite and knowledge is infinite. How hazardous it is to pursue the infinite with the finite!"[17] Thereupon those teachers of man turned away from the strenuous path of knowledge-seeking and resorted to the various ways of introspection, meditation, and contemplation in search for what they conceived to be "deeper wisdom." Some taught the ways of direct communion with God through devout contemplation. Others elaborated the stages of *dhyāna* by means of which one might attain the magic powers of the gods.[18]

There is genuine spiritual joy in the work of the scientists who seek to wring from nature her little secrets by means of rigid methods of study and experimentation. Truth is deeply hidden and never reveals itself to those insolent souls who approach nature with unaided hands and untrained sense organs. Science trains our intelligence and equips it with necessary tools and methods. It teaches us not to despair of the infinity of knowledge, for it is only through piecemeal accumulation of fragmentary information that we can hope to arrive at some knowledge of nature at all. Every piecemeal acquisition is progress, and every little step in advance gives to the worker a genuinely spiritual rapture. When

---

16. The last phrase is from *Daodejing*, Chapter 19.—Eds.

17. *Zhuangzi*, Chapter 3.—Eds.

18. *Dhyāna* is the mental focus practiced during meditation that leads to enlightenment.—Eds.

Archimedes, on jumping into the bath tub, suddenly found the solution of the scientific problem that had troubled him, he was so overjoyed that he ran naked into the streets and shouted to everybody: "Eureka! Eureka!" This has been the spiritual joy that has constantly visited every research-worker in science, every Galileo, Newton, Pasteur, and Edison—a state of rapturous spirituality totally unknown to the pseudo-prophets of the old civilization, who professed to seek the higher knowledge of the totality of things by inward contemplation and self-hypnotism.

The most spiritual element in science is its skepticism, its courage to doubt everything and believe nothing without sufficient evidence. This attitude is not merely negative, although on the negative side it has performed very great service in liberating the human mind from slavish subjection to superstition and authority. The attitude of doubt is essentially constructive and creative: it is the only legitimate road to belief; it aims at conquering doubt itself and establishing belief on a new basis. It has not only fought the old beliefs with the irresistible weapon, "Give me evidence," but also raised new problems and led to new discoveries by the same insistence on evidence. It is this spirit of "creative doubt" which has made the biographies of the great scientists such as Darwin, Huxley, Pasteur, and Koch, the most inspiring of all human records.[19] Just as credulity has made our medieval saints, so has doubt made our modern gods who overcame nature and blessed man.

IV

But the most spiritual phase of the modern civilization of the West is its new religion which, in the absence of a better name, I shall term the religion of Democracy.

Modern civilization did not begin with religion, but it has resulted in a new religion; it did not much trouble about morals, but it has achieved a new system of morals. The European powers of the fifteenth and sixteenth centuries were frankly states of piracy. The great heroes of the age, Columbus, Magellan, Drake, and their like, were great pirates who braved the stormy and unknown seas in search of gold, silver, ivory, spices, and slaves.[20] Their adventures were usually supported by genuine royal or imperial patronage, and their glory and spoils were justly shared by their state and sovereign. They had no scruples for their religion which taught love for all men, or for their morals which condemned even usury.

---

19. Thomas Huxley (1825–1895) was one of the leading proponents of Darwinian evolutionary theory, and also coined the term "agnostic." Robert Koch (1843–1910) won the Nobel Prize in Medicine and is regarded, along with Louis Pasteur (1822–1895), as one of the founders of microbiology.—Eds.

20. Magellan and Drake captained the first and second circumnavigations of the globe, respectively.—Eds.

Those acts of piracy opened up the new continents to European trade and colonization which in turn greatly enhanced the material wealth and power of some of the European states and furnished tremendous stimulus to production and invention. The Industrial Revolution which followed fundamentally transformed the methods of production and multiplied the productive powers of the European states. With the increase in the material enjoyment and the rise of a large middle class, there has been simultaneously an expansion in man's imaginative power and sympathy. And with the restoration of man's confidence in himself as the agent to control his own destinies, there have developed the various types of social consciousness and social virtues. All this leads to the rise of the new religion of democracy, by which I mean to include the individualistic ideals of the eighteenth century and the socialistic ideals of the last hundred years.

The fight for Freedom and the Rights of Man became the war-cry of the American Revolution, the French Revolution, and the Revolutions of 1848, and have vibrated through all the later revolutions. They have worked themselves into the constitutions of the new republics. They have brought about the downfall of monarchies, empires, and aristocracies. They have given to man equality before the law and freedom of thought, speech, publication, and religious belief. Above all, they have emancipated the women and made universal education a reality.

The ideals of Socialism are merely supplementary to the earlier and more individualistic ideas of democracy. They are historically part of the great democratic movement. By the middle of the nineteenth century, the *laissez-faire* policy was no longer sufficient to achieve the desired results of equality and liberty under the highly organized and centralized economic system. Compulsory education was opposed as an infringement of liberty, and legislation regulating wages and factory conditions was branded as class legislation. The time had come for a new social and political philosophy which would meet the needs of the new economic life of the age. Hence the rise of the socialistic movements which, when freed from their distracting theories of economic determinism and class war, simply mean the emphasis on the necessity of making use of the collective power of society or of the state for the greatest happiness of the greatest number. In practice, the movement has taken two main directions. On one hand, there has been the strong tendency to organize labor as the effective means for the protection of the interests of the working class, and collective bargaining and strikes have been the chief weapons. On the other hand, there has been an equally strong tendency on the part of all modem democratic governments to forestall the wasteful methods of class struggle by assimilating and putting into practice a number of socialistic ideas such as taxation on inheritance, progressive income tax, compulsory insurance of workmen against accident and old age, regulation of working hours, fixing of minimum wages, and others. By one way or another or by both, many ideas which were once regarded as dangerously socialistic, have become an integral part of the legislative and governmental program of every modern state. One may still believe in the sacred right of property, but the tax on income and inheritance has become a most important source of revenue for most governments. One may still condemn the idea of class war, but organized labor has become a fact and strikes are almost universally legalized. England, the mother country of capitalism, has had a Labor Government and may soon have another. The United States of America, the champion of individual liberty, is trying to enforce national prohibition. The world is becoming socialistic without being aware of it.

This religion of Democracy which not only guarantees one's own liberty, nor merely limits one's liberty by respecting the liberty of other people, but endeavors to make it possible for every man and every woman to live a free life; which not only succeeds through science and machinery in greatly enhancing the happiness and comfort of the individual, but also seeks through organization and legislation to extend the goods of life to the greatest number—this is the greatest spiritual heritage of the Western civilization. Is it necessary for me to remind my readers that neither the emancipation of women, nor democratic government, nor universal education has come from the so-called spiritual civilizations of the East?

V

I cannot think of a more fitting conclusion than proposing to reconsider the much misused and therefore very confusing phrases "spiritual civilization," "material civilization," and "materialistic civilization." The term "material civilization" ought to have a purely neutral meaning, for all tools of civilization are material embodiments of ideas and the wheelbarrow civilization of the East is no less material than the motor-car civilization of the West. The term "materialistic civilization," which has often been applied to stigmatize the modern civilization of the West, seems to me to be a more appropriate word for the characterization of the backward civilizations of the East. For to me that civilization is materialistic which is limited by matter and incapable of transcending it; which feels itself powerless against its material environment and fails to make full use of human intelligence for the conquest of nature and for the improvement of the conditions of man. Its sages and saints may do all they can to glorify contentment and hypnotize the people into a willingness to praise their gods and abide by their fate. But that very self-hypnotizing philosophy is more materialistic than the dirty houses they live in, the scanty food they eat, and the clay and wood with which they make the images of their gods. On the other hand, that civilization which makes the fullest possible use of human ingenuity and intelligence in search of truth in order to control nature and transform matter for the service of mankind, to liberate the human spirit from ignorance, superstition, and slavery to the forces of nature, and to reform social and political institutions for the benefit of the greatest number—such a civilization is highly idealistic and spiritual. This civilization will continue to grow and improve itself. But its future growth and improvement will be brought about only through conscious and deliberate endeavors in the direction of more fully realizing those truly spiritual potentialities which the progress of this civilization has indicated.

55. Liu Shaoqi, *On the Ethical Cultivation of Communist Party Members*

translation by Bryan W. Van Norden[21]

Liú Shǎoqí 劉少奇 *(1898–1969) was an early leader of the Chinese Communist Party, as well as a brilliant theoretician. Below are excerpts from his major philosophical work,* On the Ethical Cultivation of Communist Party Members, *which he originally gave as a series of lectures to students at the Institute for Marxism-Leninism in the Communist guerrilla base at Yan'an. In this work, Liu synthesizes Marxism and traditional Confucian methods of ethical self-cultivation. According to communist theory, China in the early twentieth century was a society still subject to the decadent and reactionary influences of "feudal" (traditional) culture, as well as that of the newly rising capitalistic bourgeois class. The Party's goal is to achieve a revolution in which power will be put into the hands of the peasant farmers and the proletariat (factory workers). Liu argues that, in order to achieve this goal, Communist Party members ("cadres") must engage in self-cultivation in order to overcome the negative influences of the bourgeois and feudal cultures that have inevitably influenced them.*

In reading these excerpts, notice how Liu not only cites Confucian texts, but also makes many of the same points as Confucians about the need for and nature of ethical cultivation. Nonetheless, Liu claims that earlier forms of cultivation failed because they were tied to the oppressive and exploitive feudal social structure from which they originated. In sections of this work not translated here, Liu quotes extensively from Marx, Lenin, and Mao Zedong (the leader of the Chinese Communists) in order to show the orthodoxy of his own views. —Eds.

Why must Communist Party members engage in ethical cultivation? People's thinking and perception is determined by their social context. The thinking and

21. Translation based on 刘少奇选集, vol. 1 (人民出版社, 1981), pp. 97–167. A complete (but awkward) translation of this work is available under the title "How to Be a Good Communist," http://www.marxists.org/reference/archive/liu-shaoqi/1939/how-to-be/, accessed 1 May 2013. All footnotes are by the translator unless otherwise indicated.

perception of different classes of people reflect their different class status and interests. Because a comparatively inexperienced revolutionary grew up and was raised in the old society, he will generally maintain all sorts of remnants of the thinking and perceptions of the old society, including preconceptions, old practices, and old traditions. Kongzi said, "At fifteen, I set my mind upon learning. At thirty, I was firmly established. At forty, I was no longer confused. At fifty, I understood the mandate of Heaven. At sixty, my ear was attuned. At seventy, I could follow my mind's desires without ever overstepping the bounds."[22] What this feudal thinker is describing is his own process of ethical cultivation.[23] Even *he* did not claim to be a Heaven-born "sage."

Similarly, Mengzi, another feudal thinker, said that figures who were going to undertake a "great responsibility" in history endured a bitter process of tempering. This is what he meant when he said, "The world will first make their minds bitter, weary their bones, starve their bodies, exhaust their selves, and frustrate their actions—all in order to perturb their minds, toughen their natures, and supply what they are lacking in themselves."[24] Communist Party members are people who will undertake the "great responsibility" of changing the world in an utterly unprecedented way. Consequently, they must emphasize ethical tempering and cultivation even more so in the revolutionary struggle.

Our ethical cultivation as Communist Party members is the cultivation necessary for a revolutionary of the proletarian class. Our cultivation cannot be separated from revolutionary practice. It may not be separated from the reality of the revolutionary movement of the broad mass of workers (especially the mass of the proletariat).

There are those who say, "One cannot acquire through learning the character and thinking of the sort of great revolutionary geniuses who created Marxism-Leninism. One simply cannot elevate one's own character and thinking to the sort of high level occupied by the creators of Marxism-Leninism." People who say this regard the creators of Marxism-Leninism as Heaven-born mystical figures. Is this sort of perspective correct? I believe that it is incorrect.

In the *Mengzi,* there is this line: "Any person can become a Yao or Shun."[25] I think this is well put. Every Communist Party member must be firmly grounded, must seek the truth from facts, make a determined effort at tempering himself, sincerely cultivate himself, and step by step, as much as he is able, elevate his own thinking and character. He should not believe that the thinking and character of the sort of great revolutionary geniuses who created Marxism-Leninism is beyond his reach. To think that way would be to become one of "those who

---

22. *Analects* 2.4, in Part III, Selection 34.

23. According to orthodox Marxism, all pre-modern Chinese society either has a "feudal" or a slave-based socioeconomic structure.

24. *Mengzi* 6B15.

25. *Mengzi* 6B2.

are destroying themselves" or "those who throw themselves away," and fail to advance out of fear.[26] If it were like this, he would become a "political mediocrity," like a "wall of dung" that "cannot be troweled."[27]

Owing to variations in the political awareness, revolutionary experience, assigned task, cultural level, and conditions of social action of our party members, there will be variations in the extent to which each comrade must particularly emphasize (or even re-emphasize) ethical cultivation.

In ancient times in China, Zengzi said, "I examine myself daily on three counts."[28] This is talking about the issue of self-examination. There is a famous saying about this: "Like cutting, like chiseling; like grinding, like filing."[29] This refers to the fact that friends must help each other, and critique each other.

What all this is explaining is that if a person wishes to succeed in advancing, he must undergo a bitter "task," and earnestly engage in self-cultivation.[30] However, what the many people in ancient times who talked about "ethical cultivation" meant was something idealistic, formalistic, abstract, and removed from social practice. They one-sidedly emphasized subjective practice, mistakenly believing that if they merely preserved their "pure knowing," they would be able to transform phenomena, transform society, and transform themselves.[31] Of course, this is an illusion. *We* cannot engage in ethical cultivation like this. We are revolutionary materialists: our ethical cultivation cannot be separated from the revolutionary practice of the mass of the people.

In order to stick to this sort of Marxist-Leninist method of cultivation, we must resolutely oppose and thoroughly eradicate one of the greatest misfortunes regarding education and learning that has been left to us by the old society: the separation of theory from practice. In the old society, there were many people who, in their education and learning, were of the opinion that what they learned was actually not something that they had to act in accordance with. Some even thought it was something that they *could not* act in accordance with. Everything they wrote and said was about "benevolence and righteousness" and "the Way of Virtue." However, in their practice they were thieves and prostitutes, through and through. The reactionary faction of the Nationalists ardently reads *The Three People's Principles* by Sun Yat-sen,[32] and chants lines from his "Last

---

26. *Mengzi* 4A10, in Part III, Selection 35.

27. *Analects* 5.10.

28. *Analects* 1.4, in Part III, Selection 34.

29. *Odes*, no. 55, cited in *Analects* 1.15.

30. "Task" (*gōngfu* 工夫, also translated as "spiritual task" or "spiritual practice") is a term emphasized by Wang Yangming. See Wang's "Reply to Inquiries Made by a Friend" in Part III, Selection 44.

31. "Pure knowing" is literally "good heart" (*shàn liáng zhī xīn*), a phrase adapted from *Mengzi* 7A15, which appears in Part III, Selection 35.

32. Sun Yat-sen (1866–1925) is revered in both the People's Republic of China (in mainland China) and the Republic of China (on Taiwan) for his role as leader of the revolution that

Testament."[33] However, in practice they are violent, corrupt, and murderous oppressors of the masses, who oppose "the nationalities of the world that treat us as equals." It has gotten to the point that they compromise with or surrender to our national enemies. There was once an old Licentiate-level graduate of the imperial examinations who said to my face that there were only two sentences from Kongzi that he had ever been able to act in accordance with: "His grain could never be refined enough. His meat could never be minced carefully enough."[34] As for the rest, he had never acted in accordance with them, and had never tried to act in accordance with them. Since they are like this, whether they were educating or learning, of what value was their "Way of the sages and worthies"? Their purpose was simply to accumulate wealth and use this "Way of sages and worthies" to oppress those whom they exploited, and use a mouthful of "benevolence and righteousness" and "the Way of Virtue" to deceive the people. This is the attitude of the representatives of the exploiting class toward the sages and worthies that they "revere." Of course, we Communist party members, who learn Marxism-Leninism and learn the best parts of our nation's heritage, absolutely cannot adopt this attitude. What we learn, we must then put into practice. We proletarian revolutionaries—who have conscientiousness, Sincerity, and purity—cannot deceive ourselves, cannot deceive the people, and cannot deceive the ancients. This is a distinguishing trait of us Communist party members, and it is an excellent trait.

---

overthrew the last Chinese imperial dynasty, the Qing, in 1911. His primary theoretical work is *The Three People's Principles* (1925), which emphasizes the importance for China of nationalism, democracy, and welfare.

33. The "Last Testament of the President" is the testament of the Chinese Nationalist President Sun Yat-sen from the period when he was gravely ill on March 11, 1925. The complete text follows: "I have exerted my utmost effort for the Nationalist revolution for forty years. Its goal is to achieve freedom and equality for China. Based on my forty years of experience, I deeply understand that if we wish to achieve this goal, we must appeal to the masses of the people, ally ourselves with the nationalities of the world that treat us as equals, and struggle together with them. At this point, the revolution has still not been completed. My comrades, you must continue the struggle to the end, in accordance with the strategy I have laid out, including the Program of National Reconstruction, The Three People's Principles, and the Manifesto I made at the First National Congress of the Nationalists. In the short term, I emphasize holding a meeting of the National Assembly and eliminating the Unequal Treaties. These must be achieved in the shortest possible time. This is my testament." [This note is in the original text.—Tr.]

34. *Analects* 10.8. The original Chinese of the *Analects* passage is ambiguous. Liu Shaoqi and the Licentiate he was talking with gave it the meaning I supply in the translation above. In contrast, Edward Slingerland's translation reflects the view of most traditional and modern interpreters: "He would not eat in excess, even when presented with refined grain or finely minced meat." See Slingerland, trans., *Confucius: Analects: With Selections from Traditional Commentaries* (Indianapolis: Hackett Publishing, 2003), p. 103.

56. Liu Shaoqi, "Self-Criticism"

anonymous translator[35]

In 1949, the Chinese Communists established the People's Republic of China (PRC) on the mainland after defeating the Nationalists, who fled to Taiwan, where the Republic of China (ROC) continues to this day. Mao Zedong had long been the undisputed leader of the Communists, and many viewed Liu Shaoqi as his staunch supporter and likely successor. However, Mao's radical economic and social programs during the Great Leap Forward (1958–1961) resulted in mass starvation. Liu was one of the first to speak out against the Great Leap Forward, and eventually succeeded Mao in the most power-ful position in government, Chairman of the Chinese Communist Party. Mao responded by launching the Cultural Revolution (1966–1976), which encouraged students to drop out of school, join the ultra-leftist Red Guards, and root out "capitalists and reactionaries" in the Party. Anything associated with traditional culture, especially Confucianism, was subjected to intense, and typically violent, criticism. Liu was purged from office based on the accusation that he was a "counter-revolutionary." Below is an excerpt from the "Self-Criticism" that Liu Shaoqi was forced to issue, in which he "con-fessed" his former errors. Liu later died in mysterious circumstances while in custody. Years after the death of Mao, Liu was officially cleared of all charges and lauded for his service by the more moderate Chinese government. —Eds.

During the fifty-odd days following June 1 of this year [1966], I made mistakes in line and in orientation in guiding the Great Proletarian Cultural Revolution. I am the one who should bear the greater part of the responsibility for the mis-takes. . . . The mistakes I had committed during this Great Cultural Revolution were again personally rectified by Chairman Mao, the great leader, great com-mander and great helmsman of our Party and the people, after his return to Beijing. . . . Why have I committed mistakes in line and in orientation during this Great Proletarian Cultural Revolution? . . .

In ideology, my bourgeois world outlook was not basically transformed; I still possessed many idealistic and metaphysical viewpoints. Hence, in my observa-tion and handling of problems, I frequently could not take a strong and clear stand, sometimes even taking a reactionary bourgeois stand. During my work, I demonstrated a conviction that I was always right and attempted to be the teacher of others.

---

35. Translation slightly adapted from "Liu Shao-chi's Self Criticism Made at the Work Con-ference of the CCP Central Committee, October 23, 1966," *Issues and Studies*, 6:9 (June 1970), pp. 90–98. Used with permission.

Most important was the fact that I did not make a good study and grasp Mao Zedong's thought, and was unable to apply Mao Zedong's thought correctly in work and struggle. I did not learn from the masses in practice, nor did I seek sufficient instructions from and make enough reports to Chairman Mao. Sometimes, I acted contrary to Mao Zedong's thought. I did not accept the correct opinions of some comrades; on the contrary, I listened to and adopted many incorrect opinions.

This is my understanding concerning the reasons for my mistakes during the Great Proletarian Cultural Revolution. This understanding is, of course, neither deep nor comprehensive enough. Continued efforts are needed for a greater understanding. I am determined to work hard to study Mao Zedong's thought and to learn from Comrade Lin Biao's example in the creative study and application of Chairman Mao's works.[36] I am determined to correct my mistakes and to exert strenuous efforts in the future to do some useful work for the Party and for the people.

57. Mou Zongsan, "Appearances and Things-in-Themselves"

translation by David Elstein[37]

Móu Zōngsān 牟宗三 *(1909–1995) is generally considered the most important Chinese philosopher of the twentieth century. An extremely prolific scholar, he wrote on almost the entire history of Chinese philosophy. He was also very interested in Western philosophy, translating Kant's three* Critiques *and Wittgenstein's* Tractatus Logico-Philosophicus *into Chinese. Mou's philosophical accomplishments were similarly diverse. Among his more notable achievements, he essentially single-handedly re-wrote the histories of both Neo-Confucian and Buddhist thought. Our first selection from Mou's writings, below, examines his idea of intellectual intuition as a foundation for morality. In his later work, Mou carried on a sustained engagement with Kant, whom he felt was the only Western philosopher who understood morality. But he was ultimately unsatisfied with leaving the foundation of morality, the free will, as a postulate. Here he tries to show that Chinese philosophy can succeed where Kant failed.*

---

36. Lin Biao was chosen by Mao to succeed Liu Shaoqi. Mao would eventually turn against Lin too, and Lin died in a plane crash, apparently while attempting to flee China for the Soviet Union.

37. This translation is based on Mou Zongsan, *Xianxiang yu wuzishen* 現象與物自身, (Taibei: Student Books, 1990).

To understand this excerpt, we need a little background in Kant's philosophy. In the Critique of Pure Reason, *Kant distinguished appearances, which we can perceive and have knowledge of, from things-in-themselves, the existents that are necessary for appearances to exist, but that we can never have knowledge of. Human beings have sensible intuition, which is issued by our sense faculties that allow us to perceive appearances. However, only God has intellectual intuition, which is a non-sensible intuition of things-in-themselves. The free will is not something we can know through sensible intuition. Appearances are subject to causal laws and we can have no perception of a free action that is not determined by causal laws. And so in his works on morality, Kant refers to freedom as a postulate. That is, on Kant's view we have to assume we are free, because otherwise morality does not exist (for we wouldn't be able to choose what we do), but we cannot have an intuition of freedom and thus know of its nature and existence (as our selves cannot be objects of the senses). This is where Mou felt Kant was inadequate.*

*Mou argues that human beings can have intellectual intuition, and so we can know we are free. He argues that the moral awareness emphasized by Confucian philosophers like Mengzi and Wang Yangming is an indication of our fundamental mind (*běnxīn 本心*), which is beyond appearances. Mou uses various terms to refer to such awareness, particularly moral feeling (*juéqíng 覺情*), illuminating awareness (*míngjué 明覺*), and illuminating awareness of intellect-in-itself (*zhītǐ míngjué 知體明覺*). These feelings give us access to our real nature, what Mou calls nature-in-itself (*xìngtǐ 性體*) to indicate that it is not part of appearances. This is intellectual intuition, intuition into our nature as a thing-in-itself. Through this intuition, we can reveal the moral self. The first step is what I have translated as "presencing" the moral mind. This is the initial step of feeling and acting on our moral nature. As these feelings become stronger and one becomes more in touch with nature-in-itself, it then "manifests," meaning it becomes completely revealed. At that point, one is a sage: one can act morally based on one's fundamental mind, with no feeling of forcing oneself. It is simply what one is. Even if most people never get to this stage, Mou believes that it illustrates what our nature actually is, and that it is possible to have intellectual intuition, thereby showing that morality is a reality after all, not merely a postulate. —Tr.*

An Enhanced Conceptualization of "Freedom"[38]

At this point, we should have a transformed way of thinking.

First, we give an appropriate and exhaustive analysis of this stipulated freedom. 1) The free autonomous will is precisely the essential functioning of the

---

38. Mou, *Xianxiang yu wuzishen*, Section 3.II.2C, pp. 76–83.

moral feelings; it is precisely the mind. 2) It is self-legislating; it is precisely Pattern (*li* 理).[39] 3) According to the meaning of the term, it is determined by an unconditional law. Actually it determines itself; it is derived from autonomy. That is to say, it is not passively and unwillingly determined by the law, but actively and willingly determines itself by the law it establishes itself. This is what Mengzi meant by saying the Pattern and righteousness please my mind, my mind takes joy in Pattern and righteousness.[40] 4) "Determination" means for the will to reveal its unique nature through its self-legislation. 5) It takes joy in the law it gives to itself, so its maxim cannot possibly conflict with morality. Therefore, it is a holy will,[41] because it is Pattern in itself. 6) Thought that is influenced by sensibility is not this free autonomous will. The former can be either good or bad: "Two possible characters under different circumstances."[42] The latter is purely good without any bad: "One turning point with two functions."[43] (The "one turning point" is the free, autonomous will and its self-legislation. The "two functions," according to Liu Jishan [Liu Zongzhou, 1578–1645] are to love good and hate bad. To put it in Kant's terms, these are a negative meaning of freedom, which is independent and does not rely on the material of law, and a positive meaning of freedom, which is a self-legislated unconditional law. Intentions can be either good or bad. The "differing characters" differ in the reality of their content.) 7) To intentions, the moral law is synthetic; to the free autonomous will, the moral law is analytic. 8) The free autonomous will is self-legislating, and so issues imperatives. Therefore, it determines duties. An imperative commands us to act according to this law, and therefore to act this way is our duty. Imperatives and duties do not apply to the free, autonomous will in itself. The self-legislation of the free autonomous will is the irresistible action of nature-in-itself, and the duties it determines are our fundamental lot. As Mengzi said, "A gentleman's lot is already settled." (Mengzi said, "It does not add to a gentleman's nature if he puts great things into effect, nor does it subtract from his nature if he lives in poverty. This is because his lot is already settled."[44] The gentleman's lot is settled by the unceasing activity of nature-in-itself. This is also called "one's natural lot" and is allotted by nature-in-itself.)

---

39. Although Mou uses the same term as in Neo-Confucian philosophy, for him it has a meaning closer to reason (*lixing* 理性).

40. *Mengzi* 6A7.

41. In Kant's philosophy, a holy will is a will free from inclination that acts purely from reason.

42. Liu Jishan [Liu Zongzhou], *Liu Zongzhou quanji*, ed. by Dai Lianzhang and Wu Guang (Taibei: Academia Sinica Institute of Chinese Literature and Philosophy Planning Committee, 1996), vol. 2, p. 485.

43. I have not found this exact quote in Liu Zongzhou's works. It may be a paraphrase from *Liu Zongzhou quanji* vol. 1, p. 718.

44. *Mengzi* 7A21. Here and below, translations of the *Mengzi* are based on Bryan Van Norden, trans., *Mengzi: With Selections from Traditional Commentaries* (Indianapolis: Hackett, 2008), with some modifications.

The above is all derived from an analysis of the concept of a free autonomous will.

Second, after having done this analysis, the question is how to make this free autonomous will into a "presence" and not merely a "postulate." ("Presence" is Mr. Xiong [Shili's] term, which accords with the tradition of Chinese philosophy.) The key here is in the shift to "intellectual intuition."

(1) The free autonomous will is just the "ontological moral feelings"[45] of the "fundamental mind." It is not just reason but illuminating awareness (*míngjué* 明覺).[46] One aspect of its self-legislating reason (what Kant said is the self-legislating of pure practical reason) is the effect of its illuminating awareness. Reason is the reason of "the fundamental mind is Pattern,"[47] not the abstract talk of reason with a purely formal meaning. (Kant sometimes took the free will to be practical reason, but he was unwilling to say it is the mind. He instead mainly treated the speculative employment of reason and the practical employment of reason as belonging to the same reason, and then said this practical employment is practical reason. This is vague.) For the illuminating awareness to self-legislate, to legislate the moral law is to be aware [of a moral action], and that awareness is the legislation. The mind legislates, which is to be aware of [a moral action], and is aware of it in the midst of legislating. Its consciousness, its awareness, which is being in this consciousness and awareness, shift to "intellectual intuition."

(2) This intellectual intuition makes universal law a concrete presence, not just a fact of reason[48] (merely a formal fact) without any intuition to support it (of course it has no pure intuition or empirical intuition, only intellectual intuition). Moreover, it is a fact that "is necessarily presenced by the ontological moral feelings of the mind itself."[49] It makes the universal law present in the responses of the moral feelings of illuminating awareness (*míngjué juéqíng* 明覺覺情). Therefore, the universal moral law is concretely universal, not abstractly universal. However, this is not to say this law is limited by empirical objects or is conditional.

(3) This intellectual intuition not only illuminates each thing and affair the moral feelings of illuminating awareness affect as things in themselves, it also reflects back on and illuminates itself. This makes "freedom" a necessary and

---

45. "Ontological" here indicates that these moral feelings are not appearances but rather belong to nature as a thing-in-itself.

46. This term comes from Wang Yangming's thought.

47. "Reason" (*lǐxìng* 理性) is closely related to "Pattern" (*lǐ* 理) in Chinese. What Mou means is that this is reason that has a particular content, the moral pattern of Neo-Confucianism. It is not just instrumental reason.

48. In the second *Critique*, Kant refers to consciousness of the categorical imperative as "a fact of reason." Immanuel Kant, *Practical Philosophy*, trans. and ed. by Mary Gregor (Cambridge: Cambridge University Press, 1996), p. 164.

49. Mou may be quoting himself, but the source is unknown.

definite presence, not a postulate. Intellectual intuition is this light radiated by the self-activity of these moral feelings of illuminating awareness. Making freedom a presence is the astonishment of self-activity, and through this astonishment it reflects back on itself and awakens itself, illuminating itself through this astonishment. By illuminating itself through this astonishment, the free autonomous will becomes a presence, and not just a presence but a manifestation. Presence is manifestation because intellectual intuition is sudden and complete, without concealing or distortion.

(4) However, human beings always have sensible existence, and therefore are often influenced, led, and controlled by sensibility, which conceals the moral feelings of illuminating awareness of the fundamental mind and makes it difficult to reveal them. So the problem of moral practice is how to presence the fundamental mind among the concealing obstacles so it becomes manifest. There is no other miraculous external method. The critical essential factor is still the self-astonishment of the moral feelings of illuminating awareness. This is the power that makes the [fundamental mind] itself well up. Through this self-astonishment, we reflect back to the fundamental mind's illuminating awareness of moral feelings. This is what I call "reflective verification." This reflection (my reflection) actually is [the fundamental mind's] awakening itself through self-astonishment. Through this reflection, it presences and then manifests. As far as the concealing obstacles, it gradually presences, it gradually manifests. In this respect, one can also speak of an infinite process. However, because of intellectual intuition it can completely and suddenly presence and manifest at any time. The more it presences the stronger it becomes, and sensibility is relegated to a passive status. Because of this, sensibility presents no challenges, but is rather acted on by [the fundamental mind]. When it is perfectly and completely presenced, the "flowing of the Heavenly Pattern," this is sagehood, or what Kant called the "holy will." However, this "holy will" is also the fully real manifestation of the fundamentally existing moral feelings of illuminating awareness, and certainly does not mean the will only a sage has. Yao and Shun had it, and so do ordinary people. That Yao and Shun could be Yao and Shun was simply because they could manifest it. Ordinary people are ordinary people simply because they have not manifested it yet. "The mind, buddha, and sentient beings—there is no difference between these three."[50] One could also say, "The mind, sage, and sentient beings—there is no difference between these three." A sentient being is a potential sage; a sage is an awakened sentient being. How is this so? Because they have the same fundamental mind.

(5) When we are controlled by sensibility, our intentions often cannot follow the moral feelings of illuminating awareness (what Wang Yangming called

---

50. This is a fairly common saying in Chinese Buddhist writings, particularly Tiantai and Huayan. Variations can be found in T33 no. 1716 *Miaofa lianhua jing xuanyi* and T36 no. 1736 *Dafang guang fo Huayanjing shu* among others.

"the illuminating awareness of intellect in itself"[51]) and therefore always have both good and bad. This is what Wang called "the arising of bodily intention."[52] But when the moral feelings of illuminating awareness gradually presence from among the concealing obstacles, and then perfectly and suddenly presence and manifest, then intentions completely transform and proceed from the illuminating awareness of the moral feelings of the fundamental mind. This is what Wang called extending knowledge to make intentions sincere, and what Liu [Zongzhou] called "transforming intentions and returning to the [fundamental] mind."[53] Transforming intentions and returning to the fundamental mind, intentions arise from the intellect and then are purely good without any badness. They are just the spread of true reality from the responses of the intellect itself. Then the will's maxim cannot conflict with the moral law; it is just the unfolding of the pure knowing of Heavenly Pattern. This is what Yang Cihu (1141–1226) called "unaroused intention" and what Wang Longxi (Wang Ji, 1498–1583) called "intentionless intention" (intention without the character of intention).[54] Intentions only come to exist when the fundamental mind has not presenced, which is when the fundamental mind is obscured and turned into the phenomenal mind, and the activity of the mind is entirely circumscribed by sensibility. But when the fundamental mind uses its own power to astonish, it will definitely presence, and because of the possibility of intellectual intuition it will definitely be perfectly and suddenly manifested. Therefore, transforming intentions and returning to the fundamental mind and "intentionless intention" are absolutely possible and attainable. The "holy will" is "intentionless intention." People, although they are finite, can certainly become infinite.

The two-step explanation above completes the large scope of "freedom is a presence and not merely a postulate."

Kant, however, never reached this point. His argument was this: considering a person as a rational being, we can postulate a pure will (only as a postulate and this postulate cannot be fully understood analytically). However, since he is a physical being, he is easily swayed by sensibility, and therefore his will, even as the postulated pure will, is not a holy will. A holy will only belongs to "the

---

51. *Zhiti mingjué* 知體明覺. This particular phrase does not actually appear in Wang's work. Wang does use *mingjué* 明覺. "Intellect" here must be understood in the sense of "intellectual intuition." The intellect itself is the fundamental mind, not the mind that is aware of phenomena.

52. Chen Rongjie, ed., *Wang Yangming Chuanxi lu xiangzhu jiping* (Taibei: Student Books, 1983), sec. 101, p. 123.

53. A nearly identical phrase is in Liu, *quanji*, vol. 2, p. 491. This exact phrase does not actually appear in Wang's work.

54. Yang Cihu, *Cihu yishu, Congshu jicheng xubian*, v. 130 (Taibei: Xinwenfeng, 1989), 13.343; Wang Longxi, *Wang Longxi quanji* (Taibei: Huawen shuju, 1970), vol. 1, p. 90.

highest intelligence" (that is, God). Human beings are determined to be finite beings and cannot be finite yet also infinite. . . .

Note: As we said in the two-part account of freedom, the free autonomous will is holy; the moral law is holy. [Free autonomous will] itself is holy because it itself is Pattern. Having established the free autonomous will, if one then says its maxim can conflict with the moral law and is thus not holy and then is not the free autonomous pure will, this is contradictory. Saying the free autonomous will is holy is not saying that because it is holy it then is "not only above all practical laws, but above all practically restrictive laws and as a result above obligation and duty."[55] It is free and autonomous, it gives the law to itself, it takes joy in the law, and so it follows the law willingly and submits to its constraints. These constraints are not passive, however, but active and so are constraints without the character of constraints. The will is like this in its reality. As soon as Kant thought of law he thought of its constraining, but this is not critical. He also thought the free autonomous will must be acted upon and constrained and therefore is not holy, but this violates freedom and autonomy. He was thinking of those "intentions" that are controlled by sensibility as the pure will. This is to make what is pure impure, what is free unfree, and this is contradictory. Therefore, having postulated its purity, one should not then think of it as "intentions" but should only think of it as pure and then analytically think of the unity of mind and Pattern. It is entirely the moral law and the moral law is entirely it. It is holy.

Obligation and duty are products of the human point of view. The will determines this duty for us and obligates us to act in this way. The will itself as beyond duty determines this duty. If it had to be compelled and obligated under a duty, then it would become an intention. Not only would this be contradictory, but we would also have to further postulate a free autonomous will [that is the source of this obligation] and this would result in an infinite regress. Otherwise, there can never be a free autonomous will and there is only the opposition of reason and intention. If it is still possible to speak of duty and obligation in regard to the will, that is duty that it determines for itself and obligation that it gives itself. Determining its duty, it can fulfill its duty. Obligating itself, it can fulfill its obligations. This is the pure knowing and pure capability that Mengzi spoke of.[56] In itself, without duty it cannot be wholly unconstrained and without obligation it cannot be completely unconstrained. It is this way in its true reality, just as if it were constrained by the law: constraint without the character of constraint, and this is the character of its holiness. In this will, the law, con-

---

55. I have translated Mou's rendering of Kant in Chinese rather than quote the English translation. Cf. Kant, *Critique of Practical Reason*, in *Practical Philosophy*, 166; Akademie numbers (hereafter "Ak") 5:32.

56. *Mengzi* 7A15, in Part III, Selection 35.

straint, duty, and obligation are not opposed to holiness. It is only when the will is seen as intention that the opposition arises. Kant could never analytically fully express the meaning of freedom he postulated and because of this it is unstable.

However, if freedom so postulated can be a presence due to the possibility of intellectual intuition and if this established freedom can be fully expressed analytically, then intellectual intuition must be possible. In this way, it is possible for human beings to be finite and yet also infinite, to become sages and buddhas. This is the full manifestation of the holy will. People influenced by sensibility in actuality are not holy, but due to the manifestation of the holy will, when they are finite yet also infinite then they are also holy. Thus, the holiness of the will is not a model or idea "which we can only approximate without end but can never attain."[57] It certainly is a "model" and also a "practical ideal"; however, it a model or ideal that can manifest, not a model or ideal which we "can only approximate without end but can never attain." As we say, the manifestation of this model can be a manifestation in an infinite process and it can also be complete, sudden, and immediate manifestation. These two modes are not in opposition. When the key moments of its responses are all particular then it manifests in an infinite process and each step is a partial manifestation and cannot be entirely complete, but when its responses are intentionless intentions and unknowing knowledge, without any thread of attachment, then it is completely and suddenly manifested. A part is the whole without any mutual obstruction.[58] Even if our sensibility sometimes sways us, the will manifests among the concealing obstructions, and here is where we say it is an endless process, not to mention a difficult one.

However, once it can be the master, it can make this arduous path into a level road. Sensibility is employed [by it] and does not obstruct, and then a partial manifestation is complete manifestation; the progressive and the complete and sudden do not obstruct each other. The three teachings of Confucianism, Buddhism, and Daoism are well acquainted with talking about this philosophical level. I have tied these together here to show this model can manifest and is not something one cannot attain, and to show where Kant is insufficient. If one understands this then one can distinguish the "moral enthusiasm" and "flattering themselves with a spontaneous good of heart" that Kant disapproved of[59] but which cannot be applied to Mengzi's thought. That is to say, Confucians are absolutely not "moral enthusiasts" and cannot be slandered for "flattering

57. Although this is in quotation marks, it is a paraphrase of Kant, *Critique of Practical Reason*, in *Practical Philosophy*, 166; Ak 5:32.

58. The identity of part and whole without mutual obstruction is characteristic of Huayan Buddhist thought. See Fazang, "The Rafter Dialogue," and "Essay on the Golden Lion," in Part II, Selections 14 and 15.

59. Kant, *Critique*, in *Practical Philosophy*, 208; Ak 5:84–85.

themselves with a spontaneous good of heart." They certainly do not "flatter themselves" for this, nor is [sagehood] a "fantasy." . . .

Intellectual intuition and illuminating awareness of intellect itself[60]

The wondrous responses[61] of the illuminating awareness of intellect itself are the free autonomous will. How can I know this intellect in itself? It is that through the illuminating awareness of intellect itself which can presence at any time (for example, when suddenly seeing a child about to fall into a well, people all have a feeling of alarm and compassion[62]), this astonishment itself can awaken us, and then through reflective verification we understand. This awakening due to astonishment is like the red sun rising out of the bottom of the sea; it is not at all sensible. Therefore, the reflective verification in question is the illuminating awareness of intellect itself reflecting its own light back onto itself and not a phenomenal mind different from itself sensibly and passively coming to cognize it, which could never reach it in itself. So this reflective understanding is purely intellectual and not the passivity of sensibility. This kind of reflective understanding is the self-illumination of intellectual intuition emitted by the light of illuminating awareness of intellect itself. "Seeing a child about to fall into a well" is a turning point. "Seeing" is vision, which belongs to sensibility, but in the turning point brought about by seeing this, the fundamental mind manifests. It is not the sensibility of the phenomenal mind producing a [sensible] intuitive apprehension and perceiving the appearance of a child falling into a well, nor is it discursive understanding thinking conceptually and thinking such an appearance, but rather the fundamental mind presencing and determining for itself a direction for unconditional action.

The self-illumination of the light of this mind is intellectual intuition. Loosely speaking, it is said to "awaken us." In reality, it is that fundamental mind awakening itself as soon as it becomes active, and reflectively becomes aware of itself. This is called the fundamental mind astonishing itself. Astonishing and awakening itself is a process of suddenly recognizing and affirming itself, and this is called the self-affirmation of the fundamental mind. Then we follow it as what we are, where we recognize and affirm this mind as our fundamental mind, the fundamental mind of the free autonomous will with wondrous responses. This identification and affirmation is what I mean by "reflective verification." Intellectual intuition is included in this reflective verification and in this way we can say that although we are finite beings, we can still have intellectual intuition.

The fundamental mind astonishes itself and reflects itself. There is no capacity

---

60. Mou, *Xianxiang yu wuzishen*, section 3.II.5, pp. 100–2.

61. This phrase is drawn from Wang Longxi, *Wang Longxi quanji*, vol. 1, p. 425.

62. *Mengzi* 2A6, in Part III, Selection 35.

for awareness or object of awareness; it simply is itself aware of itself, in the manner of "a⊂a": the capacity for awareness is its own light. The capacity is the object of awareness; the object is the light of the capacity for awareness, so the object is the capacity. As a result, the capacity for awareness melts into the object and there is no capacity, the object of awareness melts into the capacity and there is no object. There is only the fundamental mind actually manifesting.

When we speak of intellectual intuition on the basis of the fundamental mind illuminating itself and understand that our fundamental mind is free and autonomous on the basis of intellectual intuition, this understanding is not just cognitive, nor is it just a compulsion that compels us by the necessity of the moral law, but is grasped intuitively without doubt, which is to say it manifests, and this is called "knowledge by intellectual intuition." Although it is knowledge by intellectual intuition and not understanding by consciousness;[63] however, it is still objectively apodictic knowledge. This knowledge is naturally not knowledge through theoretical understanding by the phenomenal mind, but rather practical intuitive knowledge of self-illumination of the fundamental moral mind. (When Kant talked about practical knowledge it was just vacuous talk of what is "grasped by understanding" and he couldn't use the word "intuition.") For this practical knowledge we can use the word "intuition" and then freedom is not a postulate but a presence with objective necessity. When we affirm freedom this is a necessary and apodictic affirmation, yet it is not conceptual (theoretical) but practical. Intellectual understanding and phenomenal understanding are fundamentally different. Intellectual understanding does not extend phenomenal understanding. Kant only admitted phenomenal understanding and so could only talk of apodicticity of understanding in regard to objects of phenomenal understanding, which are necessarily apodictic. Freedom is not grasped by phenomenal understanding and there was no intellectual understanding, so in regard to freedom as an object he could not say its theoretical apodicticity was in fact necessarily apodictic. We, however, admit intellectual understanding, which means objective necessity, and necessary certainty need not connect to theoretical understanding and can instead connect to practical, intellectual understanding.

Intellectual intuition is the light emitted by the illuminating awareness of intellect itself; this light reflects back on the illuminating awareness of intellect itself and makes it manifest in reality, so there is no manifold to speak of in intellectual intuition. What it makes manifest and gives us is just the illuminating awareness of intellect itself. The illuminating awareness of intellect itself is pure unity and the intellectual intuition that constitutes its reflected light which makes us aware of it is also one, and being aware of it, it manifests. There is no manifold to speak of and no synthesizing a manifold to speak of, either. If in intuiting the illuminating awareness of intellect itself there is a manifold

---

63. The term Mou uses here, *shi* 識, is used to mean the faculty for knowing appearances.

that can be presented to us, then this must be sensible intuition and what it intuits must not be the illuminating awareness of intellect itself in itself but the illuminating awareness of intellect itself fallen into sensibility and transformed into embodied deluded cognition, and therefore is an appearance of *samsara*.[64]

58. Mou Zongsan, "The Principles of Authority and Governance"

translation by David Elstein[65]

The second selection is from Mou's political work. One of the goals of his earlier philosophy was to show that science and democracy do not conflict with Confucian philosophy, but are in fact required by it. He felt traditional Chinese political thought focused too much on moral virtue and not enough on developing objective institutions. He refers to this approach as "the functional presentation of reason" or "the intensional presentation of reason," and contrasts these with the Western mode of reasoning, which he variously identifies as "the structural presentation of reason" or "the extensional presentation of reason." The intensional/extensional dichotomy derives from his early interest in Bertrand Russell's philosophy, where intensional truths are subject-variant while extensional truths are subject-invariant. The functional/structural distinction is much the same. In government, the Western mode of reasoning led to distinguishing morality and politics, and a focus on abstracting government into institutions that would be efficacious regardless of who occupied them (subject-invariant). Chinese political views, in contrast, were intensional in that their efficacy depended on who held power, and political thought aimed at producing "sagely rulers and worthy ministers" instead of developing objective institutions. In Mou's view, this lack of institutional structures must be remedied.

Mou thus faces the question of how to justify such objective institutions in Confucian terms, given that they did not exist throughout the history of Confucian thought. He argues that earlier Confucians did not sufficiently appreciate the importance of institutions, which are in fact a necessary outgrowth of Confucian philosophy. This is not a logical requirement, as it is logically

---

64. In Chinese Buddhism, "samsara" refers to the phenomenal world, especially insofar as humans mistakenly regard it as real.—Eds.

65. This translation is from Mou Zongsan, *Zhengdao yu zhidao* 政道與治道, rev. ed. (Taibei: Student Books, 1991). [All footnotes are by the translator unless otherwise indicated. We have modified the translation for consistency with the conventions of this volume. We are solely responsible for any resulting errors or infelicities.—Eds.]

possible to have sage rulers without democracy. So Mou denies there is a direct connection between inner sagehood and the "new outer kingliness," which refers to science and democracy. That is, there is no direct logical connection between Confucian moral philosophy and democracy. Instead it is a dialectical, indirect connection, which must be achieved through "self-restriction," (zìwǒ kǎnxiàn 自我坎陷) a key term for Mou. Mou's own gloss for this term is "self-negation," a term that resonated with Hegel's dialectic, which served as an inspiration to Mou. Although in theory there could be virtuous rulers in the traditional system, the full realization of human nature requires democracy as a matter of practical necessity. The Chinese imperial system was not conducive to developing virtue in either the rulers or the masses. Democracy would be more successful, and so Mou argues that realizing Confucian values requires democratic politics. Since democracy does not explicitly aim at virtue—voters do not have to evaluate candidates morally—Mou describes this as a contradiction between the moral reason of Confucianism and the theoretical reason necessary to develop democratic institutions. So moral reason must restrict itself to allow for the growth of theoretical reason, which paradoxically makes it possible for moral reason to realize its goal.

Although moral reason must restrict itself to allow for the development of value-neutral political institutions, this is neither a complete nor permanent abandonment of morality in politics. Mou feels democracy absolutely has to have a moral basis, but politics and morality nevertheless need to be separated so each is independent. He is concerned about the government enforcing a particular conception of the good that would make morality lose its independence, but he does not agree with the liberal ideal of state neutrality, in which the government takes no position on values at all. He argues for a middle path, in which public education should include basic human values, which he thinks need not lead to any controversies about different ethical, metaphysical, or religious views. Most importantly, a government cannot use moral development as an excuse to coerce or harm people. Becoming a sage is a personal goal, not a political one, and even sages abide by the limits established by the constitution. Government is not neutral, but it is limited to providing basic moral education. Morality and politics are thus related, but each still maintains its own independent domain.—Tr.

Chapter 3: Reason's Functional Presentation and Structural Presentation

Section 4: How to Go from the Functional Presentation to the Structural Presentation [of Reason][66]

Sections 2 and 3 above were analytic explanations and now I will give a further synthetic explanation. We need to answer the following question: how to derive a structural presentation [of reason] from the functional presentation [which

---

66. Mou, *Zhengdao yu zhidao*, pp. 55–61.

Chinese culture has]. Functional presentation proceeds from the Virtuous nature and belongs to inner sagehood. When speaking of inner sagehood, it must extend to outer kingliness. Outer kingliness is the extension of inner sagehood. However, in the past people spoke of outer kingliness as directly derived from inner sagehood. As the *Great Learning* said,

> The ancients who desired to enlighten the enlightened Virtue of the world would first put their states in order. Those who desired to put their states in order would first regulate their families. Those who desired to regulate their families would first cultivate their selves. Those who desired to cultivate their selves would first correct their minds. Those who desired to correct their minds would first make their thoughts have Sincerity. Those who desired to make their thoughts have Sincerity would first extend their knowledge. Extending knowledge lies in getting a handle on things.[67]

Reversing this, it then says,

> Only after one gets a handle on things does knowledge reach the ultimate. Only after knowledge has reached the ultimate do thoughts have Sincerity. Only after thoughts have Sincerity is the mind correct. Only after the mind is correct is the self cultivated. Only after the self is cultivated is the family regulated. Only after the family is regulated is the state ordered. Only after the state is ordered is the world at peace.[68]

This back and forth process shows that outer kingliness is the direct extension of inner sagehood.[69] The core of inner sagehood is correcting the mind and making thoughts Sincere, and extending knowledge and getting a handle on things are assigned to the spiritual practice of correcting the mind and making thoughts Sincere.[70] Cultivating the self, regulating the family, putting the state in order, and bringing peace to the world all come out of inner sagehood. If outer kingliness is limited to putting the state in order and bringing peace to the world, then outer kingliness is also a direct extension of inner sagehood. In this way, outer kingliness just becomes an effect of inner sagehood, and is completed or realized in the "functional presentation" of the virtue of inner sagehood.

However, if outer kingliness—putting the state in order and bringing peace to the world—still has its own internal, unique construction which connects to what we now call science and democratic politics, then it is not something that can be completely realized by the functioning of inner sagehood. Obviously, we cannot directly derive science or democratic politics from the functional

---

67. *Great Learning*, Classic 4, in Part III, Selection 33.

68. *Great Learning*, Classic 5, in Part III, Selection 33.

69. That is, political order requires personal virtue.

70. "Spiritual practice" (*gōngfu* 工夫, also translated as "spiritual task") is a term emphasized in the philosophy of Wang Yangming. See Wang's "Reply to Inquiries Made by a Friend" in Part III, Selection 44.—Eds.

presentation of inner sagehood. Outer kingliness does indeed come out of inner sagehood. But there are direct connections and indirect connections. Direct connection is the way previously mentioned. Indirect connection is how we now link to science and democratic politics. We take it to be the case that [only] indirect connection is able to realize the highest attainment of outer kingliness. If it is just a direct connection, it will only become a stunted version of outer kingliness. In this way, going from inner sagehood to outer kingliness indirectly, there is a kind of transformative, sudden change and not a direct inference. That is to say, from the functional presentation of reason it is impossible directly to infer the structural presentation. Moreover, turning from the functional presentation to the structural presentation is not a direct turn but an indirect turn.

This indirect turn shows a kind of transformative, sudden change. For example, one cannot derive skyscrapers directly from mountains and rivers. Skyscrapers have their own unique construction, which requires expert engineers who also have their unique essence. Really, this is just giving a formal, necessary condition and not an actual, sufficient condition. It is just one parameter; it cannot bring about the full meaning of indirectness because obviously, without mountains and rivers there could not be skyscrapers,[71] but the existence of mountains and rivers cannot directly lead to skyscrapers. Similarly, without the Virtuous nature there could not be science or democratic politics, but just the existence of Virtuous nature cannot directly lead to them. From this idea, we say that in this process there is a transformative, sudden change.

This aspect of transformation has two meanings: first, that the Virtuous nature of inner sagehood has a relationship to science and democracy, but not a direct relationship; second, that science and democracy have their own particular natures. These two show that these are independent and yet also related. Functional presentation and structural presentation are independent and also related. How is this possible? How can we really link them together?

All direct connections are entailments, so it appears we can use logical inference to display them. For example: "All men are mortal; Kongzi is a man; therefore Kongzi is mortal."[72] This is a kind of direct link. However, in going from functional presentation to structural presentation, which is indirect, we cannot directly illustrate it using logical inference. Indirect connection is stipulated as "transformative, sudden change." The "transformative" is transformative because there is a kind of "contrary" meaning present.

The formation of this "contrary" meaning happens in the following manner. The Virtuous nature in its direct moral meaning and functional presentation

---

71. I take it that Mou's meaning is that people would not have had the inspiration to build tall structures without seeing mountains, not that mountains and rivers are necessarily sources of the physical parts of skyscrapers.

72. The stock example of deductive logic in Western thought is "All men are mortal. Socrates is a man. Therefore, Socrates is mortal." Mou cleverly gives the example a Chinese twist.—Eds.

does not include the structural presentation which results in science and democracy; however, according to its fundamental nature as moral reason, it cannot but demand science (which represents knowledge) and democratic politics (which manifests justice and fairness). Furthermore, speaking from the internal perspective of science and democracy, the fundamental nature of the "structural presentation of reason" which makes these possible infringes on the moral meaning and functional presentation of the Virtuous nature; that is, theoretical reason and practical reason conflict with each other. It is in this conflict that the "contrary" meaning displays itself. [Moral reason] requires something which conflicts with its fundamental nature. This is clearly a contradiction. The thing that it demands must start being established by [moral reason] negating itself and then transforming into an opposing thing that is contrary to its self-nature (viz. theoretical reason).

It [moral reason] requires something which conflicts with its fundamental nature. Looking at these relations superficially or horizontally, this is a contradiction, but looking at them internally and comprehensively, then if this contrariness can begin to satisfy and realize moral reason's requirements, then the contradiction melts away in the realization or satisfaction. Further, the realization is an "objective realization" and in this way the contradiction melts away in an objective realization. The dissolution [of the contradiction] and objective realization show that the connection [between Virtue and science and democracy] can be made indirectly. That is, to make this kind of connection, we have to be indirect for a moment. This is the transformative, sudden change achieved by starting from the contrary. If our virtuous nature simply stops at the functional presentation, then there will only be subjective realization or absolute realization. In order to achieve objective realization, then it must be completed in this indirect fashion. If it is just a subjective realization, then logical inference can express it. But if it is an indirect connection and from this attainment of an objective realization, this is not something that can be achieved by logical inference. At this point, we come to understand necessity in dialectical development. Dialectical expression is absolutely crucial.[73]

. . . As for democratic politics, it belongs to objective practice, so its relation to moral reason should be even more evident. The emergence of a democratic polity is a question of people self-consciously determining their direction in political life, and based on this clue we can tie it to moral reason. Because the democratic polity is part of an objective framework for objective practice, naturally it cannot be fully realized by the functional presentation of moral reason. The structural presentation of reason is internal to the democratic polity itself, and this reason forthwith loses its meaning as Virtues of character, or concretely speaking, as practical reason. It turns into amoral theoretical reason. The

---

73. Mou now turns to apply the above general account to science and democracy. We pick up with the passages on democracy below.

structural presentation of theoretical reason directly corresponds to the democratic polity. Yet the wholeness of the democratic polity in itself is demanded by moral reason, or put differently, the emergence of the democratic polity is the realization of the highest or greatest moral values. What this shows is that to realize these moral values, moral reason has no choice but to restrict itself down from the mode of functional presentation, take a step back, and transform into the structural presentation of theoretical reason.

When people perceive politics has its independent meaning internal to the perspective of this structural presentation, it naturally becomes an independent domain temporarily distinct from and seemingly unrelated to morality. In the structural presentation each element of the polity, such as the arrangement of power and definition of rights and duties, are all horizontally coordinated.[74] This is how there can be independent political science. And the discussion of each element of government can be a discussion purely as political science, striving for clear, certain, and reasonable fairness. As for the source of the values these [elements of government] project, which are the meaning of the values expressed by this "reasonable fairness," or the source of highest moral reason, it is set outside of this domain of horizontal coordination, and looked at as something to do with morality, religion, or metaphysics. When discussing each element of the polity purely as political science, the activity of reason in this discussion is also purely the activity of theoretical reason without any shred of involvement with practical, moral reason.

Because politics has its own independent meaning and domain, it is not impossible to separate out the root [of politics][75] this way, and it is also not impossible to stop at theoretical reason and discuss politics purely as political science. At this level, it is not impossible to disperse freedom into various rights and say, "Freedom means having human rights." This kind of government, with an independent meaning and domain, is characteristic of the West in the modern period. But those who are a little more familiar with what "modern" means in politics all know this bit of common sense. When I was in Tianjin twenty years ago, Luo Longji[76] once said something to me: The greatest contribution of modern politics is precisely the separation of politics from morality. This wasn't his discovery; he was just passing on a common understanding. But behind this understanding is a background of Western cultural history: the separation from morality is in fact a separation from the smokescreen of moral religion which

---

74. Mou's point is that these are not distributed according to moral desert but given to all equally.

75. I.e., moral values and moral reason.

76. Luo Longji (1896–1965) was a well-known political scientist. Starting in 1932, he taught at Nankai University in Tianjin for several years while also writing for the journal *Yishi bao*. His meeting with Mou was apparently during these years. He later held several posts in the government after the Communist revolution in 1949.

was tied up with politics under a kind of theocracy. Realistically speaking, it was a removal of those smokescreens. As far as Chinese culture, morality is purer and doesn't have the Western kind of morality where theocratic politics and religious doctrines are mixed together. However, even if it is less religious, it is still acceptable to speak of politics entering the modern period and being temporarily separate from morality.

We must understand, however, that this separation and delimitation is just because politics has its independent meaning and domain, and political science has ideas of rights and law which can be discussed in a purely political-scientific way. In this independent domain politics is not tied to metaphysical moral reason, which makes each concept in the democratic polity clear and definite. This clarity and definiteness is just for the convenience of language; for linguistic clarity and definiteness it is not necessary to get into so much and it is enough to express the facts of horizontal coordination in a defined way within the large brackets of democratic politics. This is just the standpoint of a political scientist, not the standpoint of a practitioner struggling for democracy, nor is it the standpoint of the totality of the activity of human nature or cultural ideals. So it is clear and definite just for linguistic convenience. As for talking about real clarity and definiteness, then talking about how freedom connects to moral reason and people's self-awareness is unavoidable. We can't just look at freedom in a piecemeal way: as a result, as scattered rights. This actually makes it less clear. Above I brought up observing people's awakening and struggle and looking at freedom in connection with these, and this actually makes it clearer. Democratic politics doesn't drop from the sky; getting rights is not eating a free meal that just shows up at your door all prepared. These are obtained by people struggling and bleeding for their ideals, for justice. It is obvious that freedom must connect to moral reasoning and self-awareness; there is nothing abstract or abstruse here, nor is there any metaphysical theory likely to incite controversy. This is a definite fact of practice. Rights are just the result of objectification [of these moral values]. In a democratic polity rights are guaranteed by the constitution.

People just eat their ready-made meal and forget the struggle of the people before them. They begin to stop at theoretical reason and become constrained by the standpoint of political scientists; they carve up freedom into distinct rights in a piecemeal way and think the connections talked about above are abstract, abstruse, and pointless metaphysical disputes. Not only that, they also think that talk of connecting [freedom] with moral reason and self-awareness becomes pan-moralism, which is an aid to totalitarianism. These are all one-sided thoughts that come of a piecemeal approach that only understands one aspect [theoretical reason] and doesn't understand what the other aspect [moral reason] is. This is how they get to such sweeping statements writing off [the importance of moral reason]. This is another example of what Kongzi meant by saying, "Loving wisdom without a love for study will result in the vice of excess."[77] Pan-moralism is indeed incorrect, but, unbeknownst to them, this "excess" also results in a type of pan-politicism. . . .

Chapter 7: How Politics Can Change from Mythological to Rational
Section 4: The Limits of Politics and Education and
the Separation of Politics and Morality[78]

Now the remaining problem is: under the intensional presentation of reason, we have the principle of individuality (a principle of respecting individual life) that is yielding and dispersed,[79] "each thing treated in its own terms"[80] that "realizes their individuality." On the one hand it still includes an idea of education, but on the other hand it includes the problem of separating morality and politics. Whenever one takes the approach of "the intensional presentation," there are no limitations derived from a concept of a political system as a formal entity and it becomes very difficult to separate out the unstable scope of the intensional presentation in its "totality of life" and delimit its parameters.[81] However, even if this is the case, Confucians still have their highest principle to limit it.

Earlier, I expressed that that "yielding and dispersed, each thing treated in its own terms," spirit is a kind of spirit of the benevolent that can display benevolence. In politics, foremost is to define benevolence in this kind of "yielding and dispersed" way; here, this is the only way there is benevolence. (The content of benevolence and Virtue is unlimited and inexhaustible, and the methods and domains of displaying them are likewise unlimited and inexhaustible. In other areas, they take different forms. But the "yielding and dispersed, each thing treated in its own terms" way expresses a spirit of nonattachment and changeability. No matter what, this is the fundamental meaning of benevolence and Virtue. They can be applied as appropriate in other areas, but cannot depart from this fundamental meaning.) Previous Confucian political doctrines put a great deal of weight on manifesting the benevolent spirit [*rénzhě jīngshén* 仁者精神] of benevolence, and so mainly spoke about this benevolent spirit itself and emphasized the aspect of subjective ability, because this is key to whether one has Virtue or not. Placing weight on subjective ability means emphasizing Virtue.[82] . . . One first establishes oneself with benevolence and Virtue

---

77. *Analects* 17.8.

78. Mou, *Zhengdao yu zhidao*, pp. 123–28.

79. That is, not interfering with individual development.

80. Although the quotation marks are not in the original, this is a quotation from *Chengshi yishu*, in *Er Cheng quanshu, Sibu beiyao* v. 365 (Taibei: Zhonghua shuju, 1981), 6.4a.

81. That is, it is hard to define the proper limits for morality.

82. Following in the original is a series of quotations from the *Analects* and *Mean* illustrating the importance of personal virtue for political leaders.

and then uses these to transform the people. (Fundamentally, punishments are eliminated.)

So in governing the world through Virtue, one first makes "yielding and dispersed, each thing treated in its own terms" the highest political principle, which has the further implication of transformative education (*jiàohuà* 教化).[83] The "intensional presentation of reason" necessarily leads to this conclusion, which is why above I said . . . it is difficult to delimit its parameters.[84] In the totality of life, the range of oscillation of the intensional presentation must extend to imply transformative education. Without "the extensional presentation of reason," without limitations derived from a concept of a political system as a formal entity, this will certainly be the conclusion at which it arrives. With the extensional presentation and the associated limitations of a formal concept [of government], then politics is politics and transformative education is transformative education. Politics constitutes an independent field and naturally may not interfere with transformative education. This is the first step in limiting government.

Next, based on the idea of "realizing each thing's individuality," one need only talk about freedom, equality, rights, and other such extensional, formal concepts. When these are sufficient, there is no need to talk about "the understanding of transformative education" based on "the totality of life." This is the second limitation. However, in "the intensional presentation of reason" there cannot be this limitation. The benevolent spirit that puts weight on "the subject's ability," based on the idea of "realizing each thing's individuality," will necessarily consider "the totality of life," which includes the implication of transformative education. Emphasizing the individual here cannot only be a political extensional emphasis of the individual.[85] . . .

Despite this, one cannot merely politically and extensionally emphasize the individual, but when speaking of transformative education here there is still the highest principle of the intensional presentation limiting it. That is, "first enrich the people then teach them."[86] Teaching is also a matter of fulfilling what is already in human nature and human characteristics. It is not a kind of teaching that enforces some personal ideas and imposes some concepts distant from or external to people. This is what the political meaning of transformative education according to "the intensional presentation of reason" guards against.

---

83. The Chinese term implies not just any kind of education, but education that shapes character. [Compare the statement, "'Education' means cultivating the Way," from the *Mean* 1.i, in Part III, Selection 36.—Eds.]

84. Mou quotes his entire sentence here.

85. Following in the original is a parenthetical comment that contrasts the Confucian view with Legalist ideas of government.

86. A paraphrase of *Analects* 13.9.

Therefore, this is another highest principle and education cannot violate this principle.[87] . . .

In government measures, for realizing each thing's individuality, life comes first. That means to consider everything as an "existing, living individual" which must be protected. Individuals suffering hardships without recourse, having no place—this is something the benevolent cannot bear. However, as far as an individual's "totality of life," not only does life come first, meaning obtaining material happiness, one must also obtain a life with value and meaning and become a "benevolent being." So Mengzi said, "If one is careful about providing instruction in the village schools, emphasizing the righteousness of filiality and brotherliness, those whose hair has turned gray will not carry loads on the roadways."[88] Teaching means to teach the way of filiality, brotherliness, conscientiousness, faithfulness, ritual propriety, righteousness, and a sense of shame. To sum it all up, it is what Mengzi said: "Between father and children there is affection; between ruler and ministers there is righteousness; between husband and wife there is distinction; between elder and younger there is precedence; and between friends there is faithfulness."[89] In the *Mean* it says, "The universal Way of the world has five aspects. . . . The five aspects are the relationships between ruler and minister, father and son, husband and wife, elder and younger brothers, and friends."[90] These are the minimal and universal way of benevolence, not some external concept or theory added onto people. They are based on facts and the true way of human nature and human characteristics. This is why it says these things are "universal." Education should not go beyond teaching these. It is difficult to say that a person as a human being should not have these qualities.

So within the intensional presentation, as far as the totality of life which connects to this understanding of transformative education, one cannot say it interferes with freedom. Politically as well, transformative education cannot go beyond this level; beyond this is not something with which government can be concerned. This is the limit of the political understanding of transformative education. Confucians of the past all acknowledged this of their own accord. The typical way of putting it was that one should regulate oneself[91] strictly but be tolerant of others. Implementing this in government, the first step is "first enrich the people then teach them." (This is priority according to significance, not necessarily priority in time.) The second step to teach the minimal and universal way of benevolence. Beyond this, government should not and cannot be involved. In politics, one cannot complain if people fail to become sages. This limit does not just apply to politics, but as a general rule, becoming a sage is an

---

87. Mou next quotes part of *Mengzi* 1A3.

88. *Mengzi* 1A3.

89. *Mengzi* 3A4.

90. *Mean* 20.vii, in Part III, Selection 36.

91. Reading 己 instead of 已.

individual affair, not something one can expect of others. This is what is called the Way of sympathetic understanding.[92] (Of course, teachers and friends urge each other on to advance in virtue in hopes of reaching sagehood. This is a different idea.) In this way, the separation of morality and politics can be attained as follows.

One, an individual's own moral practice: this is an infinite progression, and in both depth and breadth it has no limit. Moreover, the inner regulation of the process of practice is winding and multidimensional; it is difficult to reduce it to a single rule. Every dimension proceeds from the subjective aspect of one's own existence, progressing from a sincere and deep wish. The ultimate goal should be sagehood and becoming a sage is an infinite process. This is all internal.

Two, the morality of political and typical social transformative education. These are just rules for preserving a typical benevolent life. This can only be external preservation. It cannot be a deep internal quest, nor can it be a profound demand. This "cannot" is an impossibility in principle; this is a fundamental limitation on government.[93] (The "unity of government and teaching" in the past in China was just this kind of teaching; this cannot be disputed. It was different from the "unity of government and teaching" in the West, because in that case it was religious teaching, which brought in the problem of faith. And so later on there was the struggle over "freedom of belief." In China, freedom of belief was never an issue. The teaching in official transformative education did not relate to or interfere with faith. Its concern was just "the minimal and universal way of humanity." Under the extensional presentation politics is indeed independent, but its laws cannot fail to guarantee this. So in the understanding of transformative education in Chinese government of the past, one cannot say it turned into "pan-moralism," because there were political principles and rhythm and there were also transformative educational principles and rhythm, which were separated and limited. Here I use "separated," "limited," and "rhythm" as intensional terms according to the intensional presentation to clarify the divisions, not extensional terms according to the extensional presentation. This is because they are not formalized and defined as the extensional presentation is. Nevertheless, the separation between them is clear. Because an individual's personal practice of morality, spirit of becoming a sage, and spirit of established doctrine were not a focus of this [unity of government and teaching], if one tries to impose the unsuitable [Western model of freedom of belief], the highest political principle will vanish.)

Three, no matter how great or divine an individual's accomplishment in realizing his moral character, when it comes to expressing his character in politics he

---

92. On "sympathetic understanding," see *Analects* 15.24, in Part III, Selection 34.—Eds.

93. Mou's point seems to be that a government cannot make people into sages even if it tries, because the motivation to be a sage has to come from the agent and cannot be externally coerced.

cannot go beyond these limits (the highest principles of the political world); in fact, exactly due to his greatness, he must make these limits inviolate. In ancient times, someone who could realize these limits was called a sage-king; in the present, he is called a great statesman. Otherwise, in ancient times he was called a hegemon, tyrant, or despot.[94] In the present, he is called a dictator or autocrat.

In the above I followed the intensional presentation of reason of Confucian political thought to express the highest principles of the political world. There are just the following three:

One, in political authority to establish firmly a concept of a public world through nomination[95] and general elections (power is given by Heaven, meaning given by the people[96]) (political power proceeds from political authority).

Two, in governance to establish firmly a principle of "yielding and dispersed, each thing treated in its own terms" and "realizing each thing's individuality" (governing power proceeds from governing authority).

Three, in morality to establish firmly an educational principle of "first enrich the people then teach them" and "regulate oneself strictly but be tolerant of others" (this includes limitations on political transformative education and the separation of politics and morality).

The understanding of government encompassed by these three principles I call the intensional meaning of democracy.

---

94. The last phrase, "despot," is an echo of *Mengzi* 1B8.—Eds.

95. Mou says the process of recommendation Mengzi describes in 5A5 is equivalent to nomination in modern democracy (Mou, *Zhengdao yu zhidao*, p. 114).

96. See *Mengzi* 5A5.

ILLUSTRATION CREDITS

Tomb Painting, Han Dynasty: Gentlemen in conversation, painting on ceramic tile from a tomb near Luoyang, Eastern Han dynasty (CE 25–220).

Decorative Sculpture of an Offering Table: Offering Table, Chinese, Ming dynasty (1368–1644), glazed and painted earthenware, Frances Lehman Loeb Art Center, Vassar College, Poughkeepsie, New York. Gift from the collection of Justin G. Schiller, Kingston, NY, 1997.25.64.

The Five Phases: Diagram illustrating the generation (outer arrows) and overcoming (inner arrows) sequences of the Five Phases, contemporary rendering by Liz Wilson, Hackett Publishing.

The Eight Trigrams Arranged around the Yin-Yang Symbol: Image of the Eight Trigrams surrounding the Yin-Yang Symbol, by Benoît Stella, used under the Creative Commons Attribution-Share Alike 3.0 Unported license (http://creativecommons.org/licenses/by-sa/3.0/legalcode).

Ban Zhao: Ban Zhao, as envisioned by Shangguan Zhou, from his *Wan Xiao Tang Zhu Zhuang Hua Zhuan*, 1743.

Huineng: The Sixth Patriarch of Chan Buddhism: Huineng cutting bamboo, ink on paper, by Liang Kai, Southern Song dynasty (1127–1279).

A Representation of Indra's Web: Contemporary illustration by Melissa Van Norden.

Illustration for the *Classic of Filial Piety*: Illustration of the *Classic of Filial Piety*, ink and color on silk, attributed to Ma Hezhi (1131–1189). Image from the website https://commons.wikimedia.org/wiki/File:The_Classic_of_Filial_Piety_4.jpg.

Han Yu: Han Yu, as envisioned by Shangguan Zhou, from his *Wan Xiao Tang Zhu Zhuang Hua Zhuan*, 1743.

Cheng Hao and Cheng Yi: (left) Cheng Hao and (right) Cheng Yi, as envisioned by Shangguan Zhou, from his *Wan Xiao Tang Zhu Zhuang Hua Zhuan*, 1743.

Diagram of the Great Ultimate: Contemporary illustration of traditional design by Liz Wilson, Hackett Publishing.

Zhu Xi: Zhu Xi, as envisioned by Shangguan Zhou, from his *Wan Xiao Tang Zhu Zhuang Hua Zhuan*, 1743.

Confucian Scholar: "Jin Wei Shi Dai Xiansheng Kui," by Ren Xiong, from *Yu Yue Xian Xian Xiang Zhuan Zan*, 1856.

Lu Xiangshan: Lu Xiangshan, as envisioned by Shangguan Zhou, from his *Wan Xiao Tang Zhu Zhuang Hua Zhuan*, 1743.

Wang Yangming: Wang Yangming, as envisioned by Shangguan Zhou, from his *Wan Xiao Tang Zhu Zhuang Hua Zhuan*, 1743.

"Admonitions of the Court Instructress": Scene from "Admonitions of the Court Instructress," handscroll, ink and color on silk, attributed to Gu Kaizhi, ca. 380 CE.

Li Zhi: Li Zhi, image from http://upload.wikimedia.org/wikipedia/commons/0/00/Li_Zhi.jpg.

"Village School": "Village School," by Xu Yang, ink and color on silk, eighteenth century. Image from http://commons.wikimedia.org/wiki/File:Xu_Yang_-_Village_school.jpg.

Frame from "The Evil Life of Confucius": Frame from "The Evil Life of Confucius," a mass-produced propaganda poster from the Cultural Revolution (1966–1976). Photograph courtesy of Ken Brashier, from his website: http://people.reed.edu/~brashiek/syllabi/Poster/Title%20Page.html.

GLOSSARY

Our Translation	Alternative Translations	Chinese Term	Meaning
above with respect to form / below with respect to form	what exists before physical form / what exists after physical form; above form / below form	形而上 *xíng ér shàng* / 形而下 *xíng ér xià*	complementary phrases from the Great Appendix to the *Changes* whose meaning is disputed; most translators follow Zhu Xi's interpretation, according to which the phrases refer, respectively, to Pattern in itself, before its embodiment in *qi*, and the concrete entities, composed of Pattern as manifested through *qi*, that make up the spatio-temporal world (see "Pattern" and "*qi*"); however, equally plausible is the interpretation of Lu Xiangshan, who argues that both phrases refer to concrete entities, but the former refers to things insofar as they are in accordance with the Way (which see). See also Zhu Xi, *Categorized Conversations*, in Part III, Selection 32, and Lu Xiangshan, in Part III, Selection 37.

Our Translation	Alternative Translations	Chinese Term	Meaning
arhat		羅漢 *luóhàn*	a term for someone who has achieved Buddhist enlightenment; Mahayana Buddhists (which see) sometimes use the term to denigrate those who seek enlightenment only for themselves, in contrast with a bodhisattva (which see)
benevolence	goodness, humanity, humaneness	仁 *rén*	the disposition to feel sorrow for the suffering of others, and happiness for the well-being of others, and to act appropriately on these feelings; one of the four cardinal virtues of the Neo-Confucian tradition. See also *Mengzi* 2A6 and 6A6, in Part III, Selection 35
bodhisattva		菩薩 *púsà*	a Buddhist who has achieved enlightenment and now works to alleviate the suffering of others. See also arhat
Buddha		佛 *fó*	the Enlightened One, a title for Siddhartha Gautama, the founder of Buddhism; or a title for anyone who achieves enlightenment (e.g., the Buddha, a Buddha)

Our Translation	Alternative Translations	Chinese Term	Meaning
characteristic, phenomenon	character	相 *xiàng*	the manner in which something manifests itself to perception or consciousness; sometimes has the connotation of a misleading appearance (phenomenon), but for the enlightened it can simply refer to a useful mode of experiencing reality (characteristic). See Fazang, "The Rafter Dialogue," in Part II, Selection 14
conscientiousness	dutifulness, doing one's best	忠 *zhōng*	classically, the virtue of loyalty; for Neo-Confucians it becomes the virtue of making a diligent effort to follow the Way (which see), and then often paired with sympathetic understanding (which see). See also *Analects* 4.15, in Part III, Selection 34
dharma		法 *fǎ*	a momentarily existing phenomenon (e.g., one of the ever-changing configurations of matter or consciousness); or the teachings of Buddhism; or the causal laws governing the transformations of the universe; originally a Sanskrit word

Our Translation	Alternative Translations	Chinese Term	Meaning
embodiment, embodied disposition	temperament	氣質 *qìzhì*	the endowment of *qi* of a particular entity, which accounts for its individual traits, such as temperament, intelligence, innate character, etc.; it can be modified through ethical cultivation
exhaustively investigate the Pattern		窮其理 *qióng qí lǐ*	a phrase first found in the *Changes*, referring to a complete understanding of the structure of the universe
expedient means	skillful means	方便 *fāngbiàn*	known in Sanskrit as *upāya,* this is the technique of adapting the formulation of a teaching to the level of understanding of one's audience; it may involve stating an outright falsehood that is nonetheless useful for encouraging virtuous behavior (e.g., the claim that the Buddha is a god), or it may simply be making statements that are highly context-sensitive (e.g., encouraging a timid person to be daring, while encouraging a reckless person to be more cautious)

Our Translation	Alternative Translations	Chinese Term	Meaning
faithfulness	faith, trustworthiness	信 *xìn*	classically, the virtue of honesty, especially in dealing with friends and colleagues; for Buddhists and Neo-Confucians, the virtue of believing in and being committed to the Way (which see) with unwavering conviction
feelings	passions, emotions	情 *qíng*	desires and emotions; often specified in a general list derived from the *Rites* (happiness, anger, sadness, fear, love, desire, and dislike) or a list of specifically ethical emotions from *Mengzi* 2A6 and 6A6 (compassion, disdain, deference or respect, and approval/disapproval)
Five Phases	five elements, five agents, five forces	五行 *wǔ xíng*	Earth, Water, Fire, Metal, and Wood; a pattern of five correlations found across a wide variety of phenomena (e.g., five planets, five notes), or five stages that a process can go through. See also Selections on the Five Phases, in Part I, Selection 8

Our Translation	Alternative Translations	Chinese Term	Meaning
Function	use, operation	用 *yòng*	the distinctive or proper operation of something; the complementary term with Substance (e.g., water is Substance, a wave is Function; the eye is substance, seeing is Function)
fundamental, foundation, root	basic, original	本 *běn*	the adjective "fundamental" typically describes the underlying state of something (its "foundation"), which may be obscured by selfish desires, illusory conceptions, or its embodiment in *qi* (see "embodiment" and "*qi*"); sometimes the original sense of the term, "root," is used to draw a metaphorical distinction between "roots" and "branches" (the underlying state and its specific manifestations)

Our Translation	Alternative Translations	Chinese Term	Meaning
getting a handle on things	investigating things, rectifying things, rectifying thoughts	格物 *géwù*	a phrase from the *Great Learning* whose meaning is highly disputed; most translators follow Zhu Xi's interpretation, "investigating things" (i.e., intellectually understanding the manifestations of the Pattern in things); however, Wang Yangming's interpretation is equally plausible, "correcting things" (i.e., exercising one's innate knowledge in action); our translation aims to be neutral among the competing interpretations. See the discussions in Zhu Xi, *Collected Commentaries on the* Great Learning, in Part III, Selection 33, and Wang Yangming, "Questions on the *Great Learning*," in Part III, Selection 38

Our Translation	Alternative Translations	Chinese Term	Meaning
Great Ultimate	Supreme Ultimate, Supreme Polarity	太極 *tàijí*	a term from the Great Appendix to the *Changes*; Neo-Confucians agree that this expression refers to the Pattern in itself; however, there is a subtle disagreement over whether we should conceive of it as something conceptually prior to its embodiments in concrete things (as Zhu Xi argues), or as simply an aspect of its concrete embodiments (as Lu Xiangshan argues). See Zhu Xi, *Categorized Conversations,* in Part III, Selection 32, and Lu Xiangshan, "Correspondence on the Great Ultimate," in Part III, Selection 37.
Heaven	Nature	天 *tiān*	an impersonal higher power responsible for the structure of the universe; or one of the aspects of the universe (e.g., Heaven and Earth, or Heaven, Earth, and Humans)
Hinayana			a derogatory term sometimes used by Mahayana Buddhists to refer to Theravada Buddhists (see "Mahayana" and "Theravada")

Our Translation	Alternative Translations	Chinese Term	Meaning
karma			strictly speaking, this Sanskrit term refers to intentional action; however, it is often used loosely to refer to the "fruits of karma," the good or bad consequences that follow from intentional actions
Mahāyāna			one of the sects of Buddhism, and the version that spread to China, Japan, Korea, and Vietnam; originally a Sanskrit term meaning Great Vehicle; Mahayanists sometimes refer to Theravada Buddhists (which see) by the derogatory term Hinayana
mandate, fate	command, decree	命 *ming*	whatever is dictated by Heaven or the Pattern; specifically, what we ought to do (the mandate), or what is determined by causal factors beyond our control (fate); see Heaven, Pattern, Way. See also *Mean* 1, in Part III, Selection 36
mind	heart, heart-mind	心 *xīn*	the faculty of both thinking and feeling, as well as the physical organ of the heart
nature		性 *xìng*	the characteristics that make something the distinct kind of thing that it is, and provide a normative standard for its proper functioning

Our Translation	Alternative Translations	Chinese Term	Meaning
nirvana		涅槃 *nièpán*	the state of bliss achieved by extinguishing all selfish desires and illusory beliefs; for many Chinese Buddhists it is a state that one can achieve while alive and active in everyday life
overarching Pattern	moral principle	道理 *dàolǐ*	the Pattern considered as a whole, as opposed to the distinct manifestations of the Pattern; or the Pattern as the way things out to be
Pattern	principle	理 *lǐ*	the underlying structure of the universe, typically conceived of as fully present in each and every thing that exists; or a particular manifestation of this structure. See Fazang, "Essay on the Golden Lion," in Part II, Selection 15, and the discussion in Zhu Xi, *Categorized Conversations,* in Part III, Selection 32
Pattern is one but its manifestations are diverse	Principle is one but its manifestations are many	理一而分殊 *lǐ yì ér fēn shū*	slogan meaning that while there is only one Pattern, it is imparted to myriad things, resulting in distinctive manifestations; attributed by Cheng Yi to Zhang Zai's "The Western Inscription," but the phrase is not found in that work

Our Translation	Alternative Translations	Chinese Term	Meaning
qi	psychophysical stuff, material force, ether, vital energy, pneuma	氣 *qì*	the fundamental spatio-temporal stuff that composes concrete objects; or a particular form that this stuff takes (e.g., *yin qi*, turbid *qi*, floodlike *qi*). See also Selections on *Qi*, in Part I, Selection 6
reverence; reverential attentiveness	inner mental attentiveness	敬 *jìng*	a state of respectful mental focus on something
righteousness	rightness	義 *yì*	the disposition to disdain to do what is dishonorable, particularly a disdain to pursue profit at the expense of morality; one of the four cardinal virtues of the Neo-Confucian tradition. See also *Mengzi* 2A6 and 6A6, in Part III, Selection 35
ritual; propriety	rites, ceremony	禮 *lǐ*	ceremonies and etiquette that help us to express respect, give thanks, etc. (e.g., a ritual offering of wine and food to the spirits of one's ancestors, or bowing to greet someone); or the virtue of practicing the rituals with the appropriate motivations
Shakyamuni			Sanksrit expression meaning the sage of the Shakya tribe, another title for Siddhartha Gautama, the Buddha

Our Translation	Alternative Translations	Chinese Term	Meaning
Sincerity	genuineness, authenticity, truth	誠 *chéng*	the state of being true to one's genuine, fundamental self. See the *Mean,* in Part III, Selection 36
Substance	body, state	體 *tǐ*	the qualities or structure of something that makes it what it is; the complementary term with Function (e.g., water is Substance, a wave is Function; the eye is substance, seeing is Function)
sympathetic understanding	sympathy, understanding, altruism, using oneself as a measure to gauge others	恕 *shù*	using one's own desires and feelings as a way of determining what is appropriate in one's treatment of others; often paired with conscientiousness (which see). See also *Analects* 4.15, in Part III, Selection 34
Theravada			one of the major sects of Buddhism, and the one that spread to Sri Lanka and most of Southeast Asia; originally a Sanskrit term meaning Way of the Elders; sometimes referred to by Mahayana Buddhists (which see) by the derogatory term Hinayana

Our Translation	Alternative Translations	Chinese Term	Meaning
this mind	this heart, the heart	此心 *cǐ xīn*	a technical expression for Neo-Confucians, referring to the mind conceived of as our pure, innate, moral sense (as opposed to the mind when misled by selfish thoughts and desires); originally a phrase from *Mengzi* 1A7
ultimateless	Ultimate of Non-Being	無極 *wújí*	a phrase found in Zhou Dunyi's "Explanation of the Diagram of the Great Ultimate," taken by Zhu Xi to be an alternative name for the Great Ultimate (which see). See Zhou Dunyi, "Explanation of the Diagram of the Great Ultimate," in Part III, Selection 24; Zhu Xi, *Categorized Conversations,* in Part III, Selection 32; and Lu Xiangshan, "Correspondence on the Great Ultimate," in Part III, Selection 37
upāya			see "expedient means"
Virtue	power	德 *dé*	the moral charisma possessed by virtuous people that induces others to willingly obey them; or a term for the specific dispositions that are virtues (e.g., wisdom, courage, and benevolence)

Our Translation	Alternative Translations	Chinese Term	Meaning
Way	Course	道 *dào*	the correct manner in which to live one's life and organize society; or a fundamental metaphysical principle responsible for the nature of the universe
wisdom		智 *zhì*	practical wisdom; the disposition to correctly distinguish right and wrong and to show good judgment in practical deliberation; one of the four cardinal virtues of the Neo-Confucian tradition. See also *Mengzi* 2A6 and 6A6, in Part III, Selection 35
yin/yang		陰 *yīn* / 陽 *yáng*	terms to describe complementary opposites; generally, the well-being and proper functioning of anything depends upon mixing these in the right proportions. See Selections on *Yin* and *Yang*, in Part I, Selection 7

BIBLIOGRAPHY

General Surveys and Foundational Texts

Chan, Wing-tsit, trans. *A Source Book in Chinese Philosophy*. Princeton: Princeton University Press, 1963.

Graham, Angus C. *Yin-Yang and the Nature of Correlative Thinking*. Singapore: Institute of East Asian Philosophy, 1986.

Hutton, Eric L., trans. *Xunzi: The Complete Text*. Princeton: Princeton University Press, 2014.

Ivanhoe, Philip J. *Confucian Moral Self Cultivation,* rev. ed. Indianapolis: Hackett Publishing, 2000.

———, trans. *The Daodejing of Laozi*. Indianapolis: Hackett Publishing, 2003.

Ivanhoe, Philip J., and Bryan W. Van Norden, eds. *Readings in Classical Chinese Philosophy,* 2nd ed. Indianapolis: Hackett Publishing, 2005.

Johnston, Ian, and Wang Ping, trans. *Daxue and Zhongyong [Great Learning and Mean]: Bilingual Edition*. Hong Kong: Chinese University Press, 2012.

Legge, James, trans. *The Ch'un Ts'ew with the Tso Chuen [Spring and Autumn Annals* with the *Zuo Commentary]*. Vol. 5 of *The Chinese Classics*. Hong Kong: Hong Kong University Press, 1872.

———, trans. *Confucian Analects, Great Learning, and Doctrine of the Mean*. Reprint, New York: Dover Publications, 1971.

———, trans. *The Li Ki [Rites]*, 2 vols. Oxford: Clarendon Press, 1885.

———, trans. *The She King [Odes]*. Vol. 4 of *The Chinese Classics*. Oxford: Clarendon Press 1871.

———, trans. *The Shoo King [Documents]*. Vol. 3 of *The Chinese Classics*. London: Trübner, 1865.

———, trans. *The Works of Mencius [Mengzi]*. Oxford: Clarendon Press, 1895.

———, trans. *The Yi King [Changes]*. Oxford: Clarendon Press, 1882.

Li, Chenyang, ed. *The Sage and the Second Sex: Confucianism, Ethics, and Gender*. La Salle, IL: Open Court Press, 2000.

Liu Shu-hsien. *Understanding Confucian Philosophy*. Westport, CT: Praeger, 1998. A New Confucian perspective on the history of the tradition.

Lynn, Richard John, trans. *The Classic of Changes: A New Translation of the* I Ching *as Interpreted by Wang Bi*. New York: Columbia University Press, 2004.

———, trans. *The Classic of the Way and Virtue: A New Translation of the* Tao-te Ching *of Laozi as Interpreted by Wang Bi*. New York: Columbia University Press, 2004.

Slingerland, Edward, trans. *Confucius: Analects: With Selections from Traditional Commentaries*. Indianapolis: Hackett Publishing, 2003.

Tanner, Harold. *China: A History*. Indianapolis: Hackett Publishing, 2009.

Van Norden, Bryan W. *Introduction to Classical Chinese Philosophy.* Indianapolis: Hackett Publishing, 2011.

———, trans. *Mengzi: With Selections from Traditional Commentaries.* Indianapolis: Hackett Publishing, 2008.

Wang, Robin R., ed. *Images of Women in Chinese Thought and Culture: Writings from the Pre-Qin Period through the Song Dynasty.* Indianapolis: Hackett Publishing, 2003.

Wilhelm, Richard and Cary F. Baynes, trans. *The I Ching, or Book of Changes.* Princeton: Princeton University Press, 1967. Includes an intriguing Foreword by Carl Jung.

Ziporyn, Brook. *Zhuangzi: The Essential Writings with Selections from Traditional Commentaries.* Indianapolis: Hackett Publishing, 2009.

Han Dynasty

Csikszentmihalyi, Mark, trans. *Readings in Han Chinese Thought.* Indianapolis: Hackett Publishing, 2006.

Knoblock, John and Jeffrey Riegel, trans. *The Annals of Lü Buwei: A Complete Translation and Study.* Stanford: Stanford University Press, 2001.

Major, John S., Sarah Queen, Andrew Meyer, and Harold D. Roth, trans. *The Huainanzi: A Guide to the Theory and Practice of Government in Early Han China.* New York: Columbia University Press, 2010.

Queen, Sarah. *From Chronicle to Canon: The Hermeneutics of the* Spring and Autumn, *According to Tung Chung-shu [Dong Zhongshu].* New York: Cambridge University Press, 1996.

Wang Ch'ung [Wang Chong]. *Lun-Heng,* translated by Alfred Forke. 2 vols. Reprint. New York: Paragon Press, 1962.

Xu Gan. *Balanced Discourses,* translated by John Makeham. New Haven: Yale University Press, 2002.

Yang Xiong. *Exemplary Figures,* translated by Michael Nylan. Seattle: University of Washington Press, 2013.

Buddhism

Addiss, Stephen, Stanley Lombardo, and Judith Roitman, eds. *Zen Sourcebook.* Indianapolis: Hackett Publishing, 2008.

Cook, Francis H. *Hua-yen Buddhism: The Jewel Net of Indra.* University Park, PA: Pennsylvania State University Press, 1977.

Donner, Neal and Daniel B. Stevenson. *The Great Calming and Contemplation: A Study and Annotated Translation of the First Chapter of Chih-I's Mo-Ho Chih-Kuan.* Honolulu: University of Hawaii Press, 1993.

Dumoulin, Heinrich. *Zen Buddhism: A History.* Vol. 1, *India and China.* New York: MacMillan, 1994.

Hakeda, Yoshito S., trans. *The Awakening of Faith: Attributed to Asvaghosha.* New York: Columbia University Press, 2005.

Lusthaus, Dan. *Buddhist Phenomenology: A Philosophical Investigation of Yogacara Buddhism and the Ch'eng Wei-shih Lun.* London: RoutledgeCurzon, 2003.

Nhat Hanh, Thich. *The Heart of Understanding: Commentaries on the Prajna-paramita Heart Sutra.* Revised ed. Berkeley: Parallax Press, 2009. An accessible popular introduction to the metaphysics of Huayan and Chan.

Siderits, Mark. *Buddhism as Philosophy.* Indianapolis: Hackett Publishing, 2007. This is a helpful text for appreciating the Indian foundations of Buddhism.

Swanson, Paul L. *Foundations of T'ien-t'ai Philosophy: The Flowering of the Truths Theory in Chinese Buddhism.* Fremont, CA: Asian Humanities Press, 1995.

Watson, Burton, trans. *The Lotus Sutra.* New York: Columbia University Press, 1993.

————, trans. *The Zen Teachings of Master Lin-Chi.* New York: Columbia University Press, 1999.

Zongmi. *Inquiry into Humanity,* translated by Peter Gregory. Honolulu: University of Hawaii Press, 1995.

Neo-Confucianism

Angle, Stephen C. and Justin Tiwald. *Neo-Confucianism: A Philosophical Introduction.* Malden, MA: Polity Press, forthcoming.

Chan, Wing-tsit, ed. *Chu Hsi and Neo-Confucianism.* Honolulu: University of Hawaii Press, 1986.

————, trans. *Reflections on Things at Hand.* New York: Columbia University Press, 1967.

Gardner, Daniel K., trans. *The Four Books: The Basic Teachings of the Later Confucian Tradition.* Indianapolis: Hackett Publishing, 2007.

————, trans. *Learning to Be a Sage: Selections from the* Conversations of Master Chu, *Arranged Topically.* Berkeley: University of California Press, 1990.

Graham, Angus C. *Two Chinese Philosophers.* Reprint. La Salle, IL: Open Court Press, 1992. An introduction to the philosophy of Cheng Yi and Cheng Hao.

Ivanhoe, Philip J., trans. *Readings from the Lu-Wang School of Neo-Confucianism.* Indianapolis: Hackett Publishing, 2009.

Kim, Yung Sik. *The Natural Philosophy of Chu Hsi (1130–1200).* Philadelphia: American Philosophical Society, 2000.

Makeham, John, ed. *Dao Companion to Neo-Confucian Philosophy.* Dordrecht: Springer, 2010.

Smith, Kidder, Jr., Peter K. Bol, Joseph A. Adler, and Don J. Wyatt. *Sung Dynasty Uses of the* I Ching. Princeton: Princeton University Press, 1990.

Wang Yang-ming. *Instructions for Practical Living and Other Neo-Confucian Writings.* New York: Columbia University Press, 1963.

Wu Yubi. *The Journal of Wu Yubi,* translated by Theresa Kelleher. Indianapolis: Hackett Publishing, 2013. An example of the effort to apply Confucian teachings in one's daily life.

Late Imperial Confucianism

Elman, Benjamin. *From Philosophy to Philology: Intellectual and Social Aspects of Change in Late Imperial China.* Los Angeles: UCLA Asian Pacific Monograph Series, 2001.

Ewell, John. "Re-inventing the Way: Dai Zhen's *Evidential Commentary on the Meaning of Terms in Mencius* (1777)." Ph.D. dissertation, History, University of California at Berkeley, 1990.

Ivanhoe, Philip J., trans. *On Ethics and History: Essays and Letters of Zhang Xuecheng.* Stanford: Stanford University Press, 2009.

Nivison, David S. "Two Kinds of 'Naturalism': Dai Zhen and Zhang Xuecheng." In *The Ways of Confucianism*, David S. Nivison, ed. La Salle, IL: Open Court Publishing, 1996.

Tiwald, Justin. "Dai Zhen on Human Nature and Moral Cultivation." In *Dao Companion to Neo-Confucian Philosophy*, John Makeham, ed. Dordrecht: Springer, 2010.

Twentieth-Century Chinese Philosophy

Angle, Stephen C. *Contemporary Confucian Political Philosophy: Toward Progressive Confucianism.* Malden, MA: Polity Press, 2012.

Bell, Daniel A. *China's New Confucianism: Politics and Everyday Life in a Changing Society.* Princeton: Princeton University Press, 2008.

Hu Shih. *Chinese Philosophy and Intellectual History.* Vol. 2 of *English Writings of Hu Shih,* edited by Chih-p'ing Ch'ou. London: Springer, 2013.

Knight, Nick. *Marxist Philosophy in China: From Qu Qiubai to Mao Zedong, 1923–1945.* Dordrecht: Springer: 2010.

Liu Shao-ch'i [Liu Shaoqi]. *How to Be a Good Communist.* Peking: Foreign Languages Press, 1939. Online version at [http://www.marxists.org/reference /archive/liu-shaoqi/1939/how-to-be/index.htm].

Makeham, John, ed. *New Confucianism: A Critical Examination.* New York: Palgrave Macmillan, 2003.

Mao Tse-tung [Mao Zedong]. *The Second Revolutionary War Period.* Vol. 1 of *Selected Works of Mao Tse-tung.* Peking: Foreign Languages Press, 1967. Online version at [http://www.marxists.org/reference/archive/mao/selected-works /index.htm]. See especially the essays, "On Practice" and "On Contradiction."

Metzger, Thomas. *Escape from Predicament: Neo-Confucianism and China's Evolving Political Culture.* New York: Columbia University Press, 1977.

Mou Zongsan. *Nineteen Lectures on Chinese Philosophy: A Brief Outline of Chinese Philosophy and Its Implicated Issues,* translated by Esther C. Su, forthcoming.

Nivison, David S. "Communist Ethics and Chinese Tradition." *Journal of Asian Studies* 16:1 (November 1956): 51–74.

Sun Yat-sen. *San Min Chu I: The Three Principles of the People,* translated by Frank W. Price. Shanghai: Institute of Pacific Relations, 1927.

T'ang Chun-i [Tang Junyi]. *Essays on Chinese Philosophy and Culture.* Taipei: Student Book Company, 1988.

Xiong Shili. *New Treatise on The Uniqueness of Consciousness (Xin Weishilun),* translated by John Makeham. New Haven: Yale University Press, 2014.

INDEX OF NAMES

INDEX LOCORUM,
THE FOUR BOOKS